Organizational Change and Development

DIPAK KUMAR BHATTACHARYYA

Professor (OB/HRM)
Xavier Institute of Management
Bhubaneswar

Oxford University Press is a department of the University of Oxford.
It furthers the University's objective of excellence in research, scholarship,
and education by publishing worldwide. Oxford is a registered trademark of
Oxford University Press in the UK and in certain other countries

Published in India by
Oxford University Press
22 Workspace, 2nd Floor, 1/22 Asaf Ali Road, New Delhi 110 002

© Oxford University Press 2011

The moral rights of the author have been asserted

First published in 2011
10th impression 2020

All rights reserved. No part of this publication may be reproduced, stored in
a retrieval system, or transmitted, in any form or by any means, without the
prior permission in writing of Oxford University Press, or as expressly permitted
by law, by licence, or under terms agreed with the appropriate reprographics
rights organization. Enquiries concerning reproduction outside the scope of the
above should be sent to the Rights Department, Oxford University Press, at the
address above

You must not circulate this book in any other form
and you must impose this same condition on any acquirer

ISBN-13: 978-0-19-806646-0
ISBN-10: 0-19-806646-5

Typeset in Baskerville
by Le Studio Graphique, Gurgaon
Printed in India by Repro books Limited, Thane

For product information and current price, please visit www.india.oup.com

Dedicated to

*Tapodeep, Sudip, and Sutapa,
whose proximity helped my understanding of change and developmental issues*

Preface

Organizations today are operating in a fast-changing environment where business practices are dynamic and economies are vulnerable to market fluctuations. Potential threats from external environment require organizations to be much more dynamic in nature. In the process of survival, sustainability, and growth, organizations are initiating planned changes by re-orienting their systems, structures, and processes, particularly organizational processes. Understanding organizational change thus becomes an important area of study for organizations and for business managers. Further, the need for change in organizations is not only triggered by the environment they operate in (which is fiercely competitive), but also from within. Introduction of new technology, changing social and lifestyle patterns, career aspirations of organizational members, and frequent changes in consumer priorities have contributed to the evolution of this complex web of change. Organizations, globally, are constantly trying to devise a wide variety of strategies to cope with these changes.

Strong leadership, right policies, and effective communication are the three basic pillars of any successful change endeavour. These are directly related to organizational design and structure which, in turn, influence processes and interventions for bringing change in organizations. The design issues involve chain of command, span of control, authority, delegation, and accountability. Flexibility in design helps an organization not only in being proactive, but also to initiate change as per the environmental pressures.

The field of organizational change is a confluence of various disciplines, such as organizational psychology, sociology, action research and statistics, international trade and economics, public administration, law, finance, and many more. Managing change will thus involve an array of activities, such as creation of organizational identities, knowledge development and its institutionalization, management of diversity, constant upgradation of technology, alignment of strategic goals with economic environment, asset management, creation of appropriate cultures, restructuring of roles, coping with market competition, and management of internal as well as external crises.

Organizational development (OD), which is concerned with change interventions, is an all-encompassing ongoing process. For any organization to sustain and grow, OD intervention is an inseparable component. This further underlines the importance of change management in the field of business management education. For today's executives and aspiring managers, understanding various change and developmental issues is very important. The courses on organizational change and development are designed to provide the students exposure to some of the change management strategies that are being adopted by organizations, both in India and abroad. The idea is to help aspiring managers understand and appreciate how organizations go through the process of change along with providing clarity on the strategies and measures of change management.

This book makes an attempt to help aspiring and practising managers to understand, appreciate, and implement change management.

About the Book

There are very few textbooks available that cover the entire gamut of issues in the area of organizational change. There are a few reference books which primarily address some specific issues. Further, universities, management institutes, and various professional bodies offer this subject in different names, such as Organizational Effectiveness, Organizational Change, Organizational Development, etc. ***Organizational Change and Development*** has been developed keeping in view the curriculum requirements of all such courses in national and international universities and management institutes. With its special pedagogical features and lucid style, the book would meet the requirements of students.

The book is divided into 5 sections, namely Understanding Organizational Processes and Change, Organizational Change Management, Nature of Organizational Development, Organizational Development Interventions and Strategies, and Contemporary Issues in Organizational Development. With a strong conceptual foundation, the book takes the readers through the entire processes and stages of change as seen and experienced worldwide.

Students will find the book useful in understanding the various theories of change management and their application in organizational situations. Diagnosis, planning, and guiding change management form the backbone of OD interventions. The concepts are suitably supplemented by case studies, corporate practices, exercises, and lessons from Indian as well as global organizations. Each chapter has cases emulating the best practices of world-class organizations in India and abroad. The book has been developed keeping in view the Indian context, and holistically encapsulates the international flavour of change management as well.

The strength of the book lies in its exhaustive treatment of a wide array of topics along with various exhibits on global change management. Various snapshots of different stages/levels of change and OD in organizations worldwide and simple language add further value. Students of various MBA and PGDM programmes, particularly those who specialize in organizational behaviour (OB)/human resource (HR), would find the book immensely useful. It also caters to students who wish to gain additional insights into organizational design and strategy areas. The book strives to become an essential reading for consultants and managers as well.

Pedagogical Features

Special pedagogical features used throughout the book are as follows:

- Written in simple language, the book uses numerous exhibits and industrial examples.
- Each chapter is self-contained and gradually leads to successive levels of knowledge to ensure holistic understanding of the subject.

- Each chapter starts with an opening case or vignette which orients the readers to concepts discussed later in the chapter. The chapters also provide analytical case studies at the end for learning enhancement.
- Basic theoretical concepts are discussed with reference to corporate practices to help students understand the application of their learned knowledge.
- Each chapter has a summary, a set of key terms of the concepts discussed in the chapter, and concept review and analytical questions for revision.
- Select references are provided for each chapter which will help the readers identify material for further reading.
- Appendices, graphs, charts, illustrative tables, and models are provided in the book as additional information/resources.

After going through this book, the reader will be able to

- get clarity on various dimensions of change and development and their interconnections in business organizations;
- learn to analyse organizations holistically using a variety of systems tools;
- recognize the most common types of problems that occur in organizations and generate specific recommendations to address all such issues;
- develop complete action plans that are aligned and integrated with each other for optimum effectiveness;
- understand how to create powerful teams to collaborate and guide change in organizations;
- develop a realistic change management strategy which gets acceptance and generates sense of ownership in the organization;
- guide change according to proven principles of successful organizational change; and
- ensure ongoing motivation during change and effectively address resistance.

Coverage and Structure

The book is divided into five parts which cover the various aspects of organizational change and development. These parts are further divided across twenty-one chapters.

Part 1 Understanding Organizational Processes and Change

Chapter 1 of the book focuses on organizational systems, structure, and design. Readers will be able to understand the systems view of organizations and various relationships. The chapter covers different approaches to understand organizations and concludes with the relationship between organizational culture and design.

Chapter 2 introduces organizational change. Various models of organizational transition have been discussed. The different types of organizational change, various strategies of organizational change, and management of resistance to change are the other highlights of the chapter.

Chapter 3 deals with the organizational change process and the various theories of organizational change along with manpower redundancy aspect during the change. Organizational change processes related to mergers and acquisitions are also discussed.

Chapter 4 emphasizes on organizational change through increased effectiveness. The chapter consists of various measures on organizational effectiveness and various contemporary models of organizational excellence. Managerial skills and competencies and their contribution to organizational effectiveness and excellence in the new millennium have been highlighted.

Part 2 Organizational Change Management

Chapter 5 elaborates on the organizational improvement process through change management, implementation of change improvement systems, change management survey, process of mobilizing the organization, etc. Discussions on various types of change and the concept of change management iceberg provide useful insights. The chapter also provides guidelines for management of change, and highlights qualities of a change agent.

Chapter 6 introduces the concept of power and leadership in change management. The chapter consists of the sources of power, power and empowerment, implications of power and empowerment, and organizational politics. Transactional and transformational leadership along with leadership styles and theories have also been integrated with management of change.

Chapter 7 deals with technology management, its link with innovation, strategies, HR implications, planning, and the process of technology transfer. The chapter introduces various models of technology and discusses its influence on organizational structure and design.

Chapter 8 discusses the issues pertaining to technology and culture in organizations. Introducing the concept of proactive manufacturing culture, the chapter focuses on Hofstede's cultural orientation model, influence of culture in the workplace, the process of identification of technological culture in organizations, the process of transition from reactive to proactive culture, and the steps involved in technology transition process.

Chapter 9 covers attitude and its measurement for organizational change. Different approaches to and strategies for attitudinal change, HRD initiatives and attitudinal change, and the use of various scaling techniques to map attitude have also been elaborated in this chapter.

Chapter 10 highlights the process of achieving organizational change through change in organizational culture. Merger and its impact on organizational culture, the process of changing the organizational culture, etc. are other areas covered here. Organizational diagnostics, organizational climate, and management-directed cultural change also have been discussed in this chapter.

Chapter 11 is dedicated to performance-driven organizational change process. The chapter also emphasizes on the concept of performance metric, process of performance modelling, and the use of balanced scorecard, HR scorecard, competency mapping, and knowledge management practices to achieve the desired organizational change.

Chapter 12 emphasizes on total quality management (TQM) practices to achieve organizational change. The chapter illustrates how quality management practices exert impact on organizations to facilitate the process of organizational change.

Part 3 Nature of Organizational Development

Chapter 13 initiates discussions on OD including the concepts, strategic dimensions, and the features and characteristics of OD. The goals and steps in OD are also dealt with in detail. The chapter also discusses the action research process, leadership development, and the role of consultants in OD processes. Values and ethical issues in OD and organizational life cycle analysis are other topics covered here.

Chapter 14 introduces the process of organizational diagnosis and development. After discussing the concepts of organizational diagnosis, the chapter elaborates on its various forms as also the use of various tools and techniques available for the same.

Part 4 Organizational Development Interventions and Strategies

Chapter 15 introduces various models and intervention tools of organizational development, their usage, and effectiveness.

Chapter 16 reviews organizational change and development in the era of globalization. It discusses the various factors to promote globalization and technology transfer. The chapter finally aligns globalization with the OD processes and also helps in understanding the alignment of HR strategy with business goals in the context of globalization.

Chapter 17 reviews knowledge management and learning organization issues in the context of organizational change and development. After introducing the theoretical issues, the chapter focuses on the strategies of knowledge management and highlights its relationship with change management.

Chapter 18 discusses the change management strategies along with various principles, philosophies, and institutional framework of strategic organizational change.

Part 5 Contemporary Issues in Organizational Development

Chapter 19 introduces diversity management issues in bringing organizational change. The relation between culture and diversity has been discussed along with the methods for bringing diversity. Various challenges to ensure cultural diversity have also been highlighted upon.

Chapter 20 discusses the importance of teamwork in organizational transformation. Various teamwork practices and their usage in organizational change and development have been elaborated upon.

Finally, Chapter 21 discusses organizational change and development research and introduces the various tools and models involved. Various quantitative and qualitative change management research issues, such as data collection and analysis, use of statistical tools, framing of hypothesis and testing, etc., have been elaborated with illustrative examples, to help the readers undertake further research.

Acknowledgements

I wish to extend a special note of thanks to my students, friends, and colleagues at the Camellia School of Business Management, Kolkata, and the Indian Institute of Social Welfare and Business Management (IISWBM), Kolkata, who have always been a source of inspiration.

I take pleasure in thanking Mr N.R. Datta, Chairman of Camellia Group, Mr Partha Pal, Mr Mrinmoy Chatterjee, Dr Subshasish Sengupta, Dr Abir Chatterjee, Dr N.C. De Sarkar, Dr C.T. Bhunia of Camellia Group, and Prof. Sanjay Kumar Bhattacharyya, Director of the National Institute of Technical Teachers' Training & Research, Kolkata, for their constant support. My mentor, Prof. Sudipti Banerjea of the University of Calcutta, deserves a special mention.

The support and assistance received from the editorial team at Oxford University Press, New Delhi, in bringing out this book is gratefully acknowledged.

Last, but not the least, I wish to convey a special note of gratitude to my wife and children, without whom writing this book would not have been possible.

I would be grateful for any critical comments on my book from faculty members and students to improve future editions. Readers can send their suggestions to dkbhattacharyya@yahoo.co.in.

DIPAK KUMAR BHATTACHARYYA

Brief Contents

Preface v

PART 1 Understanding Organizational Processes and Change — 1

1. Understanding Organizational Systems, Structure, and Design *3*
2. Introduction to Organizational Change *43*
3. Organizational Change Process *82*
4. Organizational Effectiveness and Excellence *119*

PART 2 Organizational Change Management — 157

5. Managing Organizational Change *159*
6. Power, Leadership, and Organizational Change *185*
7. Technology Management *207*
8. Technology and Culture *224*
9. Attitude Measurement for Change Management *236*
10. Organizational Culture and Change *254*
11. Change through Performance Management *279*
12. TQM Practices and Organizational Change *310*

PART 3 Nature of Organizational Development — 327

13. Organizational Development *329*
14. Organizational Diagnosis and Development *358*

PART 4 Organizational Development Interventions and Strategies — 379

15. Approaches and Models *381*
16. Globalization and Organizational Change and Development *409*
17. Knowledge Management and Change *433*
18. Change Management Strategies *453*

PART 5 *Contemporary Issues in Organizational Development* 469

19. Organizational Development and Diversity Management 471
20. Organizational Transformation through Teamwork 489
21. Organizational Change and Development Research 508

Index 551

Detailed Contents

Preface v

PART 1 *Understanding Organizational Processes and Change* 1

1. **Understanding Organizational Systems, Structure, and Design** 3

   Introduction 3
   Definitions and Principles of an Organization 5
      Organization, Organizing, and Organizational Structure 6
   Systems View of an Organization 6
      Feedback Loop 7
   Organizational Structure and Systems 10
      Components of Organizational Structure 11
   Types of Organizational Structure 12
      Adhocracy and Bureaucracy: The Two Ends of a Continuum 13
      Organizational Effectiveness 14
   Systems Theory, Systems Analysis, and Systems Thinking 15
      Principles of Systems Theory 16
   Open Systems Approach to an Organization 17
   Organizational Cybernetics, Viable Systems Model, and Organizational Systems 18
      Open Systems Concepts and Orchestra Organization 19
      Chaos Theory 20
   Socio-technical Systems Thinking 22
   Systems Dynamics 23
   Business Process Approach to an Organization 23
      Michigan Model 24
      Harvard Model 24
      Guest's Model 24
      Warwick Model 24
      Elements of the Business Process Model 25
      Description of Business Process Model 25
      Normative and Descriptive Models 27
   Organizational Design 28
      Bureaucratic Model 29
      Behavioural Model 29
   Role of Critical Success Factors in Organizational Design 30
      Human Resource Information Systems and Its Usage in Organizational Design 32
      Organizational Culture and Design 35
   Business Process Re-engineering 36
      Situational Aspects of Organizational Design 36

2. **Introduction to Organizational Change** 43

   Introduction 44
   Content and Process Theories of Organizational Change 45

Need for Organizational Change 46
Philosophy of Organizational Change 47
Organizational Change, Transformation, and Renewal 49
Change Triggers 50
   Business Development-driven Change 51
   Environment-driven Change 52
   Culture-driven Change 53
   Strategy-driven Change 54
   Business Plan-driven Change 55
   Process-driven Change 55
   Competency-driven Change 55
   Performance-driven Change 55
   Innovation-driven Change 56
Key Elements for Success in Organizational Change 57
   Organizational Change through Training and Development 58
Organizational Transition 58
   Generic Change or Transition Models 59
Types of Change 62
   Planned vs Emergent Change 62
   Episodic vs Continuous Change 63
   Developmental, Transitional, and Transformational Change 63
Systems Thinking and Change 66
Strategies of Change Management 67
   Normative Re-educative Strategy 67
   Rational-empirical Strategy 67
   Power-coercive Strategy 68
   Action-centred Strategy 69
Personal Construct Psychology and Organizational Change 70
   ABC Technique and Organizational Change 71
   Integrative Approach to Organizational Change 72
Role of Organizational Change Consultants 73
Common Drawbacks in Implementing Organizational Change 74

3. Organizational Change Process   82

Introduction 83
Organizational Change Process through Personal Examination 83
Features of Organizational Change 84
Theories of Organizational Change 86
Change Processes 87
   Change Process and Its Stages of Unfreezing, Changing, and Refreezing 88
   Organizational Change Process 88
   Business Environment-led Change Process 89
   Strategic Planning-focused Change Process 90
   Customer and Market-driven Change Process 91
   Organizational Culture-driven Change Process 91
   Organizational Structure and the Change Process 93
   Leadership Performance-driven Change Process 93
   SWOT Analysis and the Change Process 95
   Environmental Scanning and Feedback-enabled Change Process 97
Role and Significance of HRD in the Organizational Change Process 98
   Focus of the HRD System 98
   Role of HRD Manager in Organizational Change Process 99
   HRD Culture and Climate 100
   Competencies as Enablers of Organizational Change Process 101
Organizational Change through Management of Manpower Redundancy 102
Mergers and Acquisitions 103
   Change Processes Involved during Mergers and Acquisitions 104
   Recent Research on Mergers and Acquisitions 106

Mergers and Acquisitions in India 109
Strategic Focusing in the Organizational Change Process 110
Scenario Planning for Effective Organizational Change Process 110
   Forces of Scenario Planning 112
   Steps for Scenario Planning 112
   Application of Delphi Technique in Scenario Planning 113
   Nominal Group Method 114

4. Organizational Effectiveness and Excellence 119

Introduction 119
Measuring Organizational Effectiveness 121
   Organizational Effectiveness Inventory 122
   OE Cycle 122
   Dashboard 122
   Open Systems Model 126
   Contemporary Models of Organizational Effectiveness and Excellence 127
   The McKinsey Way of Problem-solving Approach 131
   Excellence Model of Peters and Waterman 132
Management by Objectives for Organizational Effectiveness and Excellence 133
EFQM Excellence Model 133
Quality Management Principles for Organizational Excellence 135
Managerial Roles Theory for Achieving Organizational Effectiveness and Excellence 135
Managerial Skills and Competencies 135
   Skill Inventories 137
   Multi-skilling 138
   Skills for the New Millennium 138
   Developing Competencies for Effective Organizational Change 140
P-CMM Model for Organizational Excellence 140
Shingo Prize Model of Organizational Excellence 143
Malcolm Baldrige Model for Organizational Excellence 144
Organizational Change through Six Sigma 145
Six Sigma in Organizations 147
Lean Practices to Achieve Organizational Excellence 149

PART 2   *Organizational Change Management*   157

5. Managing Organizational Change 159

Introduction 160
Nature of Change 161
   Responsibility for Managing Change 162
Change Management Principles 162
Change Transitions for Individual Employees 163
Organization Improvement Process through Change Management 166
Implementing Change Improvement Systems 167
Change Management Survey 167
The Commitment Curve 170
   Mobilizing the Organization 171
Types of Change 171
Change Management—The Skill Requirements 172
   Political Skills 172
   Analytical Skills 172
   People Skills 173
   System Skills 173
   Business Skills 173
Change Management Iceberg 173
Change in Organizational Culture 174

Managing Organizational Change through Modification of Group Behaviour 176
Effective Change Management 178
  Explain the Need for Change 178
  Discuss in Detail the Issues Involved 178
  Facilitate the Change Programme with Training and Support 179
  Implement the Desired Change 179
  Reinforce the Change 179
Qualities of a Change Agent 180
Approaches to Change Management 180

6. Power, Leadership, and Organizational Change 185

Introduction 186
Theories of Power 187
Organizational Power and Control 189
Power and Systems of Organizational Membership 190
Sources of Power 191
  Organizational Sources 191
  Individual/Personal Sources 192
Power and Empowerment 193
  Definition and Concept of Empowerment 193
  Understanding Power and Empowerment Implications in Practice 193
  The Process of Empowerment 194
Organizational Politics 195
Transactional and Transformational Leadership 196
  Contingency Framework of Change 197
Environment and Leadership 199
  Culture and Climate of Leadership 200
  Leadership 201
Leadership and Power 201

7. Technology Management 207

Introduction 208
Concept of Technology Management 209
  Sociological Issues in Technology Management 209
  Organizational Structure and Design 210
  Economic Issues in Technological Change 211
Strategic Technology Management 211
Human Resource Management and Technology Management 213
  Design and Engineering 213
  Processing Fabrication and Assembly 214
  High Speed Machining 214
  Inspection 214
  Integration and Control 214
  Network Communications 215
Technology Planning 216
  Principles of Technology Planning 216
  Technology Transfer 217
  Technology Innovation 218
  Technology and Organizational Design 218

8. Technology and Culture 224

Introduction 224
Culture and Organizations 225
Proactive and Reactive Technological Cultures 227
  Proactive Technological Culture 227
Transition from Reactive to Proactive Technological Culture 228
  Existing Manufacturing Systems 230
  Steps in the Technology Transitioning Process 232

9. Attitude Measurement for Change Management   236

Introduction   237
Employee Attitudes in the Organizational Change Process   238
Approaches to Attitudinal Change   239
Strategies for Attitudinal Change   239
Attitude Measurement for Organizational Change   243
HRD Initiatives and Attitudinal Change   243
Use of Scaling Techniques to Map Attitude   245
    Likert Scales   246
    Other Measures of Attitudes   246
Attitude Surveys   246
    Likert's Summated Rating Scale   248
    Thurstone's Equal Appearing Intervals Scale for Attitudinal Survey   249
    Guttman's Cumulative Scale   249
    Johari Window   249

10. Organizational Culture and Change   254

Introduction   255
Organizational Culture   255
    Aspects of Organizational Culture   256
    Differences in Organizational Cultures   257
Dimensions of Cultures and Their Influence on Organizations   258
    High Context vs Low Context   258
    Monochronic vs Polychronic   258
    Future vs Present vs Past Orientation   259
    Quantity of Time   259
    Power Distance   260
    Individualism vs Collectivism   260
Definition and Characteristics of Organizational Culture   261
Organizational Culture as External and Internal Variables   262
Types of Organizational Culture   263
Organizational Culture from a Global Perspective   265
Mergers and Their Impact on Organizational Culture   266
    P&G–Gillette   267
    Tata–Corus   267
    HP–Compaq   267
    Daimler–Chrysler   268
Organizational Culture Change Process   268
    Organizational Structure   269
    Organizational Diagnostics   269
    Attitudes towards Work   269
    Organizational Commitment   270
    Organizational Climate   271
Models of Organizational Culture Change   272
    Root Metaphor   272
    External and Independent Variable   272
    Internal Variable   272
    Management-directed Cultural Change   273

11. Change through Performance Management   279

Transformation of Tata Consultancy Services (TCS)   279
Introduction   280
Overview of Performance Management   280
Dimensions of Performance   281
Performance Models   282
Performance-driven Organizational Change   284
    Performance-driven Organizational Change Process   286
Setting Standards of Performance   288
    Guidelines for Performance Standards   288

Developing a Performance Metric 290
  Performance Matrix 292
Effective Performance Modelling 294
  The Human Side of Performance Metrics 294
  Customer-focused Metrics 294
  Designing Metrics 295
  Various Dimensions of Performance 295
Managing Change through Balanced Scorecard 297
  Perspectives of Balanced Scorecard 297
HR Scorecard 301
  Process of Developing HR Scorecard 301
  Key Benefits of HR Scorecard 302
Competency Mapping and Competency Development 303
Performance Improvement through Knowledge Management Practices 304
Knowledge Management and Resource-based Competitive Advantage 305

12. TQM Practices and Organizational Change 310

Introduction 310
TQM and the Operating Environment of Organizations 311
  ISO Standards and TQM Systems 313
  Selection and Use of the ISO 9000:2000 Family of Standards 313
  Optimizing the Cost of Quality 314
Teams and Teamwork 315
Organizational Change and TQM 318
Employee Empowerment 319
  Quality of Work Life (QWL) 319
Organizational Change through Innovation and Creativity 320

PART 3 Nature of Organizational Development 327

13. Organizational Development 329

Introduction 330
Definitions and Concepts of OD 331
  Certain Clarifications about OD 333
Need for OD in Organizations 333
OD as Action Research Process 335
Strategic Aspects of OD 336
History or Evolution of OD 338
  Laboratory Stem 339
  Survey Research Feedback Stem 339
  Socio-technical Stem 339
Features of OD 340
Characteristics of OD 340
Principles of OD 341
  Individuals 341
  Groups 342
Organizations as Human Entities 342
OD in Different Types of Organizations 342
OD and Management Development 343
Goals of OD 344
Steps in OD 345
Important Triggers for OD 346
  Knowledge Explosion 346
  Rapid Product Obsolescence 346
  Changing Composition of the Labour Force 346
  Growing Concern over Personal and Social Issues 346
  Increasing Internationalization of Business 347
OD and Organizational Involvement 347
OD and Leadership Development 347

Role of an External Consultant in OD Processes   348
 Ethical Guidelines for OD Professionals   349
Organizational Life Cycle Analysis   350
OD and Business Process Re-engineering (BPR)   352

14. Organizational Diagnosis and Development   358

Introduction   359
Definitions and Concepts   359
Objectives of Organizational Diagnosis   360
The Diagnostic Cycle   360
Different Forms of Organizational Diagnosis   361
Organizational Analysis for Diagnosis   363
Areas of Measurement for Organizational Analysis   363
 Attitudes towards Work   364
 Organizational Commitment   364
 Organizational Climate   365
Organizational Health Survey   366
Questionnaire Development for Organizational Diagnosis   367
Use of Interview as a Diagnostic Tool   368
Task Forces for Organizational Development   370
Assessment Centres Approach for Organizational Diagnosis   371
Observational Methods of Organizational Diagnosis   371
 Secondary Data and Unobtrusive Measures   372

PART 4 Organizational Development Interventions and Strategies   379

15. Approaches and Models   381

Introduction   382
Different Models and Approaches of OD   382
Organizational Life Cycle Model   387
OD Models   387
 Force Field Analysis   388
 Leavitt's Model   388
 Likert's System Analysis   389
 Open Systems Theory   390
 Weisbord's Six-box Model   390
 Congruence Model for Organization Analysis   393
 McKinsey's 7-S Framework   394
 Tichy's Technical-political-cultural (TPC) Framework   394
 High-performance Programming   395
 Harrison's Model of Diagnosing Individual and Group Behaviour   396
 Burke–Litwin Causal Model   397
 ACHIEVE Model   397
 PRIMO-F Business Growth Model   398
 IDEAL Model   399
 ADKAR Model of Individual Change   400
 Bridges' Transition Model   401
 Action Research Model   401
 Dannemiller–Tyson Interactive Strategic Planning   402
 Mobius Model   402
 World Healing Model   403
Organizational Development through Competency Development   404

16. Globalization and Organizational Change and Development 409

Introduction 410
Definitions and Concepts 410
Factors Promoting Globalization 413
Technology Transfer and Globalization 414
Globalization and OD Processes through HR 415
   Aligning HR Strategy with Business Goals 415
Major Institutions Regulating Globalization 418
   World Trade Organization (WTO) 418
   International Monetary Fund (IMF) 419
   World Bank 420
   United Nations (UN) 420
   Organization for Economic Cooperation and Development (OECD) 420
   United Nations Conference on Trade and Development (UNCTAD) 420
Globalization Challenges for Managing Organizational Change and Development 421
   Managing HR 421
   Managing Diversity 421
   Interdependence 422
   Managing Ambiguity 422
Organizational Preparedness to Cope with the Challenges of Globalization 422
Review of Organizational Purpose and Values 423
Core Processes and Decentralized Authority 424
Leadership 425
Globalization and Organizational Transformation 426
   Strategic Alignment 427

17. Knowledge Management and Change 433

Introduction 433
Knowledge Management 435
   Assumptions 436
   Integral Components 437
   Benefits 438
Enablers of Knowledge Management in Organizations 438
Knowledge Management Strategy 441
   Knowledge–Strategy Link 443
Strategic Framework for Mapping Knowledge 444
Gap Analysis 446
Strategic Knowledge Management in Indian Organizations 447
   Indian Companies and Knowledge Management Practices 447
Knowledge Management and Resource-based Competitive Advantage 448
Knowledge Management and Organizational Change 449

18. Change Management Strategies 453

Introduction 454
Definitions and Concepts 455
Principles of Change Management Strategy 459
Philosophies of Strategic Change Management 461
Steps for Strategic Change Management 461
Successful Change Management Strategies 462
Strategic Organizational Change in the Institutional Framework 463
Selection of Organizational Change Strategy 464

PART 5 Contemporary Issues in Organizational Development   469

19. Organizational Development and Diversity Management   471

Introduction   472
Definitions and Concepts   472
   Gender Diversity and Modern Organizations   473
Diversity Management   473
   Contextual Issues of Diversity Management   474
Strategic Approach to Cultural Diversity Management   474
Tools for Cultural Diversity Management   476
   Productivity, Innovation, and Talent Management   476
Aspects of Diversity Management   477
   General Diversity Management   477
Different Approaches to Diversity   478
   Business Performance and Diversity   479
   Diversity as a Business Imperative   479
Cross-cultural Diversity Issues and Globalization   480
   Cross-cultural Practices in the US and India   480
Diversity and Propensities of Multinational Organizations   481
Challenges of Workforce Diversity   483
Effective Management of Workplace Diversity   483
Future Corporate Challenges for Diversity   484

20. Organizational Transformation through Teamwork   489

Introduction   490
Team Building Exercises   491
Objectives of T-group   491
Benefits of T-group Training   492
Role Analysis   493
Nature, Purpose, and Types of Teams   494
   Types of Teams   494
   Team Management Wheel—A Model for Teamwork   495
   Productive Team for Organizational Change and Development   496
Measurement of Team Effectiveness   497
   Team-building Quiz   498
   Belbin's Team Role Self-perception Inventory   498
Organizational Transition through Teamwork   501
Cross-cultural Teamwork   502

21. Organizational Change and Development Research   508

Introduction   509
Change Management Research   510
   Deriving Causal Connections   510
   Process Support through Research   511
   Implementation Help through Research   511
Different Approaches to Organizational Change Research   512
Literature Review for Organizational Change Research   512
Model Building in Organizational Change Research   513
Common Change Management Research Tools   514
   Observation as Tool   514
   Online Questionnaire   514
   Action Research   515
Standard Research Tools for Organizational Change and Development   515

Myers-Briggs Type Indicator (MBTI) Assessment 515
Strength Deployment Inventory (SDI) 515
Klein Group Instrument (KGI) 515
Pearson-Marr Archetype Indicator (PMAI) 516
Leadership Spectrum Profile (LSP) 516
FIRO-B (Fundamental Interpersonal Relations Orientation-behaviour) Assessment 516
Thomas–Kilmann Conflict Mode Instrument (TKI) 516
Work Environment Scales (WES) 516
Role of Organizational Change and Development Research 517
Understanding Organizational Change Research Tools and Techniques 518
Quantitative Paradigm 518
Qualitative Paradigm 519
Validity and Reliability 521
Data Types and Preparation for Analysis 522
Scaling Techniques 522
Other Types of Scale 525
Processing and Coding of Data 528

Making Use of Collected Data 528
Measurers of Central Tendency 528
Three Measures of Variability 529
Two Measures of Relationship 531
Four Measures of Relative Position 531
Inferential Statistics 532
Framing of Hypotheses 533
Power and Statistical Errors 535
Simple Analysis of Variance 537
Multiple Comparison of Variances 538
Analysis of Covariance 538
Research Discussion 538
Conclusion and Recommendations 539
Qualitative Research Considerations 539
Focus Group 539
Interview Technique 540
Other Types of Interview 541
Understanding Personality 544
Determinants of Personality 544
Individual Behaviour and Performance 545
Thinking and Decision-making Process 545
Measurement of Personality Traits 546

Index 551

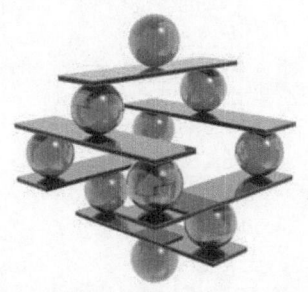

PART 1

Understanding Organizational Processes and Change

- **Understanding Organizational Systems, Structure, and Design**
- **Introduction to Organizational Change**
- **Organizational Change Process**
- **Organizational Effectiveness and Excellence**

1 Understanding Organizational Systems, Structure, and Design

Learning Objectives

After reading this chapter, you will be able to understand
- the definitions and principles of an organization
- systems view of an organization
- organizational structure and its components
- the various principles of the systems theory
- the open systems approach to an organization
- the viable systems approach to an organization
- socio-technical systems thinking
- the business process approach to an organization
- organizational design and the critical success factors
- what business process re-engineering is

Redesign while You Change Your Product Line

Sanjoy Electricals is a traditional pager service organization in Mumbai, with huge corporate accounts. The company grew at a rate of 50 per cent per annum until the early 1980s. However, it suffered a serious setback with the advent of Internet and mobile services. It required a reduction in manpower and total organizational restructuring. The company then invested in new product development, such as corporation information handling and back-office support, to educational institutions and universities (student's information handling, sending fees reminders, finalizing assignment submission dates, etc.). It redesigned the organization with no reporting relationships, empowering the accounts managers for each client to run their show as strategic business units. This helped it to regenerate and survive in a competitive market.

INTRODUCTION

In simple terms, an organization is made of a group of people with specific goals and objectives. An organization is also defined as the relation among components of a system. Organizational structure denotes these components and relations that bind people working in an organization. The three pillars of an organization are the people, the organization itself (considered as a separate entity), and technology. The people-related issues encompass education, training, and attitudes. The organizational issues cover strategy, policy, culture, and structural aspects. And technology involves hardware, software, telecommunications, and information systems. There are three different levels of organizational structure—strategic, tactical, and operational. The strategic level represents the decision-making level, that is, the corporate or the top level of an organization. The tactical or business level is the middle management level, where strategic decisions are transformed into tactics to achieve the strategic intents. The operational level represents the actual implementation, where first level employees and workers execute the tactics adopting the action plans (see Fig. 1.1).

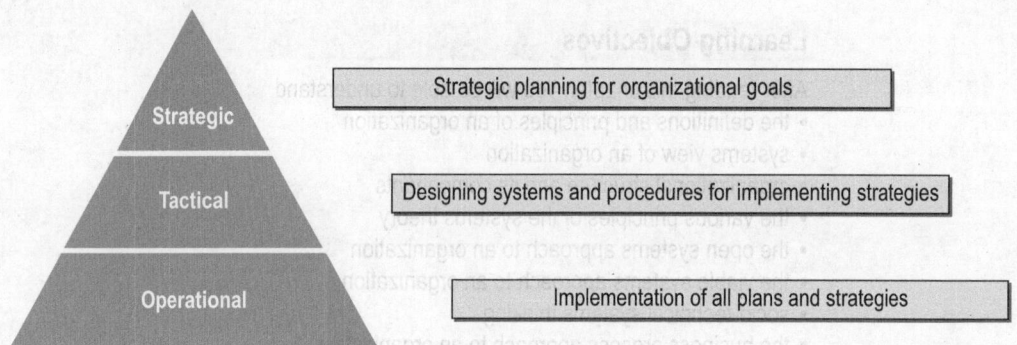

FIG. 1.1   Three organizational levels

To optimize the available resources in the organization in accordance with the plans, managers have to design and pattern work effectively. In the process, they create appropriate conditions for members of the organization to work together in order to achieve the intended goals and objectives. Thus, the function of organizing can be best described as pulling together the resources and the people to act in cooperation in order to accomplish the task. While the planning function deals with what needs to be done, the organizing function focuses on how this is to be achieved by forming proper action groups. Therefore, like planning, organizing too is another important function of management. Behavioural scientists and sociologists view organization as comprising human relationships in group activity. In an operational sense, however, organization can be considered as consisting of division of work among people and coordination of their activities towards some common objectives. Box 1.1 highlights the role of structures in fulfilling organizational activities.

> **BOX 1.1   The role of structure in organizations**
>
> Organizational structure helps to determine the authority relationships among the members of the organization, and thus influences the behaviour of individuals, groups, and divisions within the organization. Among others, the structure of an organization affects the division of tasks, communication systems, decision-making patterns, and finally, the way people relate to each other.

Global competition requires many organizations to redefine their structure and even to relocate in order to take advantage of state-of-the-art technology and communication support. With reduced trade barriers under the World Trade Organization (WTO) regime, presence in the global market is now the first priority for many organizations. Proximity to markets, new dimensions of customer support, and economy of scale in operations has led many organizations to redefine their structures. Even global majors such as IBM, Ford, Dupont, Siemens, etc. are spreading their organizational structures internationally. Global competition has also accentuated organizational turbulence, which always prompts organizations to revisit their structure and people relationships. Use of e-commerce, knowledge and information, workplace diversity, and ethical issues are other factors that prompt organizations to reform and restructure established process and systems in order to remain up to date.

DEFINITIONS AND PRINCIPLES OF AN ORGANIZATION

Robbins and Coulter (2002) defined organizing as 'determining what tasks are to be done, who is to do them, how the tasks are to be grouped, who reports to whom, and where decisions are to be made.' Allen (1958), on the other hand, defined organizing as 'the process of identifying and grouping the work to be performed, defining and delegating responsibility and authority, and establishing relationships for the purpose of enabling people to work most effectively together in accomplishing objectives.' According to Brown (1945), organizing is 'the part each member of an enterprise is expected to perform and the relations between such members, to the end that their concerted endeavour shall be most effective for the purpose of the enterprise.' Koontz (1961) considered organizing as 'the establishment of authority relationships with provision for coordination between them, both vertically and horizontally in the enterprise structure.' Organization is essentially a formal structure of people, which is set up to achieve some defined goals. Thus, a business or manufacturing unit may be termed a business or a manufacturing organization.

The key features of an organization can be described as follows:

1. It is a group of people who are organized to achieve a common purpose.
2. It is an entity, a unit, or an establishment, which utilizes resources to achieve some common purpose.
3. It shows a structure of relationships among members of an enterprise.
4. It is a process that enables people working in an enterprise to relate to tasks and facilities, and helps them achieve intended goals.

It is evident from the definitions that different theorists have used the term 'organizing' in different ways. Yet, according to Young (1975), the father of the theory of process, the term organizing can also be used as follows:

1. It is a grouping of activities.

2. It establishes authority and responsibility.
3. It describes working relationships.

Organization, Organizing, and Organizational Structure

Defining the various terms related to organization, namely organization, organizing, and organizational structure, is important. The term 'organization' is used to refer to a social group, which is deliberately created and maintained in order to achieve some intended goals. More specifically, it is defined as a formal social group. It can also be described as a process of determining activities that are required to achieve intended goals, by creating various roles, and ensuring effective operation of the total system. Organizing, on the other hand, is defined as a management process which corroborates with our earlier definition of organization as a process of identifying, classifying, grouping, and assigning various activities among members of an organization with adequately defined authority relationships to achieve set objectives. Organizational structure, however, is the outcome of the organizing process. It is a framework that defines authority and outlines the relationships which govern the activities of the people working in the organization. In fact, all these principles have emerged from the numerous definitions of organization proffered by various organizational thinkers. Box 1.2 highlights the key constituents of an organization.

> **BOX 1.2 Three pillars of an organization**
>
> People, the organization itself, and technology are the three pillars of an organization. Issues concerning people encompass education, training, and attitudes. Organizational issues relate to strategy, policy, culture, and structure, while those about technology pertain to the use of technology, communication, and information systems.

SYSTEMS VIEW OF AN ORGANIZATION

A system is a collection of parts (or sub-systems), which are integrated to accomplish some goals and objectives. Systems have inputs, processes, outputs, and outcomes, with continuous feedback among these. If one part of the system is removed, the nature of the system will change. Systems range from being very simple to very complex. Social systems also comprise numerous sub-systems, which are arranged in hierarchies and integrated to accomplish the overall goal of the system. Each sub-system, in turn, will have its own boundaries and can have its own set of inputs, processes, outputs, and outcomes.

An organization is viewed as a system or a unit, consisting of the arrangement of activities to achieve its objectives. Such arrangement requires a systems approach as it involves a study of all the management or organizational activities, rather than a single subset. That is why it is said that a systems view of any organization considers the organization in its totality.

The systems theory also provides new perspectives for managers to interpret patterns and events in their organizations, and understand the benefits of integration by focusing out of their narrow work domain. It enables them to recognize various parts of the organization and their interrelationships, and also understand how coordination takes place among different departments so that they can focus on keeping the organization as a whole in their mindset. Figure 1.2 reflects the various components to help understand this better.

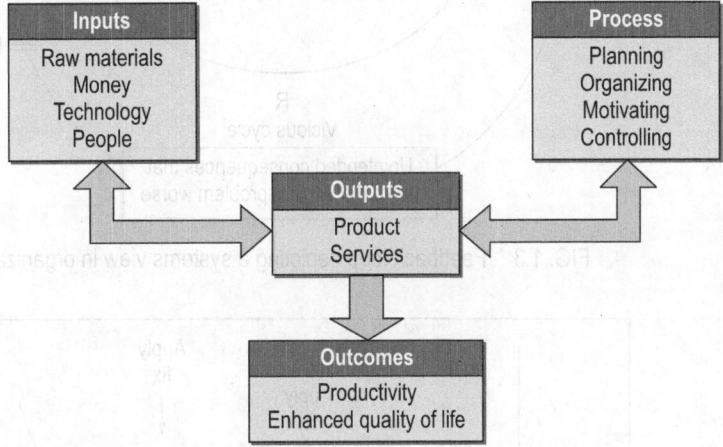

FIG. 1.2   Systems view of organizational processes

With a systems view, managers can also diagnose problems considering larger patterns of interactions in the organization, such as structure, which can provoke behaviours. To illustrate this better, let us take any organization with a number of strategic business units (SBU) based on product line or product mix. Theoretically, one SBU should not compete with another. However, managers may sense the culture of competition between SBUs and also among individuals. Without a systems view, managers may diagnose this problem by attributing commonality of product and nature of service. With a systems view, they can broaden their canvas of thoughts to issues such as probable incentive payment systems (maximum weightage on individual target achievement, rather than group and organizational target achievement), or organizational resource crunch (as SBUs are supposed to share the common resource facilities of the organization, etc.).

Feedback Loop

A generic feedback loop diagram to illustrate how a systems view of the organization helps to manage change in the organization is presented in Fig. 1.3.

In this loop we have a symptom connecting process, which balances the system to correct a problem and return it to stability. The vicious cycle on the outer side creates a reverse impact unless problems in the organizational systems and structures are fixed. Again, this cannot be done once and for all, as problems may recur repeatedly. Problem fixing is necessary each time a problem occurs, as illustrated in Fig. 1.4.

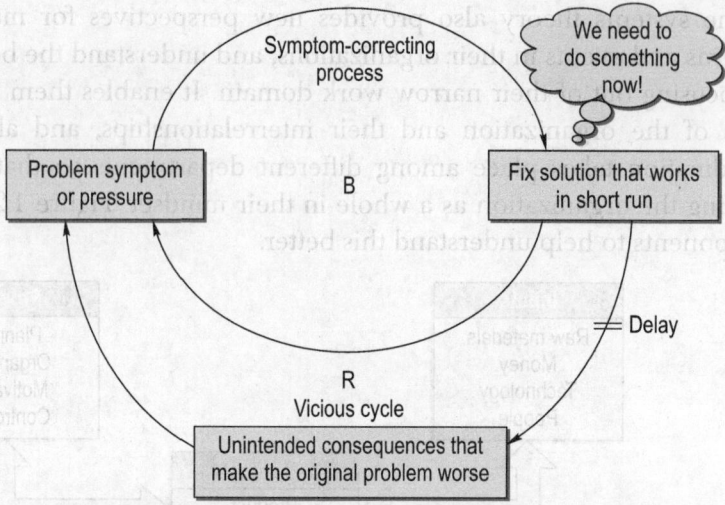

FIG. 1.3   Feedback loop depicting a systems view in organizations

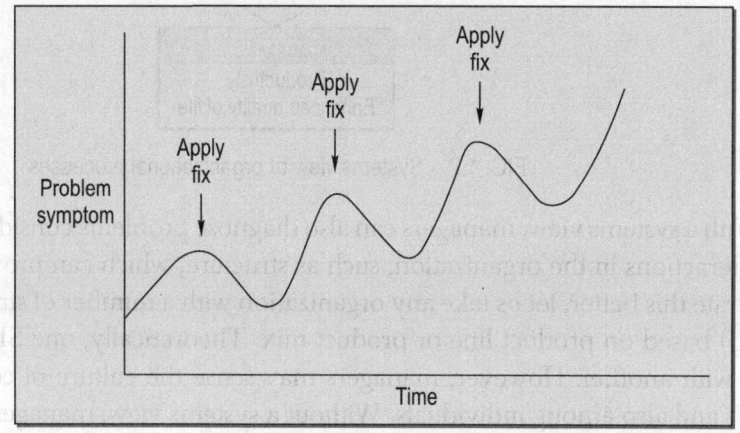

FIG. 1.4   Recurrence and fixing of organizational problems
Source: http://www.pegasuscom.com/course_preview, accessed on 20 July 2009.

Thus, every organization effectively functions through an integrated interlocking network of sub-systems and possesses the following attributes:

1. The system is goal-oriented.
2. The whole is more than the sum of all parts in a system.
3. A system is engaged in processing or transformation of inputs into output.
4. Various components of a system are interrelated and interdependent. They interact with each other.
5. A system acts upon its environment and is also acted upon by the environment.

The organization is considered to be a system, as it draws inputs from the environment along with other resources such as men, materials, machines, and knowledge processes, and then obtains the output, that is, the end product or service. Finally, through feedback, it tries to further adjust to the environmental requirements.

A systems approach is primarily followed in managing an organization because of the following reasons:

1. It emphasizes the dynamic character of business, equating it with a living organism.
2. It focuses on the interrelationship between business and the environment.
3. It stresses on the changing environment and accordingly makes an adjustment by managing the change.
4. It provides information inputs for decision-making and managerial control.
5. It guides the formulation of business objectives which are sustainable, keeping pace with the environment.
6. It subsumes the organization as a whole, considering each unit or department as part of the sub-system that are interrelated and interdependent.
7. It frames an integrated structure, incorporating each sub-system as part of the total system.

The concept of systems in organizations primarily emerged due to the interconnectedness of occurrences, which could be external or internal to the organization. With a systems approach, organizations can manage the process of transformation of inputs to outputs. Although this approach has many manifestations, we are primarily concerned here with the organizational structure, which improves when the organization is seen from a systems viewpoint. Exhibit 1.1 depicts the organizational structure system at GE.

EXHIBIT 1.1 Structure at GE worldwide

General Electric (GE) simplifies organizational structure into four segments.

- GE Technology Infrastructure—Led by Vice-Chairman John Rice, this segment includes healthcare, aviation, transportation, and enterprise solutions. These businesses have opportunities to leverage technology, software, and engineering.
- GE Energy Infrastructure—Led by Vice-Chairman John Krenicki, this segment includes energy, oil and gas, and water. These technologies work together with large customers, particularly in emerging markets.
- GE Capital—Led by Vice-Chairman Mike Neal, this segment aggregates all the financial service businesses, including commercial finance, GE Money, industry verticals (GECAS, energy financial services), and corporate treasury. This organization will improve GE Capital's opportunities to allocate capital, grow globally, and reduce cost.
- NBC Universal—Led by Jeff Zucker, this segment is unchanged and will continue to focus on its strategic evolution through globalization and diversification.

GE operates as a technology, media, and financial services company worldwide.

ORGANIZATIONAL STRUCTURE AND SYSTEMS

The structure of an organization illustrates its form, and is evident from the way various divisions, departments, functions, and people are linked together and interact. Traditionally, an organizational structure shows vertical operational responsibilities with horizontal linkages, and is represented by an organization chart. The structure of an organization is usually proportional to its size and geographic dispersion. Vertical representation of an organizational structure is synonymous to Max Weber's theory of bureaucracy (1946). However today, in a complex business environment, we find more modern forms of organizational structure, such as organic, networked, matrix, and even virtual organizations. The changing business environment not only emphasizes the change in reporting relationships and corresponding changes in the structure of an organization, but also necessitates periodic organizational restructuring, manpower downsizing, and job compositional shift, making reporting to the boss redundant. Thus, organizational structure refers to a pattern or system of grouping people and jobs in an organization. Although the terms organizational structure and organizational design are used interchangeably, the latter is much wider in scope and experience as a set of managerial decisions and structural elements to effect change in the organizational structure.

Organizational structures and systems can also be understood in terms of Greenwood and Hinings' (1993) design archetypes or holistic patterns. They have defined pattern as a function of ideas, beliefs, and values, while design archetype is described as a set of structures and systems. In the process of change, organizations follow certain change tracks and every organization moves through these tracks. Each track indicates a certain degree of a given archetype, say, some levels of strategic orientation, or certain characteristics. Tracks are therefore combinations of cognitions and behaviours. Further, Greenwood and Hinings (1993) mentioned that organizations have 'biographies', which determine the way they respond to change. Such biographies reflect the identities and strategic orientations of the organization. This observation corroborates with Miles and Snow's (1978) typology of strategic orientations as prospectors and defenders. Prospector type organizations are characterized as being dynamic with broad product lines and they always tend to innovate and explore new market opportunities. Structurally, these organizations are organic, have low levels of formalization and specialization, and high levels of decentralization. Thus, prospectors are responsive to change and the change processes in such organizations are relatively easy. Defender type organizations, however, are not dynamic and focus on achieving efficiency in the existing nature of jobs. They believe in stereotyping, and structurally they are mechanistic, formalized, and centralized. Hence, they have problems when they move for change.

Hage and Aiken (1967) identified two important features of organization structure, namely formalization and centralization. The process of formalization helps to document rules and procedures related to jobs, and enables the organization to rigidly adhere to the norms. However, this can be expressed differently, that is, to what extent are employees supervised to ensure that they do not divert from the company's rules and regulations (Hage and Aiken 1967). Centralization deals with the amount of power distributed among employees at various positions. This variable is measured in terms of hierarchy of authority and participation in decision-making. According to Hage and Aiken (1967), the former examines whether or not employees are reliant upon their supervisors for decision-making, while the latter identifies the level of employees' involvement in decisions on resource allocation and policy formation.

Components of Organizational Structure

According to Mintzberg (1981), 'organizational structure is the sum total of the ways in which it divides its labour into distinct tasks and then achieves coordination among them.' Mintzberg believed that organizational structure is a configuration of systems and relationships, and suggested six components as illustrated in Fig. 1.5.

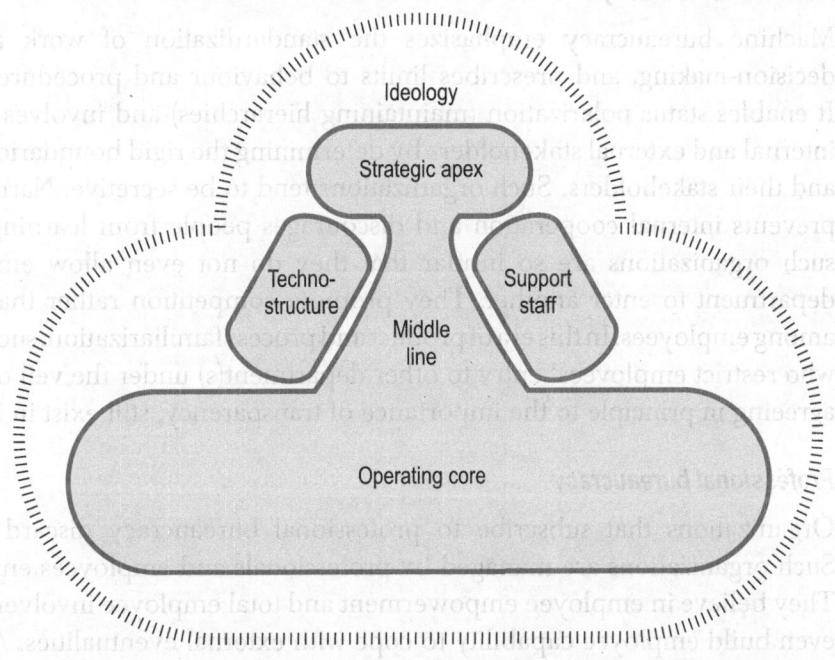

FIG. 1.5 Mintzberg's typology of organizational configurations

Source: http://www.12manage.com/methods_mintzberg_configurations.html, accessed on 20 July 2009.

People operating in the core part of the organization are involved in the production of goods and services. The strategic apex of the organization is involved with control. Middle line managers align the strategic apex with the operating core. People at the techno-structure core design, plan, change, or train the operating core. The support staff provides support to the operating core. In short, ideology includes the traditions and beliefs that make one organization distinct from another.

TYPES OF ORGANIZATIONAL STRUCTURE

Organizational structure outlines the authority relationships among members of an organization, and thus influences (and in turn is influenced by) the behaviour of individuals, groups, and divisions within the organization. Among others, the structure of an organization affects the division of tasks, communication systems, decision-making patterns, and the way people relate to each other. Organizational structures may be standardized or open. Having reviewed various components of organizational structure, Mintzberg classified these into five different types. These are (i) machine bureaucracy (standardized structure), (ii) professional bureaucracy, (iii) adhocracy or innovative forms, (iv) simple or entrepreneurial forms, and (v) divisional forms. Each form indicates a different pattern of behaviour of the organization.

Machine bureaucracy

Machine bureaucracy emphasizes the standardization of work and centralized decision-making, and prescribes limits to behaviour and procedures for members. It enables status polarization (maintaining hierarchies) and involves control of both internal and external stakeholders by determining the rigid boundaries between them and their stakeholders. Such organizations tend to be secretive. Narrow-mindedness prevents internal cooperation and discourages people from learning. Unthinkably, such organizations are so insular that they do not even allow employees of one department to enter another. They promote competition rather than collaboration among employees. In this era of product and process familiarization, such organizations, who restrict employees' entry to other department(s) under the veil of secrecy, while agreeing in principle to the importance of transparency, still exist in India.

Professional bureaucracy

Organizations that subscribe to professional bureaucracy discard formalizations. Such organizations are managed by professionals and employees enjoy less control. They believe in employee empowerment and total employee involvement (TEI), and even build employee capability to cope with external eventualities. A free and open culture promotes a learning environment; hence, such organizations can also practise knowledge management, competency development, and truly transform people into good performers.

Adhocracy

The third form of organizational structure is the adhocracy or innovative structure. Such organizations emphasize development of a distinctive corporate culture.

Characteristically, they decentralize their decision-making process and promote open communication, discussion, negotiation, and interaction among people and divisions. According to Mintzberg, such organizations demonstrate alliance-building behaviour.

Entrepreneurial form

The entrepreneurial form of organizational structure is simple, since a single person (usually the entrepreneur himself/herself) directs the activities of the firm. The major advantage of this form of organizational structure is that it can quickly build trust and change existing norms when they are found to be incompatible. However, when relationships are not built on trust, such organizations may demonstrate a great amount of instability.

Divisional form

The fifth and final type of organizational structure is the divisional form, which focuses on autonomous divisions. However, this may not always imply decentralization of decision-making. Often, it sparks intra-unit fighting and generates a 'cowboy mentality'.

Adhocracy and Bureaucracy: The Two Ends of a Continuum

To understand adhocracy, let us first understand its literal meaning. The term 'ad hoc' means 'for purpose' and the suffix 'cracy' means to 'crack down'. The term was used in 1970 by Alvin Toffler and later popularized by Henry Mintzberg. According to Waterman (1990), adhocracy is 'any form of organization that cuts across normal bureaucratic lines to capture opportunities, solve problems, and get results'. An adhocracy form of organization is innovative and capable of solving problems. Some of the characteristics of adhocracy are as follows:

- More organic structure
- Less formalization of behaviour
- Specialization-based formal training
- Encouragement of mutual adjustment
- Low standardization of procedures
- Roles are not clearly defined
- Selective decentralization
- Work organization rests on specialized team; hence, they become the power centre
- Horizontal job specialization
- High cost of communication
- Culture based on democratic and non-bureaucratic work
- Cross-departmental task forces

In adhocracy organizations people across functions have the authority to make decisions and take actions concerning organizational interests, since hierarchical barriers are absent. Box 1.3 discusses the two ends of a continuum—bureaucracy versus adhocracy.

> **BOX 1.3 Bureaucracy vs adhocracy**
>
> The structure of any organization facilitates achievement of organizational goals and objectives. Hence, decisions on the type of organizational structure are very important. We have already learnt that the most common type is bureaucracy. However, the bureaucratic model in itself is not the organizational structure; it can only provide hypothetical guidelines to create a business design that is a blueprint and descriptive in nature. Thus, bureaucracy per se is not the final product. Adhocracy, on the other hand, is a structural system that does not consider traditional ways of bureaucracy, that is, formal rules and regulations. It is flexible and quickly adapts to the dynamic environmental changes.

Each structural system has its advantages and disadvantages, and deals with each situation differently. Bureaucracy is mechanical. It approaches problems systematically through predetermined guidelines. Adhocracy, on the other hand, challenges problems with a more flexible approach, to ultimately achieve the final goals. Organizations with an adhocracy structure can respond to changes quickly, while bureaucratic organizations need more time since they are more rigid on procedural norms. Again, in an adhocracy there may be more conflict and group rivalry, while in a bureaucracy such occurrences are fewer, as interpersonal relationships are more formal and entire systems are regimented. Therefore, one cannot say that one system is better than the other; it depends on the nature and type of the activities in an organization.

Based on Weber's theory of bureaucracy, Johari and Yahya (2009) provided distinct features of formal organizations wherein tasks are distributed among various positions to enhance specialization among the staff. This encourages an effective hiring process, which is done by matching job requirements to candidates' qualifications. Another aspect discussed in this theory is related to the hierarchy of authority which takes on the pyramid shape, whereby each official is responsible for the actions of his/her subordinates, and has clear-cut authority over those under his/her supervision. In other words, authority is clearly circumscribed in such a structure. Therefore, a theoretical framework can be proposed based on the literature reviewed, as shown in Fig. 1.6.

Organizational Effectiveness

Before we define organizational effectiveness, let us first understand the term 'effectiveness'. Effectiveness is the extent to which an activity helps in achieving the long-term goals of an organization. Since effectiveness is measured for specific

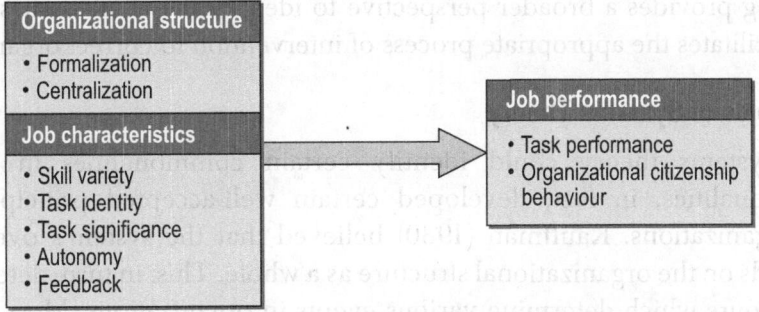

FIG. 1.6 Conceptual framework for predicting the relationship between organizational structure and job characteristics, and individual performance

activities, we can define activity-specific effectiveness as the outcome that supports the broader goals of an organization. Both qualitative and quantitative tools are required to measure the overall effectiveness. Behavioural parameters, such as values, attitudes, skills, and behaviour, are measured using qualitative tools. These are also used to measure the value and volume of output changes, customer satisfaction, changes in profitability, etc.

Khandwalla's studies (1973, 1974) developed a model of organizational structure for effective organizations, establishing the relationship between mass output orientation of manufacturing technology and three organizational variables—vertical integration, decentralization in top level decision-making, and the use of sophisticated controls. Based on subsequent research information, Khandwalla also included the size of the organization as a structural variable.

Cameron (1986) illustrated that most effective organizations can also be characterized as paradoxes, that is, contradictions, simultaneous opposites, incompatibilities, etc. Based on his findings, he tried to explain why confusion and disagreement surround effectiveness.

Organizational effectiveness is the extent to which the organization, as a whole, achieves its goals while optimizing its resources. This depends on the degree of interpersonal skills, positive attitudes, technical competencies, small group activities, etc., which together contribute to the achievement of organizational goals and objectives. Therefore, organizational effectiveness refers to the corporate management systems that produce development results of an organization. Among others, an effective organizational structure helps to achieve organizational effectiveness.

SYSTEMS THEORY, SYSTEMS ANALYSIS, AND SYSTEMS THINKING

The systems theory has unearthed the process of understanding the complex world of systems. In organizations, the systems theory is applied through systems analysis, and is, in turn, achieved through systems thinking, which helps us to study the organization, its patterns, structures, and events. Thus, like a diagnostic tool, systems thinking provides a broader perspective to identify the actual issues and its causes, and facilitates the appropriate process of intervention to correct organizational odds.

Principles of Systems Theory

The systems theory could identify certain commonalities in systems. Such commonalities, in fact, developed certain well-accepted principles of systems for organizations. Kauffman (1980) believed that the system's overall behaviour depends on the organizational structure as a whole. This, in turn, determines various behaviours which determine various events in organizations. Most managers only see and respond to events, which is more a reactionary rather than proactive approach. Breaking organizational systems only by responding to events becomes more of an effort, such as addressing organizational problems as and when they arise. Such organizations characteristically adopt incremental strategies (short-term) to fix some events.

Ackoff and Emery (1972) focused on the issues of linkage between systems thinking and human behaviour. Levin (2006) analysed the organization as an open and productive system that interacts with its environment, draws inputs, and converts them back into outputs for the environment. Thus, to analyse the organization as a system, it is necessary to relate it to its environment. Organizational systems have their own sub-systems, that is, economic, technological, socio-cultural, and politico-legal. These are explained in Fig. 1.7.

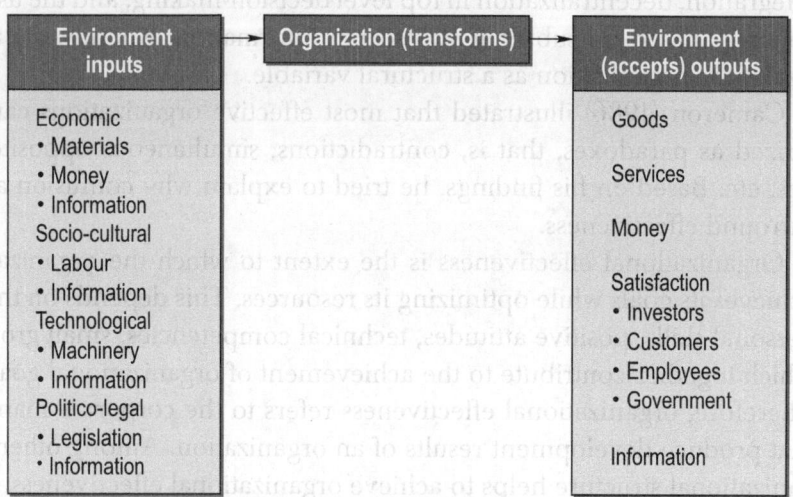

FIG. 1.7 The organizational system and sub-systems

Based on this, the systems principles can be listed as follows:
1. Organizational systems follow patterns of events in a cycle.
2. Each pattern of events indicates some specific phases and the behaviour of the organizational changes at each phase.

3. Systems interpret patterns and events in their organizations.
4. Systems seek balance with the organizational environments.
5. When systems do not interact with their environment, they become limited.
6. A circular relationship exists between the overall system and its parts.

OPEN SYSTEMS APPROACH TO AN ORGANIZATION

Traditionally, an organization is viewed as a closed system that considers everything as deterministic. Hence, depending on its preferences, an organization must outline its structure. In today's changing world, an open systems approach to an organization is considered more relevant and is characterized by importation of energy, throughput, output, cycles of events, negative entropy, information input, steady or dynamic homeostasis, differentiation, integration and coordination, and equifinality (Fig. 1.8). Such characteristics actually emerged from the consideration of the organization as a living system.

According to Boone and Kurtz (1992), in an open systems organization, a cycle of events is a process by which it receives inputs from the environment and transforms them to generate output. Negative entropy represents the ability of the organization to autonomously repair itself, and survive and grow by importing resources from its environment, and transforming them to outputs. Organizations maintain equilibrium over a period of time through steady or dynamic homeostasis, and develop structures and specialized functions through differentiation. The equifinality principle of open systems organization enables them to achieve their objectives through several different courses of action.

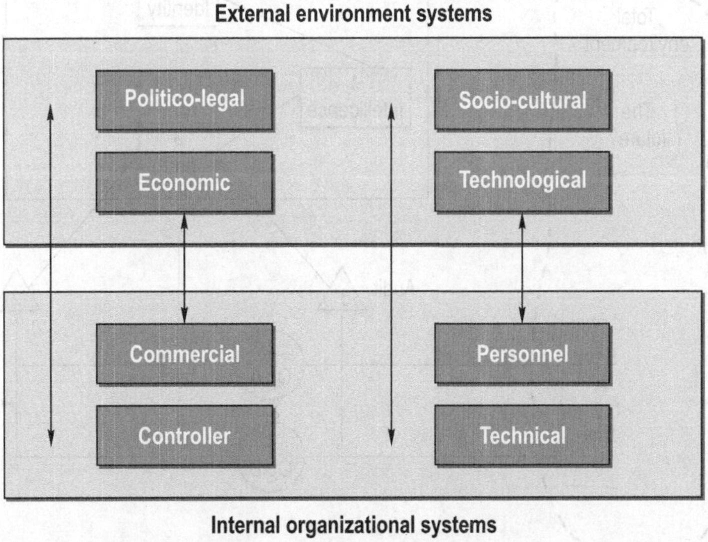

External environment systems

| Politico-legal | Socio-cultural |
| Economic | Technological |

Internal organizational systems

| Commercial | Personnel |
| Controller | Technical |

FIG. 1.8 A typical open systems model of organization

ORGANIZATIONAL CYBERNETICS, VIABLE SYSTEMS MODEL, AND ORGANIZATIONAL SYSTEMS

Organizational cybernetics has emerged as a management systems approach. It adopts cybernetic notions for organizational and social management by focusing on the viable system model (VSM) postulated by Beer (1979) (Fig. 1.9). VSM is an important instrument in the operation of organizational cybernetics. According to Beer, cybernetics is 'the science of effective organization.' A system is said to be viable when it is able to adapt effectively to environmental changes even when such changes are unforeseen. VSM thus consists of operation (O) with embedded management (M) and environment (E). It is used in organizations to diagnose different elements in designing information systems, the management structure, and even organizational vision, mission, and structure.

Thus, VSM is an organizational framework of various functions and relationships, and creates conditions through which organizations can diagnose the major dysfunctions and develop necessary intervention strategies.

Based on his study of organic systems, Beer observed that organizational systems can sustain an independent existence despite the operations of the law of requisite variety. This law describes how complexity can operate and overpower a system of management. In cybernetics, the word 'variety' denotes complexity, which is infinite. Instead of dealing with the environmental complexity, management should create appropriate operating processes which can interact with the environment and sustain

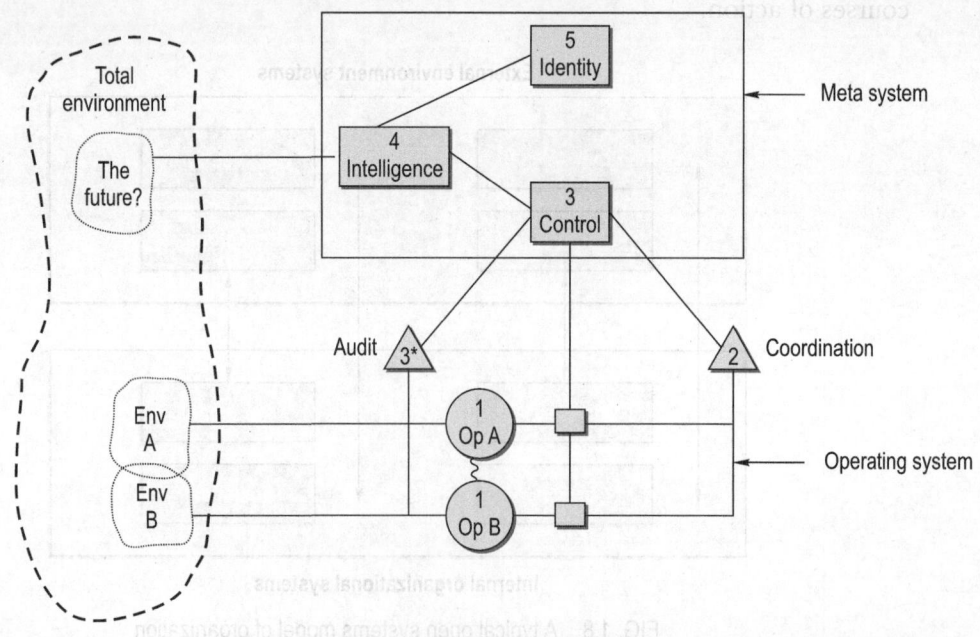

FIG. 1.9 Viable systems model

its independent existence. According to Beer (1972), operations of the law of requisite variety exhibit the following properties:

- Maintenance of identity (every organization must have a purpose and accordingly should organize its means to achieve this)
- Ability to self-repair (an organization should be sufficiently capable to self-repair and sustain)
- Self-awareness (organizations must be aware of themselves, that is, what they are comprised of)
- Self-organizing (organizational structure should be specific to the environment and context)
- Self-balancing (homeostasis)
- Open system (adaptive to extract information from their environment)
- Embody recursivity (exist within other viable systems)

The model comprises two operating systems that primarily interact with the external environment and the five attendant systems, demonstrating specific interrelationships and producing the properties of variability.

As per the model, System 5 represents the identity, that is, the total system purpose and the measures of success. System 5 passes down to System 3, which controls the policies and authority, and also governs the overall system outcomes. It balances the present and the future, external and internal perspectives, and moderates its relationship between System 3 and System 4. A change in System 3 influences System 1 (operational systems, i.e., A, and management function, i.e., B). System 3 and System 1 (A and B both parts) through interactions lead to establish agreements, that is, they are managed by System 2. System 4 examines the external environment and gains intelligence about the totality and the future. Therefore, in VSM, all of these systems operate with a cybernetic intervention at any point in time, and in the process ensure that the organization becomes a self-controlling system.

Open Systems Concepts and Orchestra Organization

The term 'orchestra organization' is used in an open systems perspective and is a complex set of interdependent sub-systems. An open systems organization takes input from the environment, processes it, and produces output. In an open system, efficient interaction with the environment and various sub-systems determines the success of an organization. An efficient organization considers relationships and reciprocal influences between itself and its environment, and even considers extending its sphere beyond the formal boundary through an efficient boundary spanning sub-system. These play the buffering role to account for external organizational uncertainty. In a typical orchestra organization, processes or throughput are specialized functions which are distinct and interdependent. Even the coordinating function is considered as throughput, as it helps to achieve the output. The job of coordination in an orchestra organization may be both formal and informal. Depending on its structure and the use of physical space, an orchestra organization may emphasize more on informal coordination. However, this depends on how it organizes its human resources.

Chaos Theory

The chaos theory has emerged from the view that there is a system even in chaos. It studies the complexity of the world to identify principles to understand organizations. It deals with the structure of turbulence, that is, a study of unpredictable complex systems simulating the weather pattern. Edward Lorenz of MIT (Hilborn 2004), a meteorologist, proposed a visual presentation to explain the theory of chaos. This is shown in Fig. 1.10.

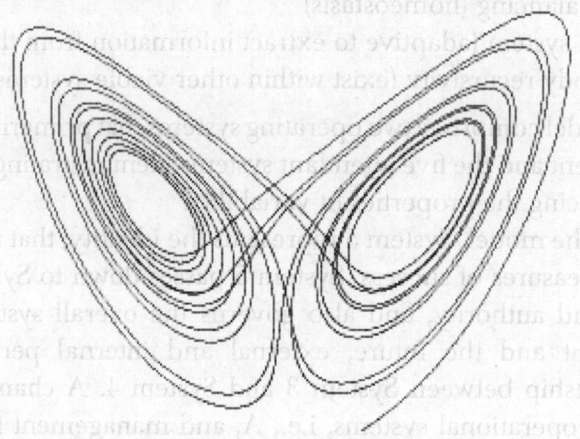

FIG. 1.10 Chaos model

The picture resembles a butterfly and is hence also known as the 'butterfly effect'. This refers to the discovery that in a chaotic system it is theoretically possible that a slight change would make no difference whatsoever; but when at a certain stage, the system is unpredictable, the future may unfold quite differently depending on whatever little difference has occurred.

The chaos theory has emerged from the Gestalt theory, which suggests that the whole is greater than the sum of its parts. The application of the chaos theory to management depicts organizations as complex and unpredictable because of numerous relations among the constituents of a system.

The following are the characteristics of a chaotic system:

Sensitive to initial conditions At the outset, a complex system reacts to different variables in unpredictable ways. Even starting with the same, exact, or slightly different variables in a model, the results or outcomes would be different if the system is complex.

Same context may not repeatedly hold good In a complex system, the same context never occurs twice. Hence, in organizations, a team with essentially identical personnel and similar characteristics will never perform exactly the same, which means that a system is never identical. A strategy or decision will also never be repeated even in the same context.

Set of values and strange attractors   In the chaos theory, the same set of values migrate over a time in a given system. This means that attractors (set of values) in the chaos theory act as the influence of gravity. Attractors can be a single fixed point, a collection of points, a complex orbit, or an infinite number of points. In organizations, attractors, that is, the set of values, cause a behaviour which alters over time depending upon the social, economical, or other forces that drive the system at a given point of time, and determine how they interact.

Chaos is fractal   Literally speaking, fractal means a curve or surface that is independent of scale. Any segment, if magnified in scale, appears identical to the whole curve. In the management analogy, it is assumed that different levels of organization resemble others like a fractal in the managerial hierarchy. A form of social structures can be examined in relation to characteristics of the whole system at the macro and micro levels.

Theory of bifurcation   Bifurcation is the sudden appearance of qualitatively different solutions to the equations for a non-linear system, as a parameter is varied. In an organization, two different patterns (groups) can emerge to address an issue differently, as complexity increases. This is often recommended as a source of creativity.

Organizations are complex and adaptive systems that have behaviours similar to those found in nature have different stages of stability and chaos. A manager is prompted to take advantage of such complexity rather than controlling it. Theorists in management and social organization now believe that organizations are also non-linear dynamic entities having the same characteristics as any natural phenomenon.

The organization is also often perceived as comprising of formal and shadow systems, and an analogy is made between chaos in natural systems and the social organization. Similarly, the long-term behaviour of the organization is unpredictable, akin to the inability to predict hurricanes far into the future. Scholars, such as Stacey (1993), addressed this issue by stating that managers must learn how to manage the anxiety that accompanies being on the edge of chaos, employing a nearly mystical concept of 'creative destruction'. Stacey ended with optimism, believing that although long-term outcomes are impossible to predict, dealing effectively with change and challenge on a daily basis will ultimately result in success.

Thus, the chaos theory is often used as a way to conceptualize management theory and other social systems. An efficient manager can plan for and expect constant change in the environment. His/her goals become not just a set of results, but a series of contingency scenarios to which he/she can react in the short-term, at some later date in the future. The same principle applies to human societies. Tiny changes in one person's state of mind can, on occasions, lead to major changes in society as a whole. Or, simple acts can lead to unintended consequences.

SOCIO-TECHNICAL SYSTEMS THINKING

Herbst (1974) pioneered the concept of socio-technical systems thinking based on the studies done on coal mining workers in the 1950s, in the UK. The major landmark in the study was recognizing that with small self-regulating work teams, organizations can get better results. According to this theory, the quality and quantity of output in any work organization depends on two distinguishable aspects—the technological system and the social structure of the work system. The social structure of the work system in an organization is partly influenced by the technological systems. Therefore, any organization can optimize its performance through suitable modification of technical and social systems. This concept is also known as 'social ecology of industry'.

Managers often fail to appreciate that several exogenous events are interrelated in a way that leads to irreversible generation in the organization (Emery and Trist, 1965). Following this, we can have four ideal types of organizational environment—placid randomized, placid clustered, disturbed reactive, and turbulent. Survival of an organization depends upon the compatibility between its strategy and the type of environment it confronts.

As per the model pioneered by the Tavistock Institute of London, the technical sub-system consists of devices, tools, and techniques, which transform inputs to outputs to enhance the economic performance of the organization. According to the model, the social system consists of employees, their knowledge, skills, attitudes, values, and needs., Organizations develop the desired structure by integrating technical and social sub-systems. Technical sub-systems, therefore, consist of technology and tasks, and social sub-systems consist of structure and people. A schematic representation of the model based on Bostrom et al. (1977), which suggests development of management information systems, integrating social and technical sub-systems, is presented in Fig. 1.11.

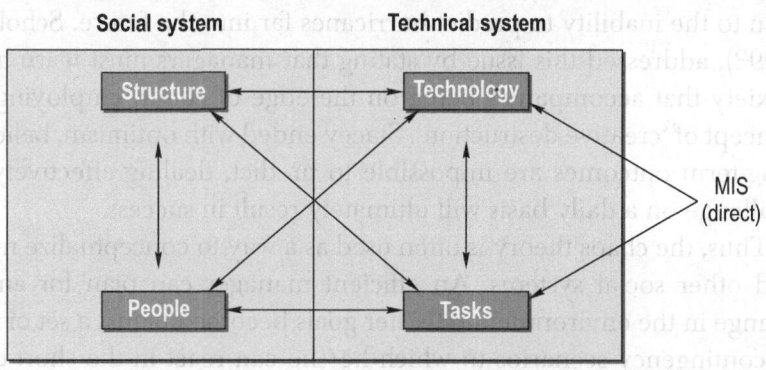

FIG. 1.11 Socio-technical systems

SYSTEMS DYNAMICS

Forrester (1958) pioneered the concept of systems dynamics (SD). This approach involved the use of the concepts and ideas of the control theory and control engineering in management and decision-making. SD is primarily orientated towards identifying (defining), modelling, and simulating a system (e.g., a factory, a city, an economy, or even an entire ecological system) in order to explicate how it will behave under different policy regimes. The SD approach deals with 'dynamic systems', that is, aggregates of physical and abstract entities which are distinguishable from their surrounding environment as purposive wholes, and which exhibit dynamic behaviour. The approach recognizes that certain dynamic systems may behave in a counter-intuitive manner, that is, an unexpected manner, due to the way they are constituted. It seeks to predict their behaviour patterns by trying to model dynamic systems and simulating them on a computer.

BUSINESS PROCESS APPROACH TO AN ORGANIZATION

Tracing history, we find that the 1980 was the era of automation. Computer numerical control (CNC), direct numerical control (DNC), numerical control (NC), flexible manufacturing system (FMS), robots, etc. were introduced in the manufacturing industry. In contrast, the 1990s were about people. Total quality management (TQM) concepts in the 1990s focused on delegation, total employee involvement, ownership, shared values, cross-functional teamwork, self-managed work teams, employee empowerment, etc. Various models of excellence such as the European business excellence model (EFQM), Shingho prize model, people capability maturity model (PCMM), etc. highlighted the role and importance of people, and the process-centred approach to manage people in organizations.

There is really no model of the organizational business process. Business process provides critical support to the key operational processes within manufacturing. In terms of organizational change and development, it is better to relate with human resource management (HRM) processes (where more weights are assigned) than business process as a whole. Hence, the subsequent part of the discussion will deal with the HRM process and its interrelationship with organizational change and development. A brief introduction to business excellence models has also been given to help readers appreciate how a structured business process supports organizational development and growth.

Broadly speaking, in organizations, there is the 'prescriptive model' and the 'normative model'. Here, we will not go into the details of such models but only review the 'Michigan model' pioneered by Fombrun in 1984, the Harvard model pioneered by Beer and others, also in 1984, and some others which are universally acknowledged.

Michigan Model

This model (Fombrun et al. 1984) has two perspectives: (a) the strategic and environmental perspective, and (b) the HR perspective. The first represents the relationship between people and the organizational strategy as well as the political, economic, and cultural forces which affect them. The second perspective provides a simple framework to show what the relationship between selection, appraisal, rewards, and training should be, and the effect on performance.

Harvard Model

This model (Beer et al. 1984) consists of two parts: (a) the HR system and (b) a map of the HRM territory. The HR system represents labour relations and personnel administration perspectives under four HR categories—employee influence, HR flow, rewards, and work systems. In the model, a map of the HRM territory shows how it is closely connected to both the external environment (i.e., stakeholder interests) and the internal organization (i.e., situational factors).

Guest's Model

This model (1987) involves seven policies for achieving the four main HR outcomes. According to Guest, these outcomes will lead to desirable organizational results. Guest's seven categories are broadly the same as those of Harvard. For example, where the Harvard model has HR flow, Guest has manpower flow and recruitment, selection and socialization; where as the former has work systems, the latter calls these organizational and job design. Both models have reward systems. Guest has three additional categories, which are policy formulation and management of change; employee appraisal, training and development; and communication systems.

Warwick Model

This model (Hendry and Pettigrew 1990) of organization consists of the inner and outer contexts, and places which require more emphasis on strategy. It is based on the Harvard model, which has business strategy in situational factors, while the Warwick model has business strategy content. The Harvard model has task-technology in the situational factors part, while the Warwick model has it in the inner context.

A major difficulty has been the confusion over types of models being used; sometimes they are normative or prescriptive, and sometimes descriptive or analytical. For example, the Harvard model is described by Torrington and Hall (1991) as an analytical model rather than normative or prescriptive. At the same time, several other scholars describe it as normative. Actually, the Harvard model is made up of both normative and analytical elements.

Another feature that adds to this confusion is the problem with the classification of various organizational models. Therefore, we find two fundamental gaps in these models:

- Lack of clarity on type of models (i.e., classifications) and their definitions
- Absence of a systems engineering-based attempt to model HRM as a business process

Elements of the Business Process Model

A well-crafted business process extends support to the organization and exists to support all other processes within the organization. Therefore, these processes strengthen the business process. Second, in supporting its customers, business process must ensure that it maximizes its contribution to the overall business objective and strategy. Business process is continuous, in line with Deming's plan—do, check, and act—of the PDCA cycle of continuous planning and improvement. The business process should therefore consist of the following sub-processes which make up the continuous cycle:

1. Plan (re-plan) HRM strategy.
2. Implement HRM strategy.
3. Monitor impact on business results.

Description of Business Process Model

The business process model consists of three sub-processes as illustrated in Fig. 1.12.

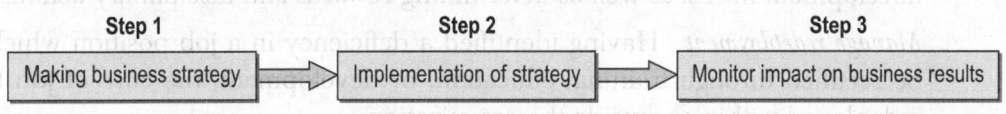

FIG. 1.12 Steps in the business process model

Each of these processes consists of a number of activities.

Step 1: Making business strategy

Make organizational strategy   Use business strategy, and the objectives and requirements of key business processes to formulate an integrated strategy, by setting objectives, establishing current capabilities, negotiating appropriate budgets for realistic implementation of the plan, and setting HR policies.

Set objective activity   Interpret business strategy, and the objectives and requirements of other key business processes to organizational requirements and objectives.

Establish current capability activity   Establish the current HR capability within the business and its key processes to meet the set objectives.

Plan activity Develop a plan, including budgets, which defines courses of action the business is going to adopt to build upon its current capabilities, and develop its HR in line with the stated HR objectives and requirements.

Negotiate budget activity Use the requirement of the plan to negotiate for financial resources which will lead to successful implementation of strategy.

Set HR policies activity Set up types of compensation, staffing methods, appraisal methods, form of training and development, and working conditions for the relevant strategic needs.

Step 2: Implementation of strategy

Implement HR management strategy sub-process Implement the HR strategy by controlling HR planning, monitoring, utilizing, recruiting, assessing, and selecting the right people in order to develop, train, and educate them. This requires managing HR performance through review and appraisal, and will also result in redeployment of HR.

Control HR Make sure that HR is planned, correctly applied, and monitored, in accordance with the objectives and requirements of the organization.

Recruit activity Bring HR positions in line with requirements from internal or external sources. This activity is concerned with upgrading people's capabilities within the business in line with its HR objectives.

Manage HR performance This involves setting targets for individuals, monitoring progress against the targets, and identifying necessary training, education, and development needs, as well as determining rewards and disciplinary actions.

Manage redeployment Having identified a deficiency in a job position which cannot be rectified through training, education, or development, the current job holder is redeployed within or outside the organization.

Negotiate for working condition This activity deals with the requirement of people and capacity of business. It is related to HR policies and plans (people terms and conditions).

Step 3: Monitoring impact

Monitor impact on business result This sub-process monitors the impact of the HRM processes on business performance by monitoring its contribution to the business strategy and objectives, and other key business processes.

Monitor impact on business strategy The impact of the HR strategy on business strategy as well as on business performance is monitored.

Monitor impact on people's satisfaction This activity is concerned with establishing how well the business satisfies its employees.

Monitor impact on process management This involves monitoring the extent to which the HRM strategy and its implementation satisfy the requirements of process management. This helps to formulate strategy and set the direction for the whole business.

Monitor impact on operating process This helps to measure the effectiveness of HRM strategy and its implementation in satisfying the requirements of the operating processes, that is, getting orders, developing products, fulfilling orders, and supporting products.

Monitor impact on support process This determines how well the HRM strategy and its implementation satisfy the requirements of support processes. These include finance and IT, and enable operation of the process functions.

Thus, by analysing the various types of business process models, we can develop a business process approach to organizations, incorporating various aspects of systems engineering principles.

Normative and Descriptive Models

Normative models of business process reflect or establish standard behaviour. These values or norms set expectations for individuals and groups. Normative models are designed to authoritatively impose what should be done in a specific case. Prescriptive research-based models make hypothetical claims that outcomes specified within the model will be achieved if certain preconditions are met. According to some researchers, the advantage of normative/prescriptive models is that first, they are more open to scientific testing, and second, when policies and practices are established in a way that is consistent with the model and integrated with the business strategy, it will lead to desirable outcomes for people and organizations.

Descriptive models describe how organizations try to reflect exactly what has or is happening when it is implemented. Legge (1995) sub-divided descriptive models into two types: (i) descriptive–functional, and (ii) descriptive–behavioural. Descriptive–functional models state 'what is' rather than 'what should be' the function of organizations. Descriptive-behavioural models state more precisely what the actual behaviours of specialists and managers engaged in organizational activities are.

Analytical models of organization refer to the use of logical reasoning about a subject or problem. Tyson (1997) summarized that analytical models of organization should be applicable to both cause and effect in terms of their influence on the relationships between people.

Thus, a normative model of business process describes what the function of the organization should be and what is good for business. The descriptive model describes 'what is' instead of 'what should be'. An analytical model describes the causes and effects of the business process through the use of logical reasoning. Therefore, an analytical model could be either normative or descriptive.

ORGANIZATIONAL DESIGN

The term 'design' is defined as a model of an object to be realized. Likewise, organizational design is a model to depict the relationship among employees and groups, and precedes the creation process, that is, realizing the organizational goals and objectives. Daft and Lewin (1990) defined organizational design as a formal architecture of culture, strategy, and employment relationships. Lewin and Stephens (1994) further considered organizational design as the macro property of organization.

Designing organizations is the process of creating a structure or chart to indicate the action for employee groups to realize some common objectives. From a traditional percept, the organizational design process starts with the division of labour. After this, it develops the mechanism of coordination of the individual along with a group of employees. Modern views on organizational design, however, reflect on the future organization of a group and appropriate design of organization, and then develop some mechanism of coordination between an individual and groups of employees. As appropriate organizational design contributes to effective performance of employees and groups, every company tries to strategically design its organization and derive the advantages of high performance. Globalization, turbulent business environments, increased competition, advanced communication systems, among others, persuade organizations to explore the best and most relevant design. Pettigrew et al. (2003), therefore consider that organizational design has strategic significance. Network organizations, virtual teams and organizations, formal and informal alliances, project-based organizations, etc. are some of the new-age designs.

It is now common for many organizations to shift from the functional organization type to a product-oriented one, focusing on self-managing groups to decrease the throughput time and costs. There are examples of organizations that have shifted from semi-independent clusters to a kind of matrix organization to respond to customization issues. For example, even an automobile manufacturer with tight assembly line-based workstations may be required to tune to the matrix structure for obvious reasons of accommodating customized car designs and manufacturing. TCS, for example, follows a mix of organizational design. Although at the corporate level they follow a functional structure, at the operations level they opt for a matrix design in order to accommodate specific customers' requirements.

In every organizational change process, we may require a new organizational design, as change triggers adopting new strategies which require a new approach to solving problems, and hence there may be a need for a new design. Both Quinn (1980) and Chandler (1962) highlighted the strategic relevance of organizational design. Burns and Stalker (1966) emphasized the need for organistic structures to cope with the turbulence of the environment. Woodward (1965) and Perrow (1967) considered the influence of technology on the organizational structure. Katz and Kahn (1966) however, conceded the impact of the environment on the organizational structure. Likewise, many other authors suggested using specialization, standardization, formalization, and age and size of the organization, as variables for organizational design. Similarly, Khandwalla (1977), Galbraith (1995), and also Burton and Obel (2004), discussed various important aspects of organizational design. Mintzberg's (1979) work on configurations, which explains the important typology of organizations, is considered to be one of the most appropriate for effective organizational design.

Effective organizational design depends on the interrelationships of principles of job specialization, departmentalization, coordination, and line and staff positions. It is defined as a total pattern of structural elements and patterns, which are used to manage the overall organization. Effective organizational design is instrumental in implementing organizational strategies for achievement of organizational goals. Broadly, organizational design rests on two models—the bureaucratic model and the behavioural model—as summarized in the following section.

Bureaucratic Model

The bureaucratic model rests on Max Weber's theory of bureaucracy, which is highlighted in Chapter 3. The basic premise of this theory rests on designing organizations by creating an absolute and clear division of labour, along with a hierarchy of positions in conformity with the principles of the scalar chain, so that the commands run from top to bottom, establishing a set of concise and consistent rules and procedures (for decisional conformity), framing policies and practices, and finally running the organization impersonally.

In the changing business environment, despite its fundamental strength in simplifying the process or organizational design, and operational efficiency and effectiveness, the bureaucratic model is criticized for the following drawbacks:

1. It cannot cope with the changing external environment.
2. Formal rules and procedures often dissuade achievement of organizational goals.
3. It often neglects the human aspects of organization, as it considers people to be an economic rational entity (primarily driven by money).
4. It traditionally considers upper management people as being more knowledgeable than those reporting to them, which may not always be true in today's global organizations.
5. It often creates 'bureaupathology' or a feeling of insecurity among people. It emerges from a typical ritualistic behavioural pattern of managers, particularly those who are in authority. Such 'pathological' behaviour may be counter-productive in achieving organizational effectiveness and growth.

Behavioural Model

The behavioural model of organizational design is an extension of the human relations school of management thought. It duly recognizes the weaknesses of the relational and mechanistic characteristics of the bureaucratic model, and emphasizes the social and psychological implications of organizational life. Socio-technical systems theory and Likert's Systems 4 organization theory are the two known behavioural models used in organizational design.

The socio-technical systems theory approach, pioneered by Trist and Bamforth (Emery 1980) with the Tavistock Institute, London, emphasized the need for balancing the human side of an organization with its technical and mechanical side while designing it. This means that every organization consists of two systems, namely social systems and technical systems. Balancing these two systems using a socio-technical model ultimately leads to effective organizational design. Social systems represent both formal and informal human interactions in organizations. Technical systems represent the tasks involved in producing goods and services. The socio-technical systems theory has been explained earlier in this chapter.

Likert's Systems 4 organization theory deals with eight characteristic processes of organization—leadership, motivation, communication, interaction, decision, goal-setting, control, and performance. According to Likert, all these characteristics ultimately lead to four different design approaches, namely Systems 1, 2, 3, and 4. System 1 is described as 'exploitive–authoritative', that is, an extreme manifestation of bureaucratic organization. In such organizations, managers take all the decisions with no participation from subordinates. System 2 represents the 'benevolent–authoritative' style, which means that managers repose trust in subordinates and allow them an upward communication. System 3 represents a 'consultative style' where managers have complete confidence and trust in subordinates, and even solicit advice from them, but retain the right to decision-making. System 4 represents a 'participative leadership' style, which is the extreme manifestation of behavioural organization.

Table 1.1 shows the two extreme forms (System 1 and System 4) of organizational design using Likert's framework.

ROLE OF CRITICAL SUCCESS FACTORS IN ORGANIZATIONAL DESIGN

Critical success factors (CSF) analysis is a method developed at MIT's Sloan School by John Rockart (1982) to guide businesses towards creating and measuring success. It is a widely used top-down methodology that is especially suitable for designing systems. It is a reductionist method for going from an abstract vision to concrete requirements.

CSF is a key area where satisfactory performance is required for the organization to achieve its goals; a means of identifying the tasks and requirements needed for success. At the lowest level, CSFs become concrete requirements or a means to prioritize requirements. The CSF analysis method starts with vision and mission statements. Hence, it is imperative to develop 5–6 high level goals, a hierarchy of goals, and their success factors.

TABLE 1.1 Likert's framework of organizational design: Extreme forms

	System 1 organization	System 4 organization
Leadership process	No trust and confidence in subordinates. Subordinates distance them from their superiors and can hardly afford to discuss their work-related problems with them.	High confidence and trust in subordinates who are free to discuss their work-related problems with their superiors.
Motivational process	Subordinates suffer from the problem of physical and monetary insecurity, and nurture unfavourable attitude towards the organization.	Subordinates feel motivated for participatory work environment and they nurture favourable attitude towards the organization, and volunteer to achieve goals and objectives.
Communication process	Distorted downward communication. Subordinates view every communication from the superior with suspicion.	Free flow of upward, downward, and lateral communication within the organization. Communication is accurate and easily understandable by all.
Interaction process	Closed and restricted. Subordinates can hardly participate or have any knowledge in departmental goals, methods, and activities.	Open and extensive. Subordinates and superiors can affect departmental goals, methods, and activities.
Decision process	Highly centralized and occurs only at the top.	Occurs at all levels; and hence, decentralized.
Goal-setting process	Located at the top of the organization; hence discourages participation.	Encourage group participation in setting high realistic objective.
Control process	Centralized and emphasizes fixing blame for mistakes.	Dispersed; emphasizes self-control and problem solving.
Performance goals	Low and passively sought by superiors who hardly put in efforts to develop the subordinates in the organizations.	High and actively sought by superiors who commit themselves to developing the subordinates through systematic training.

Source: Adapted from Likert (1967)

It leads to concrete requirements at the lowest level of decomposition (a single, implemental idea). These apart, it identifies the problems being solved and the assumptions being made. Its cross-reference usage helps to identify scenarios and problems with requirements. CSF analysis produces results that express the needs of the enterprise clearly and (hopefully) completely, and allows measuring success and prioritizing goals in a sensible way. When used together with traditional usage scenarios, it ensures that the needs of both the user and the enterprise are met.

The critical success factors (CSF) analysis provides

- objective and definable end results
- clear definition of entities and relationships
- access to source data in required formats
- understanding of data and business context
- create and analyse competency database

Therefore, it is a good idea to ensure that inputs from all the key players are considered when designing an organization. Not only does this help to identify requirements that may have been missed, but it also guarantees some degree of consistency to fit into the organizational model.

Human Resource Information Systems and Its Usage in Organizational Design

Human resource information systems (HRIS) are a range of computerized technology used to store, record, link, analyse, and present data about the human element within the organization. In HRIS, while the external environments are connected through the Internet, Intranet allows organizations to communicate from within, more rapidly and effectively. HRIS thus encompasses both internal and external information processing. Application of HRIS is now possible in all HR functions to reinforce information sharing, as HR information is now considered a strategic input.

Here we will discuss in detail the application of HRIS in human resource development (HRD). HRD represents an integrated approach to the learning of employees, which enhances the capability of an organization to survive and advance, renewing the competency of its people. It is now well established that effective HRD can enhance the competitive success of an organization. Exhibit 1.2 depicts an outline of HR vision at ONGC, a Fortune 500 company in India, and elucidates the role of HRD and the importance of an HRIS.

Hall and Torrington (1991) and Martinsons (1997) made significant contributions in the field of application of HRIS in HRD. A systematic review of the literature reveals that there are four key challenges facing the HRD function.

Challenge 1: Linking HRD with business objectives

This is the greatest challenge for HR professionals today. It involves convincing the top management about the value of HRD, questioning and revaluating the traditional perception of organizational effectiveness, and ensuring its alignment with business objectives. The process of analysing the behaviour or skills that are likely to determine the organization's survival and advancement is critical in this regard, and involves a review of existing skills and competencies, and selecting appropriate learning activities for future action. HRIS can play an important role at each of these stages. Use of Intranet or 'groupware' technology allows the key management team to confer more readily about the characteristics that are seen as necessary to move the organization forward. Newly developed HR databases can provide customized reports about existing employees on any aspect of their characteristics. In knowledge-based systems, HRIS helps to replicate the problem-solving and decision-making approaches of 'experts', that is, about a particular problem or issue. HRIS thus, also creates a knowledge infrastructure that is unique to a particular organization. Training delivery and evaluation can also be facilitated via these

EXHIBIT 1.2 HR vision and mission statements at ONGC

HR vision

'To build and nurture a world class human capital for leadership in energy business.'

HR mission

'To adopt and continuously innovate best-in-class HR practices to support business leaders through engaged, empowered and enthused employees.'

HR objectives

1. Enrich and sustain the culture of integrity, belongingness, teamwork, accountability, and innovation.
2. Attract, nurture, engage, and retain talent for competitive advantage.
3. Enhance employee competencies continuously.
4. Build a joyous workplace.
5. Promote high performance work systems.
6. Upgrade and innovate HR practices, systems, and procedures to global benchmarks.
7. Promote work life balance.
8. Measure and audit HR performance.
9. Promote work life balance. Integrate the employee family into the organisational fabric.
10. Inculcate a sense of corporate social responsibility among employees.

Measuring HR performance

HR parameters have been incorporated in the MoU by ONGC since 1994–1995, to systematically and scientifically evaluate effectiveness of HR systems, which enables and facilitates time-bound initiatives.

HR parameters of MoU for 2009–2010

- Mentoring and coaching
- HR audit
- Engagement survey
- Continuous professional education credit course for finance executives of ONGC

A motivated team

HR policies at ONGC revolve around the basic tenet of creating a highly motivated, vibrant, and self-driven team. The company cares for each and every employee and has in-built systems to recognize and reward them periodically. Motivation plays an important role in HR development. In order to keep its employees motivated, the company has incorporated schemes such as *Reward and Recognition Scheme, Grievance Handling Scheme, and Suggestion Scheme.*

Incentive schemes to enhance productivity

- Productivity honorarium scheme
- Job incentive
- Quarterly incentive
- Reserve establishment honorarium
- Roll out of succession planning model for identified key positions
- Group incentives for cohesive teamwork, with a view to enhance productivity

Training and development

An integral part of ONGC's employee-centred policies is its thrust on their knowledge upgradation and development. ONGC Academy, previously known as the Institute of Management Development (IMD), which has an ISO 9001 certification, along with 7 other training institutes, plays a key role in keeping our workforce at pace with global standards.

ONGC Academy is the premier nodal agency responsible for developing the HR of ONGC. It also focuses on marketing its HRD expertise in the field of exploration and production of hydrocarbons. ONGC's Sports Promotion Board, the apex body, has a comprehensive sports policy through which top honours in sports at national and international levels have been achieved.

Source: www.ongcindia.com/people.asp#b, accessed on 20 July 2009.

systems, building an electronically held knowledge resource for the organization. This process was empirically explored by Martinsons in 1997. Some scholars even specified general linkages between the types of HRIS used and company strategy. This work thus corroborates the belief that effective HRD (reinforced with HRIS) supports organizational strategy.

Challenge 2: Achieving integration between HRD processes and other HR initiatives

This is again an important challenge concerning the issues of integration and the practical difficulty of establishing a range of HR initiatives to support one another within the HR function, and across the organization. Performance management is the key to this type of integration. When HRIS is part of a performance management system, it can contain and record criteria and performance to achieve a 'fit' between HR processes, and can become a centralized point where each HR function is articulated and integrated. Performance management systems operate most effectively in a good, transparent environment. It can play an important role in communicating the vision articulated by top management, as it allows the rapid transfer of information.

Challenge 3: Creating an environment within which individuals can take responsibility for their own learning

HRIS also provides a huge potential for people to play an active role in their own development, provided they recognize and address the challenges. To achieve this, employees' self-service and widespread access to HRIS for training and development purposes is most significant. This can also be achieved through workstation-based interactive training that provides an opportunity to test new skills and allows people to work at their own pace.

Challenge 4: Gaining the support and commitment of line managers in the learning process

HRIS also has a great potential to allow line managers to become involved in the HRD process. They can bring together the developmental experiences of their subordinates and make informed decisions about how best to use their team. Access to related HR data, such as working patterns, absenteeism, and rewards, places the line manager in a stronger position in terms of understanding issues that may impact positively or negatively on the HRD process.

Activities which support strategic business objectives are as follows:

- Achieving integration between HRD processes and other HR initiatives
- Creating an environment within which individuals can take responsibility for self-learning
- Gaining the support and commitment of line managers in the learning process

Organizational Culture and Design

Analysis of organizational culture as an approach to organizational design is a difficult task. The culture of an organization is deep-rooted in its history and is below the surface of awareness. Any organizational culture change process follows certain well-defined and structured steps.

Although it varies from organization to organization, a tentative list of the steps that an organizational culture change process follows can be drawn as follows:

1. Identify the core values and beliefs.
2. Uncover core values and beliefs, which may include stated values and goals, but they are also embedded in organizational metaphors, myths, and stories, and in the behaviour of members.
3. Acknowledge, respect, and discuss differences between core values and beliefs of different sub-cultures within the organization.
4. Look for incongruence between conscious and unconscious beliefs and values, and resolve these by choosing the ones that the organization wishes to commit to. Establish new behavioural norms (and even new metaphor language) that clearly demonstrate the desired values.
5. Repeat these steps over a period of time. As new members enter the organization, ensure that they are surrounded with clear messages about the culture they are entering.
6. Reinforce desirable behaviour.

As culture change is an ongoing process, it is difficult to identify organizations that have 'completed' a successful culture change. We can however find examples of change-in-progress in organizations. Exhibit 1.3 reflects such an endeavour.

EXHIBIT 1.3 Culture change

A major multinational company engaged itself in a purposeful culture change process. The company had a large number of female employees on their payroll who were no less in their performance track records, but always believed they were being discriminated against. They wanted a meeting with the CEO of the company to complain about such perceived discrimination.

Meeting with the CEO and subsequent discussions with the managers ultimately revealed that discrimination, both racist and sexist, did exist. The problem was identified as a conflict with espoused values. The company then developed an 'aspiration statement', which outlined the desired beliefs, attitudes, and behaviour. The statement specified the company's commitment to communication, ethical management practices, employee empowerment, and recognition for those who contributed to the mission of the company. All these were reinforced by the training sessions on leadership, diversity, and ethics. Performance evaluation of employees has been linked with the 'aspiration statement'.

The experience of the company underscored the fact that an organization's culture change takes a long time.

BUSINESS PROCESS RE-ENGINEERING

In most organizations, these days some degree of business process engineering (BPE) or business process re-engineering (BPR) is taking place. BPR is often described as a radical redesign of strategic, value-added, business processes to achieve breakthrough performance improvements. BPR is a large-scale overhaul of basic business processes, and involves replacing old structures and practices with something new.

When BPE projects are completed properly, the end products include recommendations on what information needs to be collected and used, who will collect it, and at what point in the business cycle. Table 1.2 explains BPR.

Situational Aspects of Organizational Design

The four important situational factors in organizational design are technology, environment, size, and organizational life cycle.

Technological aspects

Technology is one of the major contingency factors that influence organizational design. Technology, per se, facilitates the conversion process, which transforms organizational inputs (materials, equipment, labour, etc.) into outputs (products and services). Rigorous technological change in Indian organizations during the post-reform days have played a crucial role in redesigning organizations, and includes even public sector enterprises and departmental undertakings. Technological issues, and organizational structure and design are discussed in later chapters.

Environmental aspects

Environmental issues also influence organizational structure and design in a large way. These are discussed in separate chapters incorporating broader issues, such as

TABLE 1.2   Business process re-engineering

Business	Process	Re-engineering
It involves the processes that support the development, production, and delivery of products and services. Re-engineering business process, such as marketing and selling, administration, logistics, and supply chain, can significantly optimize the cost for the organization. It can also lead to improvement in cycle times and enhance customer satisfaction.	It is the core of any business and comprises a collection of activities, which transform inputs to outputs, or value addition to the customer. Thus, process actually documents tasks and activities. The core of any business is a set of processes, each of which consists of a collection of activities that use inputs to create an output of value for the customer. The objective of the entire process determines which tasks and activities are to be done and how they should be arranged.	Re-engineering is a radical reform that reaches the very core of the business, and is not just a superficial rearrangement of what already exists. BPR then is a comprehensive, one-step turnaround that takes more time and effort than incremental change strategies, and often needs considerable support from systems analysis and information technology.

globalization and cultural changes. Even a bureaucratic or mechanistic organization (resembling Likert's System 1 or Max Weber's bureaucratic type organization) today needs to respond to environmental issues in order to sustain itself competitively or to survive. Even though the theory of stable and unstable environments propounded by Burns and Stalker (1961) advocated that environments might remain fairly stable over time, and organizations can survive in them without redesigning their structure, it is hardly possible now, as the environment for every organization constantly changes. Organic organizations (resembling the behavioural model or Likert's System 4), however, always prepare to face environmental uncertainties and change accordingly.

Organizational size and form aspects

Organizational size and form also play a crucial role in determining the organizational structure and design. Structural features of large and small organizations widely differ. For example, large organizations may necessarily require decentralizing, while smaller organizations may get the right fit through centralization of their activities.

Organizational life cycle aspects

The organizational life cycle hypothesis considers organizational design in its different stages, such as birth, youth, middle stage, and maturity. This theory believes that every organization elevates itself to different stages, and accordingly its structure and design varies. For example, at the birth stage organizations become more informal, where activities overlap. There may not be any rules and regulations, or structured systems of planning, performance evaluation, and coordination. At the youth stage, some decentralization in decision-making occurs when a few trusted employees are taken into confidence, though the final decision-making stake remains centralized. At the middle stage, organizations become reasonably successful and rather large. Organizational design and structure becomes bureaucratic with formalized functional departments and supporting staff departments. Authority slowly gets decentralized and largely becomes policies, rules, and regulations bound. At the maturity stage, organizations become very large, mechanistic, and specialized, with structured sets of rules, policies, and procedures. This hypothesis, therefore, mainly advocates how an organization frames its design at the different changing stages of its life cycle.

In effecting change in any organization, it is important to first understand the organization as a whole and the systems view in particular. Once it is understood in the right perspective, organizations can introduce changes in the desired way and can survive in an ever-changing competitive environment. In the next chapter, we will introduce organizational change as a concept and as a process.

SUMMARY

In this introductory chapter, we have discussed the systems view of organization and explained how organizational structure relates to the systems concept. Organization is defined as the relation among components of a system. Organizational structure denotes the components and relations that bind people working within the organization.

A system is a collection of parts (or sub-systems), which is integrated to accomplish the overall goal of an organization. Systems have inputs, processes, outputs, and outcomes, with ongoing feedback among these. If one part of the system is removed, the nature of the system is changed. Systems range from being very simple to very complex. Social systems are comprised of numerous sub-systems as well. These are arranged in hierarchies and integrated to accomplish the overall goal of the system. Every organization effectively functions through an integrated interlocking network of sub-systems.

Effective organizational design depends on the interrelationships of principles of job specialization, departmentalization, coordination, and line and staff positions. It is defined as the total pattern of structural elements and patterns which are used to manage the overall organization. Effective organizational design is instrumental for implementing organizational strategies for achievement of organizational goals. Broadly, organizational design rests on two models—the bureaucratic model and the behavioural model. However, technology, environment, size, and organizational life cycle are the four important situational factors in organizational design.

KEY TERMS

Butterfly effect Proposed by meteorologist, Edward Lorenz, it is a visual representation to explain the theory of chaos. The picture, so created, resembles a butterfly, and hence the name, 'butterfly effect'.

Critical success factor (CSF) It is a key area where satisfactory performance is required for an organization to achieve its goals.

Orchestra organization The term is used in the open systems perspective and is a complex set of interdependent sub-systems.

Systems dynamics It is primarily orientated towards identifying (defining), modelling, and simulating a system (e.g., a factory, a city, an economy, or even an entire ecological system) in order to explicate how the system might behave under different policy regimes.

Three pillars of organization The three pillars of organization are people, organization, and technology.

Viable systems model It consists of operations with embedded management and environment. It is used in organizations to diagnose different elements in designing information systems, management structure, and even organizational vision, mission, and structure.

CONCEPT REVIEW QUESTIONS

1. Explain briefly the business process models for organizational structure and design.
2. Explain the systems view of organization. How does the systems view influence organizational structure and design?
3. Discuss the difference between normative models and prescriptive models.
4. How can viable systems models and the socio-technical approach influence organizational structure and design?
5. What is HRIS? What are the key challenges before an organization for implementing HRIS in the HRD function?
6. Write short notes on the following:
   (a) Open systems approach
   (b) Cybernetics
   (c) Situational variables in organizational design

CRITICAL THINKING QUESTIONS

1. Hexagon is a global player in machine tools manufacturing. It has a presence in all major European, American, and South-East Asian countries. Its R&D unit is located in India. Hexagon is presently restructuring its multi-location units, including two in India. In one of the Indian units, based in Pune, you are one of the key members of the restructuring team. Hexagon wants you to develop a model restructuring plan, aligning its business goals with the new organizational design which focuses on a socio-technical approach, keeping in view the local culture and resource availability. Suggest your model plan.
2. An organization has approached you to investigate into their proposed plan of expansion in different locations, including abroad. The organization desires your involvement and expertise to change their existing hybrid structure and explore the possibility of converting their product lines into independent business units (IBU). As an expert in organizational systems and design, suggest your line of action with logic.
3. A multinational desktop manufacturer with a business presence all over the world, including India, follows a direct marketing approach through their network structure. Recently, however, the organization is experiencing a down turn in their sales position. Preliminary investigation attributes this to the absence of monitoring at the headquarter level. Suggest how you can ensure such control while maintaining the network structure.

CASE STUDY

Balanced Scorecard for Organizational Transformation

After the Asian currency crisis of 1997, all banks in Indonesia faced the crisis of transformation. One of the management tools used to oversee the performance was balanced scorecard. With good corporate governance and alignment within the organization, the performance measurement initiative of the bank gained momentum. Customer service, operational efficiency, and proactive HRD practices were the three focus areas in the balanced scorecard adopted by the Indonesian banks to overcome the crisis.

One of the important case studies of such a bank is Bank Universal. Bank Universal was established in the year 1990 by merging three small banks. Initially, it focused on corporate banking and later expanded to retail banking, primarily in Jakarta and other major cities of Indonesia. With 2200 employees and an asset size of US$1.2 billion, the bank virtually collapsed during the crisis of 1997. However, with the implementation of scientific performance management systems (using balanced scorecard) and sustained HR initiatives, it ultimately survived the crisis.

From a business point of view, the bank strategically focused on sector-specific financing, such as the automotive sector (mainly refinancing the suppliers, dealers, and end users of automobile industry products), coal mining (supply chain side), traders, plywood supply chains, etc. By focusing on niche retail banking, it has achieved expertise in this area. Another reason for being sector specific was to avoid mistakes in financing the large companies who became the major defaulters and major contributors to the high NPAs of the bank during the crisis period.

Introduction of the balanced scorecard helped the bank to balance its focus among its processes, customer service, learning and growth, and finance. Without efficient processes and quality of people to serve customers, it is not possible for a bank to get a good return on investment. While initially implementing the balanced scorecard at the corporate level, the bank later took this to the branch operation level and then cascaded it to the individual employee level. It implemented the balanced scorecard across the organization in four stages, with three strategic themes, such as handling past problems (related to loan portfolios), embracing a new business model (to enhance profitability), and adopting a new market strategy to develop a good banking image.

After implementation of the balanced scorecard, the bank observed that people appreciated each other. The marketing people appreciated the service people, and they appreciated the operational and process people, who in turn appreciated the HR people. All could thus collectively contributed to the performance of Bank Universal. Effective coordination and communication throughout the organization improved the performance and the bottom line.

Source: Bank Universal's website at http://www.bankuniversal.co.id as accessed on 30 April 2009.

Discussion Question

Read this case carefully and relate it to your own experience of an organization, clearly segmenting individual areas of activities and operations. Also, explore the possibility of introducing the balanced scorecard and indicate how it can augment the business results.

REFERENCES

Allen Louis, A. (1958), *Management and Organization*, McGraw-Hill, New York.

Beer, M., B. Spector, P. Lawrence, D. Quinn Mills, and R. Walton (1984), *Managing Human Assets*, Free Press, New York.

Beer, S. (1979), *Heart of the Enterprise*, John Wiley and Sons, Chichester.

———. (1972), *The Brain of the Firm*, Penguin Press, London.

Boone, Louis E. and David L. Kurtz (1992), *Management*, McGraw-Hill, New York.

Bostrom, R.P. and J.S. Heinen (1977), 'MIS problems and failures: A socio-technical perspective', *MIS Quarterly*, Vol. 1, No. 3, pp. 17–32.

Brown, Alvin (1945), *Organization: A Formulation of Principle*, Hibbert Printing Company, Trenton, N.J.

Burns, T. and G.M. Stalker (1966), *The Management of Innovation*, Tavistock, London.

Burns, T., and G. Stalker (1961), *The Management of Innovation*, Tavistock, London.

Burton, R.M. and B. Obel (2004), *Strategic Organizational Diagnosis and Design, the Dynamics of Fit*, Kluwer Academic Publishers, Dordrecht.

Cameron, Kim S. (1986), 'Effectiveness as paradox: Consensus and conflict in conceptions of organizational effectiveness', *Managemeent Science*, Vol. 32, No. 5, May, pp. 539–553, DOI: 10.1287/mnsc.32.5.539,

Chandler, A.D. (1962), *Strategy and Structure: Chapters in the History of the Industrial Enterprise*, M.I.T. Press, Cambridge (Mass).

Charlotte, Roberts and Art Kleiner (1999), 'Five kinds of systems thinking', from P. Senge et al., *The Dance of Change*, Doubleday, New York.

Child, John (1972), 'Organization structure and strategies of control: A replication of the aston study', *Administrative Science Quarterly*, June, Vol. 17, No. 2, pp. 163–177,

Daft, R.L. and A.Y. Lewin (1990), 'Can organization studies begin to break out of the normal science straitjacket? An editorial essay', *Organization Science*, Vol. 1, pp. 1–9.

Emery, F.E. (1980), 'Designing socio-technical system for greenfield sites', *Journal of Occupational Behaviours*, Vol. 1, Issue 1, pp. 19–27.

Emery, F.E. and E.L. Trist (1965), 'The causal texture of organizational environments', *Human Relations*, Vol. 18, pp. 21–32.

Fombrun, C.J., N.M. Tichy, and M.A. Devanna (1984), *Strategic Human Resource Management*, Wiley, New York.

Forrester, K.W. (1958), 'Industrial dynamics: A major breakthrough for decision makers', *Harvard Business Review*, Vol. 36, pp. 37–66.

Galbraith, J.R. (1995*)*, *Designing Organizations: An Executive Briefing on Strategy, Structure and Process*, Jossey–Bass, San Francisco.

Greenwood, Royston, and C.R. Hinings (1993), 'Understanding strategic change: The contribution of archetypes', *Academy of Management Journal*, Vol. 36, pp. 1052–1081.

———. (1988), 'Organizational design types, tracks, and the dynamics of strategic change', *Organization Studies*, Vol. 8, pp. 293–316.

Guest, D.E. (1987), 'Human resource management and industrial relations', *Journal of Management Studies*, Vol. 14, Issue 5, pp. 503–521.

Hage, J. and M. Aiken (1967), 'Program change and organizational properties: A comparative analysis', *American Journal of Sociology*, Vol. 73. No. 1, pp. 503–519.

———. (1967), 'Relationship of centralization to other structural properties', *Administrative Science Quarterly*, Vol. 12, No. 1, pp. 72–92.

Hammer, Michael and J. Champy (1993), *Re-engineering the Corporation: A Manifesto for Business Revolution*, Nicholas Brealey, London.

Hendry, C. and A. Pettigrew (1990), 'Human resource management: An agenda for the 1990s', *International Journal of Human Resource Management*, Vol. 1, Issue 3, pp. 1743.

Herbst, P.G. (1974), *Socio-technical Design: Strategies in Multidisciplinary Research*, Tavistock Publications, London.

Hilborn, R.C. (2004), 'Sea gulls, butterflies, and grasshoppers: A brief history of the butterfly effect in non-linear dynamics', *American Journal of Physics*, Vol. 72, pp. 425–427.

Hinings, C.R. and Royston Greenwood (1988), *The Dynamics of Strategic Change*, Blackwell, New York.

Johari, Johanim and Khulida Kirana, Yahya (2009), 'Linking organizational structure, job characteristics, and job performance constructs: A proposed framework', *International Journal of Business and Management*, March, Vol. 4, No. 3, pp. 145–152.

Katz, D., and R.L. Kahn (1966), *The Social Psychology of Organizations*, Wiley, New York.

Kauffman, D.L. (1980), *Systems I: An Introduction to Systems Thinking*, Future Systems, Inc, S.A. Carltorn, Minneapolis, MN.

Khandwalla, P.N. (1977), *The Design of Organizations*, Harcourt Brace Jovanivich, New York.

———. (March 1974), 'Mass output orientation of operations technology and organizational structure', *Administrative Science Quarterly*, March, Vol. 19, No. 1, pp. 74–97.

Khandwalla, P.N. (1973), 'Viable and effective organizational designs of firms', *The Academy of Management Journal*, Vol. 16, Issue 3, pp. 481–495.

Koontz, H. (1961), 'The management theory jungle', *Academy of Management Journal*, Vol. 4, Issue 3, pp. 174–188.

Legge, K. (1995), *Human Resource Management: Rhetorics and realities*, Macmillan, London.

Levin, Mark Sh. (2006), *Composite Systems Decisions*, Springer, New York.

Lewin, A.Y. and C.U. Stephens (1994). 'CEO attitudes as determinants of organizational design: An integrated model', *Organization Studies*, 15(2), pp. 183–212.

Likert, R. (1967), *The Human Organization*, McGraw-Hill, New York.

Maier, Mark W. and Eberhardt Rechtin (2000), *The Art of Systems Architecting*, Second Edition, CRC Press, Boca Raton.

Martinsons, M.G. (1997), 'Human resource management applications of knowledge based systems', *International Journal of Information Management*, Vol. 17, Issue 1, pp. 35–53.

Maturana, H.R. and F.J. Varela (1987), *The Tree of Knowledge: The Biological Roots of Human Understanding*, Shambala, Boston.

Miles, Raymond E. and Charles C. Snow (1978), *Organizational Strategy, Structure, and Process*, McGraw-Hill, New York.

Mintzberg, H. (1981), 'Organization design: fashion or fit', *Harvard Business Review*, January–February, pp. 103–166.

———. (1979), *The Structure of Organizations*, Prentice Hall, Englewood Cliffs (N.J.).

Perrow, C. (1967), 'A framework for comparative analysis of organizations', *American Sociological Review*, Vol. 32, pp. 194–208.

Pettigrew, A.M., R. Whittington, L. Melin, C. Sanchez-Runde, F. Van den Bosch, W. Ruigrok and T. Numagami (2003), *Innovative Forms of Organizing, International Perspectives*, Sage, London.

Planck, Max (1949) *Scientific Autobiography and Other Papers*, translated by Frank Gaynor, New York: Philosophical Library, p. 178. Quoted by Arthur Young in *The Reflexive Universe*, New York: Delacorte, 1975.

Prigogine, I. and I. Stengers (1984), *Order out of Chaos: Man's New Dialogue with Nature*, Bantam Books, London.

Quinn, J.B. (1980), *Strategies for Change: Logical Incrementalism*, Irwin, Homewood (Ill).

Robbins, Stephen Mary and Coulter (2002), *Organizational Behaviour*, Pearson Education, New Delhi.

Rockhart, J. (1982), 'The changing role of information systems executive: A critical success factors perspective', *Sloan Management Review*, Vol. 23, Issue 1, pp. 3–13.

Rosabeth, Moss Kanter (2001), *Evolve! Succeeding in the Digital Culture of Tomorrow*, Harvard Business, Boston.

Russell, L. Ackoff and Frederick Edmund Emery (1972), *On Purposeful Systems: An Interdisciplinary Analysis of Individual and Social Behaviour as a System of Purposeful Events*, Aldine-Atherton: Chicago.

Stacey, R.D. (1993), 'Strategy as order emerging from chaos', *Long Range Planning*, Vol. 26, Issue 1, pp. 10–17.

Thompson, James D. (2001), 'Organizations in Action', in J.M. Shafritz and J.S. Ott, *Classics of Organization Theory*, Harcourt College Publishers, Fort Worth.

Toffler, Alvin (1970), *Future Shock*, Bantam Books, New York.

Torrington, D. and L. Hall (1991), *Personnel Management: A New Approach*, Prentice Hall, Englewood Cliffs, NJ.

Tyson, S. (1997), 'Human resource strategy: A process for managing the contribution of HRM to organizational performance', *International Journal of Human Resource Management*, Vol. 8, Issue 3, pp. 277–290.

Ulrich, Karl T. and Steven D. Eppinger (2000), *Product Design and Development*, Second Edition, Irwin McGraw-Hill, Boston.

Waterman, R. (1990), *Adhocracy: The Power to Change*, Whittle Direct Books, Knoxville, TN.

———. (1988), *The Renewal Factor*, Bantam, New York.

Weber, M. (1946), Max Weber, ed H.H. Gerth, and C.W. Mills, Oxford University Press, Oxford.

Woodward, J. (1965), *Industrial Organization, Theory and Practice*, Oxford University Press, Oxford.

2 Introduction to Organizational Change

Learning Objectives

After reading this chapter, you will be able to understand
- the concept, content and process theories of organizational change
- the need and philosophy of organizational change
- the steps to successful organizational change
- the different triggers for change
- the role of training, development, and motivation in organizational change
- organizational transition and its various models
- types of organizational change
- systems thinking and organizational change
- various strategies of organizational change
- personal construct psychology and organizational change
- the role of organizational change consultants
- the drawbacks in the implementation of organizational change

Navigate and Rediscover Change in the E-world

'Flying birds feeding on marine life found marshlands where food was plentiful and easier to catch, and so began dwelling there.' Fuller (1969) used this line in his famous book, *Operating Manual for Spaceship Earth*. This analogy also applies to organizational change, as in a globally competitive world, organizations need to learn how to evolve. Portraying contemporary organizations as birds and the Internet as marshland, Kanter (2001) suggested that organizations need to shift to the e-world in order to rediscover and steer themselves through the ocean of change.

Organizations must be innovative in order to create something new if they are to thrive and evolve in the modern e-culture. This implies a shift from hierarchical bureaucracies to more aerodynamically e-suited communities and systems, and traditional organizations experience a problem in doing so. Based on a survey of 785 organizations (basically, drawing samples from such organizations), Kanter classified organizations into two types—pacesetter and laggard. The pacesetter organizations can adapt to changes quickly and in a systematic manner, while laggards are unable to adapt to genetic changes in practices and operations.

Kanter further identified four key elements of effective organizational e-culture—strategy, becoming big, becoming integrated communities, and becoming talent dependent. Strategy provides the basic business theme and enables an organization to continuously go for new products. Such organizations replace their traditional hierarchical decision-making systems by an 'internal marketplace of ideas'. Organizations grow by creating alliances, partnerships, and coalitions with other organizations. The new class of workers who specialize in making these connections are called 'collabronauts'. Kanter identified three types of cooperative relationship systems and functions of effective collabronauts, and offered advice on how to restructure for e-business. Successful e-based organizations operate as integrated communities.

The e-world requires that organizations present a seamless face to its environment, and this in turn necessitates elimination of internal boundaries. Strong employee communities lead to cooperation between divisions, shared learning, constructive dissent, and empowered employees, bound together by a common purpose. Finally, organizations become talent-dependent and talent-driven by creating a culture that attracts and retains the best people. They realize that knowledge workers today place greater emphasis on the challenges of the job, growth opportunities, and financial security, rather than on job security.

Kanter recommended the 'change wheel' model to handle change and identified 10 critical ingredients needed for successful change. These are: establishing a common vision, finding champions and sponsors, providing rewards and recognition, honing the skill sets required to perceive needs and opportunities, divergent and kaleidoscopic thinking, inspiring vision, coalition building, nurturing a working team, persistence, and spreading credit and recognition.

INTRODUCTION

Organizational change comprises four main issues, namely content, contextual, process, and criterion. Content issues focus on the substance of contemporary organizational changes. Contextual issues centre on the forces or conditions present in the external and internal environments of organizations. Process issues concentrate on the actions undertaken during the establishment of intended change. Criterion issues, on the other hand, tackle outcomes usually evaluated in organizational change.

Often, the terms organizational change and organizational development (OD) are used interchangeably. In fact, one encompasses the other. Organizations cannot avoid organizational change if they are to keep pace with the changing business scenario. Globalization has also accelerated the need for change. Increased competition, changing customer expectations, economic uncertainty, etc. are putting age-old organizational systems and practices under tremendous pressure. Organizations, therefore, need to review their internal business processes and also consider external environmental issues if they are to stay competitive.

While discussing the prospects of OD and organizational change, Sashkin and Burke (1987) identified five contemporary trends. These are (i) high integration of task and process aspects of OD (as in networked organizations), (ii) greater attention to developing the OD theory, (iii) increased interest to manage conflict (particularly in cases of mergers and acquisitions), (iv) more thrust on OD research to identify improved methodology for organizational change, and (v) greater focus on designing organizational culture to manage change. Similarly, after summarizing the recent developments in OD and organizational change, Woodman (1989) recommended seven trends. Four are similar to those suggested by Sashkin and Burke. The other three trends proposed by Woodman are (i) increasing interest in high performance and greater commitment to work systems, (ii) application of change management research to internal organizational processes, and (iii) application of change research outcomes to social movements.

Other scholars, such as Pasmore and Fagans (1992), also identified and explored issues in OD and organizational change. They have considered historical and philosophical perspectives dating back to Plato and mainly focused on increasing participation of all in these processes. Participation in OD and organizational change even accentuate individual development. Successful participation in the change process precedes knowledge and focused preparation of people. They have helped us in delineating the required knowledge and also the steps required for preparation of individuals for participation in the OD and change process. All these, therefore, suggest OD and organizational change essentially as participative processes.

CONTENT AND PROCESS THEORIES OF ORGANIZATIONAL CHANGE

Once identified, such factors help organizations to develop the right strategy mix, suitable structures, the overall mission (to achieve a sense of direction), the long-term relationship between the organization and the environment, and to delineate its scope of activities. The contextual theory of organizational change emphasizes the identification of forces and conditions in internal as well as external environments. External conditions or forces are governmental regulations, technological advances, and various competitive forces which augment market competition. Internal conditions or forces are the degree of specialization (technology-specific) level of organizational slack, and lessons from previous change issues. Contextual issues or elements of organizational change, therefore, relate to the success or failure of organizational responses to internal and external environments.

Process theories of organizational change deal with various process issues, addressing the actions taken by organizations in the course of their change initiative. Such actions might have been taken to tackle the external environment or internal environment, and even issues at the individual level. External environmental issues, such as rules and regulations of various central and state governments and local bodies, influence organizational employment practices, consumption of energy, production processes, health and safety of workers, environmental pollution, output, product safety regulations, etc. In responding to such changes, organizations need to make changes in the operating environment and in the behaviour of employees in order to achieve desired goals and objectives.

The process theory of organizational change therefore, focuses on actions or organizational responses to implement change within the organization and employees' responses to these. Hence, organizations that adopt the process theory approach of organizational change are basically concerned with developing suitable response mechanisms to the external environment components that affect their internal activities, so as to optimize employee responses.

Content theories of organizational change deal with the causes and the resultant effects of change in individual and organizational performance data. Hence, they identify the in-built transformational and transactional dynamics of successful organizational change. On one hand, transformational change factors, such as leadership, culture, mission, and strategy, identify areas that require new employee behaviours resulting from external and internal environmental pressures. Transactional factors, on the other hand, deal with the psychological and organizational variables that predict and control the motivational and performance consequences of the work group environment. These include management practices, structure, systems (policies and procedures), task requirements, and individual skills/abilities.

NEED FOR ORGANIZATIONAL CHANGE

The need for change in an organization is difficult to track, as such needs widely vary. Organizational change basically involves organic adjustments and is required for different reasons. Some of the important motives behind organizational change are as follows:

Set right the situation Organizations often need to correct situations, which they believe require some adjustment or change. For example, in a recessionary market, an existing HR policy on variable pay may seem to be incorrect when it is based on the value of total sales. The organization may amend this with fixed performance incentive till the market situation improves.

Fix things that are needed Organizations orchestrate change, often through external interventions, in order to correct poor performance areas. This may require alignment of some activities to derive strategic advantages. For example, disadvantages arising out of its location relative to its market may require an organization to set up a marketing office and relocate some staff in order to rectify this situation. Similarly, Indian multinationals, Asian Paints and Dabur, have set up manufacturing units across the nation and abroad to derive advantages of market proximity, and to optimize the cost of distribution and supply.

Seize opportunities to grow New market opportunities may motivate an organization to build new capabilities by expanding their activities or through strategic alliance, identifying business partners, etc. This requires increasing manpower strength and investing in new resource building. For example, when political pressure in the US mounted against outsourcing to India, Infosys set up units in Canada to get US-outsourced jobs, and then routed these to their Indian units.

Emerge as different entity Often organizations change to become more flexible. While adapting to new situations is essential, flexibility in operation or functions may also be required in special circumstances, for example, developing strategic business units based on product mix or type to make each product type an independent profit centre. To give each product a competitive edge over Fuji Photo Film, Kodak restructured the organization and formed 34 strategic business units.

Apart from these, there are many other requirements that may prompt an organization to change. These have been elaborated in separate sections while explaining the change triggers.

PHILOSOPHY OF ORGANIZATIONAL CHANGE

Philosophies are the value systems and guiding forces for organizational change. It is difficult to provide individual organization-wise philosophy and value systems. However, in most cases it is observed that change in organizations is motivated by the following core philosophies:

- Adaptability
- Flexibility
- Strategic
- Focus on behavioural issues
- Participative change process
- Ethics
- Balancing stakeholders' interest

To understand the implementation of these, let us examine Kotter's eight-step model of change shown in Exhibit 2.1.

EXHIBIT 2.1 Kotter's eight-step model

Kotter (1995, 2002) suggested an eight-step model to understand and manage the process of organizational change. Each step relates the responses of people to the change process, where people see, feel, and then change. This change model can be summarized as follows:

- Increase the urgency by activating people through inspiration, so that they move and appreciate the relevance of the change objectives.
- Develop a team to manage organizational change that will ensure putting the right people in the right place, address issues of emotional commitment, the right skill-mix, and hierarchical levels. This process will certify the success of any organizational change initiatives.
- Develop the right vision, which is simple, understandable, and shared by the entire change team. The real test of right vision is to understand how far it becomes a shared vision, and to what extent people can relate them to the vision of the organization. With a shared vision, people can draw the right strategy, matching their emotional and creative needs to successfully drive the organizational change process.
- Communicate the vision, more from the selling perspective, to increase the involvement of all cross sections of people in the organization, including those who are likely to be affected, so that they can respond positively to the change

(Contd)

(Exhibit 2.1 contd)

process. This would be possible only when the change initiatives respond to people's needs.
- Empower people so that they can be active in the change process, by encouraging people to participate in the change process, providing them with constant feedback and support, and recognizing and rewarding their progress and achievements.
- Pursue change with an incremental approach, that is, gradually and step-by-step. The idea is to celebrate every success in the change process and to inform people that results are being achieved. To ensure this, the organization must set aims that are easy to achieve, manageable, and the results are traceable. Strategically, organizations drive the change process with a mantra to do first things first, before embarking on the next stage of change.
- Organizational change requirements never cease to exist and are ongoing; hence, Kotter suggested that the change initiatives should not be given up. A dynamic organization always encourages change, highlights what it can achieve, and what it intends to accomplish in the future.
- Reinforce the success of change with new values and culture, and with more proactive policies in recruitment, promotion, motivation, etc. This will ensure sustaining the change process and enable the organization to truly leapfrog in this competitive world.

Some generic theories of change are discussed in Table 2.1. However, various approaches are adopted at the organizational level, keeping in view the operational feasibility, and these are discussed later in this chapter as well as in subsequent chapters on change.

TABLE 2.1 Different change theories and their key features

Change theories	Key features
Lewin's three-step change theory	Lewin (1951) introduced this model. According to it, behavioural change in people takes place by pushing employees towards the desired direction. In any change process, one encounters driving and restraining forces. While driving forces facilitate the change, the restraining forces oppose it. Lewin suggested how organizations could shift the balance of direction of the planned change. Lewin's first step requires unfreezing the existing behaviour, and then moving it to the desired direction, and finally, refreezing it.
Lippitt's phases of change theory	Lippitt et al. (1958) extended Lewin's three-step change theory and created a seven-step theory focusing more on the role and responsibility of the change agent. These are as follows: 1. Diagnose the problem. 2. Take stock of the motivation level and assess the capacity to change. 3. Understand the resources available and motivation of the change agents. 4. Select change objectives that are progressive in nature. 5. Select and clearly understand the change expectations. 6. Maintain the change. 7. Help the people to manage the process on their own.

(Contd)

Change theories	Key features
Prochaska and DiClemente's change theory	According to this theory, the change process crosses stages, such as pre-contemplation, contemplation, preparation, action, and maintenance. An individual overcomes each stage in cyclical order. Hence, this model is also called a spiral model. At the pre-contemplation stage, people are unaware about the change process (as they have not experienced it); hence, they often decline to change. At the contemplation stage, individuals raise their consciousness and decide to change their behaviour. At the preparation stage, they are ready to change their behaviour and plan accordingly. The action stage is characterized by the individual employees' sustenance of behavioural change. Finally, the maintenance stage establishes the new behavioural change.
Social cognitive theory	This is simply renaming the age-old social learning theory, which suggests that behavioural changes in individuals take place through environmental influences, personal factors, and behavioural attributes. It is like operant conditioning, that is, the proposition that behaviour is the outcome of consequences.
Theory of reasoned action and planned behaviour	This theory believes that behaviour is a reasoned or planned one. A person behaves in a particular way due to his/her intention to perform that behaviour. This would obviously be possible when the individual feels that the changed behaviour will lead to positive outcome. Also, there may be an effect on social environment or norms to exert impact on change.

ORGANIZATIONAL CHANGE, TRANSFORMATION, AND RENEWAL

Change alters the way an organization functions. Hence, change, transformation, and renewal altogether encompass organizational change. Change may vary in degree from organization to organization. Whatever the degree of change, it is necessary for survival of the organization. Change introduces new ways of working and assigns new goals to the employees. Organizations can derive strategic advantage if the change process continues.

Organizational transformation is called metamorphosis, as structure, function, organizational activities, and attitude of the people radically change with the process of transformation. The word transformation in an organizational context is more appropriate in cases of mergers, acquisitions, corporate gobbling, etc., when cultural change in organizations become imminent. In such cases, due to change in the management and the method of work, employees of the merged entity undergo a cultural shock. Organizations need to transform in order to set themselves in the right direction. Among others, such organizational transformation succeeds employee right-sizing, hiving-off of businesses, redundancies, process changes, etc. The term metamorphosis, which literally means change or transformation, describes all these collectively. Exhibit 2.2 takes us through the process of change as experienced at LG.

EXHIBIT 2.2 Process of change at LG

LG Electronics, India, emphasizes the work-life balance of its employees and carefully craft career development programmes. LG's brand name attracts quality manpower but its employee retention rate is very poor. Often, talent shortage is attributed to the high rate of attrition, but experts allege that the problem lies in the way the company handles its employees. For the Korean major, it is they, not the employees, who matter.

Recently, LG has undertaken a number of change management initiatives. To start with, it has banned working on Sundays. To ensure that old habits are permanently erased, its HR team telephones employees to make sure that they are not in office or on official assignments. Under their family ambassador programme, a dedicated mentor visits employees' homes, talks to their family, and understands their problems, to ensure that the work-life balance is not disturbed.

As a preparatory process for organizational change, LG has launched a five-year career development programme for all its executives. This is based on individual assessment, so that each executive can undergo a series of career development programmes based on his/her training needs. To ensure things go smoothly, LG has also set up a regular monitoring team.

The most senior executives of the company are taken through the flexible training programmes so that they can successfully drive the change in the present volatile market situation.

The five-year career development programme and flexible training programmes for senior executives are in tune with the changing economic systems and the market situation. LG believes this will not only develop long-term commitment of employees but also ensure successful tracking of good performers, who can be hand-picked and anchored for fast track career growth. With this, employees also feel motivated as they can meet their career aspirations, and the company can meet the talent shortage through internal grooming.

Continuous training is in-built into LG's organizational system. Once every three months it ensures that all cross sections of employees attend classroom sessions. They learn together, take tests, and share their experiences. On an average, every employee undergoes a minimum of 10 man-days training each year.

To ensure that they recruit with the right fit, LG conducts recruitment interviews using a bundle of biometric tests, background checks, negative interviews, stress interviews, and even an extensive study of body language.

By recruiting the right fit, introducing long-term career development programmes and offering 10 man-days training for all, LG believes that not only is the problem of attrition addressed, but that it would be able to consolidate its position in a fiercely competitive market.

Source: This case is based on LG's practices, as obtained through the news report from http://www.business-standard.com/india/news/shyamal-majumdar-change-management-at-lg/329490/ and the websites of LG (both in India and abroad), accessed on 20 October 2008.

CHANGE TRIGGERS

Organizational change is necessary to enable organizations to remain competitive, productive, and profitable. The change process is initiated from the top and cascades down through the workforce. It continues till it is integrated with the organization.

In the process of integration or implementation, many organizations unsuccessfully adopt a negative approach, that is, persuading people to change without sharing information with them. Such an approach creates difficulty for the organization, as change resistance percolates to all areas of activities resulting in loss of productivity and a decline in the bottom line (profitability). However, positive change initiatives lead to successful integration and implementation of the change, as people accept change voluntarily. Although there are many reasons for organizational change, some of the common ones are as follows:

- Mergers, acquisitions, and strategic alliances
- Management restructuring
- Introduction of new technology
- Relocation of business premises
- Diversification of business

All these are discussed in subsequent chapters. At this stage, it is imperative to understand that the impact of change can be striking and can affect all cross sections of employees in an organization. In some cases, such as partial technological change or process changes, only the activities, and particularly the people, in certain departments may be influenced. Whether the change initiatives are partial or all-encompassing, for them to be successful, it is important that they are reinforced through required cultural change, new strategies, business plans, process design, training and development, and effective performance management systems. For all this to happen, organizational change management must first take stock of the current situation, including the quality of people, and then design tailor-made programmes to ensure success of the organizational change process.

It is difficult to list the reasons why organizations need to change and what the controllable or uncontrollable change triggers (both internal and external to the organizations) are. Here, we will discuss some of the important change triggers that are common to all organizations.

Business Development-driven Change

In the organization, business development-driven change encompasses everything that exerts a potential influence on organizational business expansion. It precedes a well-crafted business plan, which spells out the mission, goals, objectives, and framing of strategies and action plans. Some of the potential areas of organizational change driven by business development are as follows:

- Sales development
- New product development
- New market development
- Organizational structure, systems, and processes
- Tools, equipment, plant, logistics, and supply chain

- Attitude of people
- Style of management
- Ways of communication
- Training and development activities
- Strategic collaboration and partnerships
- Distribution network
- Market focus
- Disposal process

In most organizations, business development-driven changes take place with the vision of the top corporate or strategic-level people. They envision the change imperatives in various areas, and initiate the change process to make their organization competitive. Business development-driven change process is more an art than a science, as many change initiatives are based on the hunches and intuition of top management. Some of their actions are difficult to interpret and analyse, and hence, emulating the best practices in business development-driven change is often difficult. Most CEOs in India still base their decisions on intuition.

Although we have many structured theories on managerial decision-making, such as rational, non-rational, incremental, and garbage-can models, in real-life situations managers often make a trade-off between risk return with a short-term (incremental) view. Not all are like Dick Fuld, CEO of Lehman Brothers, a Fortune 500 company, who could risk over-borrowing in the hope of better returns and profitability for the company (a garbage-can model of decision-making), that ultimately led the company into bankruptcy. CEOs in India Inc. cannot afford to gamble; attitudinally they are risk-aversive but often indulge in intuition-based decision-making with a bounded rationality approach (non-rational model of decision-making).

Environment-driven Change

For an organization, the environment is an endless canvas. In a global economy, a recessionary trend in one country (with whom we may not have any business relations) may require us to prepare for a change. Thus, adapting to environmental changes is imperative for modern organizations. Environment-driven change requires an organization to review its structure, relationships with stakeholders, organizational dependence on the environment (linked to important activities, such as buying and selling, i.e., customers and suppliers), compliance with changing government policies and programmes, etc. The degree of dependence decides the extent of adaptability.

As environmental factors are exogenous to the organization and the environment is continuously changing, organizations need to be dynamic in order to respond to even the slightest change cues. The changing taste and preferences of customers ultimately compelled many Indian organizations to produce value-added products. HLL's brand extension strategy of Lifebuoy soap with Lifebuoy Plus, Lifebuoy Gold, and the addition of moisturizers is a glaring example of customer-centric change in the product mix. Companies are observed to have made similar changes to address customers' complaints with 24 × 7 help lines or structured customer relationship packages.

Culture-driven Change

Many organizations undergo cultural change to make their organizational change process successful. Developing the desired culture enables organizations to focus on their changing goals and objectives, which may require that people re-examine their attitudes and perceptions about customers and market situations, etc. Corporate culture also develops shared values and beliefs, and addresses the diversity issues, which become more important in cases of mergers and acquisitions. When people subscribe to the corporate culture, organizations can implement their vision and values while drawing up strategies and action plans.

A successful cultural change initiative has a gradual rippling effect on all functional areas, including operational level activities. With the increasing diversity of the workforce and the pursuit of organizations to survive in a competitive market, a cultural fit with the changing systems and process becomes a regular constant necessity. An organizational change initiative becomes successful when it precedes a cultural change in the organization. Exhibit 2.3 outlines such a successful initiative.

EXHIBIT 2.3   Kellogg leadership for community change initiative

The WK Kellogg Foundation introduced a new leadership development programme to strengthen community leaders and make them capable of addressing their own local issues. The Kellogg leadership for community change (KLCC) series focuses on cultivating a group of community leaders for specific local issues.

The KLCC approach emphasizes collaborative leadership to draw upon the participants' collective strengths in their own community.

The foundation's goals for this initiative are as follows:

- Develop collaborative leadership with a new vision of learning in local communities.
- Develop a leadership action plan on issues affecting the quality and equity of teaching, with specific relevance to their community.
- Develop new leaders so that fresher and different perspectives can bring community change.

Why is the KLCC programme unique and innovative?

- It integrates a model to mobilize community action through a collaborative cadre of leaders in each community.
- It creates a framework so that each community can find itself and assess the work required.
- It combines inner reflective work to find values, courage, and hope, with concrete methods of mobilizing change through data analysis, systematic thinking, and focus on action.
- It interweaves learning and action to increase the capacity of individuals and groups over a period of time.

(Contd)

(Exhibit 2.3 contd)

- It honours the wisdom of each community to establish a national network for sharing local skills and talents, and to create a national learning community.
- It inspires commitment for long-term community leadership.
- It collectively promotes partnership—local, regional, and national connections—and experts, to resolve local issues.

Effective community leadership

- Welcomes diversity and recognizes that it is an asset.
- Cultivates learning relationships with those who think differently.
- Honours and builds on the history and culture of the community.

KLCC theory of change

KLCC's community leadership development programme has brought perceptible change and created a strong group of leaders in the community. This has facilitated informed decision-making and built the capacity to work together, mobilizing expertise and resources.

With KLCC's support, individuals from any social, ethnic, racial, and economic group in the community are now able to step into a leadership role. Communities benefit from the opportunities to collaborate, learn, and work in a multi-cultural and multi-sector setting with different stakeholders. Community leaders have now become change leaders and extended Kellogg's growth worldwide, thus enabling it to sustain, change, and improve.

Source: Adapted from http://www.iel.org/programs/klcc.html, accessed on 15 October 2009.

Strategy-driven Change

Strategy provides directions to the organization to achieve its goals and objectives. When these change, strategy also needs to change. Thus, a strategy for achieving increased sales in the domestic market will obviously not hold good for increasing sales internationally. A change in strategy requires organizational change, and organizational change, being all-encompassing, may require change in strategy. For example, product differentiation strategy through a value-added approach necessarily requires organizational change. Similarly, organizational change enforced through organizational restructuring requires change in organizational strategy.

The term strategic organizational change indicates that the organizational change process is pursued strategically in order to sustain a competitive advantage. Strategic organizational change can also be perceived as an organizational change initiative taken by the strategic, corporate, or top-level organizational members. However, as strategy is all-pervasive, the term strategic organizational change holds good at the business as well as the operational level when it addresses strategic issues, that is, those pertaining to enhancement of the competitive advantage of the organization.

To summarize, organizational strategy requires organizational change to achieve the strategic intent. Strategic organizational change indicates the initiative to change, meeting the needs of stakeholders, responding to environmental threats, developing the capability of the organization and people with a new set of competencies, and developing the shared values and vision, to seize new market opportunities.

Business Plan-driven Change

A business plan is usually drawn at the business level or by middle-echelon people in an organization. It translates strategies into specific tactics and thus facilitates the process of achieving the desired results through required change in the organization. For example, a strategy to achieve increased market share through customer retention can use tactics, such as increased level of discounts on successive buying, or repeatedly visiting customers to retain their attention. This may require change in the organizational policy on discounts. A business plan drawn after the strategic plan of the organization also induces organizational change.

A business plan also provides direction to members of the organization to pursue the desired objectives. It may be drawn to raise funds for the organization. Among others, a business plan should contain details of organizational change and development, strategies for marketing, operations, HRM, and financial management.

Process-driven Change

Organizations are often required to undergo process redesign to optimize resource utilization and to achieve increased levels of productivity and performance. Any technological change may succeed process redesign. Also, changing market requirements may require change in the way the jobs are completed. Whatever may be the reason, process redesign calls for organizational change. Effective process redesign aligned with the organizational change strategies help the organization to transform.

Competency-driven Change

Competency is an aggregate of the knowledge, skills, and abilities of the people, which together enable the organization to remain competitive in the market. Systematic competency mapping identifies the competency gap and organizations can accordingly initiate training and development activities to reduce the gap and extend support for organizational change. Competencies cannot remain fixed. With changing technology and business environment, and the degree of competition, the organization needs to revisit the competencies of its people and the organization as a whole, and initiate suitable organizational change.

Performance-driven Change

With changing market requirements, organizations need to review their objectives and accordingly alter the performance standards and key result areas (KRA) or key performance areas (KPA) for employees. This requires organizational change. Alignment of performance management systems with the organizational change initiatives yields better results. Managers responsible for organizational change should have the experience of integrating performance management into business planning. This integration is achieved by first establishing the common organizational change goals that will drive the business plans and then linking them to the roles, competencies, and performance improvement measures needed to achieve them.

Individual performance development plans include assessment of role requirements and competencies needed to achieve them, mapping careers and linking them to developmental plans, establishing performance improvement actions, and agreement on organizational resources and support requirements.

A performance management system can effectively support organizational change only if it is objective, valued by both employees and managers, judged to be fair and realistic, and proven to make a positive contribution to personal and organizational development.

Innovation-driven Change

Giving the message of change to employees, William Ford Jr, Chairman and CEO of Ford Motor Company said, '... henceforth "innovation will be the compass" to set the direction for Ford.' William adopted innovation as Ford's core business strategy. Similarly, Jeffrey Immelt, Chairman and CEO of General Electric (GE), also believed that innovation was central to the success of GE and this should drive the company's change initiatives. He used the term 'innovation imperative'. GE pursues over a hundred innovation breakthrough projects to drive change in the organization. Moving a step forward, Steve Ballmer, CEO of Microsoft, said that Microsoft could make customers happy and keep competitors at bay.

Use of innovation as a tool for organizational change is often misconstrued as a new product development, or simple research and development work. For many companies, creating value for the customer, rather than just creating new products, is the true innovation. For example, a new framework called the 'innovation radar', developed by Sawhney et al. (2006) at Dell Inc., could make it the most successful personal computer manufacturer in the world, offering user-friendly computers, quick market positioning, and process changes in supply chain management, manufacturing, and direct selling. The innovation radar considers 12 dimensions, which are as follows:

- Offerings
- Platform
- Brand offerings (what)
- Customers (who)
- Processes (how)
- Presence (where)
- Solutions
- Customer experience
- Value capture
- Organization's supply chain
- Networking

Setting the pace of change with the innovation radar benefits both the company and stakeholders. For the company, these (keeping pace with the market and changing taste and preferences of customers) benefits come in the form of enhanced competitive advantage. For customers, it provides value for money.

KEY ELEMENTS FOR SUCCESS IN ORGANIZATIONAL CHANGE

Effective organizational change is not easily achieved; it requires sustainable effort from all members of the organization with strategic focus on people-related issues. Drawing a roadmap for successful organizational change quickly, may therefore, not be possible. However, organizations can focus on some key elements drawn from best practices in change management, and emulate other successful organizations. These elements can be listed as follows:

1. Plan long-term—Broadly, a sound strategic vision rather than a specific detailed plan can help the organization to make reliable predictions. The reason is quite obvious; a detailed five-year plan becomes outdated within a short time frame due to change in the planning premises (the basis on which such plans are drawn). Hence, a long-term plan drawn with sound strategic vision and provision to review the planning premises can benefit an organization to initiate change in the desired direction.

2. Establish forums to communicate methods to review and implement change—Members of the organization (not just limited to change agents) should be urged to participate in such forums. The organization will benefit from their inputs, approval, and commitment, and this will automatically enhance their cooperation to change. However, the process may not be so simple, unless it precedes sharing of change information with the people.

3. Empower people—Decisions should be made at the operation level through delegation of power and responsibility. This can make the organizational change process much simpler, as with increased ability for problem solving, employees will volunteer for change, thus resulting in improved organizational efficiency.

4. Make the strategic change process free from autocracy and interference—Managers and executives who do not subscribe to such mindsets or attitudes should be gradually excluded from the change team; else, they may set back the change process.

5. Encourage, enable, and develop people to be active in the change process. This will enable the organization to form virtual teams and adopt the matrix organizational structure, where seniors play a more proactive role in initiating change in the organization.

6. Make effective use of information systems for effective management of change-related information with real-time sharing.

> **EXHIBIT 2.4 Change through training initiatives**
>
> Two cases where training and development brought about a positive change have been discussed here.
>
> **Case 1** 44 operators of a PSU POL major were trained on the change imperatives leading to their agreeing to redeployed job positions. These operators were in the technical grade and entrusted with the job of filling the POL products in barrels and loading them onto trucks for distribution. As part of their restructuring plan, the PSU opted for automatic filling and loading of barrels, rendering these 44 employees redundant.
>
> The company did not have a voluntary retirement scheme. They identified two possible areas for redeployment: the canteen and security jobs. Asking workers to accept these jobs had a tremendous adverse impact, as workers thought them demeaning and disgraceful in relation to their present official positions. In a two-day training programme, the author helped to break the ice and make them understand the need for change. Through training reinforcement he convinced them to accept the canteen and security jobs, as they are not demeaning but are critical service areas in the organization.
>
> **Case 2** The same approach was applied to help militant trade union leaders to understand the process of job-pricing, which subsequently helped them to realize that the company was not cheating them on incentive pay-outs.
>
> The thrust of training and development programmes to introduce change in organizations should be to help people align their personal aims, wishes, and needs to those of the organization.

7. Use workshops for all cross sections of employees to review priorities, agree on broad medium to long-term vision and aims, and agree on short-term action plans, implementation methods, and accountabilities.
8. Make adjustments in recruitment, training, and development, to accelerate the pace of development of people and enable them to contribute positively to a culture of empowerment.

All these change constructs can be grouped either under external or internal forces of organizational change.

Organizational Change through Training and Development

It is widely believed that irrespective of the nature of the organization, organizational change encompasses training and development, and motivation. These are primarily required to help people understand the need for change and gain their acceptance. Regardless of the ranks of the individual employees, it is important to make them understand that without change they will lose out to competition and reduction in the company's market share will eventually lead to job losses. Exhibit 2.4 emphasizes this through the author's experience in two organizations.

ORGANIZATIONAL TRANSITION

Scholars have used the term 'organizational transition' to imply that implementing change takes organizations to a transition state from where it can move towards future desired conditions and activities. Alternatively, one can say that organizational transition succeeds organizational change. However, Beckhard and Harris (1987) described transition as a distinct phase of organizational change, which preceded the other two conditions, namely the present and the future states. The organizational transition process starts when the organization feels the need or desire for a new future. Such needs emerge from three important sources:

- Change in external environment, which compels organizations to find faster, cheaper, and better ways to meet the changing needs of customers and other stakeholders
- Technological change, which involves introduction of new processes and which in turn, requires skill renewal and competency development of existing manpower
- Top-down change initiatives of managers and executives, who prefer to emulate the best practice

The first two involve unfreezing the organization and introducing new work methods. These are reactive approaches, as organizations opt for transition or change only after the events. The last approach is proactive, as organizations volunteer to change in order to remain competitive in the market on their own initiative.

Another model of organizational transformation pioneered by HTI (a US-based professional body and a pioneer in initiating organizational transformation) in the 1990s suggests the following steps:

- Understanding the opportunities to change
- Designing a guiding vision for change
- Measuring the organizational energy (strength) for change
- Developing a comprehensive plan and commitment to change
- Developing partnerships (specific working relationships) to implement the change plan
- Developing leadership to initiate, manage, and sustain the desired change

To understand the degree of change preparedness, HTI further suggests that organizations should measure their degree of preparedness on a five-point scale and a high value score, say, 4 top 5 in all these areas, would indicate that transformation is possible.

Irrespective of the nature of the need for organizational change, a clear perspective on the present state and the desired future state of the organization in the post-change phase facilitates better management of the organizational transition.

Generic Change or Transition Models

Although the various change models will be discussed in a separate chapter, we will deliberate on generic change or transition models here, as these provide the basic direction for organizational change programmes.

Lewis–Parker model of transition

Ralph Lewis and Chris Parker described a change concept, also called 'transition curve' in their paper, 'Beyond the Peter Principle—Managing Successful Transitions', published in the *Journal of European Industrial Training* in 1981. The Lewis–Parker transition curve model approaches personal change from a different perspective to the Fisher model, and is represented through a seven-stage graph based on an original work by Adams, Hayes, and Hopkins in their *Transition, Understanding, and Managing Personal Change* published in 1976. The seven stages in the Lewis–Parker transition curve are as follows:

- Immobilization—shock; overwhelmed mismatch: expectations vs reality
- Denial of change—temporary retreat; false competence
- Incompetence—awareness and frustration
- Acceptance of reality—letting go
- Testing—new ways to deal with new reality
- Search for meaning—internalization and seeking to understand
- Integration—incorporation of meanings within behaviours

The Lewis–Parker transition curve contains interesting parallels at certain stages with the 'conscious competence' learning model, which is another helpful perspective for understanding change and personal development.

John Fisher's personal transition curve

John Fisher's personal transition curve has several stages, which transform individuals to the ultimate stage of acceptance of organizational change. Briefly stated, these stages are as follows:

Anxiety At this stage individuals are unable to adequately visualize the future. This is primarily because they do not have enough information to see the organizational change in the right perspective.

Happiness At this stage, the awareness is increased and the viewpoint of one is shared by the others. Members of the organization get a sense of relief, as their feeling of anticipation matures and they can predict what might happen. At this stage, organizations need to manage unrealistic expectations of its members and help them perceive the change implications correctly, with increased psychological contact. Many people in an organization may feel alienated when confronted with the possibility of change. Organizations should try to avoid this to minimize the resistance to change.

Fear People also suffer from a sense of fear when the awareness of change implications increase, as they need to act differently in a changed situation.

Threat Threat comes when people perceive major lifestyle changes, which generally comes from radical alteration of their future choices and an increased feeling of uncertainty about how they will act/react in a new and alien environment.

Guilt This stage occurs with the awareness of dislodgement of the self from one's core self-perception, when a person recognizes the inappropriateness of a wrong decision he/she may have made earlier.

Depression At this phase, members of the organization suffer from a general lack of motivation and confusion. With the increased sense of uncertainty, they undermine their core sense of self and lose their identity with no clear vision.

Disillusionment This stage occurs when people in the organization understand that their values, beliefs, and goals are not compatible with those of the changed organization. As a result, they become demotivated, unfocused, dissatisfied, and gradually withdraw, both mentally and physically.

Hostility This typical syndrome occurs when people are sure about the failure of certain change initiatives based on their past experience. They continue to operate processes that have repeatedly failed to achieve successful outcomes and are no longer part of the new process.

Denial At this stage, people refuse to accept the change and deny that there will be any impact on the individual. They behave as if there has been no change and continue with their old practices and processes, and ignore any evidence or information contrary to their belief.

The transition curve in Fig. 2.1 shows that it is important for individuals to understand the impact the change will have on their own personal construct systems and be able to work through the implications for their self-perception. Any change, no matter how small, has the potential to impact an individual, and may generate conflict between existing values and beliefs, and anticipated altered ones.

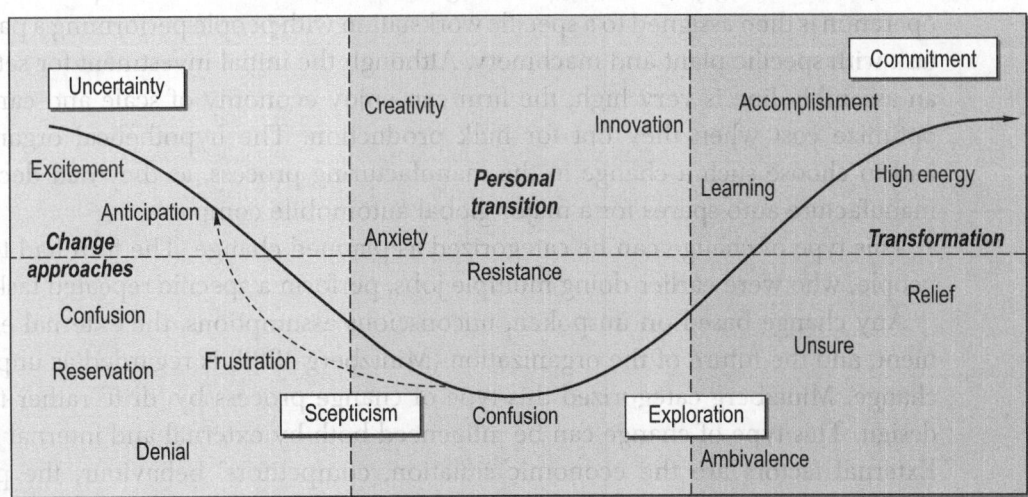

FIG. 2.1 A pictorial presentation of the transition curve

One danger for the individual, team, and organization occurs when an individual persists in operating a set of practices that has consistently failed (or resulted in an undesirable consequence) in the past, and does not help to extend and elaborate their view. Another danger area is that of denial, where people continue to operate as they always have, denying that there is any change at all. Both these can have a detrimental impact on an organization trying to change the culture and focus of its people.

TYPES OF CHANGE

Organizations adopt their change initiatives depending on the nature of change triggers discussed earlier. Such change initiatives can be classified into various types.

Planned vs Emergent Change

Planned change, on one hand, is an organizational change that is deliberate, and based on conscious reasoning and actions. On the other hand, at times and for many reasons, organizations opt for emergent change. This is also known as unplanned change. These two types of change are explained in terms of two different situations.

In the first instance, a manufacturing company changed from a job shop to an assembly line system in order to optimize cost. A job shop manufacturing process requires people with multiple skill sets, as it has the flexibility to accommodate customer-specified designs and specifications, to meet customers' varied requirements. However, the process is slow as frequent job changeover often causes problems of skill mismatch. Obviously, the cost of production becomes high and the firm cannot enjoy economy of scale. An assembly line system, on the other hand, standardizes the manufacturing process, by breaking the total job into several operations. Each operation is then assigned to a specific workstation with people performing a particular task with specific plant and machinery. Although the initial investment for setting up an assembly line is very high, the firm can enjoy economy of scale and can hence optimize cost when they opt for bulk production. The hypothetical organization had to choose such a change in the manufacturing process, as they had decided to manufacture auto spares for a major global automobile company.

This type of change can be categorized as planned change. The firm had to make people, who were earlier doing multiple jobs, perform a specific repeated task.

Any change based on unspoken, unconscious assumptions, the external environment, and the future of the organization (Mintzberg 1989) is regarded as unplanned change. Mintzberg categorized this type of change process by 'drift' rather than by design. This type of change can be influenced both by external and internal factors. External factors are the economic situation, competitors' behaviour, the political situation, legislative changes, etc. Internal factors may be the sudden power of different stakeholders or interest groups, knowledge management practices, building up the capability of people, etc.

In the second situation, after the collapse of the two hundred-year-old *Encyclopaedia Britannica*, the new promoter had to opt for product differentiation, introducing both the CD version and a single volume encyclopaedia to sustain in a competitive market.

To explain unplanned change, Dawson (1996) said that although the change process requires planned perceptive analysis, at times it cannot be isolated from the effects of coincidence, uncertainty, and chance. Thus, organizational change need not always be planned, fixed, or linear; it may be unplanned for emergent element.

Episodic vs Continuous Change

Episodic change is infrequent, discontinuous, intentional, and radical in nature (Weick and Quinn 1999). Replacement of strategy or a new product launch can be categorized under this type of change. Continuous change, on the other hand, is ongoing, evolving, and cumulative. Weick and Quinn termed episodic change as second order and continuous change as first order change process. Organizations often go for continuous change as part of their incremental or short-term strategy.

Developmental, Transitional, and Transformational Change

In terms of the extent and scope, Ackerman (1986) distinguished between three types of organizational change: developmental, transitional, and transformational.

Developmental change

This kind of change can be planned or emergent, that is, first order or incremental organizational change. It enhances or corrects existing aspects of an organization by primarily focusing on skills or process improvement.

Transitional change

Such change process tries to achieve a known desired state, different from the existing one. It is an episodic, planned, and second order, or radical change process. Most organizational change models are of the transitional type (Kanter 1983; Beckhard and Harris 1987; Nadler and Tushman 1989). However, it originated from the work of Lewin's (1951) three-stage process:

- Unfreezing the existing organizational equilibrium
- Moving to a new position
- Refreezing in a new equilibrium position

Schein (1987) further explored these three stages, suggesting that the unfreezing stage encompasses disconfirmation of expectations, creation of guilt or anxiety, and provision of psychological safety (to convert anxiety into motivation) to change. Similarly, the moving stage, which is achieved through cognitive restructuring, encompasses identification of a new role model or mentor and scanning the environment for new and relevant information. Schein suggested that the refreezing stage requires integration with the total personality and the concepts of self and relationships.

Transformational change

This kind of change is radical and second order in nature. It requires a shift in the assumptions made by the organization and its members. Transformation can result in an organization that differs significantly in terms of structure, processes, culture, and strategy. It may, therefore, result in the creation of an organization that operates in developmental mode—one that continuously learns, adapts, and improves.

To sum up the various forms of change, developmental change emphasizes improvement of existing situation; transitional change implements a known new state within a time-bound schedule; and transformational change focuses on the emergence of a new state, which is unknown till it takes shape. Exhibit 2.5 discusses change processes at Siemens AG and helps to get a better understanding of these.

EXHIBIT 2.5 Developing a high performance work culture: A study on Siemens AG

Siemens AG is a global major in electrical and electronics with a turnover of £60 billion and more than half a million people on its payroll. Based in Munich, Germany, Siemens has business presence all over the world. Today, Siemens is inseparable from our lives, as its product lines extend from traffic signal lights to MRI scanning machines. Due its global presence, Siemens needs to address cross-cultural issues and embrace those in their management practices. A high performance culture is a way of working and consists of a set of values which Siemens nurtures, to encourage people and to achieve better results. This work culture is shared by everyone.

For its sophisticated range of products, Siemens employs people with a high level of competency. Some of the skill sets required are not easily available. For example, information technology specialists, researchers, new product developers, etc. are not readily obtainable to fit its manpower requirements. But for its high-employer branding and prevalence of a performance culture, Siemens could have an edge over other competitors in sourcing the requisite skills.

To sustain the culture of performance, Siemens adopts an HRD strategy and helps people to fulfil them. People are given a choice and encouraged to identify ways to improve their careers, attend training programmes, do interesting work, and maintain a better work-life balance.

Siemens believes that total engagement of people in the workplace develops a commitment towards the organization. People become citizens of the company and when they are managed well, they feel motivated, and do a good job. Siemens regards this plan as a business strategy, which emphasizes performance, operational excellence, and responsibility towards the organization. With specific reference to people management areas, Siemens emphasizes excellence along with building and sustaining a culture of high performance. Excellence is achieved when people are given responsibility. A sense of responsibility motivates them and they feel their efforts are valued.

(Contd)

(Exhibit 2.5 contd)

A strong sense of loyalty and belonging, even in a technology intensive organization such as Siemens, makes their employees innovative. Today, innovation and creativity constitute their greatest competitive advantage. An increasing sense of value and engagement of people can best be ensured by sustaining a high performance work culture.

Engagement, both as a feeling and as a reality, is also possible through teamwork. Siemens' teamwork culture is very strong, as all operations are assigned to teams. Siemens expects true involvement of all cross sections of people in the business of the organization. Siemens' HRD strategy is drawn on four main areas. These are as follows:

- Achieving a high performance culture
- Increasing the global talent pool
- Strengthening expert careers
- Siemens' leadership excellence (SLE) programme

A high performance culture is the way of working at Siemens and involves everyone, and each person has the opportunity to develop their own specialization and acquire further expertise. The SLE provides the highest calibre leadership and management training. Siemens' talent management philosophy involves ensuring that every employee is provided with the guidance and support to achieve their full potential. This encourages them to do their best at all times. Everyone works together to achieve the organization's objectives as well as to meet their own personal goals, and they all share the same vision and dreams. For Siemens, matching talent with tasks produces a competitive advantage. Talent management enables

- job enrichment, where individuals are encouraged to take on extra tasks and responsibilities within an existing job role to make work more rewarding; and
- job enlargement, where the scope of the existing job is extended to give a broader range of responsibility, plus extra knowledge and skills development.

Talent management is a global philosophy that is a key part of supporting each of the elements of business strategy, and enables Siemens' managers to engage and motivate employees throughout the organization.

By applying talent management to all staff,

- all customer-facing staff are engaged, so that all customers benefit;
- everyone has the opportunity and choices to achieve their full potential; and
- the pipeline of high-fliers is sustained.

Siemens has created a standard process for managing the performance and development of all employees. This is referred to as the performance management process. It creates a direct link between the strategy of the whole organization and plans for each individual. Each individual is given targets based on their role and responsibility within the organization. By meeting personal targets, the individual is able to help the organization achieve its targets.

Performance management is a systematic process that creates trust and open communication by

- setting objectives,
- monitoring progress,
- creating an ongoing dialogue between each team member and his/her manager, and
- enabling forthright discussion.

Performance management in Siemens is the engine that drives talent management. It is the cornerstone of its high performance culture. When conducted in a consistent way, this system makes sure that everyone is informed about their performance. Employees are clear about the impact of their performance and what the consequences are for their development. Everyone in the organization pulls together to achieve the business strategy.

Source: Adapted from www.siemens.co.uk and www.thetimes100.co.uk, accessed on 10 June 2009.

SYSTEMS THINKING AND CHANGE

Organizational change is generally supposed to be a rational, controlled, and orderly process. However, in reality, it is very chaotic. The pursuit for organizational change involves shifting of goals, frequent discontinuity, and surprise, with unexpected change outcomes (Cummings et al. 2005; Dawson 1996). For this, change can be understood in the context of complex dynamic systems. Systems thinking originated in the 1920s, primarily from biology and engineering. To explain the concept of systems thinking, Popper (1972) introduced the concept of three Rs, namely reduction, repeatability, and refutation. Systems thinking enhances our knowledge and understanding by breaking up elements to manage the change.

A system is a set of elements connected together to form a whole, thereby possessing properties of the whole rather than of its component parts (Checkland 1981). Activity within a system is the result of the influence of one element on another. This influence is called feedback and can be positive (amplifying) or negative (balancing) in nature. Systems are not chains of linear cause-and-effect relationships but complex networks of interrelationships (Senge 1990). They can be described as being closed or open. Closed systems are completely autonomous and independent of what is going on around them. Open systems exchange materials, energy, and information with their environment. The systems of interest in managing change can all be characterized as open systems. Box 2.1 highlight the features of systems thinking in the context of change.

> **BOX 2.1 Systems thinking and change**
>
> In terms of understanding organizations, systems thinking suggests that issues, events, forces, and incidents should not be viewed as isolated phenomena but seen as interconnected and interdependent components of a complex entity. Applied to change management, the systems theory highlights the following points:
> - A system is made up of related and interdependent parts, so that any system must be viewed as a whole.
> - A system cannot be considered in isolation from its environment.
> - A system which is in equilibrium will change only if some type of energy is applied.
> - Players within a system have a view of that system's function and purpose, and players' views may be very different from each other.

From a typical organizational point of view, holistic systems thinking may be understood from the following perspectives:

- Awareness of the multiple issues involved in the organizational activities
- Interest in designing, planning, and managing organizations as living, interdependent systems committed to providing seamless attention for customers
- Recognition of the need to develop shared values, purposes, and practices, within and between organizations

- Use of large group interventions to bring together the perspectives of a wide range of stakeholders across a wider system

STRATEGIES OF CHANGE MANAGEMENT

Different strategies and procedures are used to categorize the change environment. In organizations, change strategies are adopted on the basic premise that people will volunteer to engage themselves in the change process. Normally, organizations adopt four types of change strategies. These are normative re-educative, rational-empirical, power-coercive, and action-centred. These strategies are not mutually exclusive; rather, they work and support the effective implementation plan at different stages of the change process.

Fred Nickols (2003), however, categorized four types of change management strategies differently. The first three change management strategies, that is, rational-empirical, normative re-educative, and power-coercive, are adapted from Chin and Benne's (1969) landmark contribution on changes in human systems. The fourth, that is, action-centred as referred to by other scholars, has been introduced by Nickols as environmental adaptive.

Let us try to understand these further.

Normative Re-educative Strategy

This strategy believes that changing the norms, attitudes, and values of individuals will lead to changes in their behaviour. It is based upon the core beliefs, values, and attitudes, and assumes that change will occur as individuals change their attitudes and this makes them behave differently.

The normative re-educative strategy considers people as social beings who stick to cultural norms and values. Here, change focuses on redefining the present values and norms, and making people embrace these. Characteristically, people look for culture-fit change solutions and tend to 'go with the flow'. Thus, it is for the organization to identify the flow. Charismatic and dynamic leaders can act as flow agents, as their behaviour and practices (as required for the changed situation) are emulated by their followers, that is, people in general. At times, informal organization and communities of practice work well here.

Change strategy in this case emphasizes solutions that are more consistent with the beliefs and value systems of the people, and work well when relationships are cordial and harmonious. However, the role of leadership is more important for the successful implementation of change.

Rational-empirical Strategy

The rational-empirical strategy of change management deals with the rationality of people to embrace change for their self-interest. However, this is possible only by persuasion and detailed communication. Change intents need to be clear, and organizations must understand the benefits of such change.

BHEL and NTPC used this strategy to facilitate their change process, and both achieved success.

Before an organization considers using this strategy, it must answer the following questions:

- Are the people rational?
- Do they follow their self-interest?
- Can they be reasoned logically?
- Can they set aside their value judgement when persuaded with valid reasons?

Organizations also need to provide incentives for change and guard against risk. Even rational people can oppose the change move if they perceive the benefits to be small. In such cases, organizations must make extensive use of training and communication to inform people that without change organizational sustainability will be at risk. While incentives are a short-term gain, long-term sustainability, ahead of competition, is substantially more rewarding.

Power-coercive Strategy

Organizational change often requires application of power. Employees become change-compliant when it is enforced by the top echelons of management. Hence, power coercive strategy often helps (if applied judiciously) to achieve the change intents.

In power coercive change management strategies, people are basically compliant and will generally do what they are told or can be made to do. Successful change is based on the exercise of authority and the imposition of sanctions. This can range from the iron hand in the velvet glove to downright brutality—'my way or the highway'. The basic aim here is to decrease people's options, not to increase them. Surprisingly, in many situations, people actually want and will readily accept this approach, particularly when all feel threatened and few know what to do. This is the 'stick' side of carrot-and-stick management.

Two major factors that influence the choice of this strategy are time and seriousness of the threat faced. If the organization sits astride the fabled 'burning platform', the threat is grave and the time for action is limited. The metaphor of a burning platform is useful but only if all concerned can see that the platform is on fire. This is rarely the case in an organization. Few companies have people who understand the way the business works and fewer still who appreciate the threats it faces or the opportunities it encounters.

It has been argued that change-minded leaders should create a burning platform. That idea may have merit in extreme situations but it also entails considerable risk to the organization, its people, and to the leader who attempts it.

A mitigating factor here is culture. If the culture is basically one of a benign bureaucracy that is clearly threatened, its members are likely to go along with a sensible programme, no matter how high-handed it is. Conversely, if the culture is laced with autonomy and entrepreneurship but has become complacent and contented, people will resent, and perhaps, oppose or resist authoritarian moves. In this case, key positions may have to be filled with new people.

Action-centred Strategy

Action-centred strategies focus on problem solving. Such strategies not only help to resolve the problem, but also effectively manage the change implications, particularly in the post-change phase.

Environmental adaptive strategies (or action-centred strategies) for effecting organizational change are used when people oppose loss and disruption, and demonstrate their eagerness to adapt readily to new circumstances. An organization may use change initiatives to build a new organization and transfer existing people to it. This strategy exploits the usual adaptive nature of people to smoothen the change process and thus avoids change resistance. It is also known as 'self-cannibalization' or 'die-on-the-vine' strategy. While self-cannibalization indicates that unless you do it, someone else will, the die-on-the-vine strategy assumes that people are quick in their response pattern, both in opposing the change move (when they feel it is undesirable) and in accepting or adapting to change (when they feel it is desirable).

The major consideration here is the degree of change. This strategy is best suited for situations where radical, transformative change is needed. It is not the strategy of choice for gradual or incremental change. Hence, when this strategy is used, it is often believed that it is better to dismantle the old organization and create a new one.

Exhibit 2.6 provides valuable guidelines for selection of appropriate strategies.

EXHIBIT 2.6 Strategy selection considerations

1. Degree of change—When change is radical, the environmental adaptive strategy should be selected.
2. Degree of resistance—When change is strongly resisted, use a mix of power coercive and environmental adaptive strategies. If there is weak resistance, a combination of rational empirical and normative re-educative strategies works well.
3. Population—When the population size is a combination of diverse people, all four strategies work, that is, something for everyone.
4. Stakes—When the stakes are high, a mix of all the four strategies is used, as the organization cannot afford to leave anything to chance. When the stakes are moderate, it is better to use power-coercive strategy and when they are low, any strategy will work.

(Contd)

(Exhibit 2.6 contd)

> 5. Time frame—Short time frames call for a power coercive strategy. Longer time frames require a mix of rational-empirical, normative re-educative, and environmental-adaptive strategies.
> 6. Expertise—If the expertise for making change is available, a mix of strategies is recommended, but if it is not available then the power-coercive strategy should be used.
> 7. Dependency—When an organization is dependent on its people, its ability to command and demand is limited. In the reverse case, the ability of the people to oppose is restricted. If however, the dependency is mutual, the organization can negotiate the change requirements.
>
> For all these situations, there is no single change strategy. Often the power-coercive strategy works but the right solution can be achieved through a mix of strategies.

PERSONAL CONSTRUCT PSYCHOLOGY AND ORGANIZATIONAL CHANGE

Personal construct psychology (PCP) or personal construct theory (PCT) is a concept pioneered by Kelly (1955). This theory proposes that we must understand how other people see their world and the meaning they attribute to things in order to effectively communicate and connect with them. The PCP theory is extremely relevant to develop personal emotional maturity and self-awareness in oneself and others, and for understanding the behaviour of others, and as such, its concepts augment and support many of the behavioural models and methodologies.

The PCP theory also provides a very useful and accessible additional perspective to the world and how we relate to it. It places the individual as its central focal point and is based on understanding them from within their own world view, that is, by understanding how they see the world and not according to our interpretation of it. Each of us interacts with the world from our own unique perspective and this is built up of all our past and potential future experiences, and dictates how we approach situations.

Psychological theory, generally, requires that we observe other people's behaviour and actions, and interpret them in our own way, attributing meanings based on our own past (childhood) experiences. Personal construct psychology is a more liberating theory allowing individuals to develop and grow throughout their life, constantly observing, assimilating, developing actions/reactions, experimenting, and testing beliefs. Kelly (1955) used the phrase 'man the scientist' to explain how we interact with our world.

As our nature constantly changes, we are not 'victims of our biography' and have the choice (although sometimes it may not appear so) of adopting new ways of interacting.

How we do this is a result of our past experiences and an assessment of the current situation, which is then mapped onto possible alternative courses of action; we then choose the one we think will best suit our needs. Thus, our behaviours are not static.

To interact with others, we need to have some understanding of how they perceive their world. What does it mean when someone is described as an 'extrovert'? Is it that they are the life and soul of the party, or are they considered to be loud and overbearing? How we and others treat the extrovert depends on whether it is viewed it as a positive or negative character trait.

Kelly defined his theory in a formal structured way by devising what he called the 'fundamental postulate'. Basically, this is a posh term for the statement which underpins the whole of personal construct psychology. Eleven more corollaries (or clarifying statements) were also developed which extended the theory and further elaborated the impact of the theory and how it is used. Over a period of time, as the range of the theory has developed (see Dallos 1991; Procter 1981; Balnaves and Caputi 1993), these have been expanded and additions have been made. However, these additions have not been universally acclaimed and only the original eleven are recognized.

From the organizational point of view, some constructs are more important than others. The most important ones are those that are 'core' to our sense of being. These are resistant to change and include items, such as the moral code, religious beliefs, etc., and cause significant psychological impact, if they are threatened in any way. The others are called 'peripheral' constructs and a change in them does not have the same impact. It also follows that some constructs will actually subsume other constructs as we move up the hierarchy.

There are three types of constructs. The 'pre-emptive' construct is applied in an 'all or nothing' way. For example, if an item is a ball, then it is nothing else but a ball. The second type is the 'constellate' construct. These are stereotyping constructs, for example, if this article is a ball then it must be round, made of leather, and used in football matches. The last type of construct category is 'propositional'. This one carries no implications or additional labels and is the most open form of construct. It should be noted that constructs need not have 'words' attached to them. We can, and do, have constructs which were either formed before we could speak or which have a non-verbal symbol identifying it, for example, 'gut feeling' or 'it feels right' would be a non-verbal construct. Kelly originally called these 'preverbal' constructs, but in line with others (notably Ravenette 1997).

Kelly also proposed a form of drama therapy for use by organizations. In his version, which he called 'fixed role therapy', he drew up a new character (including a new name and history) in conjunction with the client organization, and encouraged them to act as if they were this new character. This allowed the client organization to try out new ways of looking at the world in a safe environment (if it did not work they just became themselves again). Hypnotherapy has also been used to loosen (and tighten) constructs.

ABC Technique and Organizational Change

The ABC technique (Tschudi 1977) is a powerful tool for understanding why people are not willing to change. Here A is the desired change, with constructs $B1$ and $B2$

elicited; *B1* being the disadvantages about the present state and *B2* the advantages about moving to the new state. However, it is possible (if not probable) that the current situation has some advantages which may outweigh the disadvantages. Therefore, *C1* are constructs which show the negative side of moving whilst *C2* are the positive aspects of remaining the same. But, by examining the costs of not changing we can identify the barriers and introduce measures to overcome them (if necessary). Box 2.2 illustrates a model of change at the macro level proposed by Ehrlich.

> **BOX 2.2 Model of change at macro level**
>
> Paul Ehrlich (1968) has designed the change model with an equation that clarifies the magnitude of change requirement. Although the model is more appropriate at the macro-economic level, that is, for the nation as a whole, it can also be used by the organization. The equation is as follows:
> $I = P \times C \times T$ (originally $I = P \times A \times T$, where A stands for affluence)
> Here, I = impact, P = number of people, C = consumption per capita (GDP per capita) and T = technology. Reducing population in the short-run is not possible for a country and neither is the consumption. However, technological change is feasible and with efficient use of resources (according to Ehrlich, 90% more efficiently), society can ensure change. A similar analogy is also applicable for the organization.

Integrative Approach to Organizational Change

The most desirable approach of ensuring successful organizational change is to adopt the integrative approach. This approach aligns behavioural, structural, and technical strategies with organizational development strategies, and accordingly develops new behaviours, new relationships, and new processes. Figure 2.2 illustrates the integrative model of organizational change.

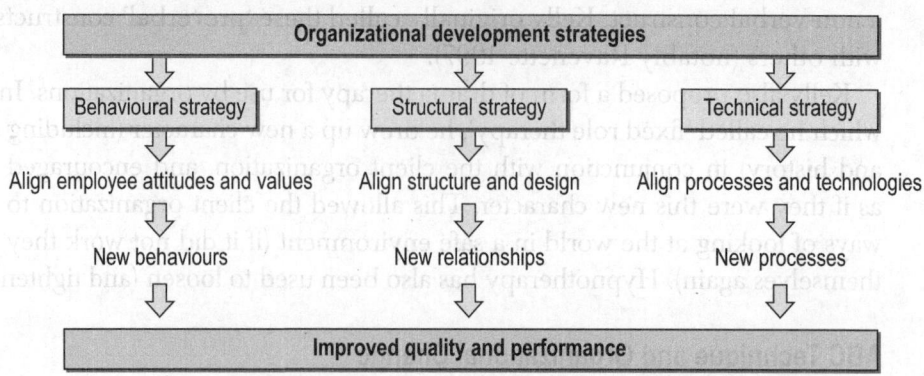

FIG. 2.2   The integrative approach to organizational change

ROLE OF ORGANIZATIONAL CHANGE CONSULTANTS

For organizational change to work, it must be a unique solution crafted either by the organization or by an outsider who will play the role of a consultant. Consultants specializing in organizational change can fill a number of needs. First, they can acquire useful information from customers, suppliers, employees, and managers. Second, they can provide and generate insights into organizational change issues not previously known or understood by senior management. Third, they can facilitate organizational change decision-making sessions that lead to clear change management action. Fourth, they can provide specialized organizational change expertise in a new procedure, technique, or way of thinking that is unknown to the organization. Please refer to Appendix 2.1 where a set of guidelines for change management has been provided. This resource would be useful for internal and external consultants while suggesting action plans.

Using a case study, Exhibit 2.7 illustrates a typical way of handling clients by organizational change consultants.

EXHIBIT 2.7   PwC's initiative with BP

The issue

The finance control and accounting function (FC&A) of BP, a gas and oil sector company, was part of the business, but in 2003 the new management framework made it a separate function.

Although this made it independent, it was still vital to maintain strong relationships with the business. The change implied a whole new set of accountabilities, relationships, and behaviours. BP quickly recognized the need to develop the function's capabilities and in 2004 it asked PricewaterhouseCoopers (PwC), which already had a long-standing relationship with BP, to work with FC&A's newly established learning faculty to design, develop, and deliver a 'great' training programme.

PwC's approach

PwC worked with BP as a partnership and helped it to develop a highly interactive programme relevant to the everyday experiences of the delegates. It combined its finance experience, training skills, and BP-specific knowledge, to produce a programme focused on behaviours and managing relationships. However, it was totally grounded in the jobs people did and used realistic control dilemmas to help people think how they would act in a given situation.

People were encouraged to put forward their views and experiences, which often meant that discussions got quite intense. When a debate took off, the facilitator ran with it, as this was one of the most valuable elements of the programme.

The outcome

The flagship 'controls excellence' programme is now being delivered globally to controllers in all BP businesses. PwC firms in the UK, US, and Singapore are assisting the faculty to deliver a further programme to embed control awareness.

The result has been excellent participant feedback, rising demand for places, and clear evidence of people taking action. 'This course has been great,' said Susan Elliott, a joint venture

(Contd)

(Exhibit 2.7 contd)

reporting manager based in Angola. 'My boss took it last year and encouraged me to come, and his boss will be taking it next year,' she said.

Martin Ludlam, an assistant business unit controller with BP in Trinidad and Tobago, agrees, 'From the business point of view, I now understand my accountabilities a lot better. It's great to discuss things and pull them together.'

The value that BP places on this programme is confirmed in PwC's client satisfaction surveys, with scores averaging nine out of ten.

Source: http://www.pwc.com, accessed on 9 September 2009.

COMMON DRAWBACKS IN IMPLEMENTING ORGANIZATIONAL CHANGE

All organizational change initiatives are not always successful. The failure rate is very high. There are many reasons for this:

- Inappropriate approach of management or not being suitable for organizational change requirements
- Inappropriate and often unrealistic expectations from organizational change
- Absence of sustained efforts over a period of time to introduce organizational change
- Incompatibility between declared change objectives, and actual behaviour and actions
- Poor understanding of the organizational change. Often many organizations construe systematic training as part of organizational change
- Lack of support and systems
- Lack of commitment to organizational change plans

Addressing and guarding against all these drawbacks can ease the process of organizational change, and make the process and the programmes smooth and successful.

SUMMARY

This chapter discussed the basics of organizational change. The subject encompasses four major issues, such as content, contextual, process, and criterion. Content issues deal with substance, contextual issues focus on external and internal environmental conditions. Process issues account for the actions taken, while criterion issues tackle the outcome of organizational change. Organizational development is now imperative for every organization to sustain in a competitive environment. Organizational change precedes the organizational development initiative in any organization. Although it is difficult to enumerate the reasons for organizational change, we have highlighted some of the motives, such as setting right something which is not in order, fixing things which are needed, grasping opportunities to derive strategic advantage, and driving the organization with a structured vision.

The chapter outlines various steps to successful change, lists the differences between organizational change, transformation, and renewal, and elaborates on different change triggers. It also focuses on different organizational change tips and the mechanism of organizational change through training and development, employee motivation, etc. Various models of organizational change, such as Lewis–Parker model, John Fisher's model, etc., have also been discussed. The chapter also outlines various types of change, the role of systems thinking in organizational change, various change management strategies, and methods of managing resistance to change.

KEY TERMS

ABC technique and organizational change Here, A is the desired change with constructs B1 and B2 elicited. B1 are the disadvantages about the present state and B2 are the advantages about moving to the new state. However, it is possible (if not probable) that the current situation has some advantages which may outweigh the disadvantages. Therefore, C1 are constructs which show the negative side of moving, whilst C2 are the positive aspects of staying the same. But, by looking at the pay-offs for not changing, we can identify the barriers and put measures in place to overcome them (if necessary).

Competency-driven organizational change Competencies for an organization cannot remain fixed. With the changing technology, business environment, and the degree of competition, organizations need to revisit the available competencies of the people and the organization as a whole, and accordingly initiate organizational change.

Environment-driven organizational change Environment-driven change requires an organization to review their structure, relationships with the stakeholders, organizational dependence on environment linked with their important activities such as, buying and selling, i.e., customers and suppliers, compliance with the changing government policies and programmes, etc. Degree of dependence decides the extent of adaptability for organizations. Environmental factors being exogenous to the organizations, and environment being continuously changing, organizations need to be dynamic to respond to even slightest change cues.

Lewis–Parker model The Lewis–Parker 'transition curve' model approaches personal change using seven stages such as, immobilization, denial of change, incompetence, acceptance of reality, testing, search for meaning, and integration. The model helps in understanding change and personal development.

Normative re-educative strategy This approach believes that changing the norms, attitudes, and values of individuals will lead to changes in their behaviours. It is based upon core beliefs, values, and attitudes. So change will occur as individuals change their attitudes and this leads them to want to behave differently.

Organizational transition Organizational transition is a distinct phase of organizational change, which starts when the organizations feel the need or desire for a new future. Such needs emerge from changes in the external environment. Technological change, and from top-down change initiatives of managers of the organization.

Transformational change Transformational change is radical or second order in nature. It requires a shift in assumptions made by the organization and its members. Transformation can result in an organization that differs significantly in terms of structure, processes, culture, and strategy. It may, therefore, result in the creation of an organization that operates in developmental mode—one that continuously learns, adapts, and improves.

Transitional change Transitional change seeks to achieve a known desired state using a three-step change process, involving
(a) *unfreezing* the existing organizational equilibrium,
(b) *moving* to a new position, and
(c) *refreezing* in a new equilibrium position.

CONCEPT REVIEW QUESTIONS

1. Why do organizations need to change? What are the important theories of organizational change?
2. Explain John Kotter's model of successful change.
3. What is organizational transition? How does it differ from organizational change and renewal?
4. Identify some of the organizational change triggers. How can a new strategy act as an organizational change trigger?
5. What are the key elements for successful organizational change? What trouble-shooting exercises are necessary?
6. Explain the Lewis–Parker and John Fisher models of organizational transition.
7. What are the different types of change? How does planned change differ from emergent change?
8. Explain the concept of systems thinking in organizational change. How does it influence change management strategy in an organization?
9. Write short notes on the following:
   (a) ABC technique
   (b) Normative strategy
   (c) Episodic change
   (d) Generic change

CRITICAL THINKING QUESTIONS

1. An Indian multinational has recently acquired a US-based company consolidating their stake by more than 51 per cent. During the acquisition, the Indian MNC agreed that there would be no job-cuts or downsizing in the US unit. At the consolidation stage, it restructured some of the job positions in the US and rendered some employees as surplus. However, these employees were offered redeployment in some newly identified job positions, after retraining. This was viewed as a violation of the initial agreement of acquisition, as US employees considered it as an attempt towards future retrenchment. Discuss this scenario in the context of the personal construct psychology (PCP) propounded by George Kelly.
2. Following the acquisition of Corus of UK, Tata Steel has to restructure organizational activities in order to achieve integration. Study the information available on websites and in newspaper reports, and critically evaluate the change process adopted by Tata Steel.
3. To achieve performance-driven organizational change, a Japanese conglomerate introduced teamwork at their industrial hub in India, with clear terms of reference to employees that they were working for the team their core objective was achieving the team goal. Although culturally congruent, as India also believes in collectivism, the Indian workers are unable to cope with the pressure and there is a high rate of absenteeism. The reasons for this are largely attributable to occupational health hazards. Suggest how the company can still ensure the performance-driven organizational change.

CASE STUDY

Change in Customer Service of Alcatel

Alcatel is the leader in the telecommunications industry in Europe. It is a $23 billion provider of telecommunication products and services. In the wake of deregulation, voice-data convergence, and rising consumer expectations for enhanced value lashing the European telecommunications industry in the 1990s, Alcatel has emerged as a winner by focusing on providing superior customer service. Alcatel executives determined that if the company were to compete and excel in a dramatically different telecommunications environment, it would have to provide superior customer service. Accenture helped Alcatel to create a new customer service operating model and interact with its highly diverse customer base more effectively. With more than 1000 employees now connected to Alcatel's customer service system, the company strengthened its competitive positioning by meeting the needs of its demanding customers more effectively.

The convergence of voice and data transmission, commoditization of equipment, deregulation, and heightened customer demand for more value were forcing telecom companies to rethink on their business. Alcatel determined through soul-searching that it was not optimally organized to respond to the new market demands. In fact, the company's approach to customer service—which was highly fragmented, with service definition, pricing, and organization, differing from country to country—was having an adverse effect on sales, and squeezing the already slim margins. Alcatel executives, the e-business group, decided that if the company were to sustain and compete, a superior customer service will be required to complement its impressive stable of products and services.

The new customer service operations model created to effectively interact with its highly diverse customer base had the following features:

- Enable most customer inquiries to be resolved over telephone. Alcatel was, till then, responding to most customer inquiries by sending field sales technicians or salespeople to the customer location, which was an expensive proposition for the company.
- Allow a high level of customer segmentation based on required service levels to optimize customer service activities. Under the previous model, customers' purchasing histories or what service activities they had agreed to pay for was not always clear.
- Provide customer service that was both standardized and personalized.

The company determined that it could create a new model to cost-effectively standardize service across its customer base, while accommodating personalized interaction with various accounts.

It believed that with these features, its new operating model would meet the dual objectives of maximizing customer satisfaction while increasing overall profitability.

A cornerstone of Alcatel's new operating model was the service factory concept, designed jointly by Alcatel and Accenture, and built on a foundation of software from Siebel Systems. The service factory comprises a three-step process for responding to customer inquiries.

In the event of a problem or inquiry, a customer contacts a welcome centre, accessed via a unique telephone number. The welcome centre staff, who has access to the customer's records, logs the reported problem and checks the service agreement details before routing the call to

- an appropriate diagnostic centre where skilled engineers access the customer site remotely, diagnose the problem, and try to solve it. If further specialized technical input (usually for hardware-related questions) is required, the diagnostic centre routes the call to the second level;
- a research and development (R&D) centre, either within Alcatel or at a relevant supplier; and
- if the situation is ultra-critical, for example; in a hospital, an engineering team would be immediately flown to the customer site to resolve the problem.

Piloted in France, the service factory concept today has been successfully rolled out in Europe, with welcome centres in many locations, including Berlin and Brussels, in addition to Paris and Lyon. Furthermore, the diagnostic centres are now organized on a skill-set basis rather than geographically. This means, for example, that the appropriate resource response for a customer enquiry from, say Denmark, may be in Germany, in which case the call will be so routed, but in such a way that the customer experiences a seamless provision of service. This approach is fully effective in responding to 80 per cent of enquiries.

Innovation delivered

To date, the results of the service factory have been impressive.

Now that all customer records are consistently, reliably, and comprehensively updated, customer satisfaction has increased as much as 86 per cent. Furthermore, the welcome centre receives more than 10,000 calls per day from across Europe, answers 93 per cent of them within 15 seconds, and loses less than two per cent of them.

Alcatel's confidence in the new service organization is reflected in its adoption of the all-in-one brand name that has encapsulated the service factory offering to external audiences across Europe.

The service factory approach, using one accessible and continually updated database, has enabled Alcatel to do away with a confusing range of catalogues and pricing structures that existed under the old country-by-country model. Now there is one pan-European model—clear, keenly priced, and reliable—that contributes to enhanced customer experiences.

With more than 1000 employees now connected to Alcatel's customer service system—including 650 in the service factory—the company has been able to strengthen its competitive positioning by more effectively meeting the needs of its demanding customers.

Source: www.acceature.com/Global/.../Customer.../ AlcatelMdel.htm, accessed on 20 October 2009.

Discussion Questions

1. Analyse the case in the light of any similar Indian telecom company which, in your opinion, requires a similar approach.
2. Explain how Alcatel's new services strategy fits into the evolving marketplace.
3. How would you describe the value proposition of Alcatel's unified communication solutions portfolio and why do you consider it unique?

REFERENCES

Ackerman, L.S. (1986), 'Development, transition or transformation: The question of change in organizations', *Organizational Development Practitioner*, December, pp. 1–8.

Balnaves M. and P. Caputi (1993), 'Corporate constructs; to what extent are personal constructs personal?' *International Journal of Personal Construct Psychology*, Vol. 6, Issue 2, pp. 119–139.

Beckhard, R. and R.T. Harris (1987), *Organizational Transitions*, Addison-Wesley OD Series, Reading, MA.

Bhattacharyya, Dipak Kumar (2007), *Human Resource Research Methods*, Oxford University Press, New Delhi.

Checkland, P. (1981), *Systems Thinking: Systems Practices*, Wiley, New York.

Chin, Robert and Kenneth D. Benne (1969), 'General strategies for effecting changes in human systems', *The Planning of Change*, Second Edition, Bennis, Warren G., Kenneth D. Benne, and Robert Chin (eds), Holt, Rinehart & Winston, New York.

Cummings, T.G. and C.G. Worley (2005), *Organization Development and Change*, Eighth Edition, South-Western Publishing, Mason.

Dallos, R. (1991), *Family Belief Systems, Therapy and Change*, Open University Press, Milton Keynes.

Dawson, S.J.N.D. (1996), *Analysing Organizations*, Macmillan, Hampshire.

Ehrlich, P. (1968), *The Population Bomb*, Ballantine Books, New York.

Fisher, John and Dr David Savage (1999), in Fisher and Savage (eds), *Beyond Experimentation Into Meaning*, EPCA Publications, Farnborough.

Ford, Bill (2005), 'Innovation key to Ford's future; Commitment to hybrids to grow', http://media. ford.com, accessed on 24 September 2008.

Kanter, R.M. (2001), *Evolve! Succeeding in the Digital Culture of Tomorrow*, Harvard Business School, Boston.

———. (1995), *World Class: Thriving Locally in the Global Economy*, Simon and Schuster, New York.

———. (1989), *When Giants Learn to Dance*, Simon and Schuster, New York.

Kanter, R.M. (1983), *The Changemasters: Innovation and Entrepreneurship in the American Corporation*, Simon and Schuster, New York.

Kelly, G.A. (1963), *Theory of Personality, Psychology of Personal Constructs*, Norton, New York.

———. (1955), *The Psychology of Personal Constructs*, Routledge, London.

Kotter, J. (1995), 'Leading change: Why transformation efforts fail', *Harvard Business Review*, Vol. 73 No. 2, pp. 59–67.

Lewin, K. (1951), *Field Theory in Social Science*, Harper and Row, New York.

Lippit, R., J. Watson, and B. Westley (1958), *The Dynamics of Planned Change*, Harcourt, Brace and World, New York.

Mintzberg, H. (1989), *Mintzberg on Management: Inside Our Strange World of Organizations*, Free Press, Chicago.

Nadler, D. and M. Tushman (1989), 'Organizational frame-bending', *Academy of Management Executive*, Vol. 13, pp. 194–202.

Nadler, D.A. (1993), 'Concepts for the management of organizational change', in Maybe, C. and B. Mayon-White (eds), *Managing Change* Second Edition, Paul Chapman, London, pp. 85–98.

Nobel, J.C. (2005), 'Ballmer: "Microsoft's priority is innovation"', 19 October 2005, www.eweek.com, accessed on 20 July 2007.

Pasmore, W. and M. Fagans (1992), 'Participation, individual development, and organizational change: A review and synthesis', *Journal of Management*, Vol. 18, No. 2, pp. 375–397.

Popper, K. (1972), *Objective Knowledge*, Oxford University Press, Oxford.

Procter H. (1981), 'Family construct psychology', in Walrond-Skinner, S. (ed.), *Family Therapy and Approaches*, Routledge and Paul Kegan, London.

Ravenette, T. (1997), *Selected papers: Personal Construct Psychology and the Practice of an Educational Psychologist*, EPCA Publications, Farnborough.

Sashkin, M. and W. Burke (1987), 'Organization development in the nineteen-eighties', *Journal of Management*, Vol. 13, pp. 393–417.

Sawhney, Mohanbir, Robert C. Wolcott, and Inigo Arroniz (2006), 'The 12 different ways for companies to innovate', *MIT Sloan Management Review*, Spring 2006, Vol. 47, Issue 3, pp. 74–82.

Schein, E.H. (1992), *Organizational Culture and Leadership*, Jossey Bass Publishers, San Francisco.

Senge, P.M. (1990), 'The leader's New York: building learning organizations', *Sloan Management Review*, Fall, pp. 7–23.

Tschudi F. (1977), 'Loaded and honest questions', in Bannister D. (ed.), *New Perspectives in Personal Construct Theory*, Academic Press, London.

Weick, K.E. and R.E. Quinn (1999), 'Organizational change and development', *Annual Review of Psychology*, Vol. 50, pp. 361–386.

Woodman, R. (1989), 'Organization change and development: New arenas for inquiry and action', *Journal of Management*, Vol. 15, pp. 205–228.

Woodward, N.H. (2007), 'To make changes, manage them', *HR Magazine*, Vol. 52, No. 5, May, pp. 63–67.

http://home.att.net/~nickols/articles.htm, accessed on 10 February 2010.

www.nickols.us, accessed on 25 December 2009.

APPENDIX 2.1
Organizational Change Guidelines

This guideline is prepared by the author, based on different organizational practices. The possible action plans that are commonly adopted by organizations seeking change are as mentioned below.

- Greater employee participation
- Greater understanding of the change
- Flexibility for informed decision-making power to people
- Inculcating trust in people throughout the change process
- Allowing employees to influence the decision-maker through a consultative process

Based on the above principles, the suggested guideline is presented below.

Step 1.0 Identification of Organizational Change

Step 1.1
The work area identifies that organizational change may be required.

To identify the need for organizational change, at the outset the employers should have dialogues with the employees, irrespective of their rank and file, and shortlist the work areas where change is imminent. At this stage, focus should be more on assimilating employees' thoughts. A good approach should precede such exercises with sharing of information about the company's present status in terms of productivity, cost, profitability, competition, and some macro-economic information. Presentation should be at their level of understanding. For example, in one case, 42 semi-skilled workers of a PSU POL major had to be re-deployed in jobs outside their job family (from operator to security and canteen staff) due to technological change (automatic loading of oil barrels). They had to be convinced of the need for change. The author first enquired as to the reason they wanted to educate their children in good schools. The answer was that education would help them to survive in a competitive job market and provide them decent and stable employment opportunities. This was used as a cue to subsequently make them understand why it was so important to their employer to re-deploy them and why canteen and security jobs were not demeaning.

Step 2.0 Determination of Significant Effects

Step 2.1
The work area determines whether organizational change will have significant effects on their employees.

Having identified the work area(s) that need change, the next step is to study the possible effects of such change in terms of existing work processes and practices, working conditions, employment practices, etc. A detailed listing of significant effects is difficult, but can be tentatively listed under the general category of redundancy. Organizational change succeeds change in the job composition, scale of company's operation (which may increase or decrease), size of the workforce, skill, knowledge obsolescence, etc. In some cases, it even reduces job opportunities, career prospects of existing employees, alteration of working hours, relocation of employees, and total job restructuring.

All these are categorized under significant effects, which evoke immediate response from employees. With such a listing, it is important for the organization to seek the peoples' mandate through collective bargaining and signing of agreements.

With the employees' consensus, the organization can move towards the next stage of change implementation.

This process is not so easy as it requires sustained efforts from the organization to cajole employees, restoring their confidence that change promises a better tomorrow. In one case, the author was involved in cajoling the deadwoods (chronically change opposing employees and non-performers) who were not prepared to believe the positive change effects. They were presented with a detailed tabulation of cost–benefit analysis of change, stressing the short and long-term cost of not implementing the change. Strategically, the company guaranteed jobs for all, provided that they were mentally prepared for redeployment in restructured jobs and ensured benchmarked performance targets (against the competing organization). All employees were taken through a compulsory skill change programme (wherever necessary). With sustained training workshops, 90 per cent of the deadwoods eventually agreed to the changes, while the other 10 per cent decided to resign.

Step 2.2
The work area documents the likely significant effects.

At this stage, a detailed listing is made of significant effects in the work areas and is available for everyone to inspect. This assures them that there are no deviations from the conditions agreed upon in the collective bargaining.

The documents should summarize the details of the proposed organizational change, the background and reasons for it, the nature and extent of change, its objectives, the likely significant effects on the relevant employees regarding the change, new direction, structure and staffing pattern, process and methods of change implementation, information sharing or communication methods of change, resources made available for the change, etc.

Step 3.0 Meeting with the Employees

Step 3.1
Formal and informal meeting with employees, particularly those who are affected by the proposed change.

Depending on the nature of the proposed change, it may be necessary to invite all employees within the relevant work area. They should be entitled to invite their employee representatives to attend the meetings. The meeting should be held as soon as possible after a need for change has been recognized. This is important as it emphasizes participation and communication, and assists in minimizing employees' uncertainty.

The purpose of the meeting is to outline the extent and nature of the proposed change, reasons for it, the aim of the change, and the proposed time frame. Employees who attend should receive a copy of the document.

In subsequent meetings, employees should be given an opportunity to discuss issues and necessary feedback on the proposed organizational change should be obtained from all of them. Based on this, a necessary list of amendments can be made on the documents.

Step 4.0 Finalizing the Change Decision and Implementation

Step 4.1
Review the amended change proposal drawn based on the employees' feedback and implement the change.

At this stage, the initial change proposal is reviewed in the context of amended change documents based on the employees' feedback, and the change document is finalized. It is then communicated in subsequent employee meetings and implemented.

It is important to remember that in order to sustain the change process, a periodic review of the change outcome is necessary, and if required, the change documents can be amended with employees' knowledge.

3 Organizational Change Process

Learning Objectives

After reading this chapter, you will be able to understand
- the basic process of organizational change
- the features of organizational change
- the various theories of organizational change
- the various change processes
- the role and significance of HRD in the change process
- manpower redundancy management in the change process
- organizational change process in mergers and acquisitions
- strategic organizational change processes
- organizational change through scenario planning

Auto India's Change Programme

Organizational change initiatives primarily focus on culture, systems, and processes. Managers and leaders need to extend support for any change initiative. These initiatives need to be ongoing in order to deliver core business of high quality. Organizations first need to make people understand the impact of change, and give them the opportunity to decide the framework of change and draw their individual action plans. Increased understanding is ensured through workshops and training sessions, which emphasize building the capability of the people to lead and manage the change process.

Auto India is facing tremendous competitive pressure from other players in India and abroad. The company now re-examines the business process and internal resource availability almost every month in order to remain competitive. Continuous change is not easy for a company with 5000 people on its payroll. To support change, the company introduced an integrated leadership development programme, which brought positive change in the attitudes, behaviour, and skills of its employees.

At the outset, the company had designed modular workshops for the key management group. These were made more interactive and experiential. The company first focused on developing appropriate strategy to successfully manage the huge tasks involved in implementing change. From the second workshop, the company gave participants a free hand to focus on business issues that were likely to change with the organizational change programme. At this stage, the key management group also reviewed the strategy. Subsequently, key management people took groups of employees through such workshops and identified the actual change agents to further the organizational change programme from among them.

INTRODUCTION

In Chapter 2, we discussed different areas of organizational change, namely content, context, process, and criterion issues. Process issues concentrate on the different actions undertaken to establish the intended change. Organizations need to focus on the internal as well as external business processes on an ongoing basis to respond to the change requirements.

The organizational change process is a broad collection of activities within the organization, which ultimately support the change initiatives it undertakes. Typically, they are evaluated from the stakeholders' viewpoint. Thus, managing the organizational change process requires proper understanding of the various stakeholders' needs and aligns these with the organizational business imperatives. It is also important to understand that change processes are classified into key processes, support processes, and sub-processes.

To ensure a continuous and successful organizational change process, certain key issues, such as targets (which should be clear and measurable), strong commitment (from all cross sections of employees of the organization), involvement (to ensure acceptance of the proposed changes), and communication (to create involvement, commitment, and target-setting), need to be considered. Building a process-oriented organizational change model can solve many problems, as members understand their individual role and get a complete picture of the organizational change process. However, it requires teamwork and a supportive work environment, where every member of the organization feels at ease to relate them to the organization.

ORGANIZATIONAL CHANGE PROCESS THROUGH PERSONAL EXAMINATION

The process of organizational change varies from one organization to another. However, at the outset, personal examination is considered to be one of the most widely known steps in the organizational change process.

To transform an organization from one state to another, it is necessary to first recognize the need for personal change and transformation. This requires personal examination. It starts with an in-depth exploration of personal beliefs, unconscious assumptions, and values, regarding the present nature of management, the organization, purposes of work, and the effectiveness of technology. It also involves an examination of alternative visions of the future. Effective change leaders are motivated by their inner vision, purpose, and mission, and thus authentically express their own being. This is not meant as an example for others to emulate. Rather, it is intended to help the people of the organization to define themselves autonomously and help them form their own opinion on the imperatives of change.

At this stage, it is also necessary to measure change from the volatility of the environment. This helps to explore the nature of change, assuming that it is not something new but a natural process for all to adopt. This new way of thinking facilitates in designing the new organizational structure and relationships.

Whether it is a subtle or dramatic way of organizational change—planned or unplanned, formal or informal, directed or non-directed, fast or slow, conscious or sub-conscious, negative or positive, visible or invisible—personal examination as explained earlier should precede the change process to minimize the risk of failure.

GAIL (India) Ltd, a public sector major in gas and oil in India, initiated an organizational change process integrating their strategic plans, performance management systems, and leadership development. This involved top management who were given the mandate to adopt a collaborative approach. With gradual de-regulation and price de-control, GAIL had to develop the new focus and organizational restructuring and introduce it to profit centres (strategic business units, SBU) and support centres (shared services). To do this, it had to assess the changing business environment, measure the performance gap, and do a SWOT analysis, and identify the critical success factors (CSF) based on these.

GAIL could list priorities to ensure organizational change within the ambit of CSF. These include improved productivity and profitability, and achieving customers' delight through improved customer services. Successful organizational change at GAIL was possible with the involvement of management, fostering innovation, focus on cross-functional communication, emulating the best practice management, and finally, by developing an entrepreneurial culture. This is called a people style of management, and is primarily characterized by horizontal coordination and support.

FEATURES OF ORGANIZATIONAL CHANGE

As explained earlier, organizational change processes vary from one organization to another. What may hold good for a manufacturing organization may not hold good for a knowledge-intensive IT company. Hence, listing the common features of organizational change is often difficult. Some of the widely recognized features of organizational change are as follows:

Invites disagreement and contradictions This is a reality that organizations need to accept. With such recognition, they can identify the strengths and weaknesses, and the degree of contradictions and disagreements, along with various other dysfunctional aspects of the change process. This facilitates early preparedness by the change leaders and often helps them to be innovative and more proactive. It is also important to understand that with contradictions, people become more amenable to acceptance once their doubts are clarified. A good example is *Encyclopaedia Britannica*. To compete against the CD of the *Encarta Encyclopaedia*, the management team decided to introduce a CD version at a lower price band. However, the salespeople opposed the move as their commission earnings were lower. Ultimately, they had to liquidate and sell their stake at less than half the price.

Ongoing and continuous process Organizations are always changing to keep pace with the dynamic business environment. These could be planned or unplanned, or directed or non-directed change. Whatever the reasons for change be, every change process needs alignment with the strategic intents of the organization to avoid any possible dysfunctional outcome. It makes members of the organization believe that they need to change in order to survive. Organizations commonly review the annual business plan several times a year to keep pace with the environmental flux. British Telecom reviews its plan eight times a year, that is, every one and a half months, thus making their organizational change process an ongoing practice.

Not always smooth sailing Every change process always get interrupted due to the mismatched perceptions of people. To avoid this, it is important to help people to form their own informed opinion on change from a positive perspective. From the organizational point of view also, it is important to be clear on the following issues, before the change process begins:

- Implications of change to the organization
- Benefits of change to the company
- Activities involved in the change process and standards of behaviour expected in the post change scenario
- Objectives of the change process
- Extent of alignment of the change process with the organizational vision and mission
- Extent of awareness of people about the change

Clarity on all these issues will benefit the organization and smoothen the change process. It is important to remember that the change process should never be imposed; rather it should be addressed respecting the sentiments and feelings of the people.

A good example is of a multinational cement major, Lafarge. Lafarge acquired and established a number of cement plants in India. In the case of one Tata cement unit acquired by Lafarge, the problem was to introduce the cement workers' wage levels. Tata Cement unit workers enjoyed the wage levels of Tata Steel workers, as the plant is located in Tata's steel city. Lafarge had a difficult time rationalizing the wage levels.

Success through collaborative inquiry and teamwork An organizational change process is essentially a group activity; it cannot succeed merely through planning and action by the top management. It is essential to pull together the energy and resource base of the people, forming cooperative teams with a shared vision, in order to implement it. Hence, it is also necessary to take decisions in collaboration with all and successfully develop a feeling of oneness. A collaborative team can only be formed when everyone connects with the organization and mentally undertakes the achievement of the common goal. The example of GAIL (India) Ltd cited earlier highlights the importance of collaborative inquiry and teamwork.

THEORIES OF ORGANIZATIONAL CHANGE

Modern approaches to organizational change relate its success or failure to some identified factors. Organizations develop alternative strategies on the gap areas based on these. When identifying such factors, emphasis is placed on long-term organizational relationship with the business environment. Accordingly, the mission or current purpose (business focus) is formulated to drive people towards achieving this and bringing in the desired changes. Such factors are classified under content issues.

Contextual issues of organizational change focus on the forces or conditions of external and internal environments that influence organizational functioning. Thus, this theory forms the context of organizational functions in given environmental constraints, both internal and external, and may vary in different organizational environments. External environmental conditions are not limited to governmental regulations. They encompass technological changes even in the global plane and dynamics of market competition. Internal conditions, on the other hand, encompass changes in the nature of the work due to technology, organizational slack, experience of previous change exercises, if any, etc. Contextual issues, therefore, leverage on the success of various internal and external components of change responses.

Process issues of organizational change are more important, as they address the detailed actions undertaken during the change process. Such actions are actual organizational responses to adjust to the external and internal environments. For example, a regulatory change in pollution control activity requires an organization to respond or act by installing effluent treatment plants (ETP). Similar regulatory norms can be imposed by the government for safety requirements, energy consumption, and employment practices, and each of these requires a different action. For example, to meet safety regulations, organizations may need to provide protective clothing to workers or reduce health hazards by re-engineering the process through technology-intensive operations. Achievement of the expected outcome also requires behaviour modification by employees.

Organizations that follow the content dimension of organizational change, generally adopt the Burke–Litwin (1992) model to predict individual and organizational performance. This model helps to deal with the cause (organizational conditions) and resultant effects, and therefore, accounts for transformational and transactional dynamics inherent in successful change efforts. Transformational factors are concerned with new employee behaviour that may be required to deal with external and internal environmental pressures. Leadership, culture, mission, and strategy are transformational factors in the organizational change process.

Transactional factors, on the other hand, are concerned with the psychological and organizational variables to predict and control employees' motivation and performance in the change process. These include management practices, style, structure, systems (policies and procedures), skills and abilities of people, and their task requirements. To make a proper distinction between the transformational and transaction factors,

Burke–Litwin developed a 150-item diagnostic questionnaire. The feedback from this can be categorized into transformational and transactional factors.

To ease the rigour of lengthy questionnaires, Vollman (1996) suggested an organizational transformation model to portray the magnitude of the organizational change process. This model is a typical eight-by-six matrix, where the rows constitute eight facets, such as (i) strategic intent (e.g., addressing the correct issues), (ii) competencies (e.g., linking current competencies to a desired transformation), (iii) processes (e.g., establishing metrics for assessing efficiency and effectiveness), (iv) resources (e.g., systematically deploying HR), (v) outputs (e.g., identifying customer expectations), (vi) strategic responses (e.g., planning action programmes), (vii) challenges (e.g., anticipating obstacles), and (viii) learning capacity (e.g., identifying new required knowledge, skills, and abilities).

These facets answer the most relevant questions in the organizational change process, such as, how to implement transformation, what the strategic intent should be, to what extent we can relate the current competencies to the transformation, and which matrices are essential to measure the efficiency and effectiveness of the organization, etc. The six columns of the matrix represent organizational dimension and the three resources that go into the process of transformational change. These are (i) culture (e.g., shared values and beliefs), (ii) configuration (e.g., organizational design), (iii) coordination (e.g., controls necessary to monitor progress), (iv) people (e.g., new behaviours), (v) information (e.g., new data requirements), and (vi) technology (e.g., new equipment required). Analysis of each column and row reveals the magnitude of a proposed transformation, and even checks the misunderstandings about the change implications which often cause people to oppose the change move.

CHANGE PROCESSES

Organizational change process is essentially a framework of problem solving. It first diagnoses the problems by scanning the premises and then draws upon well-planned actions, by setting goals at various levels and in various areas or functions. The organization then tries to gain the support and commitment of the people. This is a typical change model. However, the organizational members often perceive the word 'problem' wrongly and mistakenly assume it to be a bad or adverse situation. From a rational, analytical perspective, however, a problem is a situation that requires an action to arrive at a solution. Thus, the change process is essentially a problem-solving activity. Irrespective of the nature of the change problem (large or small), organizations must focus on the individuals and groups, as behavioural dimensions are more important than other change parameters (such as, technology, etc.). Any change process helps to achieve three goals, namely transform, reduce, and apply. Transform goals differentiate between the pre- and post-change states. 'Reduce' goals help to eliminate the differences, while 'apply' goals actually eliminate such differences through actions. In simple terms, organizational change deals with the 'how', 'what', and 'why', of change. 'How' deals with the methodology of change; 'what' pinpoints the exact areas of change; and 'why' helps to justify the need for change.

Change Process and Its Stages of Unfreezing, Changing, and Refreezing

Kurt Lewin (1951) has characterized three basic stages of change, namely unfreezing, changing, and refreezing. This view draws heavily on the adoption of the systems concept of homeostasis or dynamic stability, explained in the introductory chapter. This framework is useful as a step-ladder approach to change in organizations and provides sufficient opportunity to act before a situation arises.

The problem with this framework is that it does not allow an organization to stay unfrozen when they are in 'hang-loose' condition. Many organizations encounter this situation in the middle of the change process due to unpredictable resistance problems or non-feasibility (technically not sustainable). In other words, the core of this model is stability.

According to Kurt Lewin (1958), organizational change as depicted in Fig. 3.1, cannot occur till we unfreeze the existing systems and refreeze it with new inputs. The process of unfreezing makes the existing systems redundant and hence encounters resistance. After unfreezing, the organization reaches the transition state where it adopts a series of change initiatives and presents them to the people, and encourages them to accept these changes through increased communication and motivation. In many organizations the change process is completed half-heartedly due to non-cooperation of the people. The refreezing state is a process of stabilizing and integrating the process of change. People develop new attitudes and behavioural patterns to achieve results in the changed situation. Lewin's model is explained in Fig. 3.1.

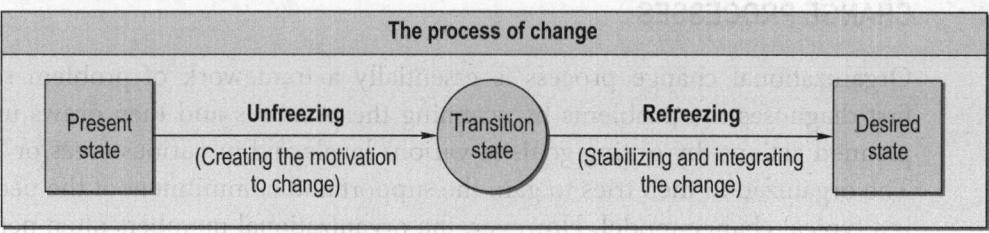

FIG. 3.1 An operational point of view of Lewin's model

Lewin's model can be related to GAIL's process of restructuring, discussed earlier in this chapter.

Organizational Change Process

The organizational change process depends on the nature of the organization and the change triggers to which it responds. For example, the change process in a textile mill and in an IT-enabled service organization would be different. Textile and jute mills largely employ unskilled and low-skilled factory workers for whom change signifies fear of job loss. They have very limited scope for job mobility. Hence, such organizations prefer to impose change in a manipulative way, without explaining fully the actual change outcome. On the other hand, participative change process (rather than coercive) will work better in an IT organization, as people employed here are largely knowledge workers.

As explained earlier, process-centric models facilitated by multiple factors consider organizational change as an ongoing exercise. Such factors act as change imperatives and facilitate the change process. Some of the important change imperatives are business leadership, strategic planning, customers and market, data/information analysis, HR, process management, and business results. These are known as the seven pillars of change.

Business Environment-led Change Process

A business has to grow within the ambit of the constraint of various factors and has to formulate its strategies so as to gain business competitiveness. We have to appreciate that business operates under some environmental imperatives and the organization has its own imperatives, which are called strategic.

In a business environment-led change process, the organization has to match, exploit, and alter the linkages between its resource competency and the environmental opportunity. The firm thus shows its preparedness to gain competitive advantage. (The decision to change or not is based on whether the organization intends to have a competitive advantage or not.) A company's competitiveness comes from functions, activities, and people, and the effective linkages between these and the culture of the organization as a whole. Through the change process, the firm establishes the relatedness and interdependence of these factors and product mix/product line, service mix/service line, and the business as a whole, supporting each other with revised strategy formulations.

While implementing a business environment-led change process, change leaders must adhere to ethical behavioural norms to meet the expectations of all stakeholders. In the name of business imperatives, organizations often tend to compromise with the external stakeholders' expectations. While the expectations of employees and customers are important, the interests of other stakeholders, such as shareholders, creditors, society, etc., are also equally important. It is, therefore, essential for the organization to step up its interactions and meetings with different stakeholders to meet all their expectations. Change leaders should also focus on building employees' capability through training reinforcement to enhance their commitment and performance as required. Similar efforts should be made in relation to customer education, building stakeholders' value through different cost-efficient strategies, etc. Thus, business environment-led change process should not be seen in isolation. It has to be drawn with a focus on all these relevant areas.

Indian BPO companies always focused on the US and other European clients for business. With the recent economic meltdown, they initially suffered a serious setback in their business volume. First Source Solutions is a BPO organization with a large foreign client base. They recently introduced a telecom vertical and obtained good business volumes from telecom majors, such as MTS, etc. Thus, a changing business environment can also present new business opportunities when the company is open to exploring new market opportunities.

Strategic Planning-focused Change Process

At times, organizations need to draw their strategic plans to set a direction for their future move. This may be required to achieve business excellence. A choice between having its own retail outlets or franchises is part of the strategic plan of many organizations. Bata India had this problem, as it found it difficult to get the pulse of the customers through franchise inputs. However, with strict franchise control (through standard operating procedures), McDonalds was very comfortable doing it. GKB Lens has only its own retail outlets. Change leaders always become future-oriented to guard against untoward events in the environment and, therefore, always draw strategic plans having reviewed the premises.

To achieve business excellence organizational strategic plans take into account customers' and suppliers' expectations, explore new business and partnering opportunities, technological developments, etc., keeping in mind the degree of their influence on the business, competition, strengths and weaknesses, and macro-level global market environment. The over 200 year-old *Encyclopaedia Britannica* had to opt for liquidation (it has been acquired by a new promoter), as it failed to understand that the *Encarta Encyclopaedia* CD from Microsoft could be a strong competitor. Dick Fuld, CEO at Lehman Brothers, failed to read the market rhythm and ventured into risky growth strategy by over-borrowing, only to end up in liquidation. Strategic plans need to be translated into specific action plans to achieve the desired changes in the listed areas of the organization.

Without strategic control, a strategic plan will not help the organization achieve the desired change objectives. A strategic plan is selected and implemented over a period of time. But as change strategies are forward-looking and designed to accomplish objectives in the future, it is necessary to enforce control over change strategy through effective strategic control systems. In organizations, this is enforced through premise control, implementation control, strategic surveillance, and special alert control.

Premise control is designed to check systematically and continuously, whether or not the premises set during the planning and implementation processes are still valid. For example, a bank may adopt an aggressive marketing strategy to achieve 15 per cent annual growth, establishing a planning premise that not more than 10 per cent would be non-performing assets. Premise control should be ensured monitoring the non-performing assets at branch level on a regular basis.

Implementation control is designed to assess whether the overall strategy results are associated with incremental steps and actions that were used to implement the overall strategy. For example, an internationally-known fast food centre decided to maintain a 3 to 1 company-owned and franchise ratio, as part of its expansion strategy to ensure control over quality of foods, rates, etc. But growing competition forced it to reverse the ratio to accelerate its ability to open new locations.

Strategic surveillance is designed to monitor a broad range of events inside and outside the organization that are likely to threaten the course of the firm's strategy.

Special alert control is exercised when a thorough, and often rapid, reconsideration of the firm's basic strategy is required based on a sudden, unexpected event.

Through such control mechanisms, the firm can achieve the objectives of its strategic plan, that is, effective organizational change.

Customer and Market-driven Change Process

Organizational change process also needs to be customer-driven, as customers are considered to be the pivot of all business. No business is possible without customers. Thus, understanding customers' present and future needs and desires, and preparing to meet these through new product designs and new service offerings is always desirable. Again, organizations cannot survive with this alone; they also need to step up customer relationship management (CRM) practices to retain customers and achieve customer satisfaction. They must recognize that cultivating and winning new customers is considerably more expensive than retaining the loyalty and goodwill of existing customers. It is therefore, important to focus on the diverse needs of customers and the market by segmentation in order to achieve organizational change.

HLL (now HUL) caters to its detergent market with product differentiation, offering various detergents at different price bands to honour its commitment to various cross sections of customers. Some of the customer-centric changes in organizational practices could therefore be product and service differentiation, CRM practices, measurement of customer satisfaction, consolidation of the market, share gain and growth, etc.

Organizational Culture-driven Change Process

In the process of working together over a period of time, people develop certain beliefs about what is right and wrong. Such beliefs establish their behavioural pattern and transform into organizational culture. Therefore, organizational culture reflects the way people work, perform their tasks, set objectives, and manage resources to achieve their goals. Culture also influences the style of decision-making, thinking, feeling, and responding to situations (opportunities and threats). Hence, the organizational change process should consider this when ascertaining the variation between the present and the future. When organizational culture itself alters due to change in business practices, be it in the local or international market, the organizational change process should account for it.

The culture-driven organizational change process requires continuous reinforcement through training and other HRD activities. Goal congruence models, Com-Be-D (communicate, behave, and demand) models, and glass wall management systems are some effective tools for cultural transformation. A goal congruence model focuses first on cultural transformation in areas where both management and employees have a common interest. Com-Be-D first emphasizes setting the desired behavioural patterns in accordance with the new culture, communicates this to employees with a message to change and behave accordingly (beginning with top management who set an example for others to emulate). Glass-wall management systems emphasize transparency through sharing all change-related information with employees, clarifying their doubts and concerns, etc.

Another good example could be the Tata–Corus merger. With the Tata acquisition of the $13.7 billion Corus Steel (a British company) in January 2007, the merged entity employed more than 84,000 people across 45 countries. Commenting on this acquisition, Mr Ratan Tata said, 'We are now a balanced company and strategically well-placed to compete at the leading edge of a rapidly changing global steel industry.' Corus suffered from a series of disruptive organizational changes in the past. This is why many industry watchers recommended that Tata must not hasten the process of change but move slowly, allowing the existing management to continue. The complete process of integration of Corus with Tata is yet to take place for obvious differences in business practices and the cultural mis-match. Corus is more a legacy-bound organization and slow to respond to change. Tata, on the other hand, though a fairly matured organization, rejuvenates itself with new ideas and changes to give a new lease of life to its business practices.

Culture, therefore, plays the most effective role in organizational change. The stronger the present culture, the more difficult it is to bring change. However, a strong culture is also an important strategic asset for the organization. Professionally managed organizations, therefore, always ensure critical culture constructs to reflect in important value systems, namely customer services, so that future cultural differences cannot dilute the internal fabric of the organization.

At times, however, it becomes difficult, particularly in cases of cross-border mergers and acquisitions. A relevant example is the cross-border merger of Advanced Micro Devices (AMD). AMD is located in Dresden, East Germany, and is a composite of three cultures—American, West German, and East German. The Americans are 'go-getters' who believe in shooting first and aiming later. West Germans are analytical, thorough, and correct, whereas the East Germans have mastered the art of innovation with limited resources. The Dresden start-up team designed a meeting format, which opened with American-style brainstorming sessions. The Americans learnt the art of deliberation and the Germans off-the-cuff dynamism.

This multicultural style gave AMD the much-needed competitive edge. AMD's case has resulted in the development of the dilemma theory (Trompenaars and

Hampden-Turner 1998), a much-discussed worldwide theory, commonly known as the THT theory. According to this, insidious culture clashes and most management problems are a result of the human habit. The challenge for corporate headquarters is to ensure that certain critically important values are reflected in all branches of the corporation, and cultural differences do not inhibit internal architecture and synergy.

Organizational Structure and the Change Process

Organization structure helps to determine the authority relationships among members of organization, and influences the behaviour of individuals, groups, and divisions within the organization. Among others, the structure of an organization affects the division of tasks, communication systems, decision-making patterns, and the way people relate to each other. Global competition now requires many organizations to redefine their structure and even to relocate, taking advantage of state-of-the-art technology and communication support.

Organizational change process, therefore, calls for revisiting the organizational structure, as structure influences several organizational variables, such as processes (communication, goal-setting, conflict resolution, socialization, leadership building, strategic planning, supporting, teamwork, behaviour, values, rituals, climate, authority (with which the role holders are imbued), and people (competence, confidence, interpersonal skills, leadership, perceptions about others). Change leaders, therefore, need to account for the organizational structure, particularly to focus on the aspects of division of work, accountabilities, and authority, which change with the organizational change process.

Structural issues encompass the organizational change process as, in the process of change organizations break down a complete task into sub-tasks, each of which is then handled by a sub-system. Hence, it needs to synthesize and synergize various processes. Thus, organizational processes need to be designed with a suitable structure to achieve the desired level of coordination, which facilitates the achievement of the organizational objectives of producing goods and services to meet the changing needs of customers through the organizational change process.

Leadership Performance-driven Change Process

Leadership plays a pivotal role in the organizational change process, as it translates vision into reality by inspiring followers to experience the change process before it actually happens. Change leaders exert influence on the members of the organization in a way that helps them to understand the importance of the change requirements for their survival and growth. This requires leaders to possess specific qualities and competencies to motivate employees, direct the systems and processes, guide the business to achieve common goals, and strengthen the organization by increasing its value.

The personal quality of leaders plays a very crucial role in a change process, as this is what actually makes people to them. Some of these personal qualities are intelligence, communication skills, emotional balance, inner drive, energy, and other managerial skills, and the requirement of these qualities depends on the change situation. Change leaders should also be able to influence people to volunteer for the change process.

In many organizations, the change leaders' power of influence helps to overcome people's resistance and regulate their behaviour, to make them believe that change is necessary. Another important aspect of the role of leadership is the consideration of situational variables. Depending on the degree and extent of change, leaders should modify the approach, keeping in view the end objective of change. A leader should also have certain characteristics, such as the ability to get others to do what the organization wants, motivate people through persuasion, the capability to provide a vision, and the ability to truly empower people to do what they want.

Leadership, being the most important enabler in the organizational change process, is instrumental in persuading people to change as well as exerting influence to perform. Some of the essential requirements of being a change leader can be summarized as follows:

Goal-setting

Good leaders should know the difference between the qualities of goals. In the context of organizational change, a leader should have extraordinary courage, dynamism, and vision to set goals that can help the organization to withstand the change pressure and succeed in total transformation, overriding competitors.

Resource allocation

Change leaders should also have rational budget-based planning power so that optimum allocation of resources between different competing needs is possible. Depending on the situation, the leader has to decide upon the priorities of resource allocation to suit the change plan.

Risk evaluation

Any change process is risky. It may or may not happen, and may even put the organizational stability at stake. As the financial and business risks are high, change leaders should be able to make a trade-off, hedging risk with the use of various risk analysis tools. Among others, leaders are required to use contingent plans to support the master change plans.

Trade-off between the short and long-term goals

Change leaders should be able to make a trade-off between short-term and long-term goals. Today's sacrifice for tomorrows benefits should be clear in measurable and traceable terms, and clearly explained to the people, or they will not volunteer for the change process.

Setting standards of performance and behaviour

Setting performance standards and expected levels of behaviour, and ensuring that people to follow these is a great challenge for leaders. A leader should lead by example, and hence should set realistic standards, so that people can achieve this with optimum levels of stretch.

Supporting processes and structure

Merely developing a structure and designing processes do not guarantee the achievement of desired levels of organizational change. Extending support to processes and structure is also important. Examples of such support could be, ensuring the flow of information through the structure to facilitate the decision-making process, sharing of information to facilitate coordination, correct analysis of performance feedback to reward the performers, etc. Thus, a change leader should also have the expertise to support the designed processes and structure.

Acculturation

Change leaders should have the expertise to design a well-planned induction and socialization process, as it is critical to transform the mindset of new recruits to adapt to the work culture environment. Similar expertise is also required for designing training workshops for existing employees so that they too develop the right attitude to adapt to changes.

SWOT Analysis and the Change Process

SWOT analysis or analysis of strengths, weaknesses, opportunities, and threats is an effective method of identifying and examining these in the change process of an organization. Often, making an analysis using this framework is enough to reveal changes that can be usefully made in an organization (Fig. 3.2). An analysis of strengths and weaknesses is internal to an organization while that of opportunities and threats

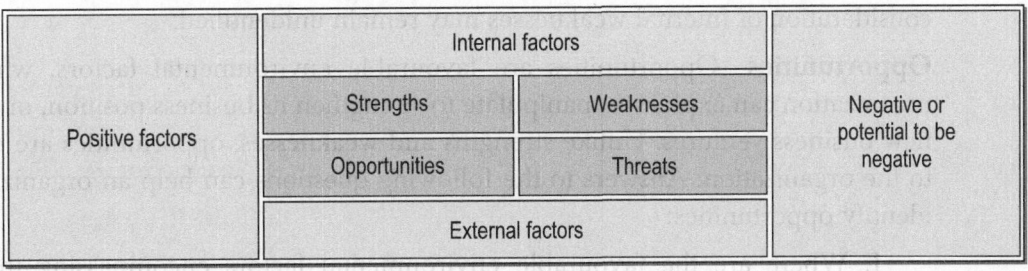

FIG. 3.2 SWOT analysis framework

are external to it. A SWOT analysis is necessary for determining the feasibility of a change process and can smoothen it, as change leaders can take decisions to minimize the risk based on the results.

Performing SWOT analysis

SWOT analysis is an effective method of identifying organizational strengths and weaknesses, and framing strategies within the ambit of the opportunities and threats facing the organization. A SWOT analysis itself could be enough to identify the change requirements. It is credited to Albert Humphrey of Stanford University, who in the 1960s and 1970s used it for strategic planning. Initially, it was known as SOFT analysis, that is, satisfactory, opportunity, fault, and threat analysis. In 1964, Urick and Orr changed the 'F' to 'W', thus, renaming it SWOT. A framework for conducting a SWOT analysis is given below and requires answers to the questions presented against each component of the analysis.

Strengths Strengths are the internal advantages. Hence, answers to the following questions categorize organizational strengths:

1. What are the organizational advantages?
2. What does the organization do well?

Answers are needed both from the organizational and from the people (whom the organization engages) point of view. They need to be realistic, and if required, drawn in the context of competitors, as this will provide a better answer. Benchmarking with competitors helps to draw the list in the context of the relative advantages of the organization. All positive tangible and intangible internal attributes of the organization are categorized as its strengths.

Weaknesses Weaknesses are the internal disadvantages. The answers to the following questions can help determine organizational weaknesses:

1. What are the areas of improvement?
2. What are the areas in which the organization fared badly?
3. What areas of dysfunction could have been avoided?

The methodology used for identification of strengths is also applicable in this case. Often people hesitate to document unpleasant truths. This should be taken into consideration or internal weaknesses may remain unidentified.

Opportunities Opportunities are favourable environmental factors, which the organization can exploit or manipulate to strengthen its business position, or identify new business ventures. Unlike strengths and weaknesses, opportunities are external to the organization. Answers to the following questions can help an organization to identify opportunities:

1. Where are the favourable environmental factors encompassing the organization?

2. What are the favourable trends which the organization can exploit to achieve stability and growth?

For today's organizations, opportunities come from both local as well as global issues. They may be in the form of policy changes, change in the social patterns, demographic trends, lifestyle changes, change in technology, or favourable economic trends.

Threats Threats are the unfavourable external factors that encompass an organization. They weaken the competitive strength of the organization, and even urge to scale down activities. Answering the following questions can help identify the threats:

1. What are the obstacles faced by the organization?
2. What are the new initiatives of competitors that can weaken the organization's position?
3. What are the changes in the products and service offerings of the organization, including change in the technical specifications, if any?
4. What is the changing technology that may threaten the organization?
5. What are the bad debt positions and the cash flow problems of the organization?

Threats are external to the organization and hence beyond the control of the organization. Depending on the severity and probability of occurrence, an organization may draw contingency plans to encounter the threats.

Its simple process of application makes a SWOT analysis a very effective tool for change management, as it can be used for problem solving, brain-storming meetings, general and strategic planning, product and service evaluation, competitor evaluation, and decision-making.

GAIL's organizational change programme; IBM's change in business focus, that is, withdrawing from desktops and entering into new business verticals, such as ITeS, Tata Steel's global acquisition programme, Videocon's business integration programmes in acquired Philips units, etc., have all used SWOT analysis to draw the action plans for organizational change.

Environmental Scanning and Feedback-enabled Change Process

This is again another enabler of the organizational change process. Like SWOT analysis, this also helps to map the environment for determining the right planning premises for organizational change. Environment scanning also helps to diagnose the change issues correctly, keeping pace with the current requirement. For example, a decision to change the existing product line of an organization cannot be effectively taken without a correct diagnosis of the problem environment scanning. Similarly, feedback analysis also facilitates organizational change and feedback from customers could be a major determinant of redesigning the customer service department, etc.

ROLE AND SIGNIFICANCE OF HRD IN THE ORGANIZATIONAL CHANGE PROCESS

Any dynamic and growth-oriented organization needs systematic organizational change to survive in a fast-changing environment. Human resource development (HRD) plays a very crucial role in this process. In India, recent economic restructuring at the macro level has influenced the need for production restructuring at the unit (micro) level, and necessitated labour restructuring vis-à-vis restructuring of HRD activities in organizations. Training, retraining, and redeployment have now become buzz words in corporate circles, as market globalization (which is an outcome of economic restructuring), de-licensing, and free flow of technology (as per the new industrial policy of July, 1991) intensified competition, rendering traditional skills and knowledge redundant. Many organizations in India are now threatened with manpower obsolescence, and to withstand this HRD activities now receive prime importance. Box 3.1 further highlights the key features for achieving organizational effectiveness.

> **BOX 3.1 Human resources and organizational effectiveness**
>
> Increased morale and motivation of employees are undoubtedly necessary to achieve productivity and functional effectiveness. But these alone cannot sustain a dynamic organization unless effort and competencies of HR are renewed constantly, and an enabling organizational culture is developed. This is possible when employees of an organization use their initiative, take risks, experiment, innovate, and make things happen.

Hence, the role and significance of HRD in the organizational change process can be appreciated when one considers the fast-changing environment coupled with technological change and intensified competition. This has necessitated the need for a renewal of the abilities of people working in the organization, which are simultaneously reinforced by changes in the organization resulting from organizational development (OD).

The role and significance of HRD can further be appreciated when we consider the different sub-systems of HRD, such as performance appraisal, career planning and development, manpower planning, management succession and development, training (which includes the role of education and development discussed earlier), OD, quality of work life (QWL), etc. All these are discussed separately in this book.

Focus of the HRD System

A review of the definition, role, significance, purpose, and objectives of HRD as explained in the foregoing chapters, shows that the HRD department of an organization focuses on the following important areas:

- Increasing the 'enabling' capabilities by developing HR, organizational health, team spirit, and increasing employment motivation and productivity.
- Balancing organizational culture by conducting periodic surveys, workshops, discussions stimulating openness, mutual trust, team spirit, creativity, initiative, mutuality, collaboration, delegation, autonomy, respect, management of mistake, management of conflict, etc.
- Learning contextual factors from different professional bodies, such as NIPM, ISTD, National HRD Network, AIMA, NIIT, etc. Through their publications, seminars, and workshops, these professional bodies share the experiences of the corporate world.
- Periodically reviewing the HRD system, which may call for redesigning performance appraisal, job rotation, reward systems, career planning, promotion, selection, induction, training and development programmes, etc.
- Integrating HRD with other corporate functions, such as production, marketing, finance, material, corporate planning, etc. Such integration will strengthen the development of an 'enabling' organization.
- Diffusion of HRD function involving line managers in various HRD aspects, such as training of subordinates, performance appraisal, promotion, placement, selection, career planning, etc. Line people by virtue of their rich experience may effectively contribute to these HRD areas. Moreover, their active association will accentuate the process of developing an integrated HRD system in an organization.
- Working with unions by taking them into confidence and collaborating with them. The fact that unions can also play a positive role in furthering the organization is evident from a number of examples, namely Syndicate Bank Employees Union very recently collaborated with the management to reduce the non-performing assets (i.e., bad debt realization).

Role of HRD Manager in Organizational Change Process

From the foregoing discussions, it is apparent that the primary goal of HRD is to increase workers' productivity and the firm's profitability, as investment in HRD improve workers' skills and enhances motivation. The other goal of HRD is to prevent obsolescence at all levels and facilitate the organizational change process. To achieve these goals, the HRD manager of any organization plays two important roles:

1. Assist people to obtain the knowledge and skills they need for present and future jobs, and to attain their personal goals even when organizational change takes place.
2. Play an 'enabling' role, providing the right context in which human performance occurs and through which the organization reaches its stated change objectives.

Organizational Change and Development

> ### EXHIBIT 3.1 Roles of an HRD manager
>
> The ASTD identified eleven roles of an HRD manager, which can be enumerated as follows:
>
> **Administrator** Providing coordination and support services for the delivery of HRD programmes and services.
>
> **Evaluator** Identifying the impact of an intervention on individual or organizational effectiveness.
>
> **Individual career development advisor** Helping individuals to assess personal competencies, values, and goals, and to identify, plan, and implement development and career actions.
>
> **HRD manager** Supporting and leading a group's work and linking it with the total organization.
>
> **Instructor/Facilitator** Presenting information, directing structured learning experiences, and managing group discussions and processes.
>
> **Marketer** Marketing and contracting programmes and services from HRD viewpoints.
>
> **Material developer** Producing written and/or electronically-mediated instructional materials.
>
> **Needs analyst** Identifying ideal and actual performance, and performance conditions, and determining the causes of discrepancies.
>
> **Organizational change** Influencing and supporting changes in organizational behaviour.
>
> **Programme designer** Preparing objectives, defining content, and selecting and sequencing activities, for a specific intervention.
>
> **Researcher** Identifying, developing, or testing new information (theory, concepts, technology, models, hardware, etc.) and translating these into implications for improved individual or organizational performance.

Exhibit 3.1 discusses the various roles of an HRD manager.

After reviewing the eleven roles of HRD as indicated by the American Society for Training and Development (ASTD), Pace et al. (1991) grouped them into four major areas, as shown in Table 3.1.

TABLE 3.1 Roles of HRD

Analytic	Developmental	Instrumental	Mediational
• Needs analyst	• Programme designer	• Instructor/Facilitator	• HRD manager
• Researcher	• Materials developer	• Organizational change agent	• Individual career development advisor
• Evaluator		• Marketer	• Administrator

Even though the specific change agent role figures in these eleven roles, other HRD roles also support the organizational change.

HRD Culture and Climate

The HRD facilitates development of an enabling culture in an organization. In a changing environment, an organization requires frequent restructuring and redesigning of activities. Without an enabling culture, it is difficult for it to withstand the change requirements. Enabling culture means creating an environment where employees are motivated to take initiatives and risk, and encouraged to experiment, innovate, and make things happen. Thus, an HRD programme that develops an enabling culture in an organization is characterized by the following practices:

- Openness
- Confrontation
- Trust
- Autonomy
- Proactiveness
- Authenticity
- Collaboration

The HRD climate is a perception by employees about the prevailing HRD culture in the organization. To understand it, organizations often institute a survey with a structured questionnaire. It is possible to map the HRD climate by analysing survey responses covering all the enabling practices mentioned earlier. Necessary remedial action, if any, can be initiated to address the gap. Some of the elements of the questionnaire can be listed as follows:

1. Does the organization consider employees as the most important resource?
2. Does the organization believe in developing competencies of all cross sections of employees and initiate action in that direction?
3. How transparent is the organization's communication?
4. Are the employees encouraged to take risks?
5. Is there a climate of collaboration, team spirit, mutual trust, and confidence?
6. Are the personnel policies supportive in nature?
7. To what extent are HRD activities development-oriented?

By consolidating the responses to this questionnaire, organizations can assess the prevailing HRD climate and design the organizational change process accordingly. Rao and Abraham (1986) believe that the HRD climate brings many positive changes in the organizations, renewing its focus on organizational activities. The HRD climate is defined as the sum total of the perceptions of the employee regarding the employee development aspects of the organization. A positive HRD climate considers all cross sections of employees as resources. It focuses on the importance of developing competencies in the employees, improves employee capabilities to cope with competitiveness, encourages transparencies in communication, and promotes risk-taking and experimentation. A positive HRD climate helps employees to identify their strengths and weaknesses, promotes a culture of mutual trust, inculcates team spirit, and ensures supportive HRD practices.

Competencies as Enablers of Organizational Change Process

Each individual acquires competencies as he/she goes along in life. These help him/her to survive, relate to different sets of peer groups, grow in stature and wealth, mark a position for him/her in the society, and leave a unique mark in his/her surroundings, which would outlast him/her. Similarly, an organizational resume helps to distinguish the organization from others. These competencies are necessary for the present as well as the future; for organizations that wish to outlive today and have a vision for tomorrow. Living organizations do acquire competencies on a day-to-day basis through its interactions with the environment and the efforts of its constituents. However, organizations with an identity of their own are aware of their competencies and take pains to build upon them, and acquire new competencies for the future.

It goes without saying that competencies are relevant in the context of the vision and values of a mature organization. Conversely, an evolving organization can create a vision for itself by becoming aware of its competencies and achieve the results.

ORGANIZATIONAL CHANGE THROUGH MANAGEMENT OF MANPOWER REDUNDANCY

In today's volatile work environment, the survival and success of organizations depend on their ability to adopt a strategic move for continual adaptation, keeping pace with the threats and opportunities of the fast-changing external environment. Technological developments, global competition, the emergence of new economies and markets, and demographic and political changes are some of the factors which influence organizations to make frequent adjustments in their existing structure, systems, and processes, and redefine their relationships with customers and other stakeholders.

The effective planning and implementation of these developments is highly influenced by people management issues particularly when changes are required to rightsize or downsize the workforce, and more specifically, manage manpower redundancy. In order to manage redundancy, the organization has to first consider what it can do to prevent it or, if that is unavoidable, how its impact can be minimized. The ideal objective is to manage HR requirements in such a way that the need for rightsizing, downsizing, or redundancy never arises. There are two aspects to avoiding redundancy avoidance—long-term or strategic and short-term action. The former can be put in place as a preventive measure, that is, before a redundancy situation occurs, whereas short-term or operational action is taken to avoid or minimize actual or imminent redundancies.

The key feature of the long-term or strategic measures is planning. Some of the characteristics of an organization facing the risk of manpower redundancies are as follows:

1. The organization has made no assessment of the likely trends affecting the viability of the business. While facing the problem of rightsizing the decisions of such an organization will eventually be reactive, that is, adopting crisis management measures, which include making sudden changes in the constitution and size of the workforce.

2. There is no clear business objective, values, or standards in the organization. In the absence, this vision will prevent it from taking long-term action to ensure suitable training and development of its people to meet future business needs. When changes become necessary in the type and mix of employees' skills, such organizations tend to make employees with old skills redundant and acquire the necessary new skills through fresh recruitment.
3. The organization would not have analysed the age and service profiles of its workforce or maintained statistics on the trends of employee turnover. Faced with the need to change the nature or size of its workforce, it will find it difficult to forecast the effect of natural wastage and may suddenly discover an imbalance in the age distribution of its staff. Such a situation will make measures, such as a voluntary retirement scheme relatively ineffective.
4. The organization would probably have a complex organizational hierarchy and rigid, centralized management systems. The risk of managerial redundancies would be relatively greater and the centralized nature of its management system will inhibit rapid operational adjustments.
5. The jobs are very closely defined with a multiplicity of work demarcations. This will inhibit the transfer of employees from one job to another to cope with changing operational pressures. Also, employees will be unwilling to accept cross-lateral job transfers.
6. Most of the workforce is permanent, full-time employees, with little or no part-timers, temporary and fixed-term contracts, or external contractors. Consequently, there is very limited scope for varying the size of the workforce to reflect fluctuations in the level of its activities, other than by redundancy or recruitment.
7. Such an organization would operate with a complicated and very detailed set of conditions of employment so that changes in working time or job duties are difficult to introduce. Although changes in employment conditions do not directly cause redundancy, inflexibility in matters, such as overtime, shift patterns, and payment systems do restrict an organization's ability to reorganize, and will therefore, have an indirect effect on its ability to avoid redundancies.
8. The organization would not have concluded any redundancy agreements with its trade unions with the result that when redundancies occur there is an immediate disagreement as to how these should be handled.

MERGERS AND ACQUISITIONS

Mergers and acquisitions result in the combination of two or more companies into one, wherein the merging entities lose their identities. Generally, the company that survives and retains its identity as the buyer, while the seller company is extinguished (Ramaiya 1977). Acquisition is a generic term used to communicate the transfer of ownership. A merger may or may not be a part of an acquisition. However, in the language of business, strictly speaking, no distinction is made between the two and is often referred to as a merger.

Based on the objective profile of an offer, business combinations such as mergers, acquisitions, or takeovers could be categorized as vertical, horizontal, circular, or conglomerate.

A *vertical combination* is one in which a company takes over or seeks a merger with another company in order to ensure backward integration or assimilation of the sources of supply, or forward integration towards market outlets.

A *horizontal combination* is a merger of two competing firms belonging to the same industry. These mergers are carried out to obtain economies of scale in production by eliminating duplication of facilities and operations, and broadening the product line, reducing investment in working capital, eliminating competition through product concentration, reducing advertising costs, increasing market segments, and exercising better control over the market.

In case of a *circular combination*, companies producing distinct products in the same industry seek amalgamation to share common distribution and research facilities in order to obtain economies by eliminating costs of duplication and promoting market enlargement. The acquiring company obtains benefits in the form of economies of resource sharing and diversification (Ansoff and Weston 1962).

A *conglomerate combination* is the amalgamation of two companies engaged in unrelated industries. It enhances the overall stability of the acquiring company, and improves the balance in the company's total portfolio of diverse products and production processes.

In yet another way, mergers and acquisitions can be categorized as rescue, partnership, adversarial, and hostile. A rescue is a financial bailout of one firm by another. Here, the acquiring organization is viewed positively. In a partnership, both the parties actively desire the combination. In an adversarial situation, only one firm takes strong interest and the other insists on a different deal. In a hostile takeover, the company, to be taken over, actively resists the acquisition.

Change Processes Involved during Mergers and Acquisitions

The mergers and acquisitions process integrates two or more organizations into a cohesive unit. These organizations espouse different values, cultures, and attitudinally different workforces. To integrate and achieve cohesion, it is necessary to adopt suitable strategies so that the process of change, particularly during the transition phase, encounters minimum dissension from the employees of both units. HR managers need to play the most crucial role in this change management process, and can be broadly classified into two types, namely pre-merger and post-merger roles.

In the pre-merger phase, HR managers need to map the strategies for both organizations. This helps to identify in advance the SWOT of mergers, and take precautionary measures in advance. Issues such as communication, power, conflict, culture, operations, etc. are carefully studied at this stage. Modern HR however requires a study of various other parameters related to the issues of change process subsequent to mergers and acquisitions. Such issues are as follows:

- Meeting various stakeholders' expectations on set goals and objectives
- Scenario planning
- Exploring options
- Investigating assumptions
- Rewards
- Integrating initiatives
- Taking stock of key processes

Based on this, the change processes in the pre-merger, integration, and post-merger phases can be summarized as follows:

Pre-merger phase

This phase consists of the following steps:

- Selection of merger and acquisition project team and leader
- Ensuring that everyone involved can learn from the process
- Performing cultural assessments of the merging businesses
- Creating practices for learning and knowledge transfer

Integration phase

The following steps come under this phase:

- Designing new teams
- Creating new structures
- Retaining key employees
- Motivating employees
- Managing the change process
- Deciding on workable HR policies
- Selecting the appropriate change agents

Post-merger phase

This phase has the following steps:

- Developing new teams
- Establishing the new culture and structure
- Solidifying leadership and staffing
- Assessing the new culture
- Assessing new strategies and structures
- Assessing the culture of the new employees

- Moulding the two new cultures into one
- Reviewing both the positive and negative lessons

Recent Research on Mergers and Acquisitions

Two major factors, namely the forces of consolidation and the forces of convergence, are the main driving features of mergers and acquisitions. With information technology revolution, the process of consolidation and convergence integrate old world assets and ideas into the new world. We can understand the nature of corporate consolidation in India by analysing some of the mega merger cases, for example, the mergers of Hindalco–Indal, Tata–Tetley, Gujarat Ambuja–DLF–ACC, and HDFC–Times Bank. In the Ambuja–DLF–ACC case, we saw a somewhat risky pre-emptive move, as it was against an international giant Lafarge, which itself was looking at acquisitions to quickly establish a national presence in the country. DLF was a straightforward cash buyout offer to the majority shareholders, similar to Hindalco–Indal. In the ACC–Ambuja case, the purpose was to double their stake.

In the banking industry, there is a great deal of share swap-based consolidation. For example, the HDFC Bank–Times Bank case in India was a share swap deal where shareholders of Times Bank got proportionate shares in HDFC Bank.

Looking at the trend, one can see that infotech, telecom, and entertainment companies are converging. The logic is that it is important to have quality content, as well as infrastructure, combined with delivery. The one single force driving the world to convergence is interconnectivity. Examples are Time–Warner and AOL, and Citibank and Travellers. One regularly hears of restructure, spin-offs, and de-mergers. Wockhardt is an example of a de-merger, where all the life sciences businesses were grouped together and de-merged, while pharmaceuticals continued as the original company. Indian Rayon, on the other hand, wrote off the assets of the Sea Water Magnesia division, which was no longer viable as a non-cash loss against accumulated profits, and is looking at disposing off the assets. It also acquired the garments division from Madura Coats for cash.

There are three classes of theories that address acquisition motives. They are (i) financial theories, (ii) resource dependence theories, and (iii) managerial and agency theories. Most researches on acquisition motives fall into the first category, namely the financial theories, and is efficiency-based. Many of these theories propose that acquisitions are driven by the search for synergy, yet it is unclear whether acquisitions are driven by synergies, as there are mixed and contradictory findings. On the other hand, resource dependence theories are more evident in cases of conglomerate mergers.

Support for resource dependence theories as an explanation for industry merger patterns can be found in the work of Pfeffer and Salancik (1978). The managerial and agency theories propose that acquisitions are driven by managerial desire for prestige, power, salary, and job security that comes with managing large companies.

Managerial theorists argue that the lack of profitability from acquisitions is no surprise, because managers of acquiring companies are paying for benefits to themselves that are of no value to shareholders. The managerial theories apply mainly as a motive for conglomerate (unrelated) acquisitions.

In most acquisition cases, organizations focus on the assessment of business risk. There are certain fundamental steps that an organization should follow to manage mergers and acquisitions, such as assess the business risk, analyse the external perimeters, pay attention to attitude, review the company's security programme, review critical applications, etc. Before a company decides to make any acquisition, it is always desirable to understand the target customers. *Harvard Business Review* reports that 70 to 80 per cent of mergers are considered failures from an acquiring shareowner's perspective. Table 3.2 lists down the top ten global acquisitions by Indian companies till 2009.

TABLE 3.2   The top 10 global acquisitions of Indian companies

Acquirer	Target company	Target country	Deal value ($ mn)	Industry
Tata Steel	Corus Group Plc	UK	12,000	Steel
Hindalco	Novelis	Canada	5982	Steel
Videocon	Daewoo Electronics Corp.	Korea	729	Electronics
Dr Reddy's Labs	Betapharm	Germany	597	Pharmaceutical
Suzlon Energy	Hansen Group	Belgium	565	Energy
HPCL	Kenya Petroleum Refinery Ltd	Kenya	500	Oil and gas
Ranbaxy Labs	Terapia SA	Romania	324	Pharmaceutical
Tata Steel	Natsteel	Singapore	293	Steel
Videocon	Thomson SA	France	290	Electronics
VSNL	Teleglobe	Canada	239	Telecom

Source: www.indianmba.com, accessed on 5 July 2009.

A review of past research screening indicates that many of the studies are more specific on defining and categorizing mergers and acquisitions rather than focusing on successful management of the acquisition by transforming the work culture.

Whether it is a case of merger, acquisition, or a takeover, transformation of the work culture immediately succeeds the process. Culture is the extent of sharing symbols, meanings, images, rule, structures, habits, values, and information, in a social system. The broad definition of culture therefore, provides a framework for understanding differences among cultural, groups in organizations and societies.

Hofstede (1980) indicated that culture includes values, which raise the question of what else is included. Culture is influenced by conscious beliefs. A significant thought of culture is the pattern of learned behaviour. Individuals are born into a culture and must subsequently learn how to behave within their society.

Undoubtedly, culture alone does not determine attitudes, intentions, and actions. Economic factors also influence behaviour. Survival is a basic human instinct that can motivate individuals to take actions contrary to social customs and habits, and may include the use of questionable or unethical behaviours, which promote self-interest or personal advantage at the expense of others or the collective good in times of economic hardship. Culture encompasses many dimensions, such as nations, occupational groups, social classes, genders, races, tribes, corporations, clubs, and social movements, which should not be led only in one direction or limited to a simple explanation.

There are six keys to successful transformation of work culture in acquired units:

- A consistent and clear driving vision
- A set of supporting processes, drawing broadly on those affected by change and often using specific institutions to refine and communicate the vision, quantify and test its reality, and translate it into implemental pieces
- A persistent and constant in-place leadership cadre, driving an ongoing sense of urgency
- The willingness and drive to re-engineer any process, doctrine, or organization, and to take risks
- Readiness to allocate the funding necessary for change and to reprioritize budget allocations
- A commitment to align the measurement system across the hierarchy and in accordance with the vision

Further, work culture change can be evolutionary or revolutionary in nature. Some authors contend that revolutionary change must be implemented at a rapid pace, while others suggest that it can be implemented in phases. Studies indicate that organizations worldwide tend to use revolutionary tactics to design change, but implement business process re-engineering (BPR) in radical stages. During the work culture change process, there is an inherent tension between the conservation of existing practices and behaviours, and innovation. Factors, such as the dysfunctional aspects of an organization, cultural inertia, and risk, can militate against revolutionary change and/or retard its implementation (Miller and Friesen 1982; Chang 1994; Jih and Owings 1995; Ahmed 1998).

In the work culture transformation phase, aligning current operating projects with long-term visions and strategies is a challenge for executives. In many companies, operating projects are pursued in a highly fragmented fashion, devoid of corporate vision and strategy. However, achieving alignment between short-term operational improvement efforts and long-term vision is central to successful transformation (Mintzberg 1994). Each organizational state comprises four strategies: fine-tuning, building, crisis, and transformation. The relative dominance of each of the four strategies will vary in line with contextual changes. When adopting a strategy of fine-tuning, an 'integrated culture' is likely to dominate. This protects and sustains core competencies, beliefs, and codes of conduct, and determines the behaviours that pervade the organization. When adopting a building strategy, a 'diffuse culture' may develop, where behaviours, codes of conduct, and values are shared within the organization. Systems are employed to deliver efficiency and add value.

In a crisis situation, a 'counter culture' may emerge. This creates conditions where decisive action is taken to suspend 'business as usual'. Work culture transformation requires an 'empowered culture' which entails continuous and uninterrupted change across the organization. According to McHugh et al. (1995), virtual relationships are formed by going beyond BPR to a state which allows the organization to 'de-invent and re-invent' itself as it faces increasingly ambiguous markets. This relationship requires open communication and total trust, as each company's unique set of core competencies and capabilities make them indispensable to the network.

Any work culture transformation initiative reforms the behaviour of the people, by reinforcing their attitude. People embrace new values after successful work culture transformation. This is explained in Fig. 3.3.

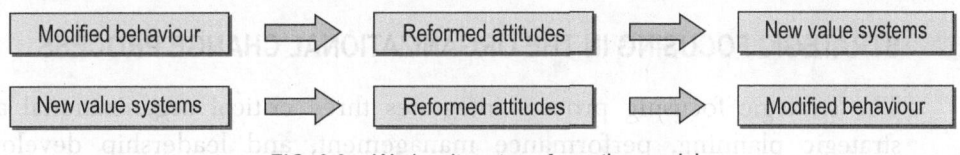

FIG. 3.3 Work culture transformation model

Mergers and Acquisitions in India

The liberalized economic policies in India have exposed Indian industry for several challenges. In response to this, the Indian economy has witnessed a sharp increase in mergers and acquisitions. The wave of mergers in the early 1990s was more a means of internal restructuring rather than an instrument for further product, market, or asset share. Today, Indian business houses increasingly resort to mergers and acquisitions as a means to growth. And, these are not limited to the domestic market.

The Tata group made two major acquisitions abroad—Tyco Global Network was bought by Videsh Sanchar Nigam Ltd (VSNL), and Singapore-based Nat Steel was acquired by Tata Steel Ltd. Yet another Tata buyout was the acquisition of South Korea-based Daewoo Commercial Vehicle Co Ltd (DWCV). Tata Consultancy Services (TCS) acquired Phoenix Global Solutions (PGS) in May 2004, and Tata Tea Ltd was also actively acquiring a couple of small plantations in the country.

Recently, Reliance had one important acquisition, namely Trevira Gmbh & Co. KG, a German speciality polyester firm, but in 2003 it made a major global acquisition of FLAG Telecom Ltd.

General Electric (GE) sold 60 per cent stake in its BPO arm, GECIS, to two strategic partners, General Atlantic Partners and Oak Hill Capital Partners. Confectionary major Candico (I) Ltd acquired a plant in Tanzania and unveiled its plans to set up another plant in Johannesburg. Pune-based Kirloskar Group acquired certain assets and businesses of UK-based SPP Pumps Ltd through a joint venture company. In

December 2004, another Pune-based company, Bharat Forge Ltd (BFL), acquired CDP Aluminiumtechnik GmbH & Co. KG (CDP AT), a German company. This is the second German acquisition by Bharat Forge, as the company had acquired the German operations of Carl Dan Peddinghaus GmbH & Co. KG in 2003, and renamed it CDP Bharat Forge GmbH.

Infosys Technologies also acquired Australia-based Expert Information Systems Private Ltd in December 2003. Indian automotive major Mahindra & Mahindra Ltd (M&M) signed a joint venture with Jiangling Motor Corporation Group (JMCG) of China to acquire 80 per cent stake in its subsidiary Jiangling Tractor Company. In December 2004, Nicholas Piramal India Ltd (NPIL) signed an agreement to acquire the global inhalation anaesthetics business of UK's Rhodia Organique Fine (Rhodia). At the same time, another pharmaceutical major, Ranbaxy Laboratories Ltd, initiated talks to acquire two firms—one in Germany and one in the US—besides planning to set up a manufacturing unit in Brazil.

STRATEGIC FOCUSING IN THE ORGANIZATIONAL CHANGE PROCESS

The strategic focusing process integrates three critical organizational activities—strategic planning, performance management, and leadership development, in an orchestrated organizational change process and benefit the organization in the following ways:

1. It aligns management and employees around a common purpose, with a clear vision for the future and meaningful goals that people can relate to.
2. It creates an innovation culture in which people are motivated and accountable for improving their personal and team performance. It aligns structures and core processes, and provides advanced leadership skills for improving people's capacity to deliver quality, service, and results. It is imperative for understanding the key principles and practices involved in developing a quality and innovation culture within the organization.
3. It helps in strategic focusing involving the top management working in teams together in a collaborative environment.

SCENARIO PLANNING FOR EFFECTIVE ORGANIZATIONAL CHANGE PROCESS

Scenarios are the alternative views of the future, primarily based on some events or changes which have occurred or are likely to occur. From the organization's point of view, it helps to identify the strategic fit for some future developments. Essentially, it reflects on future situations with some frame of references. Scenarios can also be defined as tools to prioritize our perceptions about future alternatives. Scenarios are plotted using some set of stories, and used as the basis for framing plans and strategies. Using scenarios, managers can forecast their proposed change initiatives reflecting on future situations. When planning scenarios, managers or decision-makers need to question the broadest assumptions on world functions in general, and the way the organization functions in that particular area, so that decisions can be taken in advance to meet the gap, if any. Thus, to explore the scenarios, managers essentially think about uncertain aspects to unfold any eventual happenings that may harm the organizations.

For economic globalization, it is imperative for organizations to understand the global business environment. Among others, this is affected by political changes and new emerging technologies. Such changes create discontinuity in the business and in order to sustain, organizations need to prepare for them in advance by chasing events. Scenario plans help to explore the eventualities and develop a shared understanding or commitment to strategic interventions, to change the organization before any unforeseen changes gag it.

In a turbulent market environment, organizations need to quickly adapt themselves to change. This is possible only when they are capable of preconceiving different scenarios of the environment with prior plans and programmes, and accordingly able to respond to the changes with adequate contingency plans and pre-structured strategies. Ringland (1998) and Schwartz (1991) identified that organizations worldwide were developing scenario plans to respond to unforeseen change situations. According to Schwartz (1991), scenarios are future eventualities, considering which organizations are able to determine their future directions with contingency plans.

Literally, a scenario is a script for a play. It is a tool to consolidate one's perception to track alternative future environments to take decisions at the right time. According to Wack (1985), scenario planning involves development of three or four different plots along with the associated narratives to illustrate the major driving forces for change and critical uncertainties in the environment.

Thus, scenario planning is a creative foresight of managers and decision-makers to keep pace with the changing environmental uncertainty. It is also considered a strategic planning method. The key driving forcers for the scenario plans are changing social, technical, economic, environmental, educational, political, and aesthetic (STEEEPA) trends. Globally, we find Shell and Siemens AG have made extensive use of scenario plans. Box 3.2 highlights Shell's strategy to cope with environment.

BOX 3.2 Shell's strategy for coping with oil crisis

Shell as an organization has made the most extensive use of scenario planning since 1973, primarily to cope with the oil crisis sparked by the Organization of Petroleum Exporting Countries (OPEC). Shell's strategy was to cope with the environmental turbulence often sparked by the non-compromising OPEC members, who never came to an agreement on collective price rising or production strategy. Such non-compromising attitudes of OPEC members often caused operational discontinuities in POL companies worldwide.

Peter Drucker (1954) more appropriately said that 'the greatest danger in times of turbulence is not the turbulence—it is to act with yesterday's logic'. Drucker's argument also emphasized the need for strategic forecasting making use of scenario plans to cope with the organizational change.

Forces of Scenario Planning

The major driving forces of scenario planning fall into four categories:

Social dynamics Social dynamics, in the broadest terms, incorporate major demographic trends, such as age-mix, income, education, and lifestyles, and even the change in value systems. For example, lifestyle changes now shift customers' perceptions to more value-added products and services. Customers are more informed and can question the company's products and services if they fail to meet their expectations. With more disposable incomes and change in the income level (particularly when it is on the higher side), customers seek premium-priced products and services.

Economic issues Both macro- and micro-economic trends influence the scenario plans. Macro-economic trends shape the economy as a whole. With more global interrelatedness, failure of one major multinational or transnational organization (such as Lehman Brothers) cascade failures in many organizations and also in the economy. The recent global meltdown and its effect is now an important example for us to emulate. Similarly, micro-economic issues, such as modus operandi of competing organizations could also spark the need for change and could be a basis for scenario planning.

Political issues The political beliefs and ideologies of ruling parties and strong oppositions, and legislative and regulatory changes, etc. could also be the basis for scenario plans for an organization.

Technological issues New emerging technologies influence the business per se. With the development of Plasma and LCD technology (and now, the LED technology), conventional CTVs have become almost obsolete. Similar changes in the CDMA and GSM technologies have revolutionized the mobile phone industry. In many other areas also, changes in technology have influenced change in product or service mix. Organizations that understand and gauge such changes beforehand are able to develop appropriate action plans and emerge as winners. Those who do not are languishing behind.

Steps for Scenario Planning

Having understood the key drivers for scenario plans, action has to be taken in certain steps in a sequential order. These steps, as followed by Shell, are as follows:
1. Identify the drivers for change/assumptions.
2. Draw a framework of drivers.
3. Develop some mini-scenarios, preferably seven to nine.

4. Reduce these scenarios to a manageable number, preferably two to three.
5. Prepare the draft of the scenarios.
6. List the issues arising in each scenario.

Various types of drivers for the scenarios have already been explained. To understand which driver(s) is/are important at a particular point of time, managers need to first account for the circumstances under which the organization operates, that is, make an informed assumption. Use of brainstorming, application of Delphi technique, and focus group interviews are some of the common techniques for making informed assumptions. To draw the framework of such assumptions, managers can make extensive use of their intuition or follow a structured pattern, more in the form of a flow chart. Similarly, they need to act upon each step to finally draw the scenario and use it for framing the future strategies for the organization. These steps are also known as Shell's model of scenario planning.

Application of Delphi Technique in Scenario Planning

The word 'Delphi' comes from Greece. In ancient times, it was a convention to consult an oracle—a representative of the God, Apollo, who was believed to have contact with God. The priest was only able to interpret the advice of the Oracle.

In modern times, this method is essentially a group process to achieve a consensus forecast. In scenario planning, the Delphi technique helps to significantly minimize forecasting errors, as it enables consolidating the consensus opinions of cross-functional experts. This method calls for selection of a panel of experts, either from within or outside the organization whose comments are crystallized from a series of questionnaire responses and then used as the basis of forecast. A series of questionnaires is prepared from the responses received from a prior set of questions in a sequential manner. At every stage, the information obtained from the previous questionnaire is shared among the participating members without disclosing the majority opinion to avoid any possibility of peer-group influence on the minority opinion.

The procedure of the Delphi technique may be enumerated as follows:

1. To start with, it requires selection of a coordinator and a panel of experts both within and outside the organizations.
2. The coordinator circulates questions in writing to each such expert.
3. The experts write their observations.
4. The coordinator edits those observations and summarizes them without, however, disclosing the majority opinion in his/her summary.
5. On the basis of his summary, the coordinator develops a new set of questionnaires and circulates these among the experts.
6. Experts answer the new set of questions.
7. The coordinator repeats the process until he/she is able to synthesize from the opinion of the experts.

The success of the process again depends on the following factors:
1. Experts should be chosen so that they have the requisite knowledge and skills to give the best answers.
2. Questions should be relevant to the objective.
3. The criteria for evaluating responses should be consistent, unbiased, and befitting the objectives. Although there is no universal set of criteria for evaluating responses, it is often deemed necessary to follow the guidelines indicated below and consider the assessment in terms of
   (a) the judgement of the experts in terms of their knowledge in the area,
   (b) feasibility, objectives, time, and resource requirements,
   (c) desirability, and
   (d) extraneous factors.

Nominal Group Method

Like the Delphi method, the nominal group method also involves a panel of experts. However, the major difference between the two is that while in the former technique, experts are not allowed to discuss the assessing questions, under the latter they are permitted to do so. In this method, the coordinator assumes the role of a facilitator, allowing experts to sit together to discuss their ideas, and these are recorded on a flip chart. The experts are then asked to rank their ideas according to their perceived priority. A group consensus is then derived mathematically, in terms of individual rankings. The process, therefore, affords creativity and facilitates scientific group consensus unlike consensus by qualification (where the coordinator ultimately decides the best course of action) under the Delphi technique.

Both methods, however, help to draw scenario plans, and depending on the issues and the time constraint, organizations choose the appropriate method to minimize the risk of forecasting.

SUMMARY

The chapter details various organizational change processes. In organizational change, the need to ensure personal change, such as beliefs, unconsciousness, assumptions, values, etc., is very important. This chapter discusses the various features of organizational change, theories, and organizational change process, per se, encompassing areas, such as business environment, strategic planning, customer and market focus, culture focus, organizational structure, leadership performance, etc. Here, effective use is made of SWOT analysis, environment scanning, and various HRD tools.

Organizational change also becomes imperative to manage manpower redundancy. This chapter, therefore, highlights how the organizational change process is affected by manpower redundancy and how such issues can be effectively managed. Another critical area of organizational change is to account for mergers and acquisitions, as in the post-merger phase issues related to change become more critical. Similarly, the organizational change process needs to be aligned to the strategic intents of the organization to reap strategic advantage. The chapter also details such issues.

KEY TERMS

Contextual issues It focuses on the forces or conditions of external and internal environments that influence the organizational functioning.

Implementation control It assesses whether the overall strategy results relate with incremental steps and actions that implement the overall strategy.

Premise control It systematically and continuously checks whether or not the premises set during the planning and implementation process are still valid.

Process issues It addresses the detailed actions undertaken during the change process.

STEEEPA It is a strategic planning method based on scenario plans. The key driving forces for the scenario plans are changing social, technical, economic, environmental, educational, political, and aesthetic (STEEEPA) trends.

THT theory This theory was named after F. Trompenaars and Hampden-Turner who observed that insidious culture clashes and most management problems are a result of the human habit.

CONCEPT REVIEW QUESTIONS

1. Define organizational change process. How does personal examination help in the organizational change process?
2. What are the features of organizational change process?
3. Explain Kurt Lewin's change process. Will Kurt Lewin's theory hold good in a 'hang-loose' situation? Explain.
4. What are the pillars of the organizational change process? In what type of change process can you categorize global meltdown?
5. Manpower redundancy is a burning problem for today's organization. What types of organizations are more prone to manpower redundancy?
6. Explain how mergers and acquisitions influence the organizational change process.
7. Explain the significance of scenario planning for organizational change.
8. Write short notes on the following:
    (a) Customer-centric change
    (b) Strategic planning focused change
    (c) Goal congruence model
    (d) Acculturation
    (e) Delphi technique
    (f) Nominal group method

CRITICAL THINKING QUESTIONS

1. Wal-Mart, the largest retail chain in the world, promoted the Metro 7 clothing line during Christmas 2006. Wal-Mart is traditionally identified as a grocer's shop for the masses. Their apparel stores (Metro 7) proved to be a total failure. Experts say this is due to Wal-Mart's typical identity problem in the apparel industry. Explain how scenario planning before such market expansion could have helped Wal-Mart.
2. We all know about the failure of the mergers between Daimler-Chrysler due to cultural incongruence. Browse through the available information and analyse the reasons for this. What could have been the appropriate approach for a successful organizational change process?
3. Critically examine why IBM has to reinvent itself, changing its business focus from desktop to IT-enabled services.

CASE STUDY

The Organizational Change Process in Indian Ordnance Factories

Organizational change also needs to focus on the utilization pattern of all cross sections of employees. Unless this is done, increased HR cost will reduce organizational competitiveness. With the opening of the Indian economy, public sector enterprises in India, which had earlier enjoyed captive market privileges, now face competition from private players and international level organizations in the domestic market. To survive, restructuring has now become very important for them so that almost all major organizations have had to go in for massive restructuring programmes either in terms of manpower redundancy, technology upgradation, process re-engineering, new market development, and so on.

Indian ordnance factories are categorized as departmental undertakings, as the Government of India has full stake in them. With globalization and market reform initiatives of the government, ordnance factories ceased to enjoy their erstwhile captive market privilege and had to scout for new market development opportunities, particularly in the civil market, competing with other private sector enterprises. One major hurdle for such an initiative, as envisaged by them, was cost competitiveness. Being government-controlled, they had to follow protective employment practices and, as a norm, had to appoint a large number of unskilled women workers under compulsion, for example, when any employee died prematurely before retirement. Most of these were given unskilled stationary jobs, such as filing letters, messenger duties, cooking or helping in canteens, support activities in hospitals, etc.

Rigorous technological changes in the Indian ordnance factories have taken place in the post-reform period. Almost all of them now have computer numeric control (CNC), numeric control (NC), and direct numeric control (DNC) machines. They have been compelled to switch over from single drive and special purpose machines to state-of-the-art technology to keep pace with the increasing demand of users (primarily the defence forces) for better precision, accuracy, and quality, and also for new product-mix with internationally comparable performance levels.

Cost minimization and the need to expand civil trade activities are the other two forces for technological changes in ordnance factories. Over the years, cost minimization exercises have facilitated rationalization of manpower by suitable redeployment of workers in restructured positions and by relocating surplus workers from one factory to another. Since the recruitment ban of the government still persists, manpower planning activities have been restricted to surplus and redundancy management rather than systematic planning for manpower replacement (average age-mix of workers of all ordnance factories being 55 plus). However, manpower cost is mounting in cases of unplanned recruitment, that is, recruitment of women workers on compassionate grounds. Recently, however, such recruitment has been marginally controlled after considering the economic criteria before finalizing such employment. The earlier recruitment practices so seriously jeopardized the skilled manpower replacement plan that trade apprentices (who had undergone three years systematic training) recruited ten years earlier, were still waiting their turn for employment. The ultimate beneficiaries of such huge investments on training the future manpower were obviously the private industrial units.

Many of the Group–D women workers are widows of employees, and are unskilled and not very educated. They represent 60.57 per cent of the total women (5.17 per cent) employed. Despite massive technological changes, which necessitated skill renewal training for existing workers and their redeployment in restructured positions, job compositional change, or job content change for Group–D women workers did not occur as this issue never received priority attention from the management. In spite of the fact that these women workers could have been deployed more gainfully in some gang on the shop floor, such as oilmen (who lubricate the machines), waste pickers (to pick the inorganic wastes), stores assistant, paramedical staff positions, etc., ordnance factories have so far neglected this aspect.

With skill training, such a large workforce could be placed in jobs traditionally in the male domain, such as machinist, fitter, grinder, pattern and die-maker, data entry operator, and even clerks or assistants in cash offices (for those who are reasonably literate). Organizational training programmes put very little emphasis on this aspect. Unless utilization of women workers (Group–D) receives attention from the government, with the continuance of compassionate employment policy ordnance factories will gradually become an irresponsible employer with no concern for this underprivileged class of workers, who currently only replicate their domestic duties in organizational life, that is, as orderlies (ordnance factories use this term to indicate the job of peons). This apart, they will increase the cost to the national exchequer under the veil of gainful employment, and social justice and equity.

Discussion Question

Analyse the change related issues discussed in the above case. Select a large public sector organization similar to the ordnance factories, where compassionate employment practices for women/kin are still followed or were followed in the recent past. Critically review their manpower utilization plan for such women employees and suggest your line of action for change in their effective utilization.

REFERENCES

Ahmed, P.K. (1998), 'Culture and climate for innovation', *European Journal of Innovation Management*, Vol. 1, pp. 30–43.

Ansoff, H.I. and J.F. Weston (1962), 'Merger objectives and organizational structure', *The Quarterly Review of Economics and Business*, Vol. 2, No. 3, pp. 49.

Beckhard, R. and R.T. Harris (1987), *Organizational Transitions*, Addison-Wesley OD Series, Reading, Mass.

Bhattacharyya, Dipak Kumar (2007), *Human Resource Research Methods*, Oxford University Press, New Delhi.

Burke, W. and G. Litwin (1992), 'A causal model of organizational performance and change', *Journal of Management*, Vol. 18, pp. 523–545.

Carr, C. (1996), *Choice, Chance, and Organizational Change*, Amacom, New York.

Chang, R.Y. (1994), 'Improve processes, reengineer them or both', *Training and Development*, March, pp. 54–58.

Drucker, Peter (1954), *The Principles of Management*, HarperCollins Publishers, New York.

Hofstede, G. (1980), 'Motivation, leadership, and organization: Do american theories apply abroad?' *Organizational Dynamics*, Summer, pp. 42–63.

Jih, W.J.K. and P. Owings (1995), 'From in search of excellence to business process reengineering: The role of IT', *Information Strategy: The Executive's Journal*, Winter, pp. 6–19.

Kleiner, A. (1994), 'Creating scenarios', in Senge, P., A. Kleiner, C. Roberts, R. Ross, and B. Smith, *The Fifth Discipline Fieldbook*, Doubleday, New York.

Lewin, K. (1958), 'Group decision and social change', in Maccoby, E.E., T.N. Newcomb, and E.L. Hartley, (eds), *Readings in Social Psychology*, Holt, Rinehart, and Winston, New York, pp. 213–246.

_____. (1951), *Field Theory in Social Science*, Harper and Row, New York.

McHugh, P., G. Merli, and W.A. III Wheeler (1995), *Beyond Business Process Reengineering: Towards the Holonic Enterprise*, Wiley and Sons, London.

Miller, D. (1982), 'Evolution and revolution: A quantum view of structural change in organizations', *Journal of Management Studies*, Vol. 19, pp. 131–151.

Miller, D. and P. Friesen (1982), 'Structural change and performance: Quantum vs piecemeal incremental approaches', *Academy of Management Journal*, Vol. 25, No. 4, pp. 867–892.

Mintzberg, H. (1994), *The Rise and Fall of Strategic Planning*, Prentice Hall, London.

Pace, Wayne R., Philip C. Smith, and Gordon Mills (1991), *Human Resource Development—The Field*, Prentice Hall, New Jersey.

Ramaiya, A. (1977), *Guide to the Companies Act*, Eighth Edition, Wadhwa, Nagpur.

Rao, T.V. and E. Abraham (1986), 'HRD climate in Indian organizations', Rao and Pereira (ed.), *Recent Experiences in Human Resource Development*, Oxford and IBH, New Delhi.

Ringland, G. (1998), *Scenario Planning—Managing for the Future*, Wiley, New York.

Salancik, G.R., and J. Pfeffer (1978), 'A social information processing approach to job attitudes and task design', *Administrative Science Quarterly*, Vol. 23, pp. 224–253.

Schein, E.H. (1992), *Organizational Culture and Leadership*, Jossey Bass, New York.

Schwartz, P. (1991), *The Art of the Long View*, Doubleday, New York.

Trompenaars, F. and C. Hampden-Turner (1998), 'Riding the waves of culture: Understanding diversity in global business'; Second Edition, McGraw-Hill, New York.

Vollman, T. (1996), *The Transformation Imperative*, Harvard Business School Press, Boston.

Wack, P. (1985), 'Scenarios: Shooting the rapids', *Harvard Business Review*, Vol. 63, No. 6, pp. 139–150.

4 Organizational Effectiveness and Excellence

Learning Objectives

After reading this chapter, you will be able to understand
- the meaning and concepts of organizational effectiveness and excellence
- how to measure organizational effectiveness
- various contemporary models of organizational excellence
- how managerial skills and competencies contribute to organizational effectiveness and excellence in the millennium
- relate organizational effectiveness and excellence to organizational change

TTK Group

The Rs 650 crore TTK Group has business interests ranging from pressure cookers to condoms, atlases, and maps to gripe water and surgical gloves. In a recent interview published in *The Times of India*, TTK's chairman, T.T. Jagannathan, recalled how the company's pressure cookers became a leading brand in India with thriving exports to the US as well. But post 1998, US and European exports plummeted from Rs 25 crore to a mere Rs 10 crore. Meanwhile, in India too, smaller players started to make cheaper products.

TTK was hard-hit but it learnt its lesson in good time. They closed six factories and concentrated on consumer products such as kitchen appliances, fast-moving consumer goods (FMCGs), and fee-based services such as medical care for elderly parents of NRIs, collection of rent on their behalf, planning their travel itineraries, facilitating cashless hospital entry in emergencies, and so on. Every company has to change with the passage of time. If it does not, it will be doomed. There is nothing wrong in exiting unviable areas of business.

INTRODUCTION

Before we define organizational effectiveness, let us first understand the term 'effectiveness'. Effectiveness is the extent to which an activity helps to achieve the long-term goals. As effectiveness is measured for a specific activity, we can define activity-specific effectiveness as the outcome that supports the broader goals of an organization. Both qualitative as well as quantitative tools are used to measure effectiveness. Behavioural parameters, such as values, attitudes, skills, and behaviour per se, are measured using qualitative tools. Value and volume of output changes, customer satisfaction, changes in the profitability, etc. are measured using quantitative tools.

Organizational effectiveness is the extent to which the organization, as a whole, achieves its goals while optimizing its resources. It depends on the degree of interpersonal skills, positive attitudes, technical competencies, small group activities, etc., which together contribute to the achievement of organizational goals and objectives. Therefore, organizational effectiveness refers to the corporate management system that produces the development results of an organization. Among others, an effective organizational structure helps to achieve organizational effectiveness. Box 4.1 highlights the key areas related to organizational effectiveness and change management.

> **BOX 4.1   Change and organizational excellence**
>
> People, service, and results are the foundation of a successful organization. Achieving success or excellence with focus on quality and customer satisfaction are the end results of organizational performance and members of the organization are the actual contributors in this process. Hence, organizational excellence is possible when effective people make use of effective processes, and they are effectively managed.
>
> Thus, organizations can bring positive changes through appropriate performance management practices. Among other things, this requires improvement in leadership and managerial styles, as such change initiatives bring forth new principles and practices, which also require change in the culture (both at the individual and organizational levels). Culture here is defined as the consensual validation of experience. In other words, the experiences that people agree to, believe in, and often cherish make up their culture. Every society, company, and family has a set of these experiences.

Experts consider organizational change to be a cultural change, as members of the organization are asked to validate their way of working, which is different from what they are actually used to. Teamwork, partnerships, customer focus, benchmarking with the best practice organizations, technological shift, job process changes, and environmental changes require the organization to adopt new ways of managing the business. The success of the change will depend on how effectively they are made, and how people accept the change messages. Thus, the foundation of organizational change begins with the people and intervention to support the change processes should have a people-oriented approach.

Morgan (1997) suggested numerous ways to conceptualize an organization. He suggested areas of focus that have two dimensions, namely organizational form and structure, and organizational functions and activities. Organizational design and its functions obviously have important implications for managing the processes and people. For example, managing an organization like a machine will require more managerial control while transforming it on a continuous basis will make it contextually different, as managers and the people will shape it together to sustain and grow in competition. According to Dooley (1997), traditionally organization theories believed in reductionism, determinism, and equilibrium as core principles. However, with the passage of time the paradigm shift has occurred, as today's organizations are adaptive and self-organizing, and emphasize interactions with the external environment. They practise participation, ensure workers' motivation, follow dynamic aspects of change, and learning (Morgan 1997; Wheatley 1992). Strategically, organizations now balance technicalities of organizational design with the needs and interests of the workers, and use models that meet the requirements of both. This is why, all the organizational excellence models discussed in this chapter focus on both these issues.

MEASURING ORGANIZATIONAL EFFECTIVENESS

Organizational effectiveness is measured by assessing some or all the activities an organization conducts to achieve effectiveness. Two types of evaluation are commonly used, namely formative and summative evaluation.

Formative evaluation measures the effectiveness of the change process at the initial stage. This provides data to identify possible problems and helps to adopt strategies to introduce changes in the organization effectively.

Summative evaluation consolidates the results of the organizational effectiveness after the identified strategies have been implemented, that is, after the completion of all the intervention processes. Whether formative or summative, organizational effectiveness indicators are observable and measurable. There may be both quantitative and qualitative measurement of change in the performance and behaviour of the members after organizational intervention processes.

Organizational effectiveness evaluation measures, therefore, become a reference point for organizations to judge the efficacies of intervention processes, that is, how effectively activities are carried out as planned. Effectiveness indicators can also be grouped under process indicators and impact indicators. Performance results are classified as process indicators. Impact indicators assess the degree of achievement of organizational objectives and its overall effect on the individual and group work behaviour of the people.

Irrespective of the type of measurement and effectiveness indicators, the following points must be considered when measuring organizational effectiveness:

1. There is no simple measure of organizational effectiveness.
2. Measures of effectiveness should be related to the particular context and life stage of an organization.
3. There is a need to focus on how different constituencies use the organization for different purposes.
4. It is important to differentiate between organizational levels (operational, business, and strategic).

Structured systems and metrics are used to measure organizational effectiveness. Some of the commonly used ones are highlighted here.

Organizational Effectiveness Inventory

Organizational effectiveness inventory (OEI) is a structured process of measuring organizational effectiveness and helps to evaluate the structures, systems, technologies, and skills/qualities of managers, which are construed as the causal factors of culture, and are instrumental in achieving organizational effectiveness at the individual, group, and organizational levels. Technically, OEI is capable of assessing all the internal factors that can exert or are capable of exerting influence on the organizational performance, and map the process of change or levers of change. Depending on the specific organizational requirements, it is possible to develop OEI with clear indications of measurement criteria.

According to Cooke (1997), OEI can be effectively used along with organizational cultural inventory (OCI) to assess the normative beliefs and shared behavioural expectations which reflect the abstract aspects of culture, that is, the shared assumptions and values. Thus, OEI with OCI can direct and monitor organizational change.

OE Cycle

Porter (1980) introduced the term operational effectiveness and suggested that it is difficult to achieve organizational effectiveness without this. Operational effectiveness (OE) ensures better utilization of resource inputs by reducing defects in products and developing better products. Based on this, the OE cycle, which denotes the process of managing effective operations of an organization, can be represented as in Fig. 4.1.

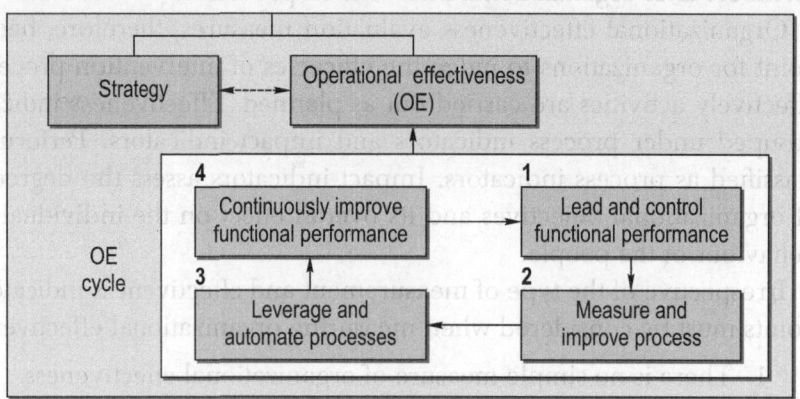

FIG. 4.1   The OE cycle

Dashboard

Dashboard is another system of measuring organizational effectiveness. It is used with reference to a Web-based technology page to collate real-time information on different spheres of organizational activities. The term dashboard is used as a technology-enabled measurement system, as it is intended to track real-time analysis on the performance of the organization, very much like an automobile dashboard which displays real-time information regarding the performance of the vehicle.

Essentially, a dashboard is a control panel as it provides a graphic presentation of performance information on a real-time basis. How well is the organization doing from an overall, divisional, and departmental perspective? Does the organization achieve performance targets? Such questions can be answered when the organization is able to design the required dashboard. Therefore, it is possible to use a dashboard as a holistic tool to measure organizational effectiveness. Box 4.2 further illustrates the use of customized dashboards.

> **BOX 4.2 Customization in dashboards**
>
> Software vendors nowadays make available customized dashboards, such as enterprise resource planning (ERP) packages. To illustrate, the finance department of any organization can use a digital dashboard and scorecard to monitor cash flows, revenues, operating profit, expenses, and other traditional financial metrics. Performance information on a dashboard can appear in a summary form.
>
> A digital dashboard can also provide signals in different colours, such as red, yellow, or green, to indicate the degree of achievement of the metrics' targets. It can facilitate departmental coordination, exchange performance information, and therefore, promote the culture of teamwork to achieve results for mutual benefit. Its technological flexibility enables manipulation of real-time information to generate different metrics. Depending on the organizational focus, it is possible to shift from one metric to another.

The successful use of dashboards as an organizational effectiveness measurement tool largely depends on developing a performance-based culture. People in the organization need to agree in principle on the key performance indicator (KPI) and its measurement through the dashboard.

Digital dashboards

Digital dashboards provide customized solutions for knowledge workers, making available consolidated information at the individual, team, and corporate level, and external information, with a single click. Thus, a digital dashboard can function as an analytical and collaborative tool, providing an integrated view to facilitate real-time decision-making.

The benefits of a digital dashboard to measure organizational effectiveness can be summarized as follows:

It focuses on critical information A digital dashboard can reduce the information overload, focusing only on vital business information. Using information filters, it can customize user-specific information, and summarize and generate relevant business reports.

It integrates information from a variety of sources It can integrate information from multiple sources. Key business data, Internet and intranet sites, team folders, and personal files can be easily organized and viewed on a digital dashboard.

It fully uses organizational knowledge Digital dashboards promote a knowledge management culture leveraging the knowledge of each one. With increasing global competitiveness, it is increasingly difficult for people to collaborate with each other. A Web-based knowledge management system enhances the capability of people gaining access to the best practice views and the underlying knowledge resources.

It is a powerful tool for change A digital dashboard facilitates organizational change, as people in the organization can use it to read their daily activities, share information, and get feedback on the organizational performance. Such information make peoples sensitive to the organizational needs and makes them feel responsible for delivering their best.

Dashboards are now very powerful tools for gaining a quick insight into the organizational performance. Depending on their requirements, organizations can customize these dashboards. The basic premise for developing dashboards is the identified key performance indicators (KPI) of the organization. KPIs highlight the trends that are essential for strategic performance and improvement of the organization as a whole. Developing and implementing a dashboard is a rigorous process and many organizations muddle this issue by identifying too many KPIs. However, it is important to restrict the KPIs to a small or manageable number of indicators, which in a true sense exerts influence on the overall performance of the organization.

A very common approach is to develop KPIs based on the critical success factors (CSF) of the organizations. This concept was pioneered by John Rockart of the Massachusetts Institute of Technology (MIT). It is possible to reduce KPIs into management numbers using the CSF by extracting the dimensions (many dimensions can be reduced to one or two), or normalization, that is, considering KPIs that are mutually exclusive and understanding the holistic performance of the organization. It is also important to understand the structure and behaviour of selected metrics to measure the KPIs. Other issues in developing KPIs are as follows:

1. Organization-wise approaches to KPIs vary in terms of hierarchy. Some organizations prefer to modularize higher level managerial KPIs into the KPIs of people down the line, while some may believe in doing it the other way round. The higher level KPIs could be the parent metrics, while the lower level KPIs could form the child metrics.
2. Approaches to aggregation of KPIs also vary from one organization to another. Some aggregate child metrics into parent metrics, while others reduce parent

EXHIBIT 4.1 Key performance indicators at Hindustan Unilever Ltd (HUL)

Wings, a well-known dashboards vendor, helped HUL to e-integrate its entire distribution network with its supply chain management (SCM) package. The FMCG major covers 1,000,000 retail outlets spread over 50,000 villages under 7000 re-distribution stockists. HUL's primary sale is to the re-distribution stockists, who make secondary sales through wholesale and retail outlets. Some of the reasons that HUL e-integrated the supply chain using a dashboard are as follows:

- Keep track of retailers to authenticate whether the sales promotional incentives reach them.
- Keep a track of stock movement, more particularly, non-moving stocks.
- Get on-time billing and reporting.

Wings' SCM provided dashboards to HUL to track all the above aspects. HUL's dashboards provide load charts, which display the quantity of each item loaded in the van for each beat with regard to the salesman, the beat, date, profit centre, product, and party-wise collection details, etc. These dashboards can provide accurate and faster data, and reports more easily with minimum manual interference.

Source: http://www.wings2000.com/cstudy, accessed on 10 January 2010.

---

metrics to child metrics. Whatever may the approach be, aggregation should be in simple understandable form, such as addition, averages, weighted averages, median, percentile, etc. depending on the information solution requirements of the company.

3. Again, in an organizational context aggregation depends on the dimensions of the information. The child metrics may have geographic dimensions (say, area-wise sales figures), which when aggregated lead to parent metrics, that is, overall sales.

Similarly, there may be other issues, namely the level of aggregation, norms to give weightages to information, direction, ownership, etc. Exhibit 4.1 helps to understand this better.

SAS/GRAPH dashboard in version 9.1.3. service pack 4

SAS/GRAPH dashboards are well-known and can deliver information as required by the organization. Some of the specific focus areas of this dashboard are indicators, such as slider chart, bullet graph, dial meter, bar chart, etc. Similarly, the types of SAS dashboards also vary. The ones most commonly used for the marketing function are telesales and marketing analysis dashboards. Telesales dashboards can monitor the real-time performance of the telesales team, browsing through information, such as call waiting time, call duration, abandoned calls, call volume, order volume, salespeople utilization rate, etc. Similarly, marketing analysis dashboards also provide various types of information to meet the needs of the organization.

A typical dashboard is appended at the end of the chapter (see Appendix 4.1).

Open Systems Model

The open system perspective emphasizes the organizational interactions with external environmental issues. Although this perspective has been popular since the 1960s, Blau and Scott (1962) and Scott (1987) have given it more prominence. Conceptually, open systems of organization established a relational chain with the inputs–throughputs–outputs. There are two aspects of these interlocking processes, morphostasis and morphogenesis (Buckley 1967). Morphostasis indicates a given form, structure, or state of a system, while morphogenesis elaborates or changes the system. A good example of morphostasis is the circulation and respiration of a biological system. For morphogenesis, it can be growth, learning, and differentiation. The other ways of viewing organizations are mechanistic and organic (Burns and Stalker 1961). Mechanistic organizations are by nature engaged in large scale, routine, and repetitive jobs. They do not require any adaptive change and are less innovative. Organic organizations, on the other hand, are characterized by highly complex work and are the right fit in a changing environment. Such organizations usually maintain an optimum level scale of activities and can quickly respond to environmental change, and also be innovative.

Organizational design, therefore, connects structures, people, processes, rewards, and tasks, to build the capabilities to gain competitive advantage (Galbraith 1973, 1994, 1995). Managerial role leashes the creativity and passion to harness these forces to achieve success for the organization (Kotter 1996; Deming 1994). Peters and Waterman's (1982) model of excellence and McKinsey's 7-S framework espouse all these values.

Organizational model of excellence

Organizational excellence is achieved through organizational effectiveness. Every organization has a competitive edge and strives to achieve excellence through systematic change initiatives. The primary enabler in achieving organizational excellence through the process of organizational change is leadership. Effective leadership requires having a sense of mission, purpose, and direction. Organizational mission emanates from the vision, which espouses the organizational philosophy and values. Leadership exerts influence individually, interpersonally, professionally, and organizationally.

Whether it is achieving excellence through quality improvement, process changes, customer satisfaction, or cost optimization, leadership acts as the major catalyst for the change process. For example, effective leadership and management bring quality in organizations. While leadership activates vision, mission, attitude, and the ability of people, management influences practices, procedures, feedback, and feeling. Whereas leadership is the heart and mind, management is the stomach and body of an organization. The mind of an organization is a metaphor for the attitude and ability of people. The heart is a metaphor for vision and mission. Practices and procedures together define the methods for an organization and represent the body, while organizational stomach means the feedback and feelings of the people. The mind, heart, body, and stomach need to interact in a balanced way to achieve excellence.

In other words, organizational excellence through effective leadership is best possible when attitude, ability, vision, mission, practices, procedures, feedback, feeling, integrate, and interact.

Contemporary Models of Organizational Effectiveness and Excellence

There are many contemporary models to achieve organizational effectiveness and excellence. These provide a framework of management practices based on more recent trends, such as globalization, theory Z concepts, McKinsey's 7-S approach, excellence models, productivity, and quality issues. With the emergence of global entities, such as the World Trade Organization (WTO) and the European Economic Community (EEC), we now operate in a global economy. Managers need to think globally even to operate in the domestic market. We are losing market shares even in the domestic market because of competition from foreign companies. Hence, it is important to understand management with a global perspective.

Some of the contemporary models of organizational effectiveness and excellence are discussed here.

Theory Z concepts

Theory Z concepts pioneered by Ouchi and Jaeger (1978) incorporated Japanese and American management culture. This theory emphasizes the need to study and adopt appropriate management practices from other countries. The concept can be understood from tabular information in Exhibit 4.2.

EXHIBIT 4.2   Theory Z practices

Type A (American)	Type J (Japanese)	Type Z (modified American)
Short-term employment	Lifetime employment	Long-term employment
Individual decision-making	Consensual decision-making	Consensual decision-making
Individual responsibility	Collective responsibility	Individual responsibility
Rapid evaluation and promotion	Slow evaluation and promotion	Slow evaluation and promotion
Explicit, formalized control	Implicit, informal control	Implicit, informal control with explicit, formalized measures
Specialized career path	Non-specialized career path	Moderately specialized career path
Segmented concern	Holistic concern	Holistic concern, including family

EXHIBIT 4.3 McKinsey's 7-S framework

Strategy	To determine allocation of scarce resources and to commit the organization to a specific course of action
Structure	To determine the number of levels (in hierarchy) and authority centres
Systems	To determine organizational processes, procedures, reports, and routines
Staff	To determine key human resource groups in an organization and describe them demographically
Style	To determine the manner in which managers should behave in order to achieve organizational goals
Superordinate goals (shared vision)	To determine the guiding concepts that an organization needs to instil in its members
Skills	To determine the abilities of people in an organization

McKinsey's 7-S framework

McKinsey's (Peters and Waterman 1982) 7-S framework identified seven independent organizational factors that today's managers need to manage. The 7-S model is a framework for analysing organizations and their effectiveness. It looks at the seven key elements that make organizations successful. Exhibit 4.3 discusses this framework.

The 7-S framework suggests that a change in any of these factors may result in an adjustment of the other factors. However, the concept of 8-S has been introduced now by adding another S—streaming. Streaming includes those areas that, either indirectly or directly, influence or shape all the 7-S.

Shared vision

This embodies the organizational vision, mission, values, and operating principles. This element of the 8-S paradigm is central to and the core of overall organizational effectiveness. The purpose of this component, as illustrated in the model, is to permeate the organizational strategy, structure, systems, style, staff, and skills. In other words, every level of the organization and each focus area should somehow embody these.

Strategy

Once a shared vision has been established at the organizational level, the process of alignment usually begins by driving the shared vision into strategy. Organizational strategy includes the approaches that a company will take to realize their shared vision. This may include gaining competitive advantage, developing new products and services for the purposes of increasing revenue, generating market share, or improving margins. They may also include being a low-cost producer, or providing product superiority through quality and customer service. The strategy needs to be linked to the shared vision.

Structure

After organizational vision and strategy have been developed, it is appropriate to put together the elements associated with the organizational structure. In other words, a company organizes itself towards its purpose and to implement strategy. Structural realignment may not make sense unless it is done within the context of an overall purpose or strategic direction. Structural changes may include anything from consolidating distribution centres to downsizing, or a host of other possibilities.

System

Shared vision, strategy, and structure work together in a somewhat sequential fashion. Once these have been established, the next step is to make sure the systems within the organization are consistent and aligned with the three other components. There are several systems in a company. These include information management systems, the personnel policies and practices system, and the replenishment system. Within these, there is a variety of processes that are critical to their functioning. To a large degree, the efficiency and effectiveness of the systems determines the successful achievement of the organizational mission.

Style

Whereas the organizational focus area is alignment, the professional area of focus pertains to the style and competency with which managers and leaders execute their particular functions. The goals, mission, direction, and alignment components of the company need to be translated by professionals within the organization in a way that ensures successful execution of the alignment. If the managerial style is not consistent with the shared vision or business strategy, there will be a major disengagement between intention and actuality. To ensure alignment, professionals need to develop, mature, and broaden their managerial effectiveness.

Staff

This is the people's component. Failures in relationships are most often due to the failures in communication. This is where teamwork issues become paramount. It also addresses the internal value chain and the partnering process. This is the critical area dealing with how people are working together towards realization of the shared vision, how they are operating within the determined structure, proceeding against the organizational strategy, and augmenting and supporting organizational systems, and is also crucial to the success of organizational alignment.

Skills

This element implies that individuals need to grow personally and professionally, and is a fundamental area in which a company addresses the development of its people. It is not as inclined towards describing communications or effectiveness, or alignment issues, as it is towards the improvement of critical business and people skills. This is where the role of training is important. Once the organizational vision, strategy, structure, and systems have been determined, it is appropriate to determine the skills that will be required to ensure alignment and accomplish the organizational mission. A well-designed curriculum approach in which all people share the same language and have the opportunity to experience training at the same time ensures a levelling experience that is slanted towards development.

Stream

The final S includes all areas outside the previously discussed elements that either indirectly or directly influence or shape them. For example, governmental regulations have an impact on organizational strategy. Certainly, the competition has an influence on structure, systems, and even vision. Another example would be what is happening in the global economy. These factors that exist outside the organization are called stream. In order to ensure alignment and development, companies need to consider not only internal components, but also what is happening outside.

A graphical representation of the model is shown in Fig. 4.2.

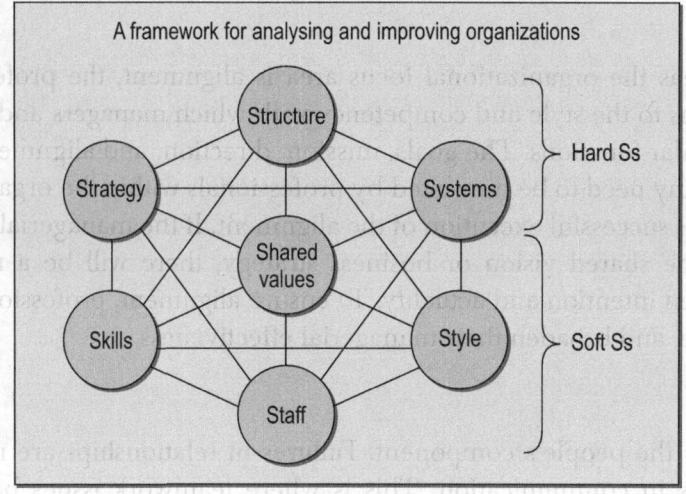

FIG. 4.2 The 7-S model

Once we understand and are familiar with the foundations and development of this model, we can outline areas of improvement. The adaptation process of this model is not so simple. It requires correct diagnosis of the elements with maximum focus on major areas of deficiency, and then drawing correct business plans and taking corrective action to improve the connectivity and integration with all the Ss. Therefore, when the complex and dynamic interrelationships between the various components are simplified, the 7-S model can serve as the most important organizational effectiveness and development tool.

The McKinsey Way of Problem-solving Approach

Based on his hands-on experience with the consulting giant, Ethan M. Rasiel, author of *The McKinsey Way*, presented the approaches and techniques they used to analyse and solve business problems. McKinsey adopts the mutually exclusive collectively exhaustive (MECE) approach. Basically, this illustrates the way it considers business problems and finds solutions, and is a time-tested McKinsey technique. As the book suggests, '…when you think you have determined the issues, take a hard look at them. Is each one a separate and distinct issue? If so, then your issue list is mutually exclusive. Does every aspect of the problem come under one (and only one) of these issues? If so, then your issues are collectively exhaustive.' According to Rasiel, MECE is a cardinal rule at McKinsey and is meticulously followed in every assignment and document.

The McKinsey 7-S framework developed by Peters and Waterman in the early 1980s still holds strong for organizations for the following reasons:

1. It improves organizational performance.
2. It examines the likely effects of future changes.
3. It aligns the departments and processes during a merger or acquisition.
4. It determines the best way to implement a proposed strategy.

Exhibit 4.4 depicts an application of this framework at Wal-Mart.

EXHIBIT 4.4 Wal-Mart and the 7-S framework

To achieve its goals, Wal-Mart employs all the three Ss, namely strategy, systems, and structure. In fact, its core strength lies in these hard Ss. Wal-Mart's objective is to provide the lowest prices and ensure that every customer gets their requirements under one roof. These two business strategies have made Wal-Mart the leader in its business segment. Another typical Wal-Mart syndrome is to embrace the market penetration model and expand even in saturated markets where there are other competing outlets. This strategy engulfs the entire company and encompasses all the Ss of the McKinsey model. The other two hard Ss, that is, systems and structure, support this strategy. We can also say that every day lower price (EDLP) has now become the style and shared values of Wal-Mart, and every member of its staff also feels committed to this. To achieve this intent, Wal-Mart establishes direct contact with the suppliers and negotiates across the table. It makes extensive use of state-of-the-art information technology systems even to connect their vendors and transmit data to them on a real-time basis so that they can follow the JIT principles and support Wal-Mart's mission to reduce the cost of holding inventory. It also works with suppliers to help them improve their efficiencies and thus contribute to cost reduction. Efficient HR systems also extend support to the hard Ss.

Thus, Wal-Mart successfully uses the McKinsey 7-S model to sustain and grow in a fiercely competitive retail industry.

Source: Compiled from www.walmart.com, accessed on 30 April 2010.

EXHIBIT 4.5 Excellence model of Peters and Waterman

A bias for action	Excellent firms make things happen
Closeness to the customer	These firms know their customers and their needs.
Autonomy and entrepreneurship	They value these in each employee.
Productivity	They achieve this through people based on trust.
Hands-on, value-driven management	They make it mandatory.
Stick to the knitting	They always deal from a position of strength.
Simple form lean staff	They develop cost-effective work teams.
Simultaneous loose–tight properties	They decentralize many decisions, while at the same time retaining tight overall control.

Excellence Model of Peters and Waterman

Peters and Waterman (1982), in their pioneering work, *In Search of Excellence*, identified some common characteristics of excellent organizations. These have now become important management principles and are presented in Exhibit 4.5.

This excellence model also serves as an important organizational development and effectiveness tool.

Organizations are composed of individuals and operate within systems. These constitute the principal units of analysis of organizational and management sciences. An effective organization can fulfil its mission through a blend of good management practices. Interpreting Peters and Waterman's model of excellence and McKinsey's 7-S model, there are two aspects that need to be examined in an organization. These are the people and the culture. People are the staff element of 7-S, while culture is a convergence of style, skills, and shared values. These exert impact, which ultimately sustains the organization, generating profit and creating value for the stakeholders. The relationship between people and the organization, and the culture is often considered dialectical. Whatever the culture created by the founders of the organization, it gets reinforced by the people who subsequently join them through their interpersonal skills and sense of accountability.

Culture ensures distributed leadership, and creates the right environment for continuous learning, openness, and decentralization. It is the soft element of 7-S. According to Peters (1982), the hard element of 7-S is fuzzy and easy to fake; the soft element is actually resilient and difficult to get right. According to him, hard is soft (easier to achieve), while the soft is hard (more difficult to achieve) in organization. Impact is the ability of the organization to achieve its goals, creating value for the stakeholders, and can attract and retain effective people, who help to preserve the culture of high performance. Effective organizations understand, measure, and communicate their impact, and use it to drive decision-making, and take a pragmatic approach to moving forward.

Management by Objectives for Organizational Effectiveness and Excellence

Drucker (1954) emphasized the organizational need for setting objectives to make performance more measurable. When objectives are set in a systematic manner, and consciously directed towards effective and efficient achievement of organizational and individual targets, it is called management by objectives (MBO). General Electric Company used the elements of MBO while reorganizing the company and introduced decentralized decision-making. In most organizations, MBO is required for performance appraisal, as it calls for active involvement of subordinates in setting the objective standards and this elicits an enhanced degree of commitment from them to achieve results. It also motivates employees because it enables them to understand their specific objectives and assess their achievement. Thus, MBO improves the process of managing by providing clarity, encouraging personal commitment, and developing effective controls.

Thus, MBO paved the way for participative management, involving people in framing objectives, aligning their individual goals with the organizational goals, or vice versa. Exhibit 4.6 further elaborates on its usage in organizations.

EFQM Excellence Model

The European Foundation for Quality Management (EFQM) excellence model was introduced in early 1992 as a framework for assessing applications for the European Quality Award. It is the most widely used organizational effectiveness framework in Europe and has become the basis for a majority of national and regional quality awards. The Energy Flow Optimization Management (EFOM) model is a non-prescriptive

---

EXHIBIT 4.6 MBO in action

A branded manufacturer of plastic moulded chairs desires a five-fold rate of growth. The owner wants to reduce day-to-day responsibilities. The management team is dissatisfied due to lack of strategic direction from the owner. Also, it is hard-pressed in relation to operational issues. By using the MBO approach, the company successfully decentralized management responsibilities and set up an internal board of management, creating new role profiles and recruiting people to fit these. With successful identification of the focus areas, internal operational difficulties were also resolved. With the new organizational structure and corporate management team, the company was able to adopt a flexible organizational design to meet internal and external challenges. Employees also felt empowered as they were able to relate how their contribution fitted in with the overall objectives of the organization. Their career development opportunities were also increased and this motivated them to view the organization from a long-term growth perspective.

framework and recognizes that there are many approaches to achieve sustainable excellence. Within this, there are some fundamental concepts which underpin EFQM and these are shown in Fig. 4.3.

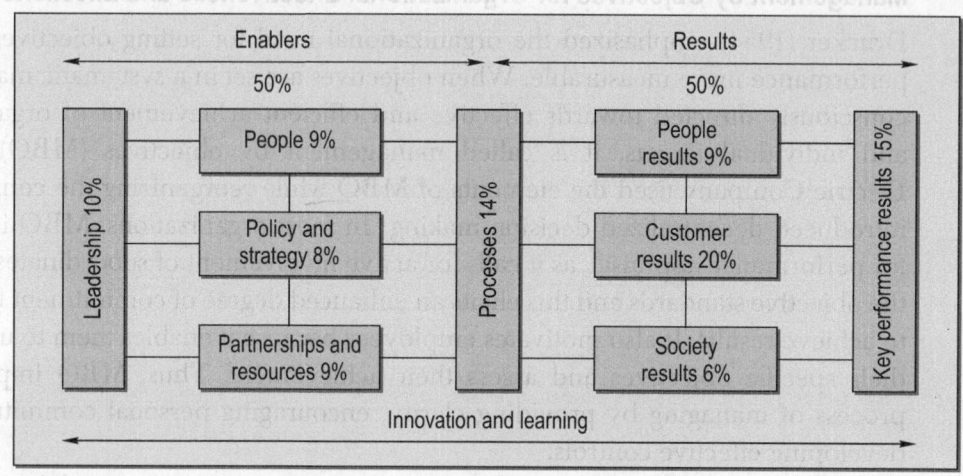

FIG. 4.3   The EFQM excellence model

A true measure of the effectiveness of the EFQM excellence model is its widespread use as a management system and the growth associated in the key management discipline of organizational self-assessment (effectiveness and excellence). It helps the organization to verify if it is on the path of excellence, identify the gaps, and find solutions. The list of fundamental concepts is not exhaustive but it can change or transform an organization towards achieving excellence. A brief outline of the fundamental concepts is as follows:

Results orientation   Achieving results that delight all the organization's stakeholders

Customer focus   Creating sustainable customer value

Leadership and constancy of purpose   Visionary and inspirational leadership coupled with constancy of purpose

Management by processes and facts   Managing the organization through a set of interdependent and interrelated systems, processes, and facts

People development and involvement   Maximizing the contribution of employees through their development and involvement

Continuous learning, innovation, and improvement   Challenging the status quo and effecting change by using learning to create innovation and improvement opportunities

Partnership development   Developing and maintaining value-adding partnerships

Corporate social responsibility Exceeding the minimum regulatory framework in which the organization operates and strive to understand and respond to the expectations of its stakeholders in society

The model is based on nine criteria. Five of these are 'enablers' and four are 'results'. The enabler criterion covers what an organization does, while the results criterion deals with what an organization achieves. Results are caused by enablers and their feedback helps to improve the enablers.

Quality Management Principles for Organizational Excellence

These aspects have been discussed separately in Chapter 12 on total quality management (TQM) but the concept is introduced here. A quality management principle is a comprehensive and fundamental rule or belief for leading and operating an organization, aimed at continually improving performance over a long period by focusing on customers, while addressing the needs of all stakeholders. With growing global competition, quality management is becoming increasingly important to the leadership and management of all organizations. Successful TQM requires both behavioural and cultural changes. It brings together two other systems, namely organizational management (OM) and human resource management (HRM), with a behavioural and cultural commitment to customer quality. Thus, TQM becomes a system within itself, either by default or choice. In a successful TQM initiative, these three management systems must be aligned.

Managerial Roles Theory for Achieving Organizational Effectiveness and Excellence

Managerial role refers to the position-specific behaviour pattern of managers. Based on his study of five organization, Mintzberg (1973) identified ten different roles of managers, classifying them into interpersonal, informational, and decisional roles. Interpersonal roles are classified into figurehead, leader, and liaison roles; informational roles are grouped as monitor, disseminator, and spokesperson roles; and decisional roles are categorized as entrepreneur, disturbance handler, and resource allocator and negotiator roles. Exhibit 4.7 elaborates these managerial roles.

Managerial Skills and Competencies

Managerial skills have become an important factor in dealing with global competitiveness at the organizational as well as at the national level. Obviously, imparting skills through training and development is not yet recognized as an important initiative at the organizational level due to the problem of quantification of its benefits and uncertainty as to whether training can truly help people to develop their skills. Skill is defined as a coordinated series of actions that serve to attain some goal or accomplish a particular task. Operationally, they are defined widely as overt responses

EXHIBIT 4.7 Mintzberg's managerial roles

Role category	Role type	Role nature
Interpersonal	Figurehead	Representing the organization to perform ceremonial duties
	Leader	Influencing subordinates to achieve their goals and objectives
	Liaison	Maintaining a horizontal chain of communication
Informational	Monitor	Collecting information concerning the organization and short-listing relevant information
	Disseminator	Sharing relevant information with subordinates
	Spokesperson	Maintaining protocol to share information with outsiders
Decisional	Entrepreneur	Focusing on innovation and change within the organization
	Disturbance handler	Managing conflicting situation by taking corrective action
	Resource allocator	Optimizing resource allocation to different competing needs within the organization
	Negotiator	Representing the organization in all major negotiations

Source: Adapted from Mintzberg, H. (1973), *The Nature of Managerial Work*, Harper and Row, New York.

and controlled stimulation. Overt responses may be verbal, motor, or perceptual. Verbal response stresses on speech (which requires memorization of words); motor responses emphasize movements of limbs and body; and perceptual responses deal with understanding sensory responses. Controlled stimulation, on the other hand, refers to energy inputs by the workers, which are expressed in units of frequency, length, time, and weight.

Technological change and skill requirements have been a subject of investigation in numerous studies across the world. While there is a general consensus that technological change alters the job, opinions differ on its nature and form. Technological changes, per se, require a broader variety and higher level of skills. Technology is also instrumental in fractioning and de-skilling of jobs. Redesigning of jobs subsequent to technological change separates the job concept from its planning and execution aspects. De-skilling and skill downgrading also occurs due to differential growth of higher versus low-skill occupations and industries. These phenomena are especially evident in India. Since the 1981 census, there has been a major occupational shift of workers from the primary to the secondary sector and from the secondary to the tertiary sector. Simultaneous structural changes in occupational patterns are also evident with a drastic reduction in the number of blue-collar workers and a significant increase in the number of white-collar workers. Another school of thought argues that de-skilling is a secondary consequence of de-industrialization, which again is prompted by technological changes.

Thus, transformations in skills due to technological change occur along two tracks. They are (a) compositional shift, that is, structural change in occupational pattern due to creation or elimination of jobs of a given skill level and the distribution of persons to jobs in a sectoral economy, and (b) changes in work content (the technical nature of work and the role relations surrounding work performance).

Internationally, the careers of the future will require greater education (more in the form of institutionalized knowledge) at the job entry level and will also demand continuing education to keep pace with technological dynamism. A greater level of technological literacy, even for lower-skilled and low-paying occupations will be in demand.

So, in the era of technological change and globalization, organization can also achieve effectiveness and excellence through skill change or upgradation.

We can thus categorize skill as a generic of technical, either entry level or advanced. Conventionally, skill can be defined as the knowledge or attributes that are deemed vital to organizational success.

There are four general types of skills as depicted in Table 4.1.

TABLE 4.1 Types of skills

Technical	Relate to specific concepts, methods, and tools, specific to an organization
Supervisory	Enable one to effectively supervise others
Interpersonal	Enable people to communicate and interact effectively
General business	Lines of business and support infrastructure

Technical skills are observable, demonstrable, and testable. The other skill types are softer, more subjective, and difficult to quantify.

Any organization intending a skill renewal or skill-change exercise needs to undertake the following tasks:

1. Profile the skills required by jobs.
2. Assess the skill levels acquired by individuals.
3. Conduct a gap analysis between the required and acquired skill.

Training should, ideally, occur before the skill is needed so that daily work can be reinforced through training.

Skill Inventories

A skill inventory is a device for pinpointing information about individuals and their suitability for different jobs. Skill inventories include the name of the employee and a listing (or inventory) of job-related skills, training, and/or experience, which could prove useful in a future assignment. The purpose of skill inventories is to provide the organization with quick, accurate information on all employees so that management can choose the best qualified person for promotion or transfer. For example, a skills inventory may consist of the following information: age, address, health, education, willingness to travel, experience in the past and present jobs, and foreign languages spoken. If an overseas assignment requires a person with the knowledge of a particular foreign language, a well-documented skill inventory can quickly identify the availability of employees with this aptitude from the organization's database and select the best candidate for the job. Thus, maintaining a skill inventory is essential for achieving organizational effectiveness and excellence, even in a changed situation.

Multi-skilling

Multi-skilling of people is very important for effective organizational change. Multi-skilling is defined as the process to train employees in a variety of skills, crossing the traditional trade-specific or craft-specific skill sets. Thus, to develop multi-skills employees require additional training to perform more jobs within the same job family or to do the entire job from a holistic point of view. Multi-skilling is often mistaken as a way of downsizing. But while downsizing occurs due to skill obsolescence among other reasons, multi-skilling aims at a holistic development of human potentialities to effectively address the requirements of changing production processes (more flexible and customized), organizational systems (decentralized control), and state-of-the-art technology (numeric control, computer numeric control, direct numeric control, etc.). Multi-skilling facilitates intra-occupational and inter-occupational job mobility, and thereby reinforces organizational effectiveness and excellence.

Skills for the New Millennium

Globally, employers are experiencing a dwindling trend in the talent pool, especially for the new skill sets required. Such skills and competencies are more focused to knowledge requirements that add value to the organization. To survive against competition, organizations need to generate new ideas, and bring out new products and services to gain customer satisfaction. Modern workplaces are technology-driven and make extensive use of information and communication. This requires employees to possess basic technical knowledge to learn and use new tools to achieve efficiencies. Again, progressive organizations are driven by a high performance work culture which requires employees to achieve superior results. They also value customer satisfaction and employees need to understand and adopt a customer-centric approach, and maximize value for all stakeholders, namely customers, suppliers, employees, and the community as a whole. So, employees need to nurture appropriate values and attitudes, team spirit, multi-skilled problem-solving attitude, and be resource-oriented.

Accordingly, new workers need to acquire people and teamwork-related skills, analytical skills, and skills to manage and handle information technology, understand the market and the changing expectations of customers, and to innovate. People skills can improve their interpersonal relationships and communication with customers. Teamwork-related skills are also embedded in people skills. Among others, it requires a teamwork attitude and willingness to achieve common goals. Analytical skills help develop problem-solving abilities, the foresight to understand and visualize the future of the organization, and plan their preparedness accordingly. Information technology-handling skills can supplement their abilities to interpret the information and data, and accordingly take decisions with minimum errors and variation. Understanding the market and customers will help to map the competitors, and change plans and programmes to achieve success. Innovation skills will help to generate new ideas and design new value-added products and services to gain competitive advantages.

In the changed global business scenario, organizations must develop the following skills in all cross sections of employees to sustain against competition and achieve excellence.

Partnerships and collaboration skills In the new millennium, all managers must understand the importance of strategic associations. It is very critical as without it, managers are unable to identify partnership and collaboration opportunities, understand the structure of working relationships with them, negotiate terms, and close deals. Organizations are forging strategic alliances to strengthen their market position at the national and international level. Even in terms of market domain, two companies can have a no-competition alliance. For example, in India, IBM and PwC do not compete for the same product-mix in the same market. Similarly, to reduce the rate of attrition IT companies have a no-poaching agreement with each other. Partnership and collaboration skills require managers to continuously scan the environment and identify such opportunities to achieve the strategic objectives.

Quick decision-making skills Developing skills for quick decision-making is also very important. Delaying response time to change leads to loss of market opportunities. Hence, managers need to master the art of quick decision-making and develop their capability to understand changed scenarios, pre-empt them, and structure suitable strategies. They understand that monitoring day-to-day operations is one aspect and making a strategic move in a changed situation (such as a global meltdown or market volatility) through quick decision-making is quite another. Even though such decisions may not always be error-free, the organization may benefit by being an early mover. With decisional flexibility, organizations can quickly reverse or change the decision, thus adjusting promptly to the situation. For example, while many organizations have their own business premises, IBM prefers to operate in rented accommodation to smoothen their exit route. This is an era of lean management which requires flexibility in operations, and a quick decision-making ability supports this.

Skills to attract and retain talent Attracting and retaining talent may not be possible only with strategic and innovative reward or compensation packages. In a knowledge-based economy, people prefer to remain in a job that gives them an opportunity to learn and grow, align their self goals with the organizational goals, provides them the right platform to incubate and nurture their creativity, and enables them to translate their creative ideas into action through innovative product or process design. Thus, a compelling workplace culture is important, and managers must create such an environment and acquire the right skills to coach and advise employees, in order to attract and retain talent.

Skills to predict the future The rate of change in the new millennium is very fast and managers must have the skills required to predict the future. They can do this by validating such insights through networking, sharing diverse assumptions with each other, etc. Many managers identify in advance certain trigger points and relate them with different scenarios to effectively predict the future.

Skills to integrate technology with the business In the new millennium, managers must be familiar with new technology and understand how it integrates with the business process. For example, an understanding of how enterprise resource planning (ERP) modules facilitate decision-making is essential if they are to succeed.

Skills to balance the stakeholders' need All organizations have diverse stakeholders and their interests often conflict. Effective managers must have the skills to balance such multiple and varied needs through stakeholder analysis.

Developing Competencies for Effective Organizational Change

Competencies are sets of behaviours which encompass skills, knowledge, abilities, and attributes. These need to be assessed at the organization as well as individual level. Individual competencies together reinforce organizational competencies. However, there is always possibility of major incongruence between them. Manpower planning helps to analyse such gaps and develop a competency model. This is a map to display a set of competencies. It is future-oriented and helps to describe an ideal workforce. When developed and documented, a competency model helps in managerial decision-making as it is well-aligned with the vision, mission, objectives, goals, and strategies of an organization. It also helps employees to understand the functional requirements and self-initiate the enrichment of their skills, knowledge, abilities, and attributes, independent of an organization-wide competency enrichment exercise. Development of competencies enables the organization to achieve successful change, effectiveness, and excellence.

P-CMM Model for Organizational Excellence

The people capability maturity model (P-CMM) is an adaptation of the capability maturity model (CMM) concepts. The motivation for P-CMM is to radically improve the ability of software organizations to attract, develop, motivate, organize, and retain the talent needed to steadily improve software development capability. However, the model is now construed as the best possible framework for organizations to successfully address their critical people-related issues. Based on the best current practices in fields, such as HR, knowledge management, and organizational development, P-CMM guides organizations in improving their processes for managing and developing their workforces. It also helps them to measure the maturity level of their workforce practices, establish a programme of continuous workforce development and integrate it with process improvement, set priorities for improvement actions, and establish a culture of excellence. Since its release in 1995, it has been widely distributed and used worldwide by organizations, small and large.

The model consists of five maturity levels each of which is a well-defined evolutionary plateau that institutionalizes new capabilities for developing the organization's workforce and avoiding introduction of practices that employees are unlikely to implement effectively.

The P-CMM includes practices in the following areas:

- Staffing (including recruiting, selection, and planning)
- Managing performance
- Training
- Compensation
- Work environment
- Career development
- Organizational and individual competence
- Mentoring and coaching
- Team and culture development

The strategic objectives of P-CMM are as follows:

- Improve the capability of software organizations by increasing the capability of their workforce.
- Ensure that software development capability is an attribute of the organization rather than of a few individuals.
- Align the motivation of individuals with that of the organization.
- Retain human assets (i.e., people with critical knowledge and skills) within the organization.

Behavioural characteristics of different maturity levels

As mentioned earlier, each maturity level is characterized by a set of interrelated practices in critical areas of workforce management and development. With the institutionalization of suggested workforce practices, organizations develop new capabilities and elevate to new levels of maturity. Thus, a P-CMM level 5 certified company is construed as a best practice organization that can achieve effectiveness and excellence with enhanced capabilities of its people.

Key process areas

Key process areas for each maturity level refer to certain particular tasks and activities, which need to be completed to gain maturity and progress. Exhibit 4.8 explains these.

The following sections explain the experiences of two IT companies who successfully achieved P-CMM level 5 certification.

P-CMM and UST

UST Global[SM] (UST) is a leading end-to-end provider of IT services and solutions to more than 1000 companies globally. It follows a client-centric global engagement model, which combines its human resources with cost, scale, and quality advantages,

EXHIBIT 4.8 Maturity level

Maturity levels	Process categories			
Level-5 Optimizing	Theme 1—Developing capabilities	Theme 2—Building teams and culture	Theme 3—Motivating and managing performance	Theme 4—Shaping the workforce
	Coaching Personal competency development	Continuous workforce innovation		
Level-4 Managed	Mentoring	Team building	Organizational performance alignment Team-based practices	Organizational competency management
Level-3 Defined	Competency development knowledge and skills analysis	Participatory culture	Competency-based practices Career cevelopment	Workforce planning
Level-2 Repeatable	Training Communication	Communication	Compensation Performance management Work environment	Staffing
Level-1 Initial	—No process initiated—			

of off-shore operations. Its six sigma practices have already imbibed a client-centric approach in the organizational DNA. With P-CMM level 5 certification in 2004, it has consolidated its foundation, that is, dedicated and qualified people to serve customers with best HR practices. UST admits that it has internally benefitted immensely from P-CMM level 5 certification and its practices. It has successfully addressed critical people-related issues and achieved overall organizational improvement. P-CMM enhanced the maturity of its people with systematic workforce development programmes, setting priorities for improvement actions, and integrating people with process improvement, establishing a culture of excellence. UST was able to build the work culture to sustain this environment.

P-CMM and WIPRO

Before opting for P-CMM level 5 certification, WIPRO elected to understand the practices in global companies. Accordingly, it extensively studied the HR policies of various companies, such as AT&T, GE, Tandem, and British Telecom. In 1999, WIPRO developed a 'competency dictionary' identifying 24 competency areas spread across the five levels of P-CMM. It also analysed the behavioural issues for each level and listed out procedures to address them.

WIPRO competes globally in critical areas of business. P-CMM level 5 certification helped to build the capabilities of its people to reach global performance standards and grow accordingly.

Thus, in UST as well as WIPRO, P-CMM level 5 certification helped to achieve excellence and effectiveness.

Shingo Prize Model of Organizational Excellence

The Shingo prize for excellence in manufacturing is named after the Japanese industrial engineer, Shigeo Shingo, who distinguished himself as one of the world's leading experts in improving manufacturing processes. He has been described as an engineering genius who helped create and comment on many aspects of the revolutionary manufacturing practices in the Toyota Production System.

The prize was established in 1988 to promote awareness of lean manufacturing concepts and recognize companies in the United States, Canada, and Mexico that achieve world-class manufacturing status. The Shingo prize philosophy is that superior business performance may be achieved through focused improvements in core manufacturing and business processes.

The Shingo prize model includes 11 key elements of world-class manufacturing. These are grouped into five categories, signifying that it is necessary to integrate them into a complete system to achieve outstanding results. The Shingo prize criteria do not prescribe specific methods, techniques, practices, or processes. Rather, for each element, the criteria list practices and techniques that might be incorporated to achieve exceptional quality, cost, delivery, and business results.

The model is illustrated in Fig. 4.4.

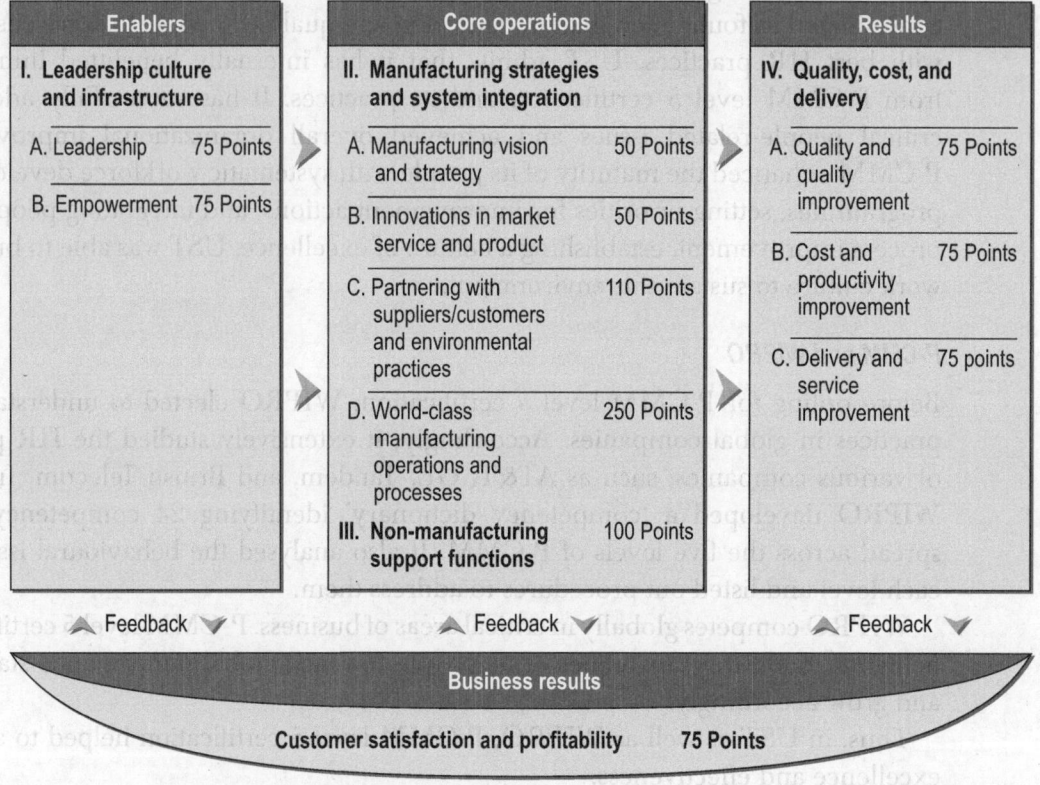

FIG. 4.4 Shingo prize model

Malcolm Baldrige Model for Organizational Excellence

This was started in 1987 as a national quality award to recognize US companies for their achievements in quality and business performance, and to raise awareness about the importance of quality and performance excellence as a competitive edge. It is not related to specific products or services. Awards are given annually in the categories of manufacturing, service, small business, and since 1999, education and healthcare.

Any organization can use the Baldrige performance excellence criteria as the basic guidelines to improve its overall performance. There are seven categories that make up the award criteria:

Leadership Examines how senior executives guide the company, and how the company addresses its responsibilities to the public and practices good citizenship.

Strategic planning Considers how the company sets strategic directions and determines key action plans.

Customer and market focus Assesses how the company determines requirements and expectations of customers and markets.

Information and analysis Examines the management, effective use and analysis of data and information to support key company processes, and the company's performance management system.

HR focus Determines how the company enables its workforce to develop its full potential, and how it is aligned with the company's objectives.

Process management Inspects how key production/delivery and support processes are designed, managed, and improved.

Business results Examines the company's performance and improvement in its key business areas, namely customer satisfaction, financial and marketplace performance, human resources, supplier and partner performance, and operational performance. The category also checks how the company performs in relation to competitors.

All types of organizations use these criteria for self-assessment and training, and as a tool to develop performance and business processes.

This has resulted in better employee relations, higher productivity, greater customer satisfaction, increased market share, and improved profitability.

The Baldrige award criteria are different from ISO 9000, as they focus on results and continuous improvement, providing a framework for designing, implementing, and assessing a process for managing all business operations. ISO 9000 is a series of five international standards published in 1987 by the International Organization for Standardization (ISO), Geneva, Switzerland. Companies can use the standards to help determine what is needed to maintain an efficient quality conformance system. ISO 9000 certification determines whether a company complies with its own quality system. It covers less than 10 per cent of the Baldrige award criteria.

Some of the important features of the Baldrige model are as follows:

- Focus more on results and service.
- Rely upon the involvement of many different professional and trade groups.
- Provide special credits for innovative approaches to quality.
- Include a strong customer and HR focus.
- Stress the importance of sharing information.

Figure 4.5 depicts the overlaps between ISO and Malcom Baldrige criteria.

Organizational Change through Six Sigma

Six sigma is a business process to improve the bottom line (profitability). This is done by designing and monitoring business activities in a way that minimizes waste and resources without compromising on customer satisfaction. The six sigma process is broader than TQM programmes. While TQM focuses on detecting and correcting defects, six sigma recreates the processes to ensure defects never arise right from the

Organizational Change and Development

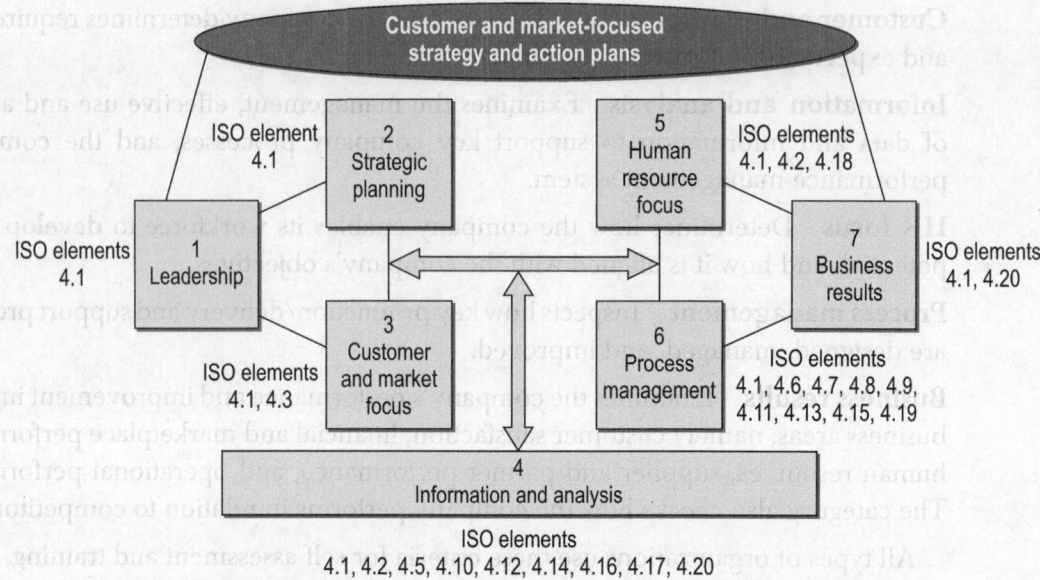

FIG. 4.5 Baldrige criteria for performance excellence framework vs ISO 9001 elements
Source: www.nist.gov/baldrige/, accessed on 20 February 2010.

beginning. From organizations' point of view, it provides maximum value in the form of increased profits and from customers' point of view, it provides maximum value in terms of high quality products and services at competitive costs.

Basic characteristics

The following are the characteristics of six sigma.

1. Sigma is a Greek alphabet and is used to denote the standard deviation of a process.
2. It was developed by Motorola in the mid-1980s and adopted by many major manufacturing organizations, including General Electric. GE Capital, the world's first service transaction-based company, introduced this in 1996.
3. It is the statistical application of TQM.
4. Sigma quality level describes the output of a process.
5. It emphasizes business process improvement in general, which includes cost reduction, cycle-time improvement, and increased customer satisfaction.
6. It implies a whole culture of strategies, tools, and statistical methodologies, to improve the bottom line of companies.
7. Higher sigma values indicate better quality products and lower sigma values represent lesser quality products. At six sigma level, products are virtually defect free, that is, it allows for only 3.4 defects per million opportunities (DPMO).

Six Sigma in Organizations

Six sigma is a process of self-assessment of organizational quality. Adopting six sigma practices in organizations can never be an overnight exercise. At the outset, the organization needs to select the process it wants to recreate as error-free. Factors that are critical to the quality of this process also have to be identified from the customers' perspectives before process recreation can start with a continuous focus on quality improvement. Some areas of improvement which six sigma helps to achieve are as follows:

- Process
- Product and services
- Investor relationship
- Design
- Supplier relationship
- Training and recruitment

A typical inverted relationship in six sigma breakthrough is depicted in Fig. 4.6.

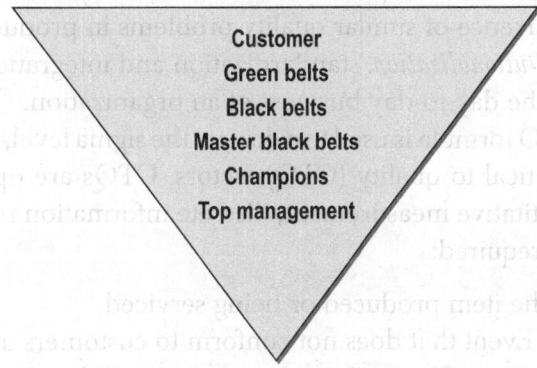

FIG. 4.6 Six sigma inverted relationship

The inverted pyramid is the top management that supports and balances the six sigma change process. Champions are executive leaders who identify individual leaders to ensure that key functions are connected to six sigma. They together form the guiding force that makes the strategy work. Champions select the master black belts to assist in dissemination of breakthrough strategy and to identify projects for improvement. They train and coach black belts and green belts, organize people, design cross-functional experiments, structure and coordinate projects and meetings, and collect and organize information. Black belts work under the master belts and apply six sigma tools and knowledge to specific projects. Green belts are employees of the organization who execute six sigma as part of their overall jobs. They dedicate only part of their time to six sigma projects unlike master black belts and black belts, who dedicate all their time to such projects.

Steps for six sigma

There are eight fundamental steps to achieve six sigma quality in the process division of an organization. These eight steps are recognize, define, measure, analyse, improve, control, standardize, and integrate. These steps are explained in the six sigma map shown as Exhibit 4.9.

In the *identification phase*, companies recognize how processes affect their profitability and what process are critical to business. The *characterization phase* helps to benchmark and provides the inputs to measure improvements. At this stage, an action plan is charted to close the gap between the current and the future, matching the company's goals for product and services. At this stage, black belts select key characteristics of one or more products/services and develop a detailed description of each step in their processes. Using process control cards, they estimate the short-term and long-term process capability.

In the *optimization phase*, design for six sigma (DFSS) is used to reconfigure products and services right from the beginning by discovering the key variables that lead to the problem, and then designing products and services eliminating such problem-generating variables. Proper control is ensured by strictly monitoring the processes to avoid recurrence of similar quality problems in products and services. In the final phase of *institutionalization*, standardization and integration of six sigma practices are done to run the day-to-day business of an organization.

The DPMO formula is used to calculate the sigma level, duly defining the customers' perceived critical to quality (CTQ) factors. CTQs are opportunities for error. Since this is a quantitative measurement, discrete information regarding the following three items is also required:

- Unit: The item produced or being serviced
- Defect: Event that does not conform to customers' requirements
- Opportunity: Chance for occurrence of a defect

EXHIBIT 4.9 The six sigma map

	Stages/Phases	Strategy steps	Objectives	
Breakthrough Strategy	Identification	Recognize and define	To identify key business issues	**Black Belts**
	Characterization	Measure and analyse	To understand level of current performance	
	Optimization	Improve and control	To initiate breakthrough improvement	
	Institutionalization	Standardize and integrate	To transform day-to-day conduct of business	

Let us take the example of examination services of an educational institute. Students consider a defect in the system when results are declared beyond three weeks. Let us assume that students have four perceived CTQs, namely speed of delivery, correct transcript of marks, adequate information about incomplete or withheld results, and proper computation of grades. These provide four opportunities for error in discrete terms. Once quantitative details about number of units and defects are made available, the following formula can be used to calculate the sigma level:

Number of Defects ÷ (Number of opportunities for error) × 1,000,000

Suppose that in our case we have 2500 results of which 10 were late due to non-availability of assignment grades and 5 were incorrect due to improper computation of grades. The calculation, therefore, would be as follows:

$$\frac{15}{(2 \times 2500)} \times 1,000,000 = 3000$$

A DPMO of 3000 almost corresponds to 4.25 sigma levels, which indicates that the institution needs to further identify the process flaws and improve the quality of service. At the six sigma level, the DPMO should be 3.4 or 3.4 defects per million.

Six sigma is a learning continuum. It reinforces the intellectual capital to continually identify the best practices, and standardize those within and across the business to create a win-win situation in a competitive world. Therefore, organizations can adopt six sigma practices to achieve excellence in quality of products and services within a minimum time frame. This requires foreseeing future skill sets with changing technology or processes. Similarly, regular competency mapping and a synergy between individual and organizational competencies need to be achieved through training and development intervention. Training employees on six sigma requires both technical and behavioural reinforcements and any skill gap requires repeated training. While all cannot be black belts and nor is this required, all should understand how important it is to improve their workmanship for defect-free products and services. Ranging from product to process familiarization, the training should focus on using statistical and analytical tools to help measure the variability and attribute reasons for failure.

Importance should also be given to compensation planning, motivation, and retention to ensure commitment and loyalty to the organization. There are many ways to design compensation and employee retention innovatively. Although it is a top-down approach, its success largely depends on the players who are catalysts for such change. It makes no sense to engage a consultant and expect results unless the initiatives are properly integrated with the HR strategy of the organization. Exhibit 4.10 illustrates the impact of the six sigma approach in an organization.

Lean Practices to Achieve Organizational Excellence

Lean production, lean management, lean thinking, and lean excellence are organizational practices to achieve excellence and effectiveness in today's highly

> **EXHIBIT 4.10 Six sigma—An experience at Cummins Inc.**
>
> Cummins Inc. saved nearly $1 billion through 5000 improvement projects in different areas of activities of the organization using three versions of six sigma (technology development for six sigma, DMAIC, and design for six sigma). Although internationally the six sigma approach is considered to be the most effective tool for improving internal production processes, Cummins extended it to every facet of their business and even beyond (bringing customers and suppliers within its scope).
>
> Cummins was established in 1919 and is a global leader in designing, manufacturing, selling, and servicing diesel engines and other related technology. It serves its customers through a network of 550 company-owned and independent distributor facilities, and 5000 dealer locations in more than 160 countries and territories. With the use of six sigma practices, Cummins was able to achieve a staggering sales figure of nearly $10 billion in 2005 and earn a profit of $550 million. For Cummins, six sigma is not just limiting its focus on shop floors; it extends to every facet of the company's business from accounting and legal departments to manufacturing units, HR, and now even to customers and suppliers. As of date, nearly 3700 employees have completed six sigma training programmes, with 500 black belts 65 master black belts, and the rest being green belts. These are assigned to three levels of the six sigma programme, namely technology development, DMAIC (define, measure, analyse, improve, and control), and design for six sigma.
>
> The company believes that six sigma has successfully cascaded to bring in a total cultural change in the organization that creates compelling pressure on employees to embrace the continuous change. With 29,000 employees, all this was not achieved without resistance and scepticism. However, a compelling work culture diffuses the opposing elements and from 2008 the company has made it mandatory for all to learn and work in six sigma to reach critical job positions through promotion.

competitive environment. It was originally developed at Toyota and is now accepted as a necessity for organizations to survive, particularly in a volatile market situation. Lean practices are characterized by world-class performances (key measures) and practices (methods and processes), and a culture of relentless continuous improvement (environment). Through lean practices, the Toyota Production System has achieved 50–70 per cent improvement in productivity, floor space, working capital, quality, and safety in an approximately three-year time frame. The fundamental philosophy of lean practices focuses on a systematic shift in the expectations, measures, performance, and vision (culture) of the company. These practices lead to operational excellence in terms of functional value, defect-free quality, outstanding delivery, and compelling price.

Transformation of an organization through lean practices starts with the value stream concept. This is a sequence of steps which an organization needs to perform, optimizing capital, material, and labour cost, to satisfy customers' needs. With a change in the value stream, it is possible to eliminate unnecessary activities that cause delays and add value to customers' satisfaction.

> **EXHIBIT 4.11 Lean management at Nestlé**
>
> Nestlé Purina Petcare (Friskies), Merseyside, UK, is a part of the Nestlé group. It manufactures dog biscuits for all the major supermarkets incorporating Bonio, Sharpes, and Specials. Committed to developing the workforce, Nestlé Purina embraced the lean management practices. With the help of a consulting team, CQM, it carried out a detailed study of the production line along with an assessment of wastage, labour utilization rate, and re-work costs, evaluated the scope of multi-shift working, and made extensive use of communication. In the process it developed tools to practise the following:
> - Team development
> - Systematic problem solving
> - Process analysis—CQM team development
> - Modern manufacturing techniques
> - Productivity measures
> - *Kaizen*/TPM/Lean manufacturing
> - Workplace organization—5S
>
> Basically, these tools strengthen lean management practices. With their use, the company could identify wastage and accordingly save costs in the production lines as well as in the processes. In addition, lean management practices helped to reduce labour costs, improve teamwork, and development of cross-functional learning. Once it is operational, the teams can further the process of its implementation autonomously.

Lean practices require creation of cells and determination of flow within these cells. The idea is to remove any work-in-process, which may otherwise deter the value-adding steps. Work-in-process within a cell is controlled via pull systems, such as *kanbans*, and production is managed through simple scheduling/replenishment systems. Pull systems are continuously developed to improve the value stream. Exhibit 4.11 illustrates how lean management practices helped Nestlé to minimize wastage.

Factors of consideration for lean management

Not every organization can effectively use lean management practices to achieve organizational excellence. This requires a thorough understanding of the processes in order to improve them at every stage, that is, every cell, keeping in mind customers' perspectives of value addition. Some of the factors which directly affect the organizational ability to become lean are as follows:

- A strategic reason to pursue the lean path *(external and motivating)*
- Active commitment of the top management team *(does the team understand the need to become lean?)*
- Cost reduction opportunity *(will a decrease in labour cost and/or working capital affect your balance sheet?)*
- Growth potential *(will increasing market share improve your bottom line?)*
- Committed owners of the company *(committed to providing tools, setting expectations, measuring performance, and affecting change)*

SUMMARY

Effectiveness is the extent of an activity that helps to achieve the long-term goals. In organizations, activity-specific effectiveness supports the broader goals of the organization. Hence, organizational change can be better achieved through organizational effectiveness. Both qualitative and quantitative tools can be used to measure organizational effectiveness. Qualitative effectiveness parameters include values, attitudes, skills, and behaviour. Quantitative effectiveness parameters are value and volume of output changes, customer satisfaction, changes in profitability, etc.

Like organizational effectiveness, organizational excellence too provides an organization a competitive edge and every organization strives to achieve excellence through systematic change initiatives. Leadership is the primary enabler in achieving organizational excellence through the process of organizational change. Effective leadership requires a sense of mission, purpose, and direction.

The chapter also discussed the various tools for measuring organizational effectiveness and the various models of organizational excellence. The nature of skills and competencies of employees and managers have significantly changed in the new millennium. Hence, organizations need to develop these. Various practices which improve organizational effectiveness have also been discussed in detail.

The chapter concludes that successful organizational change is possible in organizations that have achieved effectiveness and excellence in the way they conduct their business.

KEY TERMS

Digital dashboards They provide customized solutions for knowledge workers, making available consolidated information on individual, team, and corporate level, and the external information, instantly.

Organizational effectiveness inventory (OEI) It is a structured process of measuring organizational effectiveness.

Shared vision This embodies the organizational vision, mission, values, and operating principles. This element of the 8-S paradigm is central and core to overall organizational effectiveness.

Skill inventories A skill inventory is a device for pinpointing information about individuals and their suitability for different jobs.

Stream Stream or the 8-S includes all areas outside the previously discussed elements that either indirectly or directly influence or shape them.

Theory Z It emphasizes the need to study and adopt appropriate management practices from other countries.

CONCEPT REVIEW QUESTIONS

1. Explain the concept of effectiveness and excellence. How does organizational effectiveness and excellence relate to organizational change?
2. How can organizational effectiveness be measured? Explain the roles of OEI and digital dashboards in measuring organizational effectiveness.
3. Theory Z and 7-S are considered two important contemporary models of organizational effectiveness. Explain both the models in the context of organizational change.
4. What are the skills and competencies of managers in the millennium? How can such skills and competencies contribute to successful organizational change?
5. Explain the role of lean management for effective organizational change.
6. Write short notes on the following:
   (a) Singho prize model
   (b) Six sigma in achieving zero defects
   (c) Critical to quality factors
   (d) 8-S
   (e) Manpower redundancies

CRITICAL THINKING QUESTIONS

1. You have been retained by a company as organizational change and development consultant. The company is in the business of selling life insurance policies. It offers customized life insurance policies keeping in view the changing needs of the customers. Ninety per cent of the policies sold are customized, while 10 per cent are standard policies conforming to their structured table. Recently, the company has started having trouble in post-sales administration and operation, resulting in a serious setback in customer services. It wants you to institute six sigma practices. Explain your line of action.

2. For some unavoidable change in the business process, your company has recently experienced skills obsolescence for a large number of workers who have been with the company for a long time and are on the permanent payroll. As an expert on organizational change, suggest how you can manage this problem of manpower redundancy.

3. Emulating the lessons of the Shingo prize model, suggest how a family-managed organization can achieve excellence.

CASE STUDY

Tata Motors Commercial Vehicles Business Unit

Tata Motors have three commercial vehicle bus units (CVBUs) in India with a nationwide sales and service network. The CVBUs manufacture a wide range of commercial vehicles, such as 60-seater buses, and 6 × 4, that is, 24-seater off-road vehicles. The company serves more than 60 per cent of the Indian market and is one of the top ten truck manufacturing companies in the world. To overcome poor financial performance for two successive years, the units, which were once adjudged the world's most profitable commercial vehicle manufactures, wanted to achieve a turnaround. With their experience of having used the Malcolm Baldrige model of excellence, it framed appropriate strategy, guarding against their weaknesses. With effect from year 2000, the company began focusing on the turnaround to achieve sustainable growth and profitability as a low-cost manufacturer. It introduced the balanced scorecard, which resulted in a growth in revenue of 40 per cent between the years, 2001 and 2003. In 2005, the CVBUs reported a 25 per cent increase in sales in the domestic market against the industry growth rate of 22 per cent.

The balanced scorecard is also considered to be a business excellence framework which organizations can implement to drive continuous improvement in their business. The balanced scorecard is often mistaken as helping organizations only to capture the intricacies of performance to measure the financial outcomes, particularly those that are difficult to translate into financial terms. However, using the balanced scorecard framework with value creation maps and aligning it with the Malcolm Baldrige assessment criteria, the EFQM model or any other national and international business excellence framework yields better results.

This is exactly what happened in the case of Tata Motors' CVBUs.

The CVBUs developed a balanced scorecard and accordingly framed their strategy map putting in place a high-level steering committee consisting of functional heads and regional managers. The steering committee reported to the CEO. To activate the process of its development and implementation it appointed a core project team, keeping the final validation and ownership responsibility with the CEO.

One of the members of the steering committee is the head of the business excellence service department, whose role is to enhance the knowledge base on performance management and measurement areas of the core team members. The CVBUs prior knowledge base of Malcolm Baldrige's assessment criteria helped them to understand the weaknesses. Hence, they were able to develop the strategy map guarding against these weaknesses and make people understand its benefits. They were also able to develop more than 300 scorecards, covering almost every function. The balanced scorecard defined the overall objectives, targets, and timeframes at the company level, and then cascaded down to lower levels with proper linkages.

The CVBUs ensure continuous communication to all cross sections of employees to make them understand the vision, mission, future directions, and strategies. A CEO level communication (through personal meeting) is done annually to strengthen the process. Communication to employees is further strengthened by internal publications, intranet, and time-to-time presentations. According to the company, the critical success factors in the implementation of the balanced scorecard are as follows:

- Active and visible support of senior management
- Strong review process
- Knowledgeable team to drive and support scorecard deployment

The successful implementation of balanced scorecards for CVBUs of Tata Motors ultimately helped the group to consolidate its performance matrix and achieve efficiency with direct impact on increased revenues and profitability.

Source: This case has been extracted from Creelman, James and Naresh Makhijani (2005), *Mastering Business in Asia: Succeeding with the Balanced Scorecard,* John Wiley & Sons, Singapore.

Discussion Questions

1. Read this case carefully and comment on how Tata Motors exerted impact on its business portfolio, activating its CVBUs through balanced scorecard implementation. Did adopting the Malcolm Baldrige assessment criteria help them to achieve success in the balanced scorecard?
2. Assess the role of the top management team in any change process in the light of this case.

(*Hint: It is recommended that you visit the Tata Motors websites to get current insights.*)

REFERENCES

Amitai, Etzioni (1964), *Modern Organizations,* Prentice Hall, Englewood Cliffs, NJ.

____ (1961), *A Comparative Analysis of Complex Organizations,* Free Press, Glencoe, Ill.

Bhattacharyya, D.K. (2009), *Organization Behaviour, Concepts and Applications,* Oxford University Press, New Delhi.

____ (2007), *Human Resource Research Methods,* Oxford University Press, New Delhi.

____ (2000), 'Competency mapping and manpower redundancy—A macro level study of indian organizations', *Management and Accounting Research,* October–December, Vol. 4, Issue 2, pp. 97–105.

Blau, Peter M. and W. Richard Scott (1962), *Formal Organizations: A Comparative Approach,* Chandler Publishing Company, San Francisco.

Buckley, Walter (1967), *Sociology and Modern Systems Theory,* Prentice Hall, Englewood Cliffs, NJ.

Burns, Tom and George M. Stalker (1961), *The Management of Innovation,* Tavistock, London.

Cameron, Kim S. (2006), 'Good or not bad: Standards and ethics in managing change', *Academy of Management Learning & Education,* Vol. 5, No. 3, pp. 317–323.

Child, J. (1972), 'Organization structure and strategies of control: A replication of the Aston study', *Administrative Science Quarterly,* Vol. 17, pp. 163–177.

Cooke, R.A. (1997), 'Organizational effectiveness inventory', *Human Synergistics,* Centre for Applied Research, Arlington Heights, Ill.

Cooke, R.A. and J.C. Lafferty (1994), 'Organizational culture inventory, form–III', *Human Synergistics*, Playmouth, MI.

Denning, W. Edwards (1994), *The New Economics for Industry*, Government, Education, Second Education, Cambridge, MA.

Dooley, Kevin (1997), 'A complex adaptive systems model of organizational change', *Nonlinear Dynamics, Psychology, and Life Sciences*, Vol. 1, No. 1, pp. 69–97.

Drucker, Peter F. (1954), *The Practice of Management*, Harper and Row, New York.

Ethan, Raisel M. (1999), *The McKinsey Way*, McGraw-Hill, USA.

Galbraith, Jay R. (1995), *Designing Organizations: An Executive Briefing on Strategy, Structure and Process*, Jossey-Bass Publishers, San Francisco.

___ (1994), *Competing with Flexible Lateral Organizations*, Second Edition, Addison-Wesley, Inc., Reading.

___ (1973), *Designing Complex Organizations*, Addison Wesley, Reading, MA.

George, Eckes (2001), *The Six Sigma Revolution*, John Wiley and Sons, Inc., New York.

Kotter, John and James L. Heskett (1992), *Corporate Culture and Performance*, Free Press, New York.

Kotter, John P. (1996), *Leading Change*. Harvard Business School Press, Boston.

Kristine, Ellis (2001), 'Mastering Six sigma', *Training*, December, pp. 30–35.

Lamotte, Gaelle and Geoff Carter (2000), *Are the Balanced Scorecard and the EFQM Excellece Mode Mutually Exclusive or do they Work Together to Bring Value to the Company?* EFQM, USA.

Mikel, Harry and Richard Schroeder (2000), 'Six sigma', *Currency*, New York.

Mintzberg, H. (1973), *The Nature of Managerial Work*, Harper and Row, New York.

Mintzberg, Henry (1979), *The Structuring of Organizations*, Prentice Hall Inc., Englewood Cliffs.

Morgan, Gareth (1997), *Images of Organization*, Second Edition, Sage, Thousand Oaks, CA.

Ouchi, William G. and Alfred M. Jaeger (April 1978), 'Type Z organization: Stability in the midest of mobility', *The Academy of Management Review*, Vol. 3, No. 2.

Peters, Thomas J. and Robert H. Waterman Jr (1982), *In Search of Excellence*, Harper and Row, New York.

Porter, M. (1980), *Competitive Strategy: Techniques for Analyzing Industries and Competitors*, Free Press, New York.

Quinn, R.E. (1988), 'The competing values model: Redefining organizational effectiveness and change', *Beyond Rational Management: Mastering the Paradoxes and Competing Demands of High Performance*, Jossey-Bass, San Francisco.

Quinn, R.E. and J. Rohrbaugh (1983), 'A spatial model of effectiveness criteria: Towards a competing values approach to organizational analysis', *Management Science*, Vol. 29, pp. 363–377.

Richard, C.H. Chua (2001), 'Six sigma, A pursuit of excellence and dramatic results', *Today's Manager*, August–September, pp. 43–45.

Scott, W. Richard (1967), *Organizations: Rational, Natural and Open Systems*, Second Edition, Prentice Hall, Englewood Cliffs, NJ.

The American Society for Quality website: www.asq.org.

Weick, K.E. (1995), *Sensemaking in Organizations*, Sage, London.

Wheatley, Margaret J. (1992), *The New Science of Leadership*, Berrett-Koehler, San Francisco.

APPENDIX 4.1
Sample Dashboard

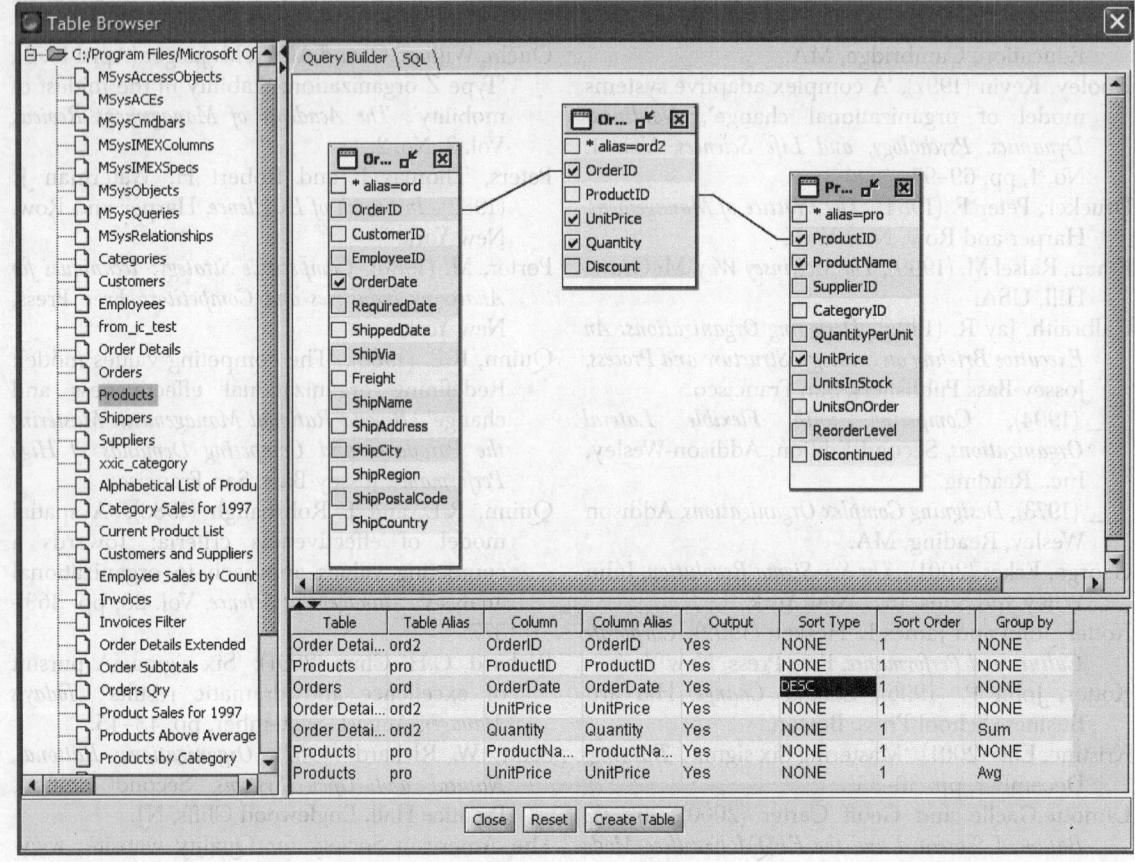

PART 2

Organizational Change Management

- **Managing Organizational Change**
- **Power, Leadership, and Organizational Change**
- **Technology Management**
- **Technology and Culture**
- **Attitude Measurement for Change Management**
- **Organizational Culture and Change**
- **Change through Performance Management**
- **TQM Practices and Organizational Change**

5 Managing Organizational Change

Learning Objectives

After reading this chapter, you will be able to understand
- change management concepts, processes, and principles
- elements and nature of change management
- organizational improvement process through change management
- implementation of change improvement systems
- change management survey
- the commitment curve
- the types of change
- the skill requirements of change management
- change management iceberg
- change in organizational culture
- effective change management
- qualities of a change agent
- different approaches to change management

Foreseeing the Problem before It is Late

With the entry of China in the WTO, large manufacturing organizations worldwide relocated their manufacturing hubs to benefit from cheap labour and relaxed labour standards. For Indian engineering major, Freedom, it is now an uphill task. The company started manufacturing machine tools during the British Raj as part of the free India movement in Ahmedabad. Today, with 50,000 employees, it has expanded its base to all the metros and is recognized as a leader in machine tools in India and other south-east Asian countries, and is known for quality and price competitiveness.

Machine tool manufacturing requires not only world-class technology but also highly skilled manpower with creative and innovative minds. With the opening of the Chinese market, many international machine tool manufacturers today enjoy cost competitiveness and have entered Freedom's market domain in India and other south-east Asian countries.

Consequently, Freedom foresees a significant drop in market shares and finds itself at the crossroads of a major organizational restructuring. Unlike others, it adopted a different approach to manage the organizational transformation. It launched a massive awareness programme about the need for change, citing examples of competitive world-class organizations. A separate corporate team was formed to keep people informed and help them to understand what was happening. This continued for two months with new clippings and news items every week around the world. The company then asked employees for their opinion regarding the desired areas of focus if it opted for change. The general opinion poll indicated that 90 per cent of the employees wanted change, but were not aware of how it should take place.

Freedom decided that it would wait and see before taking any further steps. It applied the Delphi technique to draw the change action plans. A senior managerial level change facilitator wrote to some previously identified Freedom employees asking for their blueprint for change. Within two months, they were able to identify a tentative change plan. These were then further deliberated among all cross sections of employees with the departmental heads facilitating the deliberations. Thus, the company was able to draw up a mutually acceptable action plan and successfully transform itself and can now boast, 'We always re-discover and never de-generate'.

INTRODUCTION

Change management can be defined from three different perspectives—the task of managing change, professional practice, and a body of knowledge. Tasks involved in managing change are planned and systematic in nature, and encompasses effective implementation of new systems and methods of performing jobs. For today's organizations, this is a continuous task due to the complexity of the business environment and other triggers that may be beyond their control, such as legislation, the social and political situation, competition, economic ups and downs, etc. To manage such change triggers, organizations need to adopt both reactive and proactive change strategies.

While reactive responses take place when organizations finally receive the change cues, proactive responses take the form of advance organizational preparedness, anticipating changes. In a globally competitive market situation, organizations often change autonomously, irrespective of change cue(s). Such autonomous change initiatives are evident in innovative organizations; they often come out with new products and services, and even successfully create demand for them.

Worldwide, change management is now categorized as a professional practice. It involves a series of planned tasks and activities, and requires managers (who are involved in the change management process) to act as change agents.

Change management is also considered a body of knowledge for the obvious reason that it requires professional practices. To become a successful change agent, a manager needs to possess adequate knowledge to understand the change triggers and identify appropriate change intervention tools. He/she must also understand subjects, such as psychology, sociology, economics, industrial engineering, systems engineering, organizational behaviour, and even general management. Thus, change management requires a holistic knowledge.

Therefore, we can identify the three basic elements of change management:

- The reactive or proactive task of managing change
- A professional practice
- A body of knowledge

The change management process in any organization requires all cross sections of employees to adopt new processes, technologies, systems, structures, and values. It is, therefore, a process of transition from the present state of work to the desired state, addressing various people and organization-related factors. It requires thoughtful planning and management of implementation, making effective use of the participatory approach. Involvement of the employees in the change management process is very crucial as they are the first casualty of any change intervention. As the change process affects them, they will resist it; hence, it is very important to gain their confidence, explaining the rationality of the change process, how it is going to impact on them, and how they can overcome any adverse effect resulting from it.

Organizations should also try to adopt a change strategy which people are most likely to accept. This cannot be done just by selling the idea of change. Employees can only cooperate in the change management process when they understand the need for it. Consultative communication infuses in them a sense of ownership and then they support the change process spontaneously. This apart, organizations need to arrange frequent training programmes and workshops to increase the level of awareness about the change process, the change objectives, and the proposed initiatives. The possible problem of manpower redundancy for integration or elimination of tasks also needs to be clarified.

NATURE OF CHANGE

From an operational point of view, the nature of organizational change can be categorized as process, systems, structural, and organizational change (as a whole). Organizational processes are the structured set of activities to obtain outputs. Hammer and Champy (1995) defined a business process as a collection of activities that transforms inputs to outputs and in the process adds value to the customer. Organizational processes can cut across structural boundaries, such as departments, divisions, or even firms. Organizational efficiencies are enhanced when the organizational process is managed and designed as a seamless whole.

Organizational systems are sets of procedures that are transformed to standards and followed in practice. For example, an organization may have HR systems on compensation and reward, recruitment and selection, performance appraisal, training and development, etc. In managing change, they need to bring change in the systems. Again, like systems, structure is also important in managing change. In Chapter 1, we discussed structure and systems issues and focused on the need to consider these for successful management of organizational change. Similarly, organizational change needs to be considered in the context of the organization itself to review the pattern of relationships. Organizational issues in managing change focus on relationships, pattern, and co-creating. While we understand the terms 'relationships' and 'pattern', co-creating in the context of organizational change indicates recognition of the patterns of relationships through conversations and interactions.

Responsibility for Managing Change

In managing change, the role of managers is very important. In adopting an objective or a non-judgemental stand, they facilitate the change process by helping people to have an informed choice about the change. People can only make an informed choice when they understand the reasons for change, the objectives of change, and the type of support they will get from the organization for successful implementation of change.

Organizational support is not limited to communication; it should help people to develop their capabilities to cope with the changed situation. Under no circumstances should managers impose change; rather it should be accepted through consultative communication, training and development, workshops, etc. In fact, people should be empowered to validate and refine the change process autonomously. Thus, the managerial role is enormous and managers need to be cautious in managing resistance to the organizational change process.

CHANGE MANAGEMENT PRINCIPLES

Resistance to change is a natural phenomenon. Hence, managers should effectively manage the process of organizational change following certain principles:

1. Involve people and gain their support. This is much easier when organizations seek acceptance from the people keeping in view their given system. System is the aggregation of environment, processes, culture, relationships, and behaviours (both personal and organizational). Since people are more familiar with the prevalent systems, their acceptance for change within this ambit is easier.
2. Understand the state of the organization for the present, that is, where it stands in the present context. Such mapping helps an organization to take stock of its present status.
3. Understand where the organization wants to go, and when, why, and what measures they need to take to get there. This is possible through a gap analysis between the present and the desired state.
4. Draw the plan for change with achievable and measurable terms. Any unrealistic change plan is bound to fail. So, any change plan which cannot be understood in measurable terms is meaningless.
5. Effectively communicate the change plan to people and involve them as extensively as possible. Managers can facilitate this by extending all possible support.
6. Implement the change plan undertaking job restructuring, re-deploying people in restructured positions, rightsizing through voluntary retirement schemes, etc. Along with the change plan, redesigning the process, merging, consolidating, or integrating the tasks, business units, etc. are also important

> **EXHIBIT 5.1   Important points for job restructuring**
>
> While doing the task analysis and job reorganization, it is first important for the organization to identify the extent of transferable proposals. This can be done through work breakdown analysis, which could reduce the job into several small components or elements. It now becomes much easier to identify the job commonality. Job restructuring, and keeping pace with the job commonality factors become much more effective. We also use the term 'job family' and any 'job change' aligning with the job family receives wide acceptance because of their proximity to the nature of the job.
>
> Whatever may be the process undertaken for job restructuring to implement change in the organization, people should be kept aware of all.
> Some of the tools used by organizations to undertake such tasks are as follows:
> - Flow diagrams to identify inter and intra sub-task and the extent of its variation
> - Behavioural needs analysis, along with the processes
> - Performance standards with the degree of acceptable level of ± variations, etc.

principles. The activities of the organization in implementing the change plan will depend on the particular change plan drawn, and therefore, will vary from one organization to another.

For example, Videocon, an Indian MNC, acquired a food processing unit at Siliguri, West Bengal. It was not interested in diversifying into food processing but Siliguri's strategic location in north-east India was important. It started its computer assembly hub duly retraining the workers of the erstwhile food processing unit, who felt a sense of pride in the computer assembly job. Hence, there was no resistance to the change implementation. On the contrary, when Hindustan Petroleum Ltd (HPL) tried to redeploy their technical people (who were earlier engaged in filling oil in drums) in other jobs after installing the automatic oil filling plant in its unit in West Bengal, people were highly resistant. The crisis also arose because people were not adequately informed about the change imperatives. Exhibit 5.1 lists a few important points to bear in mind before job restructuring, which is a preliminary step to any change initiative.

CHANGE TRANSITIONS FOR INDIVIDUAL EMPLOYEES

Any organizational change requires people to change so that they can willingly extend support to the change process. Reactions of people to change can be best understood in the context of their ability to understand the change, cope with it, and perceive its benefits and possible result.

There are common reactions to change and one of the key objectives of the change management is to exert influence on individuals and groups so that any scepticism and confusion can be avoided and people can be committed to the change process. Let us now understand the common reactions to change from Fig. 5.1.

Changing an organization only through a change of policies, procedures, and processes is not enough to manage change; it needs to modify the behaviour of the people. Successful organizational change, therefore, should focus on modification of the following behaviours:

- Acceptance in principle the need for change
- Value the change
- Adopt the change

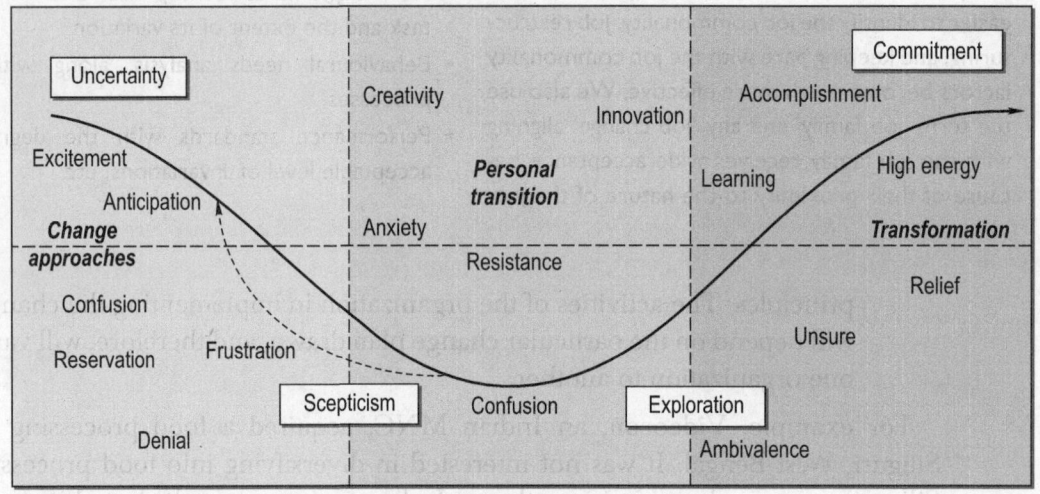

FIG. 5.1   Common reactions to change

Effective behaviour modifications require the use of tools and techniques explained earlier. Here, we will explain the process organizations adopted to understand the change management practice. One of the common practices followed is the communicate-behave-demand (Com-Be-D) process.

Organizational practices differ from one organization to another. In many of them, managers do not practise what they preach. Consequently, they fail to achieve the desired results from people down the line. In many Indian organizations, such as Murugappa Group, Bajaj, and Videocon, work culture demands that managers and executives first practise what they intend to change, so that workers can emulate their example and feel the need to change. A simple illustration of the Com-Be-D Process is given in Fig. 5.2.

FIG. 5.2   Com-Be-D process

In any change management process, managers must communicate first. Communication must be clear, direct, to the point, and ruthless. Managers must use their emotional intelligence to help people understand the change realities more objectively.

Managers must adopt the behaviour that they expect from their employees. Only then can they exert pressure on the employees to practise the changes as communicated. Here, the managers need to be tough and if required reprimand those who refuse to change. Similarly, they should reward and acknowledge the best contributions from employees.

Various issues in the change management life cycle help to address the needs of all stakeholders through effective involvement of change agents. Exhibit 5.2 summarizes specific situations in organizations during the change management process and suggests appropriate courses of action. Since these are based on organizational experiences,

EXHIBIT 5.2 Change management issues and their solution

Issues and sub-issues	Implications of issues	Solution for the issues
Crisis of leadership No visible participation of managers and leaders, ineffective decision-making, absence of vision, inappropriate involvement of people in the change process, lack of effort to resolve organizational barriers.	Change not perceived as important, slow pace of implementation, no priorities in action plans, delay in decision-making, and ultimate failure of change management process.	Proper identification of change leaders and agents, fixing their job roles and behavioural norms, coaching and guiding them to understand the courses of action, fixing responsibilities, coordination, resource planning and allocation to take the change actions, identification of change barriers, and effective enablers to remove such barriers, etc.
Crisis of building people's capability Inability to anticipate the change-related people issues, inability to understand the requirements of skills or improper identification of skills and competencies required for bringing change in organization, failure to rationalize the new requirements of the organization, etc.	High resistance to change, high employee turnover, strained employee relationships, increase in training costs (for re-training), unreasonable rise in employees' expectations, unnecessary retention of non-performers.	Early identification of people-related issues, increased level of coordination between process, technology, and team, realistic assessment of expectations from the change process, etc.
Behavioural change Lackadaisical HR attitude, under-estimation of time required for change, absence of metrics/systems to measure the difference between the previous and the present behavioural parameters, etc.	General reluctance of employees to change the behaviour, shifting of resource support to other areas of organizational activities, losing momentum to change, etc.	Open communication, adoption of people-related strategy to build capabilities, alignment of change with the organizational culture, development of appropriate metrics to measure the progress, etc.

organizations are advised to consider these aspects to minimize the risk in the change management process.

Many organizations ensure effective change management by adopting a goal congruence process. This is done by maximizing the work on overlapping areas, which are of common interest to the employees (represented by their trade unions) and the organization. This approach reduces the resistance to change and slowly builds confidence in the minds of the people who later participate voluntarily in the organizational change process. A typical goal congruence process model for a hypothetical organization is presented in Fig. 5.3.

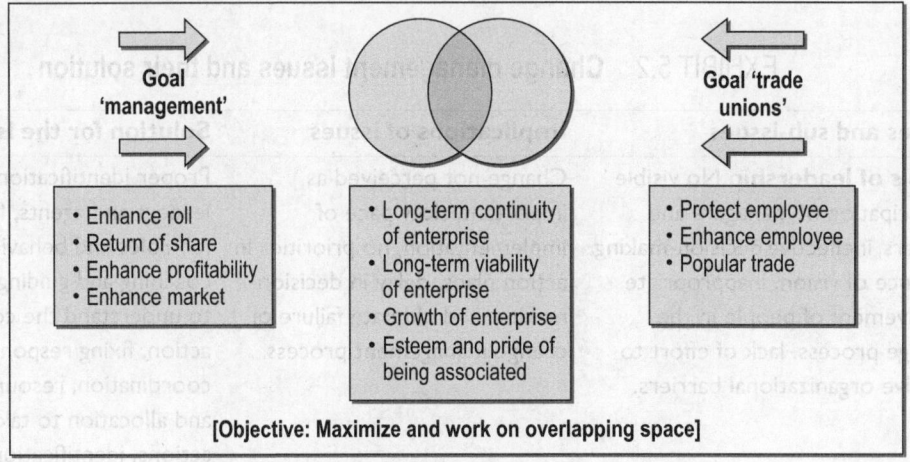

FIG. 5.3   Goal congruence process mapping

ORGANIZATION IMPROVEMENT PROCESS THROUGH CHANGE MANAGEMENT

In managing change, organizations often try to achieve improvement by following certain approaches and methodologies. Excellence and effectiveness issues have already been explained in Chapter 4. Here, we will discuss only those improvement issues which accelerate the pace of change management systems in organizations.

These are as follows:

- Lean manufacturing
- Business process management
- Appreciative enquiry
- Six sigma

Appreciative enquiry is a method of social construction of reality, which emphasize metaphors and narratives, relational ways of knowing, and the language (Hubbard 2000). It takes the idea from the social construction theory and is a strong OD practice, as it considers a radical affirmative approach to organizational change. Cooperrider and Srivastva (1987) defined appreciative enquiry as the systematic discovery of what gives life to a living system. With regard to organizational change, it focuses on apprehending, anticipating, and heightening positive potential, and initiates the desired courses of action. The appreciative enquiry process emphasizes the distinct stages of discovery, dream, design, and destiny, and systematically engages individuals to improve effectiveness. Other change improvement processes have already been discussed in Chapter 4.

IMPLEMENTING CHANGE IMPROVEMENT SYSTEMS

Whether it is a lean manufacturing, an appreciative enquiry, or any other approach, every organization must demonstrate its commitment to the system and communicate the reasons for its adoption. It requires cooperation and support from key managers. Effective use of the change improvement systems requires a structured approach. Adhocracy is prohibited in the change management process. A holistic and structured process of change management requires, among others, a well-crafted strategy with specific change intents.

It is important to communicate the approach that is adopted to the people. For example, if six sigma is considered as a possible approach to bring the desired change in the organization, simply communicating the message is not enough. The employees must understand the genesis and the philosophy of six sigma. They must appreciate that six sigma not only helps the organization to achieve zero defects by recreating a process, but also optimizes costs, improves customer satisfaction, increases profitability, and enhances organizational competitive advantages. All these result in benefits for the employees. Hence, a six sigma approach to organizational change is for the mutual benefit of the employees and the organization. Also, to achieve organizational improvement through change management process, organizations must dedicate resources for this. Resource allotment is not restricted to manpower allocation or just fixing the responsibilities of a change management team; it requires focus on training, workshops, and other awareness programmes.

Similarly, while implementing a change improvement system in organizations, it is also necessary to anticipate resistance and identify courses of action to manage this. When the resistance is in the form of general apathy and disinterest, the problem of achieving improvement in the change process increases, and the crisis deepens. Scenario planning discussed in Chapter 3 can be used in such cases.

CHANGE MANAGEMENT SURVEY

Based on people's mindset during the change process, Rosabeth Moss Kanter (a Harvard University professor) recommended the use of change management survey. results of this survey would indicate the typical mindset of people during the change transition, such as denial, emotion, resistance, acceptance, and commitment. The questionnaire she devised to track this is shown as Exhibit 5.3.

EXHIBIT 5.3 Sample questionnaire

Think about the change that is affecting you at work and tick the answer that is typical of your reaction.

	Yes	No
1. I think the changes that are happening are for the best		
2. I need to make the best of the change		
3. I am obstructive to the changes that are taking place		
4. I feel angry about the changes		
5. I would prefer to stay as we were before the change		
6. I am prepared to help others to accept change		
7. There may be benefits to be gained from change		
8. I withhold my support for change		
9. I am anxious about change		
10. I don't want to know about change		
11. My workplace will be better as a result of change		
12. I am willing to find out more about change and how it will affect me		
13. I blame management		
14. I feel frustrated that I have no control over change		
15. If I ignore change, it may not affect me		
16. I feel committed to change		
17. Change is not as bad as I originally thought		
18. I openly resist change		
19. I am upset at the need to change		
20. I can't believe that change is for the good		
21. I can see the benefits of change		
22. I accept the need to change		
23. I make my complaints known about change		
24. I feel sad at the loss of the status quo		
25. I would rather get on with what I am doing than be involved in the change		
26. We will benefit positively from the change that is happening		
27. I have started to explore what change means for me		
28. I am looking for other work possibilities that are not affected by the change		
29. I feel emotional about losing our old ways of working		
30. Change won't affect me		

How to score
Put a tick mark by each statement where you scored 'yes'. Then total the number of ticks in each column.

(Contd)

(Exhibit 5.3 Contd)

1	2	3	4	5
6	7	8	9	10
11	12	13	14	15
16	17	18	19	20
21	22	23	24	25
26	27	28	29	30
Total C =	Total A =	Total R =	Total E =	Total D =

Interpretation

The change management survey is based on the transition curve developed by Kanter. It helps to understand the following reactions to change:

C = Commitment
A = Acceptance
R = Resistance
E = Emotion
D = Denial

Look at the highest score in a category (there may be cases of similar scores in several categories). This indicates where you are on the change curve.

The survey results can help an organization to identify an overall mindset of its members, which can be categorized as follows:

Denial

A typical reaction in the early stages of change is to deny that it will take place or that it will affect you. One's reaction can manifest itself in disbelief, burying one's head in the sand, or behaving as if nothing has happened or will happen.

Emotional state

At this stage, pent-up emotions are evident. There is grieving for the loss of the status quo. Emotions can vary from expression of anger and frustration to sadness.

Resistance

Here, people outwardly show their resistance to change. This can manifest itself through outspoken dissent, unhelpful behaviour, and blame. At this stage, people who see the change in a negative light may start looking for an alternative employment.

Acceptance

People begin to see that a change is implemented and it is perhaps not all bad, and there may be ways of making the most of it.

Commitment

By this stage, people begin to support change and are committed to it. They see the benefits and make positive steps to implement it.

It is possible for people to experience emotion in the several categories. For example, they may start to accept change, yet be critical on certain aspects.

Helping people through the transition

Figure 5.4 shows a graphical presentation of the transition curve relating to productivity enhancement and the time span.

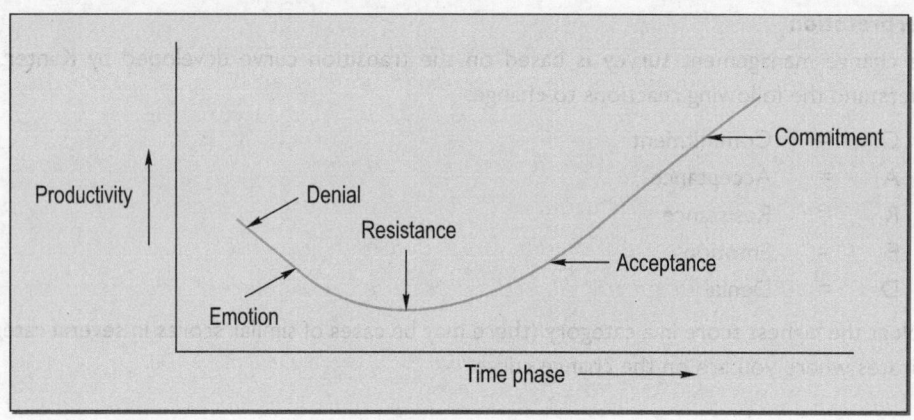

FIG. 5.4   Phases of transition

Behaviours displayed on the left side of the transition curve should not be ignored. The important aspects in effective change management are as follows:

1. Identify early on who will be the winners to change and who will be losers, what will help the change and what will hinder.
2. Let people know as much as possible about the changes taking place, and when and how the changes will affect them.
3. Give people opportunities to express their concern.
4. Consult and involve people in the changes.
5. Hold regular feedback and communication sessions. Allow negative views to be aired in a supportive way.
6. Allow adequate time for change to take place; not expecting it to happen overnight.
7. Celebrate success.

THE COMMITMENT CURVE

Organizations review their change management strategy to ensure increased levels of commitment from the people depending on their perceived mindsets. A typical commitment curve can illustrate the different stages of the change management process that people in the organization experience. However, all cross sections of employees need not experience the highest level of commitment. The hypothetical level of commitment of people in a change management process is illustrated in Fig. 5.5. With the highest level of commitment, people of the organization embrace change and implement the process spontaneously. It is the most desired stage of change adoption and is rarely achieved by the people.

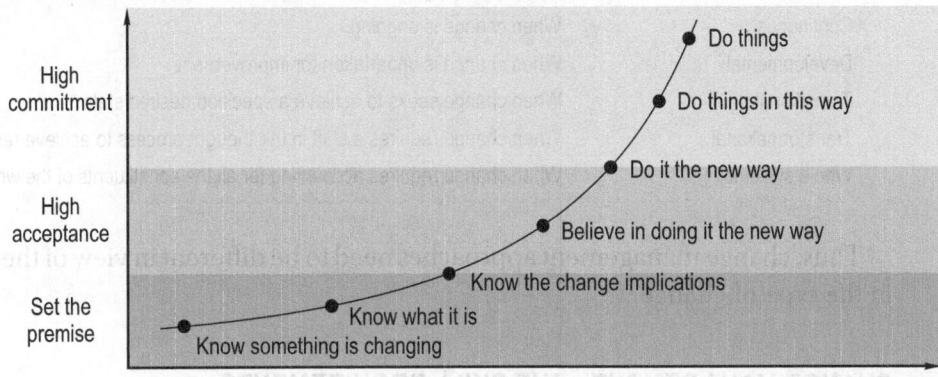

FIG. 5.5 The commitment curve

Mobilizing the Organization

A move for change in organizations requires behavioural change in the employees and this often becomes the new cultural construct for it. Frequently, this requires organizations to go against established values, practices, and systems. All these tasks of change management require mobilization of the organization, adopting a structured and systematic approach to appropriately address organizational as well as individual issues, and followed in distinctly identified stages.

The first stage is to reflect the intention and desire, and dedicate resources within a given time frame. Successful organizational mobilization becomes easier when organizations draw support from the people, and involve and empower them.

The second important aspect is to address the values and beliefs of the people. These vary widely and the change message conflicts with such variations. Hence, organizations develop shared values and shared beliefs to align people. Similarly, attention to the culture of the organization is also important.

TYPES OF CHANGE

Successful change management also requires understanding the specific types of change. All change initiatives of the organization are not planned or deliberate. Often organizations need to change to keep pace with the changing environment.

This requires that they appreciate the type of change so that appropriate intervention tools can be selected. Table 5.1 outlines the different types of change.

TABLE 5.1 Types of change

Type of change	Characteristics
Planned	When organizational change is a deliberate action
Emergent	When change is a spontaneous event to respond to the external eventualities
Episodic	When the change decision is radical, and the type of change is discontinuous
Continuous	When change is ongoing
Developmental	When change is undertaken for improvement
Transitional	When change seeks to achieve a specified desired state
Transformational	When change requires a shift in the thought process to achieve results
Whole systems	When change requires accounting for all the constituents of the whole system

Thus, change management approaches need to be different in view of the differences in the type of change.

CHANGE MANAGEMENT—THE SKILL REQUIREMENTS

Managers, leaders, and change agents need to master certain skill sets to ensure effective change management. Although it is difficult to define the extent of the skills required, one can at least highlight some of the skill sets, which all change agents must essentially possess.

Political Skills

Organizations are social systems and like any other social system, they are also political. These issues become more intense during any change process. All change agents, therefore, need to understand the change game so that any change in politics can be firmly dealt with. Power politics during the change process is evident in different hierarchical levels, particularly between trade unions and management. Many organizations often exploit the service terms of employees to transfer them elsewhere when they do not agree to change. Some organizations (especially those which are multi-locational) weaken the bargaining power of the striking workers by shifting their production to other units, or at times, even to their outsourced agents.

Analytical Skills

Change agents must also possess analytical skills as this enables rational decision-making instead of depending on intuition or gut feelings. Ambitious growth plans to consolidate the position in the market and then scaling down activities, making people redundant, and disposing of other resources are most common in today's corporate world. The recent global meltdown and subsequent collapse of many multinational financial services companies could be a good example, as leaders and managers of these companies adopted an incremental approach (short-term) while drawing their business plans. Analytical skills are important to understand the logical workflow of operations, systems, and financial analysis. Any change plan which ultimately weakens the financial status of the company is not desirable. Over-borrowing by Lehman Brothers only to accentuate profitability without truly understanding the economic strengths ultimately forced them to liquidate. Similarly in India, many Reliance units scaled down their activities and even withdrew from business.

People Skills

The third skill set for effective change is people skills. Ultimately, people are the end result in organizations and they are diverse in terms of gender, intelligence, working ability, culture, beliefs, etc. People-related skills are primarily interpersonal skills. While functional skills (namely marketing, HR, systems, etc.) make managers more knowledgeable, people skills shape them to be true performers as it helps them to get results.

System Skills

System skills also help in effective change management. The organization is viewed as a total system and its activities are its sub-systems. To acquire system skills, managers need to be well-versed on the computer operation, information processing, and various other existing systems, such as rewards, performance management, operation, etc. of the organization.

Business Skills

Possession of business skills is also important and basically, they involve understanding the work of the organization. For example, banking knowledge is a business skill for bank managers. Similarly, understanding of the steel manufacturing process can be construed as a business skill in steel manufacturing units. A holistic understanding of the organizational work is considered most important for achieving the desired results.

CHANGE MANAGEMENT ICEBERG

According to the change management iceberg concept pioneered by Kruger (2004), during the change process, organizations consider only the top of the iceberg, that is, cost, quality, and time. The bottom of the iceberg, however, is the most important aspect as it considers vital issues, such as management of perceptions and beliefs along with power and politics of management. In reality, the change management crisis lies with the submerged part of the iceberg, as interpersonal and behavioural dimensions of the change are considered more important at this stage. Figure 5.6 illustrates the change management dimensions.

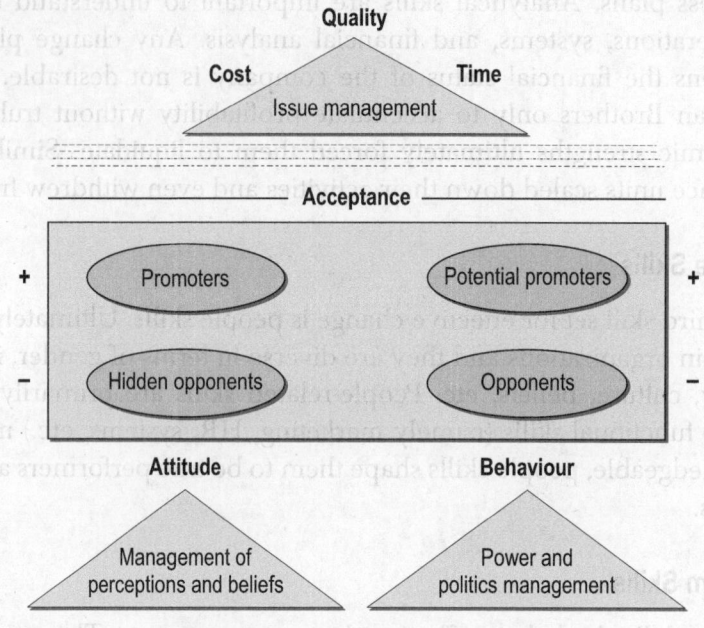

FIG. 5.6   Change management iceberg

CHANGE IN ORGANIZATIONAL CULTURE

Globalization and market economy have now made it imperative for organizations to change on a continuous basis. Today, even to operate locally, organizations need to think globally. This urges them to be more strategy-focused and agile to meet the changing expectations of customers. The upsurge of demand for lifestyle products when the economy was booming has now shifted to a demand for cheap consumables due to the economic recession. Any organization that specializes in selling premium priced products finds it difficult to master the art of selling in the mass market.

Among others, organizational change needs to be synergized with the culture of the organization as reflected in the beliefs and values that shapes the way the organization functions. This facilitates configuration of structures, policies, processes, and practices, with minimum resistance from the people. The organization thus has the advantage of bringing change in other desired areas, such as redefinition of key business processes, redesigning of workflow, development of teamwork, re-focusing on customers' needs, etc.

Some of the critical steps to manage cultural change in organizations are as follows:

1. Understand the change issues and prepare a case for change.
2. Revisit the vision, mission, and strategy, and accordingly redefine them.
3. Increase the spate of communication and involvement of people, and draw the strategy for the organization as a whole.
4. Redesign the structure of the organization, if required.
5. Draw the plan for implementation.
6. Implement the change systems.
7. Monitor and evaluate implementation progress.
8. Assess the improvement and amend the change plan, if required.

It is, however, important to understand that all these steps are essential even though their sequence may not be uniform in all cases. Similarly, the importance of a particular step may vary from one organization to another depending on the prevalent work culture of the organization. To illustrate, the work culture in the erstwhile Philips units in India was to alienate managers from the workers. This led to managers nurturing class feelings and maintaining a distinctly different set of norms for workers and for themselves. However, with the acquisition of Philips by Videocon this culture had to change, causing much dissension from the rank and file. With all the educated and highly acclaimed people on its payroll, Dell and its K-12 workforce were able to refocus its business and transform itself (from a lessor of computers) to a manufacturer and reseller.

Information on customers and other stakeholders should form the basis of change in the organization. When developing communication and strategy to increase the degree of involvement of the people, the organization must first monitor the flow of information within to guard against rumours and misinformation. While information transparency is the answer, many organizations find that when information is not communicated directly people at different levels of communication channels may prejudice it with their own bias. This is the typical outcome of the Hawthorne effect pioneered by Elton Mayo and his associates in 1933.

Often, training programmes for workers on leadership, motivation, or their participation in management are misconstrued as a deliberate attempt on the part of the management to get workers to do the job of managers without paying them the equivalent salary packages. The author faced a similar predicament while conducting such programmes for workers and trade unions. Acceptance of the tailor-made training programmes for union leaders of Hindustan Paper Corporation (HPC) was made possible by renaming the training programme as 'marketing of trade unions'. Training sessions were well-attended and some of them even opted to educate the trade union members.

During the cultural change process, the flow of communication within the organization should be enhanced by speeches of managers and supervisors, round table conferences, newsletters or in-house journals, etc.

Organizational structure and design to facilitate cultural change requires shifting from the traditional hierarchical structure to matrix structures, or forming strategic business units, etc. Such a shift clarifies the role boundaries, increases the commitment and involvement of people, and hastens the process of organizational restructuring. It is believed that a given organizational structure shapes the pattern of behaviour of the people and hence, also sets the work culture. Therefore, a shift in structure also influences the culture of the organization, which is its major construct, and therefore, has to be carefully addressed.

To implement cultural change in an organization, it is important to first understand the support systems that can facilitate implementation, monitoring, and evaluating the outcome of the change management initiatives. Important prerequisites of effective implementation are conferring the rights to question and understand the process, rights to criticize, etc.

For effective cultural change in organizations, managers must have the knowledge of human behaviour so that they can correctly identify the behaviour they need to manage. In addition, managers must also possess the requisite skills to manage any eventual behavioural consequences in the process of cultural change.

Managing Organizational Change through Modification of Group Behaviour

Both individual and group behaviour modifications are necessary to successfully bring about cultural change in the organization. Change in group behaviour must be synergized with the team effort so that all cross sections of employees perceive it as a challenge to achieve the common goals and understand that they have a common purpose. Among others, it requires setting up of mutually agreed common goals, developing a shared vision, and providing people with the opportunity to relate them to organizational strategy, individually and as members of the team.

Group behaviour modification is also possible when an organization develops the desired norms and strategies to bring a change, and provides the right direction and guidance to the people to follow such norms. When they sense the imperative to change as their personal issue, people in the group will feel empowered, enjoy the opportunity to take decisions on their own, and progress by acquiring new skills.

Strategically, organizations must step up the process of communicating and sharing information, optimizing group cohesion, developing a culture of empathetic relationships through increased levels of inter-group relationships, and providing flexibility to group members on their tasks and functions. While task and functional flexibility enhance group effectiveness, recognition and appreciation make the group a performing one. Group members with a high morale feel enthusiastic to deliver their best and the organization can thus, manage the process of change successfully.

Box 5.1 illustrates the strategic actions taken by Videocon at Phillips after the takeover.

> **BOX 5.1 Change at Phillips**
>
> Soon after it took over the two Phillips units at Kolkata, Videocon had to manage a workforce that was used to the legacy-bound culture of Phillips and resisted every attempt at change. To overcome this, Videocon gave the workers an opportunity to manage the activities and deliver results. Workers temporarily played the role of managers and supervisors (without any material change in their pay packages and official designation), and managed the workshops. However, they failed to deliver results and ultimately conceded to the management-mandated change programme. This is a typical example of learning by committing mistakes. In fact, after this, Videocon was able to successfully manage the process of transition to a culture of performance and results.

Exhibit 5.4 provides guidelines for better management of change in organizations.

> **EXHIBIT 5.4 Guidelines to manage organizational change**
>
> Although it is difficult to develop a general guideline for organizational change management, one can learn and document it from the experience of different organizations.
>
> - Develop the leadership abilities of managers and change agents who need to play a crucial role in bringing change in the organization. Every manager does not have built-in leadership quality. It is developed through the process of learning and maturity. As leaders, managers and change agents need to understand that people will emulate them. Hence, they need to embrace practices that are desirable and visible from their behaviour.
> - Revisit the mission and develop a clear sense of purpose. The mission should be as simple as possible so that it can provide a sense of direction to the people, and be candid and focus on the core business issues essential to bring about the desired change in the organization.
> - Remove hierarchical barriers and maintain a flat organizational structure so that during the process of change, people can interact informally and significantly enjoy autonomy, thereby reducing their reporting requirements.
> - Develop a team of people with a high level of energy and expertise who will play the role of catalysts or change agents, and manage the process of organizational change.
> - Review the existing systems, rules, and procedures of the organization, bring in desired modifications, and if required, even set them aside. This is very important during the process of change, so that people can express freely.
> - Design an action feedback model to enable short-term reviews to assess the change progress.
>
> *(Contd)*

(Exhibit 5.4 Contd)

This is essential to initiate modifications to the change plan, if required. For example, a shift from a hybrid organizational structure (a combination of functional and divisional structure) to a matrix structure (with dual reporting relationships) to optimize human resources and on-time completion of projects may render people direction less, as they do not have the experience of reporting to two bosses simultaneously. The action feedback model can identify such problems and may put the organization in a flux, whether the change in the structure is appropriate or not.

- Adopt a flexible approach to manage change. This is important, as during the change process, it may be necessary to alter priorities and amend the change plans.

In addition, it is also desirable to avoid a fixed mindset and maintain a log-book to document the actions initiated.

EFFECTIVE CHANGE MANAGEMENT

A negative approach to implement change, such as imposing the change without discussions with employees, selling the idea of change without any support from the employees, or even worse, unknowingly dragging employees into a change situation, is not desirable from a long-term perspective. Employees may bow down to pressure initially but will ultimately react, making the organizational change programme unsustainable. For this reason, it is desirable that organizations follow certain defined steps as detailed here.

Explain the Need for Change

Before implementing any change, it is necessary to communicate the change message to employees, clarifying why it is needed, and how it may affect them the organization, both in the short and long term. What could be the possible adverse impact if it is not implemented, both from the employee and the organizational point of view is also required to convey to the employees. While doing this, it is also important to draw the change plan with proper alignment of organizational and employees' interest. The idea is to ultimately draw a shared change programme that encounters minimum resistance from employees.

Discuss in Detail the Issues Involved

While explaining the need for a change, it is necessary to discuss the change issues in detail in order to enlighten employees on what is going to happen. At this stage, organizations should ask for suggestions and feedback from employees to map their reactions through responses and also to inculcate the feeling that they are making a constructive contribution in a crisis situation. When employees realize that they are a party to the change process, they feel more committed to cooperate and deliver results. Also, organizations can suitably enrich their change programme with mutual acceptance.

Facilitate the Change Programme with Training and Support

All employees of the organization may not be capable of keeping pace with the change programme. They may require training and support. Hence, organizations need to arrange training programmes, workshops, discussion sessions, employees' participation, etc. so that employees can take informed decisions to bring about change in the organization. This will also encourage participation and enhance general understanding of the problem, and even bring positive attitudinal change in the mindset of employees. Proper facilitation can ultimately bring success.

Implement the Desired Change

All these steps discussed so far set the premise for change after which organizations have to implement the change. However, when the change areas are wide and diverse, this has to be done in a phased manner or the change programme may be jeopardized. Further, it is also important to remember that people absorb the shock slowly; hence, persuading them to change in all spheres may ultimately ruin the effective implementation of the change programme. Professional change managers start with a small target and achieve this before moving to the next. Thus, employees can gauge the success and organizations too can sustain their change programme.

Reinforce the Change

With the success of the change implementation programme through new systems, processes, and procedures, organizations should continuously review and monitor the actual changes that have taken place to ascertain whether the change outcome has truly contributed to organizational success and achievement of its objectives, and wherever necessary, initiate corrective action.

Organization can, thus, effectively implement change without much dissension among employees. A consultative change management programme is always desirable, as it gives the best result with a high level of commitment from the people. The basic steps essential for effective change management are shown in Fig. 5.7.

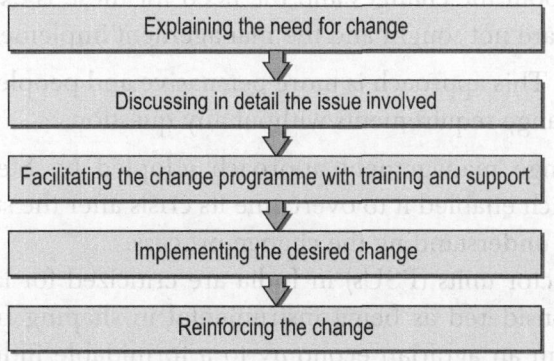

FIG. 5.7 Effective change management flow chart

QUALITIES OF A CHANGE AGENT

Change agents play a very crucial role in managing organizational change. Hence, they must possess the qualities required to mould the behaviour of people and to make the change happen. Some of the competencies and qualities of change agents are as follows:

- Mentality to accept advice
- Ability to control emotions
- Ability to solve problems
- Quality of attentive listening and positive assertion
- Effective time management
- Unbiased actions and opinions

These qualities and competencies are necessary to ease the process of managing change as change agents may have to face contradiction and disagreement.

APPROACHES TO CHANGE MANAGEMENT

All organizations do not adopt the same change approach. This may vary with the nature of the change issues. The leadership style of the change leader also has an impact on the nature of the change approach. Some of these approaches are discussed here followed with a pictorial presentation in Fig. 5.8.

Collaborative The benefits of this approach have already been highlighted. Better results can be obtained if the people who are affected by the change are involved in the change process. Collaboration is possible through successive meetings and workshops to make them aware of the change momentum.

Consultative This approach requires that information is shared and opinions sought from employees. This gives them the confidence that their issues are being duly considered in implementing the change programme.

Directive This approach requires some amount of persuasion. Here, people are informed about the changes and the need for these is explained to them. However, their views are not sought and the management implements the change.

Coercive This approach is more persuasive and people are literally told to comply with the change requirements without any question.

The change management approach adopted by Steel Authority of India Ltd (SAIL), which enabled it to overcome its crisis after the steel price was decontrolled, can help in understanding the change process.

Public sector units (PSUs) in India are criticized for lack of professionalism. Yet, they are considered as being instrumental in shaping India Inc., transforming the country from an agrarian economy to a formidable industrial power. Today, SAIL is India's largest steel manufacturing unit and along with the other PSUs, it could

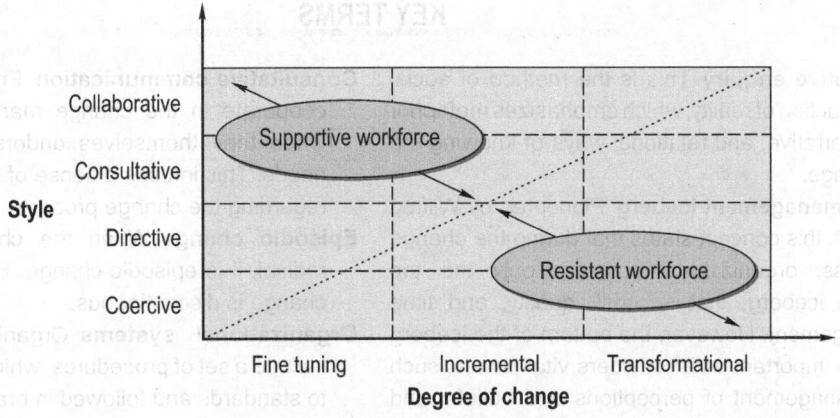

FIG. 5.8 Approaches to change management

shape the Indian economy by creating the right infrastructure to pave the process of industrialization.

SAIL embraced the best HR management practices to manage their change. Steel price decontrol created difficulties for SAIL and it had to fight for its existence in a liberalized economy while coping with competition from global players. It emerged a winner by using alternative resources for steel manufacturing and streamlining its workforce. The entire focus was on motivating employees by improving individual and team productivity. With the introduction of electronic paperless appraisal systems, the company was able to adopt a 'bell-curve approach' to identify the outstanding and below par employees. With the induction of employee satisfaction survey, TQM programme, etc., it is now able to ensure transparent communication within the organization. This change strategy helped to make SAIL a professionally managed company.

SUMMARY

Change management describes a structured approach to transition in individuals, teams, organizations, and societies that moves the target from a current state to a desired state. Stated simply, change management is a process for managing the people side of change. Recent research points to a combination of organizational change management tools and individual change management models for effective change to take place. The evolution of the change management field stems from psychology, business, and engineering. Hence, some models are derived from an organizational development perspective, whereas others are based on individual behavioural models.

Understanding individual and organizational change is necessary to implement effective change management processes and tools. In this chapter, we have discussed both these issues in detail. While individual change emphasizes behavioural and attitudinal modification of people through approaches, such as change transition curves, Com-Be-D model, goal congruence model, etc., organizational change is effected by different practices, such as lean manufacturing, business process management, appreciative enquiry, and six sigma practices. The chapter concludes with the desired qualities of a change agent and on the various approaches to change.

KEY TERMS

Appreciative enquiry This is the method of social construction of reality, which emphasizes metaphor and narrative, and relational ways of knowing the language.

Change management iceberg Pioneered by Wilfred Kruger, this concept states that during the change process, organizations consider only the top of the iceberg, that is, cost, quality, and time management. However, the bottom of the iceberg is also important as it considers vital issues, such as management of perceptions and beliefs, and power and politics in management.

Consultative communication Employees can only cooperate in the change management process when they themselves understand the change needs. This infuses a sense of ownership in them regarding the change process.

Episodic change When the change decision is radical, it is episodic change. Hence, this type of change is discontinuous.

Organizational systems Organizational systems include a set of procedures, which are transformed to standards and followed in practice.

CONCEPT REVIEW QUESTIONS

1. Define change management. What are its elements?
2. What is the nature of change? How do organizations carry out the responsibility of managing change?
3. Explain the principles of change management.
4. Explain certain change management issues and their solution.
5. Discuss how an organization can improve through effective change management. How can such change improvement systems be implemented?
6. What are the processes of mobilizing an organization through change management initiatives?
7. Explain the various types of change and their characteristics.
8. Explain the nature of skill requirements for managing change in organizations.
9. How can an organization bring about change in its culture? Discuss.
10. Explain how group behaviour modification can facilitate change.
11. List the processes of effective change management.
12. What are the approaches to change management?
13. Write short notes on the following:
    (a) Change management tools
    (b) Change transitions
    (c) Com-Be-D model
    (d) Goal congruence
    (e) Commitment curve

CRITICAL THINKING QUESTIONS

1. Your organization is planning to change the business focus from manufacturing to trading in shoes. Over the years, it has identified that manufacturing is not cost-effective. It is better to leverage the brand value and source the shoes from low-cost vendors, and sell them through various outlets spread across the country. As a change agent what would be your line of action?

2. What approach would you suggest for the organization to follow to effect change from a wide span of control to a narrow span of control?

3. List the lessons learnt from the change management process at HP-Compaq, which was ultimately a success.

CASE STUDY

Change Management

Champion International (CI) is a pulp and paper manufacturing firm with a long pedigree of traditional command and control style of management in American industry. In the mid-1980s, it became a low performer and this resulted in constrained labour relations. However, the situation improved a decade later due to the adoption of socio-technical systems. Among others, such initiatives resulted in a change in management practices. Ten out of the twelve plants could achieve excellence, with four achieving world-class status. CI's de-layering of management from 8 levels to 5, revamping the support functions, divestment of low-performing assets, improvement in information technology, and a strong customer-focused quality improvement programme helped to make them one of the most admired companies in Fortune's list for six successive years.

According to those who were engaged in the process (including one consultant), such change initiatives are more eclectic than theoretical.

Andy Sigler was the CEO when the change process started at CI. His leadership was critical for sparking and sustaining the process of transformation. Sigler's pursuit for transformation was triggered by the 1980 strike at one of CI's mills where management tried to run the plant. His statement of principles called 'The Champion Way' focused on quality circles to achieve employee involvement and helped the company to improve the work culture.

In 1985, CI's new pulp mill at Quinnesec (in Michigan) used 'The Champion Way' values as the basis for adopting a socio-technical systems approach. The plant's performance system features were self-directed work teams, pay for knowledge, and a flat management structure. The success at Quinnesec compelled CI to move away from a traditional functional structure to a more business unit focus.

Over the years, the change process focused on transformation of the work culture. Self-directed teams were formed, incentive compensation programmes were restructured and introduced for all levels, labour-management partnerships were started, new participative forms of planning were introduced, open-book management was practised, and generous amounts of training was provided. In addition, CI continued its pursuit to upgrade machinery and equipment and improved its strategic market and product focus, etc. A team of professionals managed this process of transition. CI's change process developed the conceptual model as follows:

$$W2 = A \times C \times L$$

where $W2$ refers to What Works (WW); A refers to a clear alignment of organizational change effort with business strategy, values, and core technology; C means strong capabilities that result from skilled dedicated people working together; and L signifies letting go of traditional forms of direct supervisory control.

CI's change programme initiatives and actions have been aligned with the competitive strategy of the organization, making use of core technology, and addressing the social values. This obviously led to modifications of pay systems, communications, and information technology. In fact, CI's change model leveraged the three Cs of capability, that is, competencies, commitments, and cooperation, which reinforced 3 Ss, namely style, structure, and systems.

CI continued its change pursuit even beyond and is today adjudged as the best pulp producing unit in the world.

Source: Adapted from Ault, Richard, Richard Walton, and Mark Childers (1998), *What Works—A Decade of Change at Champion International*, Jossey Bass, San Francisco.

Discussion Question

Draw lessons from the change management programmes at CI and compare it with any Indian company, to understand the degree of compatibility in their line of action. (*Hint: You can compare with Hindustan Paper Corporation.*)

REFERENCES

Aguilar, F.J. (1967), *Scanning the Business Environment*, Macmillan, New York.

Chermack T.J. and B.K. Kasshanna (2007), 'The use and misuse of SWOT analysis and implications for HRD professionals', *Human Resource Development International*, Vol. 10, No. 4, December, pp. 383–399.

Cooperrider, David L. and Suresh Srivastva (1987), 'Appreciative inquiry in organizational life', in Pasmore, W. and R. Woodman (ed.), *Research in Organizational Change and Development*, Vol. 1, pp. 129–169, Jai Press, Greenwich, CT.

Grundy, T. (2006), 'Rethinking and reinventing Michael Porter's five forces model', *Strategic Change*, Vol. 15, no. 5, August, pp. 213–229.

Hammer, Michael and James Champney (1995), *Re-engineering the Corporation: A Manifesto for Business Revolution*, Revised Edition, Nicholas Brealey, London.

Have, S.T. (2003), 'Key management models: The management tools and practices that will improve your business', *Financial Times*, Prentice Hall, London.

Hubbard, G. (2000), *Strategic Management—Thinking, Analysis, and Action*, Prentice Education, Frenchs Forest, New South Wales.

Huczynski, A. and D. Buchanan (2001), *Organizational Behaviour*, Prentice Hall, New York.

Hussey, D. (2002), 'Company analysis: Determining strategic capability', *Strategic Change*, Vol. 11, No. 1, January/February, pp. 43–52.

Jaffee, D. (2001), *Organization Theory—Tension and Change*, McGraw-Hill, New York.

Lewin, K. (1951), *Field Theory in Social Science*, Harper and Row, New York.

Orlikowski, W. and D. Hofman (1997), 'An improvizational model of change management: The case of groupware technologies', *Sloan Management Review*, Vol. 38 No. 2, pp. 11–22.

Pierce, C. (2001), *The Effective Director: The Essential Guide to Director and Board Development*, Kogan Page, London.

Robbins, S.P. (1998), *Organizational Behaviour*, Prentice Hall, New Jersey.

Turner, S. (2002), *Tools for Success: A Manager's Guide*, McGraw-Hill, London.

Wilfred Kruger (2004), www.12manage.com/methods_change_management_iceberg.html, accessed on 29 July 2009.

www.change-management.com/tutorial-improvement-systems-mod1.htm, accessed on 29 July 2009.

6 Power, Leadership, and Organizational Change

Learning Objectives

After reading this chapter, you will be able to understand
- the meaning, definition, and concept of power
- the theories of power
- organizational power and control
- power and the systems of organizational membership
- the sources of power
- power and empowerment
- organizational politics
- transactional and transformational leadership for organizational change
- environment and leadership

Power and Its Use at Workplace

Mr Thomas, the manager of a large retail chain, believes in putting pressure on newly appointed store sales representatives to get better results. He insults them and makes critical comments about their work. Sales representatives do not get any appreciation even when they exceed expected standards. Instead, they are told to 'deliver more'. He considers his habit of making open as well as behind-the-back derogatory comments about his subordinates as his core leadership strength. Retail chains now operate in a very competitive market with new players continuously entering the market.

Most of the newly recruited sales representatives are fresh out of college and consider Thomas's behaviour akin to that of a critical father who does not know how to be friendly and encourage his children to work. As a result, more than half of them resigned from their jobs within six months causing tremendous pressure on the rest to ensure satisfactory customer service. Thomas became even more ferocious in his behaviour, compelling them to undertake the additional work of those who had left the organization.

One evening, when the store was full of customers, Thomas shouted at the sales team, asking them to withdraw from their workstations and report to his office immediately to discuss the reduced sales volume of the previous week. One of the boys complained that this was a consequence of their inability to cater to customer demands due to the reduced number of salespeople. Thomas was incensed at this and would perhaps have struck the boy, but he anticipated this and caught hold of Thomas's hand. Thomas lost his balance and fell, and the young salespersons took this opportunity to attack him. The customers rescued Thomas and he was taken to hospital.

The MD of the company was informed of the situation and after conducting an enquiry, he decided to dismiss Thomas for his failure to manage the employees and for gross misbehaviour at the workplace. He observed that Thomas had threatened the professional status and personal standing of employees, and made them victims of overwork and bullying at the workplace. On recovery, Thomas took the matter to court but his plea for reinstatement was rejected.

Often managers resort to bullying at the workplace to exert power but as witnessed, this can lead to serious situations.

INTRODUCTION

Power and leadership have a significant impact on organizational change. So also does organizational politics. In this chapter, we will first discuss the concepts of power, leadership, and organizational politics, and then determine how these can influence change in organizations.

Power is the potentiality of a person to exert influence on others. In organizations, power operates principally through direct control. The right to command is granted by ownership of the means of production and is typically vested in distinct proprietary knowledge. However, this may not always be valid in all organizations. Power may be delegated from the principal to agent relation, that is, from managers who enjoy the right to command, down to other levels. Irrespective of the principal–agent relation, that is, employer–employee relation, personal or impersonal command is by nature discursive. Hence, power is often construed as stress-related strategies used by managers to achieve the superordinate (organizational) preferences. This, however, is a negative connotation of power. There are also many positive aspects.

In an organizational structure, people are working at different hierarchical levels within the organization and have reporting relationships. Power binds this hierarchical structure and the relationships between organizational members. Design of tasks and their interdependencies relate to the distribution of power, as some tasks have functional interdependence. Actual power structures in organization, therefore, conform to the organizational chart. Power need not always be discursive, or necessarily coercive; it can be used effectively by recognizing the diversity of interests of the members of the organization.

Organizational politics is another inseparable part of organizational environment. Unlike power, politics reflects the decision-making style of managers, emphasizing more on hypocrisy, veil of secrecy, rumours, and cliques. Politics is in-built within the organization due to various coalitions of people with diverse interests. Individuals and groups differ in their values, preferences, beliefs, and perceptions, and they play politics in order to influence organizational decisions to their benefit. This is natural, as for obvious reasons every organization manages to run its show with limited available resources. Thus, individuals and groups play politics to bargain for a larger pie of scarce resources.

Leadership is the relationship in which one person (the leader) influences others (the followers) to work together voluntarily to attain the goals and objectives of an organization. It is more an interpersonal influence and an art or process of influencing others to put their efforts enthusiastically and attain the goals of the organization. Thus, in the context of the organization, leadership is viewed as a managerial ability to persuade subordinates using a non-coercive method or approach. Like power and politics, leadership also greatly influences organizational change.

We will examine the influences that these have on organizational change, and hence, at the outset it is important to briefly browse through the theoretical contexts.

THEORIES OF POWER

Weber (1947) exemplified power in an organization through the process of control. He related authority to legitimacy, implying that managers enjoy it by virtue of their position in the organizational hierarchy. Although legitimate authority itself is power, an individual member of an organization without any authority can also enjoy power. Sources of authority need not always depend on legitimacy. Charismatic authority may be independent of legitimacy, as it is embedded in the outstanding characteristics of an individual. Traditional authority essentially requires respecting custom (such as a senior member of an organization is respected by others). Rational legal authority is based on the code or set of rules of an organization.

According to Weber, rational legal authority can be efficiently used by an organization through bureaucracy. This restricts managers to use rational legal authority arbitrarily. Bureaucracy binds organization with a certain set of rules. A formal set of rules can command obedience from organizational members primarily because people obey an impersonal order.

McClelland (1961) identified power as one of the three needs related to human behaviour in an organization. Achievement and affiliation needs are the other two. The need for power is an urge to control others—to make them do things. McClelland identified four stages of power:

Drawing inner strength from others This is achieved by loyally following others. Organizations ensure this through the process of empowerment.

Strengthening oneself This is done by playing the power game, using symbols signifying desired status.

Self-assertiveness This implies becoming more aggressive by manipulating situations.

Acting as an instrument of higher authority Identifying with some system of authority and emulating the methods in stages 2 and 3 can help claim formal legitimacy.

Blake and Mouton (1964) featured the kind of person who maximizes the 'authority–obedience' style of management, concentrating on result optimization through the exercise of personal authority and power. Such a manager combines a high concern for production with a low concern for people. They concentrate on maximizing production by exercising power and authority, and achieving control over people by dictating what they should do and how they should do it. Typically, such managers drive themselves and others. They investigate situations to ensure control so that others are not making mistakes. They prefer to defend their own ideas and opinions even though it may mean rejecting those of others. They deal with conflict by either trying to cut it off or winning their own position, and making their own decisions. They are rarely influenced by others, and are not afraid to pinpoint other people's weaknesses and failures. Blake and Mouton's model can be explained using the managerial grid framework shown in Fig. 6.1.

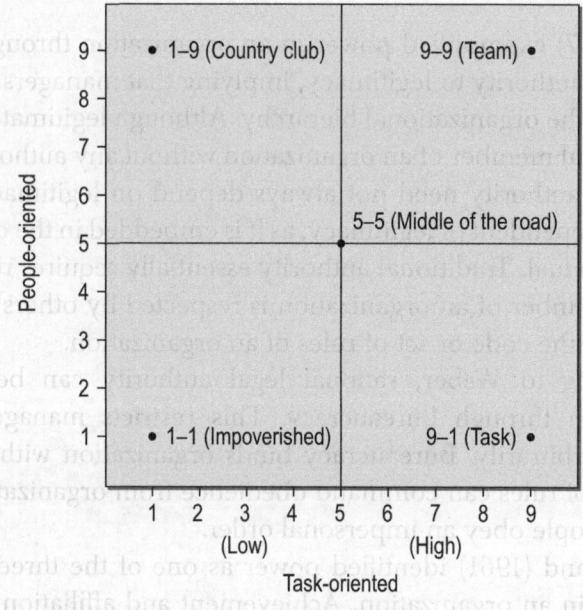

FIG. 6.1   Managerial styles

In spite of many commonalities between leadership, authority, and power, it is appropriate at this stage to clarify these terms. Leadership is the ability to influence people to willingly follow one's guidance or adhere to one's decisions. Acquiring followers, influencing them, and achieving objectives are what make a leader. In an organization, effective leadership creates a vision of the future that considers the long-term interests of all the parties involved. Leaders use power to influence group behaviour. Leadership has to cope with politics so that it does not cause disturbances within the organization.

Authority is the right to issue directives and expend resources. It is related to power but narrower in scope. Basically, authority depends on the amount of coercive, reward, and legitimate power one can exert. An individual can have expert power or referent power without having formal authority.

Power, on the other hand, encompasses both authority and leadership ability but the nature of authority is more personal than organizational.

In understanding the dynamics of the organizational change process, both power and authority are important. Leaders get things done by others by exerting power, which they may not otherwise be able to do. This means that by wielding power over people, one can get them to act in a way that may be considered in contradiction to their interests. Leaders can do so, as their power to control people bears some value either in the form of incentives, bonus, or conferring promotion, etc. This is what is called the dependency model of power.

The dependency model of power can be balanced when both the parties depend on each other. For example, a boss may be dependent on a subordinate's performance to achieve his/her targets. In this case, the subordinate controls something of value (in terms of his/her performance) which the boss wants. Hence, in a balanced dependency situation, the subordinates may not be totally powerless. In managing the behaviour of people in organizations, managers make a trade-off between their power and the power of the people reporting to them, attaching a price. Thus, this argument substantiates that there is no one in an organization who is powerless. Also, power is not the exclusive preserve of managers.

A balanced dependency model of power thus promotes a work culture of mutual trust, effectively influencing the attitudes and beliefs of people. Here, we can illustrate the experience of Videocon. The company acquired the stake of Phillips, the legacy-bound multinational. In two units in Kolkata, they faced resistance from the erstwhile Phillips employees to implement the desired organizational change, particularly in relation to tough competition from the Korean consumer electronic majors, Samsung and LG. Videocon empowered their employees to take charge of the shop floor and manage the show. The idea was to make them feel the impelling need for change and it yielded the desired results.

ORGANIZATIONAL POWER AND CONTROL

Organizational control through power implies the general ability of managers to direct and organize the efforts of the employees. In organizations, there are different types of control, such as simple, technical, and bureaucratic control.

Simple control is enforced by direct supervision and is more evident in a protocol-bound manufacturing process. Such control is the use of powers of supervisors over the jobs of the workers. Technical control is imposed by the technology used in a manufacturing process. For example, in an automated assembly-line production process, the speed of work will be important, as each job remains in a particular workstation for a fixed time and then moves to the next workstation. Supervisors control the process, imposing the timely completion of jobs by each worker within the given time limit. Through formal rules and regulations, managers enforce bureaucratic control. Bureaucratic organizations frame rules on the hours of work, entitlement to time-off under various circumstances (e.g., annual leave, compassionate leave, maternity leave, etc.), grievance procedures, and so on. There are also rules or 'standard operating procedures' that people must follow in the course of their work. This form of control is also exertion of power in a subtle form.

POWER AND SYSTEMS OF ORGANIZATIONAL MEMBERSHIP

Theoretically, organizational power is a synthesis of systems and is exerted to make people comply with the organizational requirements. While considering organizational change, it is necessary for organizations to reframe the standards of behaviour and expect compliance from people, so that the change can take place as desired. Since resistance to the change is a typical syndrome in any organizational change initiative, managers and leaders often mistakenly use their coercive power. But that may add fuel to the fire as willing people may strengthen their resistance and ultimately force the organization to withdraw their change initiative.

Prior to its liquidation and subsequent acquisition by a new promoter, *Encyclopaedia Britannica* which was priced at around US$2500 contemplated introducing a CD version of it to compete with Microsoft's Encarta priced at US$60. *Encyclopaedia Britannica's* salespeople got 10 per cent commission on every sale. Substituting the price of the printed volumes with a CD (at a price similar to Microsoft's Encarta at US$60) would reduce their earnings and hence they opposed the move.

This is why, organizations follow standards of laid-down behaviour. Goal-oriented, performance-directed organizations require the compliance of members; the problem is that deviance from these standards occurs because of weaknesses in member commitments.

Compliance is ensured by organizational control and authority structures, formal hierarchies of authority, supervision, job definitions, policies, and specified procedures. According to the bureaucratic model of Weber, these make the organization less dependent on individual variations.

There is also a motivation element to this, as structures shape the involvement of the individual within the organization that he/she belongs to. The simple proposition is that the greater the individual is committed, the less formal is the control needed. Etzioni's typology (classification scheme) includes coercive, calculative, and normative systems. We can, thus, label organizations (or parts of organizations, as we see them) adopting such systems as their prevailing cultures.

Coercive systems reflect an organization's ability to apply physical, constraining force, when people fail to meet expectations. Examples of coercive power in organizations include the ability (implied or real) to fire, demote, and transfer to undesirable positions, or strip subordinates of coveted privileges. Coercive methods nurture dysfunctional group processes with the following typical characteristics:

- Dislike and rejection
- Anger and a backlash of conflict
- Conspiracies and coalitions
- Reticence and reduced intrinsic motivation

Calculative or instrumental systems of control make use of various kinds of material or non-material rewards to secure member compliance. Organizational membership is based on the member contracting with the organization and bargaining over the desired reward in return for compliance, loyalty, reliability, and performance. Members calculate 'What's in it for me!—is it overtime, a pay raise, a promotion, a steady income, or a long-term future?' This involves shades of willingness ranging from mildly negative orientation to the calculation (what's in it for me, akin to McGregor's Theory X stick approach or Goldthorpe's affluent worker) to a positive–instrumental orientation (McGregor's carrot Theory X and normative Theory Y).

Normative or moral involvement systems of power depend on shared values which are promoted and which members subscribe to. The organization consciously generates and maintains these values, which are represented by signs and symbols—visual, verbal, behavioural, and conceptual. Commitment to the organization's ideology brings with it persuasive/suggestive power. Members internalize organizational values which become their own and guide their behaviour naturally. Individuals within the organization act as one with a very intensive commitment to the organization.

Modern business organizations invest considerable effort and resource into creating such an environment within which employees 'join as one' within a unitary, harmonious, framework of consensus to achieve organizational goals. A monastic order is an obvious example of a normative system of organizational control. But, so too is the total quality/continuous quality improvement or learning company culture.

Such systems are evident in most of the organizations. A large modern business relies heavily on calculative and normative systems. Albeit, we may conclude that in both, there is a 'motivational problem' if employees display such alleviated calculations requiring the organization to constantly bargain with individuals and groups over the substance of their rewards.

SOURCES OF POWER

French and Raven (1959) suggested five types of power based on Etzioni's power typology. Broadly, the sources of power can be categorized into two types—organizational sources and individual or personal sources.

Organizational Sources

There are three kinds of organizational sources which are discussed here.

Coercive power

Leaders exert this power to dispense punishment to those who do not comply with requests or demands. Individuals can exercise coercive power through reliance upon physical strength, verbal faculty, or through the decisions to grant or withhold emotional support from others. These provide to an individual the means to physically harm, bully, humiliate, or deny love to others.

Managers make use of several tools to manage organizational change effectively, addressing the power issues. Information sharing is the most important of these. Performance can be improved by making subordinates aware of the expected behaviour. Information can change the cognitive elements and reduce their involvement in power conflicts within the organization. By developing their expertise, managers and leaders can also create a 'halo-effect', so that subordinates feel that managers not only legitimately enjoy power because of their role position, but also deserve it because of their knowledge and expertise.

These apart, by making effective use of coercion and reward, personality, authority, and caring for the people, managers and leaders can gain the participation of people to obtain better results.

Reward power

A supervisor has reward power over staff. Through the staff appraisal process, he/she can open up doors to promotion, allocate overtime, or more interesting work. He/she can offer involvement in decision-making and thus, an enhanced status (referent power). Students will strive to complete a project to win a reward from the tutor. Such power is effective when employees believe that a direct relationship exists between effort and the achievement of the reward they value (expectancy theory). We need to recognize, however, that in most modern organizations—corporations, hospital trusts, or local authority—most managers have little scope to widely vary reward components to employees, because reward systems are governed by rules and require consistency in application.

Legitimate power

This reflects Weber's rational–legal authority. The member accepts an authority's legitimate right to require and demand compliance.

Individual/Personal Sources

Following are the two kinds of personal sources of power:

Expert power

This power derives from the recognition that the power holder has valued skills and abilities in an area critical to the members' success.

Referent (charismatic) power

This power is based on personal identification with and respect for a leader figure who is followed/supported because of his/her personal qualities or characteristics.

POWER AND EMPOWERMENT

When we refer to power, we do so from the perspective of 'power over'. On the other hand, empowerment recognizes and realizes the potential within people. Empowerment is not something given to employees by top management; rather, it is the role of top management to create a culture in which employees can use their full potential to the benefit of the organization. In this process, employees also attain a stage of maturity.

Definition and Concept of Empowerment

The word 'empowerment' is used in many different contexts and by many different organizations. The term encompasses the fields of education, social work, psychology, politics, community development, gender studies, etc. The Human Development Report (1995), stresses that empowerment is about participation. People must participate fully in the decisions and processes that shape their lives. Investing in people's capabilities and empowering them to exercise their choices is not only valuable, but is also the surest way of contributing to economic growth and overall development. For Oxfam, empowerment is about challenging oppression and inequality. Empowerment involves challenging the forms of oppression which compel millions of people to play a part in their society on terms which are inequitable, or in ways which deny their human rights (Oxfam 1995).

Gender studies stress that women's empowerment is not about replacing one form of empowerment with another. It should lead to the liberation of men from false value systems and ideologies of oppression. It should bring about a situation where each person can become a whole being regardless of gender and realize their full potential to construct a more humane society for all (Akhtar 1992 quoted in Batliwala 1994). Rowlands (1995) pointed out that empowerment is a bottom-up process and cannot be bestowed from the top.

Understanding Power and Empowerment Implications in Practice

Power conflict is natural in organizations. Power over conflict and direct confrontation between powerful and powerless interest groups in organizations are evident even in professionally managed organizations, leave aside those that lack professionalism. Organizational power for capacity building, supporting individual decision-making, leadership, etc. can best be reinforced with the process of empowerment. Thus, empowerment can also be defined as the power that people have to trigger social mobilization, build alliances and coalitions, increase self-esteem, raise awareness or consciousness, and build confidence. When people fully participate in decision-making and in the processes that benefit both the organization and its members, people empowerment is achieved in the true sense. The Human Development Report (1995) lists empowerment as one of the four essential components of the human development paradigm, the others being productivity, equity, and sustainability.

The Process of Empowerment

Empowerment is essentially a bottom-up process rather than something that can be formulated as a top-down strategy. Hence organizations, per se, cannot claim that they have empowered people; they can only facilitate the process of empowerment. This requires that the organization carefully devises coherent policies and programmes, ignoring the traditional concept of power over people. The 'power-over' concept dissuades people from developing their problem-solving capabilities and participating in decision-making. On the contrary, the 'power-with' concept encourages people to be more proactive in addressing organizational issues and pacing their individual process of development. It also encourages people to participate, acquire skills, develop their decision-making capability, and control resources. The process of empowerment can therefore be categorized as follows.

Empowering individuals directly

The process of empowering individuals directly involves the following:

1. Allow people to develop their capability to enforce self-control.
2. Allow people to participate in decision-making.
3. Develop peoples' ability to understand situations and respect their efforts.
4. Build knowledge and ability and allow people to have access to the knowledge repository.
5. Indulge people to choose their own approach autonomously.
6. Allow participation in action, development, planning, strategic, and operational processes.
7. Develop a transparent information-sharing process.
8. Allow people to develop their ability to influence.
9. Make people feel confident to express and present their viewpoints.
10. Inculcate in people a sense of responsibility for their actions.

Empowering people by changing the work environment

The process of empowerment through change in the workplace/environment involves the following:

1. Remove false assumptions.
2. Remove oppression or fear and create equality.
3. Change practices.

4. Generate communal goals.
5. Institutionalize change.
6. Enable dialogue and open communication.
7. Share responsibility.
8. Adopt democratic transparent processes.
9. Take collective action.

However, empowerment cannot be defined in terms of specific activities or end results because it involves a process whereby people can freely analyse, develop, and voice their needs and interests, without the organization pre-defining or imposing them. Organizations working towards an empowerment approach must, therefore, develop ways of enabling people to critically assess their own situation, and create and shape a transformation. This process of transformation through empowerment should be an ongoing initiative rather than a time-bound one.

At its most basic level, empowerment is defined as a process of assumption or transfer of legal power and official authority (*Webster's New World Dictionary* 1994). Empowerment is primarily a feeling or state of mind (Riger 1993; Tyne 1994), that is, assertiveness. Harp (1994) viewed empowerment of individuals as a possession of the same degree of control over one's own life and the conditions that affect it, as is generally possessed by people who are already empowered in a similar context. West and Parent (1992) defined empowerment as the transfer of power and control over decisions, choices, and values. Again, empowerment can be viewed in the context of individual people and even of groups.

ORGANIZATIONAL POLITICS

Politics is inseparable from organizations. This is obviously due to the involvement of people. Organizations overrun by politics are typically identified by the type of managerial decisions which encourage hypocrisy, secrecy, deal-making, rumours, power brokers, self-interests, image-building, self-promotion, and cliques. Such organizations lack effective teamwork. There are five possible reasons for organizational politics:

1. Organizations are coalitions composed of varied individuals and groups.
2. There are enduring differences among individuals and groups in their values, preferences, beliefs, information, and perceptions of reality.
3. Most important decisions in organizations involve the allocation of scarce resources.
4. Conflict is central to organizational dynamics and power is the most important resource.
5. Organizational goals and decisions emerge from bargaining, negotiation, and jockeying for position, among the members of different coalitions.

Besides causing problems for the individuals who work together, the end result of organizational politics can be far more devastating. Employees and managers who must concentrate on the political aspects of work may have less time to pay attention to their jobs. This translates into financial loss, which may, in turn, translate into job loss.

To reduce organizational politics, managers and leaders, make use of several strategies in their people-related decisions. All these may minimize politics but cannot guarantee elimination of it, because politics is inherent in every form wherever people come together for a purpose. Managers must emphasize performance, making a culture that employee rewards are earned and not favours granted. Similarly, promotion and pay-rise decisions should be aligned with transparent performance management systems, making people believe that the system is impersonal and reliable. A very strong weapon for reducing organizational politics is to nurture transparent communication systems. Everything that affects the workplace should be made transparent to dissuade employees to fabricate stories and spread rumours, and restrain them from deal-making and favouritism.

Thus, briefly organizational politics can be reduced when organizations

- measure performance,
- pay off on performance,
- publicize performance data,
- reveal the reasons for decisions,
- openly consider all good ideas,
- shun deal making,
- do not enter into secret deals,
- avoid all political behaviour.

We have many good examples of leaders from the corporate world who have successfully managed workplace politics. Jack Welch, former head of General Electric (GE), was one of the most impressive political players. His slogan was: 'Control your destiny or someone else will'. He chose people to push through changes and weed out 'resisters'. He replaced GE's ornate structure with a 'cartwheel'—13 spokes of business units radiating from his office.

TRANSACTIONAL AND TRANSFORMATIONAL LEADERSHIP

Change in organizations is unavoidable and it is now a business imperative to survive in competition. Although change has many manifestations, selection of the right type of change or taking appropriate change initiatives is a major leadership challenge. Two important terms often agitate one's mind—should one opt for 'transactional' or 'transformational' change? Both terms are often misconstrued as any change is classified as being transformational. However, theoretically they are different. Transactional change takes place when one goes backwards, and forward with transactions and agreements, keeping in view the immediate pursuit. Organizations that believe in transactional change can revert quickly.

Transformational change is a long-term pursuit and organizations subscribing to it do not go back. Cultural change, for example, is a transformational change as it transforms the behaviour and attitudes of the people working in an organization, and they autonomously endeavour to achieve the business outcomes. This becomes possible as people in the process of change build their capabilities. Burns (1978) first introduced the concepts of transformational and transactional leadership in his treatment of political leadership, but these terms are now used in organizational psychology as well.

Transformational leadership is one in which, one or more persons engage with others in such a way that leaders and followers raise one another to higher levels of motivation and morality. The term transformational leadership was first coined by Downton in 1973 in *Rebel Leadership: Commitment and Charisma in a Revolutionary Process*. Some of the characteristic differences between transactional and transformational leadership are enumerated.

Bass (1985) classified the behavioural characteristics of transactional leaders into four types, namely contingent reward, non-contingent reward, contingent punishment, and non-contingent punishment. The behaviour of transformational leaders on the other hand, encompasses articulation of a vision, intellectual stimulation, a high expectation of performance, providing individualized support, and providing a role model. Transactional leaders work on creating clear structures, making employees understand that they are essential, and how they will be rewarded for achieving these. They also do not hesitate to clarify, both explicitly or implicitly, the penalty for not achieving results. Transformational leaders believe in positive change, urging all to participate towards achieving positive results. Such leaders show enthusiasm for this, both for the team members and for themselves.

Organizational change consists of change in structures, systems, cultures, knowledge, and technology. Organizations envisage structural change in order to reduce the number of hierarchical levels, simplify reporting relationships, for operational feasibility, or even for manpower rationalization. Changing organizational systems requires adapting, operating, maintenance, and information systems.

Contingency Framework of Change

Change may be initiated internally or externally by managers or internal champions, or by external consultants or environmental conditions. It may be planned or unplanned, incremental or transformative, collaborative or coerced, evolutionary or revolutionary. Dunphy and Stace (1988) offered a typology of change strategies in a contingency framework. They differentiated four types of change according to collaborative or coercive modes and incremental or transformative change strategies.

Types 1 and 3 are participative evolution and forced evolution. Types 2 and 4 are charismatic transformation and dictatorial transformation. They related each type to the perceived fitness with the environment in which the organization operates. They also related it to the support available for change.

Type 1 or participative evolution is used under two conditions: (i) when an organization fits in with its environment but needs minor adjustments, or (ii) when an organization does not fit in with the environment but time is available and key interest groups favour change. Type 2 or charismatic transformation is used when organizations do not fit in with their environments and there is little time for extensive participation but there is support within the organization for radical change. Type 3 is forced evolution. This is used (i) when organizations fit in with the environment but minor adjustments need to be made, or (ii) the organizations are out of fit but time is available and key interest groups oppose change. Type 4 or dictatorial transformation is used when organizations are out of fit with the environment, there is no time for extensive participation, and no support within the organization for radical change, but radical change is vital to organizational survival and fulfilment of the basic mission. Change agents should select and use the most effective strategy and mode of change rather than relying solely on those compatible with their own personal values.

Tichy (1983) identified and brought together three dominant traditions that have guided thinking about organizations and the practice of change. These are technical, political, and cultural traditions. The technical tradition focuses on production problems amid 'environmental threats and opportunities, social, financial, and technical resources'. This tradition derives from Weberian bureaucracy, scientific and classical management, job design, and contingency theories. The political tradition centres on problems related to the allocation of power and resources.

This tradition stems from Machiavellianism, coalitional view of organizations, exchange theorists, and political science power analyses. The cultural tradition looks at 'values, objectives, beliefs, and interpretations shared by organizational members'. Sources of this tradition are studies in cultural anthropology, human relations, organizational development, and humanistic psychology.

Tichy looked at these traditions as overlapping cycles that require continual adjustment (Tichy, 1983). Strategic change, non-routine and non-incremental, starts with the recognition of problems, crises, or opportunities. His guidelines for managing transitions are as follows:

1. Review the current state diagnosis and the desired state. Design a change strategy to determine the technical, political, and cultural adjustments required by the change.
2. Project the sequence of cycles. When will the technical, political, and cultural cycles peak?
3. Plan for unbundling and uncoupling the three systems in order to manage the transition in each.

4. Plan for managing the transitions in each cycle—technical, political, and cultural.
5. Plan for re-coupling the systems—how will the technical, political, and cultural systems mesh in the desired state organization (Tichy 1983)?

Martel (1986) propounded a fivestep strategy or ways in which readers could master structural and cyclical changes: (i) recognize it, (ii) identify changes in the upstream versus downstream categories, (iii) determine the type and pattern of each change, (iv) rank them by importance and likelihood, and (v) strategically respond to structural changes, and tactically respond to cyclical changes. Martel (1986) also identified changes that offered hope for our future. These changes include (i) information becoming a valued resource, (ii) education increasing among the world's people, (iii) electronic networks of communication linking people more closely, (iv) hope for economic solutions, (v) slowing population growth rate, (vi) changing nature of work, and (vii) rising per capita and discretionary incomes.

Martel indicated that changing attitudes, preferences, and priorities were signalling greater concern for quality, health, comfort, and safety in our personal lives and environments. Juxtaposed to these structural changes, more permanent ones are cyclical; their problems include (i) periods of recession and inflation of business cycles, (ii) shortages and gluts in the demand–supply cycles, (iii) conflict and destruction of wars that enter cycles of organizational and societal behaviour, and (iv) rises in rates of family breakup and crime in cycles of social behaviour. Using his five-step strategy, he believe that the negative effects of cyclical changes could be minimized.

North Delhi Power Limited (NDPL) is a joint venture between Tata Power Limited and the government of the national capital territory. NDPL used change to its best advantage by taking over from the ailing Delhi Vidyut Board (DVB). This change management initiative could bring down the technical and commercial (AT&C) losses from over 50 to 22 per cent.

Similarly, Mangalore Refinery and Petrochemicals Ltd (MRPL) could transform itself from a near sick company to a company that could meet competitive excellence. These two Indian cases show the best way to manage organizational change by manipulating the leadership and power variables.

ENVIRONMENT AND LEADERSHIP

Every organization has a particular work environment that, to a considerable degree, dictates how its leaders respond to problems and opportunities. This is a result of the heritage of its past and present leaders. Leaders exert influence on the environment by three types of actions:

Goals and performance standards they establish Successful organizations have good leaders who set high standards and goals, such as strategies, market leadership, plans, presentations, productivity, quality, and reliability.

Values they establish for the organization Values reflect the concern the organization has for its employees, customers, investors, vendors, and surrounding community. These values define the manner in which the business is conducted and the type of business the organization will engage in.

Business and people concepts they establish Concepts define what products or services the organization will offer, and the methods and processes for conducting business.

These goals, values, and concepts make up the organization's 'personality' or how the organization is observed by outsiders as well as insiders. This personality defines the roles, relationships, rewards, and rites that take place.

Roles are positions that are defined by a set of expectations about the behaviour of any newly recruited person. Each role has a set of tasks and responsibilities that may or may not be spelt out. Roles have a powerful effect on behaviour because compensation is paid for the performance of the role, prestige is attached to it, and there is a sense of accomplishment or challenge.

Relationships are determined by tasks. Some tasks are performed alone, but most are carried out in relationship with others. Tasks determine who the role holder interacts with, how often, and towards what end. Also, the greater the interaction, the greater is the liking! This, in turn, leads to more frequent interaction. In human behaviour, it is hard to like someone with whom we have no contact and we tend to seek out those that we like. People tend to do what they are rewarded for and friendship is a powerful reward. Many tasks and behaviours that are associated with a role emerge due to these relationships. That is, new tasks and behaviours are expected of the present role holder because a strong relationship was developed in the past, either by the present or a previous role holder.

There are two distinct forces that dictate how to act within an organization. These are as follows:

Culture and Climate of Leadership

Each organization has its own distinctive culture, which is a combination of the founders, past and present leadership, crises, events, history, and size. These result in rites—the routines, rituals, and the 'way it does things'. These rites impact individual behaviour on what it takes to be in good standing (the norm) and direct the appropriate behaviour for each circumstance.

The climate is the feel of the organization, the individual, and the shared perceptions and attitudes of the members of the organization. While culture is the deeply rooted nature of the organization and is a result of long-held formal and informal systems, rules, traditions, and customs, climate is a short-term phenomenon created by the current leadership. Climate represents the beliefs about the 'feel of the organization' by its members. This individual perception of the 'feel of the organization' comes from what people believe about the activities of the organization.

Organizational climate is directly related to the leadership and management style of the leader, based on his/her values, attributes, skills, and actions, as well as his/her priorities. The ethical climate is the 'feel of the organization' regarding activities that have ethical content or aspects of the work environment that constitute ethical behaviour. The ethical climate is the belief about whether we do things right or the awareness of whether we behave the way we ought to. The behaviour (character) of the leader is the most important factor that impacts climate.

On the other hand, culture is a long-term, complex phenomenon. It represents the shared expectations and self-image of the organization, the mature values that create 'tradition', or the 'way we do things here'. Things are done differently in every organization. The collective vision that defines the institution is a reflection of its culture. Individual leaders cannot easily create or change culture because it is a part of the organization. Culture influences the characteristics of the climate by its effect on the actions and thought processes of the leader. But, everything a leader does will affect the climate of the organization.

Leadership

In the case of leadership, power is divided into six categories; however, each of these can be linked with the other as they are inter-related. Expert and informational power are concerned with skills, knowledge, and information, which the holders of such abilities are able to utilize in order to influence others. Reward and coercive power involve the ability to either reward or punish the persons being influenced in order to gain compliance. Legitimate power is the power which has been confirmed by the very role structure of the group or organization itself and is accepted by all as correct and without dispute. Referent power, on the other hand, involves the people being influenced identifying with the leader, for example, rock or film personalities using their image to enter the political arena.

Most leaders use a combination of these six types of power, depending on the leadership style used. Authoritarian leaders, for example, use a mixture of legitimate, coercive, and reward powers, to dictate the policies, plans, and activities of a group. In comparison, a democratic or participative leader would use mainly referent power, involving all members of the group in the decision-making process.

LEADERSHIP AND POWER

Leadership is the most critical element of organizational change. However, organizations frequently neglect this as they mistakenly delegate such roles to external organizational change agents. In every organization, the change agent should be the top management who should emphasize team building. Continuous team development through middle-level and line managers (who have to assume the leadership role) can streamline the change process in any organization.

However, building leadership for effective organizational change requires training of first-line managers and supervisors. With OD effort, the process gets further strengthened and everyone in the organization can understand the change intent. Leadership and OD efforts need to adopt the 'lead by example' approach when initiating the change programme, requiring top management to manage the change effort first and slowly cascade it down the line. This is what Nadler and Tushman (1990) attributed to the leadership institutional approach in the total management system of organizations.

Based on a series of experiments, Porras and Hoffer (1986) documented the specific style of leadership required for effective organizational change. These are (1) open communication (to share intentions and to listen), and (2) collaborating (making decisions in teams), etc. Similar studies by Covin and Kilmann (1990) validated such a style of leadership. Covin and Kilmann's studies further extended to the modelling of leadership behaviour in the organizational change process. At the outset, the top management demonstrates visible and consistent support for change. They should first build teams and work in a team at their level, and set an example with traceable positive outcome of change, aligning the change programme to the business needs. When people understand this in terms of increased profitability, productivity, and quality of work life, they embrace change spontaneously.

Like leadership, the effective use of power and politics, while initiating the process of change in organizations, is also important. Decisions related to change need to be logical and the management should use legitimate authority rather than non-rational use of power. Positive use of power is evident when systems that others will accept are created. As a change agent, a manager builds the arguments for change and shares the information with logic, which others cannot refute. This is a subtle way of using power.

Bradshaw–Camball (1989) recommended the use of power through a study of the organizational history and stakeholders' relationship patterns. Savage et al. (1991) also suggested a careful assessment of organizational stakeholders and categorized this into two types, that is, supportive and non-supportive. Thus, the use of power in organizational change is not prohibitive; it may, at times, be necessary. Its application can be best understood once we read the pulse of the organization and its stakeholders. Strategic use of power is possible when one is confident of developing the logical reasoning and presenting it to people who can then hardly disagree.

SUMMARY

This chapter discussed in detail the framework of organizational change in the context of power, politics, and leadership. Although all these have certain commonalities, they differ from one organization to another. All these exert significant impact on organizational change. Hence, while opting for change, organizations need to understand their inter-relations, commonalities, and differences.

The chapter explained the meaning, definition, and concepts of power, theories of power, organizational power and control, sources of power, implications of power and empowerment, organizational politics, transactional and transformational leadership for organizational change, and culture and climate of leadership. The dynamics of power and politics in an organization have been discussed. It is important for every organization to address these dynamics before initiating any change.

KEY TERMS

Bureaucracy It restricts managers to use rational legal authority arbitrarily. Bureaucracy binds the organization with sets of rules and commands obedience from organizational members.

Coercive systems They reflect the organization's ability to apply physical, constraining force to people when they fail to meet expectations.

Empathy It is generally described as a person's ability to look at things or problems from another person's point of view. It involves projecting one's self into the position of the subordinates who are being directed and led.

Normative Moral involvement systems of power This system depends on shared values which are promoted and which members subscribe to. An organization consciously generates and maintains these values, which are represented in signs and symbols—visual, verbal, behavioural, and conceptual.

Situational leadership This is linked to task and relational behaviour. Task behaviour focuses on defining roles and responsibilities, whereas relational behaviour is more about providing support to teams.

CONCEPT REVIEW QUESTIONS

1. Explain the concept of power. What are its different stages?
2. It is said that leadership, authority, and power have certain commonalities, yet they can be differentiated. Do you agree with this statement? Justify your answer.
3. Discuss the concept of power and systems of organizational membership.
4. What are the sources of power?
5. Discuss the power and empowerment implication in practice.
6. Discuss the concept of organizational politics.
7. Discuss transactional and transformational leadership for organizational change.
8. How do environment and leadership correlate? Explain with examples.
9. What are the different styles of leadership?
10. Explain leadership attitude. Why is it so important?
11. Write short notes on the follwoing:
    (a) Authority
    (b) Obedience style of management
    (c) Empowerment
    (d) Organizational climate

CRITICAL THINKING QUESTIONS

1. In the workplace how can power, politics, leadership, and the organizational change process be balanced?
2. It is often said that power is bad in effecting organizational change. However, it is also evident that strategic use of power can render better results. Identify some examples from the corporate world to explain both bad and good effects of the use of power in organizational change.
3. Your organization is a well-known steel manufacturer. To achieve cost efficiency, it has taken a long-term lease of mines. Although it appears to be a transactional change, it requires a great deal of change in the existing business processes. Suggest how this can be managed.

CASE STUDY
Lehman's Lesson

The *Fortune* magazine reports that Lehman Brothers 'ended up on the financial scrap heap because it played—and ultimately lost—a dangerous game involving high stakes, bets, and huge borrowings'. With a stupendous performance in 2007–08, its profit grew impressively. What then went so wrong that Lehman had to ultimately step down and liquidate? Experts observe and attribute this to Lehman's propensity to take more risk. It borrowed too much money, put too much of it into dubious deals, and then insisted for months that all was well when it was apparent that it was not. Lehman's bankruptcy is a sad end for a firm once regarded as prudent and well-managed.

Dick Fuld, Lehman's CEO, was bitterly opposed to the firm undertaking big, aggressive deals with its own capital. But his decision to take on the risks that he opposed in the 1980s hurt Lehman badly. Back then, Fuld's trading faction at Lehman Brothers was struggling against the firm's banking faction, led by Steve Schwarzman and Pete Peterson. The bankers wanted the firm to use its capital to do deals. The traders opposed it.

The trader–banker war weakened Lehman to such an extent that it was sold to American Express in 1984. Fuld, a Lehman lifer, stayed on, while Schwarzman and Peterson went off to found the Blackstone Group and became billionaires. In 1994, American Express gave up its 'financial supermarket' strategy and spun off a small, undercapitalized firm called Lehman Brothers, with Fuld as CEO. (That's why, despite what you read, Lehman wasn't a 158-year old firm; it was a 14-year old firm with a 158-year old name!) Lehman's leverage—borrowings relative to capital—grew, even as other firms were cutting back as the credit crunch worsened.

Very recently, with the real estate collapse well underway, Lehman (in partnership with the Tishman Speyer real estate firm) paid a whopping $22.2 billion to undertake a leveraged buyout of a big apartment developer, Archstone. Losses on the deal began to surface almost immediately. Lehman looked as if it would be able to survive more or less intact after the Federal Reserve Board announcement that it would make huge loans available to eligible investment banks. This came shortly after the Fed and the Treasury forced a fire sale of Bear Stearns, and let it be known that the timing was no coincidence.

But Lehman never fully regained market confidence, Fed and Treasury support notwithstanding. That leads us to a second Wall Street lesson from Lehman: that the Fed and Treasury can no longer control events as they once could.

Source: Adapted from Beth Kowitt, *Fortune* magazine, 13 September 2008.

Discussion Question
Analyse the case and relate it to leadership vision and issues.

REFERENCES

Amitai, Etzioni (1961), *A Comparative Analysis of Complex Organizations*, Free Press, Glencoe, Ill.

Avery, G. and E. Baker (1990), *Psychology at Work*, Prentice Hall, New York.

Bass, Bernard M. (1990), *Bass and Stogdill's Handbook of Leadership*, Free Press, New York.

—— (1990), 'From transactional to transformational leadership: Learning to share the vision', *Organizational Dynamics*, Vol. 18, Issue 3, Winter, pp. 19–31.

Bass, Bernard M. (1989), *Stogdill's Handbook of Leadership: A Survey of Theory and Research*, Free Press, New York.

Bass, B.M. (1985), *Leadership and Performance beyond Expectations*, Free Press, New York.

Bass, B.M. and B.J. Avolio (1995), *MLQ Multifactor Leadership Questionnaire for Research: Permission Set*, Mindgarden, Redwood City.

Batliwala, Srilatha (1994), 'The meaning of women's empowerment: New concepts from action', in Gita Sen, Andrienne Germain, C. Lincoln, Chan (eds), *Population Policies Reconsidered, Health, Empowerment and Rights*, Harvard University Press, Boston.

Bennis, Warren and Bert Nanus (1997), *Leaders: Strategies for Taking Charge*, Harper Business, New York, February.

Bhattacharyya, D.K. (2009), *Organization Behaviour, Concepts and Applications*, Oxford University Press, New Delhi.

____ (2007), *Human Resource Research Methods*, Oxford University Press, New Delhi.

Blake, R. and J. Mouton (1964), *The Managerial Grid*, Gulf Publishing, Houston.

Blake, Robert R. and Janse S. Mouton (1985), *The Managerial Grid III: The Key to Leadership Excellence*, Gulf Publishing Co., Houston.

Blanchard, K., J. Carlos, and W.A. Randolph (1998), *Empowerment Takes More than a Minute*, Berrett-Koehler Publishers, San Francisco.

Block, Peter (1993), *Stewardship: Choosing Service over Self-interest*, Berrett-Koehler Publishers, San Francisco.

Bolman, L. and T. Deal (1991), *Reframing Organizations*, Jossey-Bass, San Francisco.

Bolman, Lee G. and Terrence Deal (1991), *Reframing Organizations: Artistry, Choice and Leadership*, Jossey-Bass, San Francisco.

Bradshaw-Camball, P. (1989), 'The implications of multiple perspectives on power for organizational development', *Journal of Applied Behavioral Science*, Vol. 25, pp. 31–44.

Burns, James MacGregor (1978), *Leadership*, Harper and Row, New York.

Campbell, Joseph (1991), in 'The power of myth: Interviews with Bill Moyers', *Society Series*, Vol. 6, Second Edition, Basil Blackwell, Oxford.

Covin, T.J. and R.H. Kilmann (1990), 'Participant perceptions of positive and negative influences on large-scale change', *Group and Organization Studies*, Vol. 15, pp. 233–248.

Davis, Keith (1999), *Human Behaviour at Work*, Tata McGraw-Hill, New Delhi.

Dunphy, D.C. and D.A. Stace (1988), 'Transformational and coercive strategies for planned organizational change: Beyond the OD model', *Organizational Studies*, Vol. 9, pp. 317–334.

French, J.R.P. and B.H. Raven (1959), 'The bases of social power', in D. Cartwright (ed), *Studies in Social Power*, University of Michigan Press, Ann Abror.

French, W.L. (1990), *Human Resource Management*, Fourth Edition, Houghton Miffin, Boston.

Harold, Koontz, Cyril O'Donnell, and Heinz Weihrich (1993), *Essentials of Management*, Tata McGraw-Hill Publishing Company Limited, New Delhi.

Harp, H.T. (1994), 'Empowerment of mental health consumers in vocational rehabilitation', *Psychological Rehabilitation Journal*, Vol. 17, pp. 83–90.

House, R.J. and B. Shamir (1993), 'Toward the integration of transformational, charismatic, and visionary theories', in M.M. Chemers and R. Ayman (eds), *Leadership Theory and Research: Perspectives and Directions*, pp. 81–107), Academic Press, San Diego.

Kotter, John P. (1996), *Leading Change*, Harvard Business School Press, Boston, September.

Kouzes, James M. and Barry Z. Posner (1987), *The Leadership Challenge*, Jossey-Bass, San Francisco.

Lamb, L.F. and K.B. McKee (2004), *Applied Public Relations: Cases in Stakeholder Management*, Mahwah, Lawrence Erlbaum Associates, New Jersey.

Leon, Martel, (1986), *Mastering Change*, Simon & Schuster Inc, New York.

Lewin, K. (1947), 'Frontiers in group dynamics', *Human Relations*, Vol. 1, Issue 1, pp. 5–42.

Likert, R. (1967), *The Human Organisation*, McGraw-Hill, New York.

____ (1961), *New Patterns of Management*, Harper and Row, New York.

____ (1961), *New Patterns of Management*, McGraw-Hill, New York.

McClelland, D.C. and D.H Burnhan (1976), 'Power is the great motivator', *Harvard Business Review*, Vol. 54, No. 2, pp. 100–110.

McClelland, David C. (1961), *The Achieving Society*, Van Nostrand Co. Inc, Princeton.

McFarland, Lynne Joy, Larry E. Senn, and John R. Childress (1994), *21st Century Leadership: Dialogues with 100 Top Leaders*, The Leadership Press, New York.

Nadler, D.A. and M.L. Tushman (1990), 'Beyond the charismatic leader: Leadership and organizational change', *California Management Review*, Winter, pp. 77–97.

Oxfam (1995), *The Oxfam Handbook of Relief and Development*, Oxfam, Oxford.

Paul, Hersey, Kenneth H. Blanchard, and Dewey E. Johnson (2001), *Management of Organizational Behaviour—Leading Human Resources*, Pearson Education, New Delhi.

Porras, J.I. and S.J. Hoffer (1986), 'Common behaviour changes in successful organization development efforts', *Journal of Applied Behavioral Science*, Vol. 22, pp. 477–494.

Raven, B. and J. Rubin (1976), *Social Psychology: People in Groups*, Wiley, New York.

Riger, S. (1993), 'What's wrong with empowerment', *American Journal of Community Psychology*, Vol. 21, pp. 279–292.

Rowlands, J. (1995), *Empowerment Examined: Development in Practice*, Vol. 5, Issue 2, Oxfam, Oxford.

Savage, G.T., T.W. Nix, C.J. Whitehead, and J.D. Blair (1991), 'Strategies for assessing and managing organizational stakeholders', *Academy of Management Executive*, May, pp. 61–75.

Selznick, P. (1957), *Leadership and Administration*, Harper and Row, New York.

Stephen, Robbins P. (2005), *Organizational Behaviour*, Prentice Hall, New Delhi.

Tannenbaum, Robert, B. Irving, Weschler and Fred Massanick (1979), *Leadership and Organization*, McGraw-Hill, New York.

Terry, G. (1960), *The Principles of Management*, Richard Irwin Inc, Homewood, Ill.

Tichy, N. (1983), *Managing Strategic Change*, Wiley, New York.

Tyne, A. (1994), 'Taking responsibility and giving power', *Disability and Society*, Vol. 9, pp. 249–254.

UNDP (1995), *Human Development Report 1995*, Oxford University Press, Oxford.

Vecchio, Robert P. (1988), *Organizational Behaviour*, Dryden, Chicago.

Weber, M. (1947), *The Theory of Social and Economic Organization* (translated by A.M. Henderson and T. Parsons.), Free Press, New York.

Weber, Max (1947), *The Theory of Social and Economic Organization* (translated by A.M. Henderson and Talcott Parsons) Free Press, New York.

West, M. and W. Parent (1982), 'Consumer choice and empowerment in supported employment services: Issues and strategies', *Journal of Association for Persons with Handicaps*, Vol. 7, pp. 47–52.

7 Technology Management

Learning Objectives

After reading this chapter, you will be able to understand
- the concept of technology management
- various sociological issues in technology management
- strategic technology management
- human resource management and technology management
- technology planning and technology transfer
- various models of technology and their influence on organizational structure and design

Technology Investment at IFB Agro

IFB Agro is a chemical unit and produces rectified spirit, which is the core raw material for the liquor industry. This is done by processing industrial molasses, an agro-based product sourced from all over the world. The yield is highly dependent on the quality of the molasses. Rectified spirit is a controlled item and its production attracts excise duty.

The excise department in India levies duty based on the quantum of discharge on the pit. The volume of industrial molasses used in the production process determines this excise duty as there is no other suitable way to ascertain the chargeable duty on the yield, namely rectified spirit.

The company could not adjust its increased cost of production with the price of rectified spirit, as the price is controlled by the government. As a result, the company gradually became unviable, but due to the captive market privileges, it continued its production, hoping for a turnaround.

In the meantime, it received a notice from the pollution control department to install an effluent treatment plant (ETP) to reduce the carbon discharge to the environment. With its critical financial position, investment in ETP was impossible and the company decided to close down the operation. However, ETP vendors demonstrated how its installation could help the company to gain carbon deposits which could be put to profitable use. It realized that large pure carbon deposits can enable it to churn dry ice, which has a huge demand. Also, impure carbon can be used in other industrial applications. The residues too can be gainfully used as a high yielding manure.

With the use of new technology and installation of ETP, the company was ultimately able to turnaround, and from a sinking position, it rose to become an industry leader.

INTRODUCTION

The word 'technology' is often confused with diverse connotations in different commercial and industrial sectors. In the service sector, technology indicates information technology. In manufacturing, it means high-end machinery and equipment, which substitute the traditional manual work process. Yet from another perspective, technology is considered as a science and the outcome of research and development initiatives. In *Managing Technology for Corporate Success* (1970), Floyd defined technology as the practical application of scientific or engineering knowledge to the conception, development, or application of products or offerings, processes, or operations. Floyd further argued that technology is important for two critical reasons: (i) to achieve success in business and sustain competitive position, and (ii) to promote a culture of innovation through technology for long-term sustainability.

By achieving the first objective, organizations can achieve product or service differentiation, reduce costs, develop new business opportunities, and facilitate and support strategic change. By differentiating products and services, they can sustain their market share in a fiercely competitive market. Similarly, the use of technology also enables cost reduction. Organizations achieve this by acquiring new technology and integrating it through mergers and acquisitions. For example, Videocon achieved significant cost advantage in its colour television (CTV) production by acquiring Thomson's colour picture tube manufacturing technology and facilities, to remain one of the leaders in the market.

Technology also provides new business opportunities and organizations use it to drive new business. Raychem, a leader in radiation chemistry, used technology to successfully manipulate the physical properties of plastics, metals, and ceramics, leading to the introduction of memory metals, heat-resistant plastics, and specialized circuit protection devices. In India also, IFB Agro, a company that processes molasses to extract rectified spirit, used a specialized ETP to commercially exploit carbon deposition and convert it into dry ice. Today, its dry ice plant generates more revenue than its primary business of rectified spirit.

The second objective recommends the use of technology as a lever for strategic change. Hiving off its colour picture tube manufacturing facilities to Videocon is basically considered as Thomson's strategic move to LCD and plasma technology in manufacturing television sets.

Thus, using technology as a driver for organizational change, both for long-term and short-term objectives, is now more a strategic than just a technical issue. This *inter alia*, requires organizations to focus on people-related issues, considering technology as an ongoing process of change.

CONCEPT OF TECHNOLOGY MANAGEMENT

It is now clear that technology not only enhances the present competitive strength of an organization, but also creates opportunities for future growth. Thus, managing technology or technological change is an important area of concern for today's managers, who should have the vision for any investment in technology.

Innovation and technology management are intertwined. Innovation translates creative ideas into new products and services, which enhances the competitive advantage for an organization. Technology is concerned with the 'skill, knowledge, experience, tools, machines, computers, and the equipment used in the design, production, and distribution of goods and services'. Integrating innovation with technology ensures the application of technological change to products and organizations. Christensen (2003) defined technology as 'the processes by which an organization transforms labour, capital, materials, and information into products and services of a greater value'. Thus, this definition attributes innovation to a change in technology.

He added, 'Technology management is the field of study which imparts skills and knowledge designed to improve the entire process of technological change, and ranges from systems planning and design, to introduction, to evaluation of effectiveness.' Today's organization needs to manage technology, effectively integrating the human factors. The outcome is successful technological change, which enables the organization to use technology as a key driver to competitive advantage.

Technological issues in organizations encompass many concepts.

Sociological Issues in Technology Management

This aspect considers technology as the outcome of the social process, involving technology adopters (organization) and others (stakeholders) who are affected by their prevailing culture, political beliefs, and strategies. To effectively ensure technological change, the approach suggests and agreement on the social context and communication. Thus, it emphasizes innovation and communication, considering technology as a social system, and gradually adopting technological change over a period of time.

Innovation

Innovation aspects have been discussed in detail later in this chapter. Here, the focus is on some of the main attributes of innovative technology. These are relative advantage, compatibility, complexity, trialability, and observability. Relative advantage is a quantitative or qualitative measurement of innovation to understand the degree of change between the past and present innovation. If the present innovation is better, it receives an acceptance from the stakeholders and the organization also succeeds by ensuring quick adoption.

Compatibility of innovation studies the degree of consistency with the corporate value systems, past experiences, habits, and needs of the stakeholders. High compatibility ensures successful adoption, while low compatibility makes acceptance slower and even disrupts the organizational intent to achieve excellence through technology. Complexity in innovation arises due to difficulty in understanding and lack of user-friendliness. The greater the complexity, the slower is the acceptance. Trialability is the pilot testing of innovation to reduce the possible risk of technological change. Successful trials can ensure acceptance as people understand the outcome better. Observability is the degree of visibility of the outcome of technological change. A higher degree of observability means a better degree of acceptance.

Communication

Communication is the most important aspect in any technological change. Selecting the appropriate communication channels to convey the message to the receiver is a strategic decision for the organization. Whatever may be the communication channel, greater emphasis should be given to awareness. During a technological or even in a general change process, many organizations emphasize this aspect, increasing the spate of face-to-face communication, dedicating more executive time talking to people, clarifying their doubts, etc.

Social system

The social system, in the form of norms, opinion leaders, change agents, culture, political beliefs, laws, policies, etc., set the boundaries of innovation, within which the organization can bring about technological change. An incompatible social system leads to poor acceptance.

Time

Introducing, technological change in an organization in a gradual manner is not advisable because slowing the process of change reduces the opportunity to sustain competitive advantage. Therefore, the change process should be appropriately timed, bearing in mind also the degree of adaptability of the people.

Organizational Structure and Design

Technology also influences organizational structure and design. It alters the production process, systems, and even the skill sets of employees. Technology often renders workers and employees as supplementary to the production process. All this requires changes in the organizational structure. For example, in many manufacturing organizations, the production process is such that it empowers workers as independent process owners, so much so that they control their own jobs and require no supervision. The different models of technology are discussed in detail to elaborate on structure and design issues.

Economic Issues in Technological Change

In economic terms, technological change is considered from the viewpoint of feasibility in production. Hicks (1932) said that a technological change is called *Hicks neutral* when the ratio of capital's marginal product to labour's marginal product remains unchanged. Following Hicks, we have two more bifurcations of this concept, that is, Harrod neutral and Solow neutral. Harrod neutral says that if technology is labour-augmenting, it benefits labour; while Solow neutral believes that if technology is capital-augmenting, it benefits the capital (i.e., the investor).

STRATEGIC TECHNOLOGY MANAGEMENT

It is important for today's managers to learn the mechanism of successful technological change in organizations. There are three fundamental areas of practice, which facilitate technological change. First, organizations decide to work differently by quantitative assessment of performance, benchmarking against best practices, and duly appreciating stakeholders' needs. Second, they direct scarce resources to high-value uses by reengineering critical functions, and carefully controlling and evaluating expenditure through specific performance and cost measures. Third, they support major cost reduction and service improvement efforts with up-to-date professional skills, and organizational roles and responsibilities required to do the job. Managers ensure this by following certain steps, which are also considered as strategic technology management initiatives:

1. Recognize and communicate the urgency to change technology.
2. Get line management involved and create ownership.
3. Take action and maintain momentum.
4. Anchor strategic planning in customers' needs and mission goals.
5. Measure the performance of key mission delivery processes.
6. Focus on process improvement in the context of technology.
7. Manage technology as investments.
8. Integrate the planning, budgeting, and evaluation processes.
9. Establish customer–supplier relationships between line and technology vendors.
10. Position a chief technology officer to overview and manage the process of technological change.
11. Upgrade skills and knowledge of line professionals.

Strategic management of technological change requires involvement and commitment from the top. Top leadership should not only define business goals, but also initiate, mandate, and facilitate major changes in technology to support the achievement of these goals. They must appreciate the cost-benefit and risk-return trade-offs associated with the technology investments. It is also important to understand that new technology, per se, cannot improve business performance without first improving the operational process. New technology is a powerful tool to support the work processes and business decisions. Hence, if the existing work process itself is inefficient, technology cannot provide a substantive impact. Accomplishing dramatic improvements in performance usually requires streamlining or fundamentally redesigning existing work processes. Information technology projects must then be focused on improving the way the work is done rather than simply automating existing, outmoded processes.

> **Practice Assignment 7.1**
>
> Innovation is considered an important driver of technology management. Visit any organization and understand its innovative practices. Also indicate how such innovative practices translate into new technology selection.

Exhibit 7.1 illustrates how introducing new technology could enhance organizational effectiveness at Godrej.

EXHIBIT 7.1   Godrej—The Indian company who always believed in staying ahead

Godrej, like other Indian entrepreneurs, needed to subdue its change requirements at the organization level due to the reluctance of the nation as a whole, to change. A regulated economic regime literally overlooked the need to change. Customers were taken for a ride as they had to accept the shoddy products and services offered. Such inertia to change at the national level even cascaded to the individual or personal level. Attitudinally, Indians started to believe in the status quo and less commitment, and organizations too failed to promote the preferred work culture to bring about change in certain areas.

Notwithstanding all these, Godrej encouraged change from inception.

It made an extensive use of the *kaizen* systems and achieved significant increase in employee involvement and morale. With substantial cost savings, it became more flexible and was able to increase its capability to adapt to the changing needs of the environment. In terms of quantitative achievement, the company was able to reduce more than 70 per cent of its changeover time on the shop floors, and increase availability to pace manufacturing in tune with the needs of the market, while enjoying the privilege of economies of scale. It reduced its finished products and inventory holding by over 40 per cent by developing a quick market response system.

With the introduction of total productive maintenance, the company was able to reduce breakdowns, and cost of spares and repairs to about 50 per cent, from the pre-introduction phase. What is more startling is that it was able to make one of the high pressure boilers at the Vikhroli factory redundant by achieving efficiency in their energy consumption! Similarly, value analysis exercises reduced the cost of materials, while enhancing the quality of output. As in manufacturing, the company was able to bring positive changes in other functional areas, such as finance, marketing, and HR, promoting a culture of improvement. Today, employees look out for opportunities to make improvements and savings.

HUMAN RESOURCE MANAGEMENT AND TECHNOLOGY MANAGEMENT

Human resource management (HRM) has been defined as the 'process of attracting, developing, and maintaining a talented and energetic workforce to support the organizational mission, objectives, and strategies' (Schemerhorn 2001). Audretsch and Thurik (2000) argue that effective HRM practices are becoming increasingly important in the new 'knowledge-based' economy, as companies face the double challenge of the need for more highly trained employees coupled with a shortage of qualified labour.

The HR practices considered for technology management focus in the following areas:

- Human resource planning
- Systematic recruitment and selection
- Training and development programmes
- Written job description
- Regular performance appraisal
- Growth plans and strategies
- Management techniques (e.g., continuous improvement including TQM)
- Benchmarking

The advanced technologies which particularly affect the areas of organizational operations are as follows:

- Design and engineering
- Processing fabrication and assembly
- Automated material handling
- Inspection
- Integration and control
- Network communication

It is important for HR students to appreciate the nature of advanced technologies as these encompass HR practices and changing human resource development (HRD) initiatives. Advanced technologies, which are divided into the six major functional groups mentioned earlier, can further be categorized into specific areas of changes that are brought in through the technological inputs.

Design and Engineering

Changes in the design and engineering functions of an organization are implemented through the following technological reinforcement:

- Computer-aided design/engineering (CAD/CAE)
- Computer-aided design/manufacturing (CAD/CAM)
- Modelling or simulation technologies

Processing Fabrication and Assembly

In processing fabrication and assembly jobs, the following technological inputs are put into use:

- Flexible manufacturing cells or systems (FMC/FMS)
- Programmable logic control (PLC) machine(s) or process(es)
- Lasers used in materials processing (including surface modification)
- Robot(s) with sensing capabilities
- Robot(s) without sensing capabilities

High Speed Machining

High speed machining is now considered to be the most significant thrust area for an organization for achieving operational efficiency, and is ensured through the following technologies:

- Automated material handling
- Part identification for manufacturing automation, such as bar coding
- Automated storage and retrieval system (AS/RS)

Inspection

Inspection and quality checks are essential for every organization to sustain its competitive strengths. Technologies that facilitate this are as follows:

- Automated vision-based systems used for inspection/testing of inputs and/or final products
- Other automated sensor-based systems used for inspection/testing of inputs and/or final products

Integration and Control

On one hand, integration and control facilitates alignment with the organizational goals and objectives, and on the other, they ensure timely intervention to correct any deviation from the plan. Integration and control functions are enforced through the following technologies:

- Manufacturing resource planning/enterprise resource planning (MRP II/ERP)
- Computer(s) used for control on the factory floor
- Computer integrated manufacturing (CIM)
- Supervisory control and data acquisition (SCADA)
- Use of inspection data in manufacturing control
- Digital remote controlled process plant control

Network Communications

Effective network communications facilitate better coordination and enforce efficiency in organizational activities. Technologies used in network communications are as follows:

- Local area network (LAN) for engineering/production
- Company-wide computer networks (including Intranet and WAN)
- Inter-company computer networks (including Extranet and EDI)

Thus, it is clear that technologies are not just limited to the production and operation functions of an organization, but are extended to all areas, including the managerial and strategic functions. Therefore, technology should be considered an important driver for organizational growth and efficiency. And, bringing in technological change is only possible with appropriate HR intervention and with a focus on HRD issues. Exhibit 7.2 emphasizes the integration of systems with technological growth.

According to a new study by the Chartered Institute of Personnel and Development (CIPD), UK, while technology may increase productivity and efficiency it can also have a negative effect on employees, such as, a feeling of being trapped, alienated, overworked, and vulnerable. As per this report, new technologies may alienate workers because the lack of face-to-face interaction can increase work intensity, 'de-skill' manual labour by replacing traditional skills, increase surveillance and control through electronic monitoring, and create health and safety problems, such as, eye strain, backaches, and repetitive motion injuries. CIPD, therefore, suggests getting HR help in the design and implementation of new technologies.

EXHIBIT 7.2 Business growth with technology intensive HR systems at India Retail

India Retail is one of the top retail chains in India and now wants to achieve 100 per cent growth in its business. However, the company's HR support is centralized at the store level and the store manager looks after some administrative and HR issues. As store managers are always busy achieving business results, they often neglect HR issues, which ultimately leads to serious problems.

The major problem areas are irregularities in the attendance data, incomplete leave information, discrepancies in HR reports, pay-related discrepancies, mismanagement of travel expenses, and lesser focus on HRD-related activities. These have a direct bearing on the critical performance metrics of the company.

By introducing technology-intensive human resource management systems (HRMS), the company was able to automate HR systems at the store level, requiring store managers to spend only half an hour to file a report in a structured computerized format. This gives them a systematic feedback as well as suggestions to look into the deviating areas of performance and HR management.

With the introduction of technology-intensive HRMS, the company was able to successfully implement its HR policies and procedures at the store level, and also plan its HR interventions to support the business growth plan.

'It is up to HR to highlight these choices and to work with designers and implementers of new technologies to ensure there is a balance between empowerment and control,' said Graeme Martin. The major problem with organizations is that they do not involve HR in the design and implementation of new technology. However, involving HR makes employees more proactive in the change process and is therefore desirable.

> **Practice Assignment 7.2**
>
> It is now accepted that technology issues have HR ramifications. Select a particular organization and study how its HR participates in technology-related decisions. Develop your report accordingly.

TECHNOLOGY PLANNING

A technology plan serves as a bridge between established standards and organizational practices. It articulates, organizes, and integrates the content and processes of operation in appropriate technologies. It facilitates multiple levels of strategy, policy, and decision-making, and allows for resource allocations. Technology planning is an ongoing process, and translates organizational policy and technology needs into concrete actions. It allows organizations to take advantage of technology innovations while minimizing the negative impact of unexpected challenges. Technology planning provides a roadmap for the implementation of technology and can result in more efficient expenditure of limited resources, and improvement in organizational performance.

However, a technology plan by itself is not enough to ensure change. It is the processes of technology plan development, implementation, and evaluation, which are considered to be essential components of an organizational improvement plan. A well-designed technology plan is a dynamic tool providing guidance for innovation. Technology plans also represent opportunities for dialogue and professional development that encourage organizational decision-making.

Principles of Technology Planning

The basic principles of technology planning involve selecting a model and then moving the process forward. It is most helpful when used within a larger planning process and not simply as an add-on or one-time discussion. According to Hopey and Harvey–Morgan (1995), a good technology planning process can be summed up in the following six basic principles:

1. It should be organized and considered as a continuous process. It should use a simple, straightforward planning model, and result in a document that shows how technology is used to improve operations, management, assessment, and

communication. Organizations do this by taking into account their mission and philosophy, and prevailing systems and processes.
2. Be broad but realistic in scope, with economical and technically feasible solutions.
3. Involve all the stakeholders and technology experts.
4. Identify the strengths and weaknesses of the organization, and how each will impact the implementation of technology.
5. Formalize the procedures and methods for making technology decisions, including the setting of priorities and the purchase, evaluation, upgrading, and use of technology.
6. Be driven by organizational goals and objectives rather than by technological developments.

Technology Transfer

The term 'technology transfer' is used to describe a formal transferring of new discoveries and innovations resulting from scientific research conducted at universities, to the commercial sector. One way in which universities do this is through patenting and licensing new innovations. The major steps in this process include (i) the disclosure of innovations, (ii) patenting the innovation concurrent with publication of scientific research, and (iii) licensing the rights to innovations to industry for commercial development.

Technology transfer is the process by which basic technologies are developed into practical and commercially relevant applications and products. It evaluates and manages invention portfolios, oversees patent prosecution, and negotiates licensing agreements. Technology transfer activities include processing and evaluating invention disclosures, filing for patents, technology marketing, licensing, protecting intellectual property arising from research activity, assisting in creating new businesses, and promoting the success of existing firms. The results of these activities are new products, more jobs of a higher quality, and an expanded economy. The important elements of technology transfer functions are as follows:

Coordinate

Coordinating between technology users and developers, and researchers and manufactures is an important element of technology transfer. Access to relevant internal and external resources to individual projects and enterprises improves coordination.

Nurture

Proper nurturing moves technology from a research stage to an organizational usage, providing new business opportunities and entrepreneurship. An effective process of nurturing provides guidance, counselling, and resources.

Link

At this stage, the technology transfer group catalogues resources related to business enterprises and connects future entrepreneurs, researchers, and other technology developers to help pioneer new products, companies, etc. Such linkages provide referrals for individual business counselling, sources of financing, or the names of individuals who can help with a particular facet of business development.

Technology Innovation

In an organization, technological innovation leads to increased productivity, quality, sustainability, etc. As an intermediary, HR influences the pace of technological innovation, and increases employees' competencies, commitment, organizational learning, cohesiveness, etc. Successful innovation requires (bundles of) specific personnel, and organizational interventions or practices. Definitions of innovation include the process of making improvements by introducing something new, such as a new idea, method, or device, or the successful exploitation of new ideas that create a new dimension of performance. In economic terms, the change must increase either the customer value or the producer value. Innovations are intended to make someone better off and a succession of innovations provides growth to the whole economy.

The term, 'innovation' may refer to both the radical or incremental changes to products, processes, or services, or to solving a problem. In recent years, technology has done this quite well. Innovation is an important topic in the study of economics, business, technology, sociology, and engineering. As it is also considered to be a major driver of the economy, the factors that lead to innovation are critical to policy makers. In the organizational context, innovation may be linked to performance and growth through improvements in efficiency, productivity, quality, competitive positioning, market share, etc.

All organizations can innovate; however, while innovation typically adds value, it may also have a negative or destructive effect as new developments clear away or change old organizational forms and practices. Organizations that embrace innovation may destroy those that do not do so effectively.

Technology and Organizational Design

Technology as a situation aspect of organizational design has already been discussed in Chapter 1. Here, we will concentrate on some models that suggest consideration of technology factors as a situational variable for organizational design. Technology is the outcome of knowledge, equipment, and work processes used by organizations, and should not be construed merely as machines and equipment. It is a major factor for improving the quality of work. The type of technology an organization selects is an important determinant for organizational design and structure.

According to Pettigrew et al. (2003), organizational design is also influenced by technology. In fact, with the advancement of information technology, companies all over the world are now experimenting with various organizational designs to achieve the right fit with their strategies. Globally, many automobile manufacturers now focus on customized car designs to consolidate their market share. Traditionally, automobile manufacturers follow an assembly line-based production process, as every aspect of manufacturing is standardized and requires groups of workers to perform only some routine jobs at their individual workstations. However, to accommodate customized designs, automobile manufacturers are turning to a matrix structure. Due to the influence of technology, TCS also now follows an MIS approach in organizational design. At the corporate level it follows the functional structure, but at the operations level, it uses a matrix structure to accommodate the specific needs of its customers. Daft and Lewin (1990) defined organizational design as formal architecture, culture, strategy, and employment relationships. Lewin and Stephens (1994) stated that a macro property of an organization is a part of its organizational design.

We will now review two well-known models that illustrate how technology influences the organization as a whole, including its design.

Thompson's model

In 1967, James Thompson developed three classifications for technology: (i) intensive technology, (ii) mediating technology, and (iii) long-linked technology. Intensive technology is developed keeping in view a high level of uncertainty. It helps to produce the desired outcomes even in uncertain situations. Let us assume that a particular organization uses traditional dedicated technology to produce certain items, say, long-playing record players. Suddenly, customers change their taste and preferences, and switch to CDs or DVDs. This will render long-playing records obsolete. The organization will suffer as their investments in technology cannot be salvaged. However, if the organization had used intensive technology (such as flexible technology, CNC, etc.), this situation of technological obsolescence could have been avoided. Intensive technology makes workers interdependent and creative, and capable of solving their work-related problems through mutual coordination. It makes organizations more flexible in decision-making, rather than emphasizing decisions that are standard operating procedure (SOP) bound.

Mediating technology brings together individuals and/or groups to seek a mutually beneficial exchange of values. This form of technological environment is more applicable in the service industry, such as banks, financial institutions, etc.

Long-linked technology is appropriate for mass production processes, such as an automobile assembly line. It depends on highly specialized tasks in a closely controlled sequence of activities to produce the final product.

According to Thompson's model, each type of technology has specific bearings on the design and structure of the organization.

Woodward's study

Joan Woodward (1965), with her team of researchers, studied about 100 organizations in England during the 1960s to establish the linkage between the size and structure of organizations. However, they could not establish any such relationship. In their follow-up study, they found some relationship between the structure and three basic forms of technology, which they categorized as (i) small batch production technology, (ii) large batch or mass production technology, and (iii) continuous process production technology.

Small batch production technology is suitable for the production of few varieties of productions, primarily to meet the specific requirements of customers. Organizations create such facilities in order to cater to specialized demands for the defence sector. In some cases, they may demand an initial technology development cost from the customer, as such investments are dedicated only for meeting customer-specific demands.

Long batch or mass production technology is used for producing large volumes of standardized products to cater to the demand for the larger market. Such organizations automate or mechanize their production facilities, with workers being complimentary to the equipment. This type of technology helps in handling a large volume of production of high quality goods, which may require dangerous or even monotonous operations. Technology in the automobile assembly line is a good example of this.

Continuous process production technology is a completely mechanized form of production, where machines undertake all the jobs, leaving people free to focus on quality inspection and adjustment, monitoring, etc. Such technology is used in most chemical processing units, such as petroleum refineries, and chemical and nuclear power plants, where production and processing continue uninterruptedly.

From an organizational design point of view, differences in technology have different connotations. For example, more complex technology (such as continuous process) creates tall organizational structures that require more supervision and coordination. Similarly, the span of management of lower-level managers increases from small batch to mass production, and decreases from mass production to continuous process production. Also, with more technological complexity, support staff functions increase and organizations become top heavy (more managers).

SUMMARY

The effective implementation of technology is a key driver to organizational success. Technology manifests its usage in various economic and sociological issues, and all these issues deserve the attention of managers. Organizational plans and programmes suffer without proper technology management. But technology alone cannot solve all the problems; there must be a balance between technology and human intervention. It is important for HR managers to understand broadly the various technology management issues. In fact, technology today has changed the face of HR entirely, requiring the reinvention of HR, and HR professionals are now required to act as change agents in technology management.

Technology Management

KEY TERMS

Design and engineering These bring changes in the design and engineering functions of an organization, and are enforced through technological reinforcement.

Network communications These facilitate better coordination and enforce efficiency in organizational activities.

Technological innovation It leads to increased productivity, quality, and sustainability in an organization.

Technology management It is the field of study which imparts skills and knowledge designed to improve the entire process of technological change.

Technology planning It serves as a bridge between established standards and organizational practice.

Technology transfer It describes a formal transfer of new discoveries and innovations resulting from scientific research conducted at universities to the usage in the commercial sector.

CONCEPT REVIEW QUESTIONS

1. Explain why we need to understand technology management.
2. What are the sociological issues involved in technology management?
3. Explain how HR issues integrate with technology management.
4. What is technology planning? How is it done in an organization?
5. Explain the important elements of technology transfer.
6. Write short notes on the following:
   (a) Innovation
   (b) Technology transfer
   (c) Technology planning
   (d) Technology management
   (e) Economic issues of technology management

CRITICAL THINKING QUESTIONS

1. Your organization is a well-known technology provider in the country. You are looking after the technology transfer protocols. Your organization believes that technology transfer should not be absolute and outright. You have been assigned the task of drafting a technology transfer agreement for one of the clients. Draft the agreement.
2. List out the critical HR issues involved in technology transfer cases. How can such issues be resolved?
3. Using the concept of technology innovation, explain how your organization can embrace the process of technological change as an ongoing issue.
4. Explain with some recent case examples to show how technology benefits an organization.

CASE STUDY

Strategic Technological Management to Gain Market—Lifeboat's Experience

In the present business environment, technological change is taking place so fast that it is now a moving target for organizations to chase. Lifeboat is an offshoot of India's largest public sector bank, selling life insurance policies. All along, its strategic focus had been captivating customers with brand value. The premium rate is not competitive but people repose their trust in Lifeboat as it enjoys the highest brand value in India. Bank assurance is the most convenient route for selling insurance policies. Lifeboat enjoys the highest customer conversion rate among its competitors. However, its business growth is still lagging behind. Data mining with technology support is the biggest challenge for the insurance companies.

It is quite usual for the industry to track data using the opportunistic method, that is, interacting with the suppliers of the competitors, attending trade shows, sales meetings, seminars, and conferences of competitors, recruiting their ex-employees, having discussions with shared distributors, social contacts, etc. Potential customers are tapped using professional tele-salespeople and then persuaded to buy insurance policies. Lifeboat, however, discarded this approach and introduced technology-intensive data tracking systems, linking the large customer base of its bank, with targeted potential customers. In addition, the systems also track those who file their tax returns through the bank's counters, but are not account holders.

In the next phase, the company installed free debit/credit card swiping machines at retail malls, large restaurants, hotels, airline booking counters, railway ticket booking counters, etc. It was not so easy for it to get permission for this, but with financial incentives, the move was largely successful. Information on any credit or debit card swiped through these machines was automatically stored in the central database. After careful study, these were clustered into groups and then targeted to market their product. This was more beneficial than incurring huge advertisement expenses like their competitors. Thus, strategic use of technology helped it to gain a better marketing edge over its competitors.

Theoretically, strategic technology management requires an organization to follow certain steps. The first step is obviously, to ensure selection of the right players. The next step is understanding the available infrastructure and its applications. The third step is to evaluate current opportunities, and the last step is to break the priority into a series of actionable tasks that have to be accomplished within a time-bound programme.

Accordingly, the company opted for strategic management of technological change, breaking their tasks into three distinct phases as follows:

- *Market entry phase* for rapid market penetration to gain the economies of scale.
- *Innovation phase* to drive the change to achieve low cost, while ensuring value addition.
- *Commodity phase* to drive cost control to ensure the survival of the company.

In the Lifeboat case, all these steps were followed and the sequences of marketing chalked out. The process worked well and today Lifeboat enjoys the highest customer conversion rate among its competitors.

Lifeboat is now more innovative in data mining to increase its customer base. It has now introduced a customers' referral scheme, which gives existing customers certain privileges for every conversion of its referred customer, which is called customer partnering model. The latest tracking of potential customers is being done through Internet scanning, introducing the latest email management software from an internationally acclaimed vendor. The system efficiently tracks potential customers, scanning through mails it receives from existing customers and people in general. As the volume of mail is quite large, the email tracker segregates it and provides a list of potential customers, based on certain checks and balances.

Thus, Lifeboat is a perfect example of the use of technology-intensive marketing tool to sustain and grow in a competitive market.

Discussion Question
Read the above case. Study the technological change in any manufacturing industry and frame your observation to transform its manufacturing process.

Hints: Change from mono-casting to continuous-casting, from conventional lathe to CNC lathe (for machining of jobs), from hot metal hardening process to cold-swaging process, etc.

REFERENCES

Audretsch, David B. and A. Roy Thurik (2001), 'What's new about the new economy?' *Industrial and Corporate Change*, Vol. 1, No. 1, Oxford University Press, UK.

Bhattacharyya, D.K. (2007), *Human Resource Research Methods*, Oxford University Press, New Delhi.

_____ (2006), *Human Resource Management*, Second Edition, Excel Books, New Delhi.

Chartered Institute of Personnel and Development (CIPD), www.cipd.co.uk/bookstore, accessed on 8 July 2009.

Christensen, Clayton M. (2003), *The Innovator's Dilemma: The Revolutionary Book that will Change the Way You Do Business*, HarperCollins, New York.

Daft, R.L. and A.Y. Lewin (1990), 'Can organization studies begin to break out of the normal science straitjacket? An editorial essay', *Organization Science*, Vol. 1, pp. 1–9.

Hicks, J.R. (1932), *The Theory of Wages*, Macmillan, London.

Hinnings, C.R. and R. Greenwood (2002), 'Disconnects and consequences in organization theory', *Administrative Science Quarterly*, Vol. 47, Issue 3, pp. 411–421.

Hopey, C.E. and Harvey–Morgan J. (1995), *Technology Planning in Adult Literacy*, University of Pennsylvania, National Center on Adult Literacy, Philadelphia.

Kuhn, Thomas Samuel (1996), *The Structure of Scientific Revolutions*, Third Edition, University of Chicago Press, Illinois.

Lewin, A.Y. and C.U. Stephens (1994), 'CEO attitudes as determinants of organizational design: An integrated model', *Organization Studies*, Vol. 15, No. 2, pp. 183–212.

Pettigrew, A.M., R. Whittington, L. Melin, C. Sanchez-Runde, F. Van den Bosch, W. Ruigrok, and T. Numagami (2003), *Innovative Forms of Organizing International Perspectives*, Sage, London.

Rogers, Everett (2003), *Diffusion of Innovations*, Fifth Edition, Free Press, New York.

Schermerhorn, R.R. (2001), Management, John Wiley & Sons, New York.

Thompson, James (1967), *Organizations in Action*, McGraw-Hill, New York.

Weick, K.E. (1999), 'Theory construction as disciplined reflexibility: Trade-offs in the 90s', *Academy of Management Review*, Vol. 24, pp. 797–806.

Woodward, Joan (1965), *Industrial · Organization: Theory and Practice*, Oxford University Press, London.

http://www.research.cornell.edu/cotaba.html accessed on 27 July 2008.

8 Technology and Culture

> **Learning Objectives**
>
> After reading this chapter, you will be able to understand
> - the concept of culture
> - proactive manufacturing culture and how it is different from reactive manufacturing culture
> - the interface between technology and cultural issues
> - the influence of culture at the workplace
> - the process of transition from a reactive to a proactive culture
> - the steps in the technology transition process

Fusion of Technology and Culture at XYZ Co.

Today, all technology-empowered service providers including public utility services are required to give definite deadlines to deliver any service. Technology-empowered manufacturing organizations also have to meet deadlines as per the customers' requirements.

XYZ Co. is a global consumer electronics company with a presence in multilingual cultures and countries. It does not believe in outsourcing its customer services; it rather focuses on direct customer services with a 24 x 7 helpline.

With a market presence in multilingual cultures, XYZ enables customers to log complaints in their own language. The automated language interpreter registers the complaint and immediately answers back with a promise to confirm and rectify the issue within two hours. The complaints are then routed to the concerned department for quick action. This has made XYZ accessible to global customers anytime and anywhere.

XYZ's technology empowered customer service systems are tracked regularly with their e-CRM system, making the company a truly customer-driven organization. Today, XYZ understands the pulse of its customers even before they spell out their problems. This has been possible because of its employees' belief in the system and by making the customer its first priority. A proactive technology-empowered customer service system has helped the company to captivate its customers.

INTRODUCTION

A proactive manufacturing culture backed by technological advancement is an organizational weapon for gaining competitive advantage. However, without the interface of human factors, particularly human resource development (HRD) aspects, technological change is bound

> **EXHIBIT 8.1 Technology edge at CSR**
>
> Cambridge Silicon Radio (CSR) Ltd, the founder of Bluetooth chips, was able to achieve their market supremacy through technology. A 2.4 GHz, single-chip bluetooth device with integrated circuit for radio signal communication has revolutionized mobile telephones and communication systems.
>
> CSR was able to position the product, taking advantage of the fastest growing global market. It significantly achieved the market share by establishing a global value chain, and positioning over 1000 employees in the UK, US, Sweden, Denmark, France, Korea, China, Taiwan, and Japan.

to fail. Technological change and organizational improvement initiatives require a thrust in organizational change, which by default requires change in HRD initiatives. Thus, the traditional assumption that technology, per se, can enhance competitive advantage is not tenable. When an organization best utilizes its resources, it gains competitive advantage. Indisputably, productivity and quality are important for successful organizational performance. Quality improves revenue and profit, but to sustain it, organizations need to focus on HRD.

Technology creates wealth and helps to sustain jobs, and is central to our economic growth. That technology brings positive changes in the organization by significantly altering its profitability is evident from the success of CSR Ltd, a UK-based telecommunication company (see Exhibit 8.1).

Before we proceed to the broader aspects of technology and organizational change issues, we need to discuss certain basic concepts and understand how technology management has a cultural interface.

CULTURE AND ORGANIZATIONS

'Corporate culture' has been defined as 'the act of developing intellectual and moral faculties, especially through education'. The other definition of culture is 'the moral, social, and behavioural norms of an organization based on the beliefs, attitudes, and priorities of its members'. Although the first definition stresses on building culture through education, this is relevant largely in corporates that have their own unique system of emphasizing continuous learning. Many of them have their own universities, such as Sears University, Hamburger University of McDonald's, Motorola University, etc.

In India, only a few organizations focus on building a corporate culture of their own. Still, every organization has its own unique culture or value set. While some may create it consciously through induction, in others it may be unconsciously created primarily based on the value systems of the top people or the promoter.

Let us consider the example of Hewlett-Packard (HP). It successfully created a conscious corporate culture, called 'The HP Way'. HP's corporate culture is based

> **EXHIBIT 8.2 Southwest Airlines**
>
> Southwest Airlines is one of the most profitable airlines in the US. Its CEO, Herb Kelleher, defines the Southwest culture as follows:
>
> 'Well, first of all, it starts with hiring. We are zealous about hiring. We are looking for a particular type of person, regardless of which job category it is. We are looking for attitudes that are positive and for people who can lend themselves to causes. We want folk who have a good sense of humour, and people who are interested in performing as a team and take joy in team results instead of individual accomplishments. ...If you start with the type of person you want to hire, presumably you can build a workforce that is prepared for the culture you desire.
>
> Another important thing is to spend a lot of time with your people and to communicate with them in a variety of ways. And a large part of it is demeanour. Sometimes we tend to lose sight of the fact that demeanour—the way you appear and the way you act—is a form of communication. We want our people to feel fulfilled and to be happy, and we want our management to radiate the demeanour that we are proud of our people, we are interested in them as individuals, and we are interested in them outside the workforce, including the good and bad things that happen to them as individuals.'
>
> *Source:* www.southwest.com, accessed on 8 March 2009.

on (i) respect for others, (ii) a sense of community, and (iii) plain hard work (*Fortune*, 15 May 1995). This conscious culture development is sustained through extensive training of managers and all cross sections of employees. Today HP's growth and success may be traced only to their corporate culture. Exhibit 8.2 further illustrates this as a consciously-driven culture development.

An example of a more down-to-earth corporate culture is that of Sears, the second largest retail chain in the world. Sears emphasizes three Cs—compelling place to work, compelling place to shop, and compelling place to invest. It believes that this culture, when practised, takes into account the overall growth and prosperity of the organization. Incidentally, it also aligns its performance management system with the three Cs. Similarly, Wal-Mart, the largest retail chain in the world, also believes that all the employees are its associates and, therefore, as a matter of corporate culture and practices, it shares all strategic information with employees to benefit from empowerment and motivation. Wal-Mart achieves a significant rate of growth every year.

These examples illustrate how developing and sustaining a conscious culture in the organization can contribute to growth and prosperity. Corporate culture as a separate branch of management has received priority due to globalization, consequent mobility of people, and cross-cultural influences, particularly in multinational and transnational organizations.

Exhibit 8.3 lists the various applications of culture at the workplace.

EXHIBIT 8.3 Culture and its applications at the workplace

- Mergers and acquisitions
- Strategic alliances and partnerships
- Restructuring issues
- Change management
- Self-development processes
- People management skills
- Executive coaching
- Negotiation skills
- Multinational/remote/team building
- Facilitating top teams
- Project teams
- Expatriate coaching
- Sales and marketing skills
- General management training and education
- Counselling
- Leadership
- Organizational influencing

PROACTIVE AND REACTIVE TECHNOLOGICAL CULTURES

Technology and cultural issues have to be considered from different perspectives. Organization-wise, we can see variations in process design, how it is organized, and what equipment is used. However, culture-wise there is hardly any variation in areas, such as process monitoring and control, problem solving, and product quality. The existing technological culture in an organization may drive discipline; it may be well-planned, and effective for problem solving and defect prevention. One culture may provide the optimum results and the highest probability of satisfied customers, while another may result in customer dissatisfaction. Dissatisfied customers then look for other suppliers or vendors, resulting in a drop in sales. Today's customers expect consistent results and performance from their suppliers.

Two basic cultures, specific to technological issues, include a reactive technological culture and a proactive technological culture. To determine the type of culture that exists in an organization and also in a particular operation, we examine whether the organization monitors the process or the product. When the organization monitors the product, the culture is reactive in nature. Here, the organization emphasizes on finding defects. In contrast, when the organization monitors the process, it is a proactive culture because such organizations focus on preventing the defect before it arises. A proactive technological culture can only be developed and sustained through HRD.

Proactive Technological Culture

A proactive technological culture has several distinguishable characteristics. First, it focuses on prevention of defects before they occur. Second, proactive technological cultures never slow down the process improvement efforts. To make their process improvement efforts continuous, organizations adopt such programmes with specific, well-established goals. They consider quality and cycle time improvement to be an unending journey. Hence, they re-establish their goals with a focus on continuous improvement. Obviously, people working in such organizations undergo sustained HRD activities, such as training-in-process development, statistics, problem solving, project management, and new product design. Hence, the organization understands customer requirements and the desired improvement plans to sustain a high level of customer satisfaction. It acknowledges that customers are inseparable from their operation and does its best for customer integration with its business and operational plans.

Other characteristics of a proactive technological culture are as follows:

1. It invests in training its operators, supervisors, managers, engineers, and technicians in statistical process control (SPC), design of experiments (DOE), design for manufacturability (DFM), problem solving, etc.
2. It uses DOE to identify and quantify critical operating parameters or critical success factors (CSF), using statistical tools such as SPC to monitor the process.
3. It continuously monitors the process to initiate corrective action.
4. It monitors the process to prevent defects and not to find defects that have already arisen.
5. It minimizes non-value added activity. One such activity is process inspection.
6. It is focused on using timely data to drive continuous improvement.
7. It does not solve the same problems every day.
8. It involves all functions in the operation to brainstorm, evaluate, and implement effective process improvements.

Identifying proactive technological culture

Despite detailing the importance and significance of a proactive technological culture, it is not easy to identify and evaluate whether such a culture exists in an organization or not. This is perhaps due to the many constructs of proactivity that extends even to individual areas of operation. Exhibit 8.4 presents guidelines for assessment of a proactive technological culture.

TRANSITION FROM REACTIVE TO PROACTIVE TECHNOLOGICAL CULTURE

After evaluating an organization, we need to plan its transition from a reactive to a proactive technological culture. The transition process is a long journey and requires the full, active participation of management, and a great deal of dedication and work from everyone in the organization. However, the steps and processes vary from one organization to another, depending largely on their prevailing culture. While it is always desirable to involve all members of the organization to manage its own process of transition, at times outside expertise can be sought. The transition process requires a study of the following areas of the organization:

EXHIBIT 8.4 Assessing a proactive technological culture

Answering the following questions may help to assess the proactivity of a culture:

- To what extent does the organization focus on preventing or finding defects?
- How far is the organization focused on preventing defects or finding defects?
- Are the managers experts in preventing or finding defects?
- Do managers enforce control over organizational processes or is it the other way round, that is, the process controls the managers?
- Do they regularly discover the root cause of problems and initiate permanent corrective actions?
- Do managers adopt a formal problem solution approach by initiating defect prevention or do they try to escape from the customer after identifying the problem?
- To what extent are managers required to handle regular crisis management?
- Is the nature of problems regular?
- Do managers train and 'coach' operators, engineers, technicians, supervisors, etc. to understand the entire process, and to identify and solve problems?
- Do they use formal statistical tools (DOE) to identify and quantify critical operating parameters?
- To what extent do managers use formal problem-solving tools to solve problems?
- To what extent do they institutionalize problem-solving and corrective actions to ensure perpetuation of such practices?
- Do managers seek and use all available information and inputs from all levels of the organization, including suppliers and customers, to develop the optimum solutions to problems?
- Do they know how the process is performing at any particular point of time?
- To what extent managers are busy to use formal tools for developing and implementing processes and solving problems?
- Is the manufacturing operation organized in the most efficient manner and does it provide the correct resources for a particular need in the shortest possible time?
- Does the organization have both organizational and personal goals that are aimed at continuous improvement of the operation's performance and satisfy customers?
- Are these goals supported, coached, and reviewed by the management on a regular basis?
- Are customer feedbacks and suggestions used to drive corrective actions and used in process improvement projects?
- What does the customer want?
- What makes the organization win over competition?
- Does the organization have any specific detailed measurable process improvement goals and projects to achieve these goals?
- Can the organization identify the most critical elements of business operation that must be evaluated and measured to ensure that it is performing at an optimum level?
- What are the standards (metrics) for evaluating the efficiency of the manufacturing operation?
- On what basis does the organization decide and evaluate improvements, and implement this to provide the largest possible return?
- Does the organization make use of information to create a culture of continuous improvement?
- How do managers know that the implemented improvement programmes are effective and can achieve the predicted results?
- What do managers do to move to the next level of the manufacturing operation performance?

> **Practice Assignment 8.1**
>
> Use the questionnaire above and study the technological culture of any organization, based on interview responses. Use detailed explanatory notes, graphs, charts, and also some quantitative details to illustrate your findings.

Existing Manufacturing Systems

In the transition from a reactive to a proactive technology and manufacturing operation culture, the operation must first be considered as a manufacturing system. This will ensure that all the areas and issues to be evaluated are being considered. Elevation to a proactive manufacturing culture is not possible without taking a holistic view.

A 'technology system' is defined as 'the collective plans, activities, and events that are provided to ensure that products, processes, and services will satisfy given customer requirements'. The key point in considering a technology operation is to evaluate it as a system. All the factors that impact the output of a manufacturing system must be evaluated. The formal consideration and classification of the manufacturing system must include all activities that will influence the cycle time and yield of the process. It focuses on environmental safety, and housekeeping issues, new technology and product introduction, training, etc.

However, no manufacturing operation can stay competitive if it does not continually strive to improve its cycle time and yield, and the goals of the people that support the process should, therefore, be focused on this. These goals should influence their compensation and/or advancement opportunities. Exhibit 8.5 outlines all the dimensions that are used to study the manufacturing system.

The HR department has to help the operations people to view manufacturing operations as a system. Conventionally, the manufacturing function is organized with different individuals being responsible for different parts of the system. This results in conflicting goals as the organizational structure is developed with individual-centred responsibility. For example, marketing people may consider maximum order booking, improving the top line of the organization.

But the manufacturing division may fail to accommodate the increased orders. This happens because the job scheduling and order bookings are done independently without integrating both the functions with a systems approach. A reverse may also occur where the shop floor may remain idle due to the absence of orders from the marketing department.

Therefore, manufacturing improvement goals should be developed from a manufacturing system perspective, integrating the cross-functional areas.

It is now well-recognized that culture and technology are interdependent. Culture forms an important aspect in technology design, development, and utilization.

EXHIBIT 8.5 Studying manufacturing systems

As stated, a manufacturing system includes all factors and areas that impact the performance of the operation. It is difficult to develop an all-inclusive list of such factors. However, the following factors are commonly used to study the manufacturing system of any organization:

1. Process development
2. Process control
3. Process design
4. Process layout
5. Process flow
6. Process line balancing
7. Process optimization programme
8. Process tooling and fixtures
9. Process technical support
10. Process documentation and documentation control
11. Process capacity versus required capacity
12. Process scheduling and job sequencing
13. Process set up and changeover procedure
14. Operator responsibility, training, and efficiency
15. Relating process goals to personal goals
16. Management process support and performance review
17. Supplier relationships
18. Material control
19. Material flow and availability
20. Material handling
21. Preventive maintenance programme and schedule
22. Calibration control and schedule
23. Continuous improvement programme and goals
24. Industry and process benchmarking programme
25. Product design for manufacturing review process
26. New product introduction process
27. Model and prototype process and scheduling
28. Engineering change order process
29. Environmental requirements and control
30. Critical process parameter development and control

Technological changes lead to adjustments at three levels: individual, social organization, and cultural value system. Therefore, technology must be in congruence with the culture; rather, it must complement the culture. Even sociologists regard technology as part of the culture and among the inherited artefacts, goods, technical processes, ideas, habits, and values.

According to Alrusheidat (2006), some of the culture-related ergonomic aspects are as follows:

Interface design This relates to the use of human emotions in product design. It is concerned with factors, such as colour and shape. Culture-wise, the perception of colour differs. For example, red indicates danger in western countries, while it symbolizes happiness in China.

Control/display compatibility This indicates spatial movement of control and refers to the user's expectation of the stimulus–response relationship. A compatible system considers perceptual-motor behaviour, that is, differences in reading or scanning habits.

Workplace design Suitable workplace design eliminates harmful postures and improves user performance in relation to the user's biological needs, preferences, and task requirements. Variations in preferred posture influence the machine and workplace design and results into improvement in the operator's efficiency and comfort.

Design of protective equipment There are psychological and physical constraints with regard to wearing protective clothing. Some cultures may prohibit the use of helmets.

Similar culture congruent ergonomic features that influence technology could be a selection of software systems, work organization and management, design of maintenance systems, design of shift work schedules, flexibility in work schedules, etc.

> **Practice Assignment 8.2**
>
> Visit any organization and study its technological transition process. List the steps it follows and make a critical review of them.

Steps in the Technology Transitioning Process

After covering the dimensions listed in Exhibit 8.4, an organization must first initiate evaluation of the prevailing manufacturing culture. This will enable identification of strengths and weaknesses. Identified strength areas need to be leveraged to reduce the weaknesses, as weak areas will require improvement in the technology transition process. After such identification of thrust areas, it will have to follow certain steps as listed for successful technology transition.

Active management support and commitment This not only requires commitment of resources (making it available), but also active participation, sharing the experience, facilitating, and reviewing the process of transition on a regular basis. Management must listen, advise, coach, and reward the transition teams. A well-laid improvement plan outlining the estimated benefits can elicit active support and commitment from management.

Training Technology transition requires rigorous training support. Although it is difficult to list any generic training areas for technology transition in any organization, some of the common areas are the new technology process, problem-solving skills, statistics, project management, design for manufacturability, etc. Training should be need-based and there must be systems to track its efficacy, especially in the form of cost–benefit analysis (e.g., ROI).

Breaking down requirements into specific tasks A technology transition plan must have specific quantifiable goals for individual employees, teams, departments, and the organization as a whole. These must be coordinated to ensure that the transition process is moving in the right direction. For this purpose, organizations assign individuals action plans and goals.

Coaching, managing, and executing the transition plans Coaching is a very important aspect of technology transition. The transition process is always painful and complex; hence, management must continuously guide the team, leveraging their experience. Also, continuous monitoring of the progress of the teams, working with cost–benefit approach, and celebrating victory at every stage of achievement will ensure the success of the transition process.

SUMMARY

In today's organization, development of a proactive technological culture is the secret weapon for gaining a competitive advantage. Successful management of a technological culture can facilitate the process of transition in an organization. Also, it is important to integrate the people-related issues, to make the new technology a voluntarily accepted rather than an imposed one.

The transition to a proactive technological culture is not easy. It requires a great deal of work. But it is the only way to truly make measurable, meaningful, and long-term improvements that will keep the operation competitive, and most importantly, result in customer satisfaction in a very competitive environment.

KEY TERMS

Critical success factors (CSF) These determine the competitive advantage of an organization.
Proactive technological culture It is a culture that focuses on prevention of defects through continuous process improvement efforts.

Reactive technological culture This is a culture that focuses on monitoring the product to identify defects in it.
Statistical process control (SPC) It is used for quality assurance.

CONCEPT REVIEW QUESTIONS

1. Explain how technology relates to cultural issues, citing some corporate examples.
2. Explain how culture applies at the workplace. Select at least one such area of application and illustrate the process of influence.
3. What is proactive technological culture and what are its characteristics?
4. How does an organization go through the process of transition from a reactive to a proactive technological culture?
5. What are the steps involved in the technology transition process?
6. Write short notes on the following:
   (a) Proactive technological culture
   (b) Technology transition process
   (c) Coaching

CRITICAL THINKING QUESTIONS

1. Visit any workplace of your choice and identify the cultural constructs (go through their vision and mission statements and discuss with their top officials). Relate such identified cultural constructs with some of their workplace practices, illustrating more particularly how these relate to their type of technology, and products or services.

2. The technology transition process encounters resistance from people for certain reasons. What would be your appropriate action plan for managing the process of technology transition?

3. A proactive technological culture yields better results, as people quickly become adept at the process of change. Cite some examples from the corporate world.

CASE STUDY

Technology Transfer and Cultural Compatibility—Brunei–Japan Joint Ventures

Culture affects the way an organization behaves, its values, and its basic underlying assumptions. In technology transfer also, the prevalent culture of an organization can either facilitate or hinder the process.

Therefore, cultural barriers to technology transfer now require both the recipient and the donor organizations to be very cautious. This case examines the type of organizational culture that is required to achieve success in technology transfer. It also attempts to understand whether the desired culture specifications can be summed up, compared, modified, or blended with respect to the requirements of the donor organization, to facilitate technology transfer.

This case pertains to Brunei–Japan joint ventures involving technology transfer. Japan and Brunei Darussalam have certain commonality in cultures. Within the framework of modernism, Japan's culture did not change; neither did that of Brunei. Being a part of Asian culture, both believe in maintaining dignity and following the principles of humanity. Brunei's Islamic culture believes in meeting the challenges of the competitive age through science and technology, literacy, and required reforms.

Technology transfer to Brunei could take place in three different ways:

- Where technology transfer could be achieved with the absorption of the donor's culture
- Where the donor's culture was partially absorbed
- Where commonality of cultures of both the donor and the recipient countries could facilitate transfer of technology

In the first case, successful transfer of technology essentially requires acceptance of the donor's culture. Here, it was done first by physical isolation of the joint venture, creating a separate enclave, and then training the local staff on the foreign culture to facilitate cultural absorption. In the second case, the need was only to address some of the cultural components for successful operation of the joint venture. This was possible through regular training and education of the local staff in line with the Japanese style of junior and middle management operations. In the third case, technology transfer was possible at ease for minimum impact on the local culture. In such cases, the local staff members felt the necessity of technology transfer, as there was compatibility in administrative, operational, or managerial problems.

Based on the sample of Brunei–Japanese organizations located in Brunei Darussalam, the following three models of technology transfer across cultures could be developed:

In the first case, foreign direct investment (from Japan to Brunei) was facilitated in full, where a total cultural diffusion (including languages) was possible. Despite the culture shock, people embraced this as it was necessary to sustain the same work culture model of Japan due to science and technology requirements. According to the

CEO of the Brunei organization, this stage could be achieved due to the general perceptions of the people that the level of development is more important than the cultural issue. Here, perhaps economic compulsion had an overriding impact on technology transfer.

In the second case, the Brunei organization was averse to science and technology, and not prepared to change. The technology absorption capacities and capabilities of the firm could not facilitate technology diffusion.

In the third case, despite having high literacy, the science and technological culture, and consequently, the work culture of the organization did not facilitate full absorption of the technology transfer.

With these syndromes in Brunei organizations, Japanese technology transfer followed three models:

Technology transfer was possible to the fullest possible extent, in cases where absorption of the donor's culture was possible. Partial technology transfer was possible where the donor's culture was partially in line with the local culture. A minimum level of technology transfer was possible in cases where the local culture was retained.

Source: Hussain, Shabbir (1998), 'Technology transfer models across cultures: Brunei–Japan joint ventures', *International Journal of Social Economics*, Vol. 25, No. 6/7/8, pp. 1189–1198, MCB University Press.

Discussion Questions

1. Study the case carefully and relate it to any Indian organization.
2. Identify how an optimum level of technology transfer could have been achieved in the two cases.

REFERENCES

Alrusheidat, J. (2006), 'The impact of cultural dimensions on technology transfer in developing countries', *Journal of Food, Agriculture, and Environment*, Vol. 4, Issue 1, January, p. 810.

Bhattacharyya, D.K. (2009), *Cross-cultural Management*, PH Learning, New Delhi.

———. (2008), *Manpower Development and Technological Change*, Excel Books, New Delhi.

———. (2007), *Human Resource Research Methods*, Oxford University Press, New Delhi.

Entorf, Horst and Francis Kramarz (1998), 'The impact of new technologies on wages and skills: Lessons from matching data on employees and on their firms', *Economics of Innovation and New Technology*, Vol. 5, No. 2–4, pp. 165–197.

Huselid, Mark A. (1995), 'The impact of human resource management practices on turnover, productivity, and corporate financial performance, *Academy of Management Journal*, Vol. 38, No. 3, pp. 635–672.

Ichniowski, Casey, Kathryn Shaw, and Gabrielle Prennushi (1997), 'The effects of human resource management practices on productivity', *American Economic Review*, Vol. 87, No. 3, pp. 291–313.

Milgrom, Paul and John Roberts (1995), 'Complementarities and fit: Strategy, structure and organizational change in manufacturing', *Journal of Accounting and Economics*, Vol. 19, pp. 179–208.

Postman, Neil (1998), 'Five things we need to know about technological change', http://itrs.scu.edu/tshanks/pages/Comm12/12Postman.htm, accessed on 28 June 2009.

Zuboff, Shoshana (1988), *In the Age of the Smart Machine: The Future of Work and Power*, Basic Books, New York.

9 Attitude Measurement for Change Management

Learning Objectives

After reading this chapter, you will be able to understand
- the concept of attitude and its relevance in the organizational change process
- the different approaches to attitudinal change
- the strategies for attitudinal change
- the attitude measurement for organizational change
- HRD initiatives and attitudinal change
- the use of scaling techniques to map attitude

Innovative Customer Service at EMC Corporation

When a customer believes in you ... they'll stick with you almost no matter what.

–Mike Ruettgers, EMC Corporation

EMC was founded in 1979 at Hopkinton, Massachusetts. Today it is recognized as the world leader in customer service. After joining the EMC group as Vice President of operations and customer service, Mike Ruettgers found that the company's product performance failure was virtually leading it to bankruptcy. Disk drives, one of its core product lines, was witnessing the biggest challenge as customers were up in their arms not to accept this, though the company enjoyed visible market reputation in product quality and customer services.

The company's business had seriously decreased due to product unreliability. As part of a comeback strategy, Mike decided to give the customers the choice of getting a new EMC storage system or getting an IBM archival at an EMC rate (the price of the IBM equipment was higher). IBM is its biggest competitor.

This move faced severe criticism at the corporate level but Mike was convinced that this was the only way to restore customer confidence. His assumption was correct. EMC customers recognized this as an extraordinary move and EMC's commitment to its customers, and decided to continue with the company. Thus, EMC was able to make a turnaround. Technology companies, such as CISCO Systems, Sun Microsystems, Oracle, and others have reposed their confidence in EMC data archival products.

The company now has superb technologists who systematically phase out obsolete products and develop new ones to peg competition for others, and retain and expand their customer base. This initiative of new product development is further reinforced by the do-or-die sales culture improving the company's top line and helping it to recover from a deadlock situation. With 99 per cent customer retention, EMC set an example for others to emulate and was highly acclaimed by the corporate world and researchers. EMC is convinced that developing world-class problem solvers requires team players to pool the collective wisdom and solve problems on a real-time basis. Customer service requires people to be in the field and understand their real-time needs. 'Face the irate customers and dispel their apprehension'— became the mantra at EMC. Customer service and dispatch activities were centralized to bring them under the direct control of the top management. At EMC, customer service runs like any other business unit, it is implanted in the company's DNA; it is a continuous innovation.

INTRODUCTION

Attitude is a mental state of an individual which makes him/her act or respond (or be ready to respond) to or against objects, situations, etc., and to which his/her vested feeling, interest, liking, desire, etc., are directly or indirectly linked. In the course of development, a person acquires tendencies to respond to objects. These learned cognitive mechanisms are called attitudes. Change in knowledge is followed by change in attitudes. Attitudes are emotion-laden and that differentiates them from knowledge. Knowledge reinforces attitudes, and in the long-run these reinforce individual and group behaviour. Hence, attitude is neither behaviour nor the cause of behaviour but it relates to an intervening predisposition or a frame of reference which influences the behaviour of an individual.

When the interest, feeling, etc. of an individual are not connected in any way to the object or situation, his/her responses (towards the said object or situation) will then not be attitude, but opinion.

Attitudes or psychic state cannot be observed because psychological variables are dormant or latent. As it is a covert aspect, it is difficult to measure attitude. Inference, prediction from behaviour data, interviews with structured questionnaires and scales are the usual tools use to measure attitude.

It is a basic assumption that a person's attitude can be measured by asking questions about his/her thoughts, feelings, and likely actions, towards the attitude object. Attitudes can also be measured quantitatively, that is, each person's opinion can be represented by a numerical score. A particular test item, or a behaviour indicating an attitude, has the same meaning for all respondents, so that a given response is scored identically for everyone.

In a typical attitude questionnaire, respondents are asked to indicate whether they agree or disagree with a series of belief statements about an attitude object. Attitudes are arranged along an evaluative continuum ranging from *favourable* to *unfavourable*. The question that can be raised here is, 'Why not just one belief statement?' In most cases, one question will simply not address all the likely domains of an attitude. Asking only one question significantly increases the likelihood that irrelevant factors, such as the words used in the question, will create errors. If responses are summed over a number of questions, then it is a more valid measure as the error associated with individual items tends to cancel out over a number of items. Each attitude statement should represent a different and independent view about the attitude object, and cover both favourable and unfavourable attitudes, so that the nature of response to one item should not affect the response to another.

The assumption is that more extreme scale positions represent more important or more strongly held attitudes.

EMPLOYEE ATTITUDES IN THE ORGANIZATIONAL CHANGE PROCESS

An 'organization' has been defined as a complex system that produces outputs in the context of an environment, an available set of resources, and a history (Nadler and Tushman 1989). An effective organization meets the expectations of multiple stakeholders, including shareholders, employees, suppliers, customers, and the society in which it is located. It also demands the loyalty and commitment of these stakeholders for the long-term survival of the organization and of the social network in which it is embedded (Kochan and Useem, 1992).

Changes in the environment demand that organizations modify themselves from time to time. Change has become a norm for organizations as well as for the people who work with them, and who have consequently become the focal point for understanding and implementing change.

Most theorists divide change into two types according to scope: change taking place within the given system, and change aimed at modifying the system itself. Ackerman (1986) described three types of organizational change: (i) developmental change, (ii) transitional change, and (iii) transformational change. Burke and Litwin (1992) developed a model for making a distinction between transactional and transformational change. According to them, transformational change occurs as a response to the external environment and directly affects the organizational mission, strategy, leadership, and culture. In Ackerman's terminology, transactional change can be compared with transitional change.

Implementation of organizational change is considered as a step-by-step process. Lewin (1951), Beer et al. (1990), and Kotter (1998) inclined to pay more attention to the unfreezing stage. In order to reduce forces in favour of the status quo, it is necessary to persuade people regarding the need for change (Lewin 1951). In the moving stage, the forces in favour of change should be increased—attitudes, values, and behaviours should be pushed to a new level. In order to achieve this move, a change in people's mindsets is necessary (Sathe and Davidson 2000). To manage such a difficult task, people need to be interested in staying with a particular organization and committed to it.

Employee attitudes are considered to be an indicator of the future success of an organization (Hurst 1995). According to Cooper and Croyle (1984), a person's attitude influences him/her to act in a certain way. In the context of organizational change, attitude to change—the benefits of the change and the competence of managers to implement these changes—become important. At the same time, while seeking information that is relevant for decision-making, employees focus on information consistent with their attitudes (Frey 1986). Also, the role of co-workers in the formation of attitudes has not been emphasized in assessments of job satisfaction. The social information-processing approach to job attitudes argues that jobs can be interpreted in a multitude of ways and employees rely on social sources of information, and hence, cues from their co-workers contribute to the formation of job attitudes (Salancik and Pfeffer 1978).

APPROACHES TO ATTITUDINAL CHANGE

The three major approaches to attitudinal change are cognitive, social, and behavioural. Organizations can use these, either as stand-alone methods or in bundles, to bring in attitudinal change.

The cognitive approach uses sharing of information and persuasive communication, and in the process develops conflict or dissonance to bring changes in the attitude of employees. Attitudes are learnt and with new information inputs our cognitive structures get reinforced and we begin to view the world from different perspectives. Cognitive scientists believe that it is possible for us to hold two contradictory beliefs, till such time as we learn what is right or wrong. In fact, it is our cognitive dissonance that is reinforced through learning and new information inputs, and which in the process, change our attitudes.

Behavioural approaches make use of reinforcements and punishments as possible models of behavioural change. We repeat the specific behaviour or behaviours, when we understand which of these will be rewarded. Accordingly, we discriminate between types of behaviour, and discard the ones that can punish us. Gagne and Skinner are two pioneering behaviourists who recommended the use of this approach as their research, indicating that people generally repeat behaviours, opinions, and attitudes that are rewarded, and resist those that may lead to punishment.

Social approaches draw the attention of people to a role model in order to enable them to emulate him/her and nurture the desired attitude. In organizations, employees emulate leaders and tend to reinforce their own attitude by nurturing their specific attitude or attitudes. Such a propensity is further reinforced when it is used in combination with behavioural approaches. Albert Bandura, the noted social scientist, advocated that the concept of social approaches is based on the premise that our attitudes and behaviours are learnt and copied through our interactions with the social world in which we live.

STRATEGIES FOR ATTITUDINAL CHANGE

It is always desirable that organizations select appropriate strategies to bring about a positive change in the attitude of employees. However, it is difficult to determine which strategy or strategies will work, and requires a thorough understanding of the attitudinal components. Based on various inputs and leveraging the experience of the author, these strategies can be listed as follows:

Help people to release their prior commitment

A predetermined or predisposed attitude of the people often develops due to their prior commitment, which engulfs their conscious or sub-conscious mind. Organizations need to uncover this underlying commitment and emphasize on changing the attitude. Unless people's minds are released from such embedded commitments, they may not respond to the need for changing their attitude.

Provide new information

To make people understand the need for attitudinal change, it is necessary to provide information, so they can make an informed choice. Many scholars are averse to the use of the concept of 'selling the change'. But to ensure people make an informed choice to change their attitude, perhaps this needs to be followed in practice. Employees of Hindustan Paper Corporation (HPC), a public sector unit (PSU) of the Government of India, have undergone many change management programmes. In the ice-breaking sessions, to sell the idea of change emphasis was first given to mapping the employees' expectations about their children.

The analysis (based on interactions) revealed that all of them nurtured very high ambitions for their children, but preferred to maintain the status quo in the organization. Taking cues from the gap between the aspirations for their children and their position in the organization, the efforts to change, keeping in view the global, national, and industrial level scenarios, could yield the desired results. Even trade unions realized the need to change and re-focusing their strategy from a marketing perspective. Hence, the need for change must be presented to employees strategically so that they can make an informed choice.

Make positive use of fear

Employees harbour fear of unknown and unseen situations that may affect their interests. To dispel this fear, the focus should be on explaining why the present path is not necessarily the best one. When this is clearly communicated, the results will be better.

Resolve cognitive dissonance

Often the attitudes we nurture differ from our behaviour. This is called cognitive dissonance. Hence, the attitudinal change initiative of an organization must focus on resolving this dissonance, to help employees to realize that nurturing a positive attitude can not only benefit them individually, but also the organization as a whole.

Exert influence through 360-degree feedback

This strategy focuses on understanding the attitudes of employees through a 360-degree feedback and helping them to understand the areas of thrust to change this. A structured approach for regular 360-degree feedback assessment can effectively change the attitudes of the people and facilitate organizational change.

Co-opt

Organizations have used this strategy of attitudinal change with a high rate of success. Through a change management survey (explained in Chapter 6), it is possible to identify employees who resist change. Organizations intentionally put them in leadership positions, allowing them to form their own team and run the show, and then closely monitor their attitudinal change. This model has been used in some acquired units where after acquisition, employees vehemently opposed integration. These employees were given the task of managing production with a specific target to achieve. All resource support including help and guidance was provided to them. They gradually realized how difficult and challenging this was without a positive attitude and cooperation of the people, and changed their attitude.

Many organizations, however, may not like this model as they firmly believe that workers cannot responsibly run the shop floor.

Have compassion

Using compassion as a tool for attitudinal change is more a philosophical attitude and a long-drawn process. Such lessons are more evident in Buddhist philosophy, which subscribes to the notion that compassion is an effective way of building rapport and gaining peace, both for the individual self and for those who nurture negative attitudes.

Understand first

This model of attitudinal change is adopted from Stephen Covey's 7 habits (Covey 1997). Empathy (or compassion) helps us to understand the opposite view and appreciate the reasons for resistance. This helps to remove mind-blocks and develop a positive attitude, which in turn, can help to bring about change in organizations.

Have acceptance

Attitudinal change occurs consciously and unconsciously. Without displaying a negative attitude, we can at least examine matters to realize what exactly it entails. For example, until recently partnering with trade unions was never considered as a possible means to gain their cooperation. Positive results can be obtained by exploring such possibilities. A similar experience at a Kolkata-based unit manufacturing consumer electronics items was felt by author. This is detailed in Exhibit 9.1.

Have a dialogue

Organizations can also facilitate attitudinal change by opening up a dialogue with those nurturing a negative attitude. Dialogues prove an opportunity to disclose one's assumptions and develop strategies to amalgamate one's actions, which can effectively change the attitude of the people.

EXHIBIT 9.1 Employee acceptance and attitudinal change

In a Kolkata-based unit manufacturing consumer electronics goods, a serious agitation erupted after action was taken against some employees. The erring workers continued their agitation, go slow, and work-stoppages, against disproportionate wage increases, without realizing that competition from Korea could jeopardize their jobs.

While many Indian consumer electronics units had closed down due to their inability to compete in terms of price and quality, this unit was able to do so. Accommodating the workers' demand for a higher pay rise could have forced it into liquidation. Negotiations and persuasion through the unions did not yield any result.

At that stage, the CEO of the company met the union leaders with facts and figures explaining the entire scenario and the nature of the competition. Union leaders were able to appreciate this gesture and dissuade the workers from demanding a wage increase, and encouraged them to cooperate with the management to increase productivity. This example illustrates the importance of acceptance by removing mind blocks. The results in this case were quite positive, as the company not only survived the Korean competition, but was also able to increase its market share and grow substantially.

It is important to understand that attitudinal change strategies may not always work in isolation. Organizations need to adopt strategies and also create the right environment to enable employees to incubate their idea to change. Attitudinal change takes place in phases. It is not a radical panacea.

The term 'attitude' is not often used as it may attract some social stigma. Marzano (1998) used the term 'self-system', considering attitude as an interrelated system of a flow chart in beliefs and processes. Figure 9.1 illustrates the process of attitudinal change.

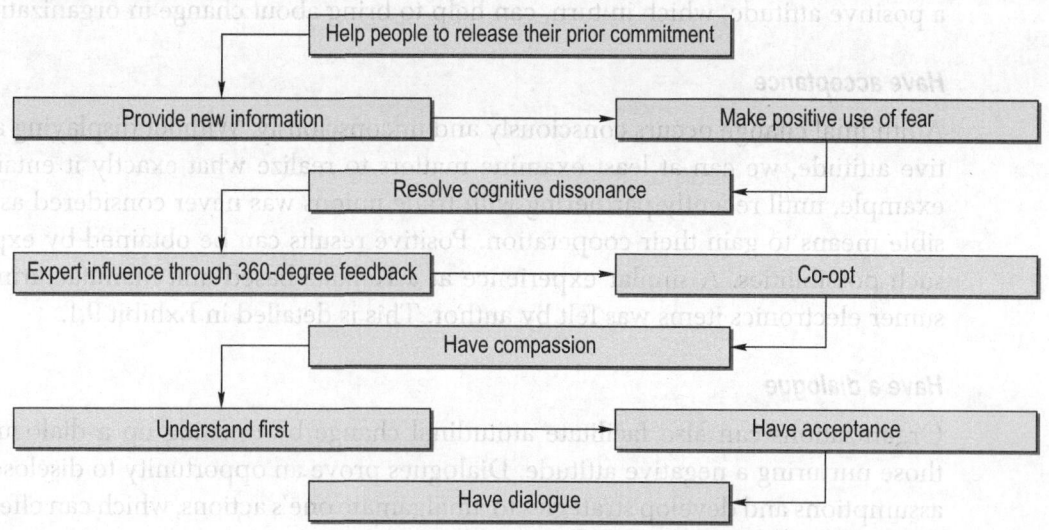

FIG. 9.1 Attitudinal changes and strategies involved

ATTITUDE MEASUREMENT FOR ORGANIZATIONAL CHANGE

Attitude measurement is usually based on the personal observation of people in their work situation and occasionally on attitudinal surveys. As attitude is the innate feeling of an individual and may not be explicit through behaviour, an attitudinal survey through an opinionated questionnaire may not yield any result. Hence, when conducting such a survey standard, reliable, and validated psychometric tools, and a structured questionnaire are used to map the attitude of employees.

Certain areas of enquiry are used when designing a questionnaire to measure employee attitudes. These are as follows:

1. This type of questionnaire seeks the degree of satisfaction of employees with the extent of information the organization has shared with them on the change aspects. Based on these responses, organizations can determine the strategy for bringing attitudinal changes in employees, to ensure that they are in conformity with the changed goals and objectives.
2. The next important attitude mapping scale measure is satisfaction with the existing leadership of the organization. Such questionnaires try to determine employees' responses to the problem-solving approach of management, the degree of trustworthiness of managerial decisions, and the facilitation role that superiors play in helping subordinates to organize their work.
3. By focusing on measuring commitment and job satisfaction, organizations can ascertain the willingness of employees to continue working with the organization and the level of satisfaction they derive from their respective jobs.
4. This type of questionnaire elicits information on employees' attitude towards the perceived benefits of change, both at the individual and organizational level.

Similarly, an attitude measurement questionnaire to measure the culture of the organization can be developed with a task and relationship orientation framework, as proposed by Vadi et al. (2002). Responses to this can help the organization to understand the extent to which employees are willing to cooperate with it to achieve common goals. Relationship orientation, on the other hand, measures the employees' sense of belonging.

HRD INITIATIVES AND ATTITUDINAL CHANGE

Changing attitudes, values, and motivations are now major issues facing organizations. They can turn such challenges into advantages through appropriate HRD interventions, ensuring that the quality of work life keeps pace with the changing human expectations. The following areas of attitudinal changes require HRD intervention:

1. Attitudes towards perceived threats to trade union legality and other large-scale efforts to reduce trade union power or cohesion.

2. Attitudes towards methods of wage negotiations, whether by collective or local bargaining.
3. Attitudes towards working conditions and any administrative machinery for the discussion or regulation of such conditions.
4. Attitudes towards worker training or promotion, and towards education in general, as a means of improving management and industrial skills.

As explained earlier, economic restructuring, market globalization, international quality system standards, etc. have, *inter alia*, prompted Indian organizations to opt for radical organizational restructuring, which, among others, calls for adoption of TQM principles in managing human resources. TQM calls for total employee involvement (TEI), employee empowerment, development of small group activities (quality circle forums), value engineering teams, etc. To translate TQM requirements into corporate practices, therefore, requires a lot of attitudinal changes at the top, such as developing flatter organizations, de-layering delegation and information, and developing an organizational culture where every employee needs to be considered as a member of a well-integrated family. To infuse attitudinal changes both at the top and lower levels, it is necessary to adopt the following HRD strategies:

Employee empowerment Empowerment is to give everyone (not just people with certain positions or job titles) the legitimate right to make judgements, form conclusions, reach decisions, and then act. Empowerment, therefore, calls for employee participation in day-to-day problem solving and innovation. Traditional participative forums (committee, joint consultative machinery, etc.) restrict employee participation in operational areas. But empowerment demands employee participation in every corporate function, to the extent that it accepts that the employee is not a mere seller of his time and labour for a contracted sum of money. The empowered employee acquires the skill and authority necessary to make decisions concerning quality and productivity. They initiate changes on their own. Empowerment changes the attitude of the employee as it develops ownership and commitment.

Promoting quality circles and total participation This strategy is used to infuse attitudinal changes and to facilitate personal involvement of employees. Quality circles (QCs) were originally defined by Japanese Union of Scientists and Engineers (JUSE) as a small group of workers, voluntarily performing quality control activities within the workshop to which they belong. These groups, with the voluntary participation of each and every member of the organization, continuously engage themselves in promoting quality control activities, irrespective of their hierarchical levels.

In reality, QCs encompass the concepts of self and mutual development, and at the same time, reinforce quality control techniques. Even though the concept of QCs originated in Japan to survive under compelling circumstances, it has now been expanded far and wide, cutting across cultural and ideological barriers. It gained popularity gradually in most of the industrialized and developing nations of the world. India, being one of the fast developing nations, is no exception.

QC can be related to increased employee motivation and productivity, and is hence used as an important HRD tool. Total knowledge, skills, creative abilities, talents, and aptitudes, together with the values, attitudes, and beliefs of the workers and/or individuals of the organization, represent the human resources in more aggressive terms. QCs ensure the total involvement of employees through a number of small group forums. Experience shows that many organizations have succeeded in improving their productivity by QC activities. Increased productivity can be achieved by increased employee motivation, and QCs ensure this better than any other method, such as complex planning, rigorous execution, etc.

Training Organizations need to focus more on training in areas, such as leadership, communication, motivation, etc. Such knowledge inputs gradually reinforce the attitude of the employees.

Team spirit This initiative helps to integrate employees with the organization and is further strengthened when a sense of belongingness is simultaneously developed among the employees.

USE OF SCALING TECHNIQUES TO MAP ATTITUDE

Different scaling techniques are used to frame questionnaires that map attitudes. The selection of such scales varies with respect to the criteria for measurement. Each scale has unique properties. Some can only establish an association between attitudinal variables, but are limited in the mathematical properties. Others have more extensive mathematical properties, and still others also hold out the possibility of establishing cause and effect relationships between variables. Without going into the details of individual scale properties, the basics of these scales are summarized in Table 9.1.

TABLE 9.1 Types of measurement

Type	Basic empirical operations	Typical usage	Typical statistics	
			Descriptive	Inferential
Nominal	Determination of equality	Classification of male-female, smoker, non-smoker, team	Percentage mode	Chi-square, binomial
Ordinal	Determination of greater or less	Rankings: Preference data, market position, attitude measurement, many others psychological measures, etc.	Median	Rank-order correlation
Interval	Determination of equality of intervals	Index numbers, attitude measurement	Mean, range, standard deviation	Product moment correlation T-test, factor analysis
Ratio	Determination of equality of ratios	Sales, units produced, number of customers, costs, age, etc.	Geometric mean	Coefficient of variation

All the above scales can map the attitude of employees but in different dimensions. The most important technique of measuring attitude is the Thurstone Scale. Its basic assumptions are as follows:

1. Attitudes lie along an evaluative continuum ranging from favourable to unfavourable.
2. Ordering of attitude statements should be such that there appears to be an equal distance between adjacent statements on the continuum, that is, judgements can be made about the degree of discrepancy among different people's attitudes.

Likert Scales

In the Likert scales, respondents place themselves on an attitude continuum:

Strongly agree	Agree	Uncertain	Disagree	Strongly disagree
1	2	3	4	5

An individual's score can be summed up and the resulting total can be used as an index of that person's attitude.

Other Measures of Attitudes

Other measures of attitudes are *overt behaviour* and *physiological dimensions,* which include skin resistance (Rankin and Campbell 1955), heart rate (Westie and DeFleur 1959), and pupil dilation (Hess 1965). These are the attitudes inferred by comparing participants' response in the presence of a neutral object and the presence of the attitude object.

Despite such problems, organizations often try to integrate the physiological dimensions of attitude with the psychological dimensions based on attitudinal surveys and accordingly map the attitude of employees, to ultimately infer the degree of compatibility of their attitudes with the organizational change management programme.

ATTITUDE SURVEYS

Attitude surveys are indispensable in factories, industries, and different organizations, for new recruits and for evaluating human relations. The study of attitudes is also important for designing a training programme, which is a core HRD function.

Attitude surveys focus on the feelings and motives of employees' opinions about their working environment. There are three basic purposes for conducting attitude surveys:

1. Compare results with other survey results.

2. Measure the effect of change that has occurred.
3. Determine the nature and extent of employee feelings regarding specific organizational issues and the organization in general.

Usually, attitude surveys are carried out by interviewing a person with a structured close-ended questionnaire. The skill of the interviewer is important for correct measurement of attitude. While framing the questionnaire, the interviewer should be cautious, as simple opinion-laden questionnaire items will not depict the attitude of the interviewee. Here, it is important to put value-laden questionnaire items, use behaviourally anchored statements, ask the respondents to rank any myth statements, etc. A sample list of such myth statements and value-laden questions is given here:

Myth statements

1. Hard work ensures better result.
2. Never say no to anyone; listen to everybody's problems.
3. One who is indispensable is efficient.

Exhibit 9.2 illustrates some survey questions followed by their interpretation.

Some organizations also use behaviourally anchored statements to measure the attitude of employees, but this may not always be possible, unless the target employees are capable of understanding the questions.

EXHIBIT 9.2 A sample survey questionnaire for attitude management

1. Do you think the expenditure on training is wasteful? (Give your answer selecting any one from the given alternatives).
   (a) To a large extent
   (b) To some extent
   (c) To a very little extent
   (d) Not at all
2. What, to your knowledge, are the major barriers to effective implementation of flexible working hours in India? (Please arrange the factors in order of your perceived preference).
   (a) Lack of awareness
   (b) Difficulty in implementation
   (c) Supervisory problems
   (d) Lack of support from workers
   (e) Lack of support from unions
   (f) Production problems
   (g) Any other (please specify)

The first questionnaire item (which reflects the attitude of a person regarding training) can be evaluated by adding the weighted value of individual responses.

Interpretation

Let the number of respondents be 15. Suppose they have given their responses to the four alternatives as follows:

Alternatives	No. of respondents
(a) To a large extent	4
(b) To some extent	4
(c) To a very little extent	5
(d) Not at all	2
Total	15

(Contd)

(Exhibit 9.2 contd)

Weighted average attitude

Alternatives	No.	Weighted	Attitude
(a)	4	4	16
(b)	4	3	12
(c)	5	2	10
(d)	2	1	2

Alternative (a) *To a large extent* is the group attitude.

The second questionnaire item allows the respondents to answer the question by selecting all alternatives in order of their perceived priority. This requires use of the factorial method for quantification of all responses.

Interpretation

Suppose the 15 respondents have responded by giving ranks to the alternative (a) as follows:

Respondent	1	2	3	4	5	6	7
Rank of (a)	1	3	5	7	1	4	3
Respondent	8	9	10	11	12	13	14	15
Rank of (a)	2	6	5	1	2	3	4	5

From the above, we get:

Priority/Rank	1	2	3	4	5	6	7
Number of respondents (Tr)	3	2	3	2	3	1	1

(Total no. of respondents = 15, No. of priorities/Ranks = 7, that is, *a* to *g*)

Weighted score value (WSV) is calculated as follows:

Priority	1	2	3	4	5	6	7
Total value	3	2	3	2	3	1	1
Weights (factorial)	7	6	5	4	3	2	1
WSV	21	12	15	8	9	2	1

In the same way, the total WSV for other alternatives can be calculated from the responses obtained against each. Suppose they are as follows:

Alternative	b	c	d	e	f	g
Total WSV	65	30	70	55	60	40

The total WSV of alternative (d) is the highest. Therefore, alternative (d) that is, 'lack of support from workers' should be the attitude/opinion of the group of respondents.

Various statistical tools can be used for measuring attitude. Since attitudes are psychological or qualitative variables, the first and foremost task for the rater is to assign numerals to objects, events, or persons. Use of the Likert type of scale, the Thurstone scale, etc. helps the interviewer to assign numbers, either discrete or continuous. Analysis of variance, correlation, chi-square test, and Kendal's co-efficient and concordance test are some useful statistical tools for measuring attitude.

Likert's Summated Rating Scale

A summated rating scale is a set of attitude statements, all of which are considered or approximated as having equal attitude value, and to each of which, subjects respond with a degree of agreement or disagreement (intensity) carrying different scores. These scores are summed and averaged to yield an individual's attitude score. Under this method, each respondent's ranking is arrived at by totalling his/her scores on all the statements (usually 5).

Likert's item analysis

In this procedure, respondents are asked to provide answers to a certain number of statements (which is usually restricted to 15). The reply to each statement is given in terms of five degrees of agreement or disagreement, namely 'strongly agree', 'agree', 'undecided', 'disagree', and 'strongly disagree'. Each statement thus becomes a scale in itself having five points on it. At one end of this scale is strong approval and the other end is strong disapproval; in between, there are many intermediate points. The respondent indicates where he/she stands on this scale with reference to each statement. The total of his/her scores on all statements is taken as a measurement of his/her attitude. The statements may be either favourable or unfavourable. For favourable statements, values given are 5, 4, 3, 2, 1, and for unfavourable statements, they are 1, 2, 3, 4, 5.

Thurstone's Equal Appearing Intervals Scale for Attitudinal Survey

This scale attempts to represent the attitudes of a group on a specified issue in the form of frequency distribution.

The construction of this scale is very cumbersome and time-consuming, and is usually avoided. Moreover, scale values assigned to statements are influenced by the attitudes, background, and intelligence of the judges, who may see things differently from the actual respondents. This scale also does not allow respondents to express the intensity of their feelings, as they can only indicate their agreement with the finally selected statements.

Guttman's Cumulative Scale

This scale is made up of a relatively small number of statements which have been tested for their one-dimensionality. A one-dimensional scale measures only one variable. The scale is known as cumulative, as the respondents who agree with the most favourable statements are theoretically presumed to agree with all other statements expressing a 'lesser' degree of favourability. Use of this scale is also avoided because of its complexity.

Johari Window

The most effective mapping of employee attitudes at the organizational level is done through the Johari Window. This (Luft and Ingham 1955) is an excellent graphical representation of the relationship between individuals and understanding oneself. It is called a window because of its four quadrants. It is also referred to as a 'disclosure/feedback model of self-awareness' and an 'information-processing tool'. The Johari Window actually represents information—feelings, experiences, views, attitudes, skills, intentions, motivation, etc.—within or about a person in relation to their group, from four perspectives. Luft and Ingham called this model 'Johari' after combining their first names, Joe and Harry. It is widely used to understand the self, to achieve personal development, improve communication, interpersonal relations, group dynamics, team development, and to strengthen inter-group relations. This model represents information for a particular group in relation to other groups.

The Johari Window has four regions—open area, open self, free area, and free self. Free self is also known as 'the arena', which includes that a person knows about himself/herself and which is also known to others. If a person is unaware about some aspect concerning himself/herself but is known to others, it is called a blind area, blind self, or blind spot. On the other hand, what others do not know about a person is called hidden area, hidden self, avoided area, avoided self, or 'façade'. Again, there may be a situation when something is unknown, both to the person and to others, which is called an unknown area or unknown self. A schematic representation of the model is shown in Fig. 9.2.

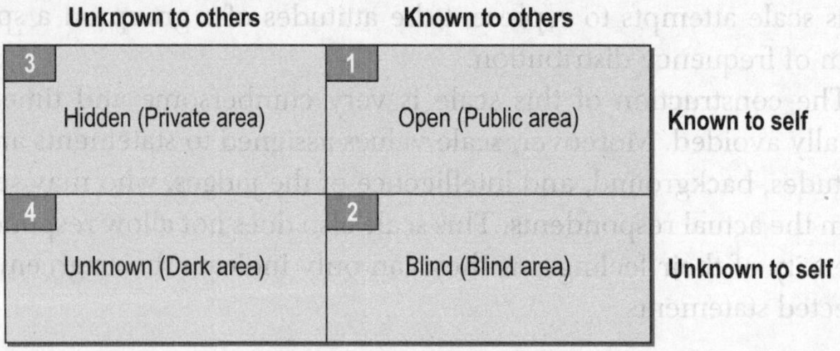

	Unknown to others	Known to others	
	3 Hidden (Private area)	1 Open (Public area)	Known to self
	4 Unknown (Dark area)	2 Blind (Blind area)	Unknown to self

FIG. 9.2   The Johari Window

Quadrant 1—'open self/area', 'free area', 'public area', or 'arena'—represents the area of free activity. When we are in this region, either individually or in a group, we are more effective and productive, because this space is for good communication and cooperation.

Quadrant 2—'blind self', 'blind area', or 'blind spot'—make us known to others but unknown to self, which results in our asking for feedback, based on which we try to reduce this area so as to increase the open area.

Quadrant 3—'hidden self', 'hidden area', 'avoided self/area', or 'facade'—indicates a situation where we know but others do not. This hidden area represents information and feelings, including sensitivities, fears, manipulative intentions, secrets, etc.

Quadrant 4—contains information, feelings, latent abilities, aptitudes, experiences, etc., which are unknown to the individual and so also unknown to others in the group.

SUMMARY

Attitudes are learned cognitive mechanisms which can be reinforced by knowledge. Attitude, per se, is not behaviour, but it develops an intervening frame of reference which influences the behaviour of an individual. Hence, understanding the attitude of employees is essential both at the time of recruitment and subsequently, when the organization plans for change.

There are four levels of attitude measurement—nominal, ordinal, interval, and ratio. These constitute a hierarchy where the lowest scale of measurement, nominal, has far fewer mathematical properties than those further up the hierarchy. Nominal scales yield data on categories, ordinal scales give sequences, interval scales begin to reveal the magnitude between points on the scale, and ratio scales explain both order and the absolute distance between any two points on the scale. Attitudes can be measured using different sets of scales. What the right scale should be will depend more on the nature of the attitude that is to be measured.

In this chapter, we have discussed the concept of attitude and its relevance to the organizational change process, different approaches to attitudinal change, strategies for attitudinal change, and achievement of organizational change through attitude measurement. The chapter also discusses how organizational change through attitudinal change can be achieved through various HRD interventions.

The chapter concluded with a detailed description of the use of various scaling techniques which readers may further explore through different sources.

KEY TERMS

Cognitive approach It is the use of sharing of information and persuasive communication, and in the process developing conflict or dissonance to bring changes in the attitude of employees.

Cognitive dissonance It is the difference in nurtured attitude and our behaviours.

Quality circles These are small groups of workers, voluntarily performing quality control activities within the workshop to which they belong. These groups are continuously engaged in promoting quality control activities irrespective of their hierarchical levels.

Semantic differential This focuses on the meaning, people give to a word or concept.

Thurstone's equal appearing intervals scale It attempts to represent the attitudes of a group on a specified issue in the form of frequency distribution. The various opinions or items on a scale are allocated to different positions in accordance with the attitudes.

Transformational change This occurs as a response to the external environment and directly affects the organizational mission and strategy, and the leadership and culture (Burke and Litwin 1992).

CONCEPT REVIEW QUESTIONS

1. Define attitude. Why is the study of attitude necessary for organizational change?
2. What are the different tools for measuring attitude? From an organizational point of view, discuss in detail at least two measurement tools with due emphasis on their relative merits or demerits in the context of organizational change.
3. Explain the different approaches to attitudinal change initiatives taken by organizations to effect organizational change.
4. What are the strategies that organizations adopt to effect attitudinal change?
5. Explain the different scaling techniques adopted by an organization to map the attitude of employees.
6. Write short notes on the following:
    (a) Equal appearing intervals scale
    (b) Cummulative scale
    (c) Summated rating scale
    (d) Employee empowerment and attitudinal change
    (e) Predictive validity

CRITICAL THINKING QUESTIONS

1. Your company has decided on a major business process restructuring, which among others, includes technology upgradation, skill renewal exercises, and change in the internal business processes. A tentative estimate indicates that to give effect to all these, major attitudinal change in the people will be required! As an expert in attitude transformation, draw a detailed action plan to suggest to the management.

2. Your company is a leading developer of software for telecom services and knowledge process outsourcing. So far, it used to get business as the approved vendor of a large multinational. Now, the company is planning to market products and services directly. The top management feels that this requires a thorough recasting of the business processes, which among others, also calls for a definite change in the attitude of employees, who are compliant with the standard operating procedures of the multinational. Suggest appropriate HRD measures that the company needs to embrace to develop positive attitudinal responses for direct marketing.

3. To become a six sigma compliant in customer services, your company wants you to introduce a 24×7 customer services help desk with a mandate to reach customers within 24 hours. As a manufacturer of water purifiers, it captivates customers with a long-term service contract. Customers often complain that their complaints are attended to only 3–4 days after they are logged several times. Meanwhile, new competitors are wooing your customers with attractive exchange offers. The company outsources customer services. Draw an action plan to make your customer service people attitudinally tuned to the new requirement.

4. You have been retained by a company to study the attitude of 50 employees on the recently introduced pension scheme. Develop at least 5 structured close-ended questionnaire items, using Likert's item analysis scale and interview the employees. Analyse all the responses using the factorial method and measure the attitude of the employees.

REFERENCES

Ackerman, L.S. (1986), 'Development, transition, or transformation: The question of change in organizations', *Organizational Development Practitioner*, December, pp. 1–8.

Augoustinos, M. (1991), 'Consensual representations of social structure in different age groups', *British Journal of Social Psychology*, Vol. 30, pp. 193–205.

Bandura, A. (1986), *Social Foundations of Thought and Action: A Social Cognitive Theory*, Prentice Hall, Englewood Cliffs.

Beer, M., R. Eisenstat, and B. Spector (1990), 'Why change programmes don't produce change', *Harvard Business Review*, November–December, pp. 158–166.

Bruner, Jerome S. (1983), *In Search of Mind: Essays in Autobiography*, Harper and Row, New York.

Burke, W. and G. Litwin (1992), 'A casual model of organizational performance and change', *Journal of Management*, Vol. 18, pp. 523–545.

Cooper, J. and R.T. Croyle (1984), 'Attitude and attitude change', *Annual Review of Psychology*, Vol. 35, pp. 394–426.

Covey, Stephen, R. (1997), *The 7 Habits of Highly Effective Families*, Golden Books, New York.

Frey, D. (1986), 'Recent research on selective exposure to information', in Berkowitz, L. (ed.), *Advances in Experimental Social Psychology*, Vol. 19, Academic Press, San Diego, pp. 41–80.

Gagné, R.M. (1985), *The Conditions of Learning and Theory of Instruction*, Fourth Edition, Holt, Rinehart, and Winston, New York.

Hess, E.H. (1965), 'Attitude and pupil size', *Scientific American*, Vol. 212, pp. 46–54.

Hess, E.H. and J.M. Polt (1960), 'Pupil size as related to interest value of visual stimuli', *Science*, Vol. 132, pp. 349–350.

Hurst, D.K. (1995), *Crisis and Renewal: Meeting the Challenge of Organizational Change*, Harvard Business School Press, Boston.

Jones, E. and H. Sigall (1971), 'The bogus pipeline: A new paradigm for measuring affect and attitude', *Psychological Bulletin*, pp. 349–364.

Kochan, T.A. and M. Useem (1992), *Transforming Organizations*, Oxford University Press, New York.

Kotter, J.P. (1998), 'Leading change: Why transformation efforts fail', *Harvard Business Review on Change*, A Harvard Business Review Paperback, pp. 1–21.

Lewin, K. (1951), *Field Theory in Social Science*, Harper and Row, New York.

Luft, Joseph and Harry Ingham (1955), 'The Johari Window: A graphical model of interpersonal awareness', Proceedings of the Western Training Laboratory in Group Development, UCLA, Los Angeles.

Marzano, Robert J. (1998), *A Theory-based Meta-Analysis of Research on Instruction*, Mid-continent Regional Educational Laboratory, Aurora, Colorado.

Moscovici, S. and M. Hestone (1983), 'Social representation from the name to the amateur scientists', in M. Hewstone (ed), *Attribution Theory, Social and Functional Extensions*, Basal Blackwell, Oxford.

Nadler, D.A. and M.L. Tushman (1989), *Organization frame Bending: Principles for Managing Reorientation*, Academy of Managment Executive, Vol. 3, pp. 194–204.

Osgood, C.E., G.J. Suci, and P.H. Tannenbaum (1957), *The Measurement of Meaning*, The University of Illinois Press, Urbana.

Petty, R.E., J.T. Cacioppo, and R. Goldman (1981), 'Personal involvement as a determinant of argument-based persuasion', *Journal of Personality and Social Psychology*, Vol. 41, pp. 847–855.

Rankin, R.E. and D.T. Campbell (1955), 'Galvanic skin response to negro and white experimenters', *Journal of Abnormal and Social Psychology*, Vol. 51, pp. 30–33.

Salancik, G.R. and J. Pfeffer (1978), 'A social information processing approach to job attitudes and task design', *Administrative Science Quarterly*, Vol. 23, pp. 224–253.

Sathe, V. and E.J. Davidson (2000), 'Toward a new conceptualization of culture change', in Ashkanasy, N.M., C. Wilderom, and M.F. Peterson (eds), *Handbook of Organizational Culture and Climate*, Sage, Thousand Oaks.

Skinner, B.F. (1938), *The Behaviour of Organisms*, Appleton, New York.

Vadi, M. J. Allik, A. Realo (2002), 'Collectivism and its consequences for organizational culture', University of Tartu, *Working Paper Series*.

Westie, F.R. and M.L. DeFleur (1959), 'Autonomic responses and their relationship to race attitudes', *Journal of Abnormal and Social Psychology*, Vol. 58, pp. 340–347.

10 Organizational Culture and Change

Learning Objectives

After reading this chapter, you will be able to understand
- the meaning, concept, and different aspects of organizational culture
- dimensions of culture and its influence on the organization
- the definition and characteristics of organizational culture
- the different types of organizational culture
- mergers and its impact on organizational culture
- organizational culture change process
- the importance of organizational structure, diagnostics, commitment, and climate in organizational change
- models of organizational culture change
- management-directed cultural change

Change Initiatives at State Bank of India (SBI)

It takes time for any new initiative to get stabilized in an institution. It also requires appropriate changes in organizational culture. SBI began to deploy technology sometime in the mid-1960s with the introduction of the punch card system of computers. With computerization across the country since 1991, the biggest challenge it faced was the discomfort its staff felt towards using keyboards. Computerization also initiated various process and workflow-related changes as the traditional manual system was very different from the computerized one.

While developing ambitious plans, the bank was also aware that new managerial roles would be a key element in achieving the desired success. The existing hierarchical management structure required a change. SBI had to find a way to reorient its experienced staff from its traditional managerial practices to fit in with the new plans for faster growth. A series of change programmes was required, which started with preliminary analysis of existing and desirable role behaviour. A variety of training programmes was designed and delivered along with employee-motivation exercises.

People at SBI began to accept computerization around 1999 and the change initiatives taken during this period finally paid off in 2003. In a seven-month period in 2003, computerization of 9000 branches across India took place with a very high degree of acceptance of the Bankmaster application by the staff. Today, it has the largest customer base and the biggest ATM network in the country, and offers its customers a diverse array of core banking solutions.

INTRODUCTION

Organizations do not operate in isolation. Every organization has to continuously interact with its environment to balance the internal environment and the mega or external environment. Contingency theories suggest that every organization has to understand the dynamics of its environment and adapt to changing demands, both outside and inside. To do this, organizations have to periodically scan the environment. Such scanning succeeds the OD initiatives. These help the organization to adapt to the changing environment and also to remain competitive. Appreciating OD requires understanding the various critical organizational issues.

Effecting organizational change through change of organizational culture has now become very significant. Therefore, every organization now tries to address the cultural issues and periodically initiates organizational development processes. To appreciate the significance of cultural issues, in this chapter we will first discuss the basic theoretical issues, and then recommend tools and their usages for effective organizational change. The chapter will also illustrate successful cases of cultural transformation and organizational change, emulating some of the best practices.

ORGANIZATIONAL CULTURE

Organizational culture has become popular since the early 1980s. There is no consensus on its definition but most authors agree that it is something holistic, historically determined and related to anthropology, socially constructed, soft, and difficult to change. It is something an organization already has. Again, organizational culture can also be viewed as what an organization is. Organizational cultures are different from national cultures. It manifests in the form of symbols, heroes, rituals, and values. National cultures differ mostly on the values level. Organizational cultures are together labelled as 'practices'.

National culture differences are reflected in solutions to organizational problems in different countries. Different national cultures have different preferred ways of structuring organizations and different patterns of employee motivation. For example, they limit the options for performance appraisal, management by objectives, strategic management, and humanization of work.

Research in organizational culture identified six independent dimensions of practices: (i) process-orientated versus results-orientated, (ii) job-orientated versus employee-orientated, (iii) professional versus parochial, (iv) open systems versus closed systems, (v) tightly versus loosely controlled, and (vi) pragmatic versus normative. The position of an organization on these dimensions is determined in part by the business or industry the organization is in. Scores on the dimensions are also related to a number of other hard characteristics of the organization. These lead to conclusions about how organizational cultures can or cannot be managed.

Managing international business means handling both national and organizational cultural differences at the same time. Organizational cultures are somewhat manageable, while national cultures are given facts for management. Common organizational cultures across borders keep multinationals together.

Culture, per se, refers to the shared beliefs, values, and norms of a group. Today's organizations emphasize more on culture, because a cultural bond gives people a sense of togetherness and when they work in a group, they deliver more.

Aspects of Organizational Culture

It is said that culture is like the inner layers of an onion. This is very appropriate for organizations also. The inner layers of an onion represent the fundamental values and these values are the crucial ingredients of culture, which shape the behaviour of people within the organization. The outer layers, such as strategies and tactics, can change quickly, rendering the prevalent culture in the organization inconsistent. This establishes the necessity for bringing cultural change in organizations, keeping in view the rationality of prevalent culture-dependent practices in the organization. In Japan, the age-old seniority-based promotion practices were based on their culture. But promoting a non-performer makes no sense, and today Japan also deviates from their culture-dependent promotional system and recognizes the performance merit. Japanese organizations have also started deviating from the practice of lifetime employment. There are also certain legacy-bound practices in old organizations that are mostly of foreign origin. In perpetuating these, some organizations lost their competitive edge and had to wind up operations. Thus, organizational culture cannot be something fixed and permanent. It has to change from time to time, keeping pace with competition, and the changing tastes and preferences of customers, etc.

Organizational culture is embedded in national culture and hence, it varies with respect to the organizations country of origin. An organization of Indian origin is culturally different from that of one originating in the US. Similarly, there is also an industry-specific culture. The culture of a manufacturing organization cannot be the same as that of an IT organization, as they belong to two different industry segments.

Another aspect of organizational culture is the degree of professionalism. For example, the culture of a family-managed organization may be different from that of a professionally-managed public limited company. The reasons are obvious; family-managed units are more closely held and the ownership rights remain with the promoter.

In organizations, culture encompasses many areas of people related issues such as the following:

- Structural system
- Compensation system

- HR policies
- Market strategy
- Client relations
- Accounting procedures
- Individual behaviour

Theoretically, organizational culture can either be bureaucratic, machine-like, or jungle-like. Each type has its advantages and disadvantages and these are explained in brief.

Bureaucratic organizational culture would be characterized by the control and governance mechanisms. An organization following bureaucratic form will lead to a culture which is rule bound with defined roles and responsibilities for its members. Hierarchies would be maintained with fewer opportunities for experimentation. A formal communication will prevail and risks would be minimized through various systems.

The *jungle-like* culture in organizations indicates professionalism, innovation, and creativity, and is the true place for unleashing the potentiality of its members. Other syndromes of jungle-like cultures in organizations could be interpersonal competition, incentives for hard work, freedom and autonomy, and risk-bearing decision-making. Despite having a high propensity of risk, organizations practising this type of culture can grow much faster than those following machine-like or bureaucratic cultures.

The *machine-like* culture prevents burn-out, lowers turnover, and smoothen financial performance. It is like a systems- or protocol-bound work environment, where every action has its roots in the standard operating procedures (SOP). While this probably minimizes costs, it requires a relatively slow-changing economic environment. When new opportunities present themselves, it moves too slowly to grasp them.

Studies show that organizational profitability is determined by the strength of its culture, but only in highly competitive markets. When the market is expanding and there are relatively few competitors, leadership does not seem to matter much. But when the market is matured and there are many powerful competitors, leadership can make a huge difference.

A strong organizational culture is internally consistent, widely shared, and clear about the appropriate behavioural requirements. Such organizations have a vision that all stakeholders understand. It acts like a mechanism of coordination; everyone in the organization works in synchronization; everyone understands the goals and also knows how to achieve them, as culture also sets the direction.

Differences in Organizational Cultures

Globalization and the changing business scenario are now increasingly shifting the business paradigm. Managers now have to deal with multiple ethnic groups representing different cultures, not only in their organization but also in global client organizations. It is important to recognize that people from diverse cultures differ in a variety of ways, including those of looking at things, dressing, communicating, and even have distinct personalities.

For example, in the US a short handshake indicates self-confidence, while a limp handshake can be interpreted wrongly. In Africa, however, a limp handshake is more acceptable. Even the duration of a handshake in Africa is longer, while in the US it takes only a few seconds.

DIMENSIONS OF CULTURES AND THEIR INFLUENCE ON ORGANIZATIONS

There are various dimensions of culture and each exerts influence on the organization. These and their implications on organizations will now be explained.

High Context vs Low Context

In a low context culture, things are concisely and candidly spelt out. As expectations are explicitly stated, people behave according to what is actually said or written. People, therefore, need to be good listeners and understand the requirements, or they may not be able to keep pace with them. In a high context culture, it is assumed that things are known to others and are relatively less spelt out, and issues remain implicit. This culture believes in communication in indirect ways. As the knowledge level of people is considered to be on par or at an equal level, it is expected that members of the organization will assume the pattern of culture and behave accordingly. Such a culture is more applicable for knowledge intensive organizations. A low context culture prevails in Germany and the Scandinavian countries, while in Japan, the Arab countries and also in France, high context culture is more dominant.

Cross-cultural interactions between low and high context culture groups often are marked with numerous difficulties. An appropriate example here would be of the interactions between the Japanese and the Westerners. Japanese believe Westerners are irritatingly dull. Westerners, on the other hand, believe that the Japanese are secretive and even deceitful. They do not like to share information. Similar perceptive mismatch is evident between the French and the Germans. As the French subscribe to a high context culture, they feel Germans (who believe in low context culture) construe their intelligence on face value. Germans, on the other hand, believe that French leaders and managers provide no direction. There are often communication breakdowns due to such mismatch particularly in low context cultures where shared understanding is more important for working in a team.

Monochronic vs Polychronic

People belonging to monochromic cultures believe in maintaining orderliness and sequence their jobs so that it does not get interrupted. They believe in doing one thing at a time. Polychronic cultures, on the other hand, believe in doing many things simultaneously. A monochronic manager is distracted and may even get annoyed when interrupted with another assignment. In contrast, a polychronic manager entertains everything together. His/her office is virtually an open door, and decision-making, meetings, and attending phones are handled simultaneously. The French and Americans subscribe to such cultures, while the Germans are monochronic in nature. The merger between Daimler-Benz and Chrysler in 1998 failed primarily due to the cultural mismatch between the two cultures.

Again, interactions between these two cultures often invite problems. The Germans who are monochronic in nature do not like the American way of conducting business meetings. During the course of meetings, Americans do not hesitate to attend to phone calls, trivial office matters, and even people. This annoys the Germans, who at times, even feel insulted. On the other hand, the Americans see Germans as cold and unfriendly, as they are very focused on their business and that too in specific terms of reference. This approach makes the Germans appear more unfriendly to the Americans.

Future vs Present vs Past Orientation

The culture of past-oriented societies subscribe to traditional values and ways of doing things. Being conservative, they respond to change slowly, and at times, believe in changing things which have already been tried and proved successful in the past. Countries, such as China, Britain, Japan, and some parts of Latin America (especially those that are Spanish-speaking) believe in a past-oriented culture. People, who believe in a present-oriented culture, characteristically look for short-term benefits as they cannot foresee the future. Some Latin American countries believe in this type of culture. People or countries belonging to the future-oriented culture are optimistic and nurture the feeling that their actions will lead to results. Their optimism is reinforced by proactive management practices. Countries, such as the US and Brazil believe in future-oriented cultures.

Quantity of Time

Perception on time value differs from country to country. Most of the industrially advanced countries believe in time value; that time lost can never be regained, and hence, effective utilization of time is very important. In traditional agrarian countries, time is not lost; it gets renewed every year. Thus, chasing time to meet deadlines is often considered unnecessary in these countries.

Characteristically, countries that believe in time value strictly enforce punctuality. Breaking punctuality is considered wasting someone else's time; hence, it is synonymous with insulting the person whose time is being wasted. When someone is unpunctual and gets away with it, he/she is wrongfully allowed to nurture a feeling of superiority. Countries such as India and Latin America, which have their roots in the old agrarian society, do not believe in time value. They do not hesitate to make people wait, do not meet them, and even ask them to come back the next day. These countries believe in doing business with mutual trust. Contrarily, countries that believe in limited time (i.e., in time value) do not develop mutual trust; rather, they establish business relations formally as a rule of law.

Power Distance

High and low power distances differentiate organizational practices. With high power distance, decision-making is centralized, organizations are structured on hierarchical lines, and people down the line hardly interact with the top bosses. With low power distance, people take decisions in a decentralized manner; they coordinate their activities and work in a team. They enjoy autonomy at work.

Countries which believe in high power distance mostly belong to old agrarian societies. Bypassing a superior is considered insubordination and can even merit disciplinary action. This is not so in countries with low power distance.

Individualism vs Collectivism

Exhibit 10.1 highlights the importance of being sensitive to different cultures. There are two kinds of culture—individualism and collectivism In individualist cultures,

---

EXHIBIT 10.1   Culture clash

An American may find it irritating and consider it as being unfriendly, if a person who has met him/her several times earlier, addresses him/her with the prefix Mr or Ms Austrians, however, consider this as normal and courteous.

Having a business meeting in an open office is often construed as lacking seriousness, but in Kuwait this is normal and often people interrupt the meeting. A Western delegation may construe it as showing less respect to the business deal.

In England, saying 'yeah' to a boss, is considered as being rude and disrespectful. An American worker may wonder what went wrong when he/she responded thus to his/her British boss. The British infer that this is a reflection of a forgetful attitude.

A Japanese business delegation wanted to express disinterest in a business deal to its Norwegian client and said, 'It will be very difficult.' The Norwegian client assumed this to mean that may be when difficulties are eased, the business deal can be finalized. So, he eagerly asked how he could help. For Japanese, saying something is 'difficult' is a polite way of saying 'no'. But in many other countries, it is construed as a 'problem'; one that can be eased with a solution.

The problems that occur in cross-cultural interaction are not exhaustive. Only some that are more relevant in a business context or situation have been included here.

Source: Bhattacharyya (2010)

importance is given to individual uniqueness and people are expected to perform their jobs with self-determination. In collectivist cultures, people work in groups and believe in loyalty and compliance. Although both cultures have good or bad implications, a good way of explaining the difference is through the experience of many international researches, particularly those who are required to generate information through cross-country surveys.

While conducting a cross-country survey, a market research organization noticed that there were more responses to mailed questionnaires from countries with an individualistic culture compared to countries that believe in a collectivistic culture. This is primarily because in a collectivist culture, the responsibility of sending the responses was given to all, while in an individualist culture this was assigned to a single official.

DEFINITION AND CHARACTERISTICS OF ORGANIZATIONAL CULTURE

Academia who studied culture have often come up with rather narrow definitions. Others have taken these definitions and combined them into new and more embracing definitions. Schein (1985) defined 'organizational culture' as 'a pattern of basic assumptions—invented, discovered, or developed by a given group as it learns to cope with its problems of external adaptation and internal integration—that has worked well enough to be considered valid and, therefore, to be taught to new members as the correct way to perceive, think, and feel in relation to those problems.' Such definitions present culture more as socially constructed realities. Another way of defining organizational culture relates to groups of people collectively, who pool together their day-to-day experiences in the work environment, and develop some practices which they believe will help the organization to survive and grow. Thus, this definition believes that culture is created in the organization, and hence, it is what people in groups develop gradually.

There are two opposing views on organizational culture. Smircich (1983) considered it as hidden attributes of 'beliefs and values'. Thompson and Luthans (1990), on the other hand, considered it as behavioural attribute, which develops with the instance of social learning. Bandura (1976, 1977) took an extended view of learning, making it the result of both direct and indirect (vicarious) means. Vicarious learning inside an organization takes place when employees interpret management actions on the basis of the treatment extended to different stakeholders. According to this theory, behaviour has two components—norms and patterns. Norms are internalized views of behaviour, while patterns are the external visible manifestations of perceived norms. Non-behavioural attributes of culture are 'heroes, rites and rituals, legends, and ceremonies'.

Behaviourism and social learning theories consider human beings as responding mechanisms. The open systems theory considers human beings as adaptive agents.

Although these mainly espouse an approach of learning and the behavioural responses, they are very significant in understanding how an organization can truly develop its culture and sell it to their employees. Smircich's (1985) typology of thinking provides a better understanding and is outlined in Table 10.1.

TABLE 10.1   Typology of thinking

Assumptions about people	Theoretical classification
Humans as responding mechanisms	Behaviourism social learning theory
Humans as adaptive agents	Open systems theory
Humans as information processors	Cybernetics
Humans as social actors	Social action theory
Humans create their realities	Ethno methodology
Humans as transcendental beings	Phenomenology

Reviewing all these approaches to organizational culture, we can, in line with Schein (1985), summarize that leaders create organizational environments that employees respond to, and in the process modify their behaviour. Finally, organizational culture primarily converges into two primary assumptions, that is, socially constructed realities and group-perceived norms and patterns.

Organizational Culture as External and Internal Variables

Organizational culture can be viewed both as an independent variable (or external variable) brought into the organization or as an internal variable, or as a root metaphor for conceptualizing organizations. Such perspectives can be modelled in line with Thompson and Luthans (1990) as shown in Fig. 10.1.

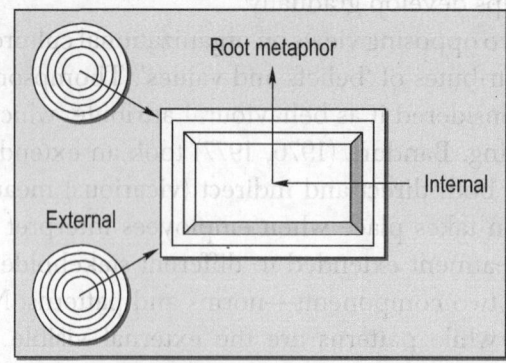

FIG. 10.1   Perspective of organizational culture

Source: Adapted from Thompson and Luthans (1990).

TYPES OF ORGANIZATIONAL CULTURE

We discussed in detail the types of organizational culture based on Prof. Greet Hofstede's world-class pioneering study on IBM. However, to understand the various types of organizational culture, we will first review the contributions of others.

Harrison (Hampden-Turner 1990) defined a four-quadrant model based on the twin axis of formulation (high–low) and centralization (high–low) to give the four cultures of role, task, atomistic (person), and power as shown in Fig. 10.2. Using a similar model, Handy (1985) named the four types of organizational culture as Apollo, Athena, Dionysus, and Zeus respectively, after the Greek gods displaying similar characteristics.

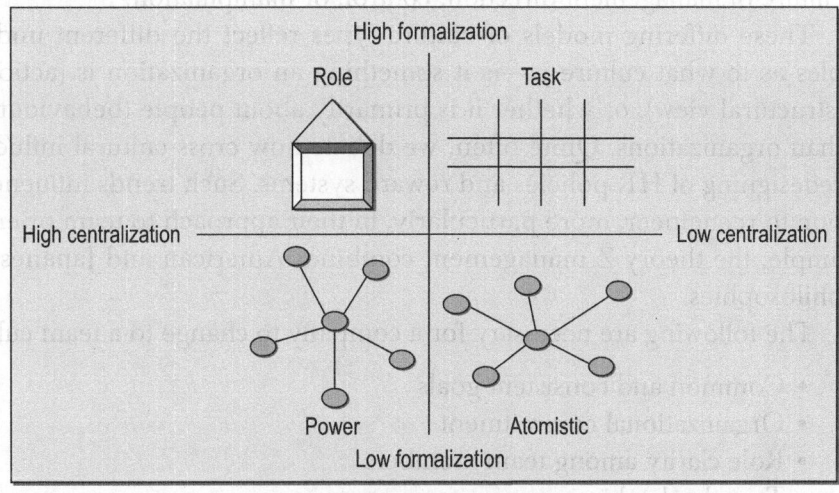

FIG. 10.2 Culture quadrants

Source: Adapted from Harrison (1972)

In yet another way, Quinn and McGrath (1985) developed the types of organization as hierarchy, market, clan, and adhocracy or hierarchical, rational, consensual, and ideological. They also proposed four types of organizational cultures and fit, alongwith leadership styles (see Table 10.2) All these are examples of classifying the culture of organizations from a structural viewpoint. A departure from such cultural classification

TABLE 10.2 Four types of fit or congruence (Quinn and McGrath 1985)

Environmental conditions	Organizational culture and form	Leadership style
High uncertainty–high intensity	Development culture (adhocracy)	Idealistic, prime mover
High uncertainty–low intensity	Rational culture (market)	Rational achiever
Low uncertainty–low intensity	Hierarchical culture (hierarchical)	Empirical expert
Low uncertainty–high intensity	Consensual culture (clan)	Existential team builder

was made by Kono (1990) based on his study of 88 Japanese organizations. Kono defined five types of organizational culture, such as vitalized, follow the leader and vitalized, bureaucratic, stagnant, follow the leader and stagnant.

Depending on the response of organizations in the marketplace, we also find a classification of types of organizational culture in the work of Deal and Kenney (1982). We can say it as 'work hard/play hard' organizational culture. Behavioural classification of types of organizational culture is seen in the work of Alvesson (1993), which is known as the metaphor concept. Based on the interpretation of the work of others, he presented ten main metaphors as cultures, namely exchange regulator, compass, social glue, sacred cow, manager-controlled rites, affect-regulator, non-order, blinder, world-closure, and dramaturgical domination. Most of these reflect a culture of management direction, control, or manipulation.

These differing models of culture types reflect the different underlying principles as to what culture is—is it something an organization is (action view) or has (structural view), or whether it is primarily about people (behavioural view) rather than organizations. Quite often, we debate how cross-cultural influence affects the redesigning of HR policies and reward systems. Such trends influence an organization to reengineer, more particularly, in their approach to team orientation. For example, the theory Z management combines American and Japanese management philosophies.

The following are necessary for a company to change to a team culture:

- Common and consistent goals
- Organizational commitment
- Role clarity among team members
- Team leadership
- Mutual accountability with the team

EXHIBIT 10.2 Application of culture at the workplace

- Mergers and acquisitions
- Strategic alliances and partnerships
- Restructuring issues
- Change management
- Self-development processes
- People management skills
- Executive coaching
- Negotiation skills
- Multinational/remote/team building
- Facilitating top teams
- Project teams
- Expatriate/Inpatriate coaching/briefings
- Sales and marketing skills
- General management training and education
- Counselling
- Leadership
- Organizational influencing

These apart, culture plays a crucial role even in operational areas. Basically, the above mentioned areas are strategically significant, where cultural areas, if not taken care of, may ultimately cause problems for the organization.

- Complementary knowledge and skills
- Reinforcement of required behavioural competencies
- Power (real and perceived)
- Shared rewards

In a competitive environment, it is difficult for organizations to survive without developing a team culture. Culture gets implemented at the workplace, encompassing almost all areas. Certain important areas of cultural applications are shown in Exhibit 10.2.

ORGANIZATIONAL CULTURE FROM A GLOBAL PERSPECTIVE

The literal definition of 'corporate culture' is the act of developing intellectual and moral faculties through education. Another definition is the moral, social, and behavioural norms of an organization that are based on the beliefs, attitudes, and priorities of its members. The first definition emphasizes building culture through education. Its relevance is more applicable in organizations that emphasize continuous learning. In Chapter 8, we have already explained that many world-class organizations have their captive learning and development centres, commonly known as corporate universities. Organizations like Motorola, McDonald's, Sears globally, and Tata, SAIL, TVS group, etc. nationally, institutionalized learning. These organizations have achieved excellence leveraging their systems of continuous learning. All these organizations pursue some specific culture, which make them different from their competitors. To make employees adaptable to their culture, such organizations emphasize on extended training and learning support, and even prolong their general induction programme. In India, Infosys and TCS, the two major players in information technology, provide time-bound long-term induction programme to make the new recruits adaptable to their culture. Therefore, every organization develops its own unique culture or set of values that differentiates them from others.

While continuous learning and extended induction programmes are some of the ways to create organizational culture, espoused values and vision of the entrepreneur or the top management also build and impact the same. Dhirubhai Ambani's Reliance, Jamshedji Tata's Tata Group, M.V. Subbai's Murugappa Group are certain examples of visionary culture in India. Later on, however, these organizations have reinforced their culture through continuous learning initiatives. We also have international examples of Jack Welch, the former CEO of GE, and Henry Ford of Ford Motors.

The spate of globalization has recently compelled many organizations to review and redefine their culture. For example, with its global presence, Hewlett-Packard (HP) has refocused their corporate culture, emphasizing on commitment to diversity, inclusion, and non-discrimination. Wal-Mart's corporate culture even extends to sharing of strategic information with the employees, to make them feel empowered and motivated.

MERGERS AND THEIR IMPACT ON ORGANIZATIONAL CULTURE

Mergers and acquisitions also bring major changes in the corporate culture and there are many examples of this across the globe. Before discussing a case in detail, let us consider certain cultural issues in the following that organizations worldwide have experienced during the post-merger phase.

- Disintegration of organizational value systems (rent-to-own store, US case)
- Low employee morale (results in poor productivity, conflicts), (rent-to-own store and Dell, US cases)
- Benefits of synergy require time (IOC and IBP, Indian cases)—IOC's market share is 54 per cent of petroleum, oil, and lubricants (POL) products but in retail business its share is 40 per cent. With IBP, IOC adds 1540 outlets to its existing 7750 outlets (IBP's market share is 8 per cent). HPCL, BPCL together now enjoy 20 per cent. The threat is from emerging new organizations.
- Rationalization and relocation of manpower may encounter problems (Blue Star, Indian case)
- Generation gap may create conflict (CMC–Tata, Bank of Madura, and ICICI)
- Flying of talents
- Different cultures (including cross-country culture)
- Rigidity to learn new things for blue collar employees
- Sentimental attachment
- Anxieties regarding redundancy (as merger follows manpower rationalization)
- Difference in HR style (e.g., Blue Star case)
- Broken faith in management due to the veil of secrecy in the merger
- Stalemate in managerial positions (one has to leave or compromise for the new group that is taking over)
- Reduces employee enthusiasm. To get a synergy of 2+2>4, it follows cost control, which may affect executive pay.

These examples illustrate how developing and sustaining a conscious culture in the organization can contribute to its growth and prosperity. Corporate culture as a separate branch has received priority due to globalization, consequent mobility of people, and cross-cultural influences, particularly for multinational and transnational organizations.

The merger mantra

Although there are many suggestions for achieving success in mergers, truly speaking, it is difficult to propose a universal mantra for the success of mergers. This is perhaps due to organization-specific issues.

Let us list some of the key findings, which perhaps have some universal character:

- Strong corporate cultures and values
- Retention of talent from the acquired company

- Leveraging of financial synergies
- Existence of a track record of success in previous cases of acquisition
- Empathetic and persuasive communication with the people of the acquired unit

With this prelude, let us now review some of the cases of merger to understand the reasons for their success and failure.

P&G–Gillette

The Cincinnati-based P&G acquired Boston-based Gillette for $57 billion to become the world's largest consumer products company with annual sales of $60.7 billion and market capitalization of $200 billion. Gillette's CEO, James M. Kilts and P&G's CEO, A.G. Lafley made this process a reality in 2005 after a series of talks and negotiations. This is a unique case of acquisition by two innovative companies to expand their product lines and strengthen their respective market position to check the growth of competitors.

Tata–Corus

The acquisition by Tata of the $13.7 billion Corus Steel, a British company, on 31 January 2007, is perhaps one of the mega acquisitions by an Indian company. With 84,000 employees in 45 countries across the world, Tata–Corus today produces 27 million tonnes of steel per annum and is the fifth largest steel producer in the world. The acquisition leader, Ratan Tata, Chairman, Tata Sons, believes that the acquisition of Corus will strategically place the company in a position to compete at the leading edge of a rapidly changing global steel industry.

Corus has witnessed a long history of disruptive organizational change and serious lack of clear strategic direction. With the centralization of functions and greater focus on profitability, more high margin products, sifting the product mix to processing and fabrication, and improving customer service, Corus could tap the potentiality of value-added growth opportunities. However, one must see what integration strategies are being taken to make Corus compatible with Tata. As of now, Tata seems to be pursuing the 'wait and watch' strategy.

HP–Compaq

In September 2001, when the CEO, Carly Fiorina, announced HP's decision to merge the business of Compaq, the stock market reacted sharply and prices fell from $23.21 to $18.87, and ended at $17.44 on 3 May 2002, the day the deal was finally consummated. From then on, the company has gradually turned around through a slow process. One of the major contributors to such a turnaround has been the smooth transition and the sound HR policies that HP followed. On the date of writing this analysis, HP stocks had closed on the previous day's trading at $45.67, a long way from the sub $18 on the day of the merger.

Due to her inability to revive the performance of the hardware businesses, Fiorina was asked to step down as the company's Chairman and CEO on 9 February 2005. The day Fiorina resigned, the shares of HP rose by 6.9 per cent on the New York Stock Exchange. However, Mark Hurd, ex-Chairman and CEO, validated the controversial merger plan of Carly Fiorina. HP is now back to its glorious past.

HP is also back on an acquisition spree. On 13 May 2008, HP and EDS (Excellerate HRO) announced that they had signed an agreement for HP to acquire Plano, the Texas-based technology company, for $13.9 billion, at $25 per share.

Industry observers say that if the merger goes through, it would provide a swath of new resources and potential clients for excellerate HRO, the jointly-owned HR outsourcing business shared by EDS and Towers Perrin. The merger would give HP the partner it has been seeking in the HR outsourcing business. Although it is too early to speculate on its impact, this merger once again reminds us that in any merger and acquisition, integration and its results cannot be expected overnight.

Daimler–Chrysler

The Daimler–Chrysler merger was announced on 7 May 1998 after a $38 billion stock deal. The *Wall Street Journal* named it the biggest industrial merger of all times, and it was announced as a merger of equals, a merger of growth, and a merger of unprecedented strength. Robert J. Eaton, Chairman and CEO, Chrysler Corporation also firmly believed that it would lead to the achievement of exciting perspectives in the growth of two very profitable automobiles companies. The new company could identify opportunities to increase sales, create new markets for Daimler–Chrysler, reduce purchasing costs, and realize economies of scale. The merger was supposed to change the entire global auto industry, but in fact, it failed. The failure is attributed to the culture incongruence between the Americans and the Germans.

ORGANIZATIONAL CULTURE CHANGE PROCESS

An analysis of organizational culture as an approach to organizational change is a difficult task. The culture of an organization is deep-rooted in its history and is below the surface of awareness. Any organizational culture change process follows certain well-defined and structured steps. Although it varies from organization to organization, we can draw a tentative list as follows:

Identify the core values and beliefs These do not just include stated values and goals, but can also be embedded in organizational metaphors, myths, and stories, and in the behaviours of members.

Consider the subcultures within the organization This is done by acknowledging, respecting, and discussing the perceived differences of organizational members in core values and beliefs.

List out the incongruence This is done between conscious and unconscious beliefs and values and resolve by choosing those that the organization wishes to commit to.

Establish new behavioural norms New behavioural norms are established (and even new metaphor language) that clearly demonstrate desired values.

Repeat these steps over a long period of time As new members enter the organization, they should be surrounded with clear messages about the culture they are about to enter.

ORGANIZATIONAL STRUCTURE

Like organizational culture, organizational structure is also one of the central issues in organizational theory in the twentieth century. Three main theories of organizational structure have emerged: (i) the archetypal bureaucracy, (ii) the stakeholder model, and (iii) newer ways of thinking, especially reflexive theories.

The archetypal bureaucracy theory stems ultimately from the theories of Max Weber. Its features are rationality, task specialization, hierarchy, and regularity, and there is a strong emphasis on structure as a controlling force. In the stakeholder model, on the other hand, rationality is abandoned and structure becomes the framework in which the various stakeholders—leaders, internal parties, and external parties—seek to achieve their own goals.

However, new research on organizational structure has focused on variables such as culture, metaphors, learning forms, dynamic organizational variants, and fields, such as total quality management (TQM), six sigma, lean production, and the related paradigm shift. Both organizational theory and organizational practice reflect on the significance and use of the concept of structure. Details of organizational structure have been discussed in Chapter 2.

ORGANIZATIONAL DIAGNOSTICS

Organizational diagnostics are measures that can apply to anyone in the organization, and can be aggregated to represent different levels of the organization, such as departments, branches, or the organization as a whole. These are useful diagnostics 'for gauging the morale of a company's workforce, testing the impact of new policies or procedures, monitoring long-term trends in the workforce, and determining where interventions are needed'. Some of the measures that are essential for an organization's growth and development are discussed here.

Attitudes towards Work

During the course of development a person acquires tendencies to respond to objects. These learned cognitive mechanisms are called attitudes. Changes in knowledge are followed by changes in attitudes. Knowledge reinforces attitudes, and in the long run, these reinforce individual and group behaviour. Hence, attitude is neither behaviour nor the cause of behaviour, but it relates to an intervening predisposition or a frame of reference which influences the behaviour of an individual.

Attitudes towards work are measured from multi-dimensional perspectives. Some sample perspectives and the way they are measured are as follows:

Job satisfaction The degree to which employees are satisfied and happy with their jobs.

Sample: *I am generally satisfied with the kind of work I do in this job.*

Role clarity Knowledge of exactly what behaviour is expected in one's job.

Sample: *I know what my job responsibilities are.*

Role conflict The extent to which two or more pressures occur together such that indulging in one would make doing the other more difficult.

Sample: *I often have to bend a rule or policy in order to carry out an assignment.*

Autonomy The extent to which employees have a say in scheduling their tasks, as well as decisions regarding the procedures to be followed and equipment to be used in their work.

Sample: *I am able to act independently of my supervisor in performing my job function.*

Participation in decision-making The extent to which employees participate in setting the goals and policies of the organization.

Sample: *I can help to make decisions which affect my work.*

Job involvement The degree to which employees are committed to and involved in their job.

Sample: *I do not mind spending a half hour past office hours if I can finish a task.*

ORGANIZATIONAL COMMITMENT

Organizational commitment is a major determinant for the performance of employees. To a great extent, it depends on the type of culture the organization nurtures. The degree of organizational commitment can be measured using the following criteria:

Job security The ability to keep a job for as long as one wants, providing one's performance is satisfactory.

Sample: *I can be sure of my job as long as I do good work.*

Loyalty The feelings of affection for and attachment to one's organization.

Sample: *If another organization offered me more money for the same kind of work, I would almost certainly accept.*

Trust in management The extent to which employees ascribe good intentions to, and have trust in the works and actions of management, and their organization.

> Sample: *Management at my location acts with sincerity.*

Identification The extent to which employees adopt, as their own, the goals and values of their organization.

> Sample: *I really feel as if this organization's problems are my problems.*

Alienation The extent to which employees feel disappointed with their career and professional development.

> Sample: *I do not feel a sense of pride or accomplishment in the work that I do.*

Helplessness The extent to which employees feel they possess few opportunities and alternatives available to them outside their organization.

> Sample: *I feel I have too few options to consider leaving this organization.*

ORGANIZATIONAL CLIMATE

It is said that the culture of an organization sets its climate. A positive organizational culture develops a climate where people are comfortable to work and give their best to achieve results. Organizational climate can be understood by measuring the following attributes:

Fairness The extent to which employees perceive their workplace to be equitable and free of bias.

> Sample: *Employees in my workplace are treated fairly, regardless of race.*

Safety The extent to which employees perceive their workplace to be safe and free of physical danger.

> Sample: *I am often in situations at work where I can easily get physically hurt.*

Support The amount of perceived emotional support employees feel from their organization.

> Sample: *Management here is interested in the welfare of its people.*

Communication The accuracy and openness of information exchange.

> Sample: *I am kept informed about the changes that affect my work.*

Tolerance for risk The degree to which the organization encourages bold action, risk, and independence of thought from employees.

> Sample: *Risk-taking is a value supported by our corporate culture.*

Flexibility The degree of adaptability and tolerance for ambiguity in an organization.

> Sample: *This organization adapts quickly to change.*

Continuous learning Perceptions of training and development opportunities in one's organization.

Sample: *There are adequate opportunities to pursue professional development activities beyond the scope of my immediate job.*

Pettigrew (1987) argued that context has more influence on organizational change than transformational leadership, which he thought was too prescriptive and whose value in terms of a firm's performance was inconclusive. Pettigrew's environmental forces are categorized into inner (political, structural, and cultural) and outer (economic, political, and competitive) types. However, like many of the objective schools, his list implies that culture is another variable, though not necessarily a directly controllable one.

MODELS OF ORGANIZATIONAL CULTURE CHANGE

From an extensive review of available studies and literature, one can identify three basic models of organizational culture change.

Root Metaphor

An organization exists and continues its existence from generation to generation of workforces. With the same analogy, culture also exists and gets perpetuated among the workforce from one generation to another. Cultural change happens, but slowly, and only through the innumerable forces between all the actors. It cannot be predetermined. Schein (1985) suggested that this was close to the situation in mid-life and mature organizations, although within the given time and the right process, he believed that cultural change was possible but not mandated.

External and Independent Variable

If one believes that culture is an external and independent variable, then there will also be the belief that there is little one can do to change it in the face of the multiplicity of external social behaviours, values, and beliefs that employees bring into the workplace. For example, religious beliefs about how to treat others, what is right or wrong, or attitudes about people of other races, etc. Over a period of time, some social changes could work in favour of some types of organizations; for example, a conservative government promoting a strong market economy (as in China).

Internal Variable

A behaviour school views that culture is an internal variable which will lead to a belief that the culture can be directed and changed. The exact methods vary but most researchers place significant emphasis on change being leader-led (e.g., Deal and Kennedy 1982) or leader-enabled (Schein 1985). However, some concentrate on the more visible symbols and artefacts, on people's behavioural patterns, and on the underlying behaviour norms, values, and beliefs of people.

MANAGEMENT-DIRECTED CULTURAL CHANGE

Cultural change through the actions and behaviour of leaders is considered as most effective, as leaders create the desired environment through a set of actions. They demonstrate the business, create the right atmosphere, shape values, and signify the business focus. They also preach the vision, coach the people, and provide a sense of direction to all. Deal and Kennedy (1982) for instance, advocated consensus building based on sharing, developing high level of trust between individuals, allowing time for people to change, setting the direction and allowing employees to work out the details, and providing training to develop the new skills needed. Within the 'atomised organization' managers 'will be both the bearers of culture as well as its promoters'. Thompson and Luthans (1990) highlighted the need for a more systematic approach: 'Changing culture in the light of this behaviour–consequence concept involves comprehensive planning and execution. Consistent messages must be conveyed through behavioural interactions and through changes in the employees' environment. Through behavioural actions people communicate ideas and values. People learn more from behaviours than from printed statements and company policies.'

Many writers, however, do introduce some form of process. Hickman and Silva (1985) advocated developing a creative insight, creating a vision of the future, and anticipating and implementing change. Patience, culture building, and matching strategy to culture are seen as important attributes of leaders. This mixing of hard strategy and soft culture is advocated by many others including Mayon–White (1993), and Benjamin and Mabey (1993).

Other scholars such as Hahn (1991), Wilson (1992), Klemm et al. (1991), Kennedy (1993), and Burack (1991) continued to provide even more systematic processes, complete with flow charts. In these approaches, culture is typically treated as another variable, almost like a resource, such as people, to be tuned and honed. Its shape is treated very much like a function of the corporate vision and mission. Burack talked about the contributory role of culture and suggested no substitute for objective strategic planning, whereas in contrast, Deal and Kennedy said that business change is cultural change.

Typically, organizational changes, such as structural changes, downsizing, plant closure, and relocation appeared to pre-empt the cultural changes, if not actually used as a lever to force through cultural change. Based on his research of 88 Japanese organizations, Kono (1990) developed a cause-and-effect approach to determine the culture, strategy, and behavioural norms. Thus, when culture is lively and vital, then it is a part of the long-range plan, and it can create an innovative strategy and in turn, create a revitalized strategy. When the culture is stagnant, either a partial plan is followed by incremental change of both strategy and culture together, or change of the culture is first followed by partial change of strategy and long-range planning, and then a comprehensive strategy change. For all these, culture can be finally defined as the actual decision-making pattern, as it is easier to observe and measure.

Despite such differing approaches, ultimately it converges to the idea that organizational culture is a long-term process and is difficult to manage. Thompson and Luthans (1990) concluded that managing culture in organizations was a process. And, it is important for the organization to communicate, and demonstrate the policies and practices to help employees to understand the process.

Schein stated that the leadership role of management was instrumental. Schein's OD approach addresses the inner characteristics of culture. Besides such a therapeutic (OD) approach, he also suggested some process models as follows:

1. General evolutionary process that ensures change from within the group, and which is natural and inevitable.
2. Adaptation, learning, or specific evolutionary process through which organizations respond to the environment and processes that people learn and adapt to.
3. Revolutionary process, where power acts as the key variable.
4. Managed process through which organizations focus on what can and cannot be changed.

It is for the leaders to consider which model to select to ensure that the members of the organization understand and adopt it with minimum confusion and disagreement.

SUMMARY

Culture includes the visible artefacts and behaviour patterns, and also the invisible behaviour norms, values, assumptions, and beliefs. Whether culture is a root metaphor embedded in organizational beliefs and values, an external uncontrollable variable, or an independent variable that can be manipulated is still debatable. The term organizational culture is generally accepted as referring to the shared meanings, beliefs, and understandings held by a particular group or organization about its problems, practices, and goals.

The concept of organizational culture is often misunderstood and confused with the related concepts of climate, ideology, and style. Organizational culture evolves from the social practices of members of organizations and, therefore, socially created realities exist in the heads and minds of organizational members as well as in the formal rules, policies, and procedures of organizational structures.

An organization's culture is either an important contributor or an obstacle to successful strategy execution. Strong organizational culture promotes good strategy execution. However, this is only possible when there is a cultural fit. Good organizations endeavour to match culture with their strategies. Organizations with strong cultural bonds cannot eliminate the deep-seated values and behavioural norms of people. A strong culture is a valuable asset when it matches strategy, but a liability when it does not. Therefore, with organizational change, a change of organizational culture also becomes necessary.

In this chapter, we discussed the meaning and concepts of organizational culture, its different aspects, and how it exerts influence on organizations. Worldwide organizations face difficulties due to cultural differences; hence, managing culture and the cultural change process are important priority areas. The chapter elaborately explains the various dimensions of culture and its influence on organizational culture, the usual problems organizations encounter due to cultural differences, the characteristics of organizational culture, organizational culture as external and internal variables, its types, and global dimension, and its process of change. The chapter concludes with a focus on the management directed cultural change process, emulating the processes suggested by different authors. For the ease of understanding, the chapter explains theoretical issues with adequate corporate examples.

KEY TERMS

Archetypal bureaucracy It stems from the theories of Max Weber. Its features are rationality, task specialization, hierarchy, and regularity, and a strong emphasis on structure as a controlling force.

Jungle-like culture It indicates professionalism, innovation, creativity, and a place for unleashing the potentiality of members. This culture promotes interpersonal competition, incentives for hard work, freedom and autonomy, and risk-bearing decision-making.

Machine-like culture This culture probably prevents burn-out, lowers turnover, and smoothes out financial performance. When new opportunities present themselves, the organization moves too slowly to win the lion's share of profits.

Monochronic cultures These value a certain orderliness and sense of there being an appropriate time and place for everything. They do not value interruptions.

Polychronic cultures These like to do multiple things at the same time. A manager's office in a polychromic culture typically has an open door, a ringing phone, and a meeting, all going on at the same time.

Root metaphor If one believes that culture is a root, then there will be a belief that there is no instant means of changing a culture which will have developed since its inception.

CONCEPT REVIEW QUESTIONS

1. Explain the concept of organizational culture. How does it differ from global and national culture?
2. What are the different aspects of organizational culture? How do these aspects make a difference among cultures of different organizations?
3. What are the dimensions of culture? How do they make a difference in the culture of an organization?
4. Explain the characteristics of organizational culture.
5. Explain the external and internal variables of organizational culture.
6. Explain the concept of organizational culture from a global perspective.
7. Explain how mergers and acquisitions exert impact on the change process of organizational culture.
8. Discuss the process of measurement of culture. What are the difficulties faced by organizations in measuring culture?
9. Explain the process of changing organizational culture.
10. Write short notes on the following:
    (a) Organizational diagnostics
    (b) Organizational climate
    (c) Role of culture in radical change
    (d) High context vs. low context culture
    (e) Power distance
    (f) Ethical issues in organizational culture

CRITICAL THINKING QUESTIONS

1. An Indian multinational with its headquarters in New Delhi recently acquired an American organization. Both companies are in consumer electronics and market leaders in their respective countries. As a cross-cultural expert, explain how the difference in national cultures and consequent

organizational cultures of these two companies can be addressed through a process of cultural integration.
2. Daiichi Sankyo of Japan has recently acquired 64 per cent stake in Ranbaxy Laboratories, India. Daiichi had reported a net loss of $3.5 billion for the year ending 31 March 2008. This loss is attributed to a sharp erosion in the share price of Ranbaxy. Although Daiichi Sankyo's perspective to acquire Ranbaxy was to establish dominance in the global generics drug market, Ranbaxy's erosion in value (primarily due to the import ban of 30 Ranbaxy products by the US Food and Drug Administration), defeated this purpose. The value erosion is further attributed to the general downturn in the global equity market after the sub-prime crisis. However, Daiichi is confident that it can overcome the crisis in the coming years. As an expert in organizational change and development, suggest what measures Daiichi could possibly take to overcome this crisis.
3. Drawing lessons from AMD's successful integration, critically examine the reasons for failure of the Daimler–Chrysler merger. As an organizational change and development expert, suggest possible action plans that could have been taken to ensure a successful integration of Daimler–Chrysler.

CASE STUDY

Unlocking Value through Operations in a Cold Rolling and Galvanizing Mill

The cold rolling and galvanizing shop is one of the profit centres of Prime Steel. The company enjoys the highest market share in galvanizing sheets. To retain this, it often has to compromise on vital efficiency measures, such as cost control, manpower optimization, and after-sales customer services. All these aspects form an important part of the performance management systems of the organization.

Recently, the company observed certain dysfunctional syndromes, which slowly reduced the market share. Some of the indicators were slow improvement of key parameters, unstructured problem-solving approach, uncontrolled consumption of raw materials, ineffective resource utilization, lack of reliability, etc.

All these had a cascading effect and began to affect the company's performance as a whole. At the individual level, however, workers achieved their performance targets, and executives and managers delivered results. The high-powered committee of Prime Steel attributed this to the present market leadership status of the company, but believed that it could not be sustained in the long run.

To ease such organizational performance problems, the company adopted a multi-pronged approach as follows:

- Identification of key value drivers
- Introduction of six sigma in a phased manner in key areas
- Introduction of total productive maintenance training to all operators
- Reframing of standard operation procedures (SOP) for protocol-bound jobs
- Installing automatic customers' complaint tracking software
- Inventory control through introduction of raw material consumption index, etc.

All the above steps ultimately led to the achievement of significant cost saving and increased revenue, optimization of raw materials consumption, energy efficiency, significant reduction in the inventory holding, and in the cycle time to respond to customers' complaints, etc.

On achieving success, the company feels that all the results are not the outcome of the efforts of people; rather they are the outcome of organizational effectiveness practices. Hence, despite the prevalence of existing systems of factoring performance incentives on organizational performance achievement, the company decided to keep such achievement results outside the purview of incentives. Employees and workers did not see anything wrong in this. However, they established their stake when the company paid 10 per cent more as annual performance incentives to managers and executives. They demanded a similar increase and threatened to go on indefinite strike if this was not granted. The company's rough estimate indicates that payment of this will outweigh the benefits accrued as a result of the recent effectiveness measures. Prime Steel is now literally in a fix.

Discussion Question

Suggest what could be your action plans to settle this impasse.

REFERENCES

Ahmed, P.K. (1998), 'Culture and climate for innovation', *European Journal of Innovation Management*, Vol. 1, pp. 30–43.

Alvesson, M. (1993), *Cultural Perspectives on Organizations*, Cambridge University Press, Cambridge.

Bandura, Albert (1977), *Social Learning Theory*, Prentice Hall, New Jersey.

———. (1976), 'Social learning theory', in Spence, J.T., R.C. Carson, and J.W. Thibuat, *Behavioural Approaches to Therapy*, General Learning Press, New Jersey, pp. 1–46.

Benjamin, G. and C. Mabey (1993), 'Facilitating redical change', in Mabey, C. and B. Mayon–White (eds), *Managing Change*, Paul Chapman, London, pp. 181–186.

Bhattacharyya, Dipak Kumar (2010), *Cross-cultural Management: Text and Cases*, PHI Learning, New Delhi.

———. (2009), *Organizational Behaviour*, Oxford University Press, New Delhi.

Burack, E.H. (1991), 'Changing the corporate culture—The role of human resource development', *Long Range Planning*, Vol. 24, No. 1, pp. 88–95.

Carr, C. (1996), *Choice, Chance and Organizational Change*, Amacom, New York.

Cummins, T. and C. Whorley (1997), *Organization Development and Change*, Southwestern College Publishing, Cincinnati.

Daft, R.L. (1995), *Understanding Management*, Harcourt Brace and Company, Orlando.

Deal, T. and A.A. Kennedy (1982), *Corporate Cultures*, Addison–Wesley, Massachusetts.

Gould, R.M. (1996), 'Getting from strategy to action: Processes for continuous change', *Long Range Planning*, Vol. 29, No. 3, pp. 278–289.

Hahn, D. (1991), 'Strategic management—Tasks and challenges in the 1990s', *Long Range Planning*, Vol. 24, No. 1, pp. 26–39.

Hampden-Turner, C. (1990), *Charting the Corporate Mind: From Dillemma to Strategy*, Basil Blackwell, Oxford.

Hampden-Turner, C. and F. Trompenaars (2000), *Building Cross-cultural Competence: How to Create Wealth from Conflicting Values*, Yale University Press, Boston.

Handy, C. (1989), *The Age of Unreason*, Century Business, London.

Handy, Charles, B. (1985), *Understanding Organizations*, Third Edition, Penguin Books, Harmondsworth.

Hickman, C.R. and M.A. Silva (1985), *Creating Excellence*, Unwin, London.

Kennedy, C. (1993), 'Changing the company culture at Ciba-Geigy', *Long Range Planning*, Vol. 26, No. 1, pp. 18–27.

Kilmann, R. (1995), 'A holistic programme and critical success factors of corporate transformation', *European Management Journal*, Vol. 13, No. 2, pp. 175–186.

Klemm, M., S. Sanderson, and G. Luffman (1991), 'Mission statements: Selling corporate values to employees', *Long Range Planning*, Vol. 24, No. 3, pp. 73–78.

Kono, T. (1990), 'Corporate culture and long range planning', *Long Range Planning*, Vol. 23, No. 4, pp. 9–19.

Leonard-Barton, D. (1992), 'The factory as a learning laboratory', *Sloan Management Review*, Vol. 34, No. 1, pp. 23–38.

Marshak, R. (1996), 'Metaphors, metaphoric fields, and organizational change', in Grant, D. and C. Ostwick (eds), *Metaphor and Organizations*, Sage Publications, London.

Mayon–White, B. (1993), 'Problem-solving in small groups: Team members as agents of change', in Mabey, C. and B. Mayon–White (eds), *Managing Change*, Second Edition, Paul Chapman, London.

Miller, D. (1982), 'Evolution and revolution: A quantum view of structural change in organizations', *Journal of Management Studies*, Vol. 19, pp. 131–151.

Orlikowski, W.J. and M.J. Tyre (1993), 'Exploiting opportunities for technological improvement in organizations', *Sloan Management Review*, Vol. 35, No. 1, pp. 13–26.

Pettigrew, A.M. (1987), 'Understanding power in organizations', in Mabey, C. and B. Mayon-White (eds), *Managing Change*, Second Edition, Paul Chapman, London.

Quinn, R.E. and M.R. McGrath (1985), 'The transportation of organizational, cultures: A competing values perspective, in Frost, P.J., L.F. Moore, C.C. Lundberg, and J.A. Martin (eds), *Organizational Culture*, Sage, California.

Schein, E.H. (1996), 'Three cultures of management: The key to organizational learning', *Sloan Management Review*, Fall, pp. 9–19.

Schein, Edgar (1985), *Organizational Culture and Leadership*, Jossey–Bass, San Fransisco.

Schoonhoven, C.B. and M. Jelinek (1990), 'Dynamic tension in innovative, high technology firms: Managing rapid technological change through organizational structure', in Tushman, M.L. and P. Anderson (eds), *Managing Strategic Innovation and Change*, Oxford University Press, New York.

Senge, P.M. (1993), *The Fifth Discipline: The Art and Practice of The Learning Organization*, Century Business, London.

Smircich, Linda (1985), 'Is the concept of culture a paradigm, for understanding organizations and ourselves', in Frost, P.J., L.F. Moore, C.C. Lundberg, and J.A. Martin (eds), *Organizational Culture*, Sage, California, pp. 55–72.

——. (1983), 'Concepts of culture and organizational analysis', *Administrative Science Quarterly*, Vol. 28, No. 3, pp. 339–358.

Thompson, K.R. and F. Luthans (1990), 'Organizational culture: A behavioural perspective', in Schneider, B. (ed), *Organizational Climate and Culture*, Chapter 9, Jessey-Bass, Oxford.

Trompenaars, F. (1993), *Riding the Waves of Culture: Understanding Cultural Diversity in Business*, Nicholas Brealey Publications, London.

Trompenaars, F. and C. Hampden-Turner (1998), *Riding the Waves of Culture: Understanding Diversity in Global Business*, Second Edition, McGraw-Hill, New York.

Tushman, M.L. and C. O'Reilly (1996), 'Ambidextrous organizations: Managing evolutionary and revolutionary change', *California Management Review*, Vol. 38, pp. 8–30.

Tushman, M.L. and E. Romanelli (1985), 'Organizational evolution: A metamorphosis model of convergence and reorientation', in Tushman, M.L. and P. Anderson (eds), *Managing Strategic Innovation and Change*, Oxford University Press, New York.

Wilson, J. (1992), 'Realising the power of strategic vision', *Long Range Planning*, Vol. 25, No. 5, pp. 18–28.

http://www.managingchange.com/bpr/bprcult/3culture.htm accessed on 5 November 2009.

11 Change through Performance Management

Learning Objectives

After reading this chapter, you will be able to understand
- the concept and overview of performance management
- the different types of performance models
- performance-driven organizational change process
- the issues related to performance standards
- the systems and processes of developing performance standards
- the concept of performance metric
- the process of performance modelling
- the importance of balanced scorecard and HR scorecard
- competency mapping and organizational change
- the role of knowledge management practices for organizational change

Transformation of Tata Consultancy Services (TCS)

To make employees responsive to internal and external factors, change their mindsets, and build capabilities, TCS focuses on empowered decision-making and inculcates in them a sense of ownership. In order to remain globally competitive, it views change as an ongoing process, revisits organizational structure and decision-making practices, and quickly responds to it. Adjustments against IP (industry practice), SP (service practice), and GM (geography matrix) are an ongoing exercise in the organization. In fact, TCS always senses this in advance. Perhaps, it is for this reason that for the first time in India, it envisaged the need to designate a chief transformation officer (CTO).

Through its learning programme, TCS ensures people capability development, which facilitates continuous mutation of the organization structure, meeting the changing employees' aspirations as well as customer delight. A glaring example of its concern about the organization structure is evident from its recent change to the matrix structure in order to keep pace with the external front. Organizational changes often cannot succeed only with the internal initiatives. TCS engaged an outsider, who acts as a change agent bringing fresh perspectives to the organization.

TCS believes in involving everyone in the process of transformation, clearly making the key concerns transparent, that is, 'why change, why now, what it means, where it will take the company, and its implications for everyone', providing a cascading effect, and making the process a great success through voluntary participation of employees. Its organizational transformation model encompasses strategic planning, change management, and alignment with project management to create business value. A performance measurement system with an economic value added (EVA) approach provides a framework to align corporate values with the performance of the constituent business units and the individual employees within it.

INTRODUCTION

Performance management systems (PMS) integrate with the strategies of the organization through the process of setting mutually decided goals or objectives, evaluation, compensation designs, promotional decisions, identification of training needs, etc. All these help the organization to achieve its strategic intents. Scientifically designed PMS are the best tools for balancing both individual and organizational needs. While at the individual level they help employees to achieve their career goals through training and other career development opportunities, at the organization level they ensure achievement of organizational goals and objectives.

Before we deliberate on issues, such as how PMS can facilitate the organizational change process, let us first understand exactly what PMS is. PMS is an ongoing process that involves both managers and employees, and works on the following lines:

1. Identifies and describes essential job functions and relates them to the mission and goals of the organization.
2. Develops realistic and appropriate performance standards.
3. Gives and receives feedback about performance.
4. Writes and communicates constructive performance appraisals.
5. Draws the required education and development programmes for employees in order to sustain, improve, and build their capability and enable the organization to sustain in competition.
6. Facilitates change in the organization.

Apart from performance management systems, balanced scorecards, HR scorecards, knowledge management practices, and competency management can also greatly help to bring in the desired organizational changes. In reality, all these measures reinforce the performance management systems of an organization.

OVERVIEW OF PERFORMANCE MANAGEMENT

The evolution of the concept of performance management as a new HRM model reflects a change of emphasis in organizations, away from command-and-control towards a facilitation model of leadership. This change has been accompanied by recognition of the importance, to the employee as well as the institution, of relating work performance to the strategic or long-term objectives and mission of the organization as a whole. Employees' goals and objectives are derived from their departments, which in turn, support the mission and goals of the organization.

The performance management process gives employees and managers an opportunity to discuss development goals and jointly create a plan for achieving them. Development plans should contribute to organizational goals as well as the professional growth of the employees. To sustain excellence in a changing environment, organizations worldwide have to make the transition from a bureaucratic to a network organization. The new organizational model emphasizes a focus on decision-making and accountability at the level where the work is done, development of a service culture that rewards team performance, and integration of operations. Critical to the success of this new model is the adoption of a customer service orientation, a flexible attitude in the face of constant change, and streamlined business processes supported by networked administrative systems.

DIMENSIONS OF PERFORMANCE

Borman and Motowidlo (1993, 1997) proposed that job performance can be divided into two categories: task and contextual performance. Theoretically, these are called the performance dimensions. Task performance activities that contribute to the organization's technical core, either directly through the implementation of the technological process or indirectly by providing the needed materials or services. Contextual performance, on the other hand, is defined as job behaviour, that is, the psychological environment in which the technical core of organizations functions.

Task performance can be characterized as follows:

1. It is a process of transforming raw materials into goods and services.
2. It replenishes the supply of raw materials through planning, coordination, supervision, or staff functions.
3. It contributes to organizational effectiveness or efficiency.

Similarly, contextual performance can be characterized as follows:

1. Enthusiasm to exert effort to complete one's own task activities successfully (includes punctuality, extra efforts, etc.).
2. Volunteering to carry out the task activities that are not a part of the job (e.g., suggestions to improve the organization, etc.).
3. Helping and cooperating with others (assisting and helping workers and customers).
4. Adhering to the organizational rules and procedures (e.g., following orders, complying with regulations, respecting authority, and organizational values and policies).
5. Endorsing, supporting, and defending organizational objectives (organizational loyalty, favourably representing the organization to outsiders, etc.).

The core difference between these two performance dimensions is that while task performance varies with the nature of the job, contextual performance remains similar across jobs.

Organizational change alters both performance dimensions, requiring employees to adapt in order to enable the organization to improve.

PERFORMANCE MODELS

There are various approaches to develop performance models. The conventional approach is to integrate the four performance variables, that is, organizational culture, people, systems, and structures. Such integration can produce a model for corporate performance management. An organization performs well in a culture-fit environment. A culture-congruent work environment makes people accountable, makes them feel responsible, and drives improvement. With a clear and common understanding of the performance areas, people can use their skills and competencies to deliver their best. The organization has to create the right performance ambience to encourage people to perform. A similar focus on organizational systems and structures can truly nurture the performance culture. Supporting systems and the collaborative structure of the organization can play a crucial role in developing the right performance culture.

A performance model can be developed using the performance triangle in Fig. 11.1.

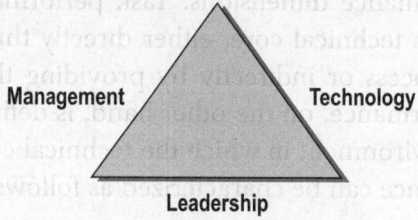

FIG. 11.1 The performance triangle

This model shows the balance between the three critical success factors in any organization. When the performance pendulum swings to the centre of the triangle, it is difficult to reach the optimum level of performance. Organizations try to balance the situation by using these critical success factors. This requires strong vision (management), passion, and energy (leadership), strengthened with technological inputs. At the organizational level, the terms 'management' and 'leadership' are often interchangeably used. But a distinction can be made by specifying certain attributes of management and leadership. The attributes of management are processes, facts, intellectual abilities, power, control, goal setting, communication, etc. On the other hand, the attributes of leadership are people, feelings, emotions, power of persuasion, commitment, positive thinking, innovation, verbal communication, etc. Management and leadership reinforced with technology can bring a positive change in the performance of the organization.

Campbell (1990) and Campbell et al. (1993) made attempts to integrate the numerous dimensions of individual performance into a comprehensive model. According to Campbell, the latent structure of job performance can be modelled using the following eight general factors:

- Job-specific task proficiency
- Non-job specific task proficiency

- Written and oral communication
- Demonstrating effort
- Maintaining personal discipline
- Facilitating peer and team performance
- Supervision/Leadership
- Management/Administration

A new conceptual framework of HRM initiatives also underscores the vital role of education, training, and development in the envisioned network organization. In such an organization, continuous learning is a prerequisite to a successful job performance and organizational effectiveness. Employees must be able to learn the work, and develop effective technical and people skills, in order to assume new responsibilities, and keep pace with and anticipate the changing nature of the work and workplace.

For managers and employees, responding to these changes requires the ability to learn, adapt to change, solve problems creatively, and communicate effectively in diverse groups. In addition, employees must take personal and proactive responsibility for their careers to ensure future employability and advancement. The realities of the contemporary workplace will continue to challenge existing paradigms and should be considered in managing the performance of employees in a dynamic work environment.

These apart, some of the organizational excellence models that also hold good for organizational performance have been discussed in Chapter 4. The balanced scorecard is discussed later in this chapter.

A manager is involved in performance management when he/she

- establishes specific job assignments,
- writes job descriptions,
- assigns responsibility for strategic initiatives,
- develops and applies performance standards,
- discusses job performance with the employee and provides feedback on the strengths and improvements needed, and
- conducts an annual performance evaluation plan for improved performance and employee development goals.

Setting the right objectives is critical for effective performance management. Objectives, such as higher profits, improved shareholder value, and customer satisfaction are understandable, but these cannot specify what managers need to do, or specify priorities and focus. Performance objectives are needed so that all cross sections of people in the organization can understand their scope of functions that contribute to the achievement of the overall objectives. From this perspective, setting the right performance objectives is very important, keeping in mind the following aspects:

- Focus on a result, not an activity
- Consistency

- Specificity
- Measurability
- Relation to time
- Attainability

These are called SMART objectives as shown in Exhibit 11.1.

Such objectives are clearer when answers to the questions are available, as shown in Exhibit 11.2.

EXHIBIT 11.1 SMART objectives

- Specific
- Measurable—that can quantify the results
- Achievable
- Relevant
- Time bound—are governed by deadlines

EXHIBIT 11.2 Self and organizational assessment to testify performance objectives

Self-assessment
- Who am I?
- What are my strengths?
- How do I work?
- Where do I belong?
- What is my contribution?

Organizational assessment
- What is its role?
- What are its resources?
- How does it function?
- What is the function within it?
- What are the functions of others?

PERFORMANCE-DRIVEN ORGANIZATIONAL CHANGE

In organizations change can either be transformational or transactional. Transformational change takes place in the process of organizational response to external stimuli, which among others, requires the organization to redefine its mission and reframe its strategy, and accordingly, adapt its culture to the changed requirements. For all these, leadership acts as the most important enabler. Transactional change, on the other hand, emphasizes internal organizational factors and processes, which organizations deliberately initiate to achieve excellence in performance. This requires consideration of structure, systems, managerial practices, and the work environment. In both types of change, as far as performance is concerned, this is what ultimately every organization aspires to achieve. Hence, ultimately organizations achieve performance excellence through change and try to sustain it. One can, thus, say that improved performance is the key driver for organizational change and development.

Based on this analogy, Burke and Litwin (1992) developed a causal model of organizational performance and change. This is shown in Fig. 11.2.

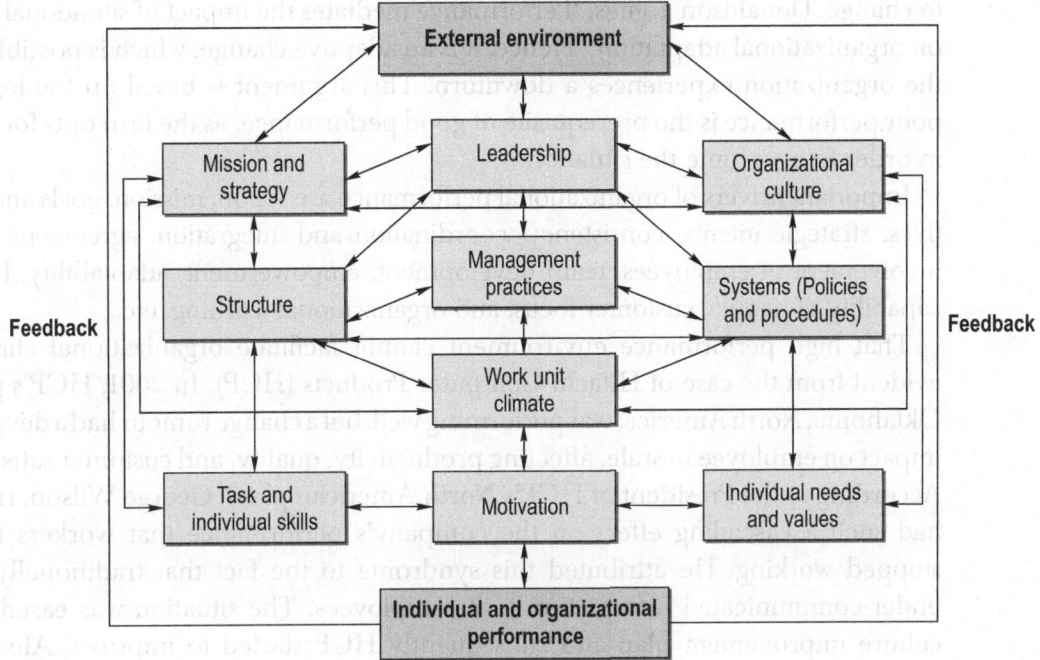

FIG. 11.2 Causal model of organizational performance and change
Source: Burke and Litwin (1992)

The casual model rests on the premise that change process in organizations is a kind of chaos (Gleick 1987) and model integrates different factors with the intention of bringing order in the process of change despite this. With the causal linkages in the process of change, the model ultimately concludes that organizations lead improved performances, both at the individual and organizational levels. The model helps to analyse, understand, and manage organizational change, and predict the change process.

According to this model, transformational and transaction change factors affect the motivation of people, which in turn, affects the performance, both at the individual and organizational levels. The feedback loop of the model directly affects the external environment. Therefore, the primary benefit of the model is that it integrates primary change factors (both external and internal), and in the process establishes a causal relationship in hierarchical order between the change elements.

The model, however, is not very specific about leadership and other internal factors that successfully transform an organization. Rather, it over-emphasizes the external environmental factors. In short, the model is complex and, therefore, difficult to practise in many organizational set-ups, particularly in legacy-bound manufacturing organizations.

However, Donaldson (1999) considered performance-driven organizational change process to be a debatable issue. It is said that high performance makes people averse to change. Donaldson argues, 'Performance mediates the impact of situational change on organizational adaptation.' Hence, it is an adaptive change, which is possible when the organization experiences a downturn. This argument is based on the logic that poor performance is the prerequisite of good performance, as the firm opts for change in order to overcome the situation.

Important drivers of organizational performance are vision, mission, goals and objectives, strategic intents, consistency, coordination and integration, agreement, values, involvement of employees, team development, empowerment, adaptability, building capability of people, customer focus, and organizational learning, etc.

That high performance environment cannot facilitate organizational change, is evident from the case of Hitachi Computer Products (HCP). In 2001, HCP's plant at Oklahoma, North America, was performing well, but a change rumour had a devastating impact on employee morale, affecting productivity, quality, and customer satisfaction. According to the President of HCP's North American plant, George Wilson, rumours had such a cascading effect on the company's performance that workers literally stopped working. He attributed this syndrome to the fact that traditionally, HCP under-communicated information to its employees. The situation was eased with a culture improvement plan and subsequently HCP started to improve. Along with this, the company introduced performance-linked pay to convey the message to the employees that individual and organizational results are interdependent. HCP was, thus, able to create a shared vision and improve the effectiveness of the organization as well. Positive employee engagement in the company's mission, values, and goals can support business success and growth. Measuring organizational culture and employee engagement is a vital step in making improvements in these areas.

Performance-driven organizational change, therefore, becomes more effective when used with other key drivers of the organization. It is always better to align changes on the customers' demand and expectations and the organizational performance as a whole. The balanced scorecard can significantly help in this regard.

Performance-driven Organizational Change Process

The process starts with the integration of PMS with the business goals and objectives of the organization. The common organizational change goals must first be identified and then linked to the roles, competencies, and performance improvement measures, to achieve the change goals. Performance improvement measures are required both at the individual and the organizational levels. While individual performance improvement measures assess the changing job roles and the competencies to achieve change in the organization, organizational performance improvement measures, through organizational development initiatives, try to bring order to the work environment. Organizational development initiatives, therefore, set the premise for both individual and organizational performance improvement.

A performance-driven organizational change process requires a series of actions and agreements at different levels. These are explained in subsequent paragraphs.

Bevan and Thompson (1992) indicated certain features of PMS to achieve performance-driven organizational change. These are as follows:

Focus on objective setting Objectives are targets which an organization sets for its employees, and is in the form of an action statement. Overall organizational objectives are decided at the strategic or corporate level. PMS helps to percolate the organizational objectives to the individual targets of employees'.

Develop systems for ongoing review of objectives PMS helps to keep a track of the achievement of objectives through the process of periodic performance review. Such a review system largely depends on the type of PMS techniques used by an organization. It may be an age-old MBO system or a 360-degree PMS (multi-dimensional), or a more recent performance tracking technique, such as a balanced scorecard. Review of objectives helps to control performance and initiates steps to correct deviations in performance or to revise the targets.

Develop personal improvement plans As PMS helps to monitor individual performance, it ensures development of personal improvement plans for employees. A particular employee may lack in performance or he/she may exceed the targets given. In both the cases, it is important to design a personal improvement plan. While in the first case, it may be important to provide performance counselling along with training and development reinforcement, in the second case, the employee may be motivated further through a proper reward system.

Alignment of training and development Since the focus of PMS is to manage and develop employee performances to sustain competitive advantage of an organization through proper alignment, it helps to identify training and development needs, and also to measure the return on investment (ROI).

Ensure formal appraisal with feedback By introducing a formal appraisal system, PMS helps to give employees a performance feedback. Both negative and positive feedback sensitize employees and help them to objectively analyse their shortfalls and positive aspects. While shortfalls can be met by learning reinforcement and setting the right direction, positive aspects can be leveraged by the employee concerned to further develop setting higher targets and to grow accordingly.

Help in pay review Performance-based pay is a modern concept. PMS helps to design compensation package for employees objectively, thus rewarding performance and reducing the variable pay (performance linked) of non-performers. Organizations can thus remain competitive by optimizing the cost of compensation.

Develop competence-based organizational capability Competence-based organizational capability helps to determine appropriate organizational change, keeping pace with competition. It also helps to plan human resources. Through qualitative and quantitative appraisals PMS can assess the prevailing competency level of employees and thus review organizational capability.

SETTING STANDARDS OF PERFORMANCE

Any organizational change, whether transformational or transactional, requires a review of the existing performance standards. If these standards are not available, they must be developed in documented form to explain the finer details of the existing jobs and the requirements of new ones. Documented performance standards not only mention the desired level of performance in terms of employee achievement, it also explains the process of doing the jobs in the best possible way. To extract the best performance from employees, it is always desirable to develop performance standards collaboratively (in participation with the employees). This is particularly important in organizational change process, as employees' support and cooperation set the pace of change and sustain it. Often performance standards are confused with job descriptions. While job description describes the functions and the tasks to be done, performance standards explain how these can be performed to meet and exceed expectations.

With the availability of documented performance standards, all cross sections of managers and employees can understand the desired performance expectation levels, and the best possible way to meet them. Effective implementation of mutually decided performance standards also requires continuous feedback and performance counselling, so that organizations can continue to sustain their momentum of change.

Performance standards can be developed through a directive or collaborative approach, or through mutual agreement. A directive approach is one in which the performance standards are formulated by the management and then shared with the employees. The sharing process also includes clarification of any pertinent issue raised by employees. A collaborative approach develops the performance standards with inputs from employees. The inputs from managers and employees are synergized and performance standards are developed in congruence with organizational change goals. This method elicits more responses because participation enhances the commitment to deliver.

Let us now consider hypothetical performance standards for different hierarchical levels for a CTV manufacturer in Exhibit 11.3.

Guidelines for Performance Standards

The following guidelines must be followed while developing performance standards:

1. Performance standards should be related to the employee's assigned work and job requirements.
2. Reporting systems should be adequate to measure and, therefore, should have more quantitative data.

EXHIBIT 11.3 Performance standards for different hierarchical levels

Level	Task description and performance standards
Level 1	Simple description of general expectation.

Example
Task description: Assemble CTVs
Standard: Put different sub-assemblies/CTVs in the assembly line

Example
Task description: Write annual reports
Standard: Annual reports will be submitted by agreed-upon date

Level 2	Simple description of specific expectations

Example
Task description: Assemble CTVs
Standard: Complete assembly of 5 error-free CTVs per minute

Example
Task description: Write annual reports
Standard: Prepare annual reports and submit them to the business heads in 7 working days before 31 March

Level 3	Description of specific expectations and success indicators

Example
Task description: Assemble CTVs
Standard: Ensure simultaneous error-free assembly of 5 CTVs per operator in 10 lines

Example
Task description: Write annual reports
Standard: Produce annual reports as per departmental format and submit to the business heads in 5 working days before 15 January

Level 4	Description of specific expectations, success indicators, and conditions, if any

Example
Task description: Assemble CTVs
Standard: Ensure 5 correct assembly of CTVs per minute per operator in 2 shop-floors and also ensure that the necessary equipments are in working order

Example
Task description: Write annual reports
Standard: Produce annual reports as per departmental format and submit to the business heads in 5 working days before 15 January

> **EXHIBIT 11.4 Checklist for performance standards**
>
> After writing the performance standards, one can check them against the questions in the following list, to ensure its appropriateness:
>
> **Are the standards realistic?** Standards should be attainable and consistent with what is necessary to get the job done. Standards for performance, which meet expectations, represent the minimum acceptable level of performance for all employees in that position.
>
> **Are the standards specific?** Standards should tell an employee exactly which specific actions and results he/she is expected to accomplish.
>
> **Are the standards based on measurable data, observation, or verifiable information?** Performance can be measured in terms of timeliness, cost, quality, and quantity.
>
> **Are the standards consistent with organizational goals?** Standards link individual (and team) performance to organizational goals and should be consistent with these goals. The success of any organization and its department's missions depends on this strategic connection.
>
> **Are the standards challenging?** Standards may describe performance that exceeds expectations. Recognizing performance that is above expectations or outstanding is crucial to motivate employees.
>
> **Are the standards clear and understandable?** The employees whose work is to be evaluated on the basis of the standards should understand them. Standards should use the language of the job.
>
> **Are the standards dynamic?** As organizational goals, technologies operations or experiences change, standards should evolve.

3. Quantifiable measures may not apply to all functions. The characteristics of performance quality that are verifiable and will meet or exceed expectations should be described in clear and specific terms.
4. Accomplishment of organizational objectives should be included where appropriate such as cost-control, improved efficiency, productivity, project completion, process redesign, or public service.

Exhibit 11.4 provides a checklist for developing standards.

DEVELOPING A PERFORMANCE METRIC

A performance metric is a standard measure to assess performance in a particular area. Metrics are the heart of a good, customer-focused process, management system, and any programme directed at continuous improvement. The focus on customers and performance standards show up in the form of metrics that assess an individual's the ability to meet customers' needs and business objectives. Most organizations use traditional performance measures, such as profit performance, return on investment, or earnings per share, to determine success. These provide reasonable estimates of whether a company achieves its ultimate goals of making profits, but does not reveal how the business achieves this position. Was it by chance? A non-recurrent situation! Should they have done much better?

Many organizations have thus created complete operating and process measures, and ratios, to track how well it manages each process and the resources. Many CEOs (particularly those who have to make quarterly business forecasts) consider performance models which integrate the measures to predict future performance. The balanced scorecard is one of the more popular conceptual modelling tools.

Developing a performance matrix and emulating examples of world-class performance excellence models help organizations to scientifically list the action plans for improving performance management systems. Based on his research, Gilbert (1978) contributed immensely in this area. A performance matrix is a construct of a performance system, which sequentially illustrates decisions to be taken to improve performance management systems in an organization. A simple model of a performance matrix deals with three levels—policy, strategy, and tactics. Some authors also call it a performance-engineering model (PEM). Like the three levels, this simplified performance matrix or PEM has three stages, namely A, B, and C. Stage A considers identification of accomplishments, decisions on important requirements, together with decisions on unit of measurement, and then developing standards. Stage B considers measurement of opportunity, duly identifying critical performance improvement plans, and measuring and analysing them. Stage C analyses the methods of accomplishment using environmental methods, people programmes, and management action.

Based on these inputs, in line with Gilbert, a sample performance matrix or PEM can be drawn as in Exhibit 11.5.

EXHIBIT 11.5 Performance engineering model (PEM)

Levels \ Stages	A Accomplishment models	B Measures of opportunity	C Methods of improvement
I Policy (Institutional systems)	Organization models: 1. Cultural goal of the organization 2. Major missions 3. Requirements and units 4. Examplary standards	Stakes analysis: 1. Performance analysis 2. Potential for improving performance (PIP) 3. Stakes 4. Critical roles	Programmes and policies: 1. Environmental programmes (data/tools/incentives) 2. People programmes (knowledge, selection, recruiting) 3. Management programme (organization, resources, standards)

(Contd)

(Exhibit 11.5 contd)

II **Strategy** **(Job systems)**	Job models: 1. Mission of job 2. Major responsibilities 3. Requirements and units 4. Exemplary standards	Job assessment: 1. Performance measures 2. Potential for improving performance (PIP) 3. Critical responsibilities	Job strategies: 1. Data systems 2. Training designs 3. Icentive schedules 4. Human factors 5. Selection systems 6. Recruitment systems
III **Tactics** **(Task systems)**	Task models: 1. Responsibilities of tasks 2. Major duties 3. Requirements and units 4. Exemplary standards	Task analysis: 1. Performance measure or observations 2. Potential for improving performance (PIP) 3. Specific deficiencies 4. Cost of programmes	Tactical instruments: 1. Feedback 2. Guidance 3. Training 4. Reinforcement

Source: Based on the model of Praxis Corporation, 1979.

PEM helps as an important guide for managers to track decisions in sequential order. Organizations can adopt this model, matching the nature and types of jobs, and the systems and process of working, in making the desired organizational change.

Performance Matrix

A 2 × 2 performance matrix can be used with a nine-point scale of importance. Areas of importance or the performance criteria vary from organization to organization. However, based on Nigel (1994), these can be drawn considering the following points:

Customers' point of view

On a scale of 1–9, the performance criteria from the customers' point of view are as follows:

1. Customers' advantage
2. Advantage with most customers
3. Useful advantage with most customers
4. Up to good industry standard
5. Up to median industry standard
6. Within the close range of the rest of the industry
7. Not usually come into customers' considerations

8. Rarely come into customers' considerations
9. Never come into consideration by customers

Competitors' point of view

On a scale of 1–9, the performance criteria from the competitors' point of view are as follows:

1. Considerably better than the nearest competitor
2. Clearly better than the nearest competitor
3. Marginally better than the nearest competitor
4. Same as competitors
5. Within striking distance of the main competitors
6. Worse than the main competitors
7. Marginally worse than most competitors
8. Usually worse than most competitors
9. Consistently worse than most competitors

Based on Nigel (1994), the 2 × 2 importance/performance matrix can be drawn as shown in Fig. 11.3.

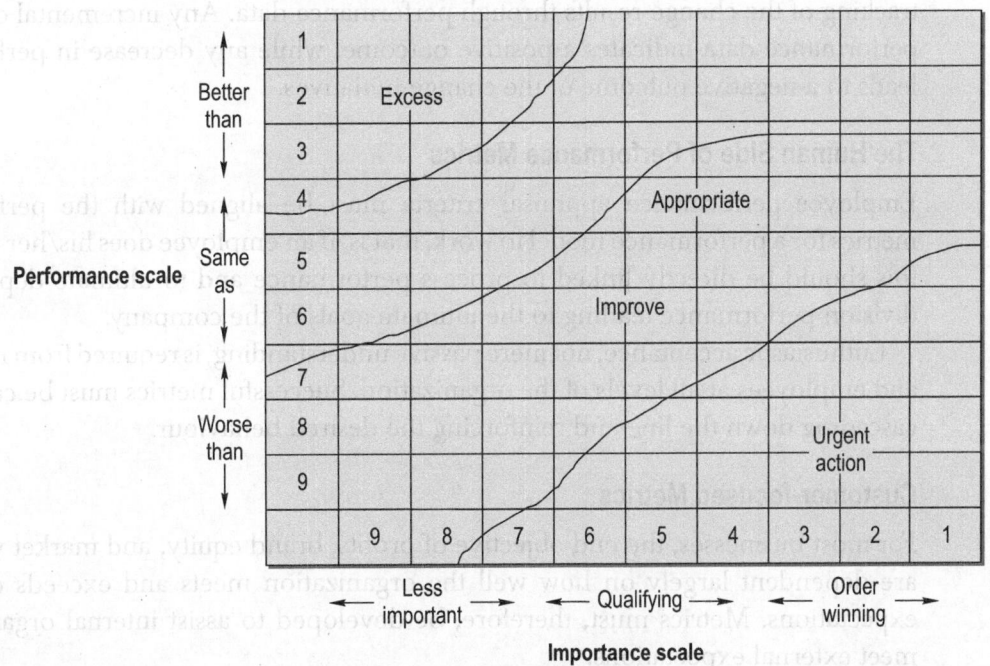

FIG. 11.3 Performance matrix

Many organizations in India and abroad make use of the performance matrix but the type and nature widely vary.

EFFECTIVE PERFORMANCE MODELLING

An effective performance model gives management the confidence that the end results are not a guesswork but a summation of the different activities and processes to attain standard performance. Such a model is required for the following reasons:

1. Establish a relevant chain of relationships, so that the process and activity metrics can ultimately result in profit enhancement, brand equity, and market valuation.
2. Ensure measurability at affordable costs.
3. Make the performance system comprehensible, so that it can be easily understood in terms of its impact analysis on the effectiveness of processes and the end results.
4. Make the model actionable, so as to ensure that a corrective action can be taken as required.
5. Motivate, people so that they work positively in the best interests of the organization.
6. Automate complaints to collect and analyse the data on time.

Meeting these requirements can effectively bring the desired change and facilitate tracking of the change results through performance data. Any incremental change in performance data indicates a positive outcome, while any decrease in performance leads to a negative outcome of the change initiatives.

The Human Side of Performance Metrics

Employee performance appraisal criteria must be aligned with the performance metrics for a performance model to work, that is, if an employee does his/her task well, this should be directly linked to process performance and to ultimate department/division performance leading to the ultimate goals of the company.

Enthusiastic acceptance, not mere passive understanding, is required from managers and employees at all levels of the organization. Successful metrics must be capable of cascading down the line and reinforcing the desired behaviour.

Customer-focused Metrics

For most businesses, the end objective of profits, brand equity, and market valuation are dependent largely on how well the organization meets and exceeds customer expectations. Metrics must, therefore, be developed to assist internal organizations meet external expectations.

The following process is important to develop customer-focused metrics:

1. Identify customers, the outputs they require, and the processes through which these outputs are created.
2. Determine customer's needs/requirements in terms of quality and service standards, and determine the existing gaps in the delivery system.

3. Determine the direct metrics that ensure meeting customer expectations.
4. Cascade these metrics horizontally and vertically through other processes that may impact their performance to develop a full suite of measures that would ensure achievement of customer satisfaction.
5. Establish current performance levels, short-term and long-term objectives, and competitive benchmarking.

Designing Metrics

Developing performance metrics, particularly in the context of organizational change, requires understanding the functioning of the organization with due re-examination of the vision, strategy, and mission of the organization. In a competitive era, performance metrics also need to be aligned with the customer expectations.

Results of the performance metrics form the basis of strategic decision-making; hence, selection of proper instruments to measure the performance is very important. Ideally, such performance measuring instruments should have the following features:

- Ability to forecast future trends both inside and outside the organization
- Objective and unbiased
- Essence of normalization to facilitate benchmarking with other organizations
- Statistically reliable
- Unobtrusive so that the persons whose performances are being measured cannot disrupt the work or trust
- Inexpensive way to collect data, ensuring that even data from a small sample size holds good
- Balanced from qualitative/quantitative and multiple perspectives
- Appropriate to measure the right things
- Quantifiable to provide ease of aggregation, calculation, and comparison
- Efficient enough to draw conclusions out of data sets
- Comprehensive to accommodate all features of the organization
- Discriminating features to track meaningful changes in the organization

Apparently, it may seem to overdo the designing of the performance metrics. However, to track the change in organizations, in terms of the performance management practices, it considerbly helps. Based on these requirements, we can develop a simple one matrix, covering some of the critical areas as in Exhibit 11.6.

Various Dimensions of Performance

The following dimensions of performance are very important for effecting organizational change through PMS:

- Output or result dimension
- Input dimension

EXHIBIT 11.6 Performance metrics

Quality	Customer satisfaction	Employee satisfaction	Finance
• Rework	• Number of complaints	• Participation rates in organization-sponsored events	• Return on investment (ROI)
• Discrepancies found	• Customer returns	• Employee turnover rates	• Cost performance index (CPI)
• Availability	• Customer survey	• Employee exit interviews/surveys	• Scheduled performance index (SPI)
• Mean (or average) time between failures	• Referrals	• Number of employee suggestions	• Return on net assets (RONA)
• Failures per hour/day/week/month		• Productivity metrics	• Estimates at completion (TC/EAC)
• Customer returns		• Incidents of violence	
• Mean time to repair		• Revenue (or sales) per employee	
• Mean time to respond to customers' complaints			
• Rate or frequency of change requirements			

- Time dimension
- Focus dimension
- Quality dimensions
- Cost dimension

An individual or a set of individuals is expected to deliver performance within a time frame. This can be stated in terms of results or effort, tasks, and quality, and a specification of the conditions under which it is to be delivered.

Results and output

The most acceptable and visible as well as measurable dimension of performance is the result or output. It describes the consequence of inputs in a summary form, or a final or semi-final product, or service form. It describes the standard and is easily measurable. Salary figures, customer numbers, financial targets, production targets, completion of tasks to meet some deadlines etc. are all stated in a result/output form. Sometimes these are also called key result areas.

Input dimension

The input dimension deals with the activities or tasks to be accomplished by the individual. The nature of activities to be undertaken, the time frame, the quality of inputs to be given, etc. constitute the input dimension. Performance can be managed better if the nature of inputs required to be put in can be envisaged without error, planned properly, and implemented.

Time dimension

Another dimension of performance is time. Performance can be defined for a task, for a day, for a week, for a month, year, or for life. The time period for performance is important. Time for information technology organizations is limited to a quarter or a three-month period. They may also be defined by tasks or project, and not by time. Time may become the target.

Focus dimension

Performance also has a focus dimension. The focus can be on anything. In defining the focus of a sales executive, the focus of performance can be on market share, profits, or new areas covered, or some or most of these. The focus of performance can be on many other dimensions, such as quality, cost, or financial dimensions, or even customers.

MANAGING CHANGE THROUGH BALANCED SCORECARD

The balanced scorecard helps to align organizational strategies with the performance of employees. So also the HR scorecard, which integrates with the organizational balanced scorecard to track the performance of employees to achieve the desired organizational change. Kaplan and Norton (1992) provided the basis of the balanced scorecard with primary focus on balancing the financial perspectives of organizations. It enables organizations to clarify their vision and strategy, and translate them into action. Through an effective feedback mechanism, it continuously improves internal business processes to achieve the desired level of strategic business performance and bring change to the organizations.

Perspectives of Balanced Scorecard

The balanced scorecard views the organization from four perspectives, and develops metrics to collect and analyse data, to track the contribution of employees to aggregate the organizational performance. They are as follows:

- Learning and growth
- Business process
- Customer
- Financial

The *learning and growth perspective* includes employee training, culture, and attitudes that relate to the improvement of individual employees as well as the organization. Organizational repositories of knowledge are now considered as the most valuable resources to survive in a climate of rapid technological change. This is particularly true for organizations that extensively make use of knowledge workers. According to Kaplan and Norton, 'learning' is more than 'training'. Learning includes the need for mentors and tutors, and free flow of communication with workers, which help them to develop problem-solving skills.

The *business process perspective* refers to internal business processes. Business process in strategic management may be either mission-oriented or support-oriented. In both these areas, organizations develop suitable metrics to understand how the business is running, and whether its products and services conform to customer requirements.

The *customer perspective* tracks the importance of customer focus and customer satisfaction in any business. Eventually, customer satisfaction is the ultimate indicator of corporate success. It is more sustainable.

The *financial perspective* emphasizes the financial details on risk assessment and cost benefit data, without disregarding the traditional financial results of an organization.

Integrating these four perspectives in the balanced scorecard helps an organization to translate strategies into action plans. The baseline for a balanced scorecard is the vision and mission, and the strategies that are developed based on the critical success factors. Thus, the balanced scorecard supports the organizational strategic intents, developing a common understanding of goals, and facilitating its assessment to review and improve strategy.

In the technological era, where organizations endeavour to sustain in a competitive market leveraging the technology, the balanced scorecard is the most important result-tracking tool to understand the extent to which the strategies are the right-fit for achieving excellence, and so also the organizational change.

A personal balanced scorecard for an export manager of a manufacturing company is presented in Exhibit 11.7. Readers are advised to develop measurement criteria for each of the initiatives/achievements, which the manager claims to have

EXHIBIT 11.7 Personal balanced scorecard for export manager

Objectives	Measures	Targets	Initiatives/Achievements
1. Financial perspective			
To turnaround the company in generating cash profit	Increase in sales and gross margin	Increase the sales to US$11 million per year from current US$8 million.	Started offering different package offers to customers with overall increased prices and margins. This helps increased sales with a gross margin of 22 per cent
		Maintain minimum gross margin of 15 per cent despite increase in purchase cost by 40 per cent due to increase in raw material cost	• Innovative approach to source new products from China and Malaysia at cheaper rates and offer the product to customers at a package • Increase in selling prices on arithmetic progression of 20 per cent each month for three months. This helps customers to absorb increase prices and helped the company to increase margins

(Contd)

(Exhibit 11.7 contd)

Objectives	Measures	Targets	Initiatives/Achievements
	Reduction in overhead cost	Reduction of financial and overhead cost by 10 per cent	Significant cost reduction, for example, Transportation: US$10,000, Travelling: US$15,000 Credit and general insurance: US$7000 p.a. Rent of store yard: US$48,000 Interest: US$7000 p.a.
		Increase the net profit to US$100,000 from current US$40,000	Increase in gross margin percentage as well as reduction of overhead and operating cost, which helped company to achieve profit of US$120,000 in financial years 2006–07.
2. Customer perspective			
To increase customer base and their satisfaction	Customer satisfaction	Survey and feedback from customers to be taken and rated. 80 per cent or more customers must be satisfied for product quality and company sales services	• Visit to customers • Feedback from customers on quality of pipes, • Understanding customer requirements, evaluating their perceptions on company's pre-sales and post-sales services
		Retain existing customers, base of 80 (local customers) and generating continuous business from them	• Attractive offers and bundled package offers with different prices are offered to customers to suit their requirements • Timely delivery • Zero defect products • Introduction of new products
	Customer retention and acquisition	To add 2 new customers every month	Flexibility in credit limit and credit period granted to customers for short-term over and above the company's standard credit terms keeping in view meeting of customers' short-term needs and developing relationship
	Market shares	To increase the sale of D.I. pipes and fittings by 10 per cent Increase the sales of other products by 20 per cent	• Focus on new government and private projects. • Close eye on competitors' movement. • Introduced and push the sales of other auxiliary products, such as gas valve, water valve. This resulted in increase of sales by 30 per cent in these products.

(Contd)

(Exhibit 11.7 contd)

Objectives	Measures	Targets	Initiatives/Achievements
3. Internal business process perspective			
Increase customers, employees, and shareholders satisfaction	Internal controls	• Zero defect documentations • Zero defect in contracts signed with customers • Monthly/weekly/daily MIS reports generation	MIS reports are generated through which operations are controlled. This helps to increase efficiencies at operational level. Hence, the productivity improves as well as customers feel delighted This minimized the chances of error in contract, execution of orders helping in reducing financial risk exposure. This has delighted the shareholders
	Monitoring of key process	• Reviewing MIS reports, assessing the outcome of operations, and suggesting the ways for improvement. • Monthly overseas travel to oversee operations and controls	Ensuring that management systems are in place on real-time basis and are sent to respective person(s) on due dates. Visiting Singapore every month to monitor the operations, helping and guiding the team
	Positive cash flow generation	To generate positive cash flow every month	Company has started generating positive cash flow for improvement in debtor's outstanding positions and for optimizing stock levels. This results into saving of substantial bank interest and improves credit ratings among banks and creditors.
	Financial and operational control	Overhead cost reduction, optimized utilization of resources	Operational control on daily basis has effectively resulted in optimum utilisation of resources which has contributed in incremental increase in rate of returns by 7 per cent
4. Learning and growth perspective			
• Increase knowledge and competency • Developing colleagues to meet business	Employee growth	Increase responsibility of colleagues by assigning at least one new job every 2 months. Employee knowledge upgradation.	Helping subordinates and colleagues to learn the process and new skills—whether technical or personal behaviour. Free knowledge sharing and exchange of views. Undergoing MBA course to increase knowledge and skill sets

(Contd)

(Exhibit 11.7 contd)

Objectives	Measures	Targets	Initiatives/Achievements
require- ments to meet company goal		Taking at least new job responsibilities of department such as in direct marketing/ operational level, etc.	To identify the areas where efforts can be put to learn and grow in the environment to meet the increasing responsibilities and demands of the job. To increase learning through front-end marketing work, operational and departmental jobs, etc. To join continuing education programmes related to the job to improve and sharpen the skills.
	Reduction in attrition rate	Employees' retentions, growth, new job assignments	Maintain harmony among sales team and finance team members. Maintain coordination with head office and subsidiary offices to optimize profit at both places. It resulted in achieving the increased profit of the holding company by 5 per cent and the subsidiary company by 20 per cent on a year-to-year basis.

taken. Although column two gives the measures, it can be made more specific with performance metrics.

HR SCORECARD

Like a balanced scorecard, the HR scorecard also aligns HR support with organizational strategy after the integration of the balanced scorecard. The HR scorecard demonstrates the value contribution of HR in achieving organizational strategic intents. It helps in the strategic alignment of HR functions by mapping critical HR supports, such as performance management systems, innovation, training, and development, etc. However, worldwide, very few organizations consider HR as a business partner.

Once integrated, the HR scorecard aligns various support functions with the business strategy. Thus, it illustrates the strategic impact of HR services and projects, and enables it to demonstrate its value through more than short-term financial outcomes. Adopting the HR scorecard as a strategic management system ensures that HR views all of its activities in terms of their contribution to the organizational goals.

Process of Developing HR Scorecard

A properly developed HR scorecard helps an organization to be more proactive in taking the required change initiatives. Organizations using a comprehensive approach can create strategic alignment between HR and the organization as a whole, in all spheres of its activities, namely framing strategy, allocating resources, budgeting, reporting, etc. They can make HR a strategic partner and effectively realize the potential of human capital.

The HR scorecard development process uses the following methodology:

Development of a business strategy A solid strategy should be aligned with the organizational goals. The HR scorecard cannot be prepared without this strategy and the organization cannot achieve the intended change.

Strategy mapping Development of a strategy map including selection of performance measures establishes targets, objectives, and identifies initiatives and ownership, to deliver the strategy.

Establish measures for each objective After translating strategy into objectives, managers and employees must know if and when objectives are being achieved. Therefore, each objective is given at least one measurement that is included in the key performance indicators.

Cascading of scorecard While developing the HR scorecard, organizations need to consider operational, managerial, and the working of front-line employees, to make the strategies happen. Hence, HR scorecards are prepared at every level in the organization, so that each of these performs. Due to its obvious cascading effect, employees can also track how their contributions meet the overall organizational goals.

Scorecard implementation This is the stage at which the scorecard design is finalized and the implementation plan drawn up accordingly.

Post implementation After the implementation of HR scorecard, a periodic review is also important to ensure that the identified core process continues to fit in with the corporate strategy.

Key Benefits of HR Scorecard

The key benefits of HR scorecard are as follows:

1. Formulates HR strategy that is aligned with the overall corporate strategy.
2. Clarifies the vision/mission of the organization.
3. Creates a consensus and ownership of the strategy in the management team.
4. Improves communication of the strategy across the enterprise.
5. Prioritizes HR initiatives by linking activities to business goals.
6. Helps support functions identifying and communicating their unique strategies.
7. Creates a framework for initiative prioritization and budgeting.
8. Aligns measurement with business goal achievement.
9. Measures HR's strategic contribution in concrete and clearly understood terms.
10. Provides real-time graphical display of key performance indicators.

The balanced scorecard and HR scorecard help an organization to effectively implement strategies, track the performance data, and achieve the desired change, be it transformational or transactional.

> **Practice Assignment 11.1**
>
> List some of the issues in learning and growth perspectives for the balanced scorecard of an organization that has undergone major technological change.

COMPETENCY MAPPING AND COMPETENCY DEVELOPMENT

Like the balanced and HR scorecards, competency mapping is another HR support tool to facilitate organizational change.

The immediate effect of new technology in an organization calls for restructuring manpower. Getting the right number of people with the right skills, experiences, and competencies, in the right jobs, at the right time is the primary objective of successful manpower restructuring in any organization. Aligning such decisions to the organization's vision, mission, goals, objectives, and strategic plan with due cognizance to budgetary constraints, make such decisions more realistic and achievable. While undertaking transformational or transactional change using the competency map, organizations can suitably identify the competencies needed in the future. By taking stock of available competencies, organizations can understand the gaps and suitably develop a competency model to provide for the future manpower requirements of the organization. Such action plans may include a right mix of new recruitment (making existing workforce redundant), training and retraining, restructuring and redeploying of existing workforce, and even rightsizing.

Competencies are sets of behaviours that encompass skills, knowledge, abilities, and attributes, and need to be assessed at the organization as well as the individual level. Individual competencies together reinforce organizational competencies. However, there is always the possibility of major incongruence between these. Workforce planning exercises help to analyse such gaps and develop and document a competency model. This helps in managerial decision-making, as it is well aligned with the vision, mission, objectives, goals, and strategies of the organization. It also helps employees to understand the functional requirements and self-initiate the enrichment of their skills, knowledge, abilities, and attributes independent of an organization-wide competency enrichment exercise.

Competency mapping is always done in the defined job context following a set of approaches, such as workforce skills analysis, job analysis, supply and demand analysis, gap analysis, and situation analysis. Skills analysis helps to describe the skills required to carry out a function. Job analysis focuses on tasks, responsibilities, knowledge, and skills required for successful job performance. Both these are done from inputs collected from surveys (through questionnaire responses), interviews with managers and employees, and benchmarking information with successful organizations. For technology intensive and machine-enabled jobs, the skill-set requirements and cycle-time for jobs (as printed in the literature) also contribute as critical input information.

Supply analysis is done considering workforce demographics (in terms of occupation, grades, structure, race, origin, gender, age, service experience, education, training, health status, retirement time, and other similar information), trends, and present workforce competencies. This, therefore, helps to understand the existing workforce status.

Demand analysis, on the other hand, helps to identify the workforce of the future in line with the vision, mission, objectives, goals, and strategies of an organization. Critical inputs from this contribute to the development of competency models for the future workforce.

With these reinforcements, organizations undertake gap analysis to understand the differences between the present and future workforce and make plans to address them accordingly.

This is done through solution analysis, taking into account both ongoing and unplanned changes in the workforce. Solution analysis also weighs different options to get the work done, either considering institutional or contractual employment. In this phase, new recruitment, restructuring, training and retraining, redeployment, and rightsizing, are all done in the light of a new competency mode.

After suitable competency mapping, the next course of action for an organization is to decide whether to downsize/rightsize or opt for training, retraining, and redeployment.

> **Practice Assignment 11.2**
>
> Visit any IT-enabled service organization, study the profile of their chief technology officer, or if that position is not available, study the profile of the chief operating officer and develop a competency map, benchmarking with other competitive organizations.

PERFORMANCE IMPROVEMENT THROUGH KNOWLEDGE MANAGEMENT PRACTICES

Early in the industrial age, workers provided motor/muscle power, leaving the thinking jobs to the management. However, with the changed environment, cognitive skills became more and more important in every area of work, be it production at the shop floor or rendering services to customers. Technology further played a crucial role in capturing and managing knowledge, making it possible for organizations to harness the potentiality of knowledge through proper development, growth, and maintenance. This, however, requires organizations to periodically retire the knowledge that is obsolete.

There are many contributors to knowledge management and learning organizations, starting with the concept of 'Gold-collar Worker' of Kelley (1985) to Argyris (1994), Drucker (1994), Peters (1992), Senege (1990), Stewart (1997), Nonaka and Takeuchi (1995), and many more. Knowledge is reinforced through learning. Therefore, before we define knowledge, it is appropriate to understand what learning is. Learning is a process of acquiring new skills or knowledge that results in new behaviour. It can take place through multiple ways, but for organizations the best way to promote learning is by exposure to new experiences. Knowledge is the ability and wisdom to use the learned experiences for achievement of individual and organizational objectives. Knowledge management, therefore, is the process of systematically and actively managing and leveraging the store of knowledge in an organization. This is important for an organization to survive in the new technological era.

Unfortunately, there is no universal definition of knowledge management and no consensus on what constitutes knowledge. Hence, knowledge management has to be considered from a broader perspective. After reviewing various definitions, one can say that knowledge management is the process through which organizations generate value from their intellectual and knowledge-based assets. Most often, generating value from such assets involves sharing them among employees, departments, and even with other companies to develop the best practices. Thus, knowledge management is a concept in which an enterprise gathers, organizes, shares, and analyses its knowledge in terms of resources, documents, and human skills. Through this, an organization gains insight and understanding from its own experience, and generates value from its intellectual and knowledge-based assets.

Knowledge Management and Resource-based Competitive Advantage

Organizational resources can be tangible or intangible. Tangible resources do not offer competitive advantage to the organization, as they can be easily duplicated by competing organizations. Intangible resources, however, can be sources of competitive advantage for an organization, as these assets are by nature inimitable. For any organization, the strongest intangible resources are organizational capabilities, which obviously represent an aggregate of individual employees' capabilities. For example, Reliance's project management and resource mobilization skills have developed their capabilities to successfully manage mega projects, even on a global scale.

Similarly, several other Indian companies, such as TVS, Mahindra and Mahindra, Hindustan Unilever (HUL), Hindalco, etc. enjoy capabilities that have given them the best competitive advantages. Procter & Gamble (P&G) the international FMCG major, literally failed to match the collective knowledge of brand management, logistics, and distribution management, and also the collective expertise and research skills of scientists and engineers at HUL. As a result, HUL continues to enjoy a competitive edge in the Indian FMCG market.

> **Practice Assignment 11.3**
>
> In this new-age technology, organizations need to use knowledge strategically. Explain this statement visiting any organization of your choice.

SUMMARY

In this chapter, the basics of performance management, duly delineating its concepts and focusing on its various dimensions have been introduced. Today, organizations consider performance management as an important and crucial function, as they are able to sustain in a competitive environment by leveraging the continuous performance improvement of employees.

In any organization, performance management systems do not just restrict its scope to employees' performance appraisal, it also integrates the individual and group performances of employees with the overall organizational performance. In this era of technological change, organizations need to use certain contemporary tools, such as the balanced scorecard, competency mapping, and knowledge management practices, to appropriately track performance and make the organization a performing one.

The balanced scorecard helps to track the performance of an organization as a whole. Competency mapping identifies the set of competencies required for human resources to keep pace with the changing job requirements. Knowledge management practices develop a culture of learning in the organization, making strategic use of both internally available and external knowledge. The performance management function, when reinforced with all these modern tools, gives better results; not just by tracking the performance scores, but also by helping employees and the organization to understand ways and means of developing the performance.

Efficient performance management is crucial for bringing in organizational change. Ultimately, change outcomes cascade to performance improvement and hence performance-driven change is a focused approach towards achieving the desired outcome. This chapter elaborates all the aspects of performance-driven change.

KEY TERMS

Balanced scorecard It is the measurement criterion balancing financial perspective.

Competency mapping This illustrates and maps behavioural parameters required in competent performance.

Financial perspective It emphasizes the financial details on risk assessment and cost-benefit data, without disregarding the traditional financial results of an organization.

HR scorecard It is the measurement criterion that ensures strategic alignment between HR and the enterprise at all levels.

Knowledge management It is the process through which organizations generate value from their intellectual and knowledge-based assets.

Performance management system It integrates with the strategies of the organization through the process of mutually decided goals or objectives setting, evaluation, compensation designs, promotional decisions, identification of training needs, etc.

CONCEPT REVIEW QUESTIONS

1. Define performance management. How can we understand if an organization practises performance management?
2. What are the important objectives of performance management? Develop SMART objectives for a change agent.
3. Define performance standards. How are such standards developed? Develop tentative performance standards for various levels of employees.
4. Explain the term 'performance metrics'. How is it developed? What are the factors that need to be considered for designing customer-focused metrics?
5. Explain the concept of performance-driven change.
6. Explain how knowledge management is strategically important for an organization, especially in the context of organizational change.
7. Explain the concept of competency. How does competency development help in organizational renewal?
8. Develop a competency map for a marketing manager of a new generation software company, clearly showing the weight distribution to different competency areas.
9. What is a balanced scorecard? What are its different perspectives? How does a balanced scorecard help to measure the impact of new technology selection?
10. Explain HR scorecard. How can it be developed? How does it support organizational change?
11. Write short notes on the following:
    (a) Collaborative performance standards
    (b) Performance modelling
    (c) Performance feedback
    (d) Competencies
    (e) Output dimensions of performance

CRITICAL THINKING QUESTIONS

1. Towers Perrin and Watson Wyatt are two international level reward and people management consultants and have recently merged. The new entity is known as Towers Watson. Both companies believe that the merger will help them to deliver better services, leveraging their mutual expertise. Both want a positive performance-driven change in the global HR consultancy market through mergers! As organizational change experts, critically comment on their merger. Develop your answer from the past experience of similar mergers, particularly when both companies are equal in stature.
2. Using a performance engineering model, critically comment on the process of organizational change for a manufacturing company specializing in value-added steel.
3. You are the HR manager of a reputed cement manufacturer in India. Your company is now going in for massive technological upgradation to gain price and quality competitiveness. Moreover, it is now facing global competitors who have also entered the Indian market. All this requires major change initiatives. You know that a performance-driven change programme will help. Explain how you can go ahead with the process.

CASE STUDY

HR Scorecard at Tata Engineering

Through the different phases of industrialization, business focus moved from both product quality to product and process quality. It continued wooing the customer by selling and marketing to cost management, then to customer focus through value for money, and, attracting the best talent to meet the above challenges.

Thus, we see the emergence of four clear business perspectives—capital management, customer management, product and process management, and talent management. However, baring world-class companies, the rest focused on one or the other business perspective as their competitive advantage/core strategy. With the simultaneous globalization of world markets and the liberalization of the Indian economy, it has become imperative for businesses to look at all the four perspectives collectively and comprehensively in order to survive.

The balanced scorecard is a tool for simultaneously aligning all four perspectives to achieve the business objective. It brings about a greater harmony of the business perspectives at the locational, functional, and divisional levels. Hence, each of these should be evaluated on the returns generated. An HR practitioner's perspective of the balanced scorecard is that of a tool that integrates the HR activities with the business perspectives leading to the achievement of objectives. A comprehensive HR balanced scorecard helps HR practitioners to deliver visible and measurable contribution to the business. It also helps to bring about change in the workplace by fostering a climate of innovation and entrepreneurship.

At Tata Engineering, the balanced scorecard initiative was undertaken at the business unit level and a comprehensive roadmap was drawn up addressing the four perspectives—financial, customer, business processes, and learning and growth. The balanced scorecard initiative also integrates the TBEM process of internal assessment, which has been institutionalized to nurture an environment of high performance, and organization-wide learning and sharing.

The business unit balanced scorecard served as the guiding force for drawing up the scorecards for different lines of business and the support functions at Tata Engineering.

HR's role on the four perspectives at Tata can be seen as

Financial: Improving the returns on the human capital employed.

Customer: Developing human resources to meet internal and external customer expectations.

Internal processes: Continuously evolving HR processes in order to meet stakeholders' expectations and contribute to the business objectives.

Learning and growth: Equip the HR team to deliver as planned.

The intent is to ensure that HR would deliver clear and quantifiable measures and thus lead, by being a role model. An attempt has been made to quantify HR by specifying the expected outcome and defining the corresponding quantifiable measure for it.

The corporate HR scorecard defines overall strategic priorities and the context which will guide the HR activities. The corporate HR scorecard is consistent with the business unit strategic agenda on the four perspectives.

Quantifiable and objective measures are identified for all HR activities and targets are based on this. A strategic initiative plan is drawn up for these measures to spell out the specific action plan, the process owner, and milestones indicating completion of a phase. Resource and budget allocations are then deployed to bridge the gap between the current performance and the target.

Discussion Question

Critically evaluate the HR scorecard system at Tata Engineering.

REFERENCES

Argyris, C. (1994), *On Organizational Learning*, Blackwell, Cambridge.

Bevan, S. and M. Thompson (1992), 'An overview of policy and practice', in Bevan, S. and M. Thompson (eds), *Performance Management in the UK: An Analysis of the Issues*, Vol. 1, IPM (now IPD), London.

Bhattacharyya, D.K. (2007), *Human Resource Research Methods*, Oxford University Press, New Delhi.

____. (2006), *Human Resource Management*, Excel Books, New Delhi.

____. (1995), 'Corporate body builder: The emerging role of HRD professional', *Indian Journal of Training and Development*, April–June.

____. (1995), 'Manpower obsolescence: A study in Indian Ordnance Factories, International Congress on Economic Transition with Human Face', *Indian Industrial Relations Association*, New Delhi.

Borman, H.C. and S.J. Motowidlo (1997), 'Task performance and contextual performance: The meaning for personnel selection research', *Human Performance*, Vol. 10, pp. 99–109.

____. (1993), 'Expanding the criteria domain to include elements of contextual performance', in Schmitt, N.C. and H.C. Borman (eds), *Personnel Selection*, Jossey Bass, San Francisco.

Burke, W. Warner and George H. Litwin (1992), 'A causal model of organizational performance and change theory and practice in organization development', La Jolla, CA: University Associates, *Journal of Management*, Vol. 18, Issue 3, pp. 187–205.

Campbell, J.P. (1990), 'Modelling the performance prediction problem in industrial and organizational psychology', in dummette, M.D. and L.M. Hough (eds), *Handbook of Industrial and Organizational Psychology*, Second Edition: Consulting Psychologists Press, Palo Alto, Vol. 1, pp. 687–732.

Campbell, J.P., R.A. McCloy, S.H. Oppler, and C.E. Sager (1993), 'A theory of performance', in Schmitt, N. and W.C. Borman (eds), *Personnel Selection in Organizaton*, Jossey Bass, San Francisco.

Donaldson, Lex (1999), *Performance-driven Organizational Change: The Organizational Portfolio*, Sage, California.

Drucker, P.F. (1994), 'The age of social transformation', *Atlantic Monthly*, November, pp. 53–80.

Gilbert, T.F. (1978), *Human Competence: Engineering Worthy Performance*, McGraw-Hill, New York.

Gleick, J. (1987), *Chaos: Making a New Science*, Viking, New York.

Kaplan, Robert S. and David P. Norton (1992), 'The balanced scorecard—Measures that drive performance, *Harvard Business Review*, January–February, pp. 80–91.

Kelley, R.E. (1985), *The Gold Collar Worker: Harnessing the Brainpower of the New Workforce*, Addison-Wesley, Reading.

Nonaka, I. and H. Takeuchi (1995), *The Knowledge Creating Company*, Oxford University Press, New York.

Peters, T. (1992), *Liberation Management*, Alfred A Knopf, New York.

Senge, P.M. (1990), *The fifth discipline: Art and practice of the learning organization*, doubleday currency, New York.

Slack, Nigel (1994), 'The importance—performance matrix as a determinant of improvement priority', *International Journal of Operations and Production Management*, Vol. 14, No. 5, pp. 59–75.

Spencer, L.M. and S.M. Spencer (1993), *Competence at Work: Models for Superior Performance*, John Wiley & Sons, New York.

Stewart, T.A. (1997), *Intellectual Capital: The New Wealth of Organizations*, Doubleday Currency, New York.

12 TQM Practices and Organizational Change

Learning Objectives

After reading this chapter, you will be able to understand
- the basics of TQM practices
- how TQM practices impact an organization
- ISO Standards, TQM systems, teams, and teamwork
- how to relate TQM to organizational culture
- the nuances of employee empowerment and quality of work life
- how to relate people-centred issues that support TQM practices
- how TQM practices facilitate organizational change

Proactive Practices and Change

In the new paradigm of quality management, organizations are required to nurture a proactive manufacturing culture that prevents defects before they can occur. It does not slow down the process improvement and establishes a culture of continuous development. Employees of such organizations receive training in process development, statistics, problem solving, project management, and design for manufacturability (DFM). There is greater focus on understanding customers and adopting customer-desired practices to achieve the highest level of satisfaction.

A traditional family-managed organization in India decided to adopt proactive manufacturing management practices. The company first streamlined its manufacturing activities, documenting the process in line with ISO requirements and then opted to develop the appropriate culture, to align people with the changing requirements. The company also appreciated the need for investment in training and took appropriate measures. With the help of an external consultant as a facilitator, serious efforts were made for helping the employees to understand the critical operation parameters, statistical process control, process of identifying non-value adding activity, etc.

INTRODUCTION

The total quality management (TQM) philosophy has now changed the business paradigm. It has a customer-centric approach and requires all members of the organization to manage its overall improvement through systematic participation in problem solving, cutting across functional and hierarchical barriers.

A process-centric approach to TQM focuses on product quality, process control, quality assurance, and quality improvement, which by default satisfy customer needs in the most cost-effective way. The human dimension of quality reinforces this process-centric approach, cascading problem solving and decision-making down the organization and allowing people to feel empowered, and take corrective action on their own to meet customer needs.

There are three opposing views on effective implementation of TQM in organizations. The first view considers it as a customer-driven organizational improvement strategy. The second view argues that it is achieved by strengthening internal efficiency and cost improvement. The third view, however, considers it as a means to introduce participative management. Managers and experts disagree about how to effectively apply TQM to their organizations. Some advise that customer satisfaction is the driving force behind quality improvement; others suggest that internal productivity or cost improvement programmes help achieve quality management. In other applications, TQM is considered as a means to introduce participative management. For example, Japan considers TQM as addressing customer satisfaction, meeting their needs and expectations. In the US, however, TQM is considered as a process for saving the cost of non-conformance (cost of quality) and making employees meet the standards agreed upon. In this context, it is also important for us to understand that processes and tasks can by default neither lead to the desired quality nor meet customer requirements. It requires the involvement of employees, change of systems and culture of the organization, and total participation.

Further understanding of the TQM philosophy is possible by differentiating between quality improvement and quality assurance. Quality assurance activities ensure that protocol-bound standards in production are met. The customer is satisfied because products are manufactured conforming to the specified requirements. Quality improvement, on the other hand, refers to the effective and efficient efforts of the members of the organization to meeting customer expectations. Thus, quality improvement, in fact, advocates the people-centric approach to TQM.

TQM AND THE OPERATING ENVIRONMENT OF ORGANIZATIONS

With the increased spate of competition and market globalization, TQM practices are now becoming important for management in all organizations. With TQM, ISO certification is often diluted. ISO, per se, enables an organization to streamline its quality assurance systems in line with ISO systems and standards, while a TQM practice, which succeeds ISO, ensures quality improvement. In line with ISO, TC176 spells out quality management and assurance. Quality management is a comprehensive and fundamental rule or belief for leading and operating an organization. It is aimed at continually improving performance over a long term, focusing on customers while addressing the needs of all other stakeholders.

This standard spells out eight quality management principles which are followed in promoting TQM culture in organizations. These are as follows:

Principle 1—Customer-focused organization Organizations depend on their customers and should, therefore, understand current and future customer needs, meet customer requirements, and strive to exceed customer expectations.

Principle 2—Leadership Leaders establish unity of purpose and direction for the organization. They should create and maintain an internal environment in which people can be fully involved in achieving the organization's objectives.

Principle 3—Involvement of people People at all levels are the essence of an organization and their full involvement enables their abilities to be used for the organization's benefit.

Principle 4—Process approach A desired result is achieved more efficiently when related resources and activities are managed as a process.

Principle 5—Systems approach to management Identifying, understanding, and managing a system of interrelated processes for a given objective improve the organization's effectiveness and efficiency.

Principle 6—Continual improvement Continual improvement should be the permanent objective of the organization.

Principle 7—Factual approach to decision-making Effective decisions and actions are based on the analysis of data and information.

Principle 8—Mutually beneficial supplier relationships An organization and its suppliers are independent, and a mutually beneficial relationship enhances the ability to create value.

Successful adoption of TQM in an organization balances the realities of organizational and HRD functions in the process of achieving the quality objectives. The organizational and human principles integrate with the organizational change process. Organizational principles are embedded with the technical aspects, while the human principles are embedded in the manner and style of meetings, decision-making, communicating, teamwork, etc. Hence, TQM is a blend of OD and HRD, which together facilitate organizational change.

Successful TQM requires both behavioural and cultural changes to fulfil the commitment of an organization towards achieving customer satisfaction. Hence, TQM principles become a management system that can be categorized into three types:

- Organization management systems
- HRM systems
- TQM systems

For organizations, successful implementation of TQM, therefore, requires integration of organization behaviour, HRD, and organizational development issues, with the quality management practices.

ISO Standards and TQM Systems

The International Organization for Standardization (ISO) is a worldwide federation of national standard bodies from more than 140 countries (one from each country). ISO standards are documented quality systems and activities, used as the basis for adoption of uniform quality systems norms for international exchange of goods and services. In fact, 'ISO' is a word derived from the Greek 'iso' meaning 'equal', which is the root of the prefix 'iso' that occurs in a host of terms, such as 'isometric' (of equal measure or dimensions) and isonomy' (equality of laws, or of people before the law). From 'equal' to 'standard', the line of thinking that led to the choice of 'ISO' as the name of the organization is easy to follow. The name 'ISO' is used around the world to denote the organization, thus avoiding a plethora of acronyms resulting from the translation of 'International Organization for Standardization' into the different national languages of members, for example, IOS in English, OIN in French, etc.

Selection and Use of the ISO 9000:2000 Family of Standards

The new ISO 9001:2000 standard is an integration of the familiar three standards ISO 9001, ISO 9002, and ISO 9003.

ISO 9001:2000 specifies requirements for a quality management system for any organization that needs to demonstrate its ability to consistently provide products that meet customer specifications and applicable regulatory requirements. It aims to enhance customer satisfaction. ISO 9001:2000 has been organized in a user-friendly format with terms that are easily recognized by all business sectors. The standard is used for certification/registration and contractual purposes by organizations seeking recognition of their quality management system.

The ISO 9000 family has many standards encompassing all areas of quality management systems. Most prominent are ISO 9000:2000, ISO 9001:2000, and ISO 9004:2000. ISO 9000 introduces quality management systems, their fundamentals, and vocabulary. It is the starting point of the standards and basically introduces the concepts. ISO 9001 introduces quality management systems and their requirements to address customer satisfaction. Certificates are issued to organizations based on this standards. ISO 9004 provides guidelines for continuous performance improvements.

ISO 9001 provides the conformance norms when an organization seeks to establish quality systems. It is now the only standard against which certification is given to an organization. As per this standard, products include services, processed materials, hardware, and software, required by the customer. ISO 9001 has five sections to clarify the activities used to supply products, quality management systems, management responsibility, resource management and measurement, analysis, and improvement. Intending organizations document all these areas in their quality manual to demonstrate their concerns for quality meeting customers' requirements.

Objectives of ISO 9001:2000 quality management systems

The objectives of ISO 9001:2000 quality management systems for an organization are as follows:

- Identify the goals that the organization intends to achieve. Goals may be efficiency and profitability, consistently meeting customer requirements, etc.
- Consistently meet customer requirements
- Achieve customer satisfaction
- Enhance market share
- Sustain market share
- Improve communication and morale in the organization
- Reduce costs and liabilities
- Increase efficiency in the production system

The organization achieves all these objectives by meeting the expectations of various stakeholders, such as customers, suppliers, shareholders, employees, and the society at large.

Optimizing the Cost of Quality

ISO documentation by itself provides an organization with the opportunity to achieve internal efficiency, influencing the attitudinal changes of the people. It helps to identify the cost of quality and reduces this cost substantially. This ultimately helps an organization to achieve cost-efficiency vis-à-vis increased profitability. To better appreciate this, let us examine some concepts on the cost of quality. It is necessary to first classify the nature of costs to analyse the cost of quality. This can be done under the following three sub-heads:

Cost of failure

Quality may fail either internally or externally, that is, in the organization or at the customers' premises. Hence, failure cost can be either internal or external. Internal failure cost includes cost of rework, cost for additional raw materials, additional payments to workmen, eventual increase in scrap, etc. External failure cost involves the cost of re-transportation, re-packaging, servicing and handling of customer complaints, and cost for loss of goodwill, in addition to the cost to be incurred for internal failure. Experience shows that this absorbs almost 70 per cent of the total cost of quality.

Cost of appraisal

Organizations have to incur expenses for verification of quality and for maintaining an inspection team. There is also a requirement for specific gadgets and tools for inspection. All the expenses incurred on this account are considered as cost of appraisal. Usually organizations spend between 28–29 per cent of the total quality cost on this.

Cost of prevention

Quality cost for prevention is incurred to reduce the quality costs on failure and appraisal. This includes expenditure on research and development, and HRD activities, and usually varies between 1–2 per cent.

Although there is no serious study on computing the cost of quality in Indian organizations, from an international perspective it can be seen that such costs, even though not accounted for under a separate heading, are as high as 40 per cent of the production cost. Indian organizations assume that there has to be some natural rejection in the normal manufacturing process. This may be as high as 22 per cent (in some cases) and is called the unavoidable rejection rate (UAR). In other developed countries, especially in Japan, the philosophy is diametrically opposite, that is, the philosophy of zero defects.

It has been seen that to substantially reduce expenditure on the cost of failure and appraisal, spending a mere 1–2 per cent more on cost of prevention can make a substantial difference. The rate of such an incremental cost benefit is as high as 70–80 per cent.

Therefore, cost of quality, though not apparent from the books of accounts, is a significant wasteful cost factor that can be greatly reduced to increase the profitability of an organization. The ISO documentation process helps to prune the cost of quality in addition to augmenting the internal efficiency of an organization. It also helps to achieve TQM in a phased manner.

Therefore, TQM can also be a good driver in bringing organizational change. Please refer to Box 12.1 for an example which illustrates this.

BOX 12.1 TQM and change

TQM practices in culture incongruent organizations can become ineffective. The Philippines nuclear power plant construction project is perhaps the best example of this. The Americans and the Filipinos are culturally so diverse that the quality manager literally had to struggle to get the consensus of workers from both the countries on quality issues. He had to spend an enormous amount of time to communicate with them and ultimately got the Americans to agree on the cultural pride within the organization. The Filipino culture of patience even in situations of conflict, slowly transformed Americans' way of treating them, and accordingly, a culture of mutual respect emerged.

TEAMS AND TEAMWORK

TQM is successful when employees at every level participate in decisions affecting their work. The most common vehicle for employee participation is a team. Teams range in scope and responsibility from problem-solving groups to self-managed work teams that schedule work, assign jobs, hire members, and set the standards and volume of output. A participative work culture is encouraged when quality becomes everybody's responsibility.

Employee involvement practices in any organization may differ in terms of organizational policies and strategies. Common employment practices are as follows:

- Suggestion systems
- Survey feedback
- Quality circles
- Formation of quality of work life teams
- Job redesign
- Formation of self-managed teams
- Formation of TQM teams

Participative management is used as the most important approach for introducing a TQM culture in any organization. People tend to live together in love and amity. This is what one of the Vedas, the *Yajurveda* (dating back to 4000 BC–100 BC) advocates. A more organized or institutionalized approach to workers' participation in management dates back to 1920, when Mahatma Gandhi advocated the principles of trusteeship in industry. This idea was further strengthened through enactment of various legislations and policy decisions. Despite the fact that organizations across the world benefited from participative management for many years, India was a little late in institutionalizing the approach. Statutory support has now made it mandatory for Indian industries to introduce the culture. Participation in some form or the other has now become virtually unavoidable for many organizations.

In the new economy, total participation of workers as opposed to statutory participation, is a must, be it through works committees, departmental councils, or other representative forums. One such way to enforce total participation is by way of forming quality circles (QC) or small group forums.

QC is an important managerial tool and can be related to increased employee motivation and productivity. Total knowledge, skills, creative abilities, talents, and aptitudes, together with values, attitudes, and beliefs of the workers and/or individuals, can represent an organization's effective HR inventory. The total involvement of employees is ensured by QCs through a number of small group forums. Organizations have succeeded in improving their productivity by QC activities that increase employee motivation, which as a result can guarantee more than any other method, such as complex planning, rigorous execution, etc.

Organizations in India have now started to train their workers and employees for successful implementation of QC concepts. They are systematic about follow-up activity in connection with setting up QC forums involving all workers, forming homogeneous groups of 8–12 employees who regularly meet once a week for at least an hour to deliberate on work-related problems, and to identify possible solutions for them. Many organizations have benefited from cost minimization, changing methods of production, work simplification, etc. Figure 12.1 explains the structure of a quality circle.

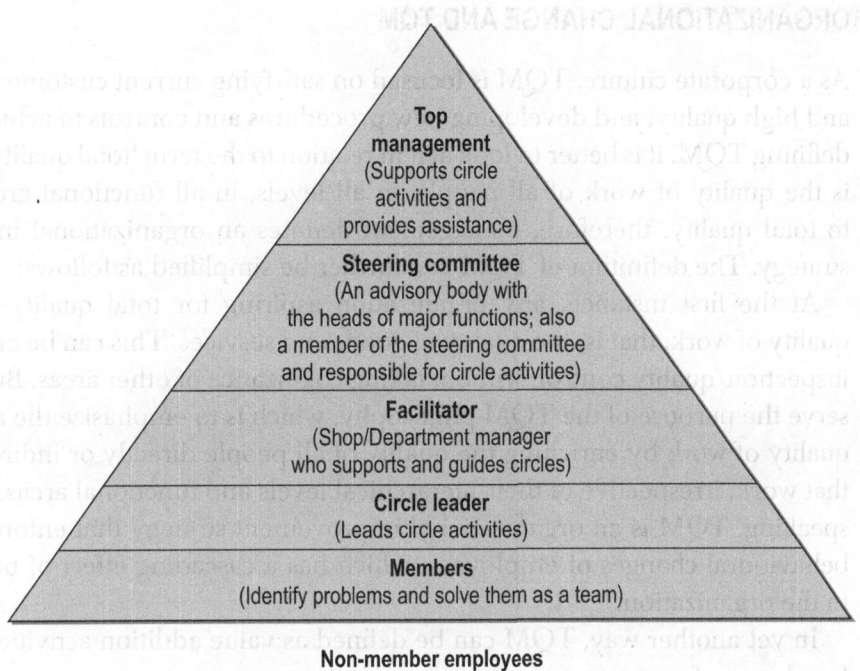

FIG. 12.1 Structure of a quality circle

Top management, sitting at the helm of corporate activities, supports the quality circles without getting directly involved in the process. Other members in the structure play their specific roles, as illustrated in the figure.

As the basic philosophy of the QCs is to involve all employees vis-à-vis workers in an organization, total involvement undoubtedly enhances the productivity of the organization. Studies conducted both in India and abroad indicate that the successful implementation of QCs is directly related to the following areas of improvement: productivity, quality, house-keeping, cost minimization, and safety, in an organization. The first precondition for effective productivity improvement through QCs is to involve trade unions, ensure total participation, institute rewards and recognition systems, and focus on continuous training. Hence, it has far-reaching implications in managing the organizational behaviour of an organization. A study of some selected ISO certified manufacturing units in India by the author, Bhattacharyya (1995) indicates how QCs can benefit the organization in developing the desired culture. To begin with, most of the organizations perceived the ISO certification process as a passport to enter foreign markets. Later, however, they realized that ISO certification by default brought certain positive changes in the culture and practices of the organization, which exerted its incremental effect on the overall performance.

QC is just one tool in bringing a TQM culture to an organization and add tremendous value to both TQM and ISO documentation.

ORGANIZATIONAL CHANGE AND TQM

As a corporate culture, TQM is focused on satisfying current customers with low cost and high quality, and developing new procedures and controls to achieve this. When defining TQM, it is better to look at it in relation to the term 'total quality'. Total quality is the quality of work of all people, at all levels, in all functional areas. In relation to total quality, therefore, management denotes an organizational improvement in strategy. The definition of TQM can further be simplified as follows:

At the first instance, any organization aspiring for total quality should ensure quality of work, that is, the quality of goods and services. This can be ensured by strict inspection/quality control, without taking cognizance of other areas. But that does not serve the purpose of the TQM philosophy, which is to emphasize the achievement of quality of work by enriching the quality of all people directly or indirectly related to that work, irrespective of their hierarchical levels and functional areas. Thus, broadly speaking, TQM is an organizational improvement strategy that enforces the desired behavioural changes of employees, which has a cascading effect of bringing change in the organization.

In yet another way, TQM can be defined as value addition activities that focus on four key performance areas in an organization:

- Quality
- Process
- Equipment
- People

Looking back, we find that the Japanese concept of total quality control has actually been renamed as TQM. Although the definition of TQM was derived from the ISO specification series, TQM per se is not a standard. It is based on total quality principles.

Learning from organizations that have successfully practised TQM, it is evident that the most commonly used technique is the formation of a short-term problem-solving group to simplify and streamline work practices. The second most commonly used technique is training. The third common practice is to have a top-down approach (quality is ultimately the responsibility of top management). The other two practices call for developing relationships with suppliers and obtaining data about customers. The first three techniques of TQM are, in fact, part of the people-centric activities in an organization. HRM practices are now emphasizing small group activities not only to enhance the problem-solving abilities of the employees, but also to provide intrinsic motivation that culminate in increased satisfaction and enhanced productivity, which in turn leads to effective change in the organization.

EMPLOYEE EMPOWERMENT

Employee empowerment is conferring legitimate rights to employees to make judgements and take decisions on their own, irrespective of the nature of their job and their hierarchical level. Hence, it can facilitate development of the problem-solving abilities of employees. Operationally, organizations first empower employees by developing their capabilities and then by condoning any errors they may make. Unlike other quality management approaches, empowerment not only calls for employee participation in the operational area, but also allows them to participate in corporate level decision-making. An empowered employee, in other words, is not a mere seller of his time and labour for a contracted sum of money, but acquires the necessary skill and authority to own.

Several multinational and national organizations have experimented with employee empowerment, involvement, and participative management as important corporate practices, and identified that employee ownership and commitment (which is possible through employee empowerment) are the two ingredients that helped achieve efficiency and productivity. Some organizations are even empowering their employees at the strategic level rather than confining their involvement only to limited operational activity.

Let us take for example, the international FMCG major, Procter & Gamble (P&G). In one of their plants at Lima, Ohio, where they make detergents, bleaches, and fabric softeners, the boundaries between managers and workers have been replaced by a team organization with only three layers—plant manager, managers, and technicians. Boland (1987) states that power is not an entity; it is dialectic and can be understood only through the process of human interaction. Thus, power is a relationship that is held between those with and those without it. This relationship can be better understood through empowerment making it possible for an organization to bring positive change. A study by the author, Bhattacharyya, in 1995 on employee empowerment in Indian banking organizations indicated that empowerment makes people more committed to their assigned tasks and they feel increasingly responsible. Thus, in a true sense, positive organizational change can to a great extent be achieved by the employee empowerment process.

Quality of Work Life (QWL)

QWL is most conventionally defined as the perceived important personal needs that an individual tries to satisfy by working in an organization. Although defined by a host of behavioural scientists, its conceptual foundations were in reality advocated by Argyris (1975) in his famous work on personality and organization. The socio-technical systems theory, pioneered by the Tavistock Institute of Human Relations, London, during the 1960s, is considered as an important QWL construct. Basic conceptual criteria for QWL incorporate growth and security as important personal needs for an individual. The possibility of furthering one's career within the organization, has therefore been identified as one of the important criteria for QWL. Although common QWL strategists place more emphasis on job redesign, formation of autonomous work groups, and worker participation in management, there are wide differences among the pioneers in this area as to what should be construed as the factors of QWL. The process of QWL can be explained with the help of the following criteria:

- Adequate and fair compensation
- Safe and healthy working conditions
- Immediate opportunity to use and develop human capacities
- Future opportunity for continued growth and security
- Social integration in the work organization
- Work and total life space
- Social relevance of working life

It is evident from studies carried out both in India and abroad that the essence of QWL is the opportunity for employees at all levels to have substantial influence over their work environment. This is a result of their participating in the decision-making process relating to their work, thereby enhancing their self-esteem and the overall satisfaction from their work. Hence, QWL calls for an open style of management, that is, sharing information and genuinely encouraging the efforts that relate to improvement of the organization. This makes it amply clear that QWL is an important managerial activity. The success of TQM programmes largely depend on appropriate OD and HRD interventions, such as emphasis on continuous training and development, encouraging participation in management through small group forums, increasing employees' motivation, looking after the career development of employees, employee empowerment, and infusing attitudinal changes at the top (such as accepting a flatter organization structure, following an democratic approach, becoming receptive to changes on a continuous basis, supporting group performance, etc.).

ORGANIZATIONAL CHANGE THROUGH INNOVATION AND CREATIVITY

Innovation is a new technique or idea encompassing product/services, process, managerial styles, and even organizational structure. It may be technology-push or demand-pull, or even a combination of both. The research and development (R&D) activities of an organization are examples of such innovation. In any organization, the need for innovation is primarily felt to keep pace with competition. It has to essentially be customer-focused as this backward linkage facilitates process-centred innovative changes. Whether it is just-in-time (JIT) inventory control, supply chain management (SCM), business process outsourcing (BPO), flexible manufacturing systems (FMS), product/service customization, strategic backward or forward integration, synergy through merger and acquisition, alliances or collaboration, organizational re-engineering,

TQM or six sigma practices, new work culture as facilitator of organizational change, or any R&D initiative for value addition, which broadly encompasses innovation; all stem from customers' explicit or implicit needs.

Mapping customers' needs and aligning them to the innovation initiative is what is needed in this competitive world. Innovation is enabled by proactive HR/OD practices and calls for creating a work environment that recognizes creativity, inter-organizational cooperation rather than competition, working as cross-functional teams, productive meetings for innovative results, introduction of formal innovation programmes, and finally, the organization's receptivity to new ideas and perspectives. Fostering innovation requires a structured approach. It has broadly to be in the given context, leadership, values, and culture. Contextual analysis helps to build the required innovation teams. Leaders facilitate these teams. Values enable adoption of principles that foster innovation and the culture provides the playing field.

At this stage, it is pertinent to define creativity as innovation and creativity are often used interchangeably in the workplace. *Webster's Dictionary* defines creativity as 'the ability or power to create, bring into existence, invest with a new form, produce through imaginative skill, make or bring into existence something new'. Creativity is, therefore, the core competency. It is the talent of employees of an organization. Competitors can replicate the strategies of an organization but not the creative talents of its employees. To encourage creativity, organizations must first create the right environment where employees feel safe even to come up with 'dumb' or 'crazy' ideas.

Creativity is often punished, as creative people spend more time getting ready for action. They are also more difficult to manage. Organizations, therefore, often see them as major time and money wasters and inhibit their creative thoughts. A review of literature on creativity helps to capture creative patterns as follows:

1. A creative process is a balance of imagination and analysis. It involves idea generation, analysis, and evaluation.
2. Creativity does not stem from the subconscious process as traditionally believed by the classical school of thought. It is a purposeful or directed attempt to generate new ideas under a controlled situation to help organizations succeed against competition. Plsek (1997) used the term more appropriately as 'directed creativity'. It is a purposeful generation of creative ideas with seriousness of its implementation whenever it matches organizational requirements. Non-implementation of even some ideas (that fit the purpose) will inhibit creativity.

Innovation is the implementation of creative ideas. Therefore, creativity is the subset of innovation. As innovation is a holistic concept, here we prefer to use the terms interchangeably.

Innovation and creativity require development of the competencies of people. These encompass skills, knowledge, abilities, and attributes. Competencies are measurable and change over time. Hamel and Prahalad (1990) attributed business success only to innovative creativity, knowledge resources, and expertise, which together create the critical potential of an organization, that is, its core competencies. Core competencies help an organization to build strategic power and are difficult to duplicate by competitors due to their obvious distinctiveness. They, are, therefore critical success factors for any organization. Although there are widespread differences regarding the constituents of core competencies and their relation to knowledge, skill, abilities, and attributes of employees, there is agreement among their proponents about how it is created and the link with the organization's goals, structure, and culture. Innovation and creativity help to develop core competencies supplementing the knowledge and skill base of the employees. In this respect, directed creativity, that is, purposeful generation of new ideas matching with organizational requirements is more relevant.

Innovation, creativity, and competencies are important facilitators for organizational change. Imperatives for organizational change basically stem from redefining business focus, re-structuring, and customer orientation—all for competitive advantage.

William Ford Jr, Chairman and CEO of Ford Motor Co., adopted innovation as the core business strategy of the company. His message to all employees speaks for itself—'Innovation will be the compass to set the direction for Ford'. Jeffrey Immelt, Chairman and CEO of General Electric (GE) also believed that innovation is the key driver of success for the company, and any change process at GE, therefore, needs to be driven by innovation. He used the term 'innovation imperative'.

SUMMARY

TQM plays a crucial role in organizational change, as adopting these practices requires the organization to change the attitudes and behaviour of its employees, and achieve complete cultural transformation. Even though some proponents of TQM believe only in the process improvement aspect to develop the quality of the products and services, there is also a human dimension to it. TQM, per se, is a complete organizational transformation process in terms of both process, and people-centric approaches. It is not possible to understand TQM without a brief appreciation of the ISO quality system standards. Although ISO is not TQM, but ISO certification (through internal changes) can pave the way for organizations to achieve TQM.

In the process of adopting a TQM culture, organizations can transform the behaviour of its people by introducing several employee involvement programmes, such as QCs, self-managed teams, employee empowerment, etc. Once TQM is achieved, organizations strive for further improvement. But all these require developing the problem-solving abilities, innovation, and creativity of people. Quality management, TQM, and six sigma practices adequately elaborate how an organization can sustain in a globally competitive market, leveraging the positive behaviour of its people.

KEY TERMS

ISO It stands for International Organization for Standardization. To ensure common quality systems standards, ISO has introduced a series of specifications.

Manpower redundancy It Implies obsolescence of skill and knowledge of people and relinquishing them from employment.

Participative management It involves all cross sections of employees in organizational functions.

TQM From an HR point of view, TQM focuses on adopting an organizational improvement strategy through development of HR.

CONCEPT REVIEW QUESTIONS

1. What is the role of quality management programme in organizational change?
2. Explain the concepts of employee empowerment and quality of work life (QWL). Also discuss how these two concepts support introduction of quality management systems in an organization.
3. As HR manager, explain how quality management principles are important areas of consideration.
4. How can innovation and creativity be nurtured in an organization? How does it support introduction of quality management systems in an organization?
5. Write short notes on:
   (a) Quality circles
   (b) QWL
   (c) Employee empowerment
   (d) Directed creativity
   (e) ISO: 9001:2000
   (f) Cost of prevention

CRITICAL THINKING QUESTIONS

1. Visit the website of Hindalco and critically comment on how their focus on quality management practices made them a global major in non-ferrous metal.
2. A people-centric approach to quality management practices can only set the order for a process-centric approach. Do you agree with this statement? Develop your answer in the context of organizational change.
3. Grasim and Marico are two Indian companies with a vibrant presence in the international market. They have also collaborated in some of their manufacturing facilities abroad. Both companies claim that innovation is their key driver for growth. Visit their websites and illustrate some of the innovative practices, which you think support both the companies' growth strategy in the international market.

CASE STUDY

Change for Renewal at Godrej

In his message in the inaugural issue of the in-house magazine, Chairman and Managing Director of the century-old Godrej & Boyce Mfg. Co. Ltd, India, Mr Jamshyd Godrej, spelt out the challenge of change for the organization.

Since its inception, Godrej has been proactive in bringing change in the organization. At the outset, the company had initiated change in their business focus. From its initial presence in law, it changed to surgical instruments, locks and safes, and even extended its business focus to vegetable oil, soaps, agricultural farming, and to many other areas, to truly transform themselves as an industrial conglomerate. All these made Godrej a true change platform as it believe that change is in its blood and embedded in its value systems.

Globalization of production and financial needs has today promoted the need for closer integration with the economies of the world, making nations highly interdependent. Nations are becoming economically multi-polar and politically uni-polar. Century-old organizations, such as Godrej, need to keep pace with such changes not only to survive but even to overtake competition.

In post-independence India, Godrej, like other Indian entrepreneurs had to subdue its change requirements at the organizational level due to the obvious reluctance of the nation as a whole to change. The regulated economic regime literally overlooked the need to change. Customers were taken for a ride, as they had to accept shoddy products and services companies offered. Such inertia to change at the national level also adversely cascaded to the need for change at the individual or personal level. Attitudinally, Indians began to believe in a status quo and less commitment, and at the same time, organizations also failed to promote the work culture necessary to bring change in the desired areas.

Notwithstanding all these, from its inception, Godrej encouraged change. Some of the change tools used by them are summarized here.

Godrej made extensive use of the *kaizen* systems and this led to significant increase in employee involvement and morale. With significant cost savings, Godrej became more flexible and could increase its capability to adapt to the changing needs of the environment. In terms of quantitative achievement, the company reduced more than 70 per cent of its changeover time on the shop floor, increased availability to pace its manufacturing in tune with the needs of the market, and yet enjoyed the privilege of economies of scale. It was able to reduce its finished products' inventory holding by over 40 per cent by developing a quick market response. With the introduction of total productive maintenance, the company reduced breakdown and the cost of spares and repairs to about 50 per cent from the pre-introduction phase. What is more startling is that the company was able to make one of its high-pressure boilers in the Vikhroli factory redundant in order to achieve efficiency in their energy consumption. Similarly, value analysis exercises reduced the cost of materials, while enhancing the quality of output. As in manufacturing, the company could bring positive change in other functional areas, such as finance, marketing, HR, promoting a culture of improvement. Today, employees look out for opportunities to make improvements and savings.

TQM movement at Godrej further renewed the change process, as among others, it brought a renewed and conscious thrust on HRM practices in the company. All the key components of TQM, namely consumer satisfaction, managing processes, changing from detecting to preventing errors, continuous improvement in the belief that there is always room for improvement, working together as a team, encouraging personal initiative, etc., were adopted. Even more dramatic were the changes in Godrej & Boyce Mfg. Co. Ltd and then at Godrej Soaps Ltd, subsequently renamed Godrej Industries Ltd. Along with the objective side of TQM—technology, product, and process improvement—embarked upon from the worker level upwards, there was the subjective aspect of TQM implying nurturing of the quality of mind on a person-to-person basis.

Greater emphasis on Indian psycho-philosophy with Indian ethos and values for all cross sections of employees further reinforced the other management initiatives, such as *kaizen* and TQM. Sensitizing managers to achieve the goal of a 'pure mind' helped the company to bring changes in the life of people, as employees were increasingly influenced by the idea of duties and obligations rather than rights and claims. These transformational experiences reflected on their behaviour towards customers (understanding their needs better), on performance and productivity, teamwork, etc.

Subsequently, as consultants, Anaar facilitated the scientific application of values, such as customers being the focus of everything, continuous improvement as essential to success, total employee involvement, dealers and suppliers to be considered as partners, and never compromising integrity—values which over the time have become a part of the Godrej philosophy.

Customers no longer expect quality, they demand it. In this context, change will involve the adoption of a whole range of 'best practices'—streamlining industrial/organizational structures to promote quicker decision-making and more effective implementation at all levels, managing industrial relations so as to effect improvements in productivity, establishing constructive government–industry coordination to enable effective and speedier response to change, identifying those capable of making the change management programme a success, selecting certain key activities to be taken up for change management, listing and distributing the criteria for a professional change team member, developing the most effective method of making known the success stories in the change management programme and above all, believing in change as a way to grow, develop, explore, and expand.

Change management in Godrej today has empowered all cross sections of employees, who now perceive the reward from organizational change as self-renewal and reinvigoration.

Source: Adapted from 'Change', *The Godrej House Magazine,* (2002), Vol. 2, Issue 5, September–October.

Discussion Question

Critically review Godrej's quality management programme after visiting their website and comment on what else it can do to bring change in the organization.

REFERENCES

Argyris, Chris (1975), 'Dangers in applying results from experimental social psychology', *American Psychologist,* Vol. 30, No. 4, pp. 469–485.

Bhattacharyya, D.K. (2007), *Human Resource Research Methods,* Oxford University Press, New Delhi.

———. (2000), 'Competency mapping and manpower redundancy—Macro level study of Indian organizations', *Management and Accounting Research,* October–December, Vol. 4, Issue 2, pp. 97–105.

———. (1995), 'Corporate body builder—The emerging role of HRD professional: A prescriptive model for success', *Indian Journal for Training and Development,* New Delhi, April–June.

———. (1995), 'Employee empowerment—A study of selected banking organizations in India, in HRD repositioning', published by the National HRD Network in their conference volume.

———. (1995), 'Manpower obsolescence—A study in Indian ordnance factories', International Congress on Economic Transition with Human Face, Indian Industrial Relations Association, New Delhi, 3–6 September.

———. (1995), 'Quality performance of some selected ISO certified manufacturing units—A third party evaluation', International Conference Proceedings on Manufacturing Excellence (MEXCEL-95), Indian Institution of Production Engineers, Mangalore, and Institution of Electrical Engineers, UK, 3–5 August.

Block, Peter (1993), *Stewardship—Choosing Service over Self-interest,* Berrett-Koehler, San Francisco.

Boland Jr, R.J. (1987), 'The In-formation of information systems', in Boland Jr, R.J. and R.A. Hirschheim (eds), *Critical Issues in Information Systems Research,* John Wiley & Sons Ltd, London.

Edward, Gordon E. (2000), *Skill Wars, Winning the Battle for Productivity and Profit,* Butterworth-Heinemann, Boston.

Hamel, G. and C.K. Prahalad (1990), 'The core competence of the corporation', *Harvard Business Review,* Vol. 68, No. 8, May–June.

James, Christiansen A. (2000), *Competitive Innovation Management,* Macmillan Business, London.

Jonne, Cesrani and Peter Greatwood (2001), *Innovation and Creativity,* Crest Publishing House, New Delhi.

Nonka, Ikujoro and Hikjiro Takeuchi (1995), *The Knowledge Creating Company,* Oxford University Press, New York.

Plsek, Paul E. (1997), *Creativity, Innovation and Quality,* Quality Press, New York.

Stolovitch, H.D. and J.G. Maurice (1998), 'Calculating the return on investment in training: A critical analysis and case study', *Performance Improvement,* Vol. 37, Issue 8, pp. 9–20.

PART 3

Nature of Organizational Development

- **Organizational Development**
- **Organizational Diagnosis and Development**

13 Organizational Development

Learning Objectives

After reading this chapter, you will be able to understand
- the meaning, definitions, and concepts of organizational development (OD)
- the need for OD in organizations
- OD as an action research process
- the strategic dimensions of OD
- the history or evolution of OD
- the features and characteristics of OD
- the principles and processes of OD
- the goals and steps of OD
- important triggers for OD
- the relationship between OD and organizational involvement; OD and leadership development
- OD and the role of consultants
- values and ethical issues of OD
- organizational life cycle analysis
- OD and business process re-engineering (BPR)

Organizational Development through Work Culture Transformation

A legacy-bound multinational electronics major in India had to revisit its business strategies due to Korean entry in industry. Being the first in India to produce conventional black and white and colour TVs, the company took pride in its captive market and believed that it offered the best to its customers. However, it had made no change in variety or models for years. With the entry of the Korean company, it had to bear the brunt of the competition in the consumer electronics industry.

The price competition rendered its products uneconomical and the multiple models introduced by the Koreans made the company's products less attractive to the customers. The employees also made demands for salary increases and other benefits.

Finally, it was taken over by another traditional Indian electronics major that had a price advantage and enabled it to compete more successfully against the Koreans. The trade unions legally challenged the acquisition and were violently opposed to it. Several workers decided not to work with the new entity. After the acquisition, the company tried to assuage the feelings of irate employees and unions, and informed them that its employment was protected with a golden parachute option, that is, the service conditions, salary, and benefits would remain unaltered. However, it did not help them to earn their confidence. Many employees took early separation and older ones opted for voluntary retirement which their original employers had offered them before the takeover. Many employees decided to wait and see.

During the first phase of operations, the company undertook rigorous communication and transparency of information with all cross sections of employees. The Chief Operating Officer spent over 80 per cent of his time meeting and talking to them, clarifying their doubts and answering queries. He met employees on the shop floor, in groups and individually in his office at designated times to discuss various issues. Thus, he set an example, not hitherto seen, for all managers and executives to be punctual and disciplined at work.

Managers demanded similar behaviour from the workers. When workers felt that things were not moving at the right pace, they were given the freedom to manage the gang level activities, deciding every aspect of their jobs on their own. Management extended support and facilitated their activities.

INTRODUCTION

Organizational development (OD) activities in an organization set the premises for bringing the desired organizational change. OD is a planned change based on the understanding of the environment and benchmarked with the best practices of organizations worldwide. Global benchmarking is necessary for the integration of economic activities. Some experts call it action-research activities. OD can also be described as a learning process. Justification for OD activities rests on the premise that with OD the organizational change process can take place holistically. It facilitates behavioural conditioning both at the individual and organizational level.

Before further deliberation on OD, let us first understand the methods of organizational change. According to Kanter et al. (1992), organizational change takes place in three directions. These are as follows:

Organizational change with respect to relationship with the environment This emphasizes the response of organizations to market changes, and the change in relations with stakeholders by restructuring or redefining the identity and boundaries through various forms of business combinations, such as mergers, acquisitions, collaborations, partnerships, etc.

Organizational change with respect to the way it operates This reviews the way people and units relate to each other, and focuses more on changes in the internal coordination, culture, and structure. This forms a part of the planned change.

Organizational change in terms of control structures This considers the way members of the organization get involved in a dominant coalition of interests, even encompassing the distribution of benefits among interest groups.

Various types of OD intervention are undertaken depending on the pattern of organizational change. Primarily, such interventions can be classified into person-centred approach, structural approach, and relationship approach. The *person-centred approach* focuses on developing the social competence, general intellectual competence, and the ability of members of the organization to innovate. The *structural approach* emphasizes the integration or re-integration of work sequences, and decentralization of decision-making. And, the *relationship approach* focuses on team development, job role negotiations, and transparent feedback mechanism. Another approach to OD that has emerged recently emphasizes organizational transformation (OT). OT-led OD basically rests on re-engineering. Often, it is argued that the term OD can be better replaced by the term OT, as OD essentially is a process of organizational transformation. But OT encounters more resistance for change as it is often linked to manpower redundancies. Nevertheless, we will discuss OT in brief in the context of business process re-engineering and explain how it can facilitate OD.

DEFINITIONS AND CONCEPTS OF OD

Based on the study on OD professionals, the American Society for Training and Development (ASTD) has identified one widely accepted definition developed by Beckhard (1969):

'An effort (a) planned, (b) organization-wide, (c) managed from the top, to (d) increase organization effectiveness and health through (e) planned intervention in the organization's processes, using behavioural science knowledge.'

Keeping in mind the magnitude of organizational change, particularly after global economic integration, organizations are now bound to build their capabilities and manage change. This necessitates more thought-provoking discussions on OD, primarily based on industry practices and the contributions of world-class OD scholars. With this perspective in mind, we will review some more definitions of OD. Neilsen (1984) and Matt Minahan of MM Associates, Silver Spring, Maryland, provided more elaborate definitions, which are shown in Box 13.1.

Similarly, Cummings and Worley (1997) stated that 'organization development is a system-wide application of behavioural science knowledge to the planned development and reinforcement of organizational strategies, structures, and processes for improving an organization's effectiveness'.

Reviewing these definitions, we can say that OD is planned as it requires systematic diagnosing of organizational change issues, developing of organizational improvement plan, and mobilization of resources to implement the improvement plans. OD is organization-wide as it involves the entire system. It is a planned intervention as it strategically makes use of behavioural science to study the existing methods of working and develops alternative methods. According to Beckhard (1969), OD requires strong commitment from the top management. They need to understand the OD programmes and actively extend support.

In summary, it is possible to understand prima facie techniques, policies, and managerial practices required for OD to improve individual members as well as the organization as a whole, so that the desired outcome is achieved. Obviously,

> **BOX 13.1 Definitions of OD**
>
> 'Organization development is the attempt to influence the members of an organization to expand their candidness with each other about their views of the organization and their experience in it, and to take greater responsibility for their own actions as organization members. The assumption behind OD is that when people pursue both of these objectives simultaneously, they are likely to discover new ways of working together that they experience as more effective for achieving their own and their shared (organizational) goals.'
>
> —Neilson
>
> 'Organization development is a body of knowledge and practice that enhances organizational performance and individual development, viewing the organization as a complex system of systems that exist within a larger system, each of which has its own attributes and degrees of alignment. OD interventions in these systems are inclusive methodologies and approaches to strategic planning, organization design, leadership development, change management, performance management, coaching, diversity, and work/life balance.'
>
> —Matt Minahan

for such all-encompassing activities, OD interventions can range from trivial work simplification to redesigning the organization as a whole, with new missions, goals, objectives, strategies, and action plans. Often, piecemeal change interventions are misconstrued as OD. For example, a management development programme (MDP) is considered synonymous with OD. But MDPs focus on development of individual managers or a group of managers. In organizational systems, a manager is part of a sub-system, whereas OD considers the system (which is all-inclusive) and not the sub-systems only.

Although some contributors emphasized the area specific issues of OD, their observations also form part of the definitions and concepts of OD. Sashkin and Burke (1987) discussed the prospects of OD duly identifying certain contemporary trends. Such trends focus on integration of task and process aspects, managing conflict in mergers and acquisitions, improving the methodology of OD research, focusing on OD theories, and intensifying efforts to design suitable organizational culture to manage change. Woodman (1989) added three more trends to discuss the prospects of OD. These are interest on high performance–high commitment work systems, application of change research in internal activities of the organization, and in social movements. Even scholars such as Pasmore and Fagans (1992) extended the origins of OD to philosophic roots of participation for individual development. In fact, their review provides in-depth treatment of various participative processes, as espoused by Sashkin and Burke (1987) and Woodman (1989).

Certain Clarifications about OD

1. OD is not sensitivity training. Sensitivity training may be a subset of OD, but OD as a whole is much more holistic.
2. OD cannot be a specific technique. If required, it may use a specific technique or techniques, based on the diagnosis of a situation.
3. OD cannot make people happy but it is concerned with the skill and competence of the organization through the individual development of people.

By quoting Lundberg (1974), we can understand the meaning and the context of OD, which requires answers to two questions, namely 'Where are we?' and 'Where would we like to be?'

Reviewing all the definitions and contexts of OD, we can define it as a comprehensive, cohesive, connected, structured, and systematic organization-wide development programme designed to meet organizational objectives.

NEED FOR OD IN ORGANIZATIONS

To sustain in a competitive world, organizations need to deliver results, nurturing a culture of performance. Organizational performance is the outcome of many factors, such as the way the organization designs, allocates, deploys, and delivers its resources. This requires members of the organization to perform both at the individual and group levels, so that an aggregation can lead to the performance of organization as a whole. Through their behavioural inputs, the members perform their job roles in accordance with the agreed standards. Organizational change requirements alter the process of doing jobs (and at times even alter their job roles), which obviously requires design of new performance standards. OD interventions are required to supplement such organizational change.

OD sets the premise for change focusing on development both at the individual and organizational levels. The primary need for OD is to facilitate organizational change and can further be understood in the context of its benefits. Both the organization and individuals benefit from OD. The nature of these benefits varies with the type of intervention. When the focus is on the development of individuals, it ensures positive behavioural change. When it is for the group or team, it brings positive change in the work culture, enhances team spirit, and makes people cultivate a sense of togetherness, which ultimately culminates in a sense of commitment to the organization.

When the focus is for the organization, OD ensures increased efficiency and effectiveness, bringing change in the work structures and processes. Thus, OD is needed to bring three-tier changes in the organization. From industry practices, it is evident that the best benefits of OD can be derived when all the three levels of benefits are combined. Porras and Berg (1978) reviewed 35 OD studies of organizations, which indicated that performance-focused OD interventions, that is, achievement of increased productivity, turnover, and profit resulted in achieving positive change in 51 per cent of the cases, while process-focused OD interventions resulted in positive change in 46 per cent. After reviewing 207 experiments, Katzell and Guzzo (1983) substantiated that individual productivity level increased in 87 per cent of the cases. With 574 OD initiatives, Golembiewski et al. (1983) observed positive outcomes in 80 per cent of the cases. All the above studies authenticate that OD interventions have a high probability of success in bringing positive change in organizations.

It is important to focus on the following areas in order to believe in and practise OD:

Human resources It is about believing that people can make a difference between the success and failure of the organization.

Workplace culture or climate This area is about believing that an appropriate culture in the workplace brings positive change. Creating and sustaining a performance-oriented work culture requires introduction of performance-based feedback systems, designing a job to ensure that workers feel a sense of accomplishment, of value and worth, and a shared vision. Often we use the term, 'workplace climate' because culture is more holistic while climate is specific to the organization.

Global market dimension Organizations now operate in ever-changing environments, the market is global, and that global players may compete even when they operate in local markets. Hence, in order to sustain and grow organizations need to partner with customers, and resolve problems in a systematic and planned manner with OD practices.

Accelerated pace of change It is about believing in an open systems approach to understand competition for resources, including people, capital, raw materials, physical resources, information, and knowledge. This is very important as without market information and knowledge organizations can lose their competitive edge to cope with the change. The liquidation of the 200 year old, *Encyclopaedia Britannica*, because it failed to understand that people can meet their information requirement through electronically available media (such as CD/DVD) in a cost-effective and efficient manner, is an example. So also the legacy-bound Philips in India, who failed to understand the Korean competition in consumer electronics and had to sell out to Videocon.

Having understood and believing in the need for change, organizations initiate OD activities either through internal change agents or by hiring external consultants. As OD expertise requires a more holistic knowledge and competence, it is desirable to retain external consultants also, so that new insights to organizational activities and the required areas of change can be properly mapped to undertake appropriate interventions. OD professionals need to be well-experienced in managing organizations.

Through a landmark study, David Gleicher developed an equation to help understand when exactly the organization is ready for change. The equation is as follows:

$$\text{Dissatisfaction} \times \text{Vision} \times \text{First steps} > \text{Resistance to change}$$

Dissatisfaction with the present situation will make an organization draw a vision for the future and translate that vision into action. Organizations need to take the first step towards reaching the future. If any of these three is missing, the product will be at zero or near zero level and the resistance to change will dominate. This model is a quick diagnostic measure to understand the possibility of change in an organization. OD can highlight these components and facilitate the process of change.

OD AS ACTION RESEARCH PROCESS

Action research is a process model for OD interventions. French and Bell (1990) described it as a 'process of systematically collecting research data about an ongoing system relative to some objective, goal, or need of that system; feeding these data back into the system; taking actions by altering selected variables within the system based both on the data and on hypotheses; and evaluating the results of actions by collecting more data'. Based on this definition, we can delineate the steps in action research as follows:

Entry This initial step requires marketing, which means finding the need for change within the organization to make people quickly understand the nature of the organization, identify the right decision-maker, and build trustworthy relationships.

Start-up and contracting This step identifies critical success factors and relates them to the culture and process of the organization, clarifying the roles of the change agents (both internal and external) and the employees. At this phase, the mechanism to tackle the resistance of change within the organization is also drawn, duly mapping the degree of formal or informal contract while defining the change process.

Assessment and diagnosis In this step, data is collected to understand the problems and opportunities within the organization. The framework of data collection can preferably be done using the model of *Dissatisfaction × Vision × First steps > Resistance to change,* as it could provide the best possible way for needs assessment. With the diagnosis, it is also possible at this stage to recommend appropriate interventions.

Feedback This is a two-way process to communicate what has been observed based on the data analysis. Feedback gives all those who have contributed an opportunity to learn about the findings of the assessment process. This encourages them to be more involved in the change process, develops their capabilities to understand and relate how their actions concern the organization, and makes them more committed to participate in selecting appropriate change interventions.

Action planning This is the step when recommendations are extracted from the assessment and feedback, and adoption of appropriate actions and intervention(s) to bring positive change in the organization are considered. As revised implementation plans, thus drawn, are based on the assessment of data, they are more logical, result-oriented, measurable, and rewarding, as they make the process of decision-making more participative.

Intervention This is the stage where the change process is actually carried out in conformity with the sequence of action plans. Intervention needs to be flexible enough so that intermediate changes, depending on the new information required, if any, can be made to modify the process.

Evaluation This stage helps in understanding the extent to which the OD process can bring a meaningful change in the efficiency and effectiveness of people and the organization as a whole. A good evaluation process not only ensures verification of the success, duly identifying needs for new or ongoing OD activities, but also facilitates the improvement of the intervention process for achieving better efficiency and effectiveness in the future.

Adoption After the evaluation step, the stage of adoption institutionalizes the OD interventions with the provision for follow-up of implementation processes, making it an ongoing organizational improvement activity. Sustaining OD activities is very important for organizations as the requirements of change never cease.

Separation Although ongoing OD activities are recommended for continuous organizational improvement, it may be necessary at times to discontinue the use of external expertise as too much consultation on the same issue may make the process counter-productive.

Although these steps have been shown as action learning steps for the OD process, following these sequential steps in real-life OD can, in fact, benefit an organization. There may be a need to reenter the process, such as back-tracking to previous steps, depending on the situational needs. Some of the major contributors on real-life OD processes in organizations are Cummings and Worley, Rothwell, Sullivan and McLean, etc.

The author extensively exercised OD in two plants of Hindustan Paper Corporation, a public sector unit in India, at a time when they were really in bad shape in terms of profitability, productivity, and even in industrial relations. Although this can partly be attributed to governmental control, which has now eased, the employees of the company were transformed and now actively partner with the management, resulting in a high degree of efficiency and effectiveness in their performance, despite the fact that they operate in a fiercely competitive environment. Exhibit 13.1 discusses this further.

STRATEGIC ASPECTS OF OD

From the discussions so far, it is clear that the OD process is a strategy, planned and managed from the top. The strategic dimensions of OD are evident from the fact

EXHIBIT 13.1 OD interventions at HPC

Hindustan Paper Corporation (HPC), a public sector unit specializing in manufacturing papers, predominantly operates in the north-eastern states of Assam and Nagaland in India. Another unit located in Kerala specializes in the production of newsprint. Pollution control norms in the paper industry are very stringent as caustic soda ash is used for bleaching. HPC units have a captive caustic soda and power unit, which gives them a substantial cost advantage.

Raw materials are sourced from forest products in the north-eastern states and this is a major problem due to issues of insurgency. HPC units source raw material largely during the peak harvesting season and even stock pile a six-month requirement, as storage of forest products is relatively easy and does not naturally deteriorate even if stored for long periods in the open. But to protect against fire, safety requirements are very high.

This is a continuous process industry and production continues 24×7 in different shifts. The units are closed only for annual maintenance. All the units of HPC produce only some specific variety of paper as changing from one variety to another can increase the machine interchangeability time. Following a production-centred approach, the units produced to their maximum capacity. However, with less focus on marketing, there was a huge stock pile of finished paper, which had a limited shelf life. It would be difficult to sell anything over six months old. HPC had hardly any control over the sale price determination as the dictum came from the ministry of heavy industries whose lack of market focus added to its woes of huge unsold stock.

Over and above this, there were problems with the trade union who felt that management did not protect workers' interests and the only option was to pressurize the management. Such a cult was also embedded in the minds of some sections of management who felt a similar antagonism towards the workers. The culture of cooperation and collaboration was totally absent.

OD interventions ultimately brought back a positive work culture to the extent of joint sharing of ideas. Trade union representatives were also taken through a series of programmes, including the ways and means of trade union marketing, negotiation, and collective bargaining. Similarly, management and all cross sections of employees were made to understand the market realities and a need to change in order to survive competition. With trade union support, HPC today is a success story of transformation.

---

that OD interventions are well-planned and structured, and based on the analysis of the change premises. Strategies, per se, provide direction to achieve the intended missions and objectives of the organization, keeping in view the resource allocation aspect, defining, and re-defining the scope of activities, and providing for uncertain situations. All these definitive contexts of strategies match with the OD processes discussed earlier and we can, therefore, also say that OD interventions have some strategic dimensions.

Burke's (1982) definition considers OD as a planned process of change. French (1990) considers OD as a long-range effort to improve the organization. Beckhard's holistic definition, that is, planned, organization-wide, and managed from the top to increase effectiveness through planned interventions, fits in perfectly with the strategies of organizations.

Beer's way of explaining OD as a method of enhancing congruence among the structure, process, strategy, people, and culture of the organization to develop the self-renewal capability, again talks about strategic dimensions.

The strategic dimensions of OD can further be understood in the context of its process of evolution. Historically, OD has emerged in the era of new economies to build capabilities of organizations to thrive in competition. Bennis (1969) viewed that OD primarily rests on three basic premises:

1. Revitalize and rebuild the organization keeping pace with the changes.
2. Create the desired climate in the organization by changing the existing systems of beliefs and values.
3. Introduce new social awareness to the people working with the organization.

All these premises, therefore, require a strategic approach to build the capability of the organization to respond to the changes through OD interventions.

HISTORY OR EVOLUTION OF OD

Lewin (1898–1947) is widely recognized as the father of OD. However, it was recognized in a more institutionalized form in the mid-1950s. Group dynamics and the action research concepts of Lewin form the basis of OD. Thus, this concept is more than half a century old. Initially, however, the term 'organizational design' was used interchangeably with the term 'organizational development'. As a result, the OD concept of the early 1970s do not hold well in today's context. For example, in the UK, OD was hardly recognized as a specialized academic or professional discipline until recently. In the US, however, it was well-recognized as a separate discipline. From an academic point of view, OD draws inputs from social psychology, sociology, psychology, and anthropology. The 'socio-technical systems' of the famous Tavistock Institute of UK, in fact, espouse the role of OD by emphasizing the need for balancing social, technical, and economic interests.

Some well-known behaviourists and organization theorists, such as Abraham Maslow, Chris Argyris, Rensis Likert, Douglas McGregor, etc., substantiate the benefits of participative methods, small group activities, etc. to motivate and increase the performance of individuals working in organizations. Some even substantiate how T-group movement can lead to achieving results through focus on group dynamics. The T-group concept attributes causal factors of behavioural problems as lying in the individual's perceptions, assumptions, and feelings concerning events and the people around. Solutions to problems can be obtained with feedback from a T-group or sensitivity group led by a non-directive trainer.

We can, thus, understand OD from three different stems. The first stem is sensitivity training or T-groups. The second is from survey, research, and feedback concepts. Both concepts primarily rest on the work of Kurt Lewin. The third stem is the socio-technical approach of the Tavistock Institute of Human Relations. Let us go into more detail about these three.

Laboratory Stem

This has its origin at the National Training Laboratories and the Research Centre for Group Dynamics of the Massachusetts Institute of Technology (MIT), under the leadership of Kurt Lewin in 1946. The process started with the research and training for community leaders, where they were brought together to discuss problems. Their discussions led to two conclusions: (a) that feedback in group interaction could be a rich learning experience and (b) that this experience could apparently lead to an organizational change through group building. In fact, this study leads to the institutionalization of T-groups in organizations to bring a behavioural change in people, which is a precursor for organizational change and development.

Survey Research Feedback Stem

This stem emerged with the use of attitude surveys to study group dynamics in 1945, in the MIT research centre mentioned earlier. It was a two-year study covering 8000 non-supervisory employees of Detroit Edison. The scope of the study was to collect data on perceptive attitudes of non-supervisory employees towards their supervisor, promotion opportunities, and work satisfaction with fellow employees. In the same line, similar reactions from first and second line supervisors and from higher levels of management have been collected, to ultimately draw the process for change.

Socio-technical Stem

Through its studies, the Tavistock Institute of Human Relations in London was able to identify the existence of a closed technical system in organizations, which make people to adopt to prevailing organizational systems. This closed system is synonymous with the traditional production and operations activities that are protocol-bound. As an alternative model, the Tavistock Institute suggested the open socio-technical system which does not consider human and technical dimensions of work in isolation but focuses on the interaction and inter-relatedness of the two.

Many international organizations embraced the Tavistock model. However, it first began in 1948 at Glacier Metal, a British company, followed by its adoption in coal mines, and even in textile mills in India. The Tavistock model was followed in the Scandinavian countries, in Great Britain, and also in many other parts of the world. However, the nature of usage differed. For example, in countries, such as Norway and Sweden its focus was on individual job enrichment, while in the US, its focus was to redesign work systems with a union management collaborative approach.

Over a period, OD theories have added many new dimensions making it a more application-oriented subject with inputs from HRM, strategic management, organizational design, and organizational theory. We can map the process of development of OD.

During the 1950s and 1960s, the focus of OD was more on the social dimensions of organizations, and on the humanistic values to promote openness, trust, and collaboration. In the 1970s, it was influenced by the organizational theory and the human side of technology, with emphasis on structural change, employee involvement, and work design. In the 1980s, OD became a theory, and many new concepts and opinions were integrated with it. The emphasis now was on the techniques for reward systems, career planning and development, and employee assistance programmes. With a management-centric OD approach, by the 1990s it became an applied discipline with action research. Today, OD is considered as the tool to achieve organizational transformation, obviously to carry out both transformational and transactional changes. Cummings and Worleys (1997) observed that the scope and dimensions of OD will continue to change with the passage of time, as future change requirements of organizations are unpredictable.

FEATURES OF OD

All the definitions discussed so far may vary in emphasis, but there are some common features:

1. OD applies to changes in the strategy, structure, and/or processes of an entire system, such as an organization, a single plant of a multi-plant firm, a department or work group, or individual role or job.
2. OD is based on the application and transfer of behavioural science knowledge and practice (such as leadership, group dynamics, and work design), and is distinguished by its ability to transfer such knowledge and skill so that the system is capable of carrying out more planned change in the future.
3. OD is concerned with managing planned change in a flexible manner that can be revised as new information is gathered.
4. OD involves both the creation and the subsequent reinforcement of change by institutionalizing change.
5. OD is orientated to improving organizational effectiveness by helping members of the organization to gain the skills and knowledge necessary to solve problems by involving them in the change process. It also requires promoting high performance, including financial returns, high quality products and services, high productivity, continuous improvement, and a high quality of working life.

CHARACTERISTICS OF OD

Although in the process of explaining OD we have already discussed its characteristics briefly, these are now explained in more detail.

OD is a planned organization change It identifies problems, diagnoses, and develops strategies for improvement. In this planned process of change, OD programmes make use of values, attitudes, culture, and team development.

OD is a planned intervention An OD intervention programme is well-structured, as the intervention strategy is developed after duly examining present working norms, values, and possible areas of conflict, considering various alternatives for better results. Some of the important areas of intervention are planning and decision-making, goal-setting, team development, organization structure, values, and culture, so that in the process it can upgrade employees' skills and abilities.

OD involves commitment from the top Unlike other change programmes through QCs (small group activities), etc., OD is essentially a top-down approach, but culminating in mutual trust and collaborative relationships with all cross sections of people in the organization. Top management must support efforts and commit themselves in the process else OD efforts are not likely to succeed.

OD makes use of social philosophy as norms of change The bureaucratic approach of OD interventions neglects the human dimensions of change. To make use of social philosophy concepts, OD interventionists need to make use of behavioural science knowledge and ensure that the process of change takes place in a humane and democratic manner.

PRINCIPLES OF OD

The OD process is influenced by many disciplines, such as psychology, sociology, anthropology, and also many modern areas, such as theories of motivation, personality, learning, group dynamics, general systems theory, leadership, power, organization design, etc. Because of such a wide spectrum of influence from various disciplines, the OD process follows certain principles for individuals, people, and organizations as a whole. Based on the work of McLean (2005), we can elaborate such principles of OD as follows:

Individuals

The principles regarding individuals are as follows:

1. Individuals have needs for personal growth and development that can be satisfied in a supportive and challenging environment.
2. Most workers can take more responsibilities and make greater contributions to organizational goals than is possible in most organizational environments. Therefore, the job design, managerial assumptions, or other factors frequently 'demotivate' individuals in formal organizations.

Groups

The principles regarding groups are as follows:

1. Groups are highly important to people and most people satisfy their needs within groups, especially the work group. This includes both peers and the supervisor, and greatly influences the individual within the group.
2. Work groups are essentially neutral and can be either helpful or harmful to the organization.
3. When working together collaboratively, work groups can greatly increase their effectiveness in attaining individual needs and organizational requirements. Group members can be more effective in assisting one another, including the exercise of leadership functions.

Organizations as Human Entities

The principles regarding organizations as human entities are as follows:

1. Since the organization is a system, changes inside a sub-system (social, technological, or managerial) will affect other sub-systems.
2. The culture of the organization tends to suppress the expression of the feelings and attitudes of most people, adversely affecting problem-solving job satisfaction, and personal growth.
3. In most organizations, the level of interpersonal support, trust, and cooperation is much lower than is desirable and necessary.
4. Although win–lose strategies can be appropriate in some situations, many such situations are dysfunctional to both employees and the organization.
5. Many personality clashes between individuals or groups are functions of organizational design rather than of the individuals involved.
6. When feelings are seen as important data, additional avenues for improved leadership, communications, goal-setting, intergroup collaboration, and job satisfaction open up.
7. Shifting the emphasis of conflict resolution from evading or smoothing to open discussion of ideas facilitates both personal growth and accomplishment of organizational goals.
8. Organizational structure and the design of jobs can be modified to more effectively meet the needs of the individual, the group, and the organization.

Exhibit 13.2 provides OD stages and methodology as followed in organizations.

OD IN DIFFERENT TYPES OF ORGANIZATIONS

Globally, some of the big companies that have engaged in OD are General Electric, General Motors, Union Carbide, Exxon, Corning Glass Works, Texas Instruments, American Airlines, DuPont, The Hotel Corporation of America, John Hancock

EXHIBIT 13.2 A typical OD methodology

Precise approaches will vary according to the circumstances but will broadly cover the following stages:
- Analyse current position within the organization
- Prepare to change (usually involving gathering information)
- Design (i.e., plan the response that will be the most effective in the situation)
- Communicate
- Deliver the change
- Evaluate (measure the effectiveness of the intervention)

Insurance Company, Polaroid, Ralston Purina, General Foods, Procter & Gamble, IBM, TRW Systems, Bank of America, and Cummins Engines. OD processes have been used in schools, communities, local and state government, and at the federal level, including the armed services. In the US army, such approaches are called organizational effectiveness (OE). Schools and universities have used both group training and survey feedback relatively early in the history of OD. OD is used in different organizations, including public and private sectors in India. Similarly, OD efforts have been applied extensively in many countries, such as Canada, Sweden, Norway, Germany, Yugoslavia, Japan, Australia, Philippines, Israel, New Zealand, and the Netherlands. It is now being used not only for development of individuals and groups, but also for proper structuring and design of the organization. Exhibit 13.3 depicts the case of Cisco which was able to transform successfully.

OD AND MANAGEMENT DEVELOPMENT

In organizations, OD is often confused with management development programme (MDP). MDP helps to develop managers, while OD improves organizational systems in totality. Thus, MDP can be considered as a subset of OD since during the OD process, organizations also make use of MDP. MDP is a scientific training process

---

EXHIBIT 13.3 Transformation at Cisco

Cisco Systems Inc. is a worldwide leader in Internet infrastructure. Cisco's OD intervention for organizational transformation was primarily through incubating future leaders and empowering them to drive the organization through change. This helped Cisco to transform from a loss-making to a profit-making venture. The quality of its leadership is a critical success factor to enable the company to tackle present and future business challenges.

The leadership and people development manager at Cisco emphasizes that the company incubates all the passions and principles of leadership to develop people. This approach is called the 'baked-in' qualities of Cisco to reinvent the organization. Such processes of developing leaders within the organization and empowering them have enabled Cisco to emerge as a very successful organization. For the last eight successive years, Cisco has been one of the *Fortune* magazine's '100 best places to work' in.

for managers and executives, to enrich their knowledge and skills to make them competent to manage their organizations effectively. Unlike general purpose training, MDPs aim at developing the conceptual and human skills of managers and executives through an organized and systematic procedure. MDP is a continuous process and encompasses the entire professional career of managers and executives.

Also, MDP is a knowledge-updating activity. It bridges this gap by enriching the functional capacity of executives and managers, and continuously updating their knowledge and skill. MDP can also be used as a vehicle for attitudinal change and development of competency.

Thus, it can help an organization to achieve the following objectives:

1. Make available managers and executives with the requisite knowledge and skills to meet the present and anticipated future needs of the organization.
2. Encourage managers to develop their full potentiality for handling greater responsibility.
3. Improve the functional competence of managers, making them more transparent and responsive to the changing needs of the organization.
4. Sustain good performance of the managers throughout their career and not allow them to develop managerial obsolescence.
5. Develop managers for higher assignments, duly replacing elderly executives.

Therefore, MDP reinforces the OD process in organizations, focusing on developing the skills and competence of managers.

GOALS OF OD

The important goals of OD are as follows:

1. The most important goal of OD is to emphasize the need for transforming from a closed to an open system by inculcating various changes in the organization. Such changes *inter alia* also include introduction of concepts of social philosophy in the organization which makes it socially more responsible and transparent.
2. To supplement authority and hierarchical roles with knowledge and skills, replacing traditional authority assigned role, creating a more congenial work environment is an important goal of OD.
3. Building mutual trust and confidence in the organization for managing people and reducing conflict is an important goal of OD.
4. Change structure and roles consistently with accomplishment of goals.
5. Encourage a sense of ownership and pride in the organization.
6. Decentralize decision-making close to the source of activity.
7. Emphasize feedback, self-control, and self-direction.
8. Develop a spirit of cooperation, mutual trust, and confidence.
9. Develop a reward system based on achievement of goals and development of people.

It is apparent from this that the goals of OD are basically to change the attitudes of people in the organization so as to enable them to identify the change areas and implement the desired organizational changes on their own.

STEPS IN OD

Blake and Mouton (1985) suggested a six-phase approach to OD:

1. Investigation by each member of the organization of his/her own managerial styles
2. Examination of the boss–subordinate relationship
3. Analysis of work team action
4. Exploring the coordination-related issues of interrelated terms
5. Identifying and defining major organizational problem areas
6. Planning for executing agreed-upon solutions that result in changes in the organization

However, OD efforts progress through a series of well-defined stages which can be enumerated as follows:

Identifying and diagnosing Required changes in relation to various units in the organization should be identified and diagnosed by examining the feedback from employees. Effective identification and diagnosis of the problem should be preceded by an employee survey.

Developing strategy While developing appropriate strategy, it is necessary to study people, sub-systems, and the organization as a total system. Strategy is the direction and scope of an organization in the long-run, matching resources, and changing the environment.

Implementing the programme The OD programme should be implemented in a phased manner, that is, it should be tried at the outset only in a small part of the organization and should gradually be implemented in the total organization only after getting positive results. Since the total organizational change precedes attitudinal change and change in the values and beliefs of the people, the initial thrust should be on training employees, improving their skills, developing self-awareness, improving interpersonal relationships, reducing conflict, etc.

Reviewing the progress of the programme In order to get an unbiased opinion, a review of the OD programme should be preferably done by a qualified person who was not involved in designing and developing it.

From the above discussion, it is evident that there are different stages of OD and organizations need to follow defined tasks at every stage, and proceed to the next stage only after the previous ones are completed.

IMPORTANT TRIGGERS FOR OD

Although it has been acknowledged that changes, per se, necessitate OD, we need to understand the important triggers of change that persuade such initiatives. Some of these are as follows:

Knowledge Explosion

Knowledge becomes obsolete with the passage of time. It is said that by the time a technology graduate passes out from his/her college, one-third of the learnt knowledge has already become obsolete. This means that even before they enter the organizations, the acquired knowledge of such graduates is outdated. This also holds good for management graduates although the degree of obsolescence for them is relatively low. Also, for organizations, the knowledge repository needs to be periodically shunned, adopting effective knowledge management practices. Among other things, this requires documentation of existing knowledge (both through internal and external benchmarking with the best performers), sharing the knowledge with others (to develop the capability of people), and finally retiring the old knowledge. Therefore, knowledge explosion, per se, requires organizations to develop continuously.

Rapid Product Obsolescence

As new knowledge is acquired, old knowledge and products quickly become redundant. Greater effort and resources are required to be put into research and development that may result in developing new products and services. Organizations gain when they quickly avert such product obsolescence through knowledge renewal and new product design. This requires organizational development. Hence, rapid product obsolescence is also an important trigger for organizational development.

Changing Composition of the Labour Force

This is also another important trigger for organizational development. New generations of workers always prefer to embrace new work processes, acquire new knowledge, skill and set of competencies, and bring innovative changes in the organization. Therefore, organizations stress on continuous development through planned OD interventions.

Growing Concern over Personal and Social Issues

New generation workers are well-informed about social and environmental issues. They expect personal changes through grabbing opportunities, and consider the organization as their vehicle to advancement. Such expectations provide a trigger for OD.

Increasing Internationalization of Business

With greater internationalization, organizations become larger and constantly need to adapt to the changes, responding to cross-cultural issues, global economic changes, etc. These apart, other changes brought in by increasing internationalization are the communications explosion, increase in professionalism, changes in the relations between line and staff, including the establishment of specialists, and the unionization of workers. OD is an important prerequisite for a manager to cope with all these.

OD AND ORGANIZATIONAL INVOLVEMENT

The scope of OD is potentially huge, encompassing both management and leadership theory and practice. Decisions as to which approach organizations should adopt and what interventions they should apply can be difficult to determine and prioritize, if the organization and individuals within it do not have a clear understanding of where they are now (present state) against where they want to be (desired state).

OD interventions are levers for change that will prompt changes in organizational behaviour to focus on performance improvement at the personal, team, or group and organizational levels. These include the following:

Organizational arrangements Goal-setting, strategic and operational planning, structure, policy and procedures, system and process design, integration and alignment of activity.

Social factors Organizational culture, individual attributes, styles and behaviours, patterns of working, partnership working and relationship building, interaction and connectivity.

Physical setting Space configuration, interior design, ambience, safety.

Technology Tools and techniques, materials, machinery and equipment, job design, workflow design, technical expertise, systems and procedures.

OD AND LEADERSHIP DEVELOPMENT

The emphasis on leadership development intensified throughout the 1990s. The importance of balancing transactional management characteristics against transformational leadership characteristics was recognized. This view was supported by Stephen Covey in his best selling book, *The Seven Habits of Highly Effective People*, where he says, '...the metamorphosis taking place in almost every industry and profession demands leadership first and management second ... no management success can compensate for failure in leadership.'

There is a highly significant relationship between the leadership style adopted by the management and the culture of the organization and, furthermore, employees' behaviour is acutely affected by their relationship with their manager. Studies have shown that the most stressful aspect of employees' roles is mostly their immediate managers, and the managers are often unaware of their effect on staff stress levels.

ROLE OF AN EXTERNAL CONSULTANT IN OD PROCESSES

OD consultants are different from management consultants at least in one major aspect, that is, while management consultants are retained by the organization to troubleshoot a single or specific aspect, for the OD consultant the client becomes the total organization. OD consultants are required to consider the interactions between processes, departments, people, customers and suppliers, board of directors, shareholders, the community, and all other stakeholders. While management consultants troubleshoot specific problems and suggest remedial measures, OD consultants need to empower employees, involve them in decision-making, create opportunities for open communication, facilitate the change process, and make people feel accountable for the change outcomes, promote the culture of collaboration, and institutionalize the culture of continuous learning.

To choose an OD consultant, it is necessary to consider certain aspects:

1. He/she must fit in with the management team and the culture of the organization. This requires consideration of personality and style, the experience, and the expertise profile of the consultant. As a person, the consultant should be attitudinally flexible to adapt to the culture of the organization.
2. He/she must be congruent with the needs of the organization. This is because organizational perspectives of OD vary. The consultant has to mould himself/herself to such requirements and be prepared to initiate OD programmes in line with organizational needs.
3. He/she must accommodate the human dimension while initiating the change process. Many organizations embrace OD interventions that do not respect the human dimensions, which often escalate tension within the organization and defeat the process of change.

Based on this, we can list the role of external OD consultants as follows:

1. Manage leadership conflicts.
2. Manage communication blocks.
3. Improve the motivation level of employees during the transition phase.
4. Ensure that people restrain themselves from becoming overconfident.
5. Ensure that customer complaints are within manageable limits during the process of transition.
6. Check decline in profit, sales, and productivity rate.
7. Avoid the risk of reduced innovation and increased bureaucracy.
8. Avoid decline in HR focus.

9. Avoid distortion of facts.
10. Avoid autocratic decisions on the change process.

An OD consultant performs all these roles through

- organizational assessment
- strategic planning
- succession planning
- scenario planning
- organizational design
- organizational culture shift
- organizational work process improvement
- integrating the organization with a group, management, and individuals

Every OD consultant performs such roles at different phases of OD to facilitate the process of change. Exhibit 13.4 explains such roles in the different phases of change.

During all these phases of change, the OD consultant must check the personal biases and listen to others. He/She must also ensure confidentiality.

Ethical Guidelines for OD Professionals

The following are the ethical guidelines for OD professionals:

1. Realize the responsibility to self.
2. Act with integrity; be authentic, and true to oneself.
3. Strive continually for self-knowledge and personal growth.
4. Recognize personal needs and desires, and when they conflict with other responsibilities seek win-all resolutions for them.
5. Assert one's own economic and financial interests in ways that are fair and equitable to one as well as to clients and stakeholders.
6. Take responsibility for professional development and competence.
7. Accept responsibility for the consequences of one's acts.
8. Strive to achieve and maintain a professional level.
9. Recognize one's own personal needs and desires, and deal with them responsibly in the performance of one's professional roles.
10. Practise within the limits of one's competence, culture, and experience to provide services and use techniques.
11. Realize responsibility to clients and significant others.
12. Serve the long-term well-being, interests, and development of the client system and all its stakeholders even when the work being done has a short-term focus.
13. Conduct any professional activity, programme, or relationship in ways that are honest, responsible, and appropriately open.
14. Establish mutual agreement on a contract covering services and remuneration.

EXHIBIT 13.4   Roles of an OD consultant

Contracting phase
- Help the organization to reflect on motivation.
- Clarify the outcomes to the organization.
- Help the organization to build realistic expectations.
- Clarify the role of consultants.
- Draw a tentative model of evaluation.
- Document the theoretical process of change.

Diagnosis phase
- Analyse the collected data to unearth the issues involved.
- Establish causal relationships.
- Establish the relevancy in relationships.
- Understand the overall impact on the organizational system.
- Communicate the likely implications to organizations.
- Assess the issues continuously.
- Remain focused drawing the borderline of OD interventions.

Planning phase
- Frame recommendations based on the data gathered.
- Evolve low cost effective solution.
- Ensure participative decision-making. Ensure commitment on agreed change from the leaderships.
- Co-create the change implementation plan.

Data gathering phase
- Determine the process of data collection.
- Determine the type of data required. Decide on the appropriate mix of data collection.
- Draw the borderlines for data confidentiality.
- Select the process to facilitate openness.
- Gather data to map the future.

Feedback phase
- Develop leadership to convey the truth.
- Involve people to start change in their own process.
- Collate the data to frame theories.
- Inculcate a non-threatening atmosphere.

Evaluation
- Develop a method to the monitor change progress during OD intervention.
- Ensure continuous feedback.
- Choose the right method of evaluation. Ensure change momentum.

15. Deal with conflicts constructively and avoid conflicts of interest as much as possible.
16. Define and protect the confidentiality of client–professional relationships.
17. Make public statements of all kinds accurately, including promotion and advertising, and provide service as advertised.

ORGANIZATIONAL LIFE CYCLE ANALYSIS

Organizational life cycle, per se, is unpredictable, but the different stages of its development can be predicted. Like human life cycles, the organizational life cycle also moves through different stages, such as infant, growth, prime, and aging or declining stage. It is important for OD professionals to understand such potential sequence of change to initiate appropriate corrective actions so that organizations can perpetuate their existence through continuous renewal.

At the *infant stage*, organizations begin with a vision and then, through environment scanning, identify the opportunities to draw their mission. These missions subsequently percolate to time-bound goals and objectives to achieve, for which they frame their strategies and action plans. With strong commitment and purpose, organizations try to achieve growth keeping their people and resources focused. The infant stage is, therefore, characterized by action-oriented, opportunity-driven, and vision-focused approaches of the organization. In the process, organizations adopt a simple informal structure, few policies, systems, and procedures. They become flexible to respond to the changes quickly in order to avoid any major crisis. This is the stage of experimentation, where decision-making is largely centralized.

At the growing or the *growth stage*, organizations formalize their vision, mission, goals, objectives, value systems, policies, and procedures. Shared vision, mission, goals, and objectives find place in the list of priorities, to partner people in the growth process. In another sense, we can call it a stage of excitement. During this phase, conflict and inconsistency become increasingly evident. Even though organizations try to decentralize and delegate authority, the absence of suitable control systems often dissuades them from doing so. Nevertheless, organizations try to increase the involvement of people.

The *prime stage* is the peak level of the organizational life cycle. This stage is characterized by high market shares, profit, and growth. With strong profit and revenues, people in the organization become more enthusiastic to deliver their best. Market leadership enhances their motivation level and organizations also accelerate their phase of growth by venturing into various activities. New product lines, new structures, high decentralization in activities, focus on performance and effectiveness, are typical syndromes of this stage of the organizational life cycle. In the process of consolidating its position at the prime stage, organizations often try to play safe to avert risk. This reduces the entrepreneurial zeal and results in their moving towards the next stage.

The *aging stage* is the stage of decline. Here, people lack ownership, reduce their sense of responsibility, commitment, and involvement. With the progress of the aging stage, people in the organization suffer from a sense of complacency, become legacy-bound, nostalgic, and question each other on their failures. Lack of coherence in actions ultimately ruins the fabric of team spirit. Organizational growth declines and slowly it becomes the prey of all-round dysfunctions. This accelerates the dying phase.

Therefore, it is important for OD professionals to understand the current stage of the organization's life cycle before initiating interventions.

Based on the inputs of Quinn and Cameron's (1983) concept of organizational life cycle, Daft (1992) explained the changes in different dimensions of an organization through the different stages of the organizational life cycle. For example, at the start-up or birth phase, the organization remains relatively small, non-bureaucratic, performs overlapping tasks, centralizes its activities, runs the business without formal rules, has less support staff, without any internal systems and task forces. At the youth stage, the size increases, the structure is pre-bureaucratic, departmentalization of activities takes place, more than one leader rules, few rules are adopted, administrative intensity increases through clerical and maintenance staff, streamlining of internal systems is done through crude budget and information systems, and top leaders are made the task forces for coordination or organizational activities. At the midlife stage, organizations become large, and bureaucratic with many departments and departmental heads; policies procedures, and manuals are developed; the number of professional staff members increases; and control systems, budgets, and performance reports are introduced. With maturity, organizations become very large and bureaucratic, jobs or tasks are broken into small areas of activity; the organization structure becomes top heavy with a high degree of formalization; there are large multiple departments; and extensive planning and teamwork starts even at the level of lower-rung employees.

To ensure their stability and growth, organizations start the change process while they reach the stage of maturity. They reinvent themselves with a series of OD interventions, introduce new products and services, and phase out (wherever necessary) the existing ones.

> **Practice Assignment 13.1**
>
> Visit the website of any major Indian company. Study their history and milestones, and identify the stage of their life cycle, detailing the state of various organizational dimensions.

OD AND BUSINESS PROCESS RE-ENGINEERING (BPR)

BPR is a major driver of organizational transformation and so also of OD. Most organizations now consider it as essential to keep pace with the global competition. Davenport and Short (1990) defined business process as 'a set of logically related tasks performed to achieve a defined business outcome'. A process is 'a structured, measured set of activities designed to produce a specified output for a particular customer or market. It implies a strong emphasis on how work is done within an organization' (Davenport 1993). In their view, processes have two important characteristics: (i) have customers (internal or external), and (ii) cross organizational boundaries, that is, they occur across or between organizational sub-units. One technique for identifying business processes in an organization is the value chain method proposed by Porter and Millar (1985).

Among others, BPR requires organizations to align with the change, and to revisit their missions and re-invent with the changing business focus. When Dell re-engineered

EXHIBIT 13.5 Applications of BPR in two organizations

Ford Motor Company

Today, Ford claims that it has re-engineered its business from just manufacturing of cars to manufacturing of quality cars. This has saved its millions of dollars on recalls and warranty repairs. The basic re-engineering was done by introducing barcodes, first in every part that goes into the car assembly, and then to scan for any missing parts in the assembled car. This has restored Ford's confidence in the quality of its cars to the extent that it offers its customers an unparalleled three-year guarantee to its customers, which has certainly helped to reposition them in a competitive worldwide market. Also, in conducting meetings Ford has introduced voice-over-IP (VoIP). This could substantially reduce the cost of conducting meetings between its branches.

Procter & Gamble (P&G) Corporation

With 300 brands worldwide, P&G is now the global FMCG major. Being an innovation-driven organization, it cannot afford to stop increasing its brand portfolio and hence re-engineered its brand management activity introducing an 'innovating innovation' programme. Knowing fully well that innovation never dies, P&G used a scorecard to evaluate which innovative idea would be better. This approach helped it to selectively introduce innovative brands to suit the market. This digital scorecard significantly improved its overall performance. Using this scorecard, P&G expects to perform 90 per cent of its R&D in virtual mode and the residual 10 per cent only for physical validation of results.

from a computer rental business to a reseller with its K-12 workforce, everybody was sceptical as to whether it would be able to run the show with the same workers. Today Dell is a success story, so much so that IBM was unable to withstand the price competition and had to change their business focus, withdrawing from desktop manufacturing and selling. But all these are not so simple and linear.

Most organizations fail in their BPR due to overfocus on issues concerning structure and process. BPR, among others, involves adoption of new strategies, redesigning of organizational structures, management style, and external relationships. But more importantly, the culture of an organization has to be thought of, as BPR also requires people to change. Globally, we have many examples of organizations that have failed in their process of transformation because they have not adequately addressed the people-related issues, for example, the case of the *Encyclopaedia Britannica* or Philips India. Therefore, BPR also helps in OD. Exhibit 13.5 illustrates how two organizations applied BPR.

SUMMARY

In this chapter, we have explained in detail the definitional and conceptual aspects of OD, first emphasizing the basic types of change and then explaining how OD can help to bring the desired change. As the definitional contexts of OD vary in approaches and applications, the OD process has been explained duly listing the steps from the action research perspective. The chapter also discussed the strategic dimensions of OD, its history or evolution, features, characteristics, principles, goals, steps, triggers, and typical methodology. Differences between OD and MDP have been explained concluding that MDP is a subset of OD.

Other important issues, such as OD and organizational involvement, leadership development, personality profiling, role of consultants, values of OD professionals, ethical guidelines for OD, organizational life cycle analysis, and OD and BPR. have been explained. All these inputs form the basis of our understanding of OD as a specialized discipline for the holistic development of organizations to ensure the desired organizational change.

KEY TERMS

Ethics and values of OD professionals OD professionals, whether in-house or external, need to follow certain professional ethics and value systems.

Management development It is virtually the development of managers. It is, therefore, concerned with upgrading of managers' skills and abilities.

OD and BPR BPR is a major driver of organizational transformation and so also of OD. BPR is essential to pace with the global competition. It is a set of logically-related tasks performed to achieve a defined business outcome.

Organizational life cycle analysis Organizations move through different stages, such as infant, growth, prime, and aging or declining stage. For OD professionals, it is important to understand such potential sequence of change to initiate appropriate corrective actions so that organizations can perpetuate its existence through continuous renewal.

CONCEPT REVIEW QUESTIONS

1. Explain the concept of OD. How is it different from a management development programme?
2. What are the important triggers for OD? In the era of globalization which trigger or triggers, in your opinion, would call for immediate OD intervention?
3. What are the steps involved in implementing OD? Why is an organizational life cycle analysis important in implementing OD measures?
4. What are the ethical issues in OD? What is the typical methodology of OD?
5. Explain the goals and steps in OD. Explain how OD and leadership development are related.
6. Discuss OD and personality profiling issues. What role do consultants play in OD?
7. Write short notes on the following:
   (a) Workplace climate
   (b) Action planning
   (c) The laboratory stem
   (d) Socio-technical stem
   (e) Product obsolescence
   (f) BPR

CRITICAL THINKING QUESTIONS

1. Explain how organizational life cycle analysis helps in proper identification of OD interventions. Develop your answer with some real-life examples.
2. Often organizations mistake OD with BPR. Drawing lessons from the corporate world, make distinctions between the two.
3. Imagine you are an OD specialist. You have been given the task of transforming an organization that is now going through major re-structuring of its business process, technology, and employees' skill and competence. Suggest your line of action.

CASE STUDY

Maxima's Transformation Process

Communicate for buy-in—this is what John P. Kotter spelt out as the fourth stage of successful change in organizations. The underlying belief at this stage is to inculcate the change vision and strategies to those people in the organization who plan for change. The process is not so easy, particularly in Indian manufacturing organizations where a large number of the people employed are an average age-mix of 50 plus and who are just sufficiently educated to perform their current job(s).

The heavy engineering giant, Maxima, number one in railway equipments and wagon manufacturing, was also influenced by the propensity for Indian organizations to heavily depend on external agencies to troubleshoot its organizational change and development process. Maxima emerged after the divestment of 72 per cent of a century-old public sector company that was originally founded by a British company and subsequently taken over by the government of India after they decided to quit India.

Immediately after acquisition, Maxima observed that the company was well-respected in the industry for the skills and ingenuity of its people. The available technology was also very good and comparable with the best in the world. As a result of quality consciousness and good workmanship, there was no dearth of orders and, in fact, the organization was booked for the next three years. Yet before acquisition it had a typical cash flow problem.

Unrealized debts reached to a level where the company did not have the resources to purchase raw materials. Staff salary payment carried a backlog of 3 to 4 months. People were restless and uncertain about government policies. Then came the news of its acquisition by Maxima.

Previously, Maxima had no experience in heavy engineering. It was in apparels and this was an unrelated business venture. Seventy-two per cent of the Government of India stake was acquired at a throwaway price of less than Rs 20 crore with the condition that people's jobs would be protected. For the government, this was the only way to absolve them from the loss-incurring PSU while gaining political mileage by divesting under the veil of job protection. Maxima underwent typical cash flow problems due to the irregular settlement of sales dues by major government-owned institutional buyers.

One of the conditions imposed by Maxima before acquisition was that the government will settle its payment dues within a time-bound schedule. Together with this, Maxima urged its major creditors (including banks who had lent the funds) to convert its debt to equity. Both conditions did wonders for it. With the booming stock market, Maxima's share was overpriced as no one was aware of its intrinsic value or fundamentals (being wholly owned by the government).

Maxima's Chairman, a typical Indian family businessman, wanted to run the show with his own vision. In his first meeting he spelt out his expectations from employees and instructed his top management to manage the company as directed by him.

Aditya, the CEO of the company was in a fix. People were restless, demoralized, and demotivated due to the non-payment of salaries, while the Chairman had a long list of expectations. At this crossroad, Aditya used his expertise of managing the company with a total participation approach. He had a quick series of meetings with the union, asking all of them to cooperate considering him as one of them, who cannot afford to let the company die. The union had tremendous confidence in Aditya who had fought for their cause and assured him that they would make the people understand the message of change.

Aditya then had meetings with the departmental heads asking them to meet their people and draw a participative vision separately for each department. The method was to be a conventional one, where each employee was asked to list his/her job priority to achieve success. Departmental heads then shortlisted common job priorities and converged them into one list that was handed over to Aditya. He met the chairman and showed him the degree of differences between his vision and the vision perceived by members of the organization. Aditya requested a permission to draw a goal congruence model with a focus on areas of common interest, which the chairman agreed to.

Aditya's first success was making employees believe that the company values their opinions and beliefs. The change process in Maxima subsequently went smoothly and the company was able to turnaround in less than two years without a single retrenchment.

Discussion Question

Read the case and critically evaluate how Aditya's efforts could effect transformation in Maxima.

REFERENCES

Argyris, C. (1994), *On Organizational Learning*, Blackwell, Cambridge.

Beckhard, R. (1969), *Organization Development: Strategies and Models*, Addison-Wesley, Reading.

Beer, M. and E. Huse (1972), 'A systems approach to organization development', *Journal of Applied Behavioural Science*, Vol. 8, Issue 1, pp. 79–101.

Bennis, W. (1969), *Organization Development: Its Nature, Origin, and Prospects*, Addison-Wesley, Reading.

Blake, Robert R. and Janse S. Mouton (1985), *The Managerial Grid III: The Key to Leadership Excellence*, Gulf Publishing Co, Houston.

Burke, W. (1982), *Organization Development: Principles and Practices*, Little, Brown & Co., Boston.

Covey, Stephen, R. (1997), *The Seven Habits of Highly Effective Families*, Golden Books, New York.

Cummings, T.G. and C.G. Worley (2005), *Organization Development and Change*, Eighth Edition, South-Western Publishing, Mason.

Daft, Richard L. (1992), *Organizational Theory and Design*, West Publishing, St Paul, Minnesota.

Davenport, T.H. and J.E. Shoot (1990), 'The new industrial engineering: Information technology and business process re-design', *Sloan Management Review*, Vol. 31, Massachusetts, pp. 11–27.

French, W. and C. Bell, Jr (1990), *Organization Development: Behavioural Science Interventions for Organization Improvement*, Fourth Edition, Prentice Hall, Englewood Cliffs.

French, W.L. (1990), *Human Resource Management*, Fourth Edition, Houghton Mifflin, Boston.

Golembiewski, Robert T., Robert J. Sutton, Reginald A. Bruce, and Stanley G. Harris (1983), *Epilogue, Human Resource Management*, Vol. 22, No. 4, pp. 467–473.

Kanter, R.M., B.A. Stein, and T.D. Jick (1992), *The Challenge of Organizational Change*, Free Press, New York.

Katzell, R.A. and R.A. Guzzo (1983), 'Psychological approaches to productivity improvement', *American Psychologist*, Vol. 38, pp. 468–472.

Kotter, J.P. (1998), 'Leading change: Why transformation efforts fail', *Harvard Business Review on Change*, A Harvard Business Review Paperback, Harvard.

Kotter, John and James L. Heskett. (1992), *Corporate Culture and Performance,* Free Press, New York.

Lewin, K. (1951), *Field Theory in Social Science*, Harper and Row, New York.

——. (1947), *Frontiers in Group Dynamics, Human Relations*, Vol. 1, Issue 1, pp. 5–42.

Likert, Rensis (1961), *New Patterns of Management*, Jossey-Bass, San Francisco.

Lundberg (1974), 'Organization development: Current perspectives and future issues', Paper presented to the Southeast Chapter of the American Institute for Decision Sciences.

McGregor, Douglas (1960), *The Human Side of Enterprise,* McGraw-Hill, New York.

McLean, Gary N. (2005), *Organization Development Principles, Processes, Performance,* Berrett-Koehler Publishers, San Francisco.

Neilson, E.H. (1984), *Becoming an OD Practitioner,* Prentice Hall, New Jersey.

Pasmore, W.A. and M.R. Fagans (1992), 'Participation, individual development, and organizational change', *Journal of Management,* Vol. 18, No. 2, pp. 375–397.

Porras, J.I. and P.U. Berg (1978), 'The impact of organization development', *Acedemy of Management Review,* No. 3, pp. 249–266.

Quinn, Robert E. and Kim Cameron (1983), 'Organizational life cycles and some shifting criteria of effectiveness', *Management Science,* Vol. 29, pp. 31–51.

Rothwell, W., R. Sullivan, and G. McLean (1995), *Models for Change and Steps in Action Research in Practicing OD: A Guide for Consultants,* Pfeiffer, San Diego.

Sashkin, M. and W. Burke (1987), 'Organization development in the nineteen-eighties', *Journal of Management,* 13, pp. 393–417.

Woodman, R. (1989), 'Organization change and development: New arenas for inquiry and action', *Journal of Management,* Vol. 15, pp. 205–228.

14 Organizational Diagnosis and Development

Learning Objectives

After reading this chapter, you will be able to understand
- the definition and concept of organizational diagnosis and development
- the objectives of organizational diagnosis
- the steps in a diagnostic cycle
- the different forms of organizational diagnosis
- the organizational analysis for diagnosis
- the areas of measurement for organizational analysis
- the organizational health survey
- use of questionnaires and interviews as a diagnostic tool
- the functions of the task forces for organizational development
- assessment centres approach for organizational diagnosis
- observational methods and use of secondary data for organizational diagnosis

Whirlpool's Way of Organizational Development

In late 1999, Whirlpool, the international white goods major, realized that it was unable to drive growth in its business. Revenues, profits, and market share were all stagnant in spite of its stupendous achievement in operational efficiency, including drastic cost cutting. With its depressing performance, in December 2000, Whirlpool reduced its international workforce by 10 per cent and simultaneously started re-structuring the workforce.

Stepping up innovation, Whirlpool also introduced new products, which gave it the edge to command premium processes as well as customer loyalty. Impelling a customer-focused culture of innovation with creative inputs from all cross sections of employees, Whirlpool gradually differentiated its offerings from that of its competitors. To institutionalize innovation, it started monthly I-Board meetings and introduced I-Box to ensure that employees' brilliant ideas reached the I-Board. Employees' creative ideas in the I-Box were selected only when these were backed by market research.

All these initiatives helped to scale up Whirlpool's business performance and by the year 2005–2006, it was able to regain its market share, and increase revenues and profits. The importance of Whirlpool's organizational development through innovation can be understood from the point of view of its high commitment to employee development. As of April 2006, its innovation pipeline had 568 projects, of which 195 were scaled up for commercial launch. With US$3.3 billion in annual sales, Whirlpool today distinctly enjoys market leadership in the white goods sector.

INTRODUCTION

While explaining the definitions and concepts of OD in Chapter 13, it has been made clear that OD strengthens organizational capability to sustain in a competitive market. The process of OD intervention, among others, requires systematic interventions, making effective use of various OD models and tools. However, the OD intervention process precedes diagnosis to understand the gap. Organizational diagnostics are measures that can be applied to anyone in the organization and can be aggregated to represent different levels of the organization, such as departments, branches, or the organization as a whole. Some of the measures seen here work equally well with teams. These diagnostics are useful for gauging the morale of a company's workforce, testing the impact of new policies or procedures, monitoring long-term trends in the workforce, and determining where interventions are needed. Such measures are essential for an organization's growth and development.

Using various diagnostic tools, we can understand three important areas of organization, based on which we can diagnose the actual gap in the organization. Without closing these gaps, one cannot achieve the desired changes. These are as follows:

- Mission/goals of the organization
- Value of the organization
- Current management style

DEFINITIONS AND CONCEPTS

According to Alderfer (1981), organizational diagnosis is a behavioural science process to collect data about the experiences of people, and feed it back to the organizational systems to promote increased understanding of the system by its members. From this perspective, therefore, organizational diagnosis establishes a shared understanding of a system and based on that understanding determines the feasibility of the change. Organizational systems align the flow of various inputs with the external environment and transform this to the flows of outputs or outcomes. Thus, organizational systems essentially include the feedback mechanisms for self-regulation. Organizational diagnosis focuses its attention on two areas: (i) sub-systems and (ii) organizational processes. Organizational sub-system areas are: (i) top management, (ii) departments, (iii) groups, and (iv) individual units, while organization processes are: (i) decision-making, (ii) communication patterns and styles, (iii) interfacing relationships between groups, (iv) conflict management, and (v) the setting of goals and planning methods.

Rather than having a specific area for improvement, organizations generally have multiple developmental needs. Hence, organizational diagnosis emphasizes the audit of areas, such as organizational culture, morale, work design, selection, and development systems. This helps to look at the organization in terms of determining gaps between the current and the desired performance, and how it can achieve its goals. Organizational diagnosis is now considered a part of the organizational development process.

Organizational diagnosis is, thus, the analysis of an organization, its structure, subsystems, and processes to identify strengths and weaknesses, and to use such outputs as the basis for future development plans of the organization. Such diagnosis can either be a routine exercise or to address some problem or problems that affect the functioning of the organization.

OBJECTIVES OF ORGANIZATIONAL DIAGNOSIS

In a competitive market, organizations need to be flexible, innovative, and make use of different techniques to diagnose their problems to improve the way they function. Diagnosis, per se, is the process of elimination or use of other analytical methods to identify the causes of organizational dysfunctional syndromes and determine the degree of its preparedness to embrace change. In every organization, there are five interactive elements, namely people, structure, technology, purpose, and task. Organizational diagnosis needs to account for all these elements in order to measure them correctly. Keeping in view these aspects, the objectives of organizational diagnosis can be framed as follows:

- Determination of organizational strengths, weaknesses, opportunities, and threats (SWOT)
- Determination of potential obstacles for improvement of the organization
- Creation of the right ambience for change
- Objective assessment of current problems
- Identification of the need for development
- Focus on areas of attention
- Competency development
- Aligning the organization with its strategic intents
- Establishing an appropriate culture for improvement

To facilitate a structured diagnosis of the organization, some of the matrices can be framed as in Exhibit 14.1. The two matrices can be used as a template to record the assessment results for future decisions.

THE DIAGNOSTIC CYCLE

Diagnosis identifies problems encompassing the organization, determines its causes, and helps the management to plan solutions. It is a powerful conscious effort towards organizational development, particularly when change becomes necessary. Some of the steps for the organizational diagnostic cycle are as follows:

- Organizational orientation
- Organizational goal-setting

EXHIBIT 14.1 Matrices for environmental and institutional analysis

Matrix 1: Environmental analysis

Categories	Opportunities	Threats
Political		
Economic		
Social		
Technological		
Geographical		
Community relations		
Informal sector network		

Matrix 2: Institutional analysis

Categories	Strengths	Weaknesses
Organizational role and profile		
Membership		
Programmes and services		
Resources and capabilities		
Management systems		
External links		

- Collection of data
- Analysis and interpretation of data
- Feedback
- Action planning
- Implementation
- Monitoring and measurement of results
- Evaluation of results

This diagnostic cycle is repetitive and reviews the activities of the organization, as organizational change and improvement plans are continuous.

DIFFERENT FORMS OF ORGANIZATIONAL DIAGNOSIS

Having understood that organizational diagnosis is an important process of organizational development, it is now vital to understand its different forms. The forms of organizational diagnosis change depending on the change situations and the areas of improvement. Organizational diagnosis may be for purposes of development or improvement, or remedial or problem solving. It is possible to have certain commonalities in the methodologies; even the diagnostic tools may be similar, but applications and outputs or outcomes may be different. Lewin (1951, 1958) played a key role in designing the process of organizational diagnosis, suggesting a three-step approach, such as planning, taking action, and measuring results. Lewin's approaches of action research, laboratory training or T-groups, survey-research methods, etc. have already been discussed in Chapter 13.

The root of laboratory training is in the Gestalt psychology perspective, which emphasizes learning with a 'here and now' approach, as in T-group learning. In both the cases, learning is more spontaneous rather than some programmed instructions. These two approaches help to identify problems in leadership, organizational structure, communication, etc., particularly when people are in a group.

Action research is a process model to systematically collect research data about the ongoing systems of the organization in order to initiate the desired actions for altering the selected variables. Two contributors in action research are John Collier and William Whyte. Survey research methods administer a different structured questionnaire to measure the attitude of people in organizations and to understand their perceptions about different organizational variables and systems. Another approach is productivity and quality of work life (QWL), developed in the 1950s by Eric Trist and others at the Tavistock Institute of Human Relations in London. This approach examines the technical and the human side of organizations and their interrelationships.

Whatever may be the form of diagnosis, it is necessary to ensure that desired outputs or outcomes are obtained, that is, the strategic fit. Let us illustrate a hypothetical situation in Exhibit 14.2.

The case in Exhibit 14.2 illustrates how perceptive differences between different hierarchical levels on some specific variable or variables exist within the organization. The degree of such variance again widens when the purpose of diagnosis changes.

Thus, the organizational diagnosis process compiles information both on the organization and its employees, its interrelationships, and the way it is perceived by

EXHIBIT 14.2 Job satisfaction and organizational diagnosis

To improve the organizational health, a public sector bank carried out a job satisfaction study on managerial, supervisory, and operational employees. The idea was to understand the perceptive differences in the job satisfaction, so as to initiate necessary action to bring positive changes in the physical environment, task environment, and the organizational climate, so that the bank could achieve improved levels of productivity and performance from all cross sections of employees.

The bank collected responses from all cross sections of employees based on a random sampling approach. Analysis of the responses indicated wide perceptive differences between managers, supervisors, and operational level employees. While managers emphasized more on organizational satisfaction and awareness, supervisors stressed on decisional autonomy and the congruent relationship between the organization and task environment. For them, positive changes in the task environment are important for job satisfaction. On the other hand, operational employees are more concerned with developing their problem-solving skills, good interpersonal relationships, mutual trust, etc. to gain job satisfaction.

the management and employees of the organization. In a true sense, making use of various tools and models, organizational diagnosis understands various dimensions of the organizational portrait.

ORGANIZATIONAL ANALYSIS FOR DIAGNOSIS

Irrespective of the nature of interventions for organizational development, organizational diagnosis follows certain sequential steps. Organizational analysis is considered the most important step of diagnosis. It is done in terms of its components and their functioning. The organization, by nature, is a total system, which obviously breaks into various sub-systems or parts. Its success or failure significantly depends on the way each sub-system or part functions. Hence, to begin with, organizational diagnosis requires a thorough understanding and analysis of organizations. This step is known as comprehensive diagnosis.

Apart from measuring the effective functioning of each sub-system and part, a detailed SWOT analysis is done to assess the degree of potentiality of each of these. Therefore, the initial step of organizational diagnosis through analysis diagnoses the various sub-systems and all the processes of the organization. Organizational analysis is carried out in various departments, units, or sub-units, to collect information on areas, such as process of goal setting, degree of role clarity, nature of culture, management styles, conflict and the way it is resolved, management of mistakes, organizational learning mechanisms, teams and teamwork, work motivation, etc.

Through preliminary organizational analysis, it is possible for the organizational change agents to get familiarized with the general functioning of the organization, plan for growth and diversification, improve organizational effectiveness, organizational problem solving, etc. However, such perspectives vary with the purpose and background of people and can be economic, political, sociological, managerial, and applied behavioural.

AREAS OF MEASUREMENT FOR ORGANIZATIONAL ANALYSIS

As already explained, organizational diagnosis is a comprehensive analysis of the critical aspects of organizational functioning, which directly relate to the effectiveness and efficiency of organizational performance. We have also explained that the areas of diagnosis vary with the requirements of organizational developmental needs. Despite this, there are certain other areas of measurement. These are understanding organizational and individual objectives, process of organizing works, infrastructural support, characteristics of behavioural reinforcements, competencies of people, capabilities of people to adapt to the environmental change, organizational vision and mission, value systems, customer rating about the organization, leadership style, employees' involvement, organizational style of communication, organizational regulatory compliance, etc. The list is so exhaustive that it is difficult to draw a line to fix the areas of interventions. Nevertheless, we can develop a framework of analysis covering some of the important areas of interventions. These areas are grouped under some major heads and then divided into some sub-areas, as follows.

Attitudes towards Work

Attitudes towards work are measured in terms of job satisfaction, role clarity, role conflict, autonomy, participation in decision-making, and job involvement.

Job satisfaction The degree of employees' satisfaction with their jobs.

Sample: *I am generally satisfied with my job.*

Role clarity Knowledge and understanding of expectations from one's job.

Sample: *I understand my job role.*

Role conflict The extent of role conflict, which generally occurs when one needs to simultaneously comply with two or more job pressures.

Sample: *I am occasionally required to deviate from the rules and policies of the organization to accomplish my job requirements.*

Autonomy The extent of employees' participation in their job scheduling, decision-making concerning the usage of tools and equipments, and the process for doing their jobs.

Sample: *I perform my jobs independently.*

Participation in decision-making The extent of employees' participation in deciding goals and objectives, and also in framing policies of the organization.

Sample: *I give my inputs in decision-making and framing of policies, relating more to my jobs.*

Job involvement The degree of employees' commitment and involvement in their jobs.

Sample: *I always prefer to finish my job before going home.*

Organizational Commitment

Organizational commitment is measured in terms of job security, loyalty, and trust in management, identification, alienation, and helplessness.

Job security The ability to continue with the job without any break, provided the performance is satisfactory.

Sample: *I can continue with my job when I perform satisfactorily.*

Loyalty The feelings or the sense of attachment with the organization.

Sample: *I can accept another job offer for the same kind of work, when I get more money.*

Trust in management The extent of trust reposed by the employees in the workings and actions of management.

Sample: *I think my management works sincerely.*

Identification The extent of employees' identification with the goals, objectives, and values of the organization.

Sample: *I consider organizational problems as my own problems.*

Alienation The extent of employees' disappointment with the career and professional development.

Sample: *I can feel a sense of pride in accomplishing my work assignment.*

Helplessness The extent of employees' feeling of helplessness at the absence of opportunities and alternatives outside the organization.

Sample: *I feel I hardly have any option outside the organization.*

Organizational Climate

James et al. (1988) defined climate as the question of personal values and culture as group values and norms. Climate, on one hand, autonomously drives individual beliefs, values, and feelings. Culture, on the other hand, is the collective beliefs, values, and feelings of the people. Katz and Kahn (1978) also pointed out the propensity of individuals to differentiate between personal and group needs. Based on these arguments therefore, we can say that organizational climate is a subset of organizational culture.

Organizational climate is measured in terms of fairness, safety, support, communication, tolerance for risk, flexibility, and continuous learning.

Fairness The extent of employees' perception of an equitable and free from bias workplace.

Sample: *I am treated fairly and equitably in my workplace.*

Safety The extent of employees' perception of a safe workplace.

Sample: *I am in a safe and danger-free workplace where I am unlikely to be physically hurt.*

Support The perceived emotional support of employees' feelings on their organization.

Sample: *I feel my management is concerned about the welfare of employees.*

Communication The extent of transparency in communication and exchange of information.

Sample: *I am always informed about the changes that affect my work.*

Tolerance for risk The extent of encouragement the organization provides employees to take bold action, risk, and think independently.

Sample: *I am allowed to take risk in my way of doing work as it is supported by my corporate culture.*

Flexibility The extent of adaptability and tolerance for ambiguity in the organization.

Sample: *I feel my organization quickly adapts to changes.*

Continuous learning The extent of training and development opportunities available in the organization.

Sample: *I get enough opportunities to do my professional development activities beyond the scope of my immediate job.*

ORGANIZATIONAL HEALTH SURVEY

Based on these lines of enquiry, one can approximate the organizational situation and accordingly decide on the improvement plans. A 55-item questionnaire to measure organizational health, commonly known as 'toxic organization survey', is included as Appendix 14.1. This is a very comprehensive and effective questionnaire to perform organizational analysis, focusing on almost all areas of organizational improvement. However, its administration and analysis requires adequate knowledge and the expertise of OD professionals.

According to this survey, when any organization scores low or moderately low in six or more issues, it is considered as toxic. This toxicity harms individual employees also. Some of the syndromes of toxic organizations are poor management/employee relations and showing little concern for employee concerns and needs. Professionally managed organizations believe in development of people and hence nurture a supportive work environment.

Some of the areas of measurement issues studied in the toxic organization survey are as follows:

Compensation/Benefits

These areas address the benefits paid to employees, in addition to their wages and salaries. As monetary benefits are the greatest motivator, dissatisfaction on this count can ultimately demotivate people, and affect the performance and productivity of the organization. A toxic organization survey can unearth such dissatisfaction and demotivation, and the organization can accordingly initiate necessary corrective action in the form of redesigning the compensation and benefits structure.

Communication

Scoring high on communication dimension indicates that the organization is high on the free flow of information upward, downward, and across the organization.

Employees in such organizations actively listen to one another and feel encouraged to express their ideas and opinions.

Customer service

Organizations with a high score on customer service focus on discovering and meeting customer's and client's needs. With active customer relationship management, such organizations can meet the needs and expectations of customers, and even develop customized products and services.

Fairness

Fairness practices by organizations directly affect the employees' perceived job satisfaction. Fairness practices require fair and equitable treatment to all cross sections of employees. Organizations ensure this by bringing desired changes in their policies and procedures, and sustaining healthy management–employee relations.

Equal employment opportunity

Equal employment opportunity in organizations can be ensured through the practice of diversity. Diversity requires consideration of gender, race, culture, and any other discriminatory variables that differentiate people. In many countries, such practices are mandatory. Diversity consideration also benefits the organization by promoting innovation and deriving benefit from strategic marketing.

Empowerment

Effective organizations empower their workforce by sharing information, being participative, soliciting employees' ideas, delegating meaningful responsibility, expressing positive expectations of employees, and rewarding performance, so that employees feel more capable and motivated to assume greater responsibility.

Similarly, an organizational health survey can also help to measure job satisfaction, the degree of trust reposed by employees on the organization and its management, consideration from management, style of supervision and leadership, employees' commitment to the organization, performance feedback, job design, safety, focus on employee development, teamwork culture, balancing, etc. In all such areas, toxicity can be measured in terms of high and low score values.

QUESTIONNAIRE DEVELOPMENT FOR ORGANIZATIONAL DIAGNOSIS

As seen in organizational health survey, many questionnaire items can be developed on several areas of organizational diagnosis. Such questionnaires can measure various dimensions of the perceptions of employees to ultimately understand the present health and the desired changes required, if any. Some important guidelines for preparing the questionnaire are as follows:

1. The purpose of the questionnaire should be clear to the respondents.
2. Often respondents may fear the problem of identification; hence, questionnaire items need to be framed so that respondents cannot be personified.
3. Respondents should have the competence and skill to answer the questions; else questions should be framed in pace with their level of understanding.
4. Respondents should trust the person(s) administering the questionnaire. Often respondents feel a lack of trust and hesitate to answer a question. Hence, at the organizational level, selection of the person to administer the question should be done very carefully.
5. The questionnaire should be very specific and brief so that respondents feel at ease.
6. The questionnaire should be structured so that responses can be tabulated to draw the desired inferences. This means that it must be close-ended to the extent possible so that respondents can identify their answer from the given alternatives.
7. For ease in administering the questionnaire, it is always better to do so in groups. People in groups feel more comfortable to answer questions.
8. Timing in administering the questionnaire should be such that details can be checked out without any distortion. For example, any questionnaire administered immediately after an event can distort the responses.

To understand the variation in the response pattern, the questionnaire should be framed so that respondents can be classified in terms of certain biographical characteristics. For example, responses can vary with respect to age groups or educational levels.

USE OF INTERVIEW AS A DIAGNOSTIC TOOL

The interview method of data collection to analyse the organization is a very popular tool and is also preferred by organizations to test the potential of success of some decisions, ideas, or actions. Interview feedback helps organizational preparedness to effectively address issues arising out of any impending change decisions. Moreover, it is more effective in generating ideas to strengthen the existing systems and processes. In the literal sense of the word, an interview means a conversation with a purpose.

There are various forms of interviews, such as patterned, indirect, or non-directive, direct planned interview, stress interview, group interview, panel or board interview, etc. All these can be either structured or unstructured.

To conduct successful interviews, the interviewer must be competent enough or the purpose of organizational analysis may be defeated. Normally, the unstructured interview method is followed for exploratory diagnosis, that is, in situations, such as identification of strengths and weaknesses, etc. It could also be used to probe a relation with certain specific organizational issues. Structured interviews are similar to administration of a questionnaire.

Questionnaire and interview methods are the most commonly used techniques for organizational analysis. However, they may not be feasible in every situation and that is why workshops and internal task forces are used. In the workshop methodology, employees of an organization assemble in groups and can be divided into sub-groups to diagnose a situation using SWOT analysis or force field analysis. While SWOT analysis assesses strengths, weaknesses, opportunities, and threats, force field analysis examines symptoms, sources, solutions, and action plans.

In workshops, the problems and issues for diagnosis are first explained to the participants. The problems may be general or specific. Some of the sample problems/ issues for diagnosis can be listed as follows:

- Improvement of general performance of employees through increased productivity and motivation
- Employees' relocation to different units of the organizations for appropriate utilization and rationalization of manpower
- Employees' low motivation and possible remedial measures to cope with it
- Employees' perceptions about the general improvement of the organization

These are all general issues. There could also be specific issues as follows:

- Changing performance appraisal systems, and possible problems and prospects in it
- High rate of absenteeism and possible ways to cope with it
- Possible ways to improve team spirit and inter-departmental collaboration
- Technological changes and upgradation in some specific job areas, and the problems and prospects involved in it

After defining the problems, either through internal change agents or external consultants, the facilitator of the workshop assesses the extent of sharing the problem among the participants present in the workshop. The preparatory work also emphasizes the composition of groups for the workshop participants, presentation, and classroom facilities. Selection of workshop participants should be made in such a way that those who are directly concerned with the problems are present.

Some of the purposes of organizational diagnosis the workshops serve are as follows:

- Legitimization of the importance of the study by top management
- Rapport-building by explaining the meaning of diagnosis, sharing experiences of other organizations, explaining the importance of the data they generate, assuring confidentiality, explaining the rationale for group formation, announcing or forming the groups on the basis of suggestions by the members, and introducing the methodology
- Group work where the groups will use force field analysis, SWOT analysis, or source–symptoms–action plan analysis

- Presentation of consolidated data and prioritization of variables for action, etc. by the groups

The atmosphere in the workshop should be free, open, and informal. The facilitator plays a major role in creating this atmosphere.

Workshop methodology could be used under the following conditions:

- When the problems are amenable for improvements
- When the organization values participative processes, and there is some amount of openness or willingness to participate and share organizational concerns
- When employees' improvement are necessary to solve the problems

TASK FORCES FOR ORGANIZATIONAL DEVELOPMENT

Apart from the above diagnostic tools, many organizations make use of task forces or internal teams for organizational development. A task force is especially constituted by the top management with a group of employees who are assigned to work on a specific task, apart from performing their job-specific roles. Every task force is formed with certain specific terms of reference, which explains the purpose of the task force, methodology to be used, flexibility in redefining the job, resource utilization, etc. The task force may work independently with some designated members of the committee or under the guidance of some top management people in the organization. Usually, task forces undertake some specific organizational development issues and not general aspects.

Let us now understand the way the task force is constituted and functions for a specific project on competency mapping of employees in the organization. Competency is the capacity of a person which leads to behaviour that meet the job demands within the parameter of the organizational environment, and which in turn, brings about desired results (Boytzis 1982). Any underlying characteristic required for performing a given task, activity, or role successfully can be considered as competency. Competencies comprise the knowledge, skills, values, and attitudes demonstrated through behaviour that results in competent and superior performance. A competency is a person-related concept that refers to the dimension of behaviour lying behind competent performance (Woodruff 1991). It is not performance—it is the qualification to perform.

Development of competency in organizations facilitates in bringing the desired changes, and reinforcing individual and organizational capabilities. A task force constituted by any organization for competency mapping and development could follow the following steps:

- Appointment of the task force committee members
- Competency requirement analysis based on the information obtained through position documentation, process documentation, personnel development resources, interviews, etc.

- Individual competency assessment primarily based on an interview using two-time tested approaches, that is, behavioural event interviews and behavioural description interviews; and also through in-basket exercises, group discussions, psychometric tools, etc.
- Gap analysis to formalize the competency requirement and availability
- Strategy formulation to design suitable strategies to address issues arising out of the competency mapping and gap analysis
- Handing over the deliverables such as competency dictionary, skill inventory, gap analysis, competency strategy, etc. to the OD group

ASSESSMENT CENTRES APPROACH FOR ORGANIZATIONAL DIAGNOSIS

The assessment centres approach is extensively used in performance and potentiality measurements of managerial employees. The approach is usually helpful to assess the decision-making styles and the power of managers in hypothetical situations. Usually, it requires managers to perform realistic managerial tasks, which experts observe for objective performance and potentiality assessment. Different simulated exercises also form a part of the assessment. For example, in-basket exercise requires managers to perform simulated jobs based on a bundle of inputs, such as reports, memos, incoming phone records, letters, etc. Similarly, leaderless group discussions, presentations, interviews, etc. could also form a part of the assessment centres.

As in performance management, the assessment centres approach can also be used for organizational diagnosis, as through the result analysis, it is possible to ascertain the perceived areas of incongruence or deficiency that requires the intervention of the organization.

OBSERVATIONAL METHODS OF ORGANIZATIONAL DIAGNOSIS

This method is most useful when an outside consultant is used for diagnosis. Insiders are most often blind to the events and data that are part of the organization. An outsider could observe a number of things. For example, the behaviour of people when work begins and at the close of working hours, the notices displayed, the work organization, the behaviour of people in meetings, the kind of memos written, tea and lunch breaks, the canteen and the way it is organized, behaviour of employees in the organization, etc. could be observed and inferences made. The main limitations of this method are as follows:

1. Not all processes are amenable to observation and the observer's own biases get reflected in these. Observation methods could be used as preliminary diagnostic tools. Unless they are supplemented with interviews or other methods, a good quality diagnosis may be different (Nadler 1977).

2. The basic strength or weakness of observations as a tool is that the observer is the data collection instrument (as opposed to a questionnaire as an observation instrument). A sensitive observer making use of an effective structure for observation can be an effective data collection tool. An observer who has little sensitivity and no guiding structure may spend hours observing, see nothing, and report no usable data.

Secondary Data and Unobtrusive Measures

Records maintained by organizations can be very useful sources of data. With easy accessibility of computers, most organizations today collect and store a lot of data. Absenteeism rates and patterns, grievances, costs, delays, work performance records, attendance at meetings, circulars, and other office communications provide ample opportunities for diagnosis.

Minutes of meetings, points of view expressed in meetings, etc. also offer enough insights. These methods unfortunately are less frequently used. For example, analysis of performance appraisal reports can give a lot of significant data about the problems and difficulties of employees, their competency gaps, and so on. Similarly, an analysis of the delays in submitting reports (MIS, budgets, appraisals, and reward recommendations), leave applications, complaints, etc. may also provide significant insights.

Unobtrusive measures are those that can ensure collection of information based on observations. As organizational diagnosis is a sensitive issue, it often becomes difficult to collect data and compile information based on direct interviews, or by administering a questionnaire. To avoid this, the required inputs are collected without the knowledge of the employees being observed, using simple indirect observation, such as understanding their behaviour at work, body language, etc.

SUMMARY

Organizational diagnoses are measures that can apply to anyone in the organization and can be aggregated to represent different levels of the organization, such as departments, branches, or the organization as a whole. Some of the measures seen here work equally well with teams. These diagnostics are useful for gauging the morale of a company's workforce, testing the impact of new policies or procedures, monitoring long-term trends in the workforce, and determining areas where interventions are needed.

By using various diagnostic tools, one can understand the important areas of organization based on which the actual gaps in the organization can be diagnosed. Every method has some advantages and some limitations. Interviews have the advantage of studying the problems in depth and offering scope for generating and testing many hypotheses. Task forces are very useful in continuous diagnosis and implementation.

Questionnaires provide systematic information and comparability with other organizations, and of the same organization at different points of time. Observations and secondary data provide direct insights into the existing situation and are factual. The quality of diagnosis is likely to improve if a number of methods are used simultaneously rather than relying on a single method.

KEY TERMS

Assessment centre It is a situation in which management candidates are asked to make decisions in hypothetical situations and are scored on their performance. It usually also involves testing and the use of management games.

Competency It is a capacity that exists in a person that leads to behaviour that meets the job demands within the parameter of the organizational environment and that, in turn, brings about desired results.

Diagnostic cycle Diagnosis identifies problems encompassing the organization, determines the causes, and helps the management to plan solutions. Organizational diagnosis follows certain pre-determined steps, which follow a cycle.

Organizational analysis It is considered to be the most important step of diagnosis. It is done in terms of its components and their functioning. Hence, to start with, organizational diagnosis requires a thorough understanding and analysis of organizations.

CONCEPT REVIEW QUESTIONS

1. Explain the concept of organizational diagnosis. What are its objectives?
2. What are the different forms of organizational diagnosis?
3. Explain the different areas of measurement for organizational analysis.
4. Explain important guidelines for framing questionnaires and conducting interviews.
5. What is the role of task forces in organizational diagnosis and development?
6. Explain the various observational methods of organizational diagnosis.
7. Write short notes on the following:
   (a) Organizational commitment
   (b) Organizational climate
   (c) Leaderless group discussions
   (d) Unobtrusive measures

CRITICAL THINKING QUESTIONS

1. Your company has outsourced the customers' complaints handling to a well-known call centre. You are a leading mobile phone manufacturer. Recently, you have observed your market share and found that profitability has nose-dived to an alarming level. As the marketing head of the company, you have been asked to draw an elaborate plan for organizational diagnosis. Develop your plan clearly detailing the methods of your diagnosis with due justification.
2. Often organizations diagnose their problems by retaining external consultants. What terms of references do you deem fit in such cases? Elaborate your answer with a draft agreement.
3. Explain how organizational diagnosis is possible using unobtrusive measures? Develop your answer with corporate examples.

CASE STUDY

Wal-Mart—The Saga of Success through Organizational Change

Goldman Sachs's analysis observes that Wal-Mart continues to deliver results even in a challenging environment. Sam Walton, founder of Wal-Mart believes, 'It makes ordinary people do extraordinary things.' Ordinary people together accomplish what even they thought they could not do. What makes Wal-Mart so great can perhaps be understood from its HR philosophy. Susan Oliver, Senior Vice-President of Wal-Mart's HR function said that in a 'labour-intensive customer service business associates (Wal-Mart employees) cannot treat customers as number one if they themselves are not treated that way'.

In the year 2006, Wal-Mart's business performance was flat. All along, its track record had shown a minimum net annual growth of 20 per cent over the general US trend. With a marginal increase of 1.9 per cent in sales, Wal-Mart had nearly reached a no-growth position. There are two aspects to this performance set-back, (i) internal operational inefficiency, and (ii) competition from two major rivals, namely Target and Costco.

During this period, Wal-Mart also expanded its international market and entered a new business segment, namely fashion. With a tag of being a cheap store, Wal-Mart could never attract affluent shoppers. Its apparel venture, Metro 7, was a total flop. Wal-Mart realized that international competitors were powerful in their respective countries and enjoyed high loyalty from their customers. Moreover, retailing is also culture-sensitive. In Germany, despite acquisition of many prestigious hypermarket chains, such as 21-store Wertkauf, Interspar, etc., Wal-Mart could not deliver results because it never got the feel of German retailing due to cultural incongruity. The German experience was repeated in South Korea.

Successive failure in new product lines, such as apparel, international expansion, etc., further worsened its position. However, Wal-Mart's rigorous practice of lean management hardly leaves any room for cost control. With RFID technology, that is, radio frequency identification, in distribution centres, it could further streamline, its supply chain.

With all these deterrents in August 2008, Wal-Mart emerged a winner. In a global meltdown when others struggled for survival, Wal-Mart tracked a 17 per cent rise in profit. The trend is upward. Although analysts worldwide could see the reason for its low prices, overall managerial efficiency is largely responsible for such success. To strengthen its position and continue its 'everyday lower price' (EDLP) philosophy, Wal-Mart achieved operational efficiency by improving the merchandise-mix, accentuating friendly customer service, and above all, by inculcating a 'cult-like' culture, binding all Wal-Martians to activate their entrepreneurial zeal and grow.

Discussion Question

Read the current state of Wal-Mart and from organizational change perspectives, suggest what else Wal-Mart could do to ensure its stability and growth. Justify your answer.

REFERENCES

Alderfer, Clayton (1981), 'Intergroup relations and organizational diagnosis', in H. Meltzer and W. Nord (eds), *Handbook of Humanizing Organizations*, John Wiley & Sons, New York.

Beckhard, Richard (1969), *Organization Development: Strategies and Models*, Addison-Wesley, Reading.

Bhattacharyya, D.K. (2009), *Organizational Behaviour—Concepts and Applications*, Oxford University Press, New Delhi.

Boytzis, R.E. (1982), *The Competent Manager: A Model for Effective Performance*, John Wiley, London.

Emery, F.E. and E.L. Trist (1965), 'The causal texture of organizational environments', *Human Relations*, Vol. 18, Issue 1, pp. 21–32.

French, Wendell L. and Cecil Bell (1973), *Organization Development: Behavioral Science Interventions for Organization Improvement*, Prentice Hall, Englewood Cliffs.

Grundy, T (2006), 'Rethinking and reinventing Michael Porter's five forces model', *Strategic Change*, Vol. 15, No. 5, August, pp. 213–229.

Harrison, M.I. (1997), *Diagnosing Organizations: Methods, Models, and Processes*, Sage, Newbury Park.

James, L.R., W.F. Joyce, and J.W. Slocum, Jr (1988), 'Comment: Organizations do not Cognize', *Academy of Management Review*, Vol. 13, No. 1, pp. 129–132.

Katz, D. and R.L. Kahn (1978), *The Social Psychology of Organizations*, Second Edition, John Wiley & Sons, New York.

Khandwalla, P.N. (1977), *The Design of Organizations*, Harcourt Brace Jovanovich Inc., New York.

Levinson, Harry (1972), *Organizational Diagnosis*, Harvard University Press, Cambridge.

Lewin, Kurt (1958), *Group Decision and Social Change*, Holt, Rinehart and Winston, New York.

____ (1951), *Field Theory in Social Science*, Harper and Row, New York.

Nadler, D.A. (1977), *Feedback and Organization Development: Using Data Based Methods*, Addison Wesley Publishing Company, Reading, Mass.

Woodruff, Charles (1991), 'Competent by any other name', *People Management*, September.

http://od.online.com/toxic_org.asp

http://www.isical.ac.in/~ddroy/odiag.html, accessed on 8 November 2009.

http://www.scribd.com/doc/14758227/Organizational-Diagnosis

www.scribd.com, accessed on 9 November 2009.

APPENDIX 14.1
OD—Organization Health Survey

Please indicate whether you agree or disagree with the statement as it applies to your company by 'clicking' on the appropriate response. There is no right or wrong answer, so please respond truthfully. Do not think too much about your answer; go with your first impression.

Statements	Strongly agree (1)	Moderately agree (2)	No opinion (3)	Moderately disagree (4)	Strongly disagree (5)
1. I am proud of the quality of the services my organization provides to its customers.	SA	MA	NO	MD	SD
2. I am satisfied with my wages.	SA	MA	NO	MD	SD
3. Management informs me about issues that are important.	SA	MA	NO	MD	SD
4. I have the authority to correct problems as they occur.	SA	MA	NO	MD	SD
5. Information flows openly between management and employees.	SA	MA	NO	MD	SD
6. Policies and procedures are explained adequately.	SA	MA	NO	MD	SD
7. My ideas and opinions count at work.	SA	MA	NO	MD	SD
8. Customer concerns get resolved quickly.	SA	MA	NO	MD	SD
9. Employees are treated fairly regardless of gender.	SA	MA	NO	MD	SD
10. Day-to-day decisions demonstrate that quality is a top priority.	SA	MA	NO	MD	SD
11. Work policies are fair.	SA	MA	NO	MD	SD
12. I am satisfied with my total benefits package.	SA	MA	NO	MD	SD
13. My performance is evaluated fairly.	SA	MA	NO	MD	SD
14. I often feel frustrated at work.	SA	MA	NO	MD	SD
15. Promotions are based upon qualifications and merit.	SA	MA	NO	MD	SD
16. Employees are treated fairly regardless of race.	SA	MA	NO	MD	SD

(Contd)

(Appendix 14.1 contd)

Statements	Strongly agree (1)	Moderately agree (2)	No opinion (3)	Moderately disagree (4)	Strongly disagree (5)
17. Achieving customer satisfaction is an everyday priority.	SA	MA	NO	MD	SD
18. I feel a strong sense of loyalty towards my organization.	SA	MA	NO	MD	SD
19. My supervisor involves me in decisions that affect my work.	SA	MA	NO	MD	SD
20. My employer provides ample opportunity for me to upgrade my skills.	SA	MA	NO	MD	SD
21. I am very satisfied with my job.	SA	MA	NO	MD	SD
22. I trust the leadership of this company.	SA	MA	NO	MD	SD
23. My values are similar to that of my organization.	SA	MA	NO	MD	SD
24. Management treats employees with respect.	SA	MA	NO	MD	SD
25. My company encourages a balance between work and outside activities.	SA	MA	NO	MD	SD
26. Management is sincere in its attempt to understand the employee's point of view.	SA	MA	NO	MD	SD
27. At work we are encouraged to solve problems as a team.	SA	MA	NO	MD	SD
28. Senior management demonstrates that employees are important to the success of the company.	SA	MA	NO	MD	SD
29. My performance reviews have been useful in helping me improve.	SA	MA	NO	MD	SD
30. I am treated fairly by my supervisor.	SA	MA	NO	MD	SD
31. My company consistently provides excellent customer services.	SA	MA	NO	MD	SD
32. My supervisor is competent at doing his/her job.	SA	MA	NO	MD	SD
33. I have enough opportunity to let management at my location know how I feel.	SA	MA	NO	MD	SD
34. Teamwork and cooperation are encouraged by my supervisor.	SA	MA	NO	MD	SD
35. I would recommend my organization to others as a good place to work.	SA	MA	NO	MD	SD
36. My supervisor is open and honest with employees.	SA	MA	NO	MD	SD
37. My organization practises its corporate values.	SA	MA	NO	MD	SD
38. Senior management provides a clear picture of where the company is headed.	SA	MA	NO	MD	SD

(Contd)

Statements	Strongly agree (1)	Moderately agree (2)	No opinion (3)	Moderately disagree (4)	Strongly disagree (5)
39. My job makes good use of my skills and abilities.	SA	MA	NO	MD	SD
40. Management practises what they preach.	SA	MA	NO	MD	SD
41. My supervisor recognizes and rewards good performance.	SA	MA	NO	MD	SD
42. I have the resources (e.g., tools, equipment, and supplies) I need to do my job effectively.	SA	MA	NO	MD	SD
43. Management can be trusted to make sensible decisions for the firm's future.	SA	MA	NO	MD	SD
44. We have enough people to get the work done.	SA	MA	NO	MD	SD
45. My supervisor sets a positive example for others to follow.	SA	MA	NO	MD	SD
46. People within my work group cooperate to get the job done.	SA	MA	NO	MD	SD
47. I am often overworked.	SA	MA	NO	MD	SD
48. My work location is safe.	SA	MA	NO	MD	SD
49. My work gives me a feeling of personal accomplishment.	SA	MA	NO	MD	SD
50. My supervisor provides adequate supervision.	SA	MA	NO	MD	SD
51. Safety is emphasized in my organization.	SA	MA	NO	MD	SD
52. I am satisfied with the career development opportunities at my company.	SA	MA	NO	MD	SD
53. Our workgroup is a collection of individuals doing their jobs, not a team with a shared task to perform.	SA	MA	NO	MD	SD
54. I balance my work priorities with my personal life so that neither is neglected.	SA	MA	NO	MD	SD
55. I have enough time to accomplish my personal and professional goals satisfactorily.	SA	MA	NO	MD	SD

Organizational Scores

Through toxic organization survey, one can measure different issues. By analysing these, we can ultimately understand the extent of organizational dysfunction or toxicity. Depending on the score values, one can understand the degree of toxicity and initiate remedial measures accordingly. Scores are considered low or high depending on the following:

- Score 1 is considered low.
- Scores equal to 2 are considered moderately low.
- Scores equal to 3 are considered moderately high.
- Scores equal to 4 are considered high.

Statements.	Strongly agree (1)	Moderately agree (2)	No opinion (3)	Moderately disagree (4)	Strongly disagree (5)
39. My job makes good use of my skills and abilities.	SA	MA	NO	MD	SD
40. Management practises what they preach.	SA	MA	NO	MD	SD
41. My supervisor recognizes and rewards good performance.	SA	MA	NO	MD	SD
42. I have the resources (e.g., tools, equipment and supplies) I need to do my job effectively.	SA	MA	NO	MD	SD
43. Management can be trusted to make sensible decisions for the firm's future.	SA	MA	NO	MD	SD
44. We have enough people to get the work done.	SA	MA	NO	MD	SD
45. My supervisor sets a positive example for others to follow.	SA	MA	NO	MD	SD
46. People within my work group cooperate to get the job done.	SA	MA	NO	MD	SD
47. I am often overworked.	SA	MA	NO	MD	SD
48. My work location is safe.	SA	MA	NO	MD	SD
49. My work gives me a feeling of personal accomplishment.	SA	MA	NO	MD	SD
50. My supervisor provides adequate supervision.	SA	MA	NO	MD	SD
51. Safety is emphasised in my organization.	SA	MA	NO	MD	SD
52. I am satisfied with the career development opportunities at my company.	SA	MA	NO	MD	SD
53. Our workgroup is a collection of individuals doing their jobs, not a team with a shared task to perform.	SA	MA	NO	MD	SD
54. I balance my work priorities with my personal life so that neither is neglected.	SA	MA	NO	MD	SD
55. I have enough time to accomplish my personal and professional goals satisfactorily.	SA	MA	NO	MD	SD

Organizational Scores

Through toxic organization survey, one can measure different issues. By analysing these, we can ultimately understand the extent of organizational dysfunction or toxicity. Depending on the score values, one can understand the degree of toxicity and initiate remedial measures accordingly. Scores are considered low or high depending on the following.

- Score 1 is considered low.
- Scores equal to 2 are considered moderately low.
- Scores equal to 3 are considered moderately high.
- Scores equal to 4 are considered high.

PART 4

Organizational Development Interventions and Strategies

- **Approaches and Models**
- **Globalization and Organizational Change and Development**
- **Knowledge Management and Change**
- **Change Management Strategies**

15
Approaches and Models

Learning Objectives

After reading this chapter, you will be able to understand
- the different models and approaches of OD
- different approaches to organizational change
- the different stages in the organizational life cycle model
- standard OD models and tools
- OD through competency development

Hitachi—Communication Conquers Rumour Mill

The production facility of Hitachi Computer Products in Norman, Oklahoma, was suddenly caught in rumour-mongering among employees that ultimately affected its productivity, quality, customer satisfaction, and even started to undermine employee morale. The Oklahoma plant is a major manufacturer of electronic products for computer, networking, communications, medical, and security industries.

The company historically follows the culture of under-communication to the employees. However, its performance was stupendous; despite many of its competitors facing the spirited challenges. Employees of Hitachi take the cues from experiences of the employees of the competing organizations and use to imagine about possible plights. To ease the situation, Hitachi conducted an organizational cultural survey and identified that organizational change would be possible through positive improvement of work culture. Accordingly, it initiated some action plans focusing on the following aspects.

Focus was on replacing the rumour mill with laid an effective communication programme. This also focused on employees' understanding the company's mission, values, and goals. All employees were exposed to information on key performance metrics, such as quality, efficiency, waste management, customer satisfaction, and profitability on a real-time basis.

Such communication linkages with the employees slowly transformed them into a unified team, and developed their shared understanding and sense of responsibility, which ultimately helped Hitachi to avoid the harmful rumour-mongering culture of its employees. Hitachi's experience helps us to understand that employees' create their own information unless the organization shares accurate information on a real-time basis with them. Communicating openly and honestly is the best tactic to deal with potentially damaging rumours.

INTRODUCTION

Chapters 13 and 14 dealt with the basics of OD and organizational diagnosis, respectively. This chapter will discuss the various models and intervention tools for conducting OD and organizational diagnosis, in addition to those mentioned in Chapter 14. OD has been defined as the process of developing internal organizational capabilities to sustain in a changing environment. Basically, OD highlights the need to achieve the organizational mission in a planned way, using different forms of behavioural science knowledge (Griffin and Cole 1984). This is a complex strategy to change the beliefs, attitudes, values, and structure of organizations so that they can adapt to new technologies, markets, and challenges (Bennis 2000). This is why OD is often considered to be synonymous with organizational effectiveness. OD is a growing field and different organizations make use of different models and tools to use it effectively. An organization with a right model depends largely on the type of intervention the organization is looking for. OD change agents (both internal and external), using different models and tools, help the organization to define and solve its problems.

Models represent cause and effect between different relationships. It is a dynamic framework to portray the key concepts and propositions of a theory. It is a representation of a process or a system and shows the most important variables in the system. The analyses of these variables lead to insights into the system. A model is not an explanation; it is a structure which discusses the functions of some aspect of a system or the system, as a whole. It may be highly conceptual or theoretical, and is tested through the process of data gathering, analysis, and reasoning.

OD models represent all these characteristics and can be categorized into explicative, schematic, or mathematical. Explicative models extend the application of well developed theories to improve our understanding of the key concepts. Schematic models are explained through the use of charts, graphs, maps of routings, networks, diagrams, etc. Mathematical models, on the other hand, show the functional relationships among different variables using mathematical symbols and equations. These apart, in OD one can also make use of descriptive and heuristic models. Descriptive models explain the situation by scaling it down to a manageable limit. Heuristic models are established decision-making procedures for solving a problem.

DIFFERENT MODELS AND APPROACHES OF OD

Various approaches may be taken to achieve organizational effectiveness through change and development initiatives depending on the specific organizational situation. Although it is difficult to explain all these approaches (or models) of organizational effectiveness and change in one chapter, here we can document the identified approaches of Field and House (1995). They highlighted all the features of different organizational change and development approaches, broadly categorizing them into nine different types. These are presented in Table 15.1.

TABLE 15.1 Organizational change approaches

Model	Effectiveness criteria	Methods	Goals	Contingencies
Rational goal	Goal accomplishment	Planning, goal-setting, and evaluation	Productivity achievement, efficiency achievement	Clear, unambiguous, mutually agreed, time-bound, and measurable goals
Human relations	To develop the capacities of employees	Cohesion and morale	Enhancing value of HR	Availability of capable people to meet the changing environmental conditions
Internal process	To ensure smooth functioning of the internal process	Information management and communication	Achieve stability and enforce control	Connectivity between organizational processes and performance
Open system	To acquire needed resources	Flexibility and organizational readiness	Acquire resources, get external support, and achieve growth	Connectivity between inputs and performance
Competing values	Achieves appropriate balance in internal vs external focus, flexibility vs control orientation, people vs organization	All previous stated methods	All previous stated goals	The organization is unclear about its own criteria or change in criteria over time
Legitimacy	Survives by acting in a manner seen by other organizations as following accepted organizational practices	Acquire the systems and structures used by other legitimate organizations	Survive and achieve external support	Organization's survival is at stake, goals and accomplishments difficult to measure, and other organizations control resources needed for survival
Strategic constituencies	All individuals and organizations of importance are at least minimally satisfied	Adapt to find at least a minimal fit with required ends	Resource acquisition and external support	Constituencies have powerful influences on the organization and it has to respond to their demands
Fault-driven	An absence of fault or traits of ineffectiveness	Measurement and quality management	Efficiency and error reduction	Criteria of effectiveness are unclear or strategies for organization improvement are needed
High performing system	Judged excellent relative to other similar organizations	Adaptability, innovation, comparison to others in and outside industry	Resource acquisition, external support, internal productivity, and efficiency	Favourable comparisons with other similar organizations are important

As per the *rational goal approach*, organizations are structures designed to accomplish specific goals. This approach is more applicable for planned organizational change. It supports the strategic view that organizations operate on decisions. Keeping in view all these, the rational goal approach model is used to bring changes to the structure of the organization or the functions based on a strategic analysis of both internal and external environments, and in the process achieve the desired level of change in the organization.

The *human relations approach* recommends the use of organizational development or the learning approach to achieve the desired level of planned organizational change. The key focus of this model is that strategic change in the organization is possible through knowledge, skills, and abilities of the people of the organization, as in this process members get the right strategic direction.

Business process re-engineering (BPR) is the *internal process approach* to organizational change. This approach targets internal processes for change, primarily analysing the operational or process-related inefficiencies. Organizations set the strategic direction for change increasing the process-related inefficiencies and replacing existing systems of working. This is categorized more as an evolutionary approach to organizational change.

The *open systems approach* emphasizes value evolution, tactics, and data-based decision-making. It is more in line with the action research model approach to planned organizational change and also requires a step-by-step approach to planned organizational change. In contrast to the BPR approach, it is evolutionary as it focuses on social rather than technical processes.

The *competing values approach* literally combines the values of the four previous approaches. The underlying belief of this approach is that the values of the organization must change to adapt to both internal and external environment. It does not concentrate on strategic or tactical directions, nor does it analyse the data, as it makes use of either revolutionary or evolutionary approaches. Often, in the process of emulating competitors, organizations embrace this model, diluting their internal value systems. Characteristically, users of this model prefer to have some immediate solutions from the organizational change.

The *legitimacy approach* believes in effecting organizational change through management development in a planned manner. The strategic, normative, and evolutionary values of this approach emphasize the need for formal education. Management practices legitimized through the management development programmes of universities is considered more strategic as the training is more focused and not general in nature.

The *strategic constituencies approach* is another planned organizational change model in which the change is carried out by dynamic and charismatic leaders with support from organizational stakeholders. Usually, organizational leaders use this approach to bring a strategic revolution. This approach is primarily built with a normative view of the organization.

Fault-driven models rest on the premise that one's lack of understanding could be the basis of one's tactical values, which can bring the desired organizational change. Total quality management (TQM), quality circles (QC), and statistical process control (SPC) are some of the approaches of this model that can facilitate the desired organizational change. All these can bring drastic changes in the organization as by nature these models are revolutionary.

High performing systems models are again planned organizational change approaches that aim at resource acquisition, external support, and internal productivity and efficiency. In this case also, organizations propel their change through adaptability, innovation, and benchmarking with others. The only difference with the competing values approach is that it relies on compatibility for smooth adaptation and hence looks for those that have compatible values. It emphasizes strong data-based decision-making.

These models of organizational change are classified in Table 15.2, based on their change approach, strategic/tactical values, evolutionary/revolutionary change, and normative/data-based values.

TABLE 15.2 Analysis of models of organizational change

Organizational effectiveness model	Organizational change approach	Strategic or tactical values	Evolutionary or revolutionary change values	Normative or data-based values
Rational goal	Functional/Structural redesign	Strategic	Revolutionary	Data-based
Human relations	Organizational development/learning	Tactical	Evolutionary	Normative
Internal process	Business process re-engineering	Tactical	Revolutionary	Data-based
Open system	Action research method	Tactical	Evolutionary	Data-based
Legitimacy	Management development	Strategic	Evolutionary	Normative
Strategic constituencies	Organizational/Cultural transformation	Strategic	Revolutionary	Normative
Fault-driven	External consultation method	Tactical	Revolutionary	Normative
High performing systems	Strategic redesign	Strategic	Evolutionary	Data-based

Apart from these, there are several other organizational change and development models. While discussing organizational diagnosis in Chapter 14, questionnaires and interview methods have been discussed extensively with some focus on workshops and force field analysis. To avoid repetition, other tools and models are discussed here. Using the Lewin's model of change, French and Bell (1973) suggested the generic model of organizational change with the action research framework as shown in Fig. 15.1.

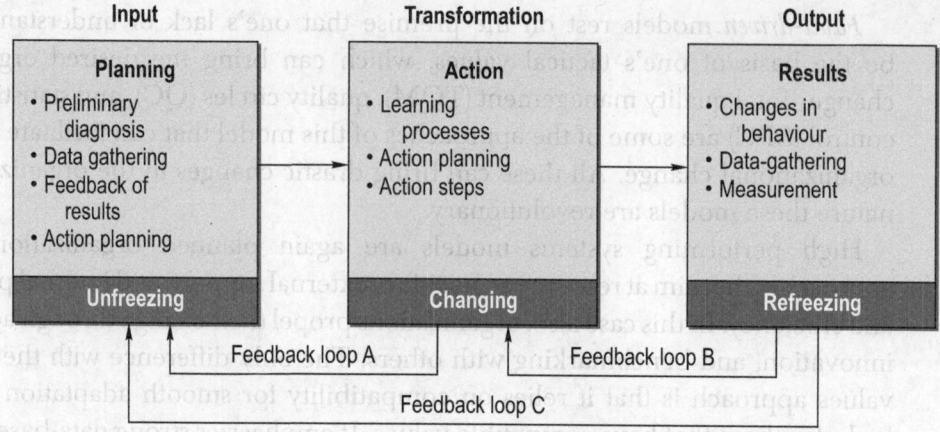

FIG. 15.1 Systems model of action-research process

Although the figure summarizes the steps and processes involved in planned change through action research, it is more valid to call it a generic model, as all other models and tools can only partially fulfil the requirements of OD. Action research as an OD process has been discussed in Chapter 13. OD interventions are defined as structured activities used individually or in combination by members of an organizational system to improve their social or task performance. There are many possible intervention strategies.

Several assumptions about the nature and functioning of organizations are made in the choice of a particular strategy. Beckhard (1969) listed six such assumptions:

1. The basic building blocks of an organization are groups (teams). Therefore, the basic units of change are groups, not individuals.
2. Relevant change goals in any organization involve the reduction of inappropriate competition between parts of the organization and the development of a more collaborative condition.
3. In a healthy organization, decision-making is distributed or decentralized, that is, it is located where the information sources are rather than in a particular role or level of hierarchy.
4. Sub-units of organizations and individuals continuously manage their affairs against goals. Controls are interim measurements, not the basis of managerial strategy.
5. One of the important goals of a healthy organization is to develop generally open communication, mutual trust, and confidence between and across levels.
6. People support what they can help to create. People affected by change must be allowed active participation and a sense of ownership in the planning and implementation of change.

Organizational change interventions encompass individuals, teams and groups, inter-group or inter-team relations, and the organization as a whole. Due to such wide coverage, it focuses on task issues (what people do) and also on process issues (how people go about doing it). Obviously for such reasons, organizational change interventions can be classified based on the mechanism of change and the emphasis put on the change issues.

ORGANIZATIONAL LIFE CYCLE MODEL

Before we further analyse OD models and tools, it is important to recapitulate the organizational life cycle concept. Like the human life cycle from birth to aging and death, some organizations too have a similar life cycle such as the infant, growth, prime, aging, and dying stages. The *infant stage* of an organization starts with a vision of strong commitment and purpose. At this stage, the organization is action-oriented, opportunity-driven, and vision-focused. At the *growing stage*, beliefs, values, goals, structure, and actions of organizations become more formalized. The *prime stage* is the upper side of the life cycle. It engulfs about two-thirds of the way to peak and is characterized by high visibility, and understanding of the common purposes and mission that drives the organization. The *aging stage* is characterized by a decline in the employees' understanding of and commitment to the organizational purpose. At this stage, the expectations for growth are lowered. And the *dying stage* is characterized by a total loss of purpose and hope. The mission is not understood and the organization becomes directionless (Adizes 1988).

There is a strong relationship between the stages of organizational life cycle and the style of leadership. An evolutionary life cycle is typical to cultures and so also to organizations. Therefore, it is important for managers and leaders in organizations to understand the potential sequence of organizational change in the context of the organizational life cycle.

The organizational life cycle concept can also be equated with the product life cycle concept. To avoid the decline phase of a product, organizations often opt for brand extension strategy, or strategy to reposition the product with new value additions. Hindustan Unilever did this to reposition 'Lifebouy' soap. But these are not successful and may result in withdrawal and even complete disruption of organizational activities.

OD MODELS

Based on the contributions of Falletta (2005), we can list the various OD models as follows:

- Force field analysis
- Leavitt's model
- Likert system analysis
- Open systems theory
- Weisbord's six-box model

- Congruence model for organization analysis
- McKinsey's 7-S framework
- Tichy's technical-political-cultural (TPC) framework
- High performance programming
- Diagnosing individual and group behaviour
- The Burke–Litwin model of organizational performance and change

A few more models which were developed in the 1990s are as follows:

- ACHIEVE model
- PRIMO-F business growth model
- IDEAL model
- ADKAR model
- Bridges, transition model
- Action research model
- Dannemiller–Tyson interactive strategic planning model
- Mobius model
- World healing model

A few OD models have been discussed in the preceding chapters. Some others are discussed here.

Force Field Analysis

This model was pioneered by Kurt Lewin in 1951. The model is simple to understand and relatively easy to visualize. It identifies both driving and restraining forces within an organization. Driving forces are primarily the environmental factors that exert pressure of change within the organization. Restraining forces, on the other hand, are organizational internal factors, such as limited resources or poor morale, and act as barriers to change. To understand the problem within the organization, the driving and restraining forces are first identified, and then defined. Goals and strategies for moving the organization towards the desired direction can then be planned.

It relies upon the change process with social implications. The basic aim of this model is to deliberately move to a state of equilibrium by adding the driving and eliminating the restraining forces, wherever appropriate. These changes are thought to occur simultaneously within a dynamic organization. Exhibit 15.1 depicts a case where OD interventions through force field analysis led to employee involvement in the organization.

Leavitt's Model

Based on Lewin's conceptualization of force field analysis, Leavitt (1965) designed another relatively simple model. This model also suggests the presence of some specific variables in the organization, which are task, structure, technological, and human variables (Burke 1994; Leavitt 1965).

> **EXHIBIT 15.1 A successful OD intervention at Click India**
>
> Click India, a software company, faced the challenges of global meltdown and consequent fall in export revenue, which forms a major part of its total revenue. The company then decided to opt for an extensive organizational change programme through OD interventions. Being a knowledge-intensive organization, the company believes in sharing the ideas of all cross sections of employees before committing to change. The company's strength was high-end banking and financial software development by customizing the requirements of major banking and financial corporations in America and Europe.
>
> In such a situation, the company used force field analysis and adopted a model of organic strategic planning, which articulates organizational vision and values to draw action plans. All the employees of the organization volunteered to accept a pay-cut to ensure that the net worth of the company does not deplete to an alarming level. Through such exercises, the company decided to develop its domestic market base and focus on new product lines, namely IT education for engineering and management graduates. This yielded results and the company was able to get over the economic sluggishness.

Structure variables are the authority, communication, and workflow systems within an organization. The technological variables are the equipment and machinery required for the task variable, and the task variables are the sub-tasks involved in making the products and services. The human variables are those that facilitate in carrying out the tasks to achieve organizational goals. Leavitt's observation is that a change in one variable affects the others. For example, change in the technological variable that occurs after the organization introduces new technology will inevitably bring changes in the task variables (as the work process and the methods change), and will also change the human variables in terms of the skill, knowledge, and competency sets required for performing the job. A change in technology may even encompass a change in the communication structure of the organization.

Leavitt considers that the variables within this model are dynamic and interdependent. However, causal relationships between these variables may not always be direct or even simple. For example, change in the human variable by default cannot bring change in other variables. There may be other causal factors that may not result in compensatory or retaliatory change in the other variables. This is particularly because unlike in force field analysis, Leavitt's model did not consider the external environmental variables that could influence the change in organizations.

Likert's System Analysis

Likert's model considers motivation, communication, interaction, decision-making, goal-setting, control, and performance (Likert 1967) as important variables. Likert's identification of variables are as follows:

System 1: Exploitative–Authoritative

System 2: Benevolent–Authoritative
System 3: Consultative
System 4: Participative group

To study the management systems operating in a given organization, Likert developed a 43-item survey instrument to measure seven organizational dimensions. The instrument measures employees' perceptions regarding the upper management, supervisors, and staff, on the various organizational dimensions. Likert provided customized scale labels to measure the response for all 43 items. Each label of question response indicates different meanings. The first response alternative indicates Likert's System 1 organization, that is, the 'exploitative–authoritative'. The second response alternative represents System 2 organization, that is, 'benevolent–authoritative', and so forth. To determine the perceived functioning of the organization, the responses of various employee groups are averaged across items and dimensions, and are understood in line with Likert's seven dimensions.

Based on Likert's study, Nelson and Burns (1984) used different terminology to name the organizations. According to them, System 1 organizations are reactive; System 2 organizations are responsive; System 3 organizations are proactive; and System 4 organizations are high-performing. Similarly, Baker (1996) refered to System 1 as 'coercive', System 2 as 'competitive', System 3 as 'consultative' (the same as Likert), and System 4 as 'collaborative'. Such terminologies, however, do not contradict Likert's viewpoint but supplement it with more contemporary names for easy identification of the organizations.

Open Systems Theory

Most of the organizational diagnostic and development models rest on the open systems theory assumptions. It is for this reason that standalone discussions on the open systems theory are avoided while introducing various organizational models. However, we need to understand the basics of the open systems theory at least at the elementary level. The premise of the open systems theory is that organizations are social systems and hence dependent upon the environmental forces for inputs (Katz and Kahn 1978). The theory allows for repeated cycles of input, transformation (that is, throughputs), output, and renewed input within organizations. A feedback loop connects organizational outputs with renewed inputs.

Weisbord's Six-box Model

For successful organizational development, Weisbord (1978) suggested six key areas. The model provides a diagnostic tool to identify these key areas and understand its complexity, interdependence, and fragmentation. The underlying assumptions of the model are that every organization operates in a dynamic business environment.

Hence, to effect change in organizations, certain structures and capabilities of people are needed.

Weisbord's six broad categories include purposes, structures, relationships, leadership, rewards, and helpful mechanisms. The purposes of an organization are its mission and goals. Weisbord refered to structure as the way in which the organization is organized; this may be by function—where people work together, or by product, programme, or project—where multi-skilled teams work together. The ways in which people and units interact is termed as relationships. Also included in the box of relationships is the way in which people interact with technology in the course of their work. Rewards are intrinsically and extrinsically associated with the work. The leadership box refers to typical leadership tasks, including a balance between the other boxes. And the helping mechanisms are the planning, controlling, budgeting, and information systems that serve to meet organizational goals. The external environment is also depicted in Weisbord's model.

Weisbord identified the various inputs as money, people, ideas, and machinery that are used to fulfil an organization's mission. The outputs are products and services. Two premises which are not apparent in Weisbord's model are crucial to understand the boxes in the model. The first refers to formal versus informal systems. Formal systems are the policies and procedures of the organization, while informal systems are the behaviours that actually occur. The bigger the gap between the formal and informal systems within an organization, the less effective is the organization. The second premise concerns the fit between the organization and the environment, that is, the discrepancy between the existing organization and the way the organization should function to meet external demands. Weisbord defined external demands or pressures as customers, government, and unions.

Diagnostic questions for Weisboard's model

Weisbord posed diagnostic questions for each box of his model. For example, he suggested that OD consultants determine whether organizational members agree with and support the organization's mission and goals within the purposes box. This question refers to his premise regarding the nature of the formal and informal systems within the organization. A sample of some of the questions he poses is as follows:

Purposes Do organizational members agree with and support the organization's mission and goals?

Structure Is there a fit between the purpose and the internal structure of the organization?

Relationships What type of relations exist between individuals and departments, and between individuals and the nature of their jobs? Is their interdependence? What is the quality of relations? What are the modes of conflict?

Rewards What does the organization formally reward, and for what do organizational members feel they are rewarded or punished? What does the organization need to do to fit in with the environment?

Leadership Do leaders define purposes? Do they embody purposes in their programmes? What is the normative style of leadership?

Helpful mechanisms Do these mechanisms help or hinder the accomplishment of organizational objectives?

The model is reproduced in Fig. 15.2.

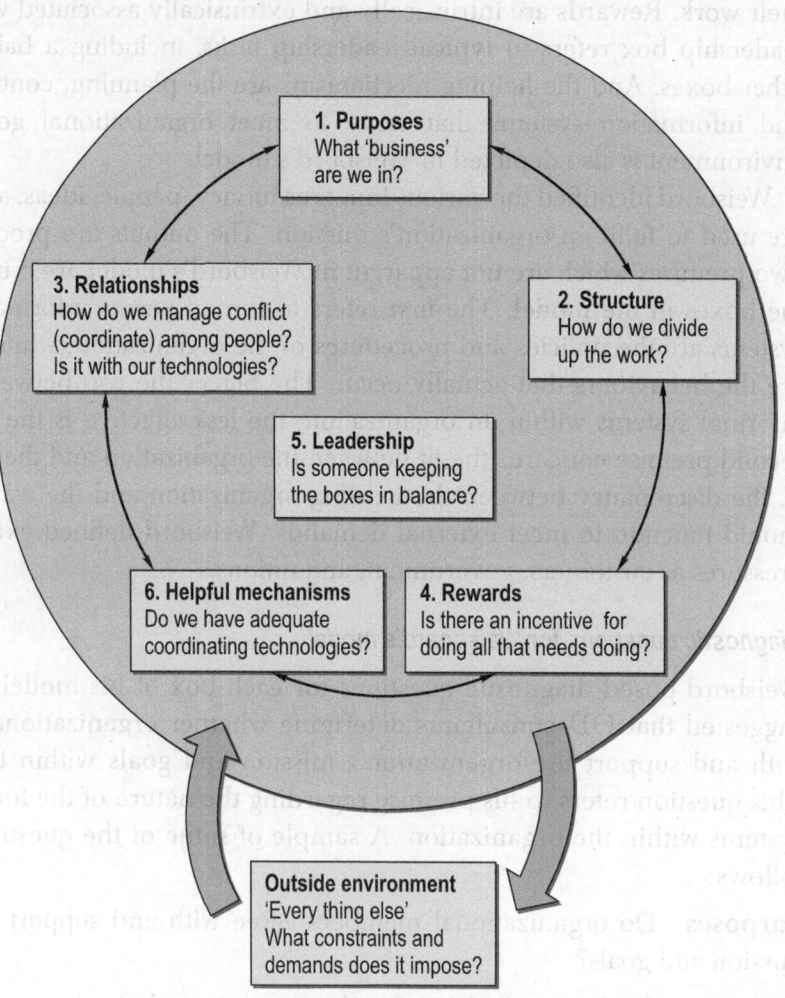

FIG. 15.2 The Weisbord model

In summary, Weisbord's model focuses on internal issues within an organization primarily by asking diagnostic questions which have to do with the fit between 'what is' and 'what should be'. The questions he posed are not predicted by the model;

rather, they are based on his OD practice. These questions serve to convict the model because they do not flow from the logic of the model.

Congruence Model for Organization Analysis

The Nadler–Tushman (1990) congruence model is a more comprehensive model, specifying inputs, throughputs, and outputs, which is consistent with the open systems theory (Katz and Kahn 1978). This model is very similar to Leavitt's model; it also retains the formal and informal systems of Weisbord's six-box model. The model is based on several assumptions that are common to modern organizational diagnostic models. These are as follows:

1. Organizations are open social systems within a larger environment.
2. Organizations are dynamic entities (i.e., change is possible and occurs).
3. Organizational behaviour occurs at the individual, the group, and the systems level.
4. Interactions occur among the individual, group, and systems levels of organizational behaviour.

The inputs within the Nadler–Tushman congruence model include such factors as environment, resources, history (i.e., patterns of past behaviour), and organizational strategies. Nadler and Tushman were explicit in their conceptualization of each of the factors. They described the resources available to the organization as HR, technology, capital, information, and other less tangible resources. While strategy is an input in the model, it is the single most important input to the organization.

The system components of the whole organizational transformation process are informal organizational arrangements, tasks, formal organizational arrangements, and individual components. Similarly, the outputs of the model include individual, group, and system outputs. Outputs may be in terms of products and services, performance, and effectiveness.

Nadler and Tushman applied the concept of congruence, describing congruence or fit as 'the degree to which the needs, demands, goals, objectives, and/or structures of one component are consistent with the needs, demands, goals, objectives, and/or structures of another component' (i.e., how well pairs of components fit together). For example, a task demands a level of skill and knowledge and similarly, the individuals available to perform the task possess varying levels of skill and knowledge. Nadler and Tushman explained that the greater the skill and knowledge match between the task and the individual, the more effective will be the performance.

The model is termed as the congruence model based on the fit between the systems components (informal organization, task, formal organizational arrangements, and individual). Six paired comparisons within the system are possible, based on the four components. Nadler and Tushman raised issues for consideration of each of these paired comparisons.

Through analysis of the congruence between the system parts, the whole organization is diagnosed as displaying relatively high or low total system congruence. The link between the 'paired fits' and the system outputs must also be considered. Nadler and Tushman (1990) explained that 'fits or lack of fits between the key components have consequences in terms of system behaviour.' For example, the fits and lack of fits can be related to behaviours observed in the system such as conflict, performance, and stress.

McKinsey's 7-S Framework

McKinsey's 7-S framework was named after a consulting company, McKinsey and Company, which has conducted applied research in business and industry (Pascale and Athos 1981; Peters and Waterman 1982). The authors worked as consultants at McKinsey and in the 1980s they used the model in over seventy large organizations. The 7-S framework was created as a recognizable and easily remembered model in business. All the seven variables which the authors term 'levers' begin with the letter 'S'. This model has been discussed in Chapter 4.

Tichy's Technical-political-cultural (TPC) Framework

Similar to some of the previous models, Tichy's model includes inputs, throughputs, and outputs, which is consistent with the open systems perspective discussed earlier. Tichy identified key variables in the model which are important to the change management process (Tichy 1983). The environment and history (broadly construed) are two major categories of input to the organization, whereas resources are a third. The throughput variables or change levers identified in the model include mission/strategy, tasks, prescribed networks, people, organizational processes, and emergent networks.

Tichy defined mission/strategy variable as an organization's approach to carrying out its mission and strategy, and criteria for effectiveness (i.e., the organization's purpose). The tasks variable refers to the technology by which the organization's work is accomplished. The prescribed networks (i.e., the formal organization) have to do with the designed social structure of the organization, such as the organization of departments, communication, and authority networks. The people variable refers to the characteristics of organizational members, including their background, motivation, and managerial style. The mechanisms which enable the formal organization to carry out the work are termed as organizational processes; these include organizational communication, decision-making, conflict management, control, and reward systems. The final throughput variable, emergent networks, refers to the structures and processes in the organization that emerge informally.

The focal point of Tichy's model is the output variable, which he termed as organizational effectiveness. Of course, the output is dependent upon the input and throughput variables. All the variables, including the input and output categories, are considered to be interrelated in the model. While some variables have a strong impact, others may have a weaker or reciprocal relationship with other variables. Tichy's overlay on the model is the technical, political, and cultural dynamics, which is abbreviated as TPC. The TPC overlay raises four questions which are vital to organizational diagnosis. These questions address the technical, political, and cultural dynamics of the organization, and are as follows:

1. How well are the parts of the organization aligned with each other for solving the organization's technical problems?
2. How well are the parts of the organization aligned with each other for solving the organization's political problems?
3. How well are the parts of the organization aligned with each other for solving the organization's cultural problems?
4. How well-aligned are the three sub-systems of the organization—the technical, political, and cultural?

The technical dynamics are the organizational production processes and also the available resources. The political dynamics are the views of dominant groups, including bargaining by powerful organizational groups. The cultural dynamics constitute shared symbols and values which make up the organizational culture. These three aspects need to be managed together with due alignment to achieve organizational change. As per Tichy's model, organizational diagnosis is quite complex. An OD consultant would begin by collecting data relevant to the four questions for each variable of the model. The data may be collected by document analysis, interviews, questionnaire, etc. In order to determine where alignment is needed, summary data would be included in a matrix, and analysed for alignment and action planning.

High-performance Programming

Nelson and Burns' (1984) high-performance programming framework assessed the current level of performance of an organization in order to plan interventions to transform the organization into a high performing system (Fuqua and Kurpius 1993; Nelson and Burns 1984). Similar to Likert's system analysis, Nelson and Burns described four organizational systems which are more or less effective. These systems or frames, as Nelson and Burns called them, include the high-performing organization (level 4), proactive organization (level 3), responsive organization (level 2), and reactive organization (level 1). To diagnose an organization, a survey instrument is used with questions related to Nelson and Burns' (1984) 11 dimensions or variables. These 11 variables are time frame, focus, planning, change mode, management, structure, perspective, motivation, development, communication, and leadership. These levels are discussed as follows:

Level 4—The high performing organization

Leaders in the high-performing organization believe in full empowerment of organizational members. They focus on organizational excellence, ensure transparency and free flow of communication throughout the organization, and allow the organization to evolve with a common vision. Members of the organization feel pride as they can identify themselves and get the opportunities to fulfil their self-actualization needs.

Level 3—The proactive organization

Leaders of the proactive organization focus on the future, duly developing the purpose for the organization. Employees of such organizations emphasize the quality of performance in order to reinforce the success of the organization. A proactive organization by nature gets involved in planning and framing developmental strategies.

Level 2—The responsive organization

A responsive organization achieves clarity of purpose and goals, and hence, is more functional. Such organizations develop the capability to quickly adapt to the changing environment. Leaders of such organizations actively coach employees to give them a sense of direction and facilitate a cohesive teamwork.

Level 1— The reactive organization

The level 1 or reactive organization lacks shared focus and people in such organizations blame each other for poor results. Employees spend time in avoiding aversive consequences and leaders are engaged in enforcing policies that lack relevance to any common purpose. Organizations with such a syndrome require immediate renewal.

The leadership activities associated with these four levels of performance in the high-performance programming framework are as follows:

1. The high-performing organization is associated with empowering leadership.
2. The proactive organization is associated with purposing leadership, that is, leaders who maintain the integrated and focused purpose for the organization.
3. The responsive organization is associated with coaching leadership.
4. The reactive organization is associated with enforcing leadership.

Harrison's Model of Diagnosing Individual and Group Behaviour

Harrison (1987) devised a model for diagnosing individual and group behaviour within organizations. This model is unique in nature as it focuses on outputs, such as organizational performance and QWL. The model represents an open systems perspective with minimum boundaries between the organization and external environment. However, the external environment is not represented by anything other than resources and feedback loops. Variables accounted for in the model are conceptualized at the organizational, group, and individual levels. The organizational level of performance represents abstract level of performance and is the function of individual performance, group performance, and QWL outcomes. The variables in the Harrison model are those that are important to performance and QWL, namely individual characteristics and individual attitudes, beliefs, and motivation. According to Harrison, the model can exert influence directly or through feedback loops. However, often it may be difficult to determine the relationship among the variables.

Burke–Litwin Causal Model

A relatively newer model, the Burke–Litwin causal model of organizational performance and change (B–L model) was developed by Litwin and others (Litwin and Stringer 1968; Tagiuri and Litwin 1968) and later refined by Burke in the late 1980s (Burke and Litwin 1992). This model includes several key features which go even beyond many of the models dealt with earlier. This model has been discussed in Chapter 13.

ACHIEVE Model

The basic premise of this model lies in the assumption that organizations can gain competitive advantage through HR; hence, it is for organizations to enhance the skills of the people and motivate them suitably. The ACHIEVE model provides appropriate ideas to efficiently manage HR to make them performers. Using a conventional performance management system, employees can only get feedback on performance problems, not on the reasons for them. The ACHIEVE model makes this possible and also helps to identify ways and means to develop suitable change strategies to solve such problems.

Therefore, the ACHIEVE model is, in essence, a performance management approach. The model has variables, such as (i) motivation, (ii) ability, (iii) understanding, (iv) organizational support, (v) environmental fit, (vi) feedback, and (vii) validity.

The following are the seven factors of the ACHIEVE model:

A—Ability

C—Clarity (Understanding)

H—Help (Organizational support)

I—Incentive (Motivation factor)

E—Evaluation (Performance feedback)

V—Validity

E—Environment

While using the ACHIEVE model (Fig. 15.3), the effect of each factor on the present and potential performance of the employee or employee group is evaluated. Through 'ability' (A), we try to assess the knowledge and skills of the employees.

C stands for clarity and measures the degree of employees' understanding or the role perception. H indicates help, that is, organizational support to the employees to help them accomplish tasks. I denotes incentive, that is, the motivation or willingness of employees to successfully accomplish tasks. E is evaluation, that is, the coaching and performance feedback. V indicates validity, or the valid and legal HR practices. Finally, E stands for environmental fit and refers to the external factors of influence on the performance of employees.

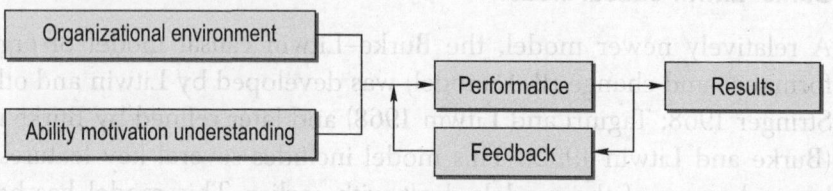

FIG. 15.3   The ACHIEVE model

Thus, the ACHIEVE model is in reality a performance management framework that integrates various concepts or the contributing factors to enhance the performance of the organization, and in the process helps to achieve the desired change.

PRIMO-F Business Growth Model

The PRIMO-F model was developed as part of a SWOT analysis of an organization. It provides a consistent framework for comparison either from within the organization or to benchmark against a previous analysis or against other organizations. The typical model is as shown in Fig. 15.4.

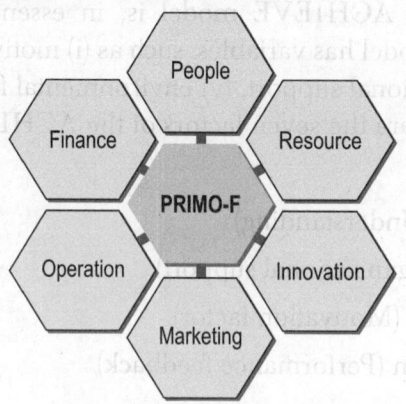

FIG. 15.4   PRIMO-F model

Here, P denotes people, R stands for resources, I stands for innovation and ideas, M stands for marketing, O indicates operations, and F denotes finance.

The model is based on the work of Durham University Business School (DUBS), and is intended to make the organizational change process effective. A mathematical interpretation of the model can be done as follows:

$$\text{Organizational growth effectiveness} = \text{Performance to date} \times \text{Potential for the future}$$

Where,

Performance to date includes finance, marketing, and operations (FiMO)

Potential for the future includes resources, experience, controls and systems, innovation, and leadership (RECoIL).

The equation does not indicate that organizations with a poor performance cannot achieve success and also does not guarantee that being successful in the past, the organization will also succeed in the future. However, it may be difficult at times for managers to differentiate between performance to date and the potential for the future.

To make use of this model for organizational change, organizations perform the framework of analysis as in Table 15.3.

TABLE 15.3 Use of PRIMO-F model in organizations

	People	Resources	Innovation/Ideas	Marketing	Operations	Finance
Rate this area on a scale of 1–10 1 = Awfully bad 10 = World-class	1--------10	1--------10	1--------10	1--------10	1--------10	1--------10
Why this score? Positives						
Why this score? Negatives						
Development priority 1—Low 10—High						

IDEAL Model

This is again another popular model for organizational change. Here, I denotes influences of internal and external factors, which exert impact on the need for organizational change. D is deciding on the key components of change. E is enabling the change. A is achieving the change, while L is the leadership. Prima facie, change management is concerned with the uncertainty and the changes in the internal and external environment of the organization.

ADKAR Model of Individual Change

The ADKAR model suggests a new implementation and improvement system. Essentially, it is an individual change management model. The model can be represented as in Table 15.4.

TABLE 15.4 The ADKAR model of individual change

ADKAR phases	Questions to consider
Awareness	Awareness on the need for the *new improvement system*: Why is the improvement system needed? What are the risks of not using this improvement system? Why is this improvement system being implemented now? What is the general nature of this change—what does it mean to use Lean? or BPM? or appreciative inquiry? or six sigma?
Desire	Desire to participate and support *the new improvement system*: What are the organizational drivers causing us to bring this new improvement system into the organization? What are my personal motivators for getting involved in Lean, or BPM, or appreciative inquiry, or six sigma (for example)?
Knowledge	Knowledge on how to use *the new improvement system*: What will be my role in using the new improvement system? What do I need to know to be successful using the new improvement system? When will I be trained on how the new improvement system works?
Ability	Ability to implement the skills and behaviours required by *the new improvement system*: What exactly will I be doing differently as a result of the new system? When will I have a chance to practise? Where do I go for support and assistance to be successful as part of this new system?
Reinforcement	Reinforcement to sustain *the new improvement system*: How do I know the organization is committed to using the new improvement system? Are senior leaders really committed to making this successful? Will this new approach be discarded next month?

Source: http://www.change-management.com/tutorial-improvement-systems-mod1.htm, accessed on 20 August 2009.

A typical ADKAR model can be drawn as in Fig. 15.5. The model was first published by Prosci in 1998 after research with more than 300 companies. Prosci released the first complete text on the ADKAR model in Jeff Hiatt's book, *ADKAR: A Model for Change in Business, Government and Our Community*. This model is intended to be a coaching tool to help employees through the change process.

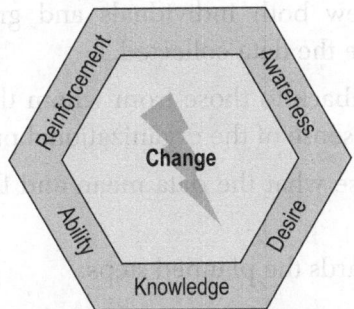

FIG. 15.5 The ADKAR model

Bridges' Transition Model

The Bridges' (1991) transition model is widely accepted by individuals and organizations as a concise and easy way to think about change and its impact. The model illustrates that transition begins with letting go—a necessary (and the most difficult) step to moving on to a new beginning. The model is actually a three-stage design and behaviours that are characteristic of all major transitions are identified.

The first stage of the model is the 'ending' or letting go of the past, which acknowledges that change begins with starting something new, but transition starts with an ending. This process can be very difficult because of the ambiguity it renders. Generally, people have difficulty letting go of the past because it is comfortable; the future is unknown. The second phase, which is referred to as the 'neutral zone' is one of transition and is marked by low stability, personal stress, and conflict. The third stage is the 'new beginning', marking a time when real change begins and there is a focus on the future. Creativity flourishes in this phase as individuals feel a sense of relief and promise.

Action Research Model

A time-tested and widely accepted process for developing and implementing a change strategy, Umstat (1984) described the action research process through data gathering, feeding data back to the client, problem solving, or dealing with issues that arise from the data, developing action plans to resolve problems, and following up to see if the action has worked as planned. Burke (1992) stated, 'Data on the nature of certain problems are systematically collected and then action is taken as a function of what the analyzed data indicate.'

By understanding what the organizational change management needs are and the impact that the change will have on the organization at large, the OD practitioner can begin to develop a change strategy and this is where the action research model can serve as a guide to thought leaders. The specific techniques used within this methodological model are as follows:

Diagnosis Interview both individuals and groups, observe the situation, then analyse and organize the data collected.

Feedback Report back to those from whom the data were obtained on the organization's collective sense of the organizational problems.

Discussion Analyse what the data mean and then plan the steps to be taken as a consequence.

Action Move towards the planned steps.

Dannemiller–Tyson Interactive Strategic Planning

Kathie Dannemiller (2000) and her co-workers used a 2 to 3 day-event of between 100 to 2300 people to roll out a new strategic direction, to be clear on their strategy, and to provide feedback to the top people in the organization. They stress planning: the use of a planning team, with much up-front advance work to make the event successful. Their approach is very task-focused and very structured, and involves interaction in small groups as part of the full-group proceedings.

The theory of the Dannemiller approach is based on a formula that Beckhard and Harris (1987) attributed to David Gleicher:

$$\text{Dissatisfaction} \times \text{Vision} \times \text{First steps} > \text{Resistance to change}$$

This means that all three components must be present to overcome the resistance to change in an organization. Dissatisfaction with the present situation necessitates the adoption of an achievable vision for the future. This is the first step towards reaching this vision. If any of the three is at zero or near zero, the product will also be at zero or near zero, and the resistance to change will dominate. The purposes of these OD interventions are to bring approaches to the organization that will enable the three components to surface so that the process of change can begin.

They also use the strategy suggested by Drucker (1974), that is, converting words into actions. They believe that there should be a common activity focus which is highly reactive, yet highly directive from above. Their focus is on results, on prioritizing choices, and on keeping the participants from feeling overwhelmed. The Dannemiller approach also sets the strategy, and gathering and processing feedback on this strategy.

Mobius Model

Stockton and Herdes (1985) developed the Mobius model for large group interaction. The model is a guide to the assessment and design of appropriate OD interventions; it is not a plan for the events themselves. It is a model which can also serve as a real-time guide to facilitating during these events. It works very well in integrating spiritual and community approaches to the technology of large-scale processes. Like a Mobius strip, the Mobius model has no difference between the inside and the outside (refer to Fig. 15.6). It promotes wholeness, there being no difference between who one is and what one does (congruence). It reflects internal dialogue as people follow their own internal voices, their anger, and their fears. It develops understanding by bringing the inside (the covert, suppressed truth) to the outside (as overt, shared data and understanding).

It is a guide for creating shared possibility, commitment, and action.

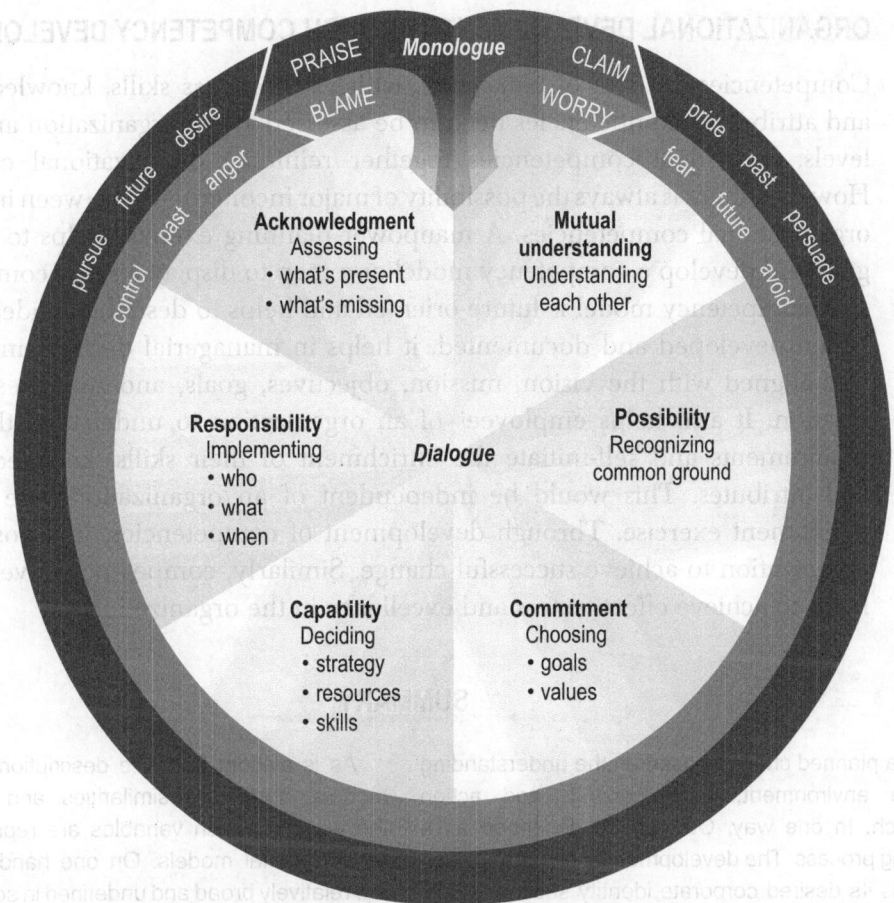

FIG. 15.6 The Mobius model

World Healing Model

Rouda (1995) has developed a revolutionary model based on a combination of ancient and modern wisdom applied to repairing the world. This begins with the progress through organizations, to communities, and our ecological system. This model ensures long-term results. The model helps to develop ecology of wellness to participate in ongoing transformation through healing the emotional, mental, physical, and spiritual dimensions of our lives.

Successful organizational change efforts require accurate diagnosis of the elements to be addressed. A good diagnostic analysis must be based on accurate perception of the situation combined with an assessment of what needs to be addressed, as well as those elements that should not or do not need to be addressed. Organizational change agents need to adopt a perspective, a collective mind (Tenbrusal 1996) that pools micro/individual processes into a more comprehensive framework.

ORGANIZATIONAL DEVELOPMENT THROUGH COMPETENCY DEVELOPMENT

Competencies are sets of behaviour, which encompass skills, knowledge, abilities, and attributes. Competencies need to be assessed at the organization and individual levels. Individual competencies together reinforce organizational competencies. However, there is always the possibility of major incongruence between individual and organizational competencies. A manpower planning exercise helps to analyse such gaps and develop a competency model or a map to display a set of competencies.

A competency model is future-oriented and helps to describe an ideal workforce. When developed and documented, it helps in managerial decision-making as it is well-aligned with the vision, mission, objectives, goals, and strategies of an organization. It also helps employees of an organization to understand the functional requirements and self-initiate the enrichment of their skills, knowledge, abilities, and attributes. This would be independent of an organization-wide competency enrichment exercise. Through development of competencies, it is possible for the organization to achieve successful change. Similarly, competency development also helps to achieve effectiveness and excellence in the organization.

SUMMARY

OD is a planned change based on the understanding of the environment, benchmarking, and action research. In one way, OD can be described as a learning process. The development of an organization towards its desired corporate identity succeeds only when the change process is undertaken holistically.

Behavioural perspectives lie within the person (qualifications, motivation) as well as outside (organizational structure, technology), and such behavioural perspectives need to be modified. The process of change is also described as a political process. Types of intervention include the person-centred approach, structural approach, and relationship approach. A new approach to organizational development is organizational transformation (OT). OT is associated with re-engineering and many feel that it could be a replacement for organization development.

As is evident from the description of the various models, there are similarities and differences in the ways in which variables are represented in the organizational models. On one hand, key variables are relatively broad and undefined in some models (for example, force field analysis model). In other models, the variables represent numerous clearly defined theoretical constructs (i.e., the congruence model for organizational analysis and Tichy's TPC framework). Some of the same constructs are represented across models, although they are termed differently. This chapter has dealt with the various models of organizational change and development. However, real application of these models in organizations depends to a great extent on the nature and type of change that the organization intends to have.

KEY TERMS

Bridges' transition model The model illustrates that transition begins with letting go—a necessary (and the most difficult) step to moving on to a new beginning. The model actually is a three-stage design, and behaviours that are characteristic of all major transitions are identified.

Competing values approach The competing values approach believes that the organization must change to adapt to both the internal and external environment. It does not concentrate on strategic or tactical directions, nor does it analyse the data, rather it makes use of either revolutionary or evolutionary approaches.

Fault-driven models It rests on the premise that our lack of understanding could be the basis of our tactical values, which can bring the desired organizational change. TQM, QCs, and statistical process control (SPC) are some of the approaches of this model, which can facilitate the desired organizational change.

Harrison's model This model is somewhat unique in that it focuses on outputs such as organizational performance and quality of work life. The model represents an open systems perspective with minimal boundaries between the organization and external environment.

High-performing systems models It is a planned organizational change approach, which aims at resource acquisition, external support, and internal productivity and efficiency.

Legitimacy approach This approach believes in effecting organizational change through management development in a planned manner. The strategic, normative, and evolutionary values of the legitimacy approach emphasize the need for formal education.

CONCEPT REVIEW QUESTIONS

1. Discuss different approaches of organizational change and development.
2. Discuss in detail the force field analysis. How does it compare with Leavitt's model?
3. Discuss the concept of organizational life cycle model. How does it relate to organizational change and development?
4. Explain in detail Weisbord's six-box model.
5. Discuss how the congruence model for organizational analysis helps in organizational change and development.
6. Explain how Tichy's technical political cultural (TPC) framework differs from high performance programming.
7. Explain in detail the contribution of the ACHIEVE model in bringing organizational change and development.
8. Explain how we can mathematically interpret the PRIMO-F business growth model.
9. It is said that the ADKAR model of individual change is the most effective one. Do you agree with this statement? Justify your answer.
10. Write short notes on the following:
    (a) PRIMO-F business growth model
    (b) Mobius model
    (c) IDEAL model
    (d) McKinsey's 7-S framework

CRITICAL THINKING QUESTIONS

1. You have been asked by your company to give strategic direction, as your company is now changing its business focus from manufacturer of desktops to ITeS. Suggest your line of action using the Dannemiller–Tyson interactive strategic planning approach.
2. Use the ADKAR model for change and suggest how this model helps to identify the issues for organizational change for a company which is planning to introduce the latest technology in food processing.
3. Explain how a competency-based approach to OD helps to understand the issues of organizational change. Frame your answer in the context of any organization.

CASE STUDY

Organizational Development at General Electric (GE)

In 2005, General Electric (GE) was one of the world's biggest conglomerates with a presence across 160 countries, 11 varied businesses, and an employee strength of around 307,000. Some of its businesses were large enough to make it to the *Fortune* 500 list on their own. GE had not only survived successfully for 133 years, but had also consistently generated great value for its shareholders despite its size. GE was the only company with a continuous listing in the Dow Jones Industrial Average since the original index was constructed in 1896. It had won many laurels as the world's most respected company in terms of its people management and sustained profitability.

One of the factors that contributed to the company's success was its ability to train and develop its multinational, diverse workforce in a successful manner. GE was one of the first companies to establish a management development centre to train and develop its employees. In the 1980s, this centre put the company on an unparallel growth route. It inspired many other renowned companies, such as Boeing, Home Depot, and Toyota Motors, to emulate their training centre model.

In the media, GE has been referred to as a 'captain of industry university' or 'the leadership factory' in recognition of its ability to produce exceptional leaders who had become the CEOs of other *Fortune* 500 companies. The mantra behind the success of GE's management development initiative lies in the fact that it went far beyond the traditional training and nurtured talent to bring out the latent potential in its employees through proper grooming.

Along with this, it had also started focusing on e-learning, introducing its online training in 1998. This initiative made GE's management development initiative more cost-effective and enabled it to maximize the value of its intellectual capital, producing the most exceptional leaders. Jack Welch, the legendary CEO of GE (1981–2001) believed that talent development at GE is a way of life. Even Prof. Nitin Nohria of Harvard University said that GE's training ground is better than that of Harvard.

Source: Kratz, Ellen Florian (2005), 'Get me a CEO from GE', *Fortune*, 18 April; Sosbe, Tim (2004), 'Bob Corcoran: The power of GE education', Chief Learning Officer, www.clomedia.com, March 2004; 'The GE talent machine', http://www.economist.com, 23 October 2003.

Discussion Question

After reading this case, suggest how GE's model of organizational change and development through manpower development can be replicated in any Indian organization. For the purpose of your answer, assume any Indian conglomerate and visit its website to collect information.

REFERENCES

Adams, J.D. (1988), 'Building critical mass for change', *OD Practitioner*, Vol. 20, No. 2, pp. 7–10.

Adizes, Ichak (1988), *Corporate Life Cycles: How and Why Corporations Grow and Die and ... It*, Prentice Hall, Englewood Cliffs.

Asch, S. (1952), *Social Psychology*, Prentice Hall, New York.

Baker III, G.A. (1996), *National Initiative for Leadership and Institutional Effectiveness: Personal Assessment of the College Environment*, Unpublished Manuscript, North Carolina State University, Raleigh.

Beckhard, R. and R. Harris (1987), *Organizational Transitions*, Addison-Wesley, Reading.

Beckhard, Richard (1969), *Organization Development: Strategies and Models*, Addison-Wesley, Reading.

Beer, M. and N. Nohria (eds), (2000), *Breaking the Code of Change*, Harvard Business School, Cambridge.

Bennis, Warren, (2000), *Managing the Dream*, Perseus Publishing, Cambridge, Massachusetts, Chapter 16, pp. 195–199.

Bhattacharyya, D.K. (2009), *Organizational Behaviour—Concepts and Applications*, Oxford University Press, New Delhi.

———. (2007), *Human Resource Research Methods*, Oxford University Press, New Delhi.

Bridges, W. (2000), *The Character of Organizations*, Davies-Black Publishing, Palo Alto.

———. (1991), *Managing Transitions*, Addison-Wesley, Reading.

Burke, W.W. (1994), 'Diagnosis models for organization development', in Howard, A. and Associates (eds), *Diagnosis for Organizational Change: Methods and Models*, The Guilford Press, New York.

———. (1992), *Organization Development: A Process of Learning and Changing*, Second Edition, Addison-Wesley, Reading.

———. (1982), *Organization Development: Principles and Practices*, Little, Brown & Co. Boston.

Burke, W.W. and G.H. Litwin (1992), 'A causal model of organizational performance and change', *Journal of Management*, Vol. 18, No. 3, pp. 523–545.

Dannemiller, K. and R. Jacobs (1992), 'Changing the way organizations change: A revolution of common sense', *Journal of Applied Behavioural Science*, Vol. 28, No. 4.

Dannemiller, K. et al. (1994), *Consultant Guide to Large-scale Meetings*, Dannemiller–Tyson Associates, Ann Arbor.

Dannemiller–Tyson Associates, (2000), *Whole-scale Change: Unleashing the Magic in Organizations*, Berrett-Koehler, San Francisco.

Drucker, P.F. (1974), *Management: Tasks, Responsibilities, Practices*, Harper and Row, New York.

Falletta, Salvatore V. (2005), *Organizational Diagnostic Models: A Review and Synthesis*, Leadersphere, Inc., accessed on 9 November 2009.

Field, R.H.G. and R.J. House (1995), *Human Behaviour in Organizations: A Canadian Perspective*, Prentice Hall Canada, Scarborough.

French, Wendell L. and Cecil Bell (1973), *Organization Development: Behavioural Science Interventions for Organization Improvement*, Prentice Hall, Englewood Cliffs.

Fuqua, D.R. and D.J. Kurpius (1993), 'Conceptual models in organizational consultation', *Journal of Counselling and Development*, Vol. 71, pp. 607–618.

Griffin, P. and M. Cole (1984), 'Current activity for the future: The zo-ped', in Rogoff, B. and J.V. Wertsch (eds), *New Directions for Child Development: No. 23: Children's Learning in the 'Zone of Proximal Development'*, Jossey Bass, San Francisco.

Hammer, Michael and James Champy (1993), *Re-engineering The Corporation: A Manifesto For Business Revolution*, Harper Business, London.

Harrison, M.I. (1987), *Diagnosing Organizations: Methods, Models and Processes*, Sage, Beverly Hills.

Hiatt, Jeffrey M. (2006), *ADKAR: A Model for Change in Business, Government and Our Community: How to Implement Successful Change in Our Personal Lives and Professional Careers*, First Edition, Prosci Research, Loveland.

Kanter, R.M. (1983), 'Empowerment', in Williamson, J.N. (ed.), *The Leader–Manager*, John Wiley & Sons, New York.

Katz, D. and R.L. Kahn (1978), *The Social Psychology of Organizations*, Second Edition, John Wiley & Sons, New York.

Kotter, J.P. (1996), *Leading Change*, Harvard Business School Press, Cambridge.

Leavitt, H.J. (1965), 'Applying organizational change in industry: Structural, technological and humanistic approaches', in March, J.G. (ed.), *Handbook of Organizations*, Rand McNally, Chicago.

Lewin, K. (1958), *Group Decision and Social Change*, Holt, Rinehart and Winston, New York.

———. (1951), *Field Theory in Social Science*, Harper and Row, New York.

Likert, R. (1967), *The Human Organization: Its Management and Value*, McGraw-Hill, New York.

———. (1957), *Some Applications of Behavioural Research*, UNESCO, Paris.

Litwin, G.H. and R.A. Stringer (1968), *Motivation and Organizational Climate*, Harvard Business School Press, Boston.

Maurer, R. (1996), *Beyond the Wall of Resistance: Unconventional Strategies that Build Support for Change*, Bard, Austin.

Miller, Lawrence, 'Barbarians to bureaucrats', published by C.N. Potter: New York. Edited by Carter McNamara, MBA, PhD, *Basic Overview of Organizational Life Cycles*, Written by Carter McNamara, MBA, PhD, Authenticity Consulting, LLC.

Nadler, D.A. and M.L. Tushman (1990), 'A general diagnostic model for organizational behaviour: Applying a congruence perspective', in Daft, R.L. and M.P. Sharfman, *Organization Theory: Cases and Applications*, St Paul.

Nelson, L. and F.L. Burns (1984), 'High performance programming: A framework for transforming organizations', in Adams, J. (ed.), *Transforming Work*, Miles River Press, Alexandria, pp. 226–242.

Pascale, R.T. and A.G. Athos (1981), *The Art of Japanese Management: Applications for American Executives*, Simon & Schuster, New York.

Peters, T. and R. Waterman (1982), *In Search of Excellence*, Harper and Row, New York.

Rouda, Robert M. (1995), *A Model for Repairing the World*, Roseville, MN, http://alumnus.caltech.edu/~rouda/background.html, acccssed on 30 September 2010.

Shepard, H.A. (1975), 'Rules of thumb for change agents', OD Practitioner, Vol. 7, No. 3, pp. 1–5.

Smith, A. (1998), *Training and Development in Australia*, Butterworths, Sydney.

Spencer, Laura (1989), *Winning through Participation: Meeting the Challenge of Corporate Change with the Technology of Participation*, Kendall/Hunt Publishing Co., Dubuque.

Stockton, W. (1985), *The Mobius Model SM*, (unpublished work), Mobius Inc, St Louis Park.

Tagiuri, R. and G.H. Litwin (1968), *Organizational Climate: Explorations of a Concept*, Harvard University Press, Cambridge.

Tenbrusal, A.E. (1996), 'Cognitions in organizations', in Clegg, S.R., C. Hardy, and W.R. Nord, *Handbook of Organizational Studies*, Sage, London.

Tichy, N.M. (1983), *Managing Strategic Change: Technical, Political and Cultural Dynamics*, John Wiley & Sons, New York.

Umstat, D.D. (1984), *Understanding Organizational Behaviour*, Second Edition, West Publishing Company, St. Paul.

Walsh, J.P. and G. Ungston (1991), 'Organizational memory', *Academy of Management Review*, Vol. 16, No. 1, pp. 57–91.

Weick, K. (1982), 'Affirmation as inquiry', *Small Group Behaviour*, Vol. 13, pp. 441–442.

Weisbord, M. and S. Janoff (1995), *Future Search—An Action Guide to Finding Common Ground in Organizations and Communities*, Berrett-Koehler Publishers Inc., San Francisco.

Weisbord, M.R. (1993), 'Diagnosing your organization: Six places to look for trouble with or without theory', in Golembiewski, R.T. (ed.), *Handbook of Organizational Consultation*, Marcel Dekker, New York.

——. (1992), *Discovering Common Ground*, Berrett-Koehler Publishers Inc., San Francisco.

——. (1987), *Productive Workplaces*, Jossey-Bass Publishers, San Francisco.

——. (1978), *Organizational Diagnosis: A Workbook of Theory and Practice*, Addison-Wesley, Reading.

Wheatley, M. (1992), *Leadership and the New Science: Learning about Organization from an Orderly Universe*, Berrett-Koehler, San Francisco.

http://www.rapidbi.com/created/organisational_assessment_tools.html, accessed on 9 July 2009.

http://www.seachange-resources.com/resources.php?sectionID=260&pageID=276, accessed on 9 July 2009.

16 Globalization and Organizational Change and Development

Learning Objectives

After reading this chapter, you will be able to understand
- the definition and concepts of globalization
- the factors promoting globalization
- technology transfer and globalization
- globalization and OD processes through HR
- the role of the major institutions monitoring globalization
- the globalization challenges for managing organizational change and development
- organizational preparedness to cope with the challenges of globalization
- organizational purpose, values, core processes, decentralized authority, and leadership
- globalization and organizational transformation
- strategic alignment

Organizational Development through Employee Development at Philip Morris USA

Organizational capability is the foundation of organizational success. Business strategies may not be properly developed or implemented without it. Creating a highly capable team requires vision, planning, and a commitment to continuous organizational development. At Philip Morris USA, organizational development efforts in the purchasing department created an internal, peer-driven organization dedicated to enhancing their organizational capability. Philip Morris USA emphasizes the value of continuous education and this is embedded in their culture. The leadership team recognized the best procurement systems and technology with smart, driven, and dynamic people. Their '10X Vision' combines technology, integrated supply chain management, and organizational capability. They call it values in action, which encompasses culture, that is, integrity, trust and respect, passion to succeed, executing jobs with quality, driving creativity into everything they do, and sharing with others.

With the '10X Vision', the purchasing department at Philip Morris focuses on three key issues, namely integrated supply management, technology, and organizational capability. The purchasing department's leadership team strongly suggested training, and senior management endorsed and sponsored a series of on-site, instructor-led training classes. The success and enthusiasm of the first class led to a second class within a year, and then to a third. Due to work schedules, family constraints, or personal choice, some employees chose to pursue their designation through independent study. The entire effort has been a great success.

INTRODUCTION

The need for organizational change and development has become more important after globalization. Globalization has changed business practices. Worldwide, globalization is interpreted as a process. Expansion of international trade, cross-border labour migration and flow of investments, cross-cultural impact on domestic businesses, re-structuring of business practices, etc. are some of the ramifications of globalization, which directly exert influence on organizations all over the world. In the post-globalization era, organizations are increasingly becoming complex. Some of the important areas of transformation are the results of changing technology with an increased spate of cross-border technology transfer, mobility of organizations and people in the global world, competition for markets and customers on a global scale, etc. The cascading effect of globalization even transcends to the task or operational environment of business organizations. Changes in operational environment require focus not only on new product or service development, but also on the skill and competency sets, attitudes, values, and culture of people. Such changes are primarily attributable to the shift in expectations of customers and the behaviour of competitors.

The consequential effect of globalization on organizations is due to the increase of alliances and partnerships rather than authority and control. This is characterized by the breakdown of tall hierarchies, increased use of teams, reorganization of functional departments into cross-functional groups, reduced centralized control, and more local autonomy. Another key aspect from the perspective of a business organization is harvesting the knowledge of the people. This is facilitated by knowledge management practices using various tools, techniques, and values, through which, organizations can acquire, develop, measure, distribute, and provide a return on their intellectual assets.

Globalization has also changed the nature of managerial work, requiring managers to increase their judgemental power, use persuasion and influence, shape the behaviour of people, etc.

DEFINITIONS AND CONCEPTS

Globalization implies an integration of world economies. It includes a rapid increase in the movement of goods, services, and capital across national borders. It is related to the increase in the significance of individual businesses that operate in a range of countries. Increasingly, these businesses see the world as a single market. One of the key drivers in globalization is the role of transnational corporations (TNCs). The United Nations defined TNC as an 'association, which possesses and controls the means of production of goods and services outside the country in which they were established'. Activities are dispersed worldwide but specialize in locations that are best suited to each of them. TNCs usually have their headquarters in one centre but have complex networks servicing their worldwide activities. Examples include General Motors, Shell, Nestlé, and Sony.

In relation to organizational change and development, globalization means a change in the way the organization works and is characterized by an unprecedented increase in international trade (Legrain 2002). It is difficult to isolate any single syndrome of globalization for an organization; it is succeeded by a series of structural changes in markets and societies. Some of these are (i) behaviour and performance of organizations which operate across several countries, (ii) relationships between firms across national boundaries, (iii) increasing ability of consumers to access international suppliers, (iv) international exploitation of intangible assets within firms (also accessible to consumers), (v) decreasing importance of geography in the choices firms make about where to carry out specific parts of their operations, (vi) how much of their operations they choose to do themselves, and (vii) how they finance them. Yip (1992) documented the effects of globalization on the behaviour and strategy of organizations. An organization's investment strategy can be either horizontal or vertical. Organizations that follow a horizontal investment strategy reproduce their own business model in a foreign country. Those with a vertical investment strategy create production chains even in foreign countries in order to get the advantage of integration. Nike is a good example of this.

Outsourcing is the most visible outcome of globalization that impacts industry structures as well as wages and income distributions (Feenstra 1998). With globalization, it is now possible for individual consumers to access international markets and make an informed choice. Customers are now able to benchmark price, quality, and services internationally and then take informed decisions. Globalization has, thus, increased international trade with appropriate trade integration in a borderless market and accentuated the spate of cross-border transactions. Inevitably, all these have an impact on organizational activities.

Organizational change and development issues now place greater emphasis on making people adaptable to change and understanding competition. Partnering people in the change process ensures this and evokes positive responses. For many organizations, the cost of labour is the most significant component of total cost. With globalization, organizations can achieve cost competitiveness through outsourcing as well as by relocating their manufacturing operations to countries where the cost of labour is cheaper. With the lowering of inter-country trade barriers, organizations can now source their requirements internationally.

Organizations anywhere in the world are now part of the global economy and are now engaged in business across borders, linking economies together into a more interconnected world. From a business perspective, globalization raises some issues of economic and managerial significance. Some of these issues are (i) Does globalization affect the economic sovereignty of poor nations? (ii) Is it a threat to jobs? (iii) Does it help to overcome poverty, or does it create more? (iv) How can the changes arising from globalization be managed both at the national and organizational levels? (v) How does it affect domestic organizations? ... and so on. It is now accepted that globalization has brought unprecedented improvements in material welfare to billions of people. It now offers unparalleled opportunities to raise living standards across the world. Again, it is also true that disparities between rich and poor are still too great. Many attribute this to globalization. However, understanding such issues is not within the purview of this chapter as it concentrates more on organizational change and development issues arising due to globalization.

In this context, globalization is cross-border and also cuts across social, cultural, and technological spheres. As a natural consequence, it increases the spheres of business and economic activities across countries, and brings changes in the culture, environment, technology, and the way organizations work. Globalization, therefore, subsumes the world into a single integrated system, and exerts influence on organizational change and development, per se. The impact of globalization on organizations can be better understood by quoting Friedman (2002), as shown in Box 16.1.

> **BOX 16.1   Definition of globalization**
>
> 'I define globalization as the inexorable integration of markets, transportation systems, and communication systems to a degree never witnessed before—in a way that is enabling corporations, countries and individuals to reach around the world farther, faster, deeper, and cheaper than ever before, and in a way that is enabling the world to reach into corporations, countries, and individuals farther, faster, deeper, and cheaper than ever before.'
>
> —Friedman

Anthony Giddens (1979) defined globalization as a decoupling of space and time, emphasizing that with instantaneous communication, knowledge and culture can be shared around the world simultaneously. Ruud Lubbers (2005), a Dutch academic, defined it as a process in which geographic distance becomes a factor of diminishing importance in the establishment and maintenance of cross-border economic, political, and socio-cultural relations. Leftists view globalization quite differently; as the dominance of some supranational corporate trade and banking institutions that are not accountable to the domestic economy of the country in which they do business. To them, globalization is an undeniably capitalist process. The recent collapse of Lehman Brothers and subsequent liquidation of several international banking corporations partly corroborate such allegations, as industrially advanced countries have been the worst affected by the economic recession of supranational organizations. However, for management students, these views are more oblique than having practical implications.

FACTORS PROMOTING GLOBALIZATION

The most important factor that promotes globalization is the decision by industrialized countries to liberalize, open, and deregulate their economies. This is done by transferring some aspects of economic governance from the public to the private sector, and placing greater reliance on market forces and market mechanisms. The justification to reduce government intervention in economic activities was mandated by the collapse of communism, which followed a centrally planned economic system, in 1989. Analysing the reasons, International Monetary Fund (IMF) says (*World Economic Outlook*, May 2000, IMF, Washington) that central planning failed on economic grounds because it could not (or would not) respond to market signals in order to guide resource allocation or permit the competition which would have put pressure on producers to raise efficiency and to innovate.

A second important factor that pushed ahead the flurry of globalization was the information and communications revolution which started in the late 1980s. This facilitated the transfer of ideas, technologies, and knowledge without time-lag across the globe and eliminated the distance barriers. This revolution has been prompted by the Internet, e-commerce, convergence of computing and telecom technologies, availability of large capacity broadband networks, and mobile communications.

A third factor is the free flow of international capital in liberalized financial markets. Due to globalization, savings can now be optimally allocated across countries to derive the best advantage from its productive use. This process was accentuated with the flexibility to invest in erstwhile protected sectors even by foreign countries, and cross-border mergers and acquisitions, apart from investments by foreign institutional investors (FIIs) and foreign direct investments (FDI).

Technology is also instrumental in enhancing the spate of globalization. State-of-the-art technologies facilitate large-scale production at a relatively cheaper rate, and new product design and development, thereby reducing product life cycles. This necessitates bigger markets to sell the products to maximize return on investment and to take care of the high cost of product development, especially in high-tech areas.

Further, globalization has also eased the process of technology transfer from one country to another. This enabled organizations to reap the advantages of production flexibility to derive comparative advantages, such as proximity to markets, availability of inputs, wage costs, etc. Thus, production flexibility is considered to be one of the important reasons for globalization as it enhances competitive advantages with reduced costs and enhanced productivity. However, technology transfer may not always yield positive results. This is evident from a real-life experience of the author shared in Exhibit 16.1. The name of the company has been deliberately changed.

Division of labour and production specializations have also increased the spate of globalization. By outsourcing, relocating the manufacturing facility, or leveraging the advantages of one country over another, organizations can now become more efficient and consumers also benefit through lower prices.

> **EXHIBIT 16.1 Globalization and technology transfer at India Steel**
>
> Globalization, among others, has accentuated the pace of technology transfer. However, technology transfer requires cultural compatibility with the recipient organization and also with the recipient country. India Steel, one of the leading steel companies in India, has used the traditional blast furnace in steel manufacturing. Here, pig iron is transported through a conveyor belt and poured in furnaces which are totally manually controlled. The molten iron with impurities is accumulated in adjacent pits, from where workers collect it in buckets and pour it from a distance to segregate the impurities. During this process workers need to be extra cautious to avoid any accidents as the molten metal is of a very high temperature.
>
> The company decided to replace these with imported remote controlled electric furnaces to make this process effective and hassle free. The vendor agency from Austria convinced the company that installation of these furnaces would make the plant more cost-effective and productive.
>
> After the initial trial run, the company installed the new furnaces in five of their ten production units. Things were moving in right earnest until one day there was a sudden total blackout due to interruption in power supply. It is important to switch off the machines during a power outing.
>
> A supervising engineer was on inspection duty but before he could switch off the machine, the power supply suddenly resumed, resulting in a huge blast that caused many casualties. The company ultimately had to shut down production permanently in order to settle the claims of the families of the deceased workers.
>
> The lesson learnt is that adopting global technology without environmental conditioning may not always provide the desirable answer. Many Indian organizations have experienced cost overruns due to technology transfer because the cost of environmental conditioning overshoots the cost of technology possession.

TECHNOLOGY TRANSFER AND GLOBALIZATION

Technology transfer is the process of sharing knowledge, technologies, skills, methods, and manufacturing, including prototypes and facilities, among different nations. As its inevitable effect, it benefits nations that suffer from the perennial problem of low technology. Technology transfer also succeeds knowledge transfer. The entire process of technology transfer is closely interconnected with globalization, hence, it is considered to be one of the major aspects of globalization. In fact, it is interdependent, and how such interdependency evolved is clear from the theoretical insights on technological determinism. The term 'determinism', denotes the causal relationship between our behaviour, cognition, and decisions, which is influenced by an unbroken chain of prior occurrences. Technological determinism, therefore, describes the relationship between social and technological aspects, which either cause or effect the cultural change. Technological determinism considers technology development and its transfer, following a predictable and traceable track to influence society. According to Veblen (1857–1929), technology is one of the important governing forces in society and, therefore, the technological development process determines social change. With the stabilization of new technology, social behaviours change, and in the process, the effect of globalization become more visible.

With the advancement of technology, the spate of globalization has increased manifold. With new technology, countries across the globe are developing new products, using technology in applications, processes, and services. This is also creating the impelling need to develop HR in the form of learning new skills, knowledge, methods, and information.

The word, technology, is embedded in the definition of globalization itself. Globalization is interweaving of markets, technology, and information. Scholars such as Friedman and others argue that globalization is not a choice. Eighty per cent of it is driven by technology which removes national and organizational barriers, resulting in its shift to different countries along with technological feasibility and economy of scales.

GLOBALIZATION AND OD PROCESSES THROUGH HR

The complexities of globalization have provoked organizations to redefine their strategies and develop multi-pronged competencies to withstand the powerful and pervasive challenges. Among others, globalization has sparked the need for transforming HR functions to develop global capabilities. OD strategies, therefore, require system-wide transformation at the structural, procedural, and cultural levels. The challenge that OD professionals face in developing the structure and strategy is to maintain a balance between global standardization and local flexibility. Hence, the OD approach requires determination of strategy, considering the relative importance of maintaining consistent principles and adapting to local culture. As globalization issues and the HR practices of organizations need to be synergized in OD programmes, the discussions here relate mostly to HR issues. Through OD programmes, not only are the people in the organization developed in line with global requirements, but the necessary changes are also made in HR practices to achieve organizational compatibility. Exhibit 16.2 highlights this need.

Aligning HR Strategy with Business Goals

To develop a global HR structure, it is important at the outset to define HR strategy in the context of overall business. Organizations can better understand the value of a global HR strategy if it is aligned with the organizational strategy. To meet the global vision, HR structure, systems, and processes should be integrated with the global business plans of the organization. This requires aligning with people, processes, and systems. To achieve its goal, HR needs to ensure that the right people are hired and motivated to do their best work, meeting global standards and requirements. A global HR framework involves certain processes that are managed centrally and benefit

EXHIBIT 16.2 Morris India—The right compensation debate

HR functions at Morris India had undergone sea changes due to expansion of its activities in the US and Europe. It has now become imperative for the company to depute its Indian employees to overseas assignments, as well as transfer their US and European counterparts on a short-term basis to its Indian units. While cultural sensitivity in both the cases is of the highest importance, the company encountered major problems in HR practices related to compensation planning and design in such transfers. The Indian employees complained that they were facing financial stricture in their assignments abroad, but their counterparts from other countries doubly benefited on Indian assignments due to differences in currency valuation. Morris then decided that for all foreign assignments, employees will continue to get the salaries they earned in their home countries, and while on deputation abroad, they would get allowances to ensure their standard of living. This meant that a suitable standard of living of Indian executives posted in the US would be protected. Such arrangements ultimately settled the impasse and Morris benefited from this change in its compensation policy for overseas assignments.

both the local and global markets. With global expansion of the organization, HR reviews and shares current practices in each region identifying the successful ones so as to leverage them globally. Each phase of the life cycle entails HR priorities considering local, regional, and organization-wide global needs. These priorities are shared with the employees in various forms to gain their commitment to the changing situation. Exhibit 16.3 helps to understand this better.

Some of the changes in HR strategy subsequent to globalization focus on the following HR practices.

EXHIBIT 16.3 HR strategy and its alignment at Dabur India

Dabur is a leading Indian consumer goods company with interests in healthcare, personal care, and foods. Dabur commenced its operation in 1884 and is today a multi-location, multi-product, global enterprise. Its products are available in more than 50 countries including the Middle East, South-east Asia, Africa, the European Union, and the US. Dabur products follow the time-tested heritage of Ayurveda backed by modern scientific trials, which ensures unfailing quality and supply. With its vision of dedication to the health and well-being of every household, and to achieve its business results, Dabur focuses on many HR issues ranging from inculcating the sense of ownership, passion for winning, people development, teamwork, innovation, and finally, emphasizes on integrity. Dabur aspires to be the most sought-after employer in India. Its HR strategy focuses on career development of employees, career mapping and management development with OD initiatives, delegation and decentralization, systematic identification of training needs, and the innovativeness and creativity of employees, and follows a system of flexible rewards. With all these HR strategies, Dabur plays the most proactive role in incremental business profit in the globalized era.

Recruitment and selection

Selection, hiring, and retaining talent is crucial as employee perceptions differ across the country. For example, in India and China, employees are influenced by family opinions and perceptions. Hence, brand and organizational reputation plays a crucial role in the employees' decision to join a company. On the contrary, employees in other countries are more influenced to join the organization where career and advancement opportunities exist, irrespective of their brand value. For the sake of career advancement in quick succession, employees of these countries do not hesitate to change jobs frequently. This causes the problem of high attrition in organizations. Obviously, this is the greatest challenge in global integration of HR. Hence, OD professionals need to focus also on organizational brand-building and developing opportunities for career growth to attract, recruit, and retain talent. Lawler and Worley (2006) suggested that while implementing strategies, the organization must develop a unique culture that is applicable globally, else they will lose the global integration, and eventually fail to retain talent. OD, therefore, requires lending support to develop HR strategy that further helps in adopting a consistent competency framework, applicable globally, to attract, recruit, retain, and develop talents.

Employee engagement

When organizations are able to improve the employee engagement, they get the opportunities to channelize their energy, passion, and commitment. Studies by Baumruk and Marusarz (2004), and Hewitt Associates, indicated strong positive relationships between employee engagement and the financial results of an organization. Improved employee engagement makes people feel accountable, improves managerial effectiveness, and creates a culture of mutual trust. Among others, OD professionals need to suggest the adoption of effective people practices and tailor-made action plans that can help create a culture of autonomous employee engagement.

Performance management

Another phase of OD interventions through HR in the context of globalization is to ensure the rigorous management of performance across the company. This requires framing of strategies to identify key talent and to manage succession to address the risk of non-availability of manpower globally, on the one hand, and nurturing a culture of superior performance, on the other. A positive performance culture with improved level of performance is an important source of competitive advantage for organizations. OD professionals must recognize this, particularly in the era of globalization, to build the capabilities of the organizations, and suggest introduction of rigorous performance management systems and processes along with a focus on evaluation and development of human resources, so that organizations can sustain in this competitive world.

Compensation and benefits

Globalization also requires companies to align their compensation and benefits plan with business strategy. Olson and Dawson (2003) suggested adoption of market-competitive rewards, balancing the risk-reward profile of the organization. OD professionals seek to align the total reward systems of the organization with the performance goals, matching these with global compatibility. To draw the compensation and benefits policy, strategically in the wake of globalization, organizations need to frame their total compensation plan in such a manner that it is uniformly applicable in all their units around the world. On the other hand, however, incentives plans can be developed locally so that local issues, such as propensity to stay beyond working hours, the urge to earn more, to move up the ladder, etc., are taken care of.

Infrastructure, training, and technology

In globalization, the other HR strategy that facilitates overall organizational development and retention of talent is to provide training opportunities, periodic job rotation for development, one-on-one mentoring, etc. Training includes leadership and technical skills along with awareness about the company culture and values (Baumruk and Marusarz 2004). Side by side, it also requires implementation technology intensive HR practices, such as introduction of human resource information systems (HRIS), and improvement of infrastructure with improved systems and processes.

Growth and development

While framing HR strategies OD professionals must also examine the growth and development aspects of organizational members, keeping pace with globalization. Opportunities for career growth, learning new skill-sets, acquiring new knowledge, etc. are very important not only for the good performers, but also for potential employees. These help to develop organizational capabilities and provide opportunities to sustain in competition.

All these HR strategies reinforce organizational preparedness to cope with the challenges of globalization, and so also help in organizational change and development.

MAJOR INSTITUTIONS REGULATING GLOBALIZATION

There are a number of international organizations that reinforce and regulate the process of globalization, creating institutional support for multi-lateral and bilateral trade. Some of these are mentioned here.

World Trade Organization (WTO)

The WTO was established in 1995 to administer the rules of international trade as agreed to by its member countries. In periodic ministerial meetings, terms of references of international trade are discussed and modalities developed to further the promotion of international trade. Before the WTO, there was the General Agreement on Tariffs and Trade (GATT). However, the scope of GATT was only limited to trading in goods. To eliminate such difficulties, it was replaced by WTO, with much more wider judicial powers to resolve international trade-related issues. WTO rules do not allow countries to favour their own organizations and protect them from imports from other countries. Similarly, it does not allow a country to favour the imports of one country over those from another. The basic premise is that the growth of trade between countries increases the wealth of everyone. International trade allows the production of goods and services by those who are most efficient, and maximizes their availability at the best competitive price and quality. The lowering of barriers, such as tariffs and import quotas helps international trade. All these come under the purview of WTO agreements. For better understanding, let us look into the details of WTO.

WTO agreements cover 12 subjects in the area of trade in goods:

- Agriculture
- Textiles and clothing
- Trade-related investment measures (TRIMS)
- Sanitary and phyto-sanitary measures (SPS)
- Technical barriers to trade (TBT)
- Anti-dumping
- Customs valuation
- Pre-shipment inspection
- Rules of origin
- Import licensing
- Subsidies and countervailing measures
- Safeguards

It also covers agreements in the following specific areas:

- General Agreement on Trade in Services (GATS)
- Agreement on Trade-related Aspects of Intellectual Property Rights (TRIPS)
- Trade Policy Review Mechanism (TPRM)
- Agreement on the Dispute Settlement Undertaking

WTO completed fifteen years of its existence in January 2010 and at present has 150 member countries.

International Monetary Fund (IMF)

IMF was established during the Second World War in 1946. Its primary purpose is to strengthen the process of globalization and provide a host of services, which are as follows:

- Promotion of international cooperation on finance
- Encourage stability in exchange rates and orderly systems for exchanging money between countries

- Provide temporary assistance for countries suffering balance of payments problems, etc.

IMF also believes that world prosperity is enhanced by greater exchange between nations and that this would be made possible when everyone agrees to abide by rules. Like the WTO, IMF has also several member countries, including India.

World Bank

The World Bank provides loans to poor countries for development projects. The bank also provides loans for investment projects, such as water and sanitation, natural resource management, education, and health. It also lends for what it calls adjustment projects, which support governments undertaking policy reforms, such as improved public sector management, etc.

United Nations (UN)

The UN was established during the concluding phase of the Second World War. It has become a promoter of globalization and argues that individual states play a dual role with responsibilities to both their own citizens and to the world society as a whole. The United Nations states that the broader global responsibility requires international institutions. It supports the case for reforms in international institutions, including its own Security Council, to make them more representative. The UN has sponsored a global compact to establish and promote a shared set of core values in the areas of labour standards, human rights, and environmental practices between the UN and the business community.

Organization for Economic Cooperation and Development (OECD)

OECD develops economic and social policy for its member countries, which includes North America, Western Europe (including Czech Republic, Hungary, and Poland), Japan, Korea, Australia, and New Zealand. It provides economic arguments for globalization, with data to demonstrate the positive contribution made by multinational corporations to economic development.

United Nations Conference on Trade and Development (UNCTAD)

This is a permanent inter-governmental body of the UN that aims to maximize the trade investment and development opportunities of developing economies, and assists their efforts to integrate into the world economy.

These apart, there are many private bodies and social organizations across the globe that promote globalization. An NGO in India, namely Liberty Institute, New Delhi, also promotes the cause of globalization.

GLOBALIZATION CHALLENGES FOR MANAGING ORGANIZATIONAL CHANGE AND DEVELOPMENT

Various challenges faced by business organizations today are now discussed under the following topics:

Managing HR

A key management challenge is to balance the short- and long-term investments. Strategically, investment in people is viewed as a long-term, strategy while the investment in business is managed with a focus on shorter-term finances. This has changed to include the long-term development of people through the creation of new jobs within the organization. Within this context, the key management challenges are to focus on the customer rather than products and services, integrate and manage the resources required to provide this focus on open systems to encourage the sharing of information and on new forms of customer–supplier relationships and organizational structure.

With globalization, another challenge for organizations is to encourage loyalty and motivate employees. Both these aspects have a direct impact on the way managers handle the human, technical, and business dimensions of the organization, and strategically manage intellectual capital. Given these challenges change can be viewed from multiple perspectives, such as the level of change (global, societal, organizational, and individual), the significance of change (deep-rooted, superficial), and the implications of change (social, management), to mention a few possibilities. One of the most significant aspects facing business organizations today is how to develop some sense out of the very fundamental changes. The increasing need for business transformation in order to position for new business represents a fundamental shift in the relationship of corporations to individuals and to society as a whole. The most important challenge of globalization is how to deal with the individuals affected by such change.

Managing Diversity

Managing diversity is another core challenge for organizations, particularly due to its complexity. The complex effect of diversity is all-encompassing, as it literally exerts influence in all aspects of organizational activities and strategies. Within the organization, diversity practices require adoption and framing of inclusive HR policies. Such policies need to value people for their talents, rather than their diversity constructs, that is, race, culture, religion, gender, language, or their countries of origin. Organizations need to be diversity-neutral in designing compensation systems, career planning, and development opportunities. Outside the organization, diversity of customers must be considered when designing products and services. Customers with different cultural constructs have different values and perceptions. The sale of hamburgers by McDonalds in countries where eating ham is a social stigma did not work and it had to differentiate its product-mix, thus deviating from its core. Similarly, stakeholder perceptions also vary with respect to diversity constructs. For all these reasons, managing diversity has become the core challenge for organizations.

Interdependence

Globalization has also increased the level of organizational interdependence and this, in turn, has changed the value webs all over the world. Increased flow of funds in the form of foreign direct investments (FDI), transfer of technology, value chains, corporate governance norms, etc. have all increased the degree of interdependence and brought major changes in business dimensions. Interdependence, on one hand, created new opportunities, and on the other, increased the complexities in the functioning of organizations.

Managing Ambiguity

Globalization has resulted in increased ambiguity for organizations with free flow of information and absence of clarity. International standards and norms are changing at regular intervals, and non-compliance with these make it difficult for organizations to address the requirements of international markets. Although cost efficiency and quality conformance are the two major value drivers for any organization, at the international level other value drivers, such as brand image, corporate social responsibility, proactive HR policies, knowledge acquisition, and privileged relationships (such as, the most favoured nations), often supersede the core value drivers mentioned earlier.

All these factors urge organizations to change. And, such change cannot be achieved through short-term solutions or simply by resolving the problems of interdependence, diversity, and ambiguity. It requires adoption of a strategic change management approach and appropriate OD interventions to renew the organization on a continuous basis.

ORGANIZATIONAL PREPAREDNESS TO COPE WITH THE CHALLENGES OF GLOBALIZATION

Global companies first react to complex business environment by creating intricate organizations. The law of requisite variety suggests that the internal complexity of an organization must match the complexity of its external environment. Framing the organization structure along product lines, geography, customers, functions, and projects, etc. are very common. For example, one of the largest conglomerates in the world, ABB Ltd had a six-dimensional matrix structure before it simplified the structure dramatically in its turnaround. The simple relation between headquarters as strategic decision-makers and subsidiaries as implementers is blurred by centres of excellence or competence, market responsibilities, joint ventures, etc.

With new structures in place, organizations are also adopting new policies to respond to changes subsequent to globalization. But these alone cannot be a panacea to move the organization forward. Often in the process of internal adjustments, organizations neglect vital external environmental cues, even to the extent of neglecting the market information. This is what happened in the case of Lehman Brothers; they failed to assess the internal economic strength and were literally overdone in reverse-mortgage marketing, ultimately leading to a global sub-prime crisis during the economic recession, and eventually into liquidation.

While internal adjustments are necessary to respond to globalization, external environmental cues are also important as real value creation is possible by exploiting external opportunities. With new product designs and servicing in the offering, organizations are developing new markets and enjoying market leadership, which not only consolidates their present growth, but also strengthens future sustainability. A good example is Tata Motor's small car, Nano. Evidently, major international automobile players are now following suit to fulfil the market demand for small cars and transform it into new business opportunities.

Therefore, organizational preparedness to cope with the challenges of globalization requires both internal and external adjustments. Strategically, it is desirable for organizations to adopt an approach of simplification in managing the complexity of change. This requires focus on the professional quality of decision-making: encouraging the simplification of organizational processes, along with emphasis on simplifying the purpose and values, core processes, decentralization, and early awareness systems. Inadequate environmental scanning and irrational forecasting of strategic outcomes cannot help organizations to survive.

With clear and consistent perceptions in line with these submissions, organizations can successfully respond to the need for change posed by globalization.

REVIEW OF ORGANIZATIONAL PURPOSE AND VALUES

Globalization requires organizations to review their vision and mission. Vision is often considered as a permanent imprint for organizations, as it guides their behaviour and value systems. However, to achieve the desired change, it is often necessary for organizations to embrace new value systems and even new behavioural approaches. For example, to adopt a customer-centric approach, a shared vision needs to be developed and embraced by all members of the organization. Therefore, to respond to the changes subsequent to globalization, it is necessary for them to develop a suitable framework to prioritize their goals. IBM's change in business focus, that is, from desktops to IT-enabled services obviously required them to redefine their business purpose, suitably changing their mission statement. A mission statement defines the purposes of the organizational existence and thus verbalizes the vision into action. For large diversified organizations the process of reviewing the purpose and values become complicated, obviously due to the problem of unification. In such cases, changes in the purposes and value systems are first achieved at the unit level, and then several unit level changes are integrated with the overall organization.

Once the purposes and value systems are redefined and shared with all members (across hierarchy) of the organization, the change process becomes simpler. As the impending business needs, priorities, etc. are clear, people can focus on actions with a consistent pattern of behaviour. For better comprehension and follow-up, it is desirable that organizations embrace not more than three or four core values based on their compelling business needs. For example, Wal-Mart's 'Every day lower prices' (EDLP), Sears three Cs, that is, compelling place to shop, compelling place to work, and compelling place to invest, and Infosys' 'Growth with imagination' are some examples of organizational values. These value statements are developed after the articulation of their compelling business needs. It is possible for these organizations to give the right sense of direction and spell out the behavioural values in line with the core values.

CORE PROCESSES AND DECENTRALIZED AUTHORITY

Like purposes and values, core processes are also an important aspect of an organization. Core processes vary from one organization to another depending on the nature of their business. For a cigarette manufacturer, such as ITC, gluing is a core process while for many FMCGs it is a non-core process. For ITC, gluing of cigarettes is a core special operation, and hence, it dissuades from outsourcing this function. For a pharmaceutical organization, research and development (R&D) is a core function, while for a consultancy organization the core process may be knowledge sharing. Organizations necessarily standardize their core processes. These may change and this involves replacement of the existing processes with new ones.

Often, changes akin to the core processes may be independent of overall organizational change. Some environmental regulations may require changes in the manufacturing process. For example, due to restriction in use of forest products, ordnance factories in India had to switch over from wooden rifle butts to plastic moulded ones. After standardizing the core processes, it is possible for the organization to decentralize the function so that at the operation level only the protocol-bound jobs are done. This ensures both consistent quality and process in carrying out the core processes. Non-core processes or activities that are not strategically very significant can be outsourced in a more cost-effective manner as the overall change impact on non-core processes is minimal. With a decentralized authority for the core processes, dispersed units of the organizations can function at equal pace and tune, bringing consistency and harmony in the total functioning of the organization.

LEADERSHIP

Leading an organization besieged with change problems subsequent to globalization requires an altogether different mindset. Traditional, hierarchy works where every level is doing something distinct and specific. However, due to the interdependencies involved during change, this may not be always possible in today's organizations. By simplifying and clarifying the vision, values, and core processes, along with decentralization of authority and institutionalization of awareness systems, hierarchy can be complemented by 'heterarchy', that is, the interdependent, networked organization in which every part reflects a different perspective of the whole, which is needed in today's global business scenario. The boss no longer needs to tell the team members what exactly to do, but rather depends on their initiative, creativity, and competence, for success.

In a networked organization, leadership means not only managing the change complexity in global organizations by providing different leadership roles and styles depending on the situation (but always consistent with the purpose, values, and core processes), but also leading different parts of a networked organization to work together and create value. The leader of a complex organization must create and communicate an understanding of the different roles played by managers, teams, business units, and bosses, in the interdependent structure. So, in complex organizations, effective communication is not only a leadership survival tool, but is also much more in terms of 'storytelling', that is, interpreting context and meaning, and investing in relationships rather than transferring dry facts or ultimatums.

It is difficult to master global complexity by following traditional management practices. The decade-long problems at General Motors (GM)—and to a lesser degree, at Ford—clearly have their roots in the long traditional control mode, leading to GM's vast bureaucracy and typical outcomes, namely mediocre products due to risk aversion, mistrust in management (reflected in the high degree of unionization), high transaction costs, and slow response. An opposite example is that of Toyota, with a very clear value set (which is now challenged as it becomes a truly global company), a simpler model of core business processes, and standardized processes throughout the world. (The famous notion that every engineer at Toyota can work in any Toyota factory in the world without having problems of adaptation, is probably slightly exaggerated, but only slightly). Another example is that of Exxon Mobile, which is driven by standardized global processes.

Research and development-driven industries, typically the pharmaceutical industry, are known for focused business models (if they have not over-compensated this by seize-through mergers). The FMCG sector and the food industry are known for strong regional decentralization but are bound together by shared processes across business lines. McDonalds, for example, follows the same quality and level of services worldwide.

Although a company may never master completely change complexity, using these principles it is possible to at least navigate through complexity and even take advantage of it. And for this to happen, leadership needs to be looked into, as leaders are the most important enablers of organizational change and development.

GLOBALIZATION AND ORGANIZATIONAL TRANSFORMATION

Organizational transformation requires a culture which questions conventional mind-sets and fosters the ability to be self-critical as well as inculcates the maturity and creativity to learn from, and act upon what is discovered. Much of this can emanate from a TQM foundation. In addition, internal systems must be flexible, yet at the same time, must incorporate the appropriate controls to facilitate radical innovation. Improvement, regardless of its nature and content, is a journey over time. As the environment changes, these external dynamics must be matched as far as possible with internal changes. There is a need to constantly evolve. Among other things, it also requires organizations to engage themselves in a self-perpetuating improvement cycle which embodies both incremental (TQM) and radical (BPR) approaches to change. Both these approaches can play a critical role in shaping an organization's capability to support its own strategy.

There are six keys to success:

- A consistent, clear, and driving vision
- A set of supporting processes, drawing broadly on those affected by change and often using specific institutions to refine and communicate the vision, to quantify and test its reality, and to translate it into implemental pieces
- A persistent and constant in-place leadership cadre, driving an ongoing sense of urgency
- The willingness and drive to re-engineer any process, doctrine, or organization, and to take risks
- The willingness to allocate the funding necessary for change and to re-prioritize budget allocations
- A commitment to align the measurement system across the hierarchy and in accordance with the vision.

There are four key transition states of organizational transformation. Each state is joined by a continuum of organizational adaptation. These forces keep the organization 'on the edge of chaos' (Handy 1989), particularly, as it transforms itself from one state to another. The transition states are separated by a step change of varying degrees of magnitude. The greatest step change is that entailed for organizations moving from the 'evolutionary zone' to the revolutionary zone'. Key variables in organizational transformation can be explained in the context of the external and organizational (internal) environment.

Factors, such as new technology, global competition, etc. make some business environments complex, turbulent, and unpredictable. Important among organizational variables is the organizational vision. A vision can highlight the opportunity for instigating change and conceptualizing the type of transformation desired. Again, depending on the nature of the environment, organizational vision can reflect a shared vision of change. Senge (1990) contend that for generative learning to take placed leaders must become stewards, designers, and teachers, rather than simply control and reward staff. The creative tension required for change comes from an informed view of current reality and a clear vision of the future.

Organizational change can be evolutionary or revolutionary in nature. Some authors posit that revolutionary change must be implemented at a rapid pace, while writers, such as Gallivan et al. (1994) suggested that revolutionary change could be implemented in phases. Studies indicate that organizations worldwide tend to use revolutionary tactics to design change, but implement BPR in radical stages. When developing espoused paradigms of change, there is an inherent tension between the conservation of existing practices and behaviours and innovation (Kondo 1996). Factors such as the dysfunctional aspects of an organization, cultural inertia, and risk can militate against revolutionary change and/or retard its implementation (Miller 1982; Miller and Friesen 1982; Chang 1994; Jih and Owings 1995; Kilmann 1995; Ahmed 1998).

Strategic Alignment

According to Davidson (1993), aligning current operating projects with long-term visions and strategies is a challenge for many executives. He stated that in many companies, operating projects seem to be pursued in a highly fragmented fashion, almost independently of corporate vision and strategy. However, achieving alignment between near-term operational improvement efforts and the long-term vision is central to successful transformation (Mintzberg 1994; Novak 1997). Gould (1996) suggested that each organizational state comprised four strategies:

1. Fine-tuning—a strategy of 'refinement' where processes and routines which build on core competencies are incrementally improved.
2. Building—a strategy of 'planning', which leads to the creation of a formal change programme. Here, core competencies are further established and made routine.
3. Crisis—where all existing routines and structures are suspended or abandoned. The structure is often accompanied by changes in leadership and power.
4. Transformation—where planning is replaced by experimentation. Staff puts to test the new directions and change is adopted in highly localized ways.

The relative dominance of each of the four strategies will vary in line with contextual changes. There are various classifications of organizational culture (Hofstede 1980; Trompenaars 1993; Chang and Wiebe 1996). Gould (1996) proposed that each of the four strategies outlined required a matching culture. When adopting a strategy of fine-tuning, an 'integrated' culture is likely to support it. This culture protects and sustains core competencies, beliefs, and codes of conduct, and determines the behaviours that pervade the organization. When adopting a building strategy, a 'diffuse culture' may help the organization to develop. This is where behaviours, codes of conduct, and values are shared within the organization. Systems are employed to deliver efficiency and add value. In a crisis situation, a 'counter culture' may emerge. This creates conditions where a decisive action is taken to suspend 'business as usual'. Transformation seems to require an 'empowered culture', which entails continuous and discontinuous change across the organization. Such organizations cannot be managed in the traditional way. Rather, acceptance of failure, devolution of responsibility and authority, empowerment of staff, and a re-conceptualization of consumers, will be required.

In the context of globalization, organizational change and development, therefore, requires organizations to master the art of change complexities, both in terms of internal and external environments. Only with a proper understanding of the change complexities, it is possible for organizations to influence change strategies and activities. In managing change, particularly after globalization, incremental business improvements cannot be the answer; it will require more sustained efforts with a long-term focus.

SUMMARY

Subsequent to globalization, organizational change and development requires managers and leaders to understand the complexities that arise in the process of transformation. While people-related issues are important, a thoughtful look into the processes, systems, and rules of organizations is also required. Organizations now need to hone the skills of their people to avoid knowledge and skills obsolescence, and also to make the best use of them by focusing on the technical and various process-related skills.

Talent management is now an important priority. Nurturing and developing talent not only requires training and development, but also enforces change in organizational cultures and practices. Playing an effective change agent's role in technology transfer, corporate leaders now balance their organizations by aligning people, business plans, and resources. It is observed that countries that successfully integrate into the global trading system enjoy faster growth, better living standards, easier access to capital and technology, higher productivity, and lower prices than countries that do not. However, global economic integration also faces the challenges of transitional problems along with various socio-cultural impacts.

Despite the global economic slowdown, many Indian organizations still enjoy competitiveness and were even able to achieve an impressive rate of growth, obviously due to appreciation of such change complexities and nurturing a long-term strategy for sustained growth. Public sector *Fortune* 500 majors, such as ONGC and IOL now operate on a global scale. Other leading public sector units, such as BHEL, NTPC, and GAIL (India) Ltd have successfully redefined their strategies to sustain their market leadership.

Major private sector units, such as Tata Steel and Aditya Vikram Birla Group, are now consolidating their global market positions through acquisitions. Many more are following suit. Thus, we have successful examples of organizational response to globalization. The lines of action described can provide a tentative guideline for achieving results.

KEY TERMS

Core processes These processes are those used by the entire company. They vary from business to business. For a manufacturing unit, it may be capital budgeting and logistics; in a pharmaceutical firm they might be research and development and go-to-market.

GATT It was a set of agreements. The role of GATT was related to the export and import of goods, particularly the reduction of tariff and elimination of non-tariff barriers.

Organizational transformations It requires a culture which questions conventional mindsets and fosters the ability to be self-critical, as well as the maturity and creativity to learn from, and act upon what is discovered. Much of this can emanate from a TQM foundation.

Performance management It is a phase of OD interventions through HR in the context of globalization to ensure the rigorous management of performance across the company. This requires framing of strategies to identify key talent and to manage succession to address the risk of non-availability of manpower globally, on the one hand; and nurturing a culture of superior performance, on the other.

CONCEPT REVIEW QUESTIONS

1. Explain the term 'globalization'. How does globalization affect organizational change and development?
2. Explain how organizations can cope with the challenges of globalization with strategic focus on HRM.
3. Who are the major players in the process of globalization? How can such players or institutional bodies influence organizational change?
4. Explain what type of organizational preparedness is necessary to cope with the challenges of globalization.
5. Discuss the process of organizational transformation in the context of globalization.
6. Discuss how, with strategic alignment, organizations can withstand the challenges of globalization.
7. Write short notes on the following:
   (a) OECD
   (b) IMF
   (c) Cultural diversity
   (d) Employee engagement

CRITICAL THINKING QUESTIONS

1. Your organization is a major manufacturer of specialized steel in India. Apart from enjoying the privilege of a captive domestic market, particularly for institutional sales to the defence, railways, and aeronautical industry, the organization also exports almost 25 per cent of saleable steel. After globalization, the organization is facing a stiff challenge from imported steel, which is cost competitive and also of better quality. This requires a major technological change in the organization. You have been assigned the task of handling the effect of globalization effect along with the challenges of technology. What would be your approach to manage such a challenge from an OD perspective?

2. Your company is a major player in the generic drugs industry. WTO issues seriously exert influence in the company's global business. Keeping in mind the recent example of Ranbaxy, explain how it can effectively manage the issues pertaining to globalization.

3. To reap the advantage of globalization your company wants to diversify through mergers and acquisitions in the unrepresented market abroad. Explain the changes required in HR strategies for such diversification.

CASE STUDY

Gimmy's Kitchen—The Change Management Approach

Like any other restaurant, Gimmy's Kitchen has also become sensitive to the external environment. To remain competitive, it had to go for a major change and be flexibile enough to react and adapt quickly to the challenges posed by the external environment. Because of its close interactions and good interpersonal relationships employees and managers, Gimmy could directly bring changes in the performance of the organization, substantially reducing the employees' resistance to change. For Gimmy, organizational change means direct physical change in operations along with changes in the behavioural dimensions of the employees. The employees are aware that they are losing their comfort zone, facing the risk of their knowledge and skills becoming obsolescent, status incongruence, and even financial insecurity, but they accept the change in order to survive and uphold the Gimmy's icon.

As a constituent of the hospitality sector, the restaurant industry is dominated by small to medium businesses. Restaurants, however, generate not less than 50 per cent of the total revenue of the hospitality industry. Moreover, it has a higher potential to generate direct employment than any other industry. Hence, change in restaurants is considered a most crucial aspect, as unsuccessful change interventions can result in liquidation. Gimmy is a big icon in Mumbai, the business hub of India, and directly employs over 2000 people in its 20 outlets spread across Mumbai and Pune. Unlike other fast food restaurants, it offers multicuisine dishes with the core philosophy of providing 'healthy food'.

Due to its focus on healthy food culture, Gimmy's clientele includes a large number of business class executives who expect to be served within a time-bound schedule. Any queuing problem can immediately create customer dissatisfaction. Gimmy wanted to reduce the queuing time of customers from 20 minutes (at present) to 10 minutes and also add a free start-up soup for all, to ensure that customers do not feel bored. It, therefore, adopted a strategy to identify the elements of commonality in each menu. A thorough study indicated an 80 per cent commonality in each menu which can be pre-made results in a substantial reduction in the queuing time and also accommodates 20 per cent customization. Any customer that asks for an item which is less common would be cajoled to wait beyond 10 minutes. A separate workstation that only cooks uncommon items on the menu will serve them.

However, 10 minutes is still very precious for busy executives and the time had to be further reduced. Moreover, customers waiting inside the restaurant reduced its reach to others who intend to visit it but are unable to do so due to paucity of time.

This *change* for Gimmy is apparently not so simple. Among others, it requires every employee to be alert and any time over-shooting is considered a gross violation of standard time requirements. Defaulting employees are counselled to improve this.

Gimmy's Managing Director now requires all cross sections of employees to share their own experiences, whereby as customers, they demand food within a time-bound schedule.

Discussion Question

You have been appointed as a facilitator in this experience sharing session. Explain how you would document such experiences, and what inputs can possibly help to bring the desired changes at Gimmy.

REFERENCES

Ahmed, P.K. (1998), 'Culture and climate for innovation', *European Journal of Innovation Management*, Vol. 1, pp. 30–43.

Baumruk, R. and T. Marusarz (2004), *Employee Engagement: Insights into Why It Matters and What You can Do About It*, Hewitt Associates, Inc.

Bhattacharyya, D.K. (2010), *Cross-cultural Management—Text and Cases*, PHI Learning, New Delhi.

———. (2009), *Organizational Behaviour: Concepts and Applications*, Oxford University Press, New Delhi.

———. (2007), *Human Resource Research Methods*, Oxford University Press, New Delhi.

———. (2006), *Human Resource Management*, Excel Books, New Delhi.

Broadbent, M and P. Weill (1997), 'Management by maxims: How business and IT managers can create IT infrastructures', *Sloan Management Review*, Spring, pp. 77–91.

Burdett, J.O. (1994), 'TQM and Re-engineering—The battle for the organization of tomorrow', *The TQM Magazine*, Vol. 6, No. 2, pp. 7–13.

Butler, Ronald E. (2004), 'Building momentum for organizational development', 89th Annual International Supply Chain Management Conference, April.

Carr, C. (1996), *Choice, Chance and Organizational Change*, Amacom, New York.

Castle, J.A. (1996), 'An integrated model in quality management, position TQM, BPR, and ISO 9000', *The TQM Magazine*, Vol. 8, No. 5, pp. 7–13.

Chang, F.S. and H.A. Wiebe (1996), 'The ideal culture profile for total quality management: A competing values perspective', *Engineering Management Journal*, Vol. 8, No. 2, pp. 19–26.

Daft, R.L. (1995), *Understanding Management*, Harcourt Brace & Company, Orlando.

Davenport, T.H. (1993), *Process Innovation: Re-engineering Work through Information Technology*, Harvard Business School Press, Boston.

Davenport, T.H., S.L. Jarvenpaa, and M.C. Beers (1996), 'Improving knowledge work processes', *Sloan Management Review*, Summer, pp. 53–65.

Davidson, W.H. (1993), 'Beyond re-engineering: The three phases of business transformation', *IBM Systems Journal*, Vol. 32, pp. 65–79.

Feenstra, R. (1998), 'Integration of trade and disintegration of production in the global economy', *Journal of Economic Perspectives*, Vol. 12, Issue 4, pp. 31–50.

Friedman, Thomas L. (2002), *Longitudes and Attitudes: Exploring the World After September 11*, Farrar Straus Giroux, New York.

Gallivan, M.J., D.J. Hofman, and W.J. Orlikowski (1994), 'Implementing radical change: Gradual versus rapid pace', Proceedings of the Fifteenth International Conference on Information Systems, pp. 325–339.

Giddens, A. (1979), *Central Problems in Social Theory: Action, Structure, and Contradiction in Social Analysis*, University of California Press, Berkeley.

Gould, R.M. (1996), 'Getting from strategy to action: Processes for continuous change', *Long Range Planning*, Vol. 29, No. 3, pp. 278–289.

Handy, C. (1989), *The Age of Unreason*, Century Business, London.

Hofstede, G. (1980), 'Motivation, leadership and organization: Do American theories apply abroad? *Organizational Dynamics*, Summer, pp. 42–63.

Jih, W.J.K. and P. Owings (1995), 'From in search of excellence to business process re-engineering: The role of IT', *Information Strategy: The Executive's Journal*, Winter, pp. 6–19.

Kilmann, R. (1995), 'A holistic program and critical success factors of corporate transformation', *European Management Journal*, Vol. 13, No. 2, pp. 175–186.

Kondo, Y. (1996), 'Are creativity and standardization mutually exclusive (Keynote)', Proceedings of the First International Conference on ISO 9000 and TQM, Luton Business School, 2–4 April, pp. 251–260.

Lawler, E.E. and C.G. Worley (2006), *Built to Change: How to Achieve Sustained Organizational Effectiveness*, Jossey-Bass, California.

Legrain, Philippe (2002), *The Truth about Globalization*, Abacus, London.

McHugh, P., G. Merli, and W.A. Wheeler, III (1995), *Beyond Business Process Re-engineering: Towards the Holonic Enterprise*, Wiley, London.

Miller, D. (1982), 'Evolution and revolution: A quantum view of structural change in organizations', *Journal of Management Studies*, Vol. 19, pp. 131–151.

Miller, D. and P. Friesen (1982), 'Structural change and performance: Quantum vs piecemeal incremental approaches', *Academy of Management Journal*, Vol. 25, No. 4, pp. 867–892.

Mintzberg, H. (1994), 'Rethinking strategic planning, part 1: Pitfalls and fallacies', *Long Range Planning*, Vol. 27, pp. 12–21.

Nevis, E.C., A.J. DiBella and J.M. Gould (1995), 'Understanding organizations as learning systems', *Sloan Management Review*, Winter, pp. 73–85.

Novak, A. (1997), 'Strategic relationship between quality management and product innovation', *The Mid-Atlantic Journal of Business*, Vol. 33, No. 2, pp. 119–135.

Olson, S. and D. Dawson (2003), 'The total compensation philosophy: New guidance for compensation committees', PricewaterhouseCoopers, LLP.

Orlikowski, W.J. and M.J. Tyre (1993), 'Exploiting opportunities for technological improvement in organizations', *Sloan Management Review*, Vol. 35, No. 1, pp. 13–26.

Ruud Lubbers (2005), 'The shift from economy to ecology', A thematic essay on the precautionary approach and globalization as they relate to principle 6, in *Earth Charter in Action*, KIT Publishers, Amsterdam.

Schein, E.H. (1996), 'Three cultures of management: The key to organizational learning', *Sloan Management Review*, Fall, pp. 9–19.

———. (1993), 'How can organizations learn faster? The challenge of entering the green room', *Sloan Management Review*, Winter, pp. 85–92.

Schoonhoven, C.B. and M. Jelinek (1990), 'Dynamic tension in innovative, high technology firms: Managing rapid technological change through organizational structure', in Tushman, M.L. and P. Anderson (eds), *Managing Strategic Innovation and Change*, Oxford University Press, New York, pp. 233–254.

Scott Morton, M.S. (1991), *The Corporation of the 1990s: Information Technology and Organizational Transformation*, Oxford University Press, New York.

Senge, P.M. (1993), *The Fifth Discipline: The Art and Practice of the Learning Organization*, Century Business, London.

———. (1990), 'The leader's New York: Building learning organizations', *Sloan Management Review*, Fall, pp. 7–23.

Sitkin, S.B., K.M. Sutcliffe, and R.G. Schroeder (1994), 'Distinguishing control from learning in total quality management: A contingency perspective', *The Academy of Management Review*, Vol. 19, No. 3, pp. 537–564.

Tapscott, D. and A. Caston (1993), *Paradigm Shift: The New Promise of Information Technology*, McGraw-Hill, New York.

Trompenaars, F. (1993), *Riding the Waves of Culture: Understanding Cultural Diversity in Business*, Nicholas Brealey Publications, London.

Tushman, M.L. and C. O'Reilly (1996), 'Ambidextrous organizations: Managing evolutionary and revolutionary change', *California Management Review*, Vol. 38, pp. 8–30.

Venkatraman, N. (1994), 'IT-enabled business transformation: From automation to business scope redefinition', *Sloan Management Review*, Winter, pp. 73–87.

Yip, G. (1992), *Total Global Strategy: Managing for World-wide Competitive Advantage*, Prentice Hall, New York.

17 Knowledge Management and Change

Learning Objectives

After reading this chapter, you will be able to understand
- the definitions and concepts of knowledge management
- the concept of data, information, knowledge, and intelligence
- the assumptions, integral components, benefits, and enablers of knowledge management
- the strategies of knowledge management
- strategic framework for mapping knowledge and gap analysis
- knowledge management practices in Indian organizations
- knowledge management and resource-based competitive advantage
- the relationship between knowledge management and change management

Siemens' ICN Knowledge Management

To develop a knowledge management programme, organizations need to consider cultural factors, duly defining its goals for success. Such organizational initiatives need to be further reinforced by process changes keeping pace with technology. Organizations further develop success metrics based on the defined goals. At the organizational level, knowledge management practices focus more on tacit knowledge (developed based on experiences and practices), documenting and sharing it with others for development.

The Siemens' ICN knowledge management case, commonly known as the ShareNet case is perhaps one of the best world-class examples for organizations around the world to emulate. Siemens' ICN, that is, the information and communication networks division is a global provider of telecommunication solutions and is active in more than 100 countries. ICN ShareNet is a community of around 18,000 sales, marketing, business development, and research and development people in Siemens. Through ShareNet networks, these globally scattered experts share and develop their knowledge to create better customer solutions. In the process, Siemens can identify and document local innovations and leverage them on a global scale.

INTRODUCTION

Early in the industrial age, motor/muscle power was provided by workers for product creation, leaving the thinking job to management. However, with the changed environment, cognitive skills became increasingly more important in every work, be it production at the shop floor or rendering services to customers. Technology further played a crucial role in capturing and managing knowledge, making it possible for organizations to harness the potentiality of knowledge by its proper development, growth and maintenance, and with an approach to periodically retire knowledge that is obsolete. There are many contributors to knowledge management and learning organizations, starting with the concept of Kelley's (1985) 'gold collar worker' to that of Argyris (1994), Drucker (1994), Peters (1992), Stewart (1997), Nonaka and Takeuchi (1995), and many more.

Knowledge management practices play a crucial role in managing organizational change. To develop the capabilities of people, it is essential to reinforce knowledge through learning. Learning is a process of acquiring new skills or knowledge that results in new behaviour. It can take place through multiple ways. But for organizations, the best way to promote learning is by exposure to new experiences. Knowledge is the ability and wisdom to use the learned experiences for achievement of individual and organizational objectives. Knowledge management, therefore, is the process of systematically and actively managing and leveraging the store of knowledge in an organization.

At this stage, it is important to understand the basic difference between skills, multi-skills, competencies, and knowledge. Skills are operational attributes to attain some goal or accomplish a particular task. It can either be generic or technical, entry level or advanced. Operationally, skill enrichment is initiated to meet present requirements. Multi-skilling is the process of training employees on varied skills across trade-specific and craft-specific skill-sets. This initiative enables employees to perform more jobs within the same job family or to do the entire job from a holistic point of view. Thus, multi-skilling optimizes manpower utilization through job enlargement and job enrichment. However, both skill enrichment and multi-skilling are intended to address the present organizational requirements. Competencies, on the other hand, encompass skills, knowledge, abilities, and attributes which are observable, measurable, and which change with the passage of time.

Organizations undertake competency mapping in a defined job context to understand the extent of its alignment with vision and mission, and to define an ideal workforce. Knowledge is a more holistic approach, which is identified, acquired, and developed for achieving organizational objectives. The Indian *gurukul* system of learning has always emphasized the importance of holistic learning. Knowledge, thus, acquired helps employees to think independently and to understand the interdependence which never gets obsolete. It becomes self-perpetuating and dynamic to address the changing objectives of organizations.

It is, therefore, evident that knowledge is a mix of the experiences, values, and information of organizations, which does not just get documented but is also translated into a regular practice to develop the capabilities of people and to bring positive change in the overall performance of the organization (Davenport et al. 1998*).* In general, however, intellectual and knowledge-based assets fall into one of the two categories: explicit or tacit. Tacit knowledge refers to knowledge that is often used but cannot be articulated or externalized, and hence, cannot be easily diffused. Explicit knowledge consists of knowledge that can be codified and presented in books, etc. and can consequently be easily transferred to others. Included among explicit knowledge are assets, such as patents, trademarks, business plans and marketing research, and customer lists.

From an organization's point of view, knowledge management is, thus, a concept in which an enterprise gathers, organizes, shares, and analyses its knowledge in terms of resources, documents, and periodically retires the old knowledge.

KNOWLEDGE MANAGEMENT

'...the truly revolutionary impact of the information revolution is not artificial intelligence, information, or the effect of computers and data processing on decision-making, policymaking, or strategy. The key to continued growth and leadership in the new economy is not electronics of computers but the cognitive skills of the "knowledge workers".'

–Peter Drucker (1994)

To understand the concept of knowledge management, it is important to know what knowledge is. Knowledge is the fact or condition of knowing something with familiarity gained through experience or association. Explicit knowledge is formal knowledge, available in the books, rules, etc. Tacit knowledge is informal knowledge, deeply rooted in an individual actions and experience, ideals, values, or cautions. The knowledge creation process requires socialization (tacit to tacit), externalization (tacit to explicit), combination (explicit to explicit), and internalization (explicit to tacit).

Unfortunately, there is no universal definition of knowledge management, just as there is no agreement as to what constitutes knowledge in the first place. For this reason, it is best to think of knowledge management in the broadest context. Theoretically, knowledge management is the process through which organizations generate value from their intellectual and knowledge-based assets. Most often, generating value from such assets involves sharing them among employees, departments, and even with other companies in an effort to devise best practices. It is important to note that the definition says nothing about technology; while knowledge management is often facilitated by IT, technology by itself is not knowledge management.

In an organizational context, knowledge management is a concept in which an enterprise gathers, organizes, shares, and analyses its knowledge in terms of resources, documents, and skills. It helps an organization to gain insight and understanding from its own experience. It is the process through which organizations generate value from their intellectual and knowledge-based assets. A knowledge manager takes the responsibility of facilitating the ongoing process of knowledge sharing and knowledge renewal. It is important to understand how knowledge is formed, and how people and organizations learn to use it wisely. The end result of a well-designed knowledge management programme is that everyone wins. Therefore, knowledge management is a newly emerging, interdisciplinary business model dealing with all aspects of knowledge within the context of the organization. It encompasses both technological tools and organizational routines in overlapping parts to include knowledge creation, knowledge codification, and knowledge sharing to promote learning and innovation, and in the process, achieve desired organizational change.

Assumptions

Before we further discuss knowledge management in an organizational context, it is important to clarify certain wrong assumptions about it. It is often believed that knowledge management is about technology, but this is not correct. Technology acts as an enabler in knowledge management functions. Knowledge is about people who collaborate and share their experience to help the organization develop its human resources. Knowledge is innovative use of information. It is the fact or condition of knowing something with familiarity gained through experience or association. From an organizational change and development point of view, knowledge may also be described as a set of models recorded in the individual brain or stored in the organizational process, products, facilities, systems, and documents (*Webster's Dictionary*). Knowledge enhances the capacity to act. It is the product of learning related to human action and more than just information.

Knowledge assets are the knowledge regarding markets, products, technologies, and organizations that a business owns or needs to own, and which enable its business processes to generate profits. Knowledge management involves identification and analysis of available and required knowledge, and the subsequent planning and control of actions to develop knowledge assets so as to fulfil organizational objectives.

Organizational information assets may include databases, documents, policies, and procedures, as well as the uncaptured tacit expertise. Organizational knowledge is the sum of the 'justified beliefs' of the employees, which diminishes with the departure of an employee. It is the major source of competitive advantage. It can never be static.

Knowledge management is important for increased competition in the marketplace. To fight against competition, organizations need to be innovative. It should focus on creation of customer value and reducing the size of the workforce.

To manage knowledge, one must identify the organizational knowledge assets, understand how knowledge can add value, specify what actions are necessary to achieve better usability and added value, and review the use of knowledge to ensure added value.

Knowledge management encompasses human capital which are (i) organizational (ii) learning, (iii) educational levels, (iv) employee empowerment, (v) management experience, and (vi) time in training. Innovation capitals are (i) copyrights and trademarks, (ii) patents (legally protected intellectual assets), (iii) new markets, and (iv) research leadership. Process capitals are (i) strategy, (ii) decisions, (iii) cycle time, and (iv) IT capacity. Customer capitals are (i) market growth and share, (ii) customer size and contact, and (iii) image enhancing customers.

At this stage, it is important to understand the meaning and context of data and information, and delineate it from knowledge management. Data may be defined as factual information, while information is useful data communication or receipt of knowledge. Knowledge may be defined as a condition of knowing something gained through experience or the condition of apprehending truth or fact through reasoning. Intelligence is the ability to understand and apply knowledge for any business solution.

From these definitional contexts, it is, therefore, clear that knowledge management techniques can be another way of effecting organizational change and development. Thus, along with other organizational change and development tools organizations can also make use of knowledge management practices to achieve the desired level of organizational change. Box 17.1 illustrates the knowledge management system at McKinsey.

BOX 17.1 Knowledge management at McKinsey

The knowledge management system at McKinsey is continuously committed to enhancing the ability to assist clients with the idea of making them more knowledgeable. It benefits McKinsey, as customers become professionals in demanding more and more and become captive. Moreover, McKinsey's expertise reduces the risk and failure in critical skill areas, such as managing mergers and acquisitions, strategic alliances, etc. Thus, knowledge management practices at McKinsey benefit both customers and the company.

Integral Components

Based on the previous discussions, we can list the integral components of KM as follows:

- Generating new knowledge
- Accessing valuable knowledge from outside sources
- Using accessible knowledge in decision-making
- Embedding knowledge in processes, products, and/or services
- Representing knowledge in documents, databases, and software
- Facilitating knowledge growth through culture and incentives
- Transferring existing knowledge to other parts of the organization
- Measuring the value of knowledge assets and/or impact of knowledge management

Benefits

The immediate benefits of knowledge management correlate to the improved bottom line of the organization. Although the basic intention of organizational change and development is to achieve the desired level of change outcome, ultimately it correlates to the improved performance of the organization. In today's information-driven economy, organizations derive opportunities and values from intellectual rather than physical capital. Today, both knowledge and information also form the inputs for any organization, and both are important enablers to renew human resources. Effective use of knowledge and information can be made through sharing with an approach of collaboration. This forms the basis of knowledge management practices. Therefore, organizational level knowledge management practices should focus on the following aspects:

1. Foster innovation by encouraging the free flow of ideas.
2. Improve customer service by streamlining response time.
3. Boost revenues by getting products and services to market faster.
4. Enhance employee retention rates by recognizing the value of employees' knowledge and rewarding them for it.
5. Streamline operations and reduce costs by eliminating redundant or unnecessary processes.

A more creative approach to knowledge management can lead to improved efficiency, higher productivity, and increased revenues in practically any business function. And, every organizational change and development initiative ultimately aspires to achieve the above results through their interventions.

ENABLERS OF KNOWLEDGE MANAGEMENT IN ORGANIZATIONS

It is impossible for competitors to imitate or copy knowledge and hence, those who possess it have a unique and inherently protected capital. This makes intellectual or knowledge assets increasingly more important, and at times, it may contribute to as much as 70 per cent of the market value of an organization. In this context, tacit knowledge plays a more crucial role as it is more difficult to imitate. With the emergence of a knowledge-based economy, many organizations today recruit a chief knowledge officer (CKO), who as a change agent encourages knowledge sharing to build a cultural climate that rewards the sharing behaviour of employees in an organization. A CKO plays a very crucial role in organizational change and development.

Both knowledge and information are the main inputs to HR. Hence, organizations believe that their knowledge management efforts should be led by the HRD. However, some organizations separately assign the knowledge management function under a CKO, independent of their HR function. In reality, however, knowledge management is more an integrated function, as knowledge encompasses all areas of organizational activities. From these perspectives, all managers, leaders, and employees of an organization could be enablers of the knowledge management function in any organization, provided the work culture sets that appropriate premise.

As an enabler of knowledge management practices in an organization, the CKO first tries to understand where the knowledge is located in the organization, or who possesses the knowledge that provides an organization its competitive advantage. We all know that knowledge is essentially created and possessed by individuals within the context of organizational interactions that allow them to use and renew knowledge. There may be very dynamic industries in which individuals may possess knowledge that may be more important and embedded in the organizational context. However, it is not possible for individuals to possess all the knowledge that is required, nor is it possible for others to substitute the knowledge of missing individuals. In such situations, individuals and the organization possess utilizable knowledge jointly and severally with the proactive support of the CKO.

Organizational learning/knowledge consists of a combination of the knowledge of all individuals in an organization and can be acquired broadly in the following ways:

- When individual members within organizations learn
- When individuals learn, it has the potential of changing the stock of knowledge in the organization, thus leading to a change in organizational knowledge
- When new knowledge comes in with new members joining the organization and old knowledge going out with those leaving it
- When there is a change in the structure and system of an organization that necessitates acquiring new knowledge
- When there are significant organizational changes requiring previously neglected knowledge to come into prominence, while some of the previously dominant knowledge may lose its importance

The knowledge management practices of the Indian power utility major, NTPC, are discussed in Exhibit 17.1.

EXHIBIT 17.1 Knowledge management system at NTPC

In 2001, National Thermal Power Corporation Limited (NTPC), the largest thermal power generating company in India took a major initiative for organizational transformation under Project Disha. This ambitious project started with a review of the goals and strategies, formulation of action plans, and finally, implementation at the various plant levels. NTPC's core business is engineering, construction, operation of power generating plants, and providing consultancy to power utilities in India and abroad. The organization aims to diversify into related businesses in the near future through horizontal and vertical integration, which is also one of its corporate objectives.

NTPC's broad strategy for realizing its overall objectives is to build on four building blocks, that is, competency, commitment, culture, and systems, derived from its HR vision of enabling its people to

(Contd)

(Exhibit 17.1 contd)

be a family of world-class professionals, and making NTPC a learning organization. To implement the above model, a knowledge management process has been initiated throughout the organization as a competency and systems building measure. NTPC's knowledge management imperatives are derived from its strategic objectives and HR vision of becoming a learning organization. It also realized that to facilitate the implementation of the business as well as HR strategy, an integrated knowledge management system is needed so that employees can transfer/share their knowledge and expertise for rapid growth and development.

A typical strategy map of knowledge management practices at NTPC is presented in Exhibit 17.2.

Based on the initial strategy map, NTPC draws its typical action plans by answering the following questions:

1. What knowledge does NTPC have?
2. Who will lead the knowledge domain?
3. Who will structure and contribute to the knowledge base?

Accordingly, stage-wise action plans of NTPC can be presented as in Fig. 17.1.

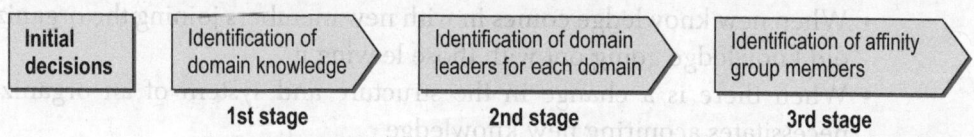

FIG. 17.1 Stage-wise action plans for NTPC's KM strategy

A typical organizational structure for knowledge management activities of NTPC can be drawn as in Fig. 17.2.

To make knowledge management an organization-wide activity, NTPC does not make KM a standalone function, but involves its core groups. In addition to their current job, employees are involved in KM activities and processes under the overall

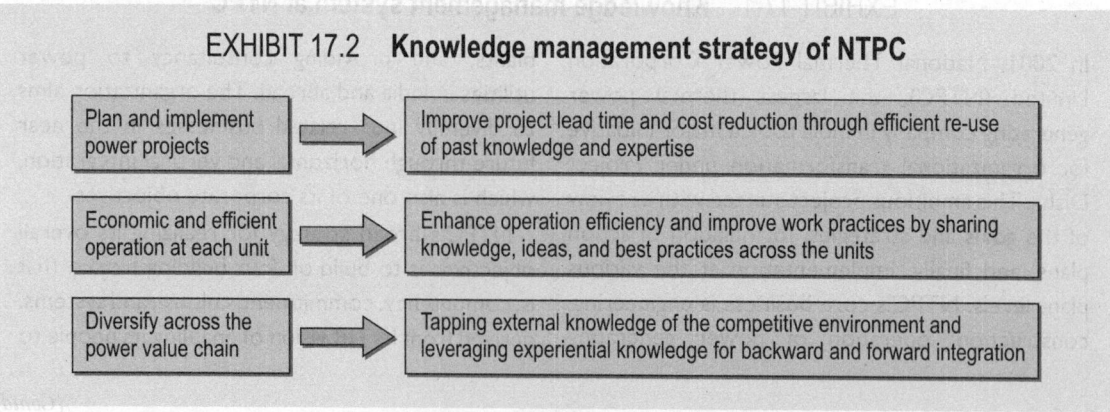

EXHIBIT 17.2 Knowledge management strategy of NTPC

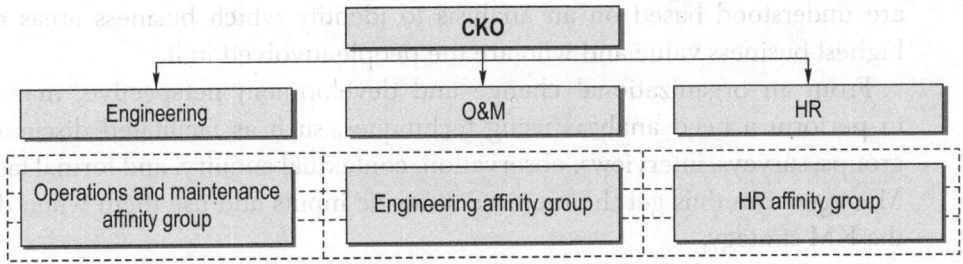

FIG. 17.2   Knowledge management structure of NTPC

support of the CKO. Among Indian companies, NTPC's KM practices are one of the best that other organizations can emulate.

KNOWLEDGE MANAGEMENT STRATEGY

Effective knowledge management helps an organization to overcome market uncertainties and ever-increasing competition. Therefore, knowledge management practices per se, could be the most effective way to bring the desired organizational change and development. To make the organization a knowledge-enabled one, it is important to manage knowledge management functions strategically.

Knowledge management strategy identifies the key needs and issues within the organization, and provides a framework for addressing these. Needs analysis ensures that the activities and initiatives that pose challenges to the organization are considered. However, the approach largely depends on organization-specific requirements. For a call centre, the most important need factor is real-time response to callers' needs. Other usual challenges faced by them are high job pressure, a closely monitored environment, high employee turnover rate, and high training costs of new recruits. Hence, the knowledge management strategy for a call centre should address these aspects. Similarly, in customer relations' jobs, it is important to ensure consistency, accuracy, and repeatability; hence, knowledge management strategy should address these needs and issues. A business managers need to support business decisions based on key information. They have to bring in organizational changes keeping pace with the market requirement. Hence, understanding accurate, complete, and relevant information, and acquiring people management skills, mentoring, and coaching skills are very important areas that deserve attention when designing the knowledge management strategy for such organizations.

While drawing up a knowledge management strategy at the macro level, the organization has to consider innovation and also its operating environment. Although the KM strategy is organization-specific, it follows two holistic approaches: top-down and bottom-up. A top-down approach considers the overall strategy of the organization, while a bottom-up approach focuses on key business processes. These are understood based on an analysis to identify which business areas deliver the highest business value and who are the people involved in it.

From an organizational change and development perspective, managers have to perform a need analysis using techniques, such as facilitated discussions, focus groups, surveys, interviews, observation, contextual enquiry, and formal task analysis. Managers can thus get the required strategic inputs and use them when drawing up the KM strategy.

Developing a knowledge management strategy provides a unique opportunity to gain a greater understanding of the way an organization operates and the challenges it faces. By focusing on identifying staff needs and issues, activities and initiatives can be recommended with the confidence that these will have a clear and measurable impact upon the organization. Supplementing this bottom-up approach with a strategic focus then ensures that the KM initiative is aligned with broader organizational directions. Taking this approach when developing a KM strategy allows limited resources to be targeted to the key needs within the organization, and delivering the greatest business benefits while positioning the organization for long-term growth and stability.

Many companies today look at knowledge management as a new process, such as TQM or customer relationship management (CRM). Concepts of TQM and CRM were earlier thought to be engineering concepts, but the world has finally come to recognize the importance of human resources in both these systems. Because of the growing importance of HR, the Shingho Prize Model talks of employee empowerment as the major component to achieve business results. Research has shown that knowledge management and transfer of best practices happen when the process is driven by an intention to create value for the business.

Another dimension along which the knowledge management strategy needs to be planned is the degree of codification and personalization. All organizations need to dynamically align their knowledge requirements based on their competitive positions and capabilities. They need to maintain a balance between creating and exploiting knowledge as well as between internal generation and bringing in knowledge from outside the organization. A company's knowledge management strategy will also be influenced by the strategies of other companies in its industry. In knowledge-intensive industries, organizations that have a more aggressive (externally-oriented) knowledge strategy tend to perform better.

As the basis of value creation increasingly depends on the leverage of intangible assets of firms, knowledge management is emerging as a powerful source of competitive advantage. However, the general recognition of the importance of KM seems to be accompanied by a technology-induced drive to implement KM with inadequate consideration of the organizational strategic objectives. Exhibit 17.3 discusses KM practices at one of the leading firms.

Penrose (1959, 1980) observed that an organization's competitive advantage rests in its superior adaptation of business conditions by effectively coordinating its

> **EXHIBIT 17.3 Knowledge management practices at Chevron**
>
> Knowledge management practices at Chevron achieved a 30 per cent productivity gain, a 50 per cent improvement in safety performance, and more than $2 billion in operating cost reductions during the 1990s. Today, Chevron believes that managing knowledge is not just a performance issue but a reputation issue as well. It helps to achieve business results and so also increases the retention of talented top employees. Using knowledge management techniques, Chevron was able to re-structure its gasoline retailing business, and drill oil and gas wells much faster and cheaper. It was also able to enhance its refinery performance. Chevron's global information link (GIL) system replaced every personal computer in the company with a common machine, software, and connective system, creating a single desktop and operating environment, worldwide. This is how Chevron achieved excellence in knowledge management.
>
> Source: Adapted from http://www.chevron.com/news/Press/Release/?id=1999-01-11&co=Chevron, accessed on 9 August 2009.

internal resources. He believed that every organization has unique knowledge-based capabilities that are economically unfeasible to replicate. Hence, growth must be based on the coordination of these resources to develop and maintain advantages based on superior use of knowledge and competency.

A recent McKinsey survey of 40 companies in the US, Europe, and South–East Asia showed that many executives think that KM 'begins and ends with sophisticated IT systems' (Hauschild et al. 2001). KM efforts have been primarily focused on developing new applications of information technology, supplemented to a lesser degree with implementing new organizational forms. The link between an organization's knowledge and business strategy has been widely ignored in practice (Davenport et al. 1998). If knowledge management is to take hold rather than become merely a passing fad, it will have to be solidly linked with the creation of economic value and competitive advantage. This can be accomplished by grounding KM within the context of business strategy.

The creation of unique strategic knowledge takes time, forcing the organization to balance short-term and long-term strategic resource decisions. Hence, the organization must determine whether it should focus on knowledge creation, exploitation, or both. Only then should it balance its knowledge resources and efforts accordingly. The firm must determine properties of knowledge and the processes for its creation, transfer, and utilization that provide a competitive advantage yet are not easily imitated by other firms.

Knowledge–Strategy Link

A linkage between knowledge and strategy can be established in the strengths, weaknesses, opportunities, and threats (SWOT) framework. Based on the strategic opportunities, organizations map their knowledge resources, leveraging their strengths, and guarding against weaknesses (internal to the organizations) and threats (external to the organizations). Knowledge, like information, is now considered an essential resource input for organizations. Hence, while exploiting new opportunities organizations need to strategically use their knowledge resources to gain competitive edge over others. To illustrate, after acquiring a government-managed food-processing unit, Videocon transformed it into a computer assembly shop, redeploying its traditional workers in computer assembly jobs. To do this, Videocon exploited its existing knowledge base for LCD TV manufacturing. Changing market environments now requires every organization to innovate. Hence, a new product or service development is a great challenge.

Strategic use of knowledge resources helps greatly in this respect. Organizations need to make many such strategic choices, leveraging their knowledge resources. This may extend to selection of technologies, designing manufacturing processes, differentiating products and services, etc. Internationally, Wal-Mart is a great example for strategic use of knowledge resources. Wal-Mart leverages the focused knowledge of its vendors, asking them to share their perceived consumption habits, needs, and practices with the retailers. Wal-Mart's retail shops act as knowledge integrators to meet the expectations of its customers in a better way. However, it is now experiencing difficulty as there is increased competition from two major rivals—Target and Costco—and is trying hard to re-invent its strategies with a back-up of knowledge resources.

STRATEGIC FRAMEWORK FOR MAPPING KNOWLEDGE

Assessing an organization's knowledge position requires cataloguing its existing intellectual resources by creating what is commonly called a knowledge map (Dyer et al. 2001). The task of categorizing or describing what a business firm knows (or what it must know) in order to remain competitive in the industry is not easy. Although firms within particular industries and maintaining similar competitive positions, or those employing similar technologies and other resources often share some common knowledge, there are no simple answers regarding what a firm must know in order to be competitive. Even if there were, there would be no sustainable advantage. In fact, each organization has a unique way of linking knowledge and strategy which itself provides them an advantage.

Knowledge can be categorized into *core, advanced,* or *innovative* (Davenport and Prusak 1997). *Core knowledge* is the minimum scope and level of knowledge required just to 'play the game'. Having that level of knowledge and capability will not assure long-term competitive viability of a firm, but does present a basic industry knowledge barrier to entry. Core knowledge tends to be commonly held by members of an industry and, therefore, provides little advantage other than over non-members.

Advanced knowledge enables a firm to be competitively viable. Although the firm may have the same level, scope, or quality of knowledge as its competitors, the knowledge content will often vary among competitors, enabling knowledge differentiation (Gurteen 1999).

Innovative knowledge is knowledge that enables a firm to lead its industry and competitors, and to significantly differentiate itself from its competitors. Innovative knowledge often enables a firm to change the rules of the game. Based on its extensive knowledge of cost accounting and economics, KPMG challenged the traditional way of accounting, and introduced strategic finance and corporate governance to measure the financial value and performance of its clients. Not only did this create confusion among competitors and an advantage for KPMG but it also allowed the firm to identify many profitable opportunities passed over by competitors while avoiding potentially unprofitable ventures.

Knowledge is not static and what is innovative knowledge today will ultimately become the core knowledge of tomorrow. Thus, defending and nurturing a competitive position requires continual learning and knowledge acquisition.

The ability of an organization to learn, accumulate knowledge from its experiences, and re-apply that knowledge is itself a skill or competence that may provide strategic advantage over and above the core competencies directly related to delivering its product or service (Patnaik 2003).

Using the strategic knowledge framework shown in Fig. 17.3, organizations can compare its desired strategic knowledge profile (to assess its internal gaps) to that of its competitors (to assess its external knowledge gaps). Additionally, it can be used to plot an organization's past knowledge path as well as the desired future state. The framework may be applied by an area of competency or, taking a more traditional strategic perspective, by strategic business units (SBU), product line, function, or

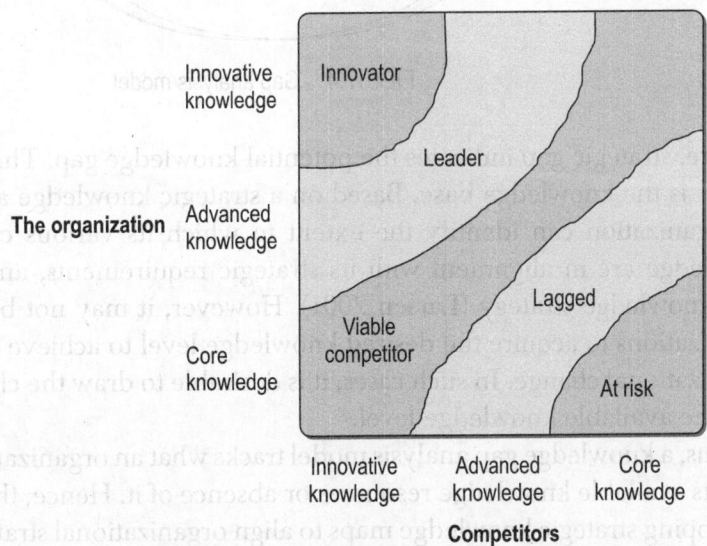

FIG. 17.3 Strategic knowledge framework

market position. Regardless of the particular way each organization categorizes its knowledge, each category can be further broken down into elements that are core, competitive, or innovative, to produce a strategic knowledge map.

GAP ANALYSIS

A gap analysis as presented in Fig. 17.4 can be performed after mapping an organization's competitive knowledge position. The gap between what an organization must do to compete and what it actually *is* doing represents a strategic gap. In line with the SWOT framework, strengths and weaknesses represent what the organization can do; opportunities and threats direct what it must do. Strategy, then, represents how the organization balances its competitive position to develop and protect its strategic niche (Mentzas 2003).

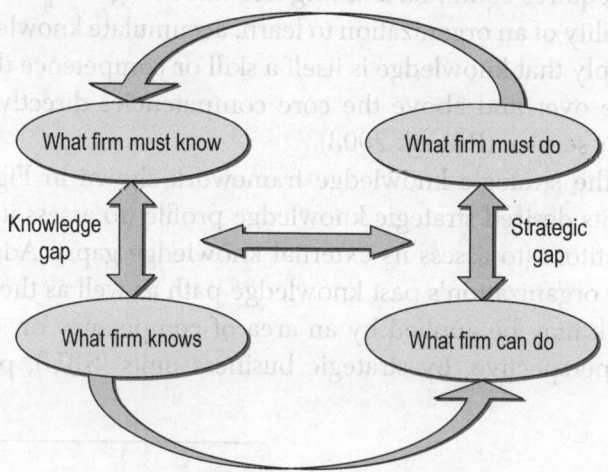

FIG. 17.4   Gap analysis model

Here, strategic gap indicates the potential knowledge gap. The greater the gap, the poorer is the knowledge base. Based on a strategic knowledge and capabilities map, an organization can identify the extent to which its various categories of existing knowledge are in alignment with its strategic requirements, and accordingly, draw up a knowledge strategy (Larsen 2001). However, it may not be always feasible for organizations to acquire the desired knowledge level to achieve the intended level of organizational change. In such cases, it is desirable to draw the change strategy in line with the available knowledge level.

Thus, a knowledge gap analysis model tracks what an organization can or cannot do with its available knowledge resources or absence of it. Hence, the model is useful for developing strategic knowledge maps to align organizational strategies. Organizations which pursue aggressive knowledge management strategies can outperform their rivals. Based on Snowden (1999), knowledge strategy integration with exploitation versus exploration orientation is illustrated in Fig. 17.5.

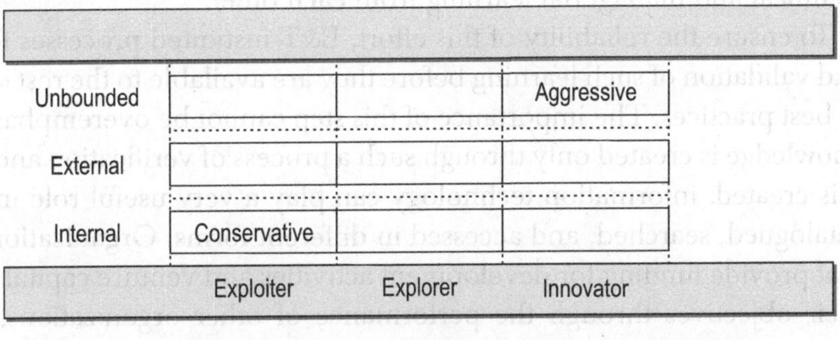

			Aggressive
Unbounded			
External			
Internal	Conservative		
	Exploiter	Explorer	Innovator

FIG. 17.5 Knowledge strategy with exploitation vs exploration orientation

In cases where organizational knowledge significantly lags behind that of its competitors or the organization is defending a knowledge position, an aggressive knowledge strategy will be required to remain competitive.

STRATEGIC KNOWLEDGE MANAGEMENT IN INDIAN ORGANIZATIONS

An Indian company with an evolving KM strategy that reflects these concerns is the picture tube manufacturer, Samtel. Since the deregulation of the economy in the early 1990s, Samtel realized that it could not be a long-term competitor in the display technology business without having a strong technological capability of its own.

Tata Steel, another Indian company, is also making extensive use of the knowledge management process to remain globally competitive. The central theme of knowledge management in Tata Steel is to leverage and re-use knowledge resources that already exist in the organization so that people will seek out the best practices rather than re-invent the wheel. It benefits the company by making expertise available throughout the organization, reducing loss of intellectual capital from people leaving the company, minimizing redundancy of knowledge-based activities, increasing knowledge productivity by disseminations, and gaining competitive advantage in the marketplace by turning intellectual capital into values through innovation.

In BHEL, knowledge management helped the company achieve process improvement, increase employee capabilities, leverage intellectual capital, gain customer market information, develop new product, manage successful customer relation, transfer best practices, open new markets, and start new businesses.

Indian Companies and Knowledge Management Practices

Indian companies have so far tended to look at knowledge management more from the exploitation angle than from the perspective of exploration and creation. Part of what is happening under the rubric of knowledge management is actually information storage and retrieval, albeit in more sophisticated and user-friendly forms than before.

Some companies are, however, graduating to real KM. Engineering major, Larsen & Toubro (L&T) is creating a knowledge base of major projects undertaken by it with technical and managerial learning from each other.

To ensure the reliability of this effort, L&T instituted processes for the verification and validation of such learning before they are available to the rest of the organization as best practices. The importance of this step cannot be overemphasized because true knowledge is created only through such a process of verification and validation. Once it is created, information technology can play a very useful role in allowing it to be catalogued, searched, and accessed in different forms. Organizations, such as NGOs that provide funding for development activities and venture capital firms that achieve their objectives through the performance of other organizations, are also looking towards knowledge management as a way of learning from success stories, identifying best practices, and transferring this to other organizations within their networks.

Just as any other strategy needs to be aligned with the structure and systems of an organization for it to be effective, knowledge management strategy also needs some organizational conditions if it is to succeed. Functional or divisional silos, hoarding of information, and poor communication are anathema to knowledge management. Knowledge management is generally associated with decentralized decision-making, and a belief in specialization and the value of deep expertise. Many Indian organizations will, therefore, have to change their entire way of thinking, structure, and culture, to make knowledge management work to their benefit.

Today, when firms in India are subject to competition from the best companies in the world on their home turf, paying greater attention to knowledge and its management is inevitable.

KNOWLEDGE MANAGEMENT AND RESOURCE-BASED COMPETITIVE ADVANTAGE

Organizational resources can be tangible, such as land, buildings, plants, and machinery, or intangible, such as brands and reputations. Tangible resources are unlikely to be the basis for competitive advantage, for the simple reason that they can often be easily duplicated by anyone who has money. Intangible resources are much more likely to meet the tests of inimitability, slow depreciation, difficulty of substitution, and competitive superiority. Perhaps, the strongest intangible resources are organizational capabilities. Reliance's legendary capability to conceive and implement mega-projects based on its ability to think on a global scale, its skills in project management, and its resource mobilization abilities meets all these tests.

Understanding what capabilities need to be created and taking the necessary steps to create them is again an exercise in knowledge management. For example, the tractor and utility automobile manufacturer, Mahindra and Mahindra (M&M) realized that to compete effectively, it would have to create a stream of new products on a continuous basis. Given its limited resources and global ambitions, it identified good project management skills as a key ingredient and initiated an organization-wide process, guided by external consultants, to create a robust project management capability.

Another company that has taken a conscious approach to create organizational capabilities is the two-wheeler manufacturer, TVS Motor Company. Like M&M, the TVS Motor Company realized that a strong product development capability was essential for its survival and growth. However, it saw the essential requirements as being the ability to match user needs to product concepts and seamlessly transfer designs. It is useful to note that a single resource, however strong, is often not a good basis for strategy. The sustained performance of Hindustan Unilever Limited (HUL) is the result not only of strong brands, but also of leveraging its collective knowledge of brand management, logistics, and distribution management, and expertise and research skills of its scientists and engineers.

KNOWLEDGE MANAGEMENT AND ORGANIZATIONAL CHANGE

Organizational change raises a conflict because of its potentiality to imbalance the relationship between employers and employees. According to Kubr (1993), employees can cope with organizational change when they see the benefit and purpose in doing so. Knowledge management as a tool can reduce the resistance through identifying and analysing both the definable and indefinable parameters of individual behaviour. According to Hayek (1953), the way something is perceived depends on a process of cognitive reflection and involvement. The essential components of this process are interpretation based on personal interests and categorization, which puts the decision object into a contextual framework.

The important point is that decisions are not only defined by the result of rational choice behaviour, but also by procedural rule behaviour. This means identifying the context in which something happens and connecting the actual event with the environmental configuration. In this sense, decision-making is a holistic process of perception, interpretation, and evaluation within a framework of rules.

Chandler (1991) indicated that individual competence is configured by knowledge and motivation. Hence, knowledge has to be managed in a way that both the individual and the organization can get the benefits of synergy. Hence, knowledge management, per se, is not to motivate people but to awaken the individual motivation by nurturing an environment, which enables people to relate themselves with the organization. For individual employees, knowledge management defines individual performance through the analysis of specialization and work experience, which can be subsequently measured in terms of observed abilities, such as professional, communicative, and social competence.

When organizational change (due to the changing environment) is imperative, individual employees' knowledge becomes the critical success factor for organizations. Management of knowledge, therefore, is crucial to successfully implement changes in organizations to sustain them in a globally competitive economy.

SUMMARY

Knowledge is the fundamental basis of competition. Competing successfully on knowledge requires either aligning strategy to what the organization knows, or developing the knowledge and capabilities needed to support a desired strategy. Knowledge management practices play a very crucial role in organizational change and development. To effect successful change organizations strategically assess their knowledge resources and capabilities in order to conceptualize their knowledge strategy, so as to reduce the knowledge gaps.

Today, knowledge management as a strategy is practised globally. Knowledge management is all about people and providing them with an environment that can contribute to enhancing their existing knowledge base and help them to develop. Organizational competitive advantages ultimately rest on its knowledge resources, as it is difficult to copy. To effect organizational change, knowledge management as a technique is extensively used by organizations across the globe. To successfully bring change through knowledge management practices, organizations need to align their strategies with the current knowledge base of the people, and develop knowledge to build the capabilities of people to successfully embrace change wherever the gap exists.

KEY TERMS

Gap analysis It is the gap between what organizations must do to compete and what it is actually doing.

Knowledge analysts They collect, organize, and disseminate knowledge, usually on demand.

Knowledge engineers They convert explicit knowledge to instructions and programmes, systems, and codified applications.

Knowledge management strategy This strategy identifies the key needs and issues within the organization, and provides a framework for addressing these.

Innovative knowledge It is that knowledge that enables an organization to lead its industry and competitors, and to significantly differentiate itself from the latter. Innovative knowledge often enables a firm to change the rules of the game.

Thinking skills These skills deal with the vision of how the product or the company can be improved.

CONCEPT REVIEW QUESTIONS

1. Define knowledge management. Indicate its benefits.
2. Explain how a knowledge organization can be created.
3. Explain how knowledge management is strategically important for organizational change and development.
4. What are the important challenges faced in a knowledge management initiative? How can such barriers be overcome?
5. Give a brief outline of knowledge management initiatives in some Indian and foreign organizations.
6. Write short notes on the following:
   (a) Chief knowledge officer (CKO)
   (b) Knowledge gap analysis
   (c) Strategic knowledge management
   (d) Resource-based competitive strategy
   (e) Enablers for knowledge management practices

CRITICAL THINKING QUESTIONS

1. A consumer electronics major would like to introduce new product lines, starting a completely new vertical. The company is known for being a low-cost manufacturer of conventional CTVs in the country. Recently, it has acquired the global manufacturing facilities of the world's number one TV manufacturer. The strategy behind the acquisition is to benefit from the cost

advantage as the acquired company has world-class picture tube manufacturing facilities. The company believes that this will ensure its low-cost manufacturing identity as the picture tube is the most important and costly component in the CTV. The company has now expanded into a new product line, that is, manufacturing of desktops. The CEO firmly believes that the synergy between LCD TVs (its new product mix) and desktops will give them competitive edge over others. Explain how knowledge management strategy can help the company to position the new product.

2. Explain what knowledge management practices would be important for your organization for the expansion of knowledge process outsourcing (KPO) business.

3. Relate knowledge management with organizational change keeping in view some recent cases from the corporate world.

CASE STUDY

Organizational Change through CRM Practices—Multi-stores

Globally, organizations are focusing on customer-centric strategy as product-oriented strategy, per se, cannot help them to survive. This requires extensive use of customer relationship management (CRM). Organizational change through CRM practices can be better understood from industry practices. It is more often called relationship marketing. For any organization, focus on CRM requires consideration of three aspects, namely, applications, infrastructure, and transformation.

Realizing the importance of IT-enabled CRM packages, the FMCG major in India, Multi-stores, introduced services to bring radical changes in the overall culture of the organization.

Multi-stores introduced CRM solutions with the expectation that the organization will become more customer-focused and would be able to derive increased level of customer satisfaction and retention, with incremental effect on its sales and revenues. A review of the results, however, did not spell out the benefits. Instead, Multi-stores failed to map the requirements of the customers for new value-added products, resulting in the deteriorating sales of the existing product-mix of detergent powder. Its rivals understood such a need and were extensively engaged in new product development to come out with more value-added detergent packs, resulting in defeat. All necessary precautions had been taken to successfully implement the customized CRM solutions, retaining the best vendor. People were trained, and taught how to use data and information to draw decisional inferences, etc. With huge investment in e-CRM packages, Multi-stores now began to believe that the traditional way of collecting and compiling information through its own salespeople could have worked better and given the company, the early signal for change.

The company retained an expert to understand the real problem and suggest what actually went wrong. The analysis of the expert indicated the following lapses in the process of e-CRM implementation:

1. Before introduction of e-CRM, it did not adequately focus on the study of job descriptions; hence, the job roles were not clear to the employees.
2. Multi-stores did not pay any attention to structuring its compensation systems, giving people the signal that they could be a partner in the progress of the organization and share the incremental benefits derived from introduction of the e-CRM packages.
3. The company did not invest adequately in training programmes to develop the capabilities of the people to meet customer's needs.

Discussion Questions

1. Study the recommendations of the expert and offer your comments. What else could be done to improve the implementation of e-CRM solutions?
2. With the realization (in this case) that the traditional way of collecting information works better, please suggest a knowledge management strategy for Multi-stores.

REFERENCES

Argyris, C. (1994), *On Organizational Learning*, Blackwell, Cambridge.

Bhattacharyya, D.K. (2009), *Organizational Behaviour—Concepts and Applications*, Oxford University Press, New Delhi.

Chandler, M. (1991), 'Alternative readings of the competence performance relation', in Chandler, M. and M. Chapman (eds), *Criteria for Competence*, Lawrence Erlbaum Associates, New Jersey.

Davenport, T., S. Jarvenppa, and M. Beers (1996), 'Improving knowledge work processes', *Sloan Management Review*, Summer, pp. 53–66.

Davenport, T.H. and L. Prusak (1998), *Working Knowledge*, Harvard Business School Press, Boston.

———. (1997), *Working Knowledge: How Organizations Manage What They Know*, Harvard Business School Press, Boston.

Drucker, P.F. (1994), 'The age of social transformation', *Atlantic Monthly*, November, pp. 53–80.

Dyer, G. and B. McDonough (2001), *The State of Knowledge Management*, Communicator E Newsletter, www.distinationcrm.com/km/dcrm–km–article.asp

Gurteen, David (1999), 'Creating a knowledge sharing culture', *Knowledge Managment Magazine*, Vol. 2, Issue 5.

Hauschild, S., T. Licht, and W. Stein (2001), 'Creating a knowledge culture', *McKinsey Quarterly*, No. 4.

Hayek, F.A. (1952), *The Sensory Order: An Inquiry into the Foundations of Theoretical Psychology*, Routledge and Paul Kegan, London.

Kelley, R.E. (1985), *The Gold Collar Worker: Harnessing the Brainpower of the New Workforce*, Addison-Wesley, Reading.

Kubr, M. (1993), *How to Use and to Select Consultants*, International Labour Office, Geneva.

Larsen, J.N. (2001), Knowledge, 'Human resources and social practice: The knowledge-intensive business service firm as a distributed knowledge system, *The Services Industries Journal*, Vol. 21, pp. 81–102.

Mentzas, G. (2003), *Research Directions for Knowledge Management in e-Government, Issues and Experiences from KM in Business Settings*, Fourth International Conference on KM in Electronic Government, Rhodes, Greece, May 26–28.

Nonaka, I. and H. Takeuchi (1995), *The Knowledge Creating Company*, Oxford University Press, New York.

Penrose, E.T. (1959), *The Theory of The Growth of the Firm*, Basil Blackwell Publisher, US edition, M.E. Sharpe, Inc., White Plains, New York, 1980.

Peters, T. (1992), *Liberation Management*, Alfred A Knopf, New York.

Porter, M.E. (1980), *Competitive Strategy: Techniques for Analyzing Industries and Competitors*, Free Press, New York.

Prahalad, C.K. and G. Hamel (1990), 'The core competence of the corporation', *Harvard Business Review*, May–June, pp. 79–91.

Rastogi, P.N. (2001), 'Dynamics of knowledge management and intellectual capital', *Productivity*, January–March, pp. 559–567.

Snowden, D. (1999), 'Storytelling: An old skill in new context', *Business Information Review*, Vol. 15, Issue 1, pp. 30–37.

Stewart, T.A. (1997), *Intellectual Capital: The New Wealth of Organizations*, Double-Day Currency, New York.

Zack, M.H. (1999), 'Developing a knowledge strategy', *California Management Review*, Vol. 41, No. 3, Spring, pp. 125–145.

18 Change Management Strategies

Learning Objectives

After reading this chapter, you will be able to understand
- the definitions and concepts of change management
- the principles of change management strategy
- the philosophies of strategic change management
- the steps for strategic change management
- strategies for successful change management
- strategic organizational change in institutional framework
- the factors that decide selection of change strategies

Change Management Strategies at GAIL (India) Ltd

In 1995, the Government of India set up a strategic planning group to formulate strategies for restructuring the oil and gas sector to make the hydrocarbon sector internationally competitive. To start with, the government increased the autonomy of public sector oil and gas units. This was followed by a gradual phasing out of administered price mechanism. Such mandates from the government subsequent to globalization necessitated change in the organizational structure followed by the need to search for new business opportunities globally in order to increase market share and achieve business growth.

In addition, the hydrocarbon sector PSUs had to focus on achieving higher productivity, adopt long-term future proof strategies, redefine the organizational values and processes with a customer-centric approach, focus on innovation and knowledge management practices, and invest in technology. Along with this came the disinvestment and partial privatization in PSUs of the Government of India. All these prompted GAIL (India) Ltd to prepare for the changing scenario. The first initiative of GAIL was to align its organizational structure with the business process in the most effective and efficient manner to implement its strategic plans and missions. To do this, it had focused on these aspects:

- Prepare for economic situation in the country and global market in general
- Evaluate the changing impact of the economy on its business
- Assess the macro level business environment in the country
- Perform organizational analysis to understand the core strength, strategic strength, and opportunities versus the profitability of various businesses
- Re-engineer business processes based on identified critical success factors
- To decide on investment and disinvestment for resource optimization, productivity achievement, increased profitability, and customer's delight through improved services.

This strategic organizational change process at GAIL integrated innovation into their daily business practices. The management of GAIL also took part in fostering innovation for long-term success. More importance was placed on cross-functional innovation. GAIL became more receptive to outside ideas. With the formation of strategic business units (SBUs), it was able to develop an entrepreneurial culture within the organization and empowerment at all levels.

To GAIL, people are the heart of organizational capabilities. SBUs and the flatter organizational structure enabled it to extract the best from its people and institutionalize the spirit of entrepreneurship. It is a common syndrome in organizations that opportunities for personal growth and learning attract the best people. And the best people always seek ownership, which the organization can provide by developing an entrepreneurial culture. With more horizontal coordination and support, network in people management system can be developed. With all these, GAIL has created a culture of excellence, developed the skill of their manpower, and made them the champions of tomorrow's global oil and gas business.

INTRODUCTION

Strategy is the long-term direction and scope of an organization matching its resources to its changing environment and in particular its markets, customers, or clients, so as to meet stakeholders' expectations. Strategy defines the scope of organizational activities, matches these with the environment, allocates resources, influences operational decisions, coordinates them with the values and expectations of stakeholders, and finally provides a long-term direction. In organizations, strategies are framed at all hierarchical levels, that is, the corporate level, competitive or business level, and operational level.

Strategies for organizational change and development are framed at the top or the corporate level and cascaded to all levels down the line, as change management essentially is a top-down approach. Change agents within the organization cascade the corporate level change management strategies down the line adopting various action plans. Organizational change and development, per se, benefit the organization in terms of enhancing the capabilities of people, and improving the systems and processes, which ultimately contribute to enhancement of organizational competitive advantages.

Organizations are constantly changing either as a result of some events external to them or for planned process improvements, adoption of new technology, restructuring programmes, or even for mergers. The biggest challenge for organizations is to implement the change programme to achieve desired behavioural and cultural outcomes, and to derive certain benefits required to sustain and grow in competition. Behavioural change in organizations does not just happen, it occurs over a time period with proper direction, leadership, and setting clear goals and benefits for the key stakeholders. When all these are communicated well in a timely manner, people feel integrated with the process of change and start cooperating. To ensure successful organizational change and development, therefore, the entire process or programme needs to be managed strategically. Strategic change management requires creative planning, skilful communication, and development of coherent change programmes to drive, achieve, and sustain the real change.

DEFINITIONS AND CONCEPTS

Organizations develop various strategies to sustain in competition. Such strategies, among others, also facilitate the desired organizational change and development. Using various critical analysis tools, organizations identify key areas of change that affect their long-term success and then develop suitable action plans to enforce the change. Action plans are developed within the resource constraint.

Strategic organizational change and development, therefore, identify the strategic strengths, weaknesses, opportunities, and threats, and then develop strategies to move the organization in the desired direction. Other important tools and techniques used for strategic organizational change and development programmes are strategic planning, training and development, facilitating change implementation teams, developing change management plans, identifying metrics to measure change outcomes, harnessing tacit knowledge, applying critical analysis tools, etc. This list is not exhaustive; it involves many more tools and techniques and largely depends on the nature of change the organization intends to achieve.

The strategic organizational change and development processes integrate three critical organizational activities, namely strategic planning, performance management, and leadership development. One of the most generic organizational change processes emphasizes organizational change through competency development. Competencies are necessary for every organization and are developed through its interactions with the environment. Based on the vision and values, competencies are developed to build organizational capabilities.

The critical organizational activities mentioned earlier help to align the management and employees around a common purpose. This requires a clear vision for the future, communicating this to all, and adoption of meaningful goals. Also, such activities focus on creation of an innovative work climate and culture through which people can be motivated, and made accountable to improve their personal and team performance. It aligns structures, core processes, and leadership skills to improve the capacity of the people to deliver quality, service, and results. Strategic organizational change requires that the top management work together in a collaborative manner.

Strategic plan is a process of thinking through the current mission of the organization with due cognizance of current environmental conditions, both external and internal. Such plans, therefore, set guidelines for future decisions and results, and facilitate organizational change and development. Functional strategies guide functional actions to implement grand strategy. This provides general direction while functional strategies give managers specific guidance for accomplishing annual objectives. Functional strategies, therefore, translate grand strategy at the business level into action plans for the organization. Operating or functional managers develop such strategies taking into cognizance the organizational change and development programmes. Hence, the time horizon for such strategies may be a year or less. Grand strategies, on the other hand, are framed with a long-term perspective at the corporate level.

At the outset, formulating functional strategies at each operational level requires identification of critical success factors. For example, marketing strategies need to focus on product, price, marketplace, and market promotion. Finance strategies may focus on capital acquisition, allocation, dividend, and working capital management. Research and development (R&D) strategies focus on basic research, commercial development, time horizon, organizational fit, and basic R&D posture. R&D posture may be defensive, offensive, and innovative or development focused. Both functional and grand strategies are essential for organizational change and development.

Strategic planning is the process by which an organization envisions its future and develops the necessary procedures and operations to achieve it. The basic steps of strategic planning process include information gathering and analysis, identification of critical issues facing the organization, development of a strategic vision, mission review/revision, and development of strategic goals and strategies.

The basic reasons why organizations undertake strategic planning are to take future decisions and enforce better control over the external forces. Also strategic plans help to ensure optimum resource allocation, bring together the people, functions, units, and departments of the organization, so that the change and development programmes run on the same wavelength. Therefore, strategic plans play a very crucial role in organizational change and development programmes. A template for a strategic plan is presented in Exhibit 18.1.

Similarly, performance management is considered very crucial in organizational change and development programmes, as through this developmental function organizations can sustain in the long-run. Moreover, performance management systems provide organizations with the essential inputs to take crucial people-related decisions and also help them to align their business goals with the performance of their people. Understanding performance management systems and strategies, therefore, has now become important for managing organizational change and development programmes.

Performance management involves thinking through various facets of performance, identifying critical dimensions of performance, planning, reviewing and developing, and enhancing performance and related competencies. It is an ongoing communication process that involves both the manager and the employee in identifying and describing essential job functions and relating them to the mission and goals of the organization, developing realistic and appropriate performance standards, and giving and receiving feedback. Based on this, an organization can plan education and development opportunities for people to bring the desired change in the organization

EXHIBIT 18.1 Strategic planning process for organizational change

Develop the mission statement → Develop the vision statement → Conduct SWOT analysis → Identify issues → Prioritize the issues and craft goal statements → Identify and articulate core values → Develop action plans

Develop organizational mission and vision statements

The mission and vision statements help us to see the baseline for the organization. When the mission and vision statements are clearly articulated, members of the organization understand the purpose of the existence of the organization and also get the direction to which they want to move.

The strategic mission statement of the organization defines its purpose of existence, while the strategic vision statement espouses the value systems and the philosophy of the organization, mainly articulating the long-term perspectives.

Scan environment

Using various tools, the organization can identify and prioritize the issues affecting the growth of the business. This clarifies whether the organization is going to achieve the vision and the mission.

Along with this environmental scan, using the SWOT or even PEST analysis helps the organization to design the desired action plans to achieve the desired change in the organization.

Identify the organizations' core values, goals, objectives

With the defined goals and objectives, organizations can develop the measurable outcomes and later understand the degree of achievement through the implementation of the change management programme.

---

and to sustain it. Thus, to sustain the competitive advantage globally, organizations must not only recruit the best fit and systematically train and develop them, but also monitor their performance to track their improvement on an ongoing basis. Else, organizational change and development programmes will lose their significance.

In any work situation, when two or more people come together to work for a goal, a structure or a group develops and leadership emerges.

In the process of integration of the three critical areas mentioned earlier, namely strategic planning, performance management, and leadership, for strategic organizational change, organizations also need to consider the issues of competency development, which have now assumed criticality in any change management process. Competencies are sets of behaviours that encompass skills, knowledge, abilities, and attributes. They need to be assessed at the organizational and individual levels. Individual competencies together reinforce organizational competencies. However, there is always the possibility of major incongruence between individual and organizational competencies. Workforce planning exercises help to analyse such gaps and develop a competency model.

A competency model, when developed and documented, helps in managerial decision-making as it is well-aligned with the vision, mission, objectives, goals, and strategies of an organization. It also helps employees of an organization to understand the functional requirements and self-initiate the enrichment of their skills, knowledge, abilities, and attributes. This is independent of an organization-wide competency enrichment exercise. In organizational change and development, HRD initiatives, such as training and development, organizational development, etc. are taken to meet the gap and to sustain the change, based on the developed set of competencies and its deficiencies (ascertained through gap analysis).

Competency development programmes significantly help in skill renewal and in managing manpower redundancies. Incidentally, it is important to mention that these are two burning issues that organizations face in any change programme. Transformations in skill due to organizational and technological change occur along two tracks: (i) compositional shift, that is, structural change in occupational pattern due to creation or elimination of jobs of a given skill level, and the distribution of persons to jobs in a sectoral economy, and (ii) changes in work content (the technical nature of work and the role relations surrounding work performance). Competency development helps to manage such transformations, making people more competent.

The effectiveness of strategy-driven organizational change can be understood when all members of the organization move in the same direction. After outlining the strategic plan, it is extremely important to communicate to the people what the organization intends to achieve, particularly the mission of the organization. Crafting an attainable mission with a realistic strategic plan is considered as having accomplished half the organizational change process. A realistic strategic plan is possible when it is drawn within the ambit the existing structure, culture, and processes, ensuring a strategic fit. But this may not always be possible, particularly when organizational change takes place in response to external environmental variables. In such cases, members of the organization are taken through behavioural and attitudinal modifications to make them flexible to new forms of structure, culture, and processes. To get the best results of organizational change, all these three drivers must support the strategy.

Team building, conflict management, decision-making, problem-solving abilities, and communication are some of the human process intervention areas that can ease the implementation of organizational change. These are further reinforced by management development programmes and organizational learning. Technical or operational interventions bring changes in the production, marketing, finance, logistics, technology, etc. and require content expertise, that is, knowledge and skill specific to the function. In the organizational change process, the change agents play the role of process facilitators. They are not the content experts.

Thus, the key drivers for organizational change are strategy, structure, culture, and human processes, and all these need to be aligned in order to get the best results.

To achieve excellence in business performance and results, most organizations worldwide align their strategies with their performance management systems. Organizations have adopted strategies to achieve their defined goals and objectives.

A well-developed strategy map for any organization gives all cross sections of organizational members a sense of direction. Linking such strategies with the individual performance goals in the form of key performance areas (KPA) and key result areas (KRA) helps the organization to gain competitive advantage through the high performance level of organizational members.

Strategy-aligned PMS facilitate organizations not only to transform the people by cascading the strategic objectives but also to effectively utilize corporate strategy and get more from the people. To do this, it is important for top management in organizations to be committed and involved in the process, and to have an understanding of the organizational vision, mission, strategy, values, and life cycle. Organizations can pursue their strategy to achieve a unique edge in a competitive market by using a balanced scorecard.

Before alignment of strategies with the PMS, it is important to identify, analyse, and prioritize the core business processes and key customers. Effective analysis and definition of key customer requirements, ensure shortlisting of critical business drivers and measures, which can then be cascaded to individual employees' goals and objectives (against the identified key drivers), and a well-drawn scorecard can provide a measurement tool, using which the company can identify the gaps between their plans and execution. Thus, in any organization an effective balanced scorecard should align its strategy with its performance management systems, identifying its business process and definable customer requirements.

With the emergent need to improve performance in order to survive the onslaught of Japanese automobile majors, General Motors Europe (GME) developed a balanced scorecard encompassing all the functions and operations of the organization across all eight business units. This has strengthened its strategic performance management because it has helped all operating units across GME to focus on and understand how their performance and capabilities impact on business strategy.

PRINCIPLES OF CHANGE MANAGEMENT STRATEGY

Strategic change management is a basic skill required for managers and leaders to ensure desired change and development programmes in organizations. To master such skill-sets, managers and leaders need to follow certain principles. These principles can be applied in any change management programme to minimize the risk of failure and are as follows:

1. People working in the same organization react differently to change.
2. Through organizational change and development, it is necessary to address the common needs of all. Congruence or commonality in needs can be understood through an analysis of survey results. No change management programme can accommodate everybody's needs; hence, focus is laid on meeting the fundamental common needs.

3. Organizational change need not always benefit the people. It is more for the long-term sustainability of the organization. Hence, it is important also to point out what their loss may be to people affected by the change, making use of a 'loss curve'.
4. Expectations of the organizations need to be managed realistically
5. Fears of people need to be assuaged, showing the long-term perspectives.

Strategies applied by organizations to meet the above principles while managing change are as follows:

1. Share information with people in an open and honest manner, so that they do not nurture unrealistic expectations.
2. Develop an effective communication strategy to ensure efficient dissemination of information, so that employees need not speculate through grapevine information. This also ensures effective management of individual reaction to change.
3. Ensure that people get the opportunity to make an informed choice.
4. Ensure that people get an opportunity to express their views.
5. Focus on developing people through coaching, counselling, and information sharing, so that they can take an informed decision and truly understand their position in the loss curve.
6. Tell the people what they can do to help avoid loss. This can assuage their potential fears of organizational change.
7. Ensure good managerial practices to make it possible for employees to have informal discussions and feedback.

Strategic change management programmes require that organizations view each such programme as an independent project. This can ensure the application of all project management skills in the change process and enhance the rate of success in change management programmes.

In change management programmes, the loss curve helps to map the extent of loss, so that employees can understand the potentiality of losses and the type of initiatives they need to take, in terms of learning, knowledge management, and competency development to minimize such loss. However, in reality such situations may not always exist. Some people may be made redundant either due to their knowledge and skill obsolescence or to major compositional shift in their job nature. Hence, they may suffer loss in terms of income, job security, and working relationships. Even in such situations, they need to be informed about such losses. A typical loss curve is presented in Fig. 18.1.

There are many types of loss curve that may have to be communicated to employees. However, the common factors are to map the initial feelings of employees with respect to the change management programmes.

Communicating the real business problem to the employees and getting them to accept the reality is a great task. That is what happened in the case of Jet Airways.

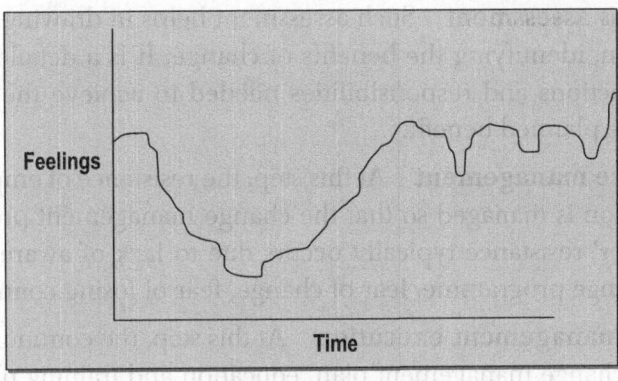

FIG. 18.1 Loss curve

Source: Adapted from http://www.teamtechnology.co.uk/changemanagement2.html, accessed on 19 July 2009.

Asking more than 1000 employees to leave and then reinstating them the next day is perhaps the type of corporate decision that does not merit any appreciation. In such a case, use of a loss curve could have helped the company to manage expectations realistically. The loss curve, as a change management tool, helps a company to deal with the fear of employees and take change decisions that may have an adverse impact on them.

PHILOSOPHIES OF STRATEGIC CHANGE MANAGEMENT

From the discussions so far we can list the philosophy of change management programmes as follows. The basic principles of strategic change management programmes mentioned earlier lies in these philosophies.

1. Strategic change management is a means to an end, and not a goal, per se. The end is improvement in organizational performance through the desired changes.
2. Strategic change management identifies and communicates the vision, allowing employees to understand their expected role to realize the desired benefits.
3. Strategic change management considers people as the greatest asset and draws the change programme accommodation, to the extent possible, towards the needs and expectations of people.

STEPS FOR STRATEGIC CHANGE MANAGEMENT

There are many strategies and techniques to support strategic change management. Such strategies exert impact on the values, attitudes, and habits of individual employees, which they demonstrate while working in the organization. Some of the steps for strategic change management are as follows:

Readiness assessment Such assessment helps in drawing up a realistic implementation plan, identifying the benefits of change. It is a detailed plan documenting the primary actions and responsibilities needed to achieve the required change and to realize the planned benefit.

Resistance management At this step, the resistance of employees at all levels of the organization is managed so that the change management programme is not affected. Employees' resistance typically occurs due to lack of awareness about the organizational change programme, fear of change, fear of losing control, and so on.

Change management execution At this step, the communication plan, implementation of change management plan, education and training plan, and active resistance management plan are drawn. The communication plan suitably draws the mechanism to communicate the change programme to the employees. Implementation of the change management plan monitors the actions to assess progress and revise the plan if required. The education and training plan aims to provide employees with the requisite skills, tools, and techniques to implement the change. The active resistance management plan provides for actively listening to and monitoring the feedback of planned changes in the process of implementation, and duly identifies the areas of resistance to suitably address them.

Change management reinforcement At this step, focus is given to sustain the change management programme. This is done through a series of activities as follows:

1. Measuring benefits to understand the results and achievements.
2. Gap identification and managing the resistance to understand the extent of unrealized benefits, so that appropriate action can be taken to meet the gaps.
3. Reinforcing change based on measurement of benefits and gap identification through new behaviours, processes, and practices.

All these steps systematically monitor the change management programme and help to identify the gaps to reinforce corrective actions to achieve the desired organizational changes. Such regular monitoring enhances the rate of success in introducing the change management programme in organizations.

SUCCESSFUL CHANGE MANAGEMENT STRATEGIES

Based on Chin and Benne (1969), certain successful change management strategies can be drawn.

Successful change management strategies rest on certain premises. The most important one is based on the assumption of empirical-rational people, who always believe in pursuing their self-interest. This change management strategy, therefore, calls for *communication of change information* to the people and offering them incentives for making the desired change happen. As they are an economic rational entity, people may put their value judgement aside and embrace change. But this strategy will only work when change programmes are attractive and do not require adopting any step prejudicial to the current interests of the employees. In reality, however, this may not always be the case. Organizational change programmes may also require altering the existing systems and procedures, which may largely affect the interests of the employees.

The second change management strategy, therefore, focuses on *balancing the incentives and risk management*. To offset the risk, organizations guard against an uncertain future with various attractive schemes, such as skill and knowledge upgradation, better career progression path, increased level of earnings, etc. Such options often encourage employees to cooperate with the change programmes.

Another change management strategy is to *make people aware of the dark aspects of the present situations or the state of affairs*. Once this aspect is clearly communicated to them and they are aware that they have limited shelf life, they make an informed choice about the change. Those who opt for change can play the role of thought leaders and influencers who persuade others to subscribe to change.

STRATEGIC ORGANIZATIONAL CHANGE IN THE INSTITUTIONAL FRAMEWORK

A resource-based view (RBV) of the organization within the institutional framework helps one's perceptions of resource characteristics, choice, determinism, and certainty within an organizational field that drives the selection of change strategies. Research indicates that organizations in the same field adopt similar change strategies. This is more because of the similarities of perceptions rather than emulating the best practices. DiMaggio (1986) suggested that the position of an organization within the same field may influence the effect of perceived variables. The possible reasons for this may be either the similar structural position of the organization or the network of ties of the organization.

Thus, perceived choice, determinism, and uncertainty are the three key variables that influence the strategic choices of the change management variables of an organization. They form the basis of the institutional framework of organizations. Organizational choices regarding strategic change options within the institutional framework, therefore, converge to certain common change approaches, as explained earlier. Integration of the resource-based view of the organizations with the institutional framework helps to better understand reasons for such convergence.

Greenwood and Hinings (1996) argued that the institutional theory suggests that firms change to align themselves with other similar organizations in their environment. Change management strategies within the institutional framework, therefore, dissuade the organization from improving its response to perceived opportunities and threats. Rather, it suggests maintaining competitive parity with organizations within the same field. Such reconfiguration facilitates the organization to change in order to sustain in competition.

Summarizing all these change management strategies, we can now tabulate them in line with Bennis, Benne, and Chin as in Table 18.1.

TABLE 18.1 Four basic strategies of change management

Strategy	Description
Rational-empirical	People are economic rational entities; hence, the organization can bring change by communicating the change information to people and offering them incentives to motivate to accept change.
Normative-re-educative	People are social beings and hence they believe in cultural norms and values. They can only subscribe to change when they feel satisfied after redefining and reinterpreting the existing norms and values.
Power-coercive	People by nature are compliant and normally do what they are told to do. Hence, organizational change is possible through the exercise of authority and the imposition of sanctions.
Environmental-adaptive	People can adapt readily to new circumstances. Hence, people can accommodate the new organizational change programme.

Practice Assignment 18.1

Manual filling of petroleum products in oil drums has now been replaced by automatic filling in one of the oil installation plants of a public sector petroleum and oil company. Such change in the process rendered around 50 technical staff members (those who used to fill petroleum products manually) surplus. Although they were all designated as technical staff members, they were in fact people who were qualified below Secondary School Learning Certificate (SSLC) and could rise to this level from the position of unskilled labour. Redeploying these surplus staff members became the most crucial issue for the company. None of them were prepared to opt for voluntary or early retirement and opposed the move to mechanize the process. As a change management expert, suggest what strategy would work in this case with justification.

SELECTION OF ORGANIZATIONAL CHANGE STRATEGY

Which strategy will work in a particular change situation is difficult to ascertain. However, leveraging the experience and emulating the practices of other organizations, managers, leaders, and agents, barring those who believe in drawing change strategies based on an institutional framework decide the strategy within the structure, culture, and the human process of the organization. In this context, therefore, it is meaningless to draw any selection guideline for framing any organizational strategy.

However, some of the factors that merit consideration before deciding the strategy-mix for organizational change can be listed as follows:

Degree of resistance Select either power-coercive or environmental-adaptive strategies when resistance is very strong. In the reverse case, that is, when resistance is weak, a combination of rational-empirical and normative re-educative strategies works better.

Target population When organizational change affects a large number of people, a mix of all four strategies can be used as it can accommodate everybody's needs and fulfil everybody's expectations.

The stakes High stakes require a mix of all four strategies as the organization cannot leave anything to chance.

The time frame When the time frame is short, that is, the change requires immediate implementation, one can use the power-coercive strategy. If a longer time frame is available, one can mix the rational-empirical, normative re-educative, and environmental-adaptive strategies.

Expertise With the availability of high change management expertise a mix of rational-empirical, normative re-educative, and environmental-adaptive strategies can be used. With less expertise, however, organizations can force the change using the power-coercive strategy.

Dependency When the degree of dependency on people is high, organizations' change abilities weaken. When such dependency is less, they strengthen. When it is a case of mutual dependence, change negotiations become more fruitful.

This is, however, a sweeping generalization of the selection of organizational change strategies. In real-life situations, it requires a more in-depth analysis using the tools mentioned earlier to diagnose the change issues and draw the intervention plans.

SUMMARY

Globally, organizations are constantly changing. This could either be because of some events external to the organization, or for planned process improvements, adoption of new technology, re-structuring programmes, or even for mergers. Strategies for organizational change and development are framed at the top or the corporate level, and cascade to all levels down the line, as change management is essentially a top-down approach. Change agents do this by adopting various action plans. The context of strategic change management can be explained with the analogy that strategies are directions that lead to the adoption of various action plans to ultimately enhance the competitive advantages of the organization.

Organizations develop various strategies to sustain in competition. Such strategies, among others, also facilitate desired organizational change and development. Using various critical analysis tools, organizations identify key areas of change that affect their long-term success and then develop suitable action plans to enforce the change. Action plans are developed within the resource constraint. Strategic organizational change and development, therefore, identify the strategic strengths, weaknesses, opportunities, and threats, and then develop strategies to move the organization in the desired direction.

Other important tools and techniques used for strategic organizational change and development programmes are strategic planning, training and development, facilitating change implementation teams, developing change management plans, identifying metrics to measure the change outcomes, harnessing the tacit knowledge, applying critical analysis tools, and analysing, the institutional framework.

KEY TERMS

Competency development For every organization, competencies are necessary and developed through its interactions with the environment.

Institutional framework It helps our perceptions of resource characteristics, choice, determinism, and certainty within an organizational field that drive the selection of change strategies.

Loss curve It facilitates in mapping the extent of loss, so that employees can understand the potentiality of losses, and the type of initiatives they need to take in terms of their learning, knowledge management, and competency development.

Readiness assessment It is a detailed plan to document the primary actions and responsibilities to achieve the required change and to realize the planned benefit.

Resistance management At this step, the resistance of employees at all levels of the organization is managed so that the change management programme does not get affected.

Strategic plans These plans are processes of thinking through the current mission of the organization with due cognizance of current environmental conditions, both external and internal.

CONCEPT REVIEW QUESTIONS

1. Explain why organizational change issue is strategically relevant.
2. Define strategic organizational change and development. What are the key drivers for strategic organizational change and development?
3. Develop a hypothetical framework for strategic planning process for an organization contemplating change from a traditional to modern technology.
4. What are the principles of change management strategy? How can adherence to such principles minimize the risk of failure in organizational change and development?
5. What are the steps involved in strategic change and development in organizations?
6. Write short notes on the following:
    (a) Strategic planning
    (b) SWOT analysis
    (c) Grand strategy
    (d) Competencies

CRITICAL THINKING QUESTIONS

1. You are playing the role of a change agent in an organization engaged in manufacturing technology-intensive lifestyle products. Your organization is now facing competition from many global players and hence contemplating major re-structuring to change the product line. Do you think such a change programme can be categorized as strategically important for your organization? Give supporting arguments.
2. Draw a strategic change management programme for your organization, which is trying to respond to change in the product line to address the demand for new lifestyle products.
3. Using the strategic planning model suggested in the chapter, draw an outline of change process, considering its implementation will be subject to acceptance by all members of the organization.

CASE STUDY

Change Management Strategy—Lessons from IBM's Study

IBM Global Business Services' change management research across the globe emphasizes improving customer satisfaction, sales and revenue growth, reducing costs, innovating processes, implementing technology, and entering new markets. IBM believes in strategic, organizational, operational, and technology-based change to survive and strive in today's competitive environment. For IBM, managing change is now a core competence.

The CEOs of companies surveyed by IBM largely believed that change is essential to survive and grow. The study revealed that despite companies' focus on continuous change, the gap between actual change capability and needed capability widens. This involves significant costs to companies. Failed change initiatives bring in budget overruns, disgruntled customers, and demoralized employees.

The IBM study reports that most CEOs consider themselves and their organizations as being largely ineffective at bringing about change. The change practitioners themselves reported the following change programme success rates:

- 41 per cent fully met objectives
- 44 per cent missed at least one objective
- 15 per cent missed all objectives or aborted

In all, 59 per cent of change initiatives failed to meet their objectives. The study reveals that the top 20 per cent organizations are successful 80 per cent of the time. Conversely, the bottom 20 per cent only manages to achieve their change objectives 8 per cent of the time. The top 20 per cent of companies are ten times more likely to lead a successful change initiative than the bottom 20 per cent.

Clearly, under-achieving organizations can draw important lessons from the top achievers. They can successfully identify the barriers to change and list the key success factors, to leverage them to achieve success. In this way, poorly performing organizations can improve their change management practices.

Some of the barriers to change identified by the IBM study are as follows:

- 58 per cent changing mindsets and attitudes
- 49 per cent corporate culture
- 35 per cent complexity is underestimated
- 33 per cent shortage of resources
- 32 per cent lack of commitment of higher management
- 20 per cent lack of change know-how
- 18 per cent lack of transparency because of missing or wrong information
- 16 per cent lack of motivation of involved employees
- 15 per cent change of process
- 12 per cent change of IT systems
- 8 per cent technology barriers

Analysis of the above factors reveals that people-related aspects account for the top three challenges, that is, four out of the top five. IBM's study suggests the following key ingredients for successful change based on the examples of top performers:

- 92 per cent top management sponsorship
- 72 per cent employee involvement
- 70 per cent honest and timely communication
- 65 per cent corporate culture that motivates and promotes change
- 55 per cent change agents (pioneers of change)
- 48 per cent change supported by culture
- 38 per cent efficient training programme
- 36 per cent adjustment of performance measures
- 33 per cent efficient organization structure
- 19 per cent monetary and non-monetary incentives

The lessons from IBM, therefore, help to develop a change management scorecard, understanding the forces for and against change. Such a scorecard helps to frame strategies that can weaken the barriers against change and strengthen the key success factors, respect and develop our own skills as a change leader, and invest in the skills development of the change team. And the core learning is that it is the people who matter most in managing change in organizations.

Source: Adapted from IBM Corporation (2008), 'Making change work study', www-935.ibm.com/services/us/gbs/bus/pdf/gbe03100-usen-03-making-change-work.pdf, accessed on 19 July 2009.

Discussion Question
From the IBM study list out the important issues of strategic organizational change and development. To what extent do you feel this study is relevant for Indian organizations?

REFERENCES

Bedeian, Arthur G. (1980), *Organizations: Theory and Analysis*, The Dryden Press, New York.

Beitler, M.A. (2005), *Strategic Organizational Learning*, Practitioner Press International, Greensboro.

Bhattacharyya, D.K. (2009), *Organizational Behaviour—Concepts and Applications*, Oxford University Press, New Delhi.

Blake, R.R. and J.S. Mouton (1964), *The Managerial Grid*, Gulf Publishing, Houston.

Champy, J. and N. Nohria (1996), *Fast Forward: The Best Ideas on Managing Business Change*, Harvard Business School Press, Boston.

Chin, Robert and Kenneth D. Benne (1969), 'General strategies for effecting changes in human systems', in Bennis, W.G., Kenneth D. Benne and Robert Chin (eds), *The Planning of Change*, Holt, Rinehart & Winston, New York.

DiMaggio, P.J. (1986), 'Structural analysis of organizational fields', in Staw, B.M. and L.L. Cummings (eds), *Research in Organizational Behaviour*, JAI Press, Greenwich, pp. 335–370.

Giddens, A. (1979), *Central Problems in Social Theory: Action, Structure, and Contradiction in Social Analysis*, University of California Press, Berkeley.

Greenwood, R. and C.R. Hinings (1996), 'Understanding radical organizational change: Bringing together the old and the new institutionalism', *Academy of Management Review*, Vol. 21, No. 4, pp. 1022–1054.

Hersy, P. and K.H. Blanchard (1993), *Management of Organizational Behaviour: Utilizing Human Resources*, Prentice Hall, Englewood Cliffs.

PART 5

Contemporary Issues in Organizational Development

- **Organizational Development and Diversity Management**
- **Organizational Transformation through Teamwork**
- **Organizational Change and Development Research**

19 Organizational Development and Diversity Management

Learning Objectives

After reading this chapter, you will be able to understand
- the definitions and concepts of diversity and organizational culture
- importance of diversity and diversity management
- cultural diversity management strategy
- the approaches to diversity
- cross-cultural diversity issues and globalization
- diversity and propensities of multinational organizations
- challenges of workforce diversity
- effective management of workforce diversity
- future corporate challenges for diversity

Barclays Bank PLC—Global Operation through Diversity Management

As part of its global expansion plan Barclays Bank PLC, adopted strategies, such as consolidation and expansion of UK banking operations, development of new international markets, development and introduction of value-added world-class products, and focus on achieving operational excellence. To globally expand business, Barclays Bank focused on its core business products, namely credit cards and loans. Accordingly, to expand the business internationally, the company went through joint ventures, acquisitions, and even organic growth. Such global business expansion brought new challenges for Barclays' HR function.

Apart from achieving stability in people management processes with focus on governance and control, the HR function also had to ensure flexibility in global and local decisions. The idea was to establish the processes, structures, and frameworks for generic guidance, but with adequate flexibility to accommodate local cultural, legal, and social issues.

Another important priority for the HR function was to develop a global mindset amongst the senior leadership team of the organization. As its business was more global, this was imperative. The company initiated a series of workshop modules to facilitate the understanding of cultures. The workshops were based on creating an extensive range of country profiles through external research and the internal knowledge pool from Barclays' employees working overseas. The workshops raised individual understanding of their own personal behaviours and the cultural challenges faced in each country. Cross-cultural training interventions and focus on language courses ultimately helped the company to add real value to its global business operations.

INTRODUCTION

Globalization, technological change, an aging workforce, and demand for new skills and education now influence the employment landscape. Today, there are people from different countries working together in an organization (ethnic diversity). Similarly, the increasing participation of women in economic activities worldwide also increased the induction of female employees. A modern approach to diversity considers different dimensions, such as race, age, religion, ethnicity, or gender, and also personality factors, work styles, and socio-economic and educational background. Any organizational change and development process, among others, requires addressing diversity issues.

Theoretical perceptions of organizations emphasize convergence issues, such as collective goals, objectives, issues, problems, and results, which require that people come together irrespective of their religion, caste, race, and gender. It is for organizations to unite such diverse entities to pursue common goals. Managing diversity requires strict conformance to the principles of uniformity. A truly diverse organization is capable of achieving efficiency and competitiveness, pooling the collective efforts of a diverse workforce. Diversity also ensures innovation. It must be carefully and constantly nurtured because creating an organization is a lot like levelling ground. Both activities create new space where the initial staffing or first species will attempt to dominate and control diversity.

The very act of establishing and staffing an organization initiates a process of limiting diversity, unless diversity is genuinely valued and vigilantly nurtured. Diversity is the attempt to bring together competing interests into a single whole. Without constant nourishment, vibrant and productive diversity will eventually fade into ineffective, unfulfilling uniformity. Organizations with high levels of uniformity are ineffective and stagnant—ultimately producing inbred corporate cultures that lack new perspectives, pioneering capabilities, and fresh ideas necessary to survive.

DEFINITIONS AND CONCEPTS

In a landmark study on 'Workforce 2020' by Richard Judy and Carol D'Amico in 1987, it was predicted that rapid technological change, globalization, demand for skills and education, an aging workforce, and greater ethnic diversification in the labour market are forever changing the employment landscape. The definition of diversity now extends beyond gender and race issues. A broader definition of diversity even includes personality and work style, and all other visible dimensions of differences in people. Even secondary influences, such as religion, socio-economic status, and education, contribute to diversity.

Often we consider diversity too narrowly and limit our focus to addressing diversity issues at the organizational level to the extent of complying with government guidelines. But strategic diversity management practices, in reality, can benefit organizations, fostering a culture of innovation and creativity. Also, gender diversity balances the workforce and is often considered important from the marketing point of view. It is for these reasons that while going for change and development, organizations need to focus on successfully addressing the diversity issues.

Gender Diversity and Modern Organizations

Gender diversity has a strategic imperative. A balanced workforce gives men and women an environment in which they feel comfortable and perform their best. The interests and ambitions of the organization and its employees coincide, and the employees' abilities match the demands the organization makes from them. Diversity is also vital for marketing and strategic reasons. The degree to which businesses, government organizations, and non-profit institutions operate effectively depends largely on how well they anticipate and respond to social changes. Leadership today requires creativity, flexibility, solid communication skills, and an understanding of the diversity and complexity that typify modern society. Management gains innovation strength when there are women in senior positions. Women can contribute to the skills, experience, and networks that are vital to today's economies based on knowledge and service. They can add crucial inputs to existing management teams, which are frequently homogeneous in nature. Investing in gender diversity is, therefore, a strategic imperative for businesses.

Organizations that appoint women to senior management positions also have access to a much larger potential workforce. The aging of the population and the persistent labour shortage means that no employer can afford to miss this opportunity. Organizations that do not make efforts to retain female employees are letting a good investment slip away. Exhibit 19.1 depicts Wipro's policy on diversity management.

DIVERSITY MANAGEMENT

As discussed earlier, diversity refers to the ways in which people differ or are similar. Diversity management includes all cross sections of people in an organization. A

EXHIBIT 19.1 Wipro and diversity management

Wipro seeks to build a climate that welcomes, celebrates, and promotes respect for the entire human race. In their commitment to diversity, they welcome people from all backgrounds and seek to include knowledge and values from various cultures. The concept and dimensions of diversity are advanced and incorporated into every aspect of the organization. Dimensions of diversity include, but are not limited to, the following: race, ethnicity, religious belief, sexual orientation, sex/gender, disability, socio-economic status, cultural orientation, national origin, and age. The implementation of the commitment to diversity rests with the organization as a whole. However, in addition to this personal commitment and involvement, they instituted a diversity committee to implement effectively the philosophy and intent of the organization with respect to diversity.

further extension to this definition of diversity management is that it is the art of capturing the diversity dividend, that is, the organizational benefits meeting the needs of diverse groups, both internal and external stakeholders. There are two main drivers of diversity management practices in organizations—the compliance aspect and the value-adding aspect. The compliance aspect is driven by legislative requirements, due diligence, fear of penalty, loss of goodwill, increase in grievances, and even negative employer branding. The value-adding aspect is driven by the need to increase competitiveness and the fear of loss due to faulty work processes.

Contextual Issues of Diversity Management

Cultural and ethnic diversity is not an autonomous demographic development. Rather, it is the manifestation of a global society. There are many aspects of contextual issues on diversity management. The first issue is obviously the social and political dynamics. The second issue pertains to the different values and behaviour of different diversity groups. The third issue is the inequities in opportunities and outcomes for their members.

A contextual approach to manage diversity is needed for several reasons. First, an organization is not a passive reflection of some broader society; it is an active social construction guided by the rules of organizational survival, and constitutes a social and cultural world of its own. Specific organizational contexts give varying meanings to differences in such general characteristics, as qualifications, cultural, and ethnic backgrounds often form the basis of social inequality.

To manage diversity problems in the workplace, it is important to have an informed idea on how the structural arrangements, cultural patterns, core business, external relations, and the strategic mission of a given organization shape such meanings and valuations. This calls for a thorough and detailed organizational analysis. It is necessary to adopt tailor-made approaches in specific organizational settings. Second, the aspect of contextual approach is to understand the status of ethnic minorities who need to be brought into the mainstream of organizational activities. Third, an inclusive approach is to be adopted with respect to diversity management. Consideration of all these will benefit the organization in terms of innovation, conflict management, problem solving, and even in gaining competitive advantages. Exhibit 19.2 depicts IBM's policy on diversity management.

STRATEGIC APPROACH TO CULTURAL DIVERSITY MANAGEMENT

Five main influences on contemporary approaches to cultural diversity management are discussed below.

General diversity management A strategic approach to diversity management in general, provides an enabling framework to deal with cultural diversity in particular.

> **EXHIBIT 19.2 Diversity management at IBM**
>
> IBM, the US-based leading IT company in the world, is always appreciated for diversity management practices. IBM's diversity management practices can be listed as follows:
> 1. Provide an understanding of diversity and its significance at the workplace.
> 2. Provide insights on how an organization can leverage diversity to gain competitive advantage.
> 3. Understand the concept of talent management and its importance.
> 4. Provide insights into how talent management initiatives can complement an organization's recruitment and retention policy.
>
> IBM is able to attract and retain talent due to its obvious focus on valuing diversity. IBM recruits people with disabilities, ensures work-life balance to value diversity, recruits women in the workplace, practises talent management, and treats diversity as a part of its business strategy.

Organizations which proactively learn from diversity and integrate the varied perspectives and ways of working in a holistic manner can fully unleash the benefits of a diverse workforce. Key organizational features contributing to the success of diversity management are openness, communication, and flexibility.

International businesses Research on managing across cultures has a major impact on our understanding of culture, and how it affects individual and organizational behaviours. National cultures have significant influence on management assumptions and on the way the business is conducted. Among other activities, business negotiation, marketing, sales, and purchasing are all facilitated through knowledge and understanding of cultural differences.

Multicultural marketplaces In the context of cultural diversity, market segments may reflect ethnic and language minorities, etc. In large diverse markets, the critical mass of minority purchasing power has also been the driving force behind this approach. Internationally, it is observed that there are clear benefits of employing immigrant workers to address the needs of the multicultural marketplace; the danger of pigeonholing individuals exists whether the target market is within the country or abroad. Strategic diversity management stresses upon the importance of looking holistically at the entire skills bundle and potential of individuals.

Human resource management (HRM) HRM has become strategically important with recognition of employees as a source of building core competence and competitive advantage. As HRM has risen to a strategic level, it brings cultural diversity management as part of its bundle of practices. Cultural diversity management interacts with other strategies, and an HRM strategy can play a key role in achieving improved productivity and innovation through effective talent management.

Globalization Globalization reflects the increased ease of mobility and communications for organizations and individuals. A positive consequence of globalization is

> **EXHIBIT 19.3   Diversity management at Domino's**
>
> Domino's Pizza's diversity philosophy is embedded in its vision. Domino's believes that workplace diversity gives it a competitive advantage. With an inclusive philosophy, the company is able to create opportunities and leverage the talents of all cross sections of employees. Some of the core diversity philosophies of the organization are as follows:
>
> 1. We demand integrity.
> 2. Our people come first.
> 3. We take great care of our customers.
> 4. We make 'perfect ten' pizzas everyday.
> 5. We operate with smart hustle and positive energy.
>
> By creating a diverse high-performance culture, the company is able to make the organization a compelling place to work in. Domino's ensures all cross sections of employees understand that diversity is beyond affirmative action and understand it as a compelling need to create value. To ensure complete adoption of diversity philosophies in day-to-day work, Domino's emphasized formalized work measures with quarterly reporting to the top management, formalized mentoring, formalized policies and procedures, and a formalized culture.
>
> *Source*: Adapted from Diversity Report and Case Studies: Research Report and Case Studies', Richard Willard, President, Management Resources International, IEA Educational Foundation, http://www.franchise.org/files/diversity.pdf, accessed on 20 July 2009.

a radically changed workforce as new skills have been imported. An example of this is Ireland, where diversity has given it the potential to be among the most innovative and dynamic places in the world to work in.

Exhibit 19.3 depicts Domino's take on diversity at the workplace.

TOOLS FOR CULTURAL DIVERSITY MANAGEMENT

Management models are means of creating a vision for organizations and of developing a strategy which is comprehensive, coordinated, purposeful, pragmatic, and integrated with other strategies. Many models start with awareness training of one's own culture as a necessary and enabling step towards understanding others. Many such tools and models have been discussed in Chapters 13, 14, and 15. Although they have been discussed in the context of organizational change and development, they are also applicable for cultural diversity management.

Productivity, Innovation, and Talent Management

Improving productivity, innovation, and talent management are economic imperatives that are intrinsically interwoven. Effective cultural diversity management contributes to the achievement of these imperatives through improved employee satisfaction, resulting in greater commitment and productivity, and higher retention rates. Work-life balance, training and development, and proper matching of immigrants' occupation

> **EXHIBIT 19.4 Diversity management at Tata Steel, India**
>
> Tata Steel recognizes that diversity in the workplace exerts a positive impact on business. To promote diversity in the workplace, the company ensures equal employment opportunities and provides training. The company's commitment to diversity can be understood from the following objectives:
>
> 1. Tata Steel will volunteer its training resources to the extent possible to improve employability of disadvantageous sections of society. The company will encourage business entrepreneurs from socially disadvantageous communities through monitoring and inclusion in the supply chain on the basis of equal merit.
> 2. Tata Steel will assist in upward mobility of talented youth from marginalized communities by increasing its access to quality higher education.
> 3. Tata Steel will report affirmative action initiatives in its annual sustainability report.

to their skills and talent, all contribute to productivity. Multicultural workplaces are more creative and innovative. Effective management of existing talent will not only increase productivity and innovation, but will also enable organizations to continue to attract more talent. Exhibit 19.4 portrays Tata Steel's policy on diversity management.

ASPECTS OF DIVERSITY MANAGEMENT

There are many aspects to human diversity management. Some of these are as follows:

- Ensuring that the correct diversities are represented in the workplace without damaging the business or breaking down team morale
- Managing an existing and diverse group of people
- Reducing racial conflicts
- Reducing cultural conflicts
- Reducing personality conflicts
- Understanding diversity
- Understanding one's self

Managing a group of diverse people is often a huge challenge. It can be very stressful and is often very challenging. The focus could be:

- Clearing conflicts
- Taking out backbiting and gossip
- Reducing stress in management and in the team
- Increasing ownership and accountability

General Diversity Management

General diversity management, which developed through anti-discrimination, affirmative action, and equality legislation as well as workplace ethics, views culture as one of the many facets of diversity, including race, ethnicity, gender, religion, age, etc. Historically, this approach developed in the US with affirmative action policies designed to overcome the dominance of white males in the workforce.

Diversity management cannot succeed in the presence of discrimination and in the context of immigration, it is necessary to ensure that the rights of the immigrant employee are not violated, that he/she is fully aware of these rights, and is capable of exercising them. However, current diversity management is not confined to such a compliance-driven or rights-based approach. Although these will be integral to its process, it takes a holistic approach to strategically use the diversity of individuals to achieve organizational and business benefits. The basic approach of diversity management lies in the fact that the workforce consists of diverse people, and diversity consists of their visible and non-visible differences. Hence, it is for the organization to harness such differences to create a congenial work environment, where everybody performs.

DIFFERENT APPROACHES TO DIVERSITY

There are three basic approaches to diversity management—a deficiency approach that makes deficits in qualifications the central issue; a discrimination approach focusing on subordination; and a differentiation approach that stresses on cultural differences.

The *deficiency approach* rests on the premise that people who are in a minority in terms of any diversity issue are a problem for the organization. The reason for this is that certain jobs require some specific knowledge and skill-sets, which these people may lack. Thus, the deficiency approach subscribes to the view that people can only join an organization when they are confident of speaking the language required and can adapt to the business logic.

The *discrimination approach* concentrates on prejudice and ethnic exclusion in enterprises. Discrimination, rather than deficiencies in qualifications, is seen as the main explanation for the marginal position of ethnic minorities. This approach, therefore, requires racism awareness programmes to enable the organization to remove inequality in the organizational structures and strategic positioning of people in important job roles, suitably developing them to take responsibilities. Cohen (1992) has formulated the 'relative autonomy rule' to fight against this approach. This rule calls for adjusting the structural forms to remove prejudices.

The *differentiation approach* to diversity management is very dominant in international organizations. The notion lies on the premise that cultural traditions bind people and hinder them in international organizations. Thus, cultural differences can be an impediment that is difficult to overcome, but can be handled with a focus on learning and training.

Whatever be the approach to diversity in an organization, the best way to manage it is through culturalization, learning, increased levels of awareness, and adoption of diversity inclusion strategy.

Business Performance and Diversity

Diversity improves performance when group members and leaders are trained to deal with group process issues, particularly those involved in communicating and problem solving in diverse teams. Presumably, HR practices for recruiting, selecting, training, motivating, and rewarding employees determine whether team members and leaders are skilled in communicating to and coordinating members of diverse teams. When HR practices support the creation of a workforce that has the skills needed to turn diversity into an advantage, diversity is more likely to lead to positive performance outcomes. In some organizations, however, HR practices may inadvertently result in teams that are diverse, but unskilled in diversity management. Such organizations are more likely to experience negative outcomes, such as disruptive conflict and increased turnover, which can harm performance.

Team-focused processes relating to building commitment and group spirit, change-focused processes relating to innovation and exploring new perspectives, and career-focused processes relating to career advancements and professional success exemplify constructive group processes.

Diversity as a Business Imperative

Issues concerning workplace diversity have generated an enormous amount of activity in organizations. Through various government actions, discriminatory employment practices based on race, colour, religion, age, disability, gender, and ethnicity have now been prohibited worldwide. With diverse workforces, organizational culture also becomes complex. Hence, organizations need to change to accommodate the principles of 'valuing diversity'. Among others, this requires focus on changing employees' attitudes and eliminating behaviours that reflect more subtle forms of discrimination and exclusion, which often inhibit effective interactions among people. To encourage employees to value the widespread physical, cultural, and interpersonal differences, many organizations now emphasize systematic training on diversity. Many authors, however, believe that such training does not lead to changes in desired attitudes and behaviour (Bezrukova and Jehn 2001). Companies, such as Hewlett-Packard (HP) acknowledged the need for valuing workplace diversity in the early 1990s.

Lew Platt, former CEO of HP acknowledged that diverse teams produce better results. However, diversity is extremely difficult to study in organizational settings because it raises sensitive, difficult-to-discuss issues. In addition, organizations are reluctant to share their experiences or data, given the legal climate and the potential for litigation. Another reason for the lack of evidence, linking workforce diversity to business performance, may be that the relationship between diversity and the bottom line is more complex.

Research on the effects of diversity within teams and small groups indicate that it can have negative as well as positive effects. Empirical literature does not support the simple notion that more diverse groups, teams, or business units necessarily perform better, feel more committed to their organizations, or experience higher levels of satisfaction. Diversity simultaneously produces more conflict, and more creativity and innovation. Creativity and innovation help organizations to come out with better products and services, which enable them to sustain and thrive in a competitive environment.

Whether diversity has a positive or negative impact on performance will depend on several aspects of an organization's strategy, culture, and HR practices. With proper facilitating conditions, diversity is associated with positive group or team processes and is, therefore, beneficial to performance, whereas under inhibiting conditions, it is associated with negative group or team processes and is, therefore, detrimental to performance.

CROSS-CULTURAL DIVERSITY ISSUES AND GLOBALIZATION

The difference in culture among different countries comes under the purview of cross-cultural diversity. Cultural diversity, however, deals with cultural differences within the nation. Cross-cultural management is effective interaction and understanding of people who represent different cultures. The way things are done in one culture may not hold good for another. Also, the same activity performed in two different cultures may carry different meanings and give different results. Hence, cross-cultural management can be defined as managing people across cultures.

In managing an organization, the cross-cultural issues must be understood and managed effectively to reap benefits. A good example is HP, which proclaims that cultural diversity gives it competitive strength, as it gets the best creative solutions and can be more innovative with divergent ideas from people across cultures. Wherever HP operates, it absorbs the local culture to reinvent management practices.

Cross-cultural Practices in the US and India

For better appreciation, let us understand some management practices in the US and India on two cultural aspects.

Right fit In the US, achievement is the only basis for promotion and reward. In India, the stress is on organizational compatibility, that is, the degree of fit between employees and the organization. When employees are the right fit for the organization, performance becomes the next criterion.

Wealth creation Another cultural construct which differentiates business and management practices between the US and India is the perceived connotation of business itself. In the US, doing business means creating wealth for the organization. Hence, hiring and firing is more prevalent not only on account of performance, but also on business failure (even in the short term). In India, however, business is not just creation of organizational wealth; it is the creation of individual wealth also.

As Indian organizations look for more organizational compatibility to get the right fit, recruitment is a process of rejection. On the contrary, for the US, companies recruitment is selection.

Cross-cultural influence on organizations due to globalization is primarily because people come from different countries with divergent cultural and administrative biases. Globalization has accentuated the pace of inter-cultural exchanges and even made it imperative for organizations to understand the diversity issues from cross-cultural perspectives. In fact, focus on diversity issues in organizations have received more attention due to increase in cross-cultural exchanges.

Traditionally, culture is understood in terms of geographical dispersion. Cross-cultural issues take culture in terms of geography, which varies from country to country and from organization to organization.

However, culture is not limited to nations. Rather, it is a unique characteristic of a social group; the values and norms shared by its members set it apart from other social groups. Culture concerns economic, political, social structure, religion, education, and language. It is the common sharing of symbols, meanings, images, rule structures, habits, values, and information processing, and even the process of organizational transformation.

Hofstede (1980) reinforced this argument stating that 'the essence of culture is the collective programming of the mind'. This dynamics of sharing as being a central element to culture is well supported by many other experts. The definition of culture could be broad, yet the operative words provide a robust framework for understanding differences among cultural groups in organizations and societies. Additionally, Hofstede (1980) indicated that culture includes values, which raises the question of what else is included. Culture is also influenced by conscious beliefs. Further, culture is also defined as the pattern of learned behaviour and encompasses many dimensions, such as nations, occupational groups, social classes, genders, races, tribes, organizations, and also social movements. Thus, globalization has further accentuated the manifestation of culture.

DIVERSITY AND PROPENSITIES OF MULTINATIONAL ORGANIZATIONS

Based on the degree of propensities, multinational organizations can either be categorized into ethnocentric, polycentric, geocentric, or regio-centric. Such propensities shape the managerial practices, attitudes, and overall business pattern of multinationals. The ethnocentric or parochial attitude of multinational organizations influences their belief that the best work approach and practices are those that they follow in their home country. On the contrary, a polycentric attitude embraces the practices of the host country, as those are the best fit for running the business in that country. A geocentric attitude emulates the best practice of global organizations, irrespective of their countries of origin. A regio-centric approach of multinationals, however, focuses on variation of HRM practices, by matching the specific norms and practices of particular geographic areas.

Managers of global organizations, therefore, must be sensitive enough to manage the diversity by keeping pace with the degree of propensities. Not only do such propensities vary with managerial practices, but also sensitize us regarding cross-cultural issues, thus making diversity management a complex process. The term 'multinational organization' is used in a more generic sense as any organization operating in multiple countries by default becomes multinational. But depending on the variation of attitudes (influenced by the above propensities), multinational companies can be multi-domestic (when they subscribe to polycentric approach), centralized (ethnocentric), or a borderless transnational (geocentric). Cultural diversity, which emerges from the variation of such propensities, therefore, becomes the most crucial issue and poses a challenge to do business in a globalized business world.

In the context of these discussions, let us now understand how HRM practices in multinationals vary. Ethnocentric and polycentric approaches are two opposing phenomena. An ethnocentric approach emphasizes global HRM strategy, and therefore, does not localize the management team. A polycentric approach, on the other hand, adopts HRM strategy that empowers the local management team.

Based on the scholarly researches of Dowling et al. (2004), the variation in HRM practices of multinational organizations with respect to the approaches can be listed as in Table 19.1.

TABLE 19.1 Various approaches and HRM practices

Type of approach	Nature of practices
Ethnocentric	Leverages the experience of the home country to standardize production; trains the employees of the host country on the organization's areas of core competency under the guidance of expatriate managers; creates a corporate culture independent of the culture of the host country.
	HRM practices differentiate between the employees of the host and home countries. The host country's employees often get demotivated, while the cultural myopia of expatriate managers fail to grab market opportunities.
	Thus, characteristically, the home country managerial practices prevail in such cultures. For such obvious reasons, key decisions are taken by the headquarters of this organization from its home country and the employees of the home country adorn the top and even middle-level managerial positions. The host country set-up becomes subsidiary and pursues the managerial practices followed at the headquarters in the home country.
Polycentric	Organizations with polycentric propensities emphasize profit maximization by embracing local managerial and business practices. The host country's pricing, production, product life cycle, and socio-economic conditions set the premise for business plans and activities of this type of organization. Even they may vary in the products and services offered, suiting the host country's market requirements. A good example is McDonald's introduction of chicken burgers in India instead of its core competent product—hamburgers. As expatriate managers are not at the helm of managerial activities, the adverse effect of cultural myopia is relatively rare in this type of organization.
	However, as subsidiaries are managed locally with local employees and heads, and with local HRM practices, synergy with the headquarters of the home country often cannot be achieved. It may even lead to corporate inertia.

Type of approach	Nature of practices
Geocentric	This type of organization applies globally integrated business strategies to manage the employees on a global basis. Strategically, these companies employ and develop HR from diverse countries. A good example is Electrolux. These employees and managers are deployed in different countries on the need basis. One major problem for this type of organization is huge investment in training and development, particularly in cross-cultural issues.
Regio-centric	This type of organization adopts policy, by keeping pace with its product and business strategies. Due to sensitivity to local conditions, this type of organization affects inter-regional transfers and achieves synergy through increased interaction between executives.

Francesco Gold (1998) documented the HRM practices in multinational organizations in line with these approaoches. Thus, depending on the degree or propensities, diversity management practices vary in multinational organizations. Managers need to first understand this aspect and then select the best approaches for managing such organizations.

CHALLENGES OF WORKFORCE DIVERSITY

Diversity is a key HR strategy. Therefore, by ensuring diversity, organizations not only comply with legislation, but are also able to select and retain talent to drive their businesses successfully. Also, a diversity inclusion strategy develops an appropriate organizational culture that fosters innovation and creativity. Such organizations understand the need of diverse consumers and develop their products and service-mix accordingly. Thus, diversity issues cannot be separated from business requirements. The future of the organization holds many challenges for all those who are involved in diversity. Hence, integration of diversity issues in every field of organizational activities truly provides opportunities to sustain competitive strength.

In an era of international networking and mobility, the social and cultural composition of communities in which people live and work is becoming increasingly diverse. This means that organizations today are confronted with a variety of individuals and groups in the labour market from where they recruit their employees, and so also have to cater to diverse consumers of their products and services.

EFFECTIVE MANAGEMENT OF WORKPLACE DIVERSITY

Dealing effectively with diversity has two important aspects: the knowledge base and the awareness of legal requirements. Some of the effective ways to manage workplace diversity are as follows:

Meticulous attention Attention should be paid to events to understand them and take appropriate actions since one cannot always witness all the events. If even the minutest discriminatory behaviour is ignored, the company may suffer at a later stage as this may culminate in low morale, conflict, legal suits, or other serious problems.

Avoiding favouritism. If for any reason someone is given a particular facility it must be based on some logical reason, else problems will occur.

No prejudices One's personal beliefs should not influence one's actions. Many contentious issues, such as race, religion, or sexual orientation, may prejudice our decisions. Such opinions may cause problems.

Being careful about the communication One should avoid the off-the-cuff remarks as these may cause ill feelings. One needs to carefully consider what is said or written. Employees mimic the way managers talk and behave, and therefore any ambiguity in communication or statements may spark their sentiments, sensitize their emotions, and even lead to some untoward incident.

Responding quickly Managers should respond to employees' concerns about workplace discrimination. It is necessary to resolve such issues at the earliest. This requires clear policy guidelines, a mechanism to gather intelligent information, and honest discussions with the person who has lodged the complaint.

Educating employees Employees should be educated about workplace discrimination. Self-education is necessary as well. Practices prevailing in industries and reports and published information should be studied to stay updated about the information.

Framing a policy document spelling out the consequences of workplace discrimination, and making it public to draw the attention of everyone in the organization as well as other stakeholders are important steps towards managing workplace diversity. A formal declaration of such policy documents in the company's website also adds tremendous value.

FUTURE CORPORATE CHALLENGES FOR DIVERSITY

In a multinational company, HR professionals are given the responsibility of hiring, retaining, motivating, and rewarding employees in different countries across the world. Ideally, an HR person who knows the local customs and cultures in different countries is most suitable for such jobs. However, it is often difficult to recruit people who have exposure in cultural diversity. In such cases, it is necessary to groom HR professionals by exposing them to different culture situations. Multinationals can do this more effectively through job rotation, but others require sustained training and knowledge reinforcement. Also, to accommodate cross-cultural diversity issues, it is necessary to adequately frame policies and guidelines which take into account culture issues.

Let us assume that a Thailand-based company wants female workers to work night shifts in India as it does in its country. This is a very culture-sensitive issue, as night shift work for female workers in India is not only culturally unsuitable but also legally not tenable, and may, therefore, pose a problem. Hence, unless there is adequate cultural compatibility, culture-specific policies and guidelines may be required. An example of Softco India in Exhibit 19.5 will further elucidate this issue.

EXHIBIT 19.5 Softco at the crossroads

This case explains the process of managing cross-cultural outsourcing and provides guidelines for effective cross-cultural interaction in a similar situation. A Bangalore-based Indian software major, Softco, had been doing business with Japan for quite sometime. The company first faced the hurdle of using Japanese, which is one of the most difficult languages to learn. Cross-cultural differences on certain other issues made it difficult for Softco employees (Indians) to adapt to the Japanese culture. Even the Japanese way of explaining the software requirements made it difficult to sign off.

The company initiated a few processes to counter this situation. It first tried to train the Indian software developers to speak Japanese, at least at the elementary level. It then tried to make them adapt to Japanese culture, and their food and drinking habits. The Japanese way of briefing their requirements is very short. It is for the people to extract more information to understand their requirements and design products accordingly. Moreover, the requirement needs vetting from top management as well as the line managers and users. The company sensitized Softco employees about the Japanese style of management and business methods. These endeavours finally paid off and global integration was achieved.

Similarly, when developing global pay strategies, companies need to address the fact that these strategies will be implemented across a broad range of different cultures. HR professionals need to ensure that the global strategy and the work culture it drives do not conflict with practices and perceptions in specific national cultures. Major global companies must recognize that policies need to be managed with the broad context of business strategy and integrated into the work culture with the support of all elements of HRM. The ultimate shape of the package of HR programmes and practices, starting from management processes to the kind of people the organization selects, is dependent on the national cultures of the various countries in which they operate.

Moreover, the company's strategy should be to have each country's operation expand within its own potential, although not necessarily within its own boundaries. From that perspective, there is no need for common HR processes or reward programmes. Each country and its own international operations do what is reasonable in terms of the local managers' perceptions. Organizations now accommodate national cultural differences while preserving work culture principles that encourage people to effectively execute the company's strategic objectives.

SUMMARY

Diversity is the experience of human differences and commonalities, and organizations globally are confronting these issues both internally (among all cross sections of employees) and externally (among customers, suppliers, etc.). Diversity management is the process of harnessing the positive potential of diversity, reassessing the organizational structures and processes, and developing awareness on diversity among people.

Diversity management practices are dealt with differently in different countries. Affirmative action, equal opportunity, gender mainstreaming, etc. are some of the alternative terms used to indicate diversity management practices.

Diversity management practices become necessary when business strategy, governmental policy, productivity, performance improvement issues, and social justice need to be converged to organizational functioning. Apart from other diversity issues, cultural diversity is now recognized as an important driving force for development and overall social upliftment. It is crucial for achieving sustainable development. By valuing cultural diversity, organizations can prevent segregation and fundamentalism, and promote innovation.

To promote cultural diversity, organizations need to reaffirm that culture is a set of spiritual, material, intellectual, and emotional features of any social group. Culture encompasses all spheres of our social life, our value systems, traditions, and beliefs. It establishes identity, social cohesion, and the development of a knowledge-based economy.

Organizations need to respect diversity of cultures through tolerance, dialogue, and cooperation. This is possible by creating a climate of mutual trust and understanding, demonstrating solidarity to other culture groups, and by developing inter-cultural exchanges. Cultural diversity widens the range of options open to everyone; it is one of the roots of development, understood not only in terms of economic growth but also as a means to achieve a more satisfactory intellectual, emotional, moral, and spiritual existence.

In this chapter, we have also discussed various dimensions of diversity with specific emphasis on cultural diversity. Also, guidelines for managing diversity have been explained with references to organizational practices.

KEY TERMS

Gender diversity at workplace This is possible through gender mainstreaming, which requires elimination of discrimination based on gender and providing equal opportunity to men and women. Only enforcing rules against gender discrimination in the workplace is not enough.

Multicultural marketplaces In the context of cultural diversity, these market segments may reflect ethnic and language minorities, etc. In large diverse markets, the critical mass of minority purchasing power has also been the driving force behind this approach in the past.

Team-focused process This relates to building commitment and group spirit, change-focused processes relating to innovation and exploring new perspectives, and career-focused processes relating to career advancements and professional success.

CONCEPT REVIEW QUESTIONS

1. Explain the concepts of diversity in the context of organizational culture.
2. What are the relations between culture and diversity? How can one ensure cultural diversity in organizations?
3. Explain the concept of diversity management. Why does an organization need cultural diversity management?
4. Discuss the approaches to workplace diversity. How do organizations address such challenges?
5. Discuss how diversity relates to the business performance of an organization.
6. Write short notes on the following:
    (a) Barriers to cultural diversity
    (b) Contextual issues of diversity management
    (c) Diversity and HR practices

CRITICAL THINKING QUESTIONS

1. United Bank of India (UBI) is a multi-locational public sector bank in India with over 5000 branches. The bank operates from its Kolkata headquarters, where board level decisions on performance management systems are taken. To ensure that its workforce reflects the communities it serves, the company aggressively recruits candidates from all backgrounds. In its overall performance measures, the bank has decided to give weightage to diversity issues. However, it is

facing the problem of data collection to assess the extent of diversity compliances at the branch levels. Please suggest to the bank some possible ways and means of collecting the required data.
2. It is alleged that diversity is not yet a high priority for India Inc. The World Economic Forum ranks India 114th out of 134 countries in the gender gap. However, with diversity inclusion strategy, India Inc. could have performed better. Identify some Indian organizations that could achieve positive results by adopting a diversity inclusion strategy.
3. What is the best way to manage the workplace diversity in an electronic assembly unit with more than 50 per cent female workforce and high cultural incongruence? Develop your answer by drawing lessons from the corporate world.

CASE STUDY

Cultural Diversity Experiences of IBM Australia and Aditya Vikram Birla Group, India

Cultural diversity, per se, provides a number of opportunities to organizations. Here, we will explain the experiences of two organizations which have successfully integrated cultural diversity with their business practices, following an inclusion strategy, and claim that they have benefited immensely.

The experience of IBM Australia and Aditya Vikram Birla Group, India, can be emulated by others to derive benefits from cultural diversity.

In 1953, IBM's CEO, Thomas J. Watson, made a statement clarifying the company's approach to diversity. Watson said, 'It is the policy of IBM to hire people who have the personality, talent, and background necessary to fill a given job, regardless of race, colour, or creed.' With such a strong foundation, IBM Australia conducted an employee opinion survey in 2001 to map how different ethnicities fared within the culture of the organization. The findings traced the impact of cultural issues between the line and staff functions. This prompted IBM Australia to develop a strategy for cultural awareness and acceptance among the employees. 'Respect for the individuals' has been adopted as the corporate value. Three pillars of IBM's diversity strategies are as follows:

- Work-life balance
- Advancement of women
- Integration of people with a disability

Through a series of programmes, including awareness sessions, the diversity team at IBM Australia were able to make employees believe that embracing diversity is more like investing in business, and hence, good commercial sense.

Under the guidance of an in-house diversity council, IBM Australia conducted a series of cultural diversity employee round tables with a focus on collection of face-to-face feedback and ideas. In this process, IBM's cultural diversity strategy raised the general level of awareness of different cultural groups within the organization. The entire process of IBM's cultural diversity programme can be summed up as follows:

1. Understand the present state of diversity issues within the organization through survey research.
2. Collect the best practices information on diversity management.
3. Identify champions at different hierarchical levels within the organization.
4. Introduce diversity management programmes involving the champions.
5. Focus on training and awareness.
6. Collect feedback both from the champions and the participating employees.
7. Collect feedback from the respective workstations of employees, to assess the extent of their diversity practices.
8. Bring changes in programmes and trainings, if required.
9. Communicate the success.

Under Mr Kumar Mangalam Birla, the Aditya Birla Group has morphed into a modern multicultural transnational with more than 72,000 people drawn from 20 different countries. To transform the organization, the group also adopted cultural diversity. Departing from the traditional perceptions of Indian business houses, for the first time it believed in a heterogeneous mix of people while going through the process of change.

Through heterogeneity, the organization improved the quality of constructive dissent and decision-making; and both these played an effective role in bringing positive changes in the organization.

The group also found that engaging people from different cultures, in fact, provides better opportunity to leverage the varied skill-sets. Similarly, the group also benefitted from the practice of cultural diversity in its business expansion plans abroad.

Source: www.ibm.com/au/en/-Australia, accessed on 20 July 2009; www.adityabirla.com, accessed on 20 July 2009.

Discussion Question

Study the experiences of both these organizations in diversity practices. Identify some other organizations and document their diversity practices, duly listing the differences in approach, if any.

REFERENCES

Abbasi, S.M. and K.W. Hollman (1991), 'Managing cultural diversity: The challenge of the 90s', *Records Management Quarterly,* Vol. 25, pp. 24–32.

Allport, G.W. (1954), *The Nature of Prejudice,* Doubleday, New York.

Amott T.L. and J. Matthaei (1991), *Race, Gender, and Work,* South End Press, Boston.

Anderson C.M. and S. Stewart (1983), *Mastering Resistance: A Practical Guide to Family Therapy,* Guilford Press, New York.

Anderson J.A. (1993), 'Thinking about diversity', *Training & Development,* Vol. 47, pp. 59–60.

Bantel, K.A. and S.E. Jackson (1989), 'Top management and innovations in banking: Does the composition of the top team make a difference?' *Strategic Management Journal,* Vol. 10 (special issue), pp. 107–124.

Castells, Manuel (1997), *The Power of Identity,* Blackwell, Oxford.

Cohen, H. (1998), 'Studying industries and their people', *Perspectives on Work,* Vol. 2, Issue 1, pp. 13–17.

Cohen, J. (1992), 'A power primer', *Psychological Bulletin,* Vol. 112, pp. 155–159.

Dowling P.J., R.S. Schuler, and D.E. Welch (1994), *International Dimensions of Human Resource Management,* Wadsworth, Belmont.

Ely, R.J. and D.A. Thomas (2001), 'Cultural diversity at work: The effects of diversity perspectives on work group process and outcomes', *Administrative Science Quarterly,* Vol. 46, pp. 229–273.

Francesco, A.M. and B.A. Gold (1998), *International Organizational Behavior,* Second Edition Prentice Hall, New Jersey.

Hofstede, Greet (1980), *Culture's Consequences: International Differences in Work-related Values,* Sage, Beverly Hills, California.

Rao, A., R. Stuart, and D. Kelleher (1999), *Gender at Work: Organization Change for Equality,* Kumarian Press, Connecticut.

Richard, Judy and Carol D'Amico (1987), *Workforce 2020,* The Hudson Institute of Indianapolis, Indianapolis.

Thomas, D. and R. Ely (1996), 'Making differences matter: A new paradigm for managing diversity', *Harvard Business Review,* September–October, pp. 79–91.

Trompenaars, F. (1993), *Riding the Waves of Culture: Understanding Cultural Diversity in Business,* Nicholas Brealey Publications, London.

http://www.nytimes.com/marketing/jobmarket/diversity/div.html (For Hudson Institutes Study on Diversity), accessed on 23 June 2009.

20 Organizational Transformation through Teamwork

Learning Objectives

After reading this chapter, you will be able to understand
- the concept and definition of team building and teamwork
- T-groups (or sensitivity training) as a team-building exercise
- role analysis as a team-building exercise
- nature, purposes, and types of teams
- team management models and RIDO scales
- productive team for organizational change and development
- measurement of team effectiveness
- team-building quiz and Belbin's team role inventory
- organizational transition through teamwork
- cross-cultural teamwork

Teamwork at Modern Pharma

Modern Pharma is in the business of formulating over the counter (OTC) lifestyle medicinal products. OTC products are sold through aggressive marketing, such as the fast moving consumer goods (FMCG) sector. The company believes that its sales position can be improved through effective teamwork. Accordingly, the company formed customer-centric teams consisting of sales, service, product development, and operations personnel, to work seamlessly to create a perfect customer experience. To make the team effective, the company also integrated inputs from other stakeholders, such as physicians, nurses, social workers, and health administrators. With all these, Modern Pharma aspired to reach excellence in achieving business results.

In the meanwhile, however, Modern Pharma faced certain issues as follows:

1. Team members were not comfortable dealing with difficult issues.
2. Teams were getting polarized, particularly in terms of their geographical location.
3. The company achieved business results, but could not deliver to its full potential.
4. Conflict and disagreement between teams were on the rise.
5. Dissatisfaction was high at the personal level due to long, stressful hours of work.

To ease the problem, the company adopted a two-pronged approach: inter-group team meetings without referring to the issues of differences and extensive coaching at the individual level to develop interpersonal relations. The approach was focused on developing a forum and language, which elicits constructive criticisms and yields positive results. This approach is quite against the conventional T-group approach, where team members are encouraged to discuss issues causing them discomfort without any binding. Modern Pharma's initial focus was to first make people adaptable to working in a team and then to exert performance results.

INTRODUCTION

Team building is the most commonly used technique for organizational change and development. It emphasizes binding people together to achieve the common goals of the organization and in the process, develop a shared vision to provide common direction to all. In simplistic terms, a team consists of a group of people who work together to accomplish some common goals. In that context, it has two common aspects: the task aspect and the people or relationship aspect. The task aspect defines the task or the job to be done or carried out, including its subsets. The people or relationship aspect focuses on interaction and working together. It includes communication, mutual responses, leadership, conflict management, etc. The task aspects can also be defined as aspects that cover the content, while people or relationship aspects focus on the process of teamwork. Teams focus primarily on the following issues:

- Intra-team task focus, that is, the content aspect
- Intra-team people focus, that is, the process aspect
- Inter-team task focus within the organization
- Inter-team people focus within the organization

According to Shaw (1981), a team represents a collection of people who interact with each other and who are interdependent, to achieve common goals. Thus, the key elements of a team are sharing common goals, interdependence, commitment, and accountability. Woodcock (1986) further elaborated the conditions for team building, and explained the nature of a team and team building. These conditions are as follows:

- Clear objectives and agreed goals
- Openness and confrontation
- Mutual support and trust
- Mutual cooperation and conflict
- Structured procedures
- Appropriate leadership
- Regular review
- Individual development
- Effective inter-group relations

Such definitions and conditions of team and team building further get expanded in the light of contributions made by Beer (1976), Argyris (1966), and Blake and Mouton (1969), who summarized the approaches to team building as follows:

- Goal-setting approach
- Interpersonal approach
- Managerial grid model
- Self-evaluation
- Perceptions about mode of functioning
- New behaviour and performance goals
- New styles of teamwork
- Individual behaviour
- Role model

Thus, team building helps organizational change and development as it eliminates many harmful interpersonal relational problems and ultimately strengthens the problem-solving abilities of people, leveraging the benefits of synergy.

TEAM BUILDING EXERCISES

At the organizational level, various team building exercises are used by focusing more on T-group and role analysis exercises. T-group or sensitivity training is an experiential learning approach. Here, a small unstructured group of people learn from their own interactions on issues pertaining to interpersonal relations. With 10–12 participants, the T-group meets with a facilitator without any specific agenda; the agenda evolves in the course of discussions. The purpose is to understand interpersonal relationship and how each of them perceives it. The group evolves like a learning laboratory as knowledge is acquired in the process of experiencing (each other), reflecting, hypothesizing, experimenting, and conceptualizing. The T-group helps essentially in two different ways:

- Understanding about self and achieving personal growth (more interpersonal focus)
- Understanding group dynamics and relationships between members

Objectives of T-group

The primary objective of the T-group is to enhance understanding about the self, gaining insights into one's own behaviour, and analysing its impact on others. One can understand how one's behaviour integrates or gels with that of others. This apart, the other objectives of the T-group in the context of organizational change and development can be enumerated as follows:

1. Enhance the understanding and awareness of group and inter-group processes.
2. Facilitate and inhibit group effectiveness.

> **EXHIBIT 20.1 Effectiveness enhancement through team interventions**
>
> The marketing team of a major FMCG organization in India introduced a day-long experiential learning programme with two objectives: understanding the individual preferences of team members and the extent of difference between individual and team preferences. The purpose was to increase the response to customers with sensitivity so that brand recall is enhanced. The programme had several modules:
>
> 1. In the first phase, the Myers-Briggs Type Indicator (MBTI) instrument was administered to the participating members electronically. The results depicted individual team member's frame of mind.
> 2. The classroom sessions emphasized on encouraging collaboration and sharing of best practices. This also helped the company to understand the individual team member's preferences.
> 3. In the next phase, team members were transferred from one team to another hypothetically to simulate the challenges faced due to the absence of the team member and to evolve possible solutions.
>
> These exercises led to an increase in accountability of team members and increased team effectiveness—a prerequisite to achieve the desired organizational change.

3. Increase greater awareness of self-behavioural processes.
4. Increase diagnostic skills in interpersonal and inter-group situations.
5. Help discover one's dominant potential, thus transforming learning into action.

Laboratory experimentation helps to develop new behaviours, which in the process help the organization bring in the desired change and develop the capabilities of people to perform. Exhibit 20.1 discusses similar interventions in an organization and their effects.

Benefits of T-group Training

As discussed previously, in organizational change and development T-group is beneficial at individual, group, and organizational levels.

Benefits at the individual level are spontaneous perceptions of behaviour with a reduced level of stress, which releases the potentiality of mental and physical health, and decreases defensive behaviour. Perceptual clarity makes people more realistic and achievement-oriented. It enhances self-esteem, and develops the capability of people to explore options and enhance the power of decision-making. People also feel motivated due to strengthening of their internal locus of control.

Interpersonal level benefits are developing insights to understand others. With enhanced self-esteem, people can comfortably communicate with each other, and become more supportive and productive in relationships. With the increase of mutual trust and respect, one can subdue aggression and develop better relationships, which pave the way for effective teamwork. The collaborative behaviour increases one's interdependence, and facilitates both individual and organizational growth through improved interpersonal relations.

Organizational level benefits of T-group training are increase in openness, trust, and interdependence, which together culminate into a conducive work environment that exerts the potential from all. With the recharged or reinforced capabilities of people, organizations can successfully manage future challenges.

ROLE ANALYSIS

Role analysis clarifies and prioritizes the role expectations from the perspective of both the role senders and the role occupiers. A role is defined as the pattern of behaviour expected from a particular job position in the organizational hierarchy. A specific job position confers a job role and the person who occupies this position is the role occupier. A job position is conferred by the organization maintaining a specific hierarchy. A role occupier works under an immediate boss who becomes the role sender and expects some specific performance and desired behaviour from him. Some of the role expectations are task, job, work, and position. Task roles are the basic job elements; job role is the component of work; work role is the expected performance standards; while positional role is the hierarchical level as per the structure of the organization, which is related to others and also to the self-role tasks expected.

From the above perspectives, therefore, a role can be differentiated from a job description. The major point of distinction is that while a job description is static and impersonal, a role is dynamic and personal. The role occupiers' personal qualities, growth, perceptions, motivations, ambitions, values, etc. are some of the major determinants of their role. Hence, despite being in the same job role, role deliverables vary from person to person.

Organizational change and development through role analysis is important as it helps in establishing clarity, in terms of expected levels of performance and behavioural inputs in the changed circumstances. The idea behind this is that in changed circumstances, organizations need to adjust the job role. Such changed expectations can be measured and communicated to role occupiers through role analysis.

Some of the important areas of role analysis are as follows:

- Detailed understanding of the coverage in terms of the function and level
- Setting up a core task force to carry out the role analysis
- Selection of persons for specific task forces
- Understanding the role sender and the changing role expectations for preparation of key performance areas (KPAs) for the role occupier
- Identification of the required set of competencies for a specific job role
- Identification of performance gaps through competency mapping and developing plans for closing the performance gaps

With all the discussed perspectives, role analysis is carried out either by engaging OD consultants or through in-house resource persons or a combination of both. Accordingly, the core task force is given the task to perform the analysis and suggest changes in the role expectations, keeping in view the required level of organizational change and development. All these need to be done within budgetary constraints in a given time frame. Simultaneously, systems, procedures, work instructions, etc. are developed or updated, and wherever necessary, powers are delegated.

NATURE, PURPOSE, AND TYPES OF TEAMS

In every organization, effective teamwork helps to attain a defined purpose and makes people feel committed, both at the individual and the collective level. This becomes possible, as team-building exercises reinforce individuals and the collective intentions of people to pursue a team purpose. The specific purpose of teams can be listed as follows:

- Building relationships
- Overcoming barriers to effective performance
- Building trust and confidence

Types of Teams

The purposes of teams mentioned earlier holds well in organizational change and development as team building often is the key to effective change. Different types of teams can be formed depending on the organizational need (for specific change requirements). For example, top management teams, commonly known as organizational teams, are formed to achieve the overall organizational objectives. Work teams are self-contained and are formed to achieve some common purpose at the specific team and individual levels. Project teams are formed to accomplish a specific task. Such teams are disbanded once the task is accomplished. Ad hoc teams are set up to troubleshoot a problem. They are short-lived and operate more like a task force.

These apart, we can also classify different types of team as follows:

Parallel team In this type of team, members are temporarily assigned some tasks to accomplish. They are selected from different functional areas and on completion of the assigned tasks, goals, or projects, they are sent back to their mother department.

Process team This type of team is formed primarily based on the test of homogeneity. Such team members collectively carry out a process, which is a part of the total system.

Hybrid team This type of team is a mixture of process, parallel, project, and full-time teams. It is formed to tackle complex organizational change and developmental issues.

Cross-functional team This type of team is represented by employees who perform different functions but try to achieve a common goal.

Determination of the type of team for a specific organizational change and development situation depends on the requirements, which are not only situation-specific but also vary with respect to time.

Team Management Wheel—A Model for Teamwork

The Margerison–McCann team management wheel depicted in Fig. 20.1 is a model which describes the team roles necessary for teams to operate at their best. Each division of the wheel is measured in terms of the RIDO scale to understand individual team management skills. Here R indicates one's power of relating to others and is measured in terms of extrovert–introvert continuum. I indicates one's ability to gather information in a practical–creative continuum. D indicates the power of making decisions in an analytical–beliefs continuum; and finally, O indicates the power of organizing one's work in a structured–flexible continuum.

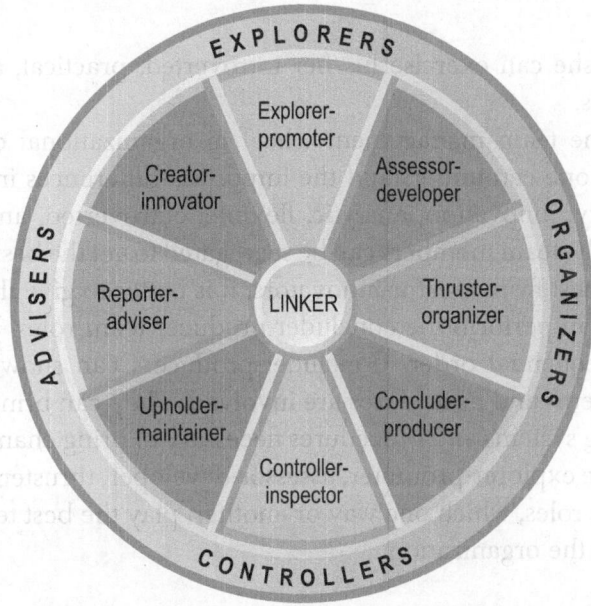

FIG. 20.1 Margerison–McCann team management wheel

A typical RIDO scale to measure the team roles appears as shown in Fig. 20.2.

All the team roles are measured using a RIDO scale in a work situation comparing them with others. One's team role preferences at work may not be the same. For example, one may look for work where one can exercise his/her 'extroverted, creative, analytical, and flexible' preferences; while another person may choose jobs

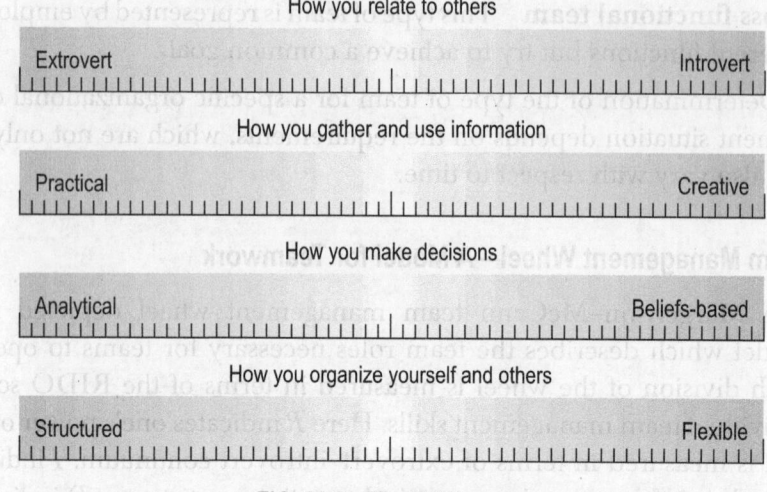

FIG. 20.2 The RIDO scale

Source: Adapted from team management systems', http://www.tms.com.au/tms12-3h.html, accessed on 9 November 2009.

where he/she can exercise his/her introverted, practical, analytical, and structured preferences.

Using the team management wheel in organizational change and development processes, one can understand the important differences in team members in terms of creativity, innovation, analytic, flexible, extroverted, and structured preferences. Accordingly, team members can be segregated to get the best from them. For example, to get the best from creator-innovators, it is better to give them the controller role so that they can perform the concluder-producer team roles, by organizing the data in the best sequential order. Concluder-producers can show high levels of creativity where systems and procedures are involved. They can bring major improvements in the existing systems and procedures necessary to bring change in the organization. So also can the explorer-promoter, assessor-developer, thruster-organizer, and upholder-maintainer roles, which one way or another, play the best team roles to bring desired changes in the organization.

Productive Team for Organizational Change and Development

Team building is an effort to work together and create a climate that encourages and values contributions from each and every team member. Through team building, organizations can harness the energies of team members for effective organizational change, which, among others, requires problem-solving abilities, task effectiveness, and maximizing the potential of each and every member. Productive team building can harness such potentials and derive the benefit of synergy from the collective efforts of people. This is subject to fulfilment of the following conditions (Francis and Young 1979):

1. There is a high degree of interdependence among the team members. Hence, for productive teamwork, it is important to exact a commitment from each team member to achieve the results.
2. The leaders of a productive team should have good people skills, strong commitment, and the attitude to invest time in team building activities. They must appreciate that team management is a shared function; hence, each team member should be given the opportunity to contribute his/her best, leveraging his/her experiences and skills.
3. Each team member must be capable and willing to contribute to information, skills, and to achieve the team purposes.
4. The team must endeavour to develop and nurture a climate of mutual trust, open communication, and a relaxed or flexible work culture.
5. The team and even its individual members must be allowed to take risks so that they can develop their abilities and skills.
6. The team must have a clear vision to set the common directions and performance targets to achieve desired change in the organization.
7. Team members' roles are defined; effective ways to solve problems and communicate are developed and supported by all team members.
8. Team members are able to examine team and individual errors and weaknesses without making personal attacks, to facilitate learning from experiences.
9. The team must ensure that team efforts are devoted to the achievement of results, and team performance is evaluated from time to time to understand the degree of fulfilment of team objectives.
10. The team must enjoy the flexibility and so also the capabilities to contribute new ideas, and translate such ideas into actions in terms of new product development, new process development, etc. Organizations must also ensure that new ideas are rewarded.
11. Team members must enjoy the power to influence the team agenda to achieve the desired results.

With all these, a truly functional productive team can significantly contribute to organizational change and development. In a true sense, team building will occur when all the team members collectively work on the task of mutual importance. Every team member should enjoy the flexibility to contribute their mite (in terms of their knowledge, skills, and experiences) to solve the impending need for change.

MEASUREMENT OF TEAM EFFECTIVENESS

From time to time, it is necessary to conduct some surveys to measure team effectiveness in the process of organizational change and development. There are many questionnaire models but their individual efficacies can only be understood while applied in specific organizational situations. Some of the common questionnaire items to measure team effectiveness are as follows:

1. Understanding how the team goals are developed. The preferred style is to decide on team goals through a group process, with adequate interaction and agreement among the team members. This process exhorts commitment from all team members to contribute their best.
2. Understanding whether all team members actively get involved in sharing their ideas. This is important to inculcate a sense of togetherness and develop a shared direction to achieve the desired level of organizational change and development.
3. Understanding whether feedback is given, and also asked for by the individual team members. This not only measures team performance but also clarifies to individual team members their weaknesses, and accordingly helps them to improve upon.
4. Understanding whether team decision-making is participative.
5. Understanding whether team leadership is distributed and shared among team members and individuals willingly contribute their resources as needed.
6. Understanding whether problem solving, discussing team issues, and critically evaluating team effectiveness are encouraged by all team members.

Similarly, several other issues, such as the process of dealing with and managing the conflict within a team, full utilization of knowledge, skills and experiences of team members, encouragement of creativity and risk-taking behaviour, etc., may be considered while framing the questionnaire items. Even so, the list is not exhaustive.

Let us now understand team-building effectiveness measurement using the most commonly used team-building quiz as shown in Exhibit 20.2. This questionnaire was administered by the author in several organizations, and the results were quite reliable as decisions based on the results yielded positive changes in the organizations.

Team-building Quiz

Change is constant in today's fast-paced world. Organizations require appropriate strategies, people, culture, and capabilities, to survive and thrive in such changing environment. Team building is one of the most effective tools for achieving the desired organizational change and development.

Belbin's Team Role Self-perception Inventory

Belbin's team role defines the behavioural pattern which characterizes one's behaviour in relation to another and helps understand what we can assess about the progress of a

EXHIBIT 20.2 Team and its effectiveness

To understand how effective team building in an organization is, we can administer the following questionnaire. The responses measure innovation, open communications, build teamwork, and strengthen the trust.

1. We have a clear vision and we understand the same.
   (a) Everyone understands (b) Most understand (c) Some understand
2. We understand our roles and our contribution to the organizational bottom line.
   (a) Everyone understands (b) Most understand (c) Some understand
3. Our teams have clear and appropriate goals.
   (a) Most of the time (b) Some of the time (c) Rarely
4. Our organization encourages free and open communication.
   (a) Most of the time (b) Some of the time (c) Rarely
5. Our organization conducts business according to a clear set of values.
   (a) Most of the time (b) Sometimes (c) Values are not articulated
6. Innovation is encouraged.
   (a) Most of the time (b) Some of the time (c) Rarely
7. We have the freedom to perform without micro-management issues.
   (a) Most of the time (b) Some of the time (c) Rarely
8. Our organization rushes to action without taking time to plan.
   (a) Rarely (b) Some of the time (c) Most of the time
9. In our team, a few people tend to dominate meetings.
   (a) Rarely (b) Some of the time (c) Most of the time
10. Our managers help us to develop our full potential.
    (a) Most of the time (b) Some of the time (c) Rarely
11. We enjoy the opportunity to handle honest, straightforward confrontation.
    (a) Most of the time (b) Some of the time (c) Rarely
12. Our team has the right mix of people and skills to achieve top performance.
    (a) Most of the time (b) Some of the time (c) Rarely
13. Our team members look forward to coming to work.
    (a) Most of the time (b) Some of the time (c) Rarely
14. Our employee attrition rate is:
    (a) Among the lowest in our industry (b) About average (c) Higher than most
15. Our organization measures the performance results.
    (a) Most of the time (b) Some of the time (c) Rarely
16. In our organization, mutual respect and trust is
    (a) High (b) Moderate (c) Low

Answer Key

Score 3 points for each (a), 1 point for each (b), and subtract 2 points for each (c) as a response.

A score of 35 or better indicates a high-performing organization, where the desired organizational change is possible with ease. A rewarding culture can further take the organization to new heights of performance.

A score of 21 to 34 indicates a competitive organization. Such organizations need to strengthen team performance with specific emphasis on training in the areas of weaknesses.

A score of 20 or less indicates serious competitive weaknesses in the organization. For such organizations, it is important that they review the mission, vision, values, and strategies, and re-draw the change plan.

team. It helps us to self-assess and accordingly make adjustments, keeping pace with the demand of a changed organizational situation. Based on their study of managerial behaviours from all over the world, Meredith Belbin and his team of researchers at Henley Management College, England, developed this psychometric tool, which encompasses different core personality traits, intellectual styles, and behaviours of leaders in nine different clusters. These team roles can be classified in the following broad categories:

- Action-oriented roles—Shaper, implementer, and completer/finisher
- People-oriented roles—Coordinator, teamworker, and resource investigator
- Cerebral roles—Plant, monitor evaluator, and specialist

In line with Belbin, these roles are explained in Exhibit 20.3.

EXHIBIT 20.3 Belbin's team role types

Belbin team-role type	Contributions	Allowable weaknesses
Plant	Creative, imaginative, unorthodox. Solves difficult problems.	Ignores incidentals. Too pre-occupied to communicate effectively.
Coordinator	Mature, confident, a good chairperson. Clarifies goals, promotes decision-making, delegates well.	Can often be seen as manipulative. Off-loads personal work.
Monitor evaluator	Sober, strategic, and discerning. Sees all options. Judges accurately.	Lacks drive and ability to inspire others.
Implementer	Disciplined, reliable, conservative, and efficient. Turns ideas into practical actions.	Somewhat inflexible. Slow to respond to new possibilities.
Completer/Finisher	Painstaking, conscientious, anxious. Searches out errors and omissions. Delivers on time.	Inclined to worry unduly. Reluctant to delegate.
Resource investigator	Extrovert, enthusiastic, communicative. Explores opportunities. Develops contacts.	Over-optimistic. Loses interest once initial enthusiasm has passed.
Shaper	Challenging, dynamic, thrives on pressure. The drive and courage to overcome obstacles.	Prone to provocation. Offends people's feelings.
Teamworker	Co-operative, mild, perceptive, and diplomatic. Listens, builds, averts friction.	Indecisive in crunch situations.
Specialist	Single-minded, self-starting, dedicated. Provides knowledge and skills in rare supply.	Contributes only on a narrow front. Dwells on technicalities.

For a detailed application of Belbin's Team Role Self-inventory, readers may refer to Bhattacharyya, D.K. (2007), *Human Resource Research Methods*, Oxford University Press, New Delhi.

For organizational change and development, it is helpful to measure or evaluate team performance using these tools so that team progress can be measured from time to time and the organization can initiate appropriate strategy to make the change plan more effective.

Adams (1987) suggested that a focused team approach helps to achieve organizational change and development. It makes the teamwork more rewarding and productive, as team members can be more proactive with clarity of their job roles. Team members can align with the organizational purpose and accomplish the job roles with adequate traceability to understand how their contributions bring the desired organizational change.

The role of team leaders is very important in bringing organizational change as they exert powerful forces to take team members forward to achieve results. For successful organizational change through teamwork, it is necessary to involve team leaders in framing vision and purpose so that they can successfully percolate these to individual team members. Also, team leaders must enjoy the power and privilege to influence the selection of team members. In the process, they can ensure that a team is selected based on their willingness, knowledge, skills, and competencies.

ORGANIZATIONAL TRANSITION THROUGH TEAMWORK

According to Beckhard and Harris (1987), organizational change involves three distinct conditions—the future, the present, and the transition states. The future state is the position that the organization wants to get to. The present state indicates where the organization currently is, and the transition state indicates the conditions and activities it requires to fulfil in order to reach the future. The process of transition begins with a desire for the future state and the direction towards which the teams should move. To survive in competition, today's organizations need to respond to the external environment and look for cost-effective ways to move towards the future to meet the changing needs of the customers. At times, with the change in technology, organizations try to achieve the desired future state. Analysis of the future and the present states can be made synonymous with the category of the unfreezing state of Lewin (1951). However, these two states are very important, as clarity in understanding them helps organizations to manage the process of transition successfully.

For better understanding of the future state the Tavistock Institute of London has developed a guideline to teamwork in manufacturing (Neumann, Holti, and Standing 1995). It identified three core performance dimensions:

1. Management of core short-term responsibilities considering the competence, individual and team motivation, personnel administration, and special competences.
2. Management of wider short-term responsibilities jointly with others through coordination with like groups, liaison with unlike groups, and setting targets for performance.

3. Managing operational process and people development through the development of organizational process, work organization, and people.

CROSS-CULTURAL TEAMWORK

Cross-cultural teamwork has now become important globally for workplace diversity. In this post globalization era, organizations are operating on a global scale, which, among others, requires hiring people from different cultural backgrounds. This is often construed as an organizational problem, as many fail to manage such workplace diversity. However, successful organizational practices can promote collaboration and innovation through cross-cultural teamwork. It is now well-established that the value systems of people belonging to different cultures vary significantly.

People with diverse cultural backgrounds nurture different attitudes towards hierarchy, achievement orientation, and perception, and in many other areas where they work with others. Also, their use of technology and approaches to time management significantly vary. As organizational change and development initiatives are now bound to keep pace with culturally diverse people, it is important to understand their process of work. Based on the industry practices, one can recommend the following approaches for effective cross-cultural teamwork:

1. One must not make any presumptions about the style of working of people representing different cultures. One needs to observe them and develop tacit knowledge to understand them and only then decide the way they work.
2. When one needs to visit any country that is culturally different, it is better to do some homework, and study that country's culture-related issues and how they influence the country's business practices. Otherwise, one will not understand the culture cues that may have some adverse impact on teamwork. This was what happened in the case of Mazda Motors of Japan when they entered the US market after acquiring a pre-existing manufacturing facility at Detroit. Setting a team goal and compelling American workers to deliver within the time frame, even when some of the team members were absent, could not be sustained, and Mazda was eventually compelled to withdraw from the US. On the contrary, Toyota and Honda, who entered the US market later, could make it a success as they integrated local culture issues with their own and created the concept of theory 'Z', blending the US and Japanese cultures.
3. It is important to understand that the countries which believe in individualist cultures may not endorse the teamwork culture in spirit. Hence, cross-cultural team members who represent individualist cultures need to be taken through the teamwork concepts and made to understand how a collective achievement could also give them individual satisfaction. It has to be emphasized that their individual contribution multiplies when they work in a team as a result of synergy, that is, 1 plus 1 is greater than 2.

4. When one communicates with a cross-cultural team, it is important to ensure that the information is clearly understood as the same words or statements have different meanings in different cultures and can be misconstrued. The best way of communicating with a cross-cultural team is to put the communicator in the role of the other person. Again, one needs to be alert in selecting the medium of communication. In many cultures, sharing information through electronic mail may not be appreciated and may even be misunderstood. Face-to-face or direct communication, though not akin to all cultures, may work better while communicating with the cross-cultural team.
5. While organizing meetings with the cross-cultural team, it is important to appreciate the language barriers; hence, the team should comprise people who understand the language, and the doubts of culturally different people should be earnestly clarified. It is important to remember that people believe in a high or low context, depending on their culture. Hence, sharing information with culturally different team members must be done accordingly. For some, understanding information contextually may not be possible. They may like information sharing in clear terms.
6. It is also important to familiarize oneself with the style of working of culturally different team members. One has to remember that every style of working has some meaning and significance. Hence, the desired style of teamwork should be drawn so that it gets acceptance from all.

Thus, cross-cultural teamwork benefits both the team members and the organization. Team members get the benefit of increasing their knowledge as they get exposed to a variety of experiences. Similarly, they can increase their interpersonal skills in the process of working with people from different cultures. Individually, they gain self-confidence and enrich themselves with valuable experiences. Organizations, on the other hand, derive the following benefits from international teamwork:

Setting a common goal for cross-border operations All members of the cross-cultural team remain focused to pursue the same goals and objectives.

Keeping pace with global changes This becomes possible with the sharing of knowledge and access to a wide range of information. Moreover, if the cross-cultural team is formed for international projects, team members also get exposure to better international level quality and processes.

Better knowledge management practices A knowledge pool provides a good international level knowledge and experience mix. Hence, cross-cultural teamwork ensures better knowledge management practices and helps the organization to develop competencies to stay competitive.

Fostering innovation and creativity It is now well established that a heterogeneous work group is more creative than a homogeneous one. This is because a heterogeneous group is exposed to a broader range of perspectives than a homogeneous one, and in the process is capable of generating a wide range of creative ideas. Also, they can better explore these ideas and translate them into innovative ways of doing things through process simplification. This may translate into innovative product designs or service offerings.

Continuous improvement Being heterogeneous, cross-cultural team members are able to explore new opportunities, by effectively utilizing their knowledge pool. In the process, they achieve continuous improvement and help the organization sustain competition.

Therefore, effective organizational change and development is also possible through cross-cultural teams.

SUMMARY

A team represents a group of people working together to achieve common organizational goals. Organizations try to achieve their goals and optimize resources through teamwork. Organizations are now shifting towards teamwork as it provides enhanced performance. To achieve effective organizational change and development, it is important to make use of teamwork strategy. However, team building is not so easy. It requires organizations to take initiatives in the right direction. People nurture different attitudes and perceptions, and accordingly behave differently in workplaces.

Individual working cannot benefit the organization to achieve the desired results. Moreover, to bring changes it may often be necessary for the organization to form cross-functional teams, to pull together the knowledge, skills, and experiences of people. Therefore, teamwork is required for organizational change and development. In this chapter, we have discussed the ways and means of team formation, suggesting a need for developing a shared vision to ensure that people get a common direction to achieve the goals of the organization.

KEY TERMS

Belbin's team roles This test defines the behavioural pattern that characterizes one's behaviour in relation to another, and understanding how one can assess the progress of a team.

Hybrid team This type of team is a mixture of process, parallel, project, and full-time teams. It is usually formed to tackle complex organizational change and development issues.

Parallel team In this type of team, members are temporarily assigned some tasks to accomplish.

They are selected from different functional areas and on completion of the assigned tasks, goals, or the projects, are sent back to their mother department.

T-group T-group or sensitivity training is an experiential learning approach. Here, a small unstructured group of people learn from their own interactions and issues pertaining to their interpersonal relations.

CONCEPT REVIEW QUESTIONS

1. Explain the concept of team building. Also discuss how it facilitates organizational change and development.
2. Discuss the role of a T-group for effective team building. How is it different from role analysis?
3. Discuss the concept of the team management wheel. How can this be interpreted using the RIDO scale?
4. Explain the concept of a productive team in the context of organizational change and development. What are the important conditions for its success?

5. Discuss the norms for measurement of team effectiveness.
6. Explain how organizational transition is possible through teamwork.
7. What is cross-cultural teamwork? Why is it important for organizational change and development?
8. Write short notes on the following:
   (a) Team leader
   (b) Belbin's team role self-inventory
   (c) Productive team
   (d) Role analysis

CRITICAL THINKING QUESTIONS

1. Leaders worldwide agree that managing organizational change and the reactions it evokes among employees are vital issues. Over two-thirds of global organizations participating in a survey commissioned by the American Management Association (AMA) acknowledged having experienced some sort of disruptive change. Individuals obviously cannot avoid change. Organizations worldwide try to ease the change process through teamwork. Your organization is going for a major change introducing the latest technology, which requires switching to Computer Numerical Control (CNC) machining centres, replacing the conventional lathe machines. Among others, this requires a major compositional shift in the skill-set of employees. Explain your action plans in the context of teamwork to achieve success in this change process.

2. We have seen instances of the success and failure of cross-cultural teamwork in the corporate world in the cases of Mazda, and Toyota and Honda in the US. In a country, such as India, where cultural diversity is very high even among people within the country, what cross-cultural teamwork model do you feel will work better? Justify your answer with corporate examples.

3. Developing a productive team for organizational change and development is the essential prerequisite for organizational success. Do you agree with this? Elucidate your answer with corporate examples.

CASE STUDY

Transforming through Teamwork—DSP, Durgapur

In a teamwork culture, it is essential for the organization to promote group dynamics so that people can largely be involved in managing discussions that pertain to achieving organizational goals. A successful transformation of the attitude of employees is a prerequisite for the success of organizational change initiatives. The positive attitude of employees cascades to the effective group dynamics and ultimately enhances the decision-making capability of people and their competency.

Having realized this, Durgapur Steel Plant (DSP), a public sector steel manufacturing unit of Steel Authority of India Limited (SAIL), promoted the culture of teamwork. The integrated steel plant, one of the largest industrial complexes in the state of West Bengal spread over an area of 6.5 sq km, employs a workforce of about 16,000 people. The plant has the rated capacity to produce 2.1 MT of hot metal, 1.9 MT of crude steel, and 1.6 MT of saleable.

With a tremendous setback in its performance in successive years, DSP had huge accumulated losses for years together. The problem increased during the first phase of economic globalization and deregulation with price decontrol mechanism, announced by the Government of India. From a privileged captive market situation, SAIL units including DSP, suddenly witnessed a sea change in the market dynamics. This required that the company quickly respond to the change, transforming the entire organization, including the attitude of employees. To promote group dynamics, at the outset SAIL emphasized on developing a shared vision, urging all its plants and employees to nurture this

> **BOX 20.1 SAIL's vision**
>
> 'To be a respected world-class corporation and the leader in Indian business in quality, productivity, profitability, and customer satisfaction.'
> The guiding principles on which the vision statement is based are as follows:
> 1. We build lasting relationships with customers based on trust and mutual benefit.
> 2. We uphold the highest ethical standards in conduct of our business.
> 3. We create and nurture a culture that supports flexibility and learning, and is proactive to change.
> 4. We chart a challenging career for employees with opportunities for advancement and rewards.
> 5. We value the opportunity and responsibility to make a meaningful difference in people's life.

and to reflect it in their day-to-day work. Box 20.1 outlines SAIL's vision.

DSP's organizational objectives are based on this vision and reflect the organizational intents in its journey towards excellence. Every employee of DSP was given the extensive message of change in the market scenario, and was systematically provided with information on the detailed, stage-by-stage change initiatives taken at the corporate level, to enable them to understand organizational preparedness to compete with the environment. Rigorous in-house training made employees understand the need for change with a positive outlook. *Kaizen* with five S, TQM, QCs, etc. reinforced their change initiatives, which among others, also helped in transforming the attitude of the employees.

Among all SAIL units, DSP today proclaims to be the most successful in reaping the advantage of transformation through attitudinal change and group dynamics. The year 2007–2008 results were as follows:

Four figure profit in 2007–2008 for the first time in its history. The plant achieved a profit before tax of Rs 1009 crore or 62 per cent more than the previous year's growth of Rs 624 crore. The plant achieved the highest ever sales turnover of Rs 5275 crore or 23 per cent higher that the previous year's figure of Rs 4288 crore. According to officials, the DSP concluded the 2007–2008 fiscal with an 'all-time best' performance in all the major areas of production, such as hot metal, crude steel, and saleable steel.

Discussion Question
In the context of the above case study, explain the role of teamwork in bringing a positive change in business results at DSP.

REFERENCES

Adams, John D. (1988), 'The role of the creative outlook in team building', *Team Building*, Reddy, W. Brendan, and Kaleel Jamison (eds.), University Associates, California.

Argyris, C. (1966), 'Interpersonal barriers to Decision-making', *Harvard Business Review*, Vol. 44, pp. 84–97.

Beckhard, R. and R.T. Harris (1987), *Organizational Transitions*, Addison-Wesley OD Series, Reading.

Beer, M. (1976), 'The technology of organization development', in Dunned, M.D. (ed.), *Handbook of Industrial and Organizational Psychology*. Rand McNally, Chicago, pp. 937–993.

Belbin, R.M. (1981), *Management Teams: Why they Succeed or Fail*, Heinemann, London.

Bhattacharyya, D.K. (2009), *Organizational Behaviour: Concepts and Applications*, Oxford University Press, New Delhi.

Bhattacharyya, D.K. (2007), *Human Resource Research Methods*, Oxford University Press, New Delhi.

Blake, R.R. and J.S. Mouton (1969, *Building a Dynamic Corporation through Grid Organization Development*, Addison Wesley, Reading.

Borrelli, G., J. Cable, and M. Higgs (1995), 'What makes teams work better?', *Team Performance Management*, Vol. 1, No. 3, pp. 28–34.

Francis, Dave and Don Young (1979), *Improving Work Groups*, University Associates Inc., California.

Higgs, M. and R. Phelps (1990), 'Does culture matter?', *Banking and Financial Training*, Vol. 6, No. 3, pp. 14–17.

Higgs, M.J. and D. Rowland (1992), 'All pigs are equal?', *Management Education and Development*, Vol. 23, No. 4, pp. 349–362.

Higgs, Malcolm (1996), 'Overcoming the problems of cultural differences to establish success for international management teams', *Team Performance Management*, Vol. 2, No. 1, pp. 36–43.

Hirschorn, L. (1984), *Beyond Mechanization*, MIT Press, Cambridge.

Hofstede, Geert (1980), *Culture's Consequences: International Differences in Work-related Values*, Sage, Newbury Park.

Lewin, K. (1951), *Field Theory in Social Science*, Harper and Row, New York.

Neumann, J.E., R. Holti, and H. Standing (1995), *Change Everything at Once*, Management Books 2000 Ltd, London.

Pareek, Udai Rao and T. Venkateshwara (1981), *Designing and Managing Human Resource Systems*, Oxford University Press, New Delhi.

Senge, P. (1990), *The Fifth Discipline*, Doubleday, New York.

Shaw, M.E. (1981), *Group Dynamics: The Psychology of Small Group Behaviour*, McGraw-Hill, New York.

Trompenaars, F. (1993), *Riding the Waves of Culture: Understanding Cultural Diversity in Business*, Economist Books, London.

Woodcock, M. (1986), *Team Development Manual*, Gower Press, Aldershot, London.

21 Organizational Change and Development Research

Learning Objectives

After reading this chapter, you will be able to understand
- organizational change and development research
- the approaches to organizational change research
- literature review for organizational change research
- model building in organizational change research
- common and standard change management research tools
- the role of organizational change and development research
- the various tools and techniques of data collection
- quantitative and qualitative change management research
- data collection and preparation for analysis
- processing and coding of data
- tools for qualitative analysis
- personality measurement

SaraIndia's Customer Feedback Analysis

To consolidate its business position in the CTV market, SaraIndia made a series of acquisitions in India and abroad, which included outright purchase of US and Korean companies and Japanese brands. Apart from SaraIndia and Korean majors in the Indian CTV market, there are some local players but they do not enjoy economy of scale and often do job work for the market leaders.

Recently, SaraIndia has experienced serious problem in counter-productive communication from customers, which resulted in customer dissatisfaction, particularly in after-sales service. Customer relationship management (CRM) for SaraIndia is handled by a local outsourced vendor. SaraIndia systematically collects CRM data and tries to do serious research investigation to ascertain the market pulse. Based on the latest information inputs, it retained the services of professional image developers and developed a customer satisfaction index. The recent rating is abysmally poor; it is 2 on a 5-point scale. While benchmarking this information with competitors (mostly Korean majors), it realized that it was in a very bad shape.

The marketing team of SaraIndia attributes this to mishandling of customer calls by the outsourced CRM service provider. However, it cannot withdraw this service provider as it is a business interest in it, in terms of equity participation. Preliminary investigation into the problems of communication indicated the following aspects:

1. Customer care executives cannot handle stressful circumstances, particularly when customers are very harsh and allege poor quality. Many customers have also complained

that quite often they get information which is contradictory.
2. Customer care executives have emulated the communication habits of their managers who always focus on the quantitative target achievement of subordinates, such as effective reduction of talking time per call received, handling of more calls within a given time, reducing the queuing problem, that is, putting calls on hold, etc. At times, managers are too harsh if customer care executives fail to deliver as per the target plan.
3. Customer care executives lack adequate product information and fail to extend online help to solve minor problems.

INTRODUCTION

Organizational change refers to the process by which organizations move from the present state to a desired future state in order to increase their effectiveness. According to Kanter (1991), change may be viewed in terms of alteration in the activities and tasks of an organization. Today's organizations survive only by changing continuously. We have already learnt that organizational change and development programmes can be either autonomous or induced. Organizations undertake autonomous changes on their own volition. This is called voluntary internal change initiatives. However, there are some change initiatives that organizations are forced to adopt. These are primarily because of changes in the external environment.

Although such change issues have been discussed in the preceding chapters, we will consider them briefly once again to set the pace of discussions in this chapter. External forces of organizational change are government regulations, degree of competition, new perceptions and attitudes of people, technology, change in political environment and government, change in demographics of the population, global economic change, advancements in communication and transportation, and many other issues over which an organization has little or no control.

For example, many public sector banks in India have delayed their responses to provide technology-intensive customer services, namely computerized banking facilities, Internet banking, electronic fund transfer, credit and debit cards, etc. As a result, they have experienced a customer shift, that is, losing the business of customers. Similarly, FMCG companies are now focusing on new lifestyle products ranging from deodorants to male fairness creams, to chewing gums. Today, a chewing gum perceptively gives confidence, as people believe that it gives freedom from bad breath.

Similarly, internal factors also influence change in an organization. As a routine measure, organizations may require to review and change their policies on compensation, employees' discipline, promotional decisions, performance standards setting, measurement criteria, etc. Organizations may also need to make changes in their structure, processes, and managerial practices. For example, many organizations now convert their individual product line or product mix into strategic or independent business units, by breaking away from their traditional hierarchical functional or divisional structure.

Some of the potential targets for organizational change, irrespective of the nature of internal or external drivers are (i) the structure of the organization, (ii) behaviour and attitude of the people, (iii) change in technology, and (iv) change in product and services. All these areas directly relate to organizational performance. Hence, ineffective changes may ultimately harm the organization. Thus, whatever be the causal factors of change, any change initiative must be supported by an adequate research backup, not just to diagnose the problems that may develop in the process of change, but also to select appropriate intervention tools.

CHANGE MANAGEMENT RESEARCH

Research is a scientific endeavour. It explores unknown facts and applications of theory from which we build knowledge and decide on its practical applications. Organizational change research helps to develop relevant approaches for successful management of change in organizations through the process of identification, critical examination, generalization, and dissemination of useful practical experiences. Like any other research, therefore, it too is a rigorous scientific activity. It is a systematic development and acquisition of knowledge and is tailored to specific change management needs to answer specific questions within a given time frame. It is now a subject of study to understand how organizations are structured and how they function, the practices of decision-making, the factors that affect organizational operations, and the strategies that contribute to the enhancement of strategic advantage of an organization.

Deriving Causal Connections

Organizational change research reveals causal connections between variables, that is, to demonstrate one variable as a cause of another. When such a causal relationship is established, one can control the 'effect' (caused) variable to achieve intended goals and objectives. Such control may be to change the causal variable, for example, eliminate or strengthen it. This apart, management research is sometimes carried out for descriptive purposes also. However, the results of descriptive research are rarely of great interest. For example, a manager may wonder why the cost of some operations is higher in one unit than in another and may collect data relevant to analyse this further. If this can be determined, he/she may be able to intervene and reduce the excess cost, bringing desirable changes in the operation.

Globally, the failure rate of organizational change and development initiatives is very high. This is primarily attributed to the failure of the organization to carry out well-planned and systematic assessments through collection and compilation of accurate data. This requires sustained research efforts with adequate knowledge on the tools and techniques of organizational research. In carrying out organizational change and development research, the research focus can be either on quantitative or qualitative assessment. Quantitative research focuses on measurement, categorization, and summarization of a situation, using numbers and labels. Qualitative research, on the other hand, focuses on informal descriptive analysis of the situation, not necessarily quantifying the results.

Process Support through Research

Research helps to carry out the process of organizational change and development, to accurately track the problems, and then design strategies for its implementation. Some issues may be measured in quantitative terms, using certain standard scales, for example, values, beliefs, and the attitude of people towards the change. However, certain issues, such as sense of commitment, level of participation in the change process, etc. can be measured better in qualitative terms. Some change issues can be measured just by observation, while others require administration of structured questionnaires.

Implementation Help through Research

Research is particularly important to carry out a planned organizational change. These are directed with certain unintentional biases, as the choice of methods is influenced by preconceived notions and values. These ultimately lead to the failure of organizational change and to guard against these, it is necessary not to prejudice the change plans with personal feelings and biases but determine it through research-based assessment of the situation. For example, a particular change agent may feel that structuring an organization based on strategic business unit (SBU) percepts, that is, on product line concept, helps to introduce the intended change plan. This is based on an unfounded truth, as in a given situation, it may not yield results; instead, it may deteriorate the change process. It is for this reason that one requires a change plan backed by research.

Organizational development has strategic imperatives, and systematic research on organizational development using various intervention tools and models helps an organization to achieve excellence. Intervention tools and models have been discussed in earlier chapters. One of the important issues in organizational change and development is personality research. Understanding individual personalities helps the organization to get the right fit, by matching with the requirements of the organization.

Effective change management research is the product of several processes. At the outset, it is important to understand the organizational issues, diagnose them with respect to the change impact both at the individual employee and at the organization level, and then frame a strategic change management programme for effective intervention and results. All these aspects including the use of various tools and models, have been intensively discussed in the previous chapters. Hence, in this chapter the discussion will centre around various other quantitative and qualitative change management research tools and techniques, with greater emphasis on the usage of statistical tools, questionnaire framing, response analysis, etc.

DIFFERENT APPROACHES TO ORGANIZATIONAL CHANGE RESEARCH

While the process of management follows a typical structure, approaches may be different and vary from situation to situation. They may be purely academic or theoretical or action-oriented. But what approach is appropriate for a given situation largely depends on the specific needs of a researcher. Five types of management research are popular. These are as follows:

Pure basic This research intends to develop a basic discipline by resolving, illuminating, and exemplifying a theoretical issue. Therefore, its basic purpose is to enhance knowledge and understanding. The results of such research become the source of knowledge for practising managers. Most of the core management concepts have developed from pure basic research.

Objective This research focuses on how to overcome a general problem in the application of an established knowledge. It is, however, not intended to solve a specific management problem. To conduct such research, the researcher frames certain clear objectives and hypotheses, and then tests the validity of established knowledge in a given situation.

Evaluative In contrast, this research assesses some aspects of the organizational function by analysing the effectiveness of a given problem, such as the effects of performance-linked pay over fixed pay on workers' motivation, the effects on change in organizational culture in post and pre-merger situations, etc. This type of research is most common in organizations as it helps practising managers to develop 'scientific neutrality' to look into some issues and devise a framework for future management.

Applied This type of research is more specific to solving a particular problem within an organization by application of appropriate knowledge. To illustrate, existing knowledge on leadership may be applied to identify the most appropriate style for knowledge workers, suitably changing the existing style in an organization. Since it is more specific to solving a given organizational problem, it is often alleged that such research does not add to existing knowledge. However, others may emulate the experience of one organization as 'best practice management' concepts.

Action In this research, action (i.e., solution of a problem) is both an outcome and a part of the research process. Its main purpose is to improve the stock of knowledge by tackling a problem, which has relevance to theory. However, as the researcher in such a case changes the research during the process, it is often alleged that the outcome cannot be replicated and this puts a constraint on testing the validity of the research in another situation. Thus, it may prevent development of general knowledge.

LITERATURE REVIEW FOR ORGANIZATIONAL CHANGE RESEARCH

A literature review is a summary of previous research on a particular topic. Literature reviews can be part of a larger report of a research project, a thesis, or a bibliographic essay that is published separately in a scholarly journal. Literature review is undertaken to understand the research problem better. One also tries to find any knowledge gap, degree of agreement on the topic, past debates, problems identified in the past, the current status of research on the topic, etc.

In organizational change and development research, literature review helps to collect information inputs from various secondary or published sources. It also helps the organization to access the documented best practices of world-class organizations. The purpose of a literature review is to convey the knowledge and ideas that have been established on a topic, and their strengths and weaknesses. It allows one to remain up-to-date regarding the state of research in the field, and familiarizes one with any contrasting perspectives and viewpoints on the topic, if any. Box 21.1 gives the uses of a literature review.

BOX 21.1 Need for literature review

Before starting a research, a literature review is always desirable for the following reasons:
- See what has been and has not been investigated
- Develop general explanation for observed variations in a behaviour or phenomenon
- Identify potential relationships between concepts and to identify researchable hypotheses
- Learn how others have defined and measured key concepts
- Identify data sources that other researches have used
- Develop alternative research projects
- Discover how an organizational change research project is related to the work of others

---

MODEL BUILDING IN ORGANIZATIONAL CHANGE RESEARCH

In management research, it is important to build models to represent cause, effect, and other relationships. A model is basically a dynamic framework or scheme to portray the key concepts, propositions, etc. of a theory. It is a representation of a process or a system, and shows the most important variables in the system in such a way that analysing it leads to insights into the system. However, it must be understood that a model is not an explanation; it is only the structure or functions of some aspect of a system, or the system as a whole. It may be highly conceptual or theoretical (theory itself being a model), developed at the start of a research and then tested through the process of data gathering, analysis, and reasoning.

A model can also be the end result of a research (in cases where there may be a weak conceptual framework at the beginning of the research). Model building is a sophisticated process. A researcher has to leverage his/her research findings to develop a model. Description, explication, and simulation are the three major functions of modelling. Quite often, computers and advanced statistical tools are used to develop the model.

Various types of models are used in management research:

Verbal/Written/Descriptive/Physical These models are categorized under one group because of their commonality to explain the situation by scaling down to a manageable limit. Verbal/Written/Descriptive models explain a situation in words (e.g., the behaviour of elements in a system), while physical models explain a situation by a physical replica, duly scaling down a machine or a structure. Physical models are also known as iconic models.

Explicative These models extend the application of well-developed theories or improve one's understanding of key concepts.

Schematic These models are shown by charts, graphics, maps of routings, network diagrams, etc.

Mathematical These models show functional relationships among different variables using mathematical symbols and equations. In management, the most commonly used mathematical models are as follows:

- Optimization models, which help to analyse problems and suggest solutions
- Heuristics models, which are some established decision-making procedures to solve a problem

COMMON CHANGE MANAGEMENT RESEARCH TOOLS

Common research tools for organizational change and management are primarily those that are used as intervention tools, such as observation, online questionnaires, action research, etc.

Observation as Tool

Observation is used to track the frequency counts of desirable or undesirable behavioural syndromes of people, particularly in teamwork, meetings, training sessions, focused group interviews, etc. For the purpose of research, the roles and desired behaviours need to be listed, and the number of times the undesired behaviour occurs has to be tallied. It is important to remember that items for observation or the behavioural attributes need to be compatible with the hierarchical levels of the people that are being observed. In a virtual environment, it is better to have two observers, to ensure more than one source of data. This helps to validate the observations. Observational research helps to determine the appropriate intervention tools based on a validated listing of attributes.

Online Questionnaire

This is synonymous with the paper and pencil test, barring its method of administration. It is administered online and can be customized, based on the requirements of the virtual team. The advantage of an online questionnaire is that it can be administered to a large population and ensures a wide reach. However, for a unitary organization to effect change and development, this may not be suitable as it requires proximity to the people affected by the change.

Action Research

The various steps (nine in all) in action research are entry, start-up and contracting, assessment and diagnosis, feedback, action planning, intervention, evaluation, adoption, and separation.

Action research for organizational change has been discussed in detail in Chapter 13.

STANDARD RESEARCH TOOLS FOR ORGANIZATIONAL CHANGE AND DEVELOPMENT

Apart from the common change management research tools mentioned, various psychometric tools are often used to supplement research. Reliable and validated psychometric tools can effectively contribute to change management research. However, selection of such tools largely depends on the change agents. Analysis of the results of these tools is not always easy. It requires skill and experience of the person who administers it. A few selected standard research tools are mentioned here.

Myers-Briggs Type Indicator (MBTI) Assessment

The Myers-Briggs type indicator (MBTI) assessment is based on Carl Jung's theory of psychological types, and is the most widely administered and researched personality assessment tool in use today Jung (1971). The MBTI assessment is based on the theory that we all have inborn preferences in the way we gather information, make decisions, energize, and orient ourselves to the outer world. Through the use of forced choice questions, the MBTI assessment identifies an individual's personality preferences across four dichotomous scales.

Strength Deployment Inventory (SDI)

Based on the relationship awareness theory, the strength deployment inventory (SDI) focuses on describing the different values that motivate relationships and interactions with others. The SDI is unique in its ability to describe different approaches to conflict, as it reveals preferred styles both when things are going well and in different stages of conflict.

Klein Group Instrument (KGI)

This is a self-administering tool designed to explore the specific kinds of leadership, negotiation, task, and interpersonal skills needed to be successful in today's team-driven workplaces. KGI assists people in defining, assessing, and developing both leadership and team membership skills. It is a Class A instrument that anyone can purchase and administer.

Pearson-Marr Archetype Indicator (PMAI)

Archetypes denote recurring stories, patterns, or forms, which shape our experiences and attach meaning to the context of our life. Based on Jung's concept of archetypes, PMAI may be defined as a well-researched assessment tool that provides a practical way to measure the presence of archetypes in individuals. Some of these archetypes may not match with our life experiences; however, it is considered as one of the best instruments for a complete understanding of the human potential.

Leadership Spectrum Profile (LSP)

The LSP is designed to assess a leader's priorities encountered along an organization or project life cycle. Thus, during the organizational change process the LSP outlines a results-driven framework that reflects the different demands that teams and leaders face when implementing any initiative. It also provides a practical way to influence the chain of command to gain the project support.

FIRO-B (Fundamental Interpersonal Relations Orientation-behaviour) Assessment

Schutz (1966) developed this instrument to help understand how we can manage our behaviour as a leader, recognize the sources of conflict, stagnation, and acknowledge the contributions of all members of the organization. There are people who may like to work in a team and those who may not. FIRO-B assesses three interpersonal needs, that is, inclusion, control, and affection, in expressed and wanted terms. People with expressed interpersonal needs are those who initiate the behaviour, while those with wanted interpersonal needs prefer to be recipients of the behaviour.

Thomas–Kilmann Conflict Mode Instrument (TKI)

Thomas–Kilmann conflict mode instrument (TKI) identifies a person's approach to conflict. The different conflict styles are derived from two independent variables: assertiveness and cooperativeness.

Work Environment Scales (WES)

This tool focuses on developing diagnostic metrics across a broad range of workplace and team dynamics. It is a quantitative survey with 90 questions across 10 scales in three major categories. It gathers data in two dimensions: the real state and the ideal state.

ROLE OF ORGANIZATIONAL CHANGE AND DEVELOPMENT RESEARCH

Organizational change research has now become important for a number of reasons. First, for the organization to remain competitive, it has to keep pace with the external change cues. Second, to achieve excellence, it needs to enforce changes, more in the nature of internal changes, in the processes, systems, structures, etc. The basic model for organizational change research is as follows:

- Conduct research to understand the source of the problem.
- Construct a feasible plan for solving the problem.
- Implement the plan and evaluate results.

Basic organizational change research helps to understand the relationship between various variables. For example, in designing a suitable compensation structure, it may be necessary to understand the teamwork and its linkage with performance. Therefore, to take proper decisions, organizational change practitioners must learn how to read and evaluate the results of such research. Thus, knowledge on basic organizational change research is extremely important for today's organizations. While this helps to understand the interrelationship between various variables, the applied organizational change research helps to solve an immediate problem (i.e., tackling the reasons for certain phenomena and then finding the solution for them).

Front-line managers also play a very crucial role in organizational change research. They perform various tasks, such as the following:

- Employee management
- Management of operational costs
- Allocate work
- Monitor work progress
- Coaching
- Performance evaluation
- Discipline and grievance handling
- Recruitment and selection

Organizations can ensure a work-life balance by leveraging all the roles of line managers. Involving them in applied organizational change research benefits an organization in many ways due to its proximity to employees. Exhibit 21.1 discusses how OD practices at Rockwell helped achieve organizational goals.

EXHIBIT 21.1 OD practices at Rockwell

Aggressive competition, demanding customers, new technologies, global markets, and the global meltdown were all putting unprecedented pressure on Rockwell International, a California-based organization specializing in space shuttle modification. Rockwell is a technology-intensive,

(Contd)

(Exhibit 21.1 contd)

knowledge-driven company and executes high-end projects for space stations. As a part of its business project, the company undertook a $60 million modification of the Atlantis Orbiter. For Rockwell, every such project is client-specific and requires customized expertise.

With technological excellence and high-end scientific expertise, the company undertook the project, embracing organizational development practices. OD practices emphasized on developing the capabilities of people and unleashing their potentialities. The need for customers' service, on-time delivery, and unparalleled quality level were some of the thrust areas for the organization that were so skilfully embedded in the minds of the people. Ultimately, this led to Rockwell's success in executing the site modification plans of Atlantis Orbiter much ahead of its schedule. The company managed the entire project spending much less than budgeted with no expenditure on overtime.

Perhaps the most stupendous achievement was the optimization of manpower. Rockwell achieved success in this project with only 20 per cent of manpower than its previous level. By transforming people, the company improved customer relations, introduced self-directed work teams, and trained employees in team skills and so on. However, in the process of transformation, the company did receive enthusiastic support of the workers' union.

In the entire process of OD implementation, Rockwell followed certain steps, such as gaining commitment from top leadership, charting the process keeping pace with the mission and purpose, and allocating resources for this. Along with these, Rockwell also developed a transparent communications plan to keep employees updated with the changing process. This helped the employees to develop a customized design and align it with the culture of high performance to achieve business results.

UNDERSTANDING ORGANIZATIONAL CHANGE RESEARCH TOOLS AND TECHNIQUES

To conduct research on organizational change issues, it is essential to understand various tools and techniques of data collection and its analysis. Organizational change research can follow either quantitative or qualitative paradigms or even a mix of both.

Quantitative Paradigm

Quantitative research is descriptive. Corelational, causal, comparative, and experimental researches are covered under quantitative organizational change research. This requires collection of numerical data to explain, predict, and control phenomena. Analysis of quantitative organizational change research requires statistical knowledge.

Quantitative data collection methods require random sampling and structured data collection instruments to fit the samples into predetermined response categories, and produce results for subsequent summarization, comparison, and generalization. Quantitative research requires framing and testing hypotheses for correct estimation of the phenomenon of interest. Hypotheses are pre-assumptions and are derived from existing theories on the research premises. Based on the research issue, samples can be randomly subjected to different treatments to draw inferences. Where this is not possible, the researcher may collect data on sample characteristics and other situational variables, and statistically analyse the influence on the dependent or outcome variable. The researcher employs probability sampling to select the samples, if the observations are required to hold good for the population (for the whole organization).

Typical quantitative data gathering strategies include the following:

- Experimental/clinical trials
- Observing and recording events
- Obtaining relevant data from ERP/MIS
- Administering surveys with structured closed-ended questions, etc.

Qualitative Paradigm

Qualitative data collection methods play an important role in impact evaluation and assessing changes in employees' perceptions. Qualitative methods can also be used to improve the quality of quantitative evaluations by generating hypothesis and clarifying quantitative evaluation results. Qualitative research includes historical research. It collects narrative data to understand phenomena by verbal synthesis. These methods will have the following attributes:

1. It is open-ended and less structured. As it is flexible, researchers can change the data collection strategy to suit the research purpose.
2. It is primarily based on interactive interviews; thus, to clarify a concept and ensure reliability of the data, the same respondents may be interviewed several times for a particular issue.
3. Qualitative research also helps to check the authenticity of the evaluations as the researcher, being flexible, can make use of multiple data collection methods. Thus, it enhances the credibility of the evaluations.
4. Qualitative research findings have limited scope for generalization. Each research produces unique results, which the researcher uses to understand a general pattern.

Irrespective of the data collection method, qualitative research is time-consuming. The researcher applying this method needs to make use of any potential sources, such as field notes, projective instruments, such as sketches, audiotapes, and photographs conforming to ethical principles of research.

Types of quantitative researches

There are various types of quantitative research. The organization has to select a particular type keeping in view its specific requirements.

Descriptive Descriptive research involves data collection and testing of hypothesis to determine and report the current phenomena. For example, if employee satisfaction level has to be measured, the researcher has to collect employee's responses on a structured questionnaire and then analyse the hypothesis to draw inferences on the degree of satisfaction or dissatisfaction.

Correlation Correlation research determines the degree of relationship between two or more quantifiable variables using a correlation coefficient (which varies between 0 and 1). However, it should not be construed as a tool to establish cause–effect relationship, which one often tries to infer through correlation research. For example, one may want to measure the correlation coefficient between the incentives value and performance output of employees.

Causal-comparative Causal-comparative research establishes the cause–effect relationship, comparing two relationships. However, in this research, one cannot manipulate the cause. For example, if a cause–effect relationship between the number of women employees and absenteeism is to be established, the gender (i.e., cause) cannot be manipulated, but the effect (absenteeism) certainly can, by extending some organizational support to women employees (such as crèches, flexible working hours, etc.).

Experimental In experimental research, the cause–effect relationship is established by comparison, and in this, the cause can be manipulated. Here, cause, that is, the independent variable, makes the difference and the effect is dependent on the cause. In the earlier case, if the organization decides to change its policy on recruitment of female employees (cause) to contain absenteeism (effect variable), then it is called experimental research.

Ethical considerations in quantitative research

There are three major ethical considerations as follows:

1. The subjects should not be harmed in any way (physically or mentally) in the name of scientific research. If an experiment involves any risk to the subjects, they should be completely informed about the nature of the risk and permission for participation in the experiment should be acquired from them in writing or from persons legally responsible for them.
2. The subject's privacy should be strictly maintained. Individual scores should never be reported or made public.
3. Ethical principle in the conduct of research with human participants is the most definitive source of ethical guidelines for a researcher. It is prepared and published by the American Psychological Association (APA) thus: '...with respect and concern for the dignity and welfare of the people who participate, and with cognizance of federal and state regulations and professional standards governing the conduct of research with human participants.' This is out of 'respect and concern for the dignity and welfare of the people who participate'.

Conducting quantitative research

Before conducting a quantitative organizational change research, it is essential to understand the following aspects:

Drawing a research plan A research plan should be developed much before the research starts. This becomes the blueprint for the research and helps to give guidance for the research and its evaluation. The components of a specific research plan are introduction, method, data analysis, time schedule and budget.

Introduction Here, the problem is introduced by developing a suitable statement. For doing so, it is important to focus on the relevance of the problem (i.e., selling the problem). Existing literature is also reviewed to establish the research premise, and the introduction part ends with a statement of hypothesis.

Method In this part, one explains how the research is carried out, by detailing the subjects (samples), instruments, and the research design.

Data analysis Here one mentions how the collected responses, observations, etc. are analysed using various statistical tools and techniques.

Time schedule This sets the deadline for completion of the research and also lists various activities involved in various phases of a research. It also ensures control at different stages. Time-bound research is every essential particularly in organizations, as most organizational change-related researches are intended to adopt strategic decisions.

Budget For organizational change research, it is important to draw a tentative budget detailing all the expenses involved and obtain approval to ensure that the research pursuit is not affected at any stage due to paucity of fund allocation.

There are three major ways to collect quantitative data: (i) administrate a standardized instrument, (ii) administrate a self-developed instrument, and (iii) record naturally available data. Standardized instruments may include existing validated instruments such as FIRO-B, Belbin team role self-perception inventory, change management, survey of Rosabeth Moss Kanter, etc. Self-developed instruments are designed by the researcher to address the research problem, while naturally available data may be performance records, absenteeism data, etc.

VALIDITY AND RELIABILITY

Whatever may be the ways of data collection, it is always desirable to test validity and reliability.

Validity is the degree to which a test measures what it intends to and, thus, allows appropriate interpretation of results. A test measure is designed keeping in view the specific purposes; therefore, validity can be evaluated only in terms of test purpose. For example, one may be interested to know how the measures on samples hold well on population on a specific issue, or how the scores predict success of a future task, or how a particular instrument measures a characteristic. These are examples of content, predictive, and construct validity. These apart, there is also concurrent validity.

Reliability measures the dependability or trustworthiness of an assessment instrument. It is the degree to which a test consistently measures whatever it intends to measure. The three aspects of reliability are equivalence, stability, and internal consistency.

Reliability is expressed numerically in terms of a coefficient. A high coefficient indicates high reliability, and this in turn indicates minimum error variance. Reliability is easier than assessment of validity. Test-retest, equivalent-forms, and split-half reliability are all determined through correlation. Test-retest reliability is the degree to which scores are consistent over time. Reliability can also be expressed in terms of the standard error of measurement (degree of variance), which is an estimate of how often one can expect errors of a given size.

A small standard error of measurement indicates high reliability and a large standard error of measurement indicates low reliability. How employees' performance scores are affected by the presence of an organizational change audit team, which do not relate to the characteristic, is measured by test-retest reliability. Similarly, in a multi-rating system, how different raters score employees' performance is determined by scorer reliability or inter-rater reliability. How the different parts of a single assessment instrument lead to similar conclusions about employees' achievement is measured by internal consistency reliability.

DATA TYPES AND PREPARATION FOR ANALYSIS

Different kinds of data results represent different scales of measurement. There are four types of measurement scales—nominal, ordinal, interval, and ratio. It is important to know which type of scale or data is collected for the research and which statistics are appropriate for data analysis.

Scaling Techniques

While doing research, it is often necessary to collect responses from the samples. The nature of responses largely depends on the type of scale used by the researcher. Respondents communicate their feelings, attitudes, opinions, and evaluations in some measurable form. Developing a proper scale helps us to measure the responses. Each scale has unique properties. Some scales can only establish an association between variables but are limited in their mathematical properties. Other scales have more extensive mathematical properties and some can also hold out the possibility of establishing cause and effect relationships between variables.

The various types of scales used in research fall into two broad categories: comparative and non-comparative. In comparative scaling, the respondent is asked to compare one brand or product with another. In non-comparative scaling, respondents need only evaluate a single product or brand. Non-comparative scaling is frequently referred to as monadic scaling and is the more widely used scale in commercial marketing research studies. There are four levels of measurement, namely nominal, ordinal, interval, and ratio.

Nominal scale

A nominal scale represents the lowest level of measurement. Such a scale classifies persons or objects into two or more categories. In other words, nominal data are those that are based on classification and categorization. When a nominal scale is used, the data simply indicates how many subjects there are in each category. Thus, this scale classifies individuals, companies, products, brands, or other entities into categories without any order. Hence, this scale is often referred to as a categorical scale. It simply counts the frequency of the cases assigned to the various categories.

An example of a nominal scale is depicted in Table 21.1.

TABLE 21.1   Nominal scale ratings

Q. What type of organizational change will you resist? (Please tick)		
Participative change	Change without alteration of present benefits	Change which enhances the learning opportunities
	Change which strengthens the future of the organization	Change which improves the quality of life

These numbers have no arithmetic properties and the only measure is the mode. This is because by using this scale, one simply tries to get a set of frequency counts. Testing of hypothesis can be done based on these data in the nominal form.

Ordinal scales

An ordinal scale puts the subjects in order from the highest to the lowest and from the most to the least. Although ordinal scales indicate that some subjects are higher or better than others, they do not indicate how much higher or better. Ordinal scales, therefore, involve ranking along the continuum of the characteristic being scaled. For example, we may ask the respondents to rank the desired change endeavours in their organization in order of their preference.

An example of an ordinal scale is depicted in Table 21.2.

TABLE 21.2   Ordinal scale rankings

Order of preference	Change mode
1	Participative change
2	Discussed change
3	Change without alteration of present benefits
4	Change which strengthens future of the organization
5	Change which enhances the learning opportunities
6	Change which improves the quality of life

This table gives the researcher the order of preference but does not provide any information about how much more one type of change is preferred to another. This is called the interval between any two methods of change. In addition to the information that is made available through a nominal scale by using an ordinal scale, one can compute the median, quartile, and percentile.

Interval scales

An interval scale has all the characteristics of a nominal and ordinal scale. In addition, it is based upon predetermined equal intervals. Most of the tests used in educational research, such as achievement tests, aptitude tests, and intelligence tests, represent interval scales. Interval scales, however, do not have a true zero point. They typically have an arbitrary maximum score and an arbitrary minimum score, or zero point. If an IQ test produces scores ranging from 0 to 200, a score of 0 does not indicate the absence of intelligence, nor does a score of 200 indicate possession of the ultimate intelligence. Interval scales may be either numeric or semantic.

Examples of interval scales in numeric and semantic formats are depicted in Table 21.3.

TABLE 21.3   Interval scale formats

Please indicate your views on organizational change methods by scoring them on a scale of 5 down to 1 (that is, 5 = Excellent; 1 = Poor) on each of the criteria listed.						
When change is						Circle the appropriate score on each line
Participative	5	4	3	2	1	
Discussed	5	4	3	2	1	
Do not alter the present benefits	5	4	3	2	1	
Strengthens the future of the organization	5	4	3	2	1	
Enhances the learning opportunities	5	4	3	2	1	
Improves the quality of life	5	4	3	2	1	

Or

Please indicate your views by ticking the appropriate responses below:					
When change is	Excellent	Very good	Good	Fair	Poor
Participative					
Discussed					
Do not alter the present benefits					
Strengthens the future of the organization					
Enhances the learning opportunities					
Improves the quality of life					

Ratio scales

A ratio scale represents the highest and most precise level of measurement. A ratio scale has all the advantages of the other types of scales as well as a meaningful, true zero point. Height, weight, time, distance, and speed are some of the examples. The highest level of measurement is a ratio scale. This has the properties of an interval scale together with a fixed origin or zero point. Examples of variables which are ratio-scaled include weights, lengths, and times. Ratio scales permit the researcher to compare both differences in scores and the relative magnitude of scores. For instance, the difference between 5 and 10 minutes is the same as that between 10 and 15 minutes, and 10 minutes is twice as long as 5 minutes.

Other Types of Scale

There are several other types of scale, which are commonly used in research on organizational change and development. These are discussed below.

Semantic scales

This type of scale makes extensive use of words rather than numbers. Respondents describe their feelings about the products or brands on scales with semantic labels. When bipolar adjectives are used at the end points of the scales, they are called semantic differential scales.

Likert scales

A Likert scale is also called a summated instrument scale (see Table 21.4). This means that the items that make up a Likert scale are summed upto produce a total score. In fact, a Likert scale is a composite of itemized scales. Typically, each scale item will have 5 categories with scale values ranging from –2 to +2 with 0 as neutral responses.

TABLE 21.4 The Likert scale

When change is	Strongly agree	Agree	Neither	Disagree	Strongly disagree
Participative	1	2	3	4	5
Discussed	1	2	3	4	5
Do not alter the present benefits	1	2	3	4	5
Strengthens the future of the organization	1	2	3	4	5
Enhances the learning opportunities	1	2	3	4	5
Improves the quality of life					

Most organizational change researchers treat Likert scales as yielding interval data. These apart, there are other types of scales, such as the Thurstone scale.

Thurstone scale

It is the first major technique of attitude measurement. Its basic assumptions are as follows:

1. Attitudes lie along an evaluative continuum ranging from favourable to unfavourable.
2. Ordering of attitude statements should be such that there appears to be an equal distance between adjacent statements on the continuum, that is, judgements can be made about the degree of discrepancy among different people's attitudes.

Likert's summated rating scale

A summated rating scale is a set of attitude statements of which all are considered or approximated as equal attitude value and to each of which subjects respond with a degree of agreement or disagreement (intensity) carrying different scores. These scores are summed up and averaged to yield an individual's attitude score. Under this method, each respondent's ranking is arrived at by totalling his/her scores on all the statements (usually 5).

This is illustrated in Table 21.5.

TABLE 21.5 Sample summated rating scale

Sl No.	Statement	Agree	Disagree
1.	Advertising promotes sales	1	0
2.	Organizational change is exploitation of people	1	0
3.	Hard work increases productivity	1	0
4.	Effective time management reduces idle hours	1	0
5.	Money and other physical benefits are the only motivations	1	0

Likert's item analysis

In this procedure, respondents are asked to respond to a certain number of statements (which is usually restricted to 15). The reply to each statement is given in terms of five degrees of agreement or disagreement, namely 'Strongly agree', 'Agree', 'Undecided', 'Disagree', and 'Strongly disagree'. Each statement thus becomes a scale in itself, having five points on it. At one end of this scale is strong approval, and at the other is strong disapproval; between these, there are many intermediate points. The respondent indicates where he/she stands on this scale with reference to each statement. The total of his/her scores on all statements is taken as the measurement of his/her attitude. A statement may be either favourable or unfavourable. Values given for favourable statements are 5, 4, 3, 2, 1, and for unfavourable statements, they are 1, 2, 3, 4, 5.

The examples in Table 21.6 will illustrate this.

TABLE 21.6 Sample item analysis

Statement	SA	A	U	D	SD
Management is a science	5	4	3	2	1
Management is not a science	1	2	3	4	5

Thurstone's equal appearing intervals scale

This scale attempts to represent the attitudes of a group on a specified issue in the form of frequency distribution. The various opinions or items on a scale are allocated to different positions in accordance with the attitudes they express. The following steps are necessary to construct a Thurstone attitude scale:

1. Brief statements expressing attitudes about a particular issue are gathered from current literatures or are especially prepared for this purpose. The statements should cover different ranges of attitudes from extremely favourable to extremely unfavourable and also include neutral statements.
2. Statements are given an arbitrary number for identification and a group of judges are asked to sort those into several piles.
3. After sorting, a complete tabulation is made to determine the number of times each statement is included in the several piles.
4. The scale values for each statement are determined graphically in the form of an ogive or cumulative frequency curve.
5. The final scale is then made, selecting 15 to 20 statements (preferably those on which judges have had least disagreement).
6. Respondents then are asked to check only those statements with which they agree.

As the construction of this scale is very cumbersome and time-consuming, it is usually avoided. Moreover, scale values assigned to statements are influenced by the attitudes, background, and intelligence of judges who may see things different from the actual respondents. This scale also does not allow subjects to express the intensity of their feelings as they have only the choice to indicate their agreement with the finally selected statements.

Guttman's cumulative scale

This scale is made up of a relatively small number of statements which have been tested for their uni-dimensionality. A uni-dimensional scale measures only one variable. The scale is known as cumulative, as respondents agreeing with the most favourable statements are theoretically presumed to agree with all other statements expressing a 'lesser' degree of favourability. Use of this scale is also avoided due to its complexity.

Another scale for measuring attitude is the social distance technique of Bogardus, which is normally used to measure highly subjective attitudes.

PROCESSING AND CODING OF DATA

For scoring, administered instruments are consistently and accurately measured following the same procedures and criteria as in each subject's test. There must be more than one scorer for a reliability check except in the case of objective type items. For such items, correctness and accuracy of the score must be ensured. Coding requires developing a system of data identification for subsequent analysis. This is important when a large number of subjects and variables have to be managed. All data regarding variables and subjects are converted into numerical values and then entered into a selected database programme for subsequent manipulations. Essentially, coding is required for analysis of data using computerized research packages as software protocols may not permit long entries.

Various statistical packages, such as SPSS, SAS, WINKS, and STATISCA 7, can be used for organizational change research.

Making Use of Collected Data

After collection of data, it is important for the organizational change researcher to understand how to make use of it. The univariate analysis technique is used to analyse data involving a single variable. This analysis focuses on the level (average) and distribution (variance) of the phenomena. Bivariate analysis on the contrary helps to examine the relationship between two or more variables. Statistical tools, such as chi-square, correlation, rank correlation, regression analysis, and analysis of variance, are used for bivariate analysis. Multivariate analysis, on the other hand, examines simultaneous relationships among three or more phenomena. Multiple linear regression, non-linear regression, and discriminant analysis are some of the tools used for multivariate analysis. At a fairly advanced level, multivariate analysis makes use of factor analysis, cluster analysis, canonical analysis, conjoint measurement, and latent structure analysis. Once the research survey is over, the organizational change researcher has to organize and summarize the data, and the best way to do that is by constructing a frequency distribution table. The process starts by recording the number of times a particular value of a variable occurs. Let us look at an example of the performance scores of 10 executives in Exhibit 21.2.

Next we may want to look at how close or far the results are from the centre. This calls for the measures of central tendency and measures of dispersion.

Measurers of Central Tendency

There are three ways to measure the central tendency:

- Mean
- Mode
- Median

EXHIBIT 21.2 Calculation of scores and distribution of score range and frequency

Score range	Frequency
50–60	2
61–70	3
71–80	2
81–90	2
91–100	1

Frequency is the number of executives who scored within the specific score range.

In the next stage, we need to construct a percentage distribution table as under.

Score range	Frequency	Percentage of executives scoring within the range
50–60	2	2/10 × 100 = 20%
61–70	3	3/10 × 100 = 30%
71–80	2	2/10 × 100 = 20%
81–90	2	2/10 × 100 = 20%
91–100	1	1/10 × 100 = 10%

Here is how to calculate each:

Let us assume that we have the following variables: 7, 2, 11, 2, 8, 3, 2

Mean = Σ 7, 2, 11, 2, 8, 5, 3/n = 35/7 = 5

Mode = The value that occur most. In our example, it is 2.

Median = To get the median value, we require to first arrange the variables either in ascending or descending order and then find the mid-point or the fiftieth percentile value.

2, 2, 3, 5, 7, 8, 11

In this example, the mode is, therefore, 5.

Three Measures of Variability

Central tendency measures may not be adequate for analysing a set of data. Various measures of variability are used for this. Let us examine the following data set:

Set A: 49, 49, 49, 50, 51, 51, 51

Set B: 20, 30, 40, 50, 60, 70, 80

The mean of both the data sets is 50 and the median is 50, but set A is different from set B. If we observe carefully, the data set B has more variation than data set A. To understand the degree of variability one usually measures the range, the quartile deviation, and the standard deviation. But before making a selection, it is necessary to understand which measures of variability suits what type of data. Range and quartile deviations are used for ordinal data, while standard deviation is used to measure the variability of interval or ratio data.

Range

Range measures the difference between the highest and the lowest score in a data set. Hence, for data set A, the range is 51 − 49 = 2, while for the data set B, the range is 80 − 20 = 60. Such differences in the ranges of two data sets obviously indicate the degree of variation between the two, despite the fact that both data sets have the same mean and median.

Quartile deviation

Quartile deviation is one-half of the difference between the upper quartile and the lower quartile in a data set. If the upper quartile is in 80th percentile, it means that there are 80 per cent scores below that point. Or else, 80th percentile is in the top 20 per cent bracket. Variability is measured by subtracting the lower quartile from the upper quartile and then dividing the result by two. Quartile deviation is a more stable measurement of variability than the range.

Standard deviation

The most appropriate measures of variability for interval or ratio data is standard deviation. This is the square root of the variance and the distance of each score from the mean. Like quartile deviation, it is also the most stable measure of variability. The steps for calculating standard deviation are as follows:

1. Find out N, the number of subjects.
2. Calculate the sum of the scores, square each score.
3. Add all the squares to get the sum of squares of the scores.
4. Square the sum of the scores and divide by the number of scores (we have a measure of variability called variance).
5. Subtract the variance from the sum of the squares of scores to get the sum of the squares (SS).
6. Divide the SS by $N − 1$.

A small standard deviation indicates the scores are close together and a large standard deviation indicates that the scores are more spread out.

$$SD = \sqrt{\frac{SS}{N-1}}, \quad SS = \Sigma X^2 - \frac{(\Sigma X)^2}{N}$$

Normal distribution

If a variable is normally distributed, then the following will be true:

1. Fifty per cent of the scores will be above and 50 per cent will be below the mean.
2. The mean, the median, and the mode are the same.
3. Most scores are near the mean.

4. The same number, or percentage of scores is between the mean and plus on standard deviation $(X + 1\ SD)$ as is between the mean and minus on standard deviation $(X - 1\ SD)$, and similarly for $X+$ or $-2\ SD$, and $X+$ or $-3\ SD$.

When a distribution is not normal, it is considered as skewed. If the extreme scores are at the lower end of the distribution, the distribution is negatively skewed; if the extreme scores are at the upper or higher end of the distribution, the distribution is positively skewed.

Two Measures of Relationship

The two most frequently used correlation analyses are the rank difference correlation coefficient, usually referred to as the 'Spearman rho' and the product moment correlation coefficient, usually referred to as the 'Pearson r'.

The Spearman rho: The Spearman rho is appropriate when the data represents an ordinal scale (although it may be used with interval data) and is used when the median and quartile deviation are used.

The Pearson r: The Pearson r is the most appropriate measure of correlation when the sets of data to be correlated represent either interval or ratio scales. The relationship is expressed by correlation coefficient, which is a number between 0.00 and 1.00.

$$r = \frac{\Sigma XY - \frac{(\Sigma X)(\Sigma Y)}{N}}{\sqrt{\left[\Sigma X^2 - \frac{(\Sigma X)^2}{N}\right]\left[\Sigma Y^2 - \frac{(\Sigma Y)^2}{N}\right]}}$$

Four Measures of Relative Position

Measures of relative position indicate where a score is in relation to all other scores in the distribution. It indicates how well an individual has performed as compared to all others. If a student scores 40 in reading, and 35 in Maths, it does not mean he/she did better in reading. In the reading test, 40 may be the lowest score and 35 may be the highest score in the Maths test.

Two most frequently used measures of relative positions are percentile ranks and standard scores (z score, t score, and stanines–standard nine).

A *percentile rank* indicates the percentage of scores that fall at or below a given score. If a score of 65 corresponds to a percentile rank of 80, the 80th percentile, this means that 80 per cent of the scores in the distribution are lower than 65. A *standard score* is a derived score that expresses how far a given raw score is from some reference point, typically the mean, in terms of standard deviation units. The most commonly reported and used standard scores are z scores, t scores, and stanines.

A z score is the most basic standard score to express how far a score is from the mean in terms of standard deviation units. If a score is exactly on the mean, its z score will be 0; if the score corresponds exactly to 1 standard deviation, its score is 1; if the score is exactly 2 standard deviations below the mean its z score will be -2. An example in Table 21.7 will illustrate this.

TABLE 21.7 Sample z scores

	Raw score	Mean x	SD	z	Percentile
Reading	50	60	10	−1.00	16th
Maths	40	30	10	+1.00	84th

$z = X$ (raw score) − mean (x)/SD.

T score is nothing more than a z score expressed in a different form $T = 10 \times z + 50$. Stanines are standard scores that divide a distribution into nine parts. Stanine stands for 'standard nine'. Stanine equivalencies are derived using the formula $2 \times z + 5$ and rounding resulting values to the nearest whole number. Like percentiles, stanines are very frequently used for standardized tests. They may be used as the criteria for selecting samples for special programmes.

Inferential Statistics

Inferential statistics helps to draw inferences about populations based on the observations of samples. At the organizational level, when the population is large, it may not always be feasible to carry out a study following the complete enumeration method. This is particularly true when the organization decides to opt for some changes in the policy concerning employees and wants to study the possible implications of policy changes. In this case, inferential statistics help to determine the likely results based on the observation of the samples.

Concept of standard error

When we randomly select a number of samples from the same population and compute the mean, it may be possible that means are different from each other and not identical to the population mean. Let us take an example. Suppose the average age of employee population in an organization is 40 years. Now we have drawn five groups of samples from five different departments or shop floors to test the implication of the companies changed policy on terminal benefits. It may soon happen that the means of the age group of five departments are different and none of the means corresponds to the population mean, that is, 40 years. This occurs due to chance variation, and is referred to as a sample error. However, it would be the researcher's duty to find out how far such a difference is the result of sampling error. It may be also a reflection of the true difference.

It is interesting to mention that we get such errors despite the fact that samples are normally distributed and sample means are very close to the population mean.

We make use of standard deviation of sample means to measure sampling errors or standard error of the mean. Standard error of mean indicates the difference in sample means which we may get when we draw the other samples from the same population. In terms of normal curve percentages, about 68 per cent of the sample means fall between ± 1 standard error, 95 per cent between ± 2 standard errors, and 99 per cent between ± 3 standard errors.

Once we get the standard deviation of sample means, we can compute the standard error by dividing it by the square root of the sample size, that is, SE (mean) = SD/square root of $(N-1)$. When a sample mean is 40 and the SE mean is 1.00, if we say that the population mean falls between 39 and 41, we have approximately 68 per cent chance of being correct; if we say that the population mean falls between 38 and 42, we will have approximately a 95 per cent chance of being correct; if we say that the population mean falls between 37 and 43, we will have approximately a 99 + per cent chance of being correct. In other words, the probability of the population mean being less than 37 and larger than 43 is less than 1 per cent.

A small standard error indicates less sampling error. Standard error of the mean is largely affected by the sample size. The standard error of the mean decreases with an increase in sample size. The other factor that affects the standard error of the mean is population standard deviation. With a large population standard deviation, populations are by default spread out. Hence, the sample means will also be spread out. To understand whether the difference between the samples mean and the population mean truly represents the population difference, we estimate standard error of the difference between the two means.

Framing of Hypotheses

Hypotheses are assumptions which we want to validate through some testing measures. We may have a number of null or alternative hypotheses depending on our research objectives. Proving or disproving a hypothesis requires formal statement of the research assumptions and also use of appropriate statistical tools. Without familiarity with the testing measures, it is always advisable to avoid it. Let us illustrate this for better comprehension. A particular scholar wants to study the 'determinants of savings behaviour in India'. His/Her formal statement of hypothesis would be:

'Savings in India is functionally related to the growth rate of income, per capita GDP, expected rate of inflation, etc.'

After developing the hypothesis, he/she has to illustrate the model using which he/she will to test these. In the present, case he/she has to first define the variables, such as growth rate of income, per capita GDP, expected rate of inflation, etc. Then he/she has to specify suitable forms of its estimation, developing an equation. In its final form of derivation, he/she may use an auto-regressive model showing aggregate savings as the behaviour or function of the different variables stated earlier. This is an econometric model. By subsequent use of non-linear least squares estimation technique, he/she may test the significance of various determinants or variables in influencing the general savings behaviour.

Now, this is one way of framing hypotheses, and defining the models and estimation tools. Depending on the nature of research, the models, estimation, and statement, per se, on the hypotheses, may vary. For example, the statement of one of the hypotheses to study the influence of various factors that motivate an employee to prefer inter-organizational career movement may be as follows:

'Unhealthy personnel practices accentuate the pace of inter-organizational career movement'.

Now to capture unhealthy personnel practices, we have to first identify different variables. A simple measure for this may be inter-correlation and then testing the negative or positive influence of each such variable.

For doing research in organizational change areas, testing of hypothesis plays a very crucial role. Before taking a decision replicating an existing system or model organizational change, researchers may need to authenticate their decisions in the context of hypothesis testing. Hypothesis is written in simple and plain language.

To illustrate, an organizational change researcher may frame a hypothesis, such as 'employee groups are different from each other with respect to Scanlon plan of incentives' or 'increased productivity raises employees' expectation to get higher incentives'. There can be two possibilities:

1. Nothing happened—We call this the null hypothesis—H_0
2. Something happened—We call this the alternative hypothesis—H_a

When we test a statistical hypothesis we try to see if something has happened and compare it against the possibility that nothing happened.

To elaborate null hypothesis, (H_0) means null = nothing = zero, that is, we did not find an effect, which means we did not find that employee groups are different with respect to the Scanlon plan of incentives, or that increased productivity and employees' expectation to get higher incentives are not related. It is important to note that we test our sample statistic against the value based on the null hypothesis sampling distribution. Thus, sample statistic and null hypothesis sampling distribution values are close. We conclude that they are not different; we did not find an effect in our study.

The alternative hypothesis means alternative = something = more than zero, that is, we did find an effect, which means that we did find that employee groups are different with respect to the Scanlon plan of incentives, or that increased productivity and employees' expectation to get higher incentives are related. In this case, however, our sample statistic is against the value based on the null hypothesis sampling distribution. Hence, sample statistic and null hypothesis values are not close, they are different.

Hypothesis tests

In hypothesis testing, the logic is to think backward, that is, we try to disprove the null hypothesis, or we try to disprove that nothing has happened. If we disprove that nothing has happened, then we conclude that something has happened. This is why hypothesis testing is said to be counter-intuitive. For example, we try to prove that the Scanlon incentives plan has a different effect on different employee groups, that is, we try to disprove that employee groups do not differ.

The simple steps of hypothesis testing are as follows:

1. Generate a hypothesis.
2. Calculate summary statistics, that is, mean standard deviation, etc.
3. Determine the statistical test to compare summary statistics against the null hypothesis.
4. Calculate the test statistic using summary statistics.
5. Calculate how far the sample is from the null hypothesis, making use of standard error of the mean.
6. Derive the appropriate sampling distribution.
7. Choose the cut-off value on sampling distribution. Cut-off values are alpha level or significance level.
8. Decide whether we are able to reject or fail to reject the null hypothesis. We do this by comparing test statistic to the cut-off value.
9. Draw a conclusion. If we reject the null hypothesis, our result becomes statistically significant, that is, it did not happen by luck or chance. If we fail to reject the null, we conclude that we did not find an effect or difference in this study.

Power and Statistical Errors

We may make an error or two when we test our hypotheses. We may conclude that things are different when they are not. This may also happen when a relationship that really exists has been missed. These are called Type I and Type II errors, respectively. Type I errors occur when we conclude that there is a difference when there is not. Type II errors occur when we conclude that there is no difference when there is. Based on a test of significance, the researcher will either reject or not reject the null hypothesis as a probable explanation for results. Here are four possible situations:

1. The null hypothesis is true (A = B), and the researcher concludes that it is true, no difference exists between A and B.
2. The null hypothesis is false (A not = B), and the researcher concludes that it is false, difference exists between A and B.
3. The null hypothesis is true (A = B), and the researcher concludes that it is false, difference exists between A and B.
4. The null hypothesis is false (A not = B), and the researcher concludes that it is true, no difference exists between A and B.

In 1 and 2, the researcher is making the correct conclusion. However, in the case of 3 and 4, the researcher is making a wrong conclusion and is, therefore, making an error. In case 3, the researcher rejects a null hypothesis that is really true and is making a Type I error. In case 4, the researcher fails to reject the null hypothesis that is really false and is making a Type II error.

Statistical power is the probability of correctly detecting a difference between the sample and the population. In any study, we want to maximize the probability of detecting a true difference. Power is to find out real differences or relationships, that is, power of the probability of correctly rejecting a false null hypothesis. It means the chance of finding what we are looking for. The previous situation is like a statistical test. We look for a difference. This is like going to the doctor to see if we are sick. It is when the H_o (null hypothesis) is false. The statistical test is like the doctor. It might say there is a difference when there is one. This is statistical power.

To increase statistical power, we can refer to the points given as follows:

1. Try to increase the effect, size, or strength of the relationship.
2. Decrease experimental error.
3. Use a higher alpha level (say 0.05 as compared to 0.01). Note that this increases power but also Type I error.
4. Increase sample size.
5. Use matched samples or co-variance techniques.

Test null hypothesis

We always test a null hypothesis, against an alternative/research hypothesis. When the difference between the two means (sample and population) is considered as the true difference, we consider this cause is attributable to treatment and not to chance. A chance explanation for the difference is called the null hypothesis. In essence, this means that there is no difference or relationship between parameters in the populations and that any difference or relationship found for the samples is the result of sampling error. The research hypothesis usually states that one method is expected to be more effective than another. Utilizing the null hypothesis is a more conclusive support for a positive research hypothesis.

Test of significance

In order to test a null hypothesis, we need a test of significance selecting a probability level to indicate the degree of risk in our decision. After the experimental research study when there is little difference between the group means, the researcher needs to decide whether the difference is significant or not in order to conclude that they represent a true difference.

The test of significance is made at a pre-selected probability level and allows the researcher to state that he/she has rejected the null hypothesis. The level is usually set at 0.05 or 0.01. This means that the researcher will have 5 per cent or 1 per cent times to find the difference by chance. There are a number of different tests of significance that can be applied in research studies, such as the t test, analysis of variance, and chi square, etc.

The researcher makes the decision to reject or not to reject the null hypothesis with a given probability. The probability of being correct is referred to as the significance level or probability level of the test of significance, i.e., 0.05 or 0.01. If 0.05 is set, the researcher will have a 5 per cent probability of making a Type I error, whereas, if 0.01 is selected, the researcher will have only 1 per cent probability of committing a Type I error. In other words, working at 0.05, the researcher has 95 per cent chance of making a correct decision; and working with 0.01 the researcher will have a 99 per cent chance of making a correct decision.

Concept of significance level

Obviously, for the researcher it is important to decide which level of significance is better, 0.01 or 0.05, and which level one must select for a particular research. As 0.01 is obviously smaller than 0.05 the chances of committing a Type I error decreases if .01 is selected. But this will increase the probability of committing a Type II error. Quite often, there is a notion that a research hypothesis can be proved or substantiated by rejecting a null hypothesis. But this is not correct. It does not support the research hypothesis. Hence, the conclusion that a significant difference exists between the variables cannot be attributable to the research hypothesis; so also rejecting the hypothesis does not mean that it is wrong.

One-tailed and two-tailed tests

A two-tailed test computes the difference that may occur in either direction, that is, either a group mean may be higher than the other (A > B or B > A). For computing significance with a t test at the 0.05 level, the two-tailed test will have the possibility of a positive t and a negative t. $(0.25 + 0.25 = 0.05)$. While a one-tailed test shows that a difference can only occur in one direction, that is, the null hypothesis proves that one group is not better than another (A is not > B).

Tests of significance are mostly two-tailed. For a one-tailed test of significance, the researcher has to be clear that a difference can only occur in one direction.

Simple Analysis of Variance

Simple analysis of variance is done through one-way analysis of variance (ANOVA). ANOVA determines the significance of difference between two or more means at a defined level of probability. Through ANOVA, we compute the F ratio. By comparing the computed F ratio with the table value of F, we can measure the significance of difference. The table value of F is determined based on the defined probability level and degrees of freedom. The formula for a one-way analysis of variance is as follows:

Total sum of squares = Between sum of squares + Within sum of squares

$$SS_{total} = \Sigma X^2 - \frac{(\Sigma X)^2}{N}$$

$$SS\text{(total)} = SS\text{(between)} + SS\text{(within)}$$

$$SS_{between} = \frac{(\Sigma X_1)^2}{n_1} + \frac{(\Sigma X_2)^2}{n_2} + \frac{(\Sigma X_3)^2}{n_3} - \frac{(\Sigma X)^2}{N}$$

Multiple Comparison of Variances

One-way ANOVA holds well when the computed F ratio, which is obtained by comparing with the table value of F, is not significant. However, if it is significant, it indicates that more than two means are involved. In such a situation, we need to determine which means are significantly different from other means. This requires the use of multiple comparison procedures. Here, the Scheffe test is more appropriate although it is prone to committing Type I errors. A Type I error occurs as it tries to find no significant difference with the given means even when F is significant. The formula for multiple comparison of variance is as foloows:

$F =$ Square of $(X_1 - X_2)/\text{MS (within)} \times (1/n_1 + 1/n_2) \times (K-1)$ with $df = (K-1), (N-K)$

$$F = \frac{(\bar{X}_1 - \bar{X}_2)^2}{MS_w \left(\frac{1}{n_1} + \frac{1}{n_2} \right)(K-1)} \text{ with } df = (K-1), (N-K)$$

Analysis of Covariance

Analysis of covariance (ANCOVA) adjusts post-test scores for initial differences on some variables and compares adjusted scores to increase the power of a statistical test by reducing within-group (error) variance. To increase the power of a statistical test, a simple solution is to increase the sample size. But practically, this is not possible as increasing the sample size involves both money and time constraints. Hence, the researcher may feel compelled to restrict the sample size. ANCOVA is basically a control technique and is used in both causal-comparative studies and experimental studies. Causal-comparative studies need not always involve equal groups. Similarly, in experimental studies either existing group or randomly formed groups are involved. As computation of ANCOVA is a lengthy procedure, the researchers often avoid it by restricting the sample size.

Research Discussion

In this part, we detail results of our interpretation and generalize the implications through our discussions. When the results' interpretation supports the hypotheses, it is quite simple to discuss. But when they do not, we need to justify it by detailing the reasons for such variation. When null hypotheses are rejected it indicates that the research hypotheses are supported but not necessarily proven. Conversely, when null hypotheses are rejected the research hypotheses are not supported. This however, does not make the research wrong, as null hypotheses may be true. In all organizational change research, we may not frame hypotheses. It may also not be possible. But some apparent relationships may exist. As a researcher, it is our duty to analyse such relationships and present the results without bothering about the reasons for not having framed our hypotheses earlier.

It is also important for a researcher to understand that when the results are statistically significant by default, it does not establish a hypothesis. Statistical significance largely depends on sample size. When the sample size is very large, even a small correlation coefficient may be construed as significant but we may not consider this. Similarly, with a large sample size, the t ratio tends to increase even with a small mean difference. Smaller samples always increase the chance of rejecting null hypotheses; while large samples may not. Large samples, in fact, help to find some important relationships.

While interpreting results, it is also important to assess how far the results may be replicated, that is, whether the study can be done again. It also establishes validity and reliability when the same results are obtained in subsequent studies. Replication may be essential when some unusual relationship is found in a research.

Conclusion and Recommendations

Conclusion and recommendations emanate from a detailed analysis of results, that is, from the research findings. Conclusions can be drawn by summarizing the results. Recommendations are given in a chronological form, addressing the research objectives. Both the conclusion and recommendations should follow logic and must have some practical significance.

QUALITATIVE RESEARCH CONSIDERATIONS

Qualitative research includes formal and informal focus groups, round tables, feedback forms, seminars, usability studies, etc. It involves a small number of samples. These meetings can include internal participants (sales, management, customer service, engineering, etc.) or external participants such as analysts, the press, existing customers, prospects, governing committees, and others. This leaves qualitative research or studies involving a small number of individuals, such as focus groups or in-depth one-on-one interviews. The primary tool in qualitative research is the focus group, but it can also include modern variations on the focus group idea, such as online focus groups and teleconferences. Qualitative researchers can use one-on-one interviews to delve deep into various topics.

Focus Group

For qualitative organizational change research, we make use of a focus group. A focus group is a round table discussion session. It usually consists of 6–10 individuals who come to a central location to sit around a table to answer questions from a trained moderator or facilitator. Respondents here are participants. Focus groups are usually held in pairs, in a series. For example, a study could consist of two or more groups in one unit of organization followed by another two in some other unit of the organization. Using multiple focus groups, the research conclusions become more relevant.

One-on-one interviews

Instead of bringing ten people together in a two-hour focus group, researchers can spend 20 minutes interviewing ten respondents individually. The in-depth interview produces more comment from each participant than the group environment, and also provides individual comments uninfluenced by group reactions. Such interviews can also be conducted over the phone.

Observational research

Rather than interacting with respondents verbally, researchers simply observe how employees make decisions about strategic issues or perform some actions. This often yields better results as the researcher can draw conclusions based purely on his/her observations. An observational research is an important source of qualitative data collection. The major advantages of observational research are that it guards against inadvertent omission, helps in getting a comprehensive view, and helps in leveraging the knowledge and experience of the researcher.

Document review

The researcher here looks for contents to authenticate his/her research. Often this method is used to supplement observational fieldwork through documentary evidences. For organizational change research, we may be interested in performance records, attendance records, organizational change reports, various compliance reports pertaining to rules and regulations, etc. These are the important sources for information collection and compilation.

Interview Technique

In research, there are two main types of interviews—structured and unstructured. The unstructured or informal interview is mostly conducted on a pilot basis for framing hypotheses. However, for certain types of research, for example, understanding the quick response of employees on a changed organizational change policy, such as change in attendance system, transfer, relocation, etc., we also may make use of this type of informal interview. This is primarily due to time and money constraints or perhaps to get a quick feel of the people working in the organization. Unstructured interviews are not controlled. Here the researcher is guided by certain pre-assumptions to map the reaction of people on certain issues. The major problem is to consolidate the response of the subjects. However, at times, it helps in critical management decisions. Focus group interview is one such example. Whatever may be the purpose, the unstructured interview inputs ultimately help to frame the structured interview questionnaire and also refine the thought process.

A structured interview is conducted with a set of specific questionnaires. In most quantitative research, collection of primary source information is made using this type of interview. The process requires administering a structured set of questionnaire items in an orderly manner on samples and then draws the necessary inferences as per our hypotheses. During the interview process, the respondents are asked uniform questions and their responses are recorded in the questionnaire itself for subsequent quantitative analysis. Since respondents do not get flexibility to add, remove, or to alter questionnaire items, the interview processes become structured.

Other Types of Interview

We have many other types of interview. Some of these are explained here.

Depth interviews

Depth interviews are face-to-face encounters. Normally, for this type of interview, the interviewer uses an unstructured or semi-structured approach to unearth innate sentiments, emotions, and attitudes. It is our experience that respondents often try to evade sensitive issues when they are required to give direct answers against structured questionnaire items. At times, their responses may even be misleading. The success of this type of interview largely depends on the skill of the interviewer, specifically on psychometric tools and psychoanalysis.

Telephone interviews

Telephone interviews are mostly conducted in marketing research. It may be done to assess the likely success or failure of a new product launch, map customers' satisfaction levels, or for some other critical marketing issues, such as pricing, quality level, expectations from product or services, etc. This type of interview is used more in the developed world. But its success is questionable as response rates may be very poor, sampling is difficult, and may not also represent the population. Moreover, the interviews may be more unstructured as respondents may not like to answer all the questions raised by the interviewer.

Focus group interviews

Focus group interviews are very powerful survey research instruments in qualitative research. Avoiding a one-to-one interview approach focus group interviews emphasize collection and compilation of information from a target group of people. The interviewer plays the role of a moderator and always tries to keep the group focused on the issues of concern. As a moderator, he/she is playing the role of a psychotherapist to generate more information by raising brief provocative statements. The interviewer here is more a listener than a talker. See Exhibit 21.3.

> **EXHIBIT 21.3 Sample questionnaire of a focus group for organizational change research for assessing problem of absenteeism**
>
> Moderator (organizational change Manager): Hello, you all are here today as per your company's short-listing. I will ask you some questions.
>
> 1. Did you remain absent from duties without prior approval of your leave in last one year?
>   (a) Yes   (b) Continue
>   (c) No   (d) Exclude
> 2. Did you participate in a group discussion or survey on absenteeism by us in the last six months?
>   (a) Yes   (b) Exclude
>   (c) No   (d) Continue
> 3. Did you remain absent for more than 10 days without prior approval during the last six months?
>   (a) Yes   (b) Continue
>   (c) No   (d) Exclude
> 4. Are you currently under any medical treatment, which prevents you from being regular at present?
>   (a) Yes   (b) Exclude
>   (c) No   (d) Continue
> 5. Now I am giving you some statements on possible problem of absenteeism. Select the statements as per your perceived priority giving the order of rank on a 5-point scale.
>   (a) I remain absent due to frequent illness.
>   (b) I remain absent for my household priorities.
>   (c) I remain absent for undergoing advanced level study.
>   (d) I remain absent for visiting my native place.
>   (e) I remain absent due to poor job satisfaction.
> 6. (For moderator): Please distribute age-group of your participants as per following:
>   Above 60   Exclude
>   50–60
>   40–50
>   30–40
>   20–30
>   Less than 30   Exclude
> 7. Sex (please record it by observation only)
>   Male   Female

Even though the questionnaire is more structured to help the focus group moderator to facilitate the discussions, the moderator can also think of following a more unstructured approach, provoking discussions and then suggesting points of interest to understand the cause of absenteeism. However, to start with, it is always desirable to follow a structured approach by developing a structured questionnaire to set the pace of discussion.

OD is a planned change based on the paradigm of understanding the environment, benchmarking, and action research. OD can, thus, be described as a learning process. The active development of an organization towards its desired corporate identity succeeds only if this change process is undertaken holistically. From a behavioural perspective this means, for example, that the behavioural conditions that lie within the person (qualifications, motivation) as well as those lying outside the person (organizational structure, technology) must be modified. The process of change is also described as a political process. Lastly, the change process is often examined in terms of whether and how basic assumptions within an organization can be decoded through analysis of symbols.

Types of intervention include the person-centred approach, the structural approach, and the relationship approach. The person-centred approach requires the development of both a social competence that fosters cooperation and a general intellectual competence that promotes innovation. The structural approach requires moves to reintegrate segregated work sequences and attempts to decentralize decision-making. The relationship approach requires team development, role negotiations, and survey feedback methods.

As organizational development has strategic imperative, systematic research on organizational development using various intervention tools and models help an organization to achieve excellence. Intervention tools and models have been discussed in earlier chapters.

One of the important research issues in organizational change and development is personality research. Understanding individual personalities helps the organization to get the right fit, matching with the requirements of the organization. Exhibit 21.4 discusses OD interventions in a Kolkata-based BPO.

EXHIBIT 21.4 OD in BPO

A new generation BPO in sector-V of Salt Lake City, Kolkata, has outnumbered its competitors in business growth and profitability within three years of its operation. The BPO has a large number of educational institutes in the vicinity and enjoys the privilege of captive recruitment of people with knowledge of the BPO industry. This also gives it a tremendous advantage in terms of substantial saving in the cost of hiring manpower. The company caters to the telecom clients worldwide. For this, it has multiple verticals, including a technical support vertical.

Recruitment in technical support functions are essentially made from youngsters with an engineering background. The technical support group functions by forming teams (essentially based on clients' accounts) consisting of 12–15 associates with an average age-group of less than 25 years. The company has recently started to face a huge rate of attrition in this vertical, despite offering a well-calibrated compensation package and a better work environment compared to competitors. Grooming technical support executives for the telecom vertical is expensive due to client-specific training, which often takes more than three months after induction.

Before OD interventions, data was collected from different stakeholders of the company to assess the reasons for attrition in one of the verticals; in the other, such attrition is within control. The analysis revealed that poor man management skill of the team leaders is the major attributing factor for attrition. Due to an obvious skill-gap in managing people, team leaders are unable to understand the aspirations of young minds. With initial training on the basics of human resource management practices, the author took them for out-bound training to experience real-life issues and gain expertise in managing these.

Participating team leaders were taken through rigorous exercises, such as decision-making in crisis situations, scenario planning, adventure tours without any guide-map, and many simulation exercises and T-group trainings. Subsequent post-training follow-up with mentoring helped them to implement this knowledge and skill in successfully managing people under them. Ultimately, they were able to understand and successfully manage the aspirations of the team members and in the process reduce the rate of attrition.

UNDERSTANDING PERSONALITY

To understand organizational change and then initiate appropriate organizational development measures, it is first necessary to understand individual behaviour. The nature and personality of an individual is the root cause of his/her behaviour. The word 'personality' is derived from the Latin word 'persona'. It denotes the masks, which used to be worn by theatrical players in ancient Greek dramas. Hence, personality is the superficial social image that we adopt. Further, we can also view personality as the reflection of the most dominant characteristics in behaviour of an individual that are observable (namely aggressiveness or shyness). Through his/her personality an individual makes an overall impression on others in various social settings, which also encompass organizations.

Some of the important characteristics of personality are as follows:

Stability of characteristics Stable personality characteristics develop consistent patterns of behaviour. Characteristics, such as warm, friendly, cold, hostile, aggressive, emotional, etc., are often found as stable in some individuals and influence their personality.

Commonalities and differences in behaviour Personality characteristics may be either common or different. Hence, to understand what an individual has in common and what is different, we try to assess certain aspects as follows:

- Like all other people
- Like some other people
- Like no other people

Personality induces people to behave in a particular manner in order to respond to social and biological pressure. It is an abstraction based on inferences that we derive from behavioural observation. It is often some uniqueness in characteristics that differentiate one individual from another. It is an evolving process, as it develops through internal and external influences, which includes genetic and biological influences, social experiences, and changing environmental stimulus.

Determinants of Personality

There are several factors that influence the shaping of our personality. By observing the behaviour of a person, one can understand the kind of influence a particular behaviour has on the personality characteristics of an individual. Such personality characteristics are briefly reviewed here:

Heredity Some characteristics of our behaviour are genetic and are inherited. Some of these are physical height, slimness, dexterity, intellectual capacity, ability to learn, logical power, etc. All these have a significant influence on our behavioural patterns.

Family background The socio-economic status of the family and education of the parents and other family members shape the personality of an individual to a considerable extent. In fact, family members themselves try to influence the behaviour of children in their desperate attempt to personify their values, roles, etc.

Nature of people with whom we interact People influence each other and this also shapes personality. For this reason, it is often said that personality is evolving and is shaped throughout one's life.

Culture This shapes our personal values and predispositions. Culture is the unique characteristic of a social group; the values and norms shared by its members set it apart from other social groups. The essence of culture is the collective programming of the mind. According to anthropological concepts, culture relates to a shared system of beliefs, attitudes, possessions, attributes, customs, and values that define group behaviour. Values are assumptions about 'how things ought to be' in the group. Thus, culture has a significant role in influencing the behaviour of an individual.

Individual Behaviour and Performance

Individual performance is primarily the result of three important characteristics. These are an individual's capacity to perform, his/her willingness to perform, and organizational support. In fact, because of the influence of behaviour on the performance of an individual, the subject 'organizational behaviour' has started to receive greater importance and has now become a core lesson for management students.

The most important personality attributes that may influence organizational behaviour are locus of control, Machiavellianism, self-esteem, self-monitoring, and risk-taking. Locus of control means both internal and external controlling power. Machiavellianism is an individual's propensity to manipulate people to satisfy his/her interest. With high Machiavellianism, an individual tends to be cool, logical, pragmatic, maintains emotional distance, and tries to control people, events, and situations. Self-esteem, whether high or low, also determines the behaviour of people in an organization. With high self-esteem, people may like more challenging assignments, while those with low self-esteem tend to show susceptibility to external influences.

The power of self-monitoring enables an individual to adjust his/her behaviour to external factors and situations, and makes him/her adaptable to situations, etc. Again, a risk-taking propensity also reflects in managerial behaviour in decision-making. High risk-taking managers take more rapid decisions and do not make use of elaborate information when making a decision. Low risk-taking managers, on the other hand, believe in routine decisions that may lead to known outcomes.

Thinking and Decision-making Process

Due to differences in individual personalities, perceptions, attitudes, and thinking, the decision-making process differs from one manager to another. For obvious behavioural significance in decision-making, we need to understand the behavioural implications and the differences in information processing which ultimately lead to decision-making.

Of the three different roles of managers, that is, interpersonal, informational, and decisional, decision-making is very significant and is in fact the real test of a manager. Information processing is essentially a cognitive process. Pre-existing systems of knowledge and experiences, which also include beliefs, propositions, schemes, and theories, develop our interpretative capability to attach meaning to any information. These processes follow three major approaches: (i) The Lens model of information processing, which is a normative approach. It develops a response capability in an individual to achieve some intended objectives (associated with a task). (ii) cognitive approach to information processing, frequently referred to as cerebral competency, which uses expectancy, demand, and incentives that drive an individual to process information, and (iii) the process-tracing approach, which obtains measures of events (processes) between information the input and output stages, that is, between the information received from the task environment and the end result.

Measurement of Personality Traits

There are many studies on primary personality traits but effective measurement of personality traits for identification and classification is widely done using the Myers–Briggs type indicator (MBTI) and the big-five model. MBTI is essentially a 100-question personality test to understand the feelings and actions of people in a given situation. The responses are classified into four major types, namely extroverted vs introverted, sensing vs intuitive, thinking vs feeling, judging vs perceiving, and then combined into 16 personality types, such as ESTJ, INFP, ESFP, INTJ, ESFJ, INTP, ENFP, ISTJ, ESTP, INFJ, ENFJ, ISTP, ENTJ, ISFP, ENTP, ISFJ. Attributes of some of the types are as follows. Despite the wide popularity of MBTI, its result is not always foolproof. Many researchers recommend its use only for self-awareness.

The big-five model, in contrast, has strong application support and often researchers feel it is a better alternative. The big-five personality factors are as follows:

- Extroversion
- Agreeableness
- Conscientiousness
- Emotional stability
- Openness to stability

Other common psychological tests to measure personality factors are 16PF (sixteen personality factors), DISC (drive, influence, steadiness, compliance), Thomas profiling, FIRO-B, Belbin team role profiling, etc. These are only some of the personality measurement tools that can be used in organizational research, particularly in regard to organizational change and development.

Japanese scientists have recently made very interesting observations relating to blood group with personality type. However, we do not have adequate research information to validate this.

SUMMARY

Organizational change research knowledge helps to appreciate the interrelationship between various organizational change variables. Today, at the organizational level the scope of organizational change research encompasses even line functions. In many organizations, even line managers are involved in organizational change research. While doing this, the researcher has to comply with many ethical issues. Such requirements may vary from organization to organization. However, all organizational behaviour researchers must comply with at least two generic requirements, that is, 'informed consent' and 'maintenance of confidentiality'.

In doing organizational change research, both quantitative and qualitative, various tools and techniques need to be understood. Quantitative tools require data collection from various experimental/clinical trials, observation and recording of events, and obtaining data from ERP/MIS and from questionnaire responses. Qualitative data, on the other hand, requires collection of narrative data through historical research, focus group discussions, etc.

Depending on the nature of research, quantitative organizational change research may either be descriptive, corelational, cause-comparative, or experimental. Similarly, qualitative organizational change research may be formal or informal, focus groups, round tables, feedback forms, seminars, usability studies, etc. A structured approach has to be followed for both quantitative and qualitative organizational change researches.

An organization has to understand the dynamics of its environment in order to be able to adapt to the changing demands of the outside and inside (within the organization) world. There are many different ways of scanning the organizational environment. After this, it is imperative to opt for OD in order to match with the requirement to stay updated in a competitive environment. However, to understand OD, it is imperative to understand various other issues, such as the corporate culture, etc. It is imperative to opt for organizational diagnostics and a planned change based on the paradigm of understanding the environment, benchmarking, and action research, that is, OD to gauge the morale of the company's workforce. OD can thus be described as a learning process. In this chapter, we have discussed this area very extensively. We have also discussed the framing of hypotheses and use of various data analysis techniques, introducing several statistical tools.

KEY TERMS

Conjoint analysis This analysis is also called the multi-attribute compositional model. Today, it is used in many of the social sciences and applied sciences including marketing, product management, and operations research.

Informed consent Employees can be selected as a research subject only if they give their consent for participation in the research.

Interval scale It has all the characteristics of a nominal and ordinal scale; in addition, it is based upon predetermined equal intervals.

Nominal scale A nominal scale represents the lowest level of measurement. Such a scale classifies persons or objects into two or more categories.

Ordinal scale An ordinal scale puts the subjects in order from the highest to lowest, from the most to the least.

Quartile deviation This is one-half of the difference between the upper quartile and the lower quartile in a data set.

Ratio scale A ratio scale represents the highest and the most precise level of measurement. It has all the advantages of the other types of scales and in addition it has a meaningful true zero point.

Reliability This refers to the reproducibility of a measurement. We quantify reliability simply by taking several measurements on the same subjects.

Semantic differential scale When bipolar adjectives are used at the end points of the scales, it is called a semantic differential scale.

Thurston scale This scale attempts to represent the attitudes of a group on a specified issue in the form of frequency distribution.

Unobtrusive data collection It is called unobtrusive because conducting research does not require asking any question or interview samples to collect such data.

Validity This refers to the agreement between the value of a measurement and its true value. We quantify validity by comparing our measurements with values that are as close to the true values as possible.

CONCEPT REVIEW QUESTIONS

1. What are the various types of data collection? Which method would you recommend for collection of data relating to organizational change and development? Justify your recommendation.
2. Develop a questionnaire using a 5-point scale for measuring the attitudes of workers. Also explain how you are going to analyse the collected responses to define the attitudes of workers.
3. What are the ethical issues in organizational change research?
4. Explain the different scaling techniques for organizational change research.
5. Explain the different types of quantitative researches. How does quantitative research differ from qualitative organizational change research?
6. Write short notes on the following:
   (a) Null hypothesis
   (b) Nominal scale
   (c) Qualitative research
   (d) Evaluation design
   (e) Estimation methods

CRITICAL THINKING QUESTIONS

1. Conduct a focus group interview with some selected identified issues and suggest how you are going to interpret the outcome of your discussions.
2. Frame a hypothesis for testing employees' preference or otherwise about various incentive schemes. Explain how you have developed this hypothesis? Also explain how you are going to test it.
3. Suggest some common change management tools that can be used for organizational change and development research.

CASE STUDY

Assignment for Class Discussion

As HR is the ultimate source of competitive advantage for an organization and has strategic relevance, systematic organizational change research at the corporate level has now become very significant. Organizational change research is even gaining importance for academic and professional interests. While methodological issues for organizational change research are not very different from other management research, yet it is important for a scholar to understand the basics, keeping in view the specific requirements of the organizational change area.

Many organizational change decisions may be taken at the corporate level based on the outcome of the organizational change research. Similarly, to arrive at a decision organizations may emulate many models, theories, and findings on organizational change research at the macro level. Hence, it is important to develop a separate knowledge depository for organizational change research. Here, however, the intention is only to spell out some general issues.

Research is widely defined as 'finding out things in a systematic way in order to increase knowledge'. If this definition is carefully reviewed, one can observe that it also holds good for organizational change research. In the true sense, organizational change research cannot be differentiated from other management research. However, there are some definite reasons why organizations should pursue systematic organizational change research. Some of these are as follows:

1. In organizations, people are now considered as the strategic resource to sustain and achieve competitive advantage. Hence, it is imperative to understand them and the best way for scientific understanding is systematic organizational change research.
2. Systematic organizational change research helps to align the organizational change initiatives of an organization with the organizational strategy.
3. For better management of HR it is necessary to design and implement a scientific organizational change system. Organizational change research can provide inputs for designing scientific organizational change systems, specific to organizational needs.
4. Systematic organizational change research in organizations helps to understand manpower requirement with the right set of competencies, who can help achieve organizational objectives.

These apart, organizational change systems are related to organizational outcomes. Hence, we need organizational change research to develop, implement, and evaluate organizational change programmes, and also to enhance accountability. Organizational change departments, per se, are also required to justify their existence duly mapping their ROI, which is not possible without systematic organizational change research. It also adds value by making available research findings, which can be leveraged by other departments to improve performance and productivity in their respective domains.

Organizational change research involves systematically enquiring into organizational change issues to increase knowledge and underpin effective action. It, therefore, enhances the quality of organizational change actions, scientifically understanding the people and processes involved in the organization. Pure organizational change research focuses on gaining knowledge, finding causes, examining the relationships between variables, and developing and testing theories. Applied organizational change research, by contrast, is more concerned with solving problems, predicting effects, and developing actions and interventions in discrete organizational contexts.

A recently concluded survey by the online community of HR professionals, HR.com, identifies the top ten areas of interest in HR research. This survey was conducted at the international level. The outcome of the survey with their respective weights is presented as Exhibit 21.5. This has been compiled by HR.com and is based on a global survey. Organizational change researchers can pick their research ideas from these areas, which have an international significance.

Discussion Question
Interpret the percentage distributions given in Exhibit 21.5 and derive a conclusion. Also mention whether the method of presentation is correct.

EXHIBIT 21.5 **Top ten areas of interest of organizational change**

Areas	Percentage	Areas	Percentage
1. Performance management	65	6. Assessment and measurement	52
2. Leadership development	63	7. Indicators and metrics	48
3. Career and succession planning	59	8. Culture assessment	45
4. Change management	59	9. Talent management systems	31
5. Talent retention	55	10. Recognition, awards, incentives	39

(Contd)

(Exhibit 21.5 contd)

Other important topics on organizational change research:

Areas	Percentage
1. *Compensation and benefits*	
Healthcare cost containment	38
Executive compensation	34
Job analysis, evaluation, and grading	25
Employee benefits	23
Benefits outsourcing	17
Retirement and pensions	15
2. *Employment selection/staffing*	
Pre-employment and employee testing	28
Job boards, online media, print media	20
Background investigations	18
3. *HRIS (Human Resource Information Systems)*	
Workforce analytics	20
Employee self-service	15

Areas	Percentage
Benefit administration and communication tools	13
4. *Organizational planning and development*	
Employee surveys	35
Mergers and acquisitions	20
5. *Training and development*	
Assessment	38
Mentoring	31
E-learning	24
Diversity	24
Distance learning	18
Learning management systems	15
6. *Others*	
Research and best practices	38
Organizational change management	30
International and global organizational change	14
Labour relations	14

REFERENCES

Bhattacharyya, D.K. (2009), *Organizational Behaviour—Concepts and Applications*, Oxford University Press, New Delhi.

———. (2007), *Human Resource Research Methods*, Oxford University Press, New Delhi.

Brinkerhoff, R.O. (1987), *Achieving Results from Training*, Jossey-Bass, San Francisco.

Dunne, Clare (2000), *Carl Jung: Wounded Healer of the Soul*, Parabola Books, New York.

Gilbert, T. (1988), 'Performance engineering', *What Works at Work: Lessons from the Masters*, Lakewood Books, Minneapolis.

Jung, C.G. (1999), *Memories, Dreams, Reflections*, Revised edition, Jaffé, Aniela (ed.), Vintage Books, New York.

———. (1971) Psychological Types (*Collected Works of C.G. Jung*), Vol. 6, Chapter 10.

Kanter, Rosabeth Moss (2001), *Evolve! Succeeding in the Digital Culture of Tomorrow*, Harvard Business, Boston.

Kanter, Rosabeth Moss (1991), 'Transcending business boundaries: 12,000 world managers view change', *Harvard Business Review*, Vol. 69, No. 3, pp. 151–164.

———. (1983), 'The change-masters: Innovation and entrepreneurship in the American corporation', Simon and Schuster, New York.

Schutz, W. (1989), *FIRO, A Three-dimensional Theory of Interpersonal Behaviour*, Will Schutz Associates, Mill Valley.

———. (1966), *The Interpersonal Underworld (FIRO)*, Science and Behaviour Books, Palo Alto.

Schwab, D.P. (1999), *Research Methods for Organizational Studies*, Lawrence Erlbaum Associates, Publishers, Mahwah.

Stout, D. (1995), *Performance Analysis for Training*, Niagara Paper Company, Niagara.

Index

ABC Technique and Organizational Change 71
   Change Equation 72
   Integrative Approach to Organizational Change 72
Analysis of Covariance 538
Approaches to Change Management 180
Areas of Measurement for Organizational Analysis 363
   Attitudes towards Work 364
   Organizational Climate 365
   Organizational Commitment 364
Aspects of Diversity Management 477
Assessment Centres Approach for Organizational Diagnosis 371
Attitude 237
   Measurement for Organizational Change 243
Attitude Surveys 246
   Guttman's Cumulative Scale 249
   Johari Window 249
   Likert's Item Analysis 249
   Myth Statements 247
   Questionnaire 247
   Thurstone's Equal Appearing Intervals Scale 249
   Use of Likert's Summated Rating Scale 248

Benefits of T-group Training 492
Business Performance and Diversity 479
   Diversity as a Business Imperative 479
Business Process Approach to Organization 23
   Guest's Model 24
   Harvard Model 24
   Michigan Model 24
   Warwick Model 24

Challenge for Workforce Diversity 483
Change in Customer Service of Alcatel 76
Change in Organizational Culture 174
   Modification of Group Behaviour 176
Change Management 160
   Iceberg 173
   Research 510
   Research Tools 514
Change Management Principles 162
   Job Restructuring 163

Change Management Strategies 67
   Action-centred 69
   Normative Re-educative 67
   Power Coercive 68
   Rational Empirical 67
Change Management Strategy—Lessons from IBM 466
Change Management Survey 167
   Helping People through Transition 170
   Sample Questionnaire 168
Change Management—The Skill Requirements 172
   Analytical Skills 172
   Business Skills 173
   People Skills 173
   Political Skills 172
   System Skills 173
Change of Organizational Culture 272
   External and Independent Variable 272
   Internal Variable 272
   Root Metaphor 272
Change Process 87
   Business Environment-led 89
   Customer and Market Focus 91
   Leadership Performance-driven 93
   Organizational Culture Focus 91
   Organizational Structure and the Change Process 93
   Strategic Planning Focus 90
   Unfreezing, Changing, and Refreezing 88
Change Transitions for Individual Employees 163
   Change Management Issues and Their Solution 165
Change Triggers 50
   Business Development-driven 51
   Business Plan-driven 55
   Competency-driven 55
   Culture-driven 53
   Environment-driven 52
   Innovation-driven 56
   Kellogg Leadership for Community Change Initiative 53
   Performance-driven 55
   Process-driven 55
   Strategy-driven 54
Chaos Theory 20

Change Management Research Tools 514
　Action Research 515
　Observation as a Tool 514
　Online Questionnaire 514
Coercive Power 192
Commitment Curve 170, 171
Competency Mapping and Competency Development 303
Conclusion and Recommendations 539
Core Processes and Decentralized Authority 424
Cross-cultural Diversity Issues and Globalization 480
　Practices in the US and India 480
　　Right Fit 480
　　Wealth Creation 480
Cross-cultural Team Work 502
Culture and Organizations 225
　Assessing a Proactive Technological Culture 229
　Control/Display Compatibility 231
　Design of Protective Equipment 232
　Existing Manufacturing Systems 230
　Identifying Technological Culture 228
　Interface Design 231
　Proactive and Reactive Technological Cultures 227
　Process of Transitioning from Reactive to Proactive 228
　Studying Manufacturing Systems 231
　Workplace Design 232

Data Types and Preparation for Analysis 522
Deriving Causal Connections 510
Description of Business Process Model 25
　Implementation of Strategy 26
　Making Business Strategy 25
　Monitor Impact 26
　Normative and Descriptive Models 27
Developing a Performance Metric 290
　Performance Engineering Model 291
　Performance Matrix 292
Diagnostic Cycle 360
Different Approaches to Diversity 478
　Deficiency 478
　Differentiation 478
　Discrimination 478
Different Approaches to Organizational Change Research 512
　Action 512
　Applied 512
　Evaluative 512
　Objective 512
　Pure Basic 512
Different Forms of Organizational Diagnosis 361
　Job Satisfaction and Organizational Diagnosis 362

Dimensions of Cultures and Its Influence on Organizations 258
　Future vs Present vs Past Orientation 259
　High Context vs Low Context 258
　Individualism vs Collectivism 260
　Monochronic vs Polychronic 258
　Power Distance 260
　Quantity of Time 259
Dimensions of Performance 281
Diversity 472
　Gender Diversity and Modern Organizations 473
　Wipro and Diversity Management 473
Diversity and Propensities of Multinational Organizations 481
　Ethnocentric 482
　Geocentric 483
　Polycentric 482
　Regio-centric 483
Diversity Management 473
　at IBM 475
　Contextual Issues of 474
Drawbacks in Implementing Organizational Change 74
　PwC's Initiative with BP 73

Effective Change Management 178
　Guidelines to Manage Change 177
　Implement the Desired Change 179
　Issues Involved 178
　Need for Change 178
　Reinforce the Change 179
　Training and Support 179
Effective Management of Workplace Diversity 483
Effective Performance Modelling 294
　Customer Focused Metrics 294
　Designing Metrics 295
　Human Side of Performance Metrics 294
　Performance Metrics 296
EFQM Excellence Model 133
Elements of the Business Process Model 25
Employee Attitudes in the Organizational Change Process 238
　Different Approaches to Attitudinal Change 239
Employee Empowerment 319
　Quality of Work Life (QWL) 319
Enablers of Knowledge Management in Organizations 438
　Knowledge Management at NTPC 439
Ethical Guidelines for OD Professionals 349

Factors Promoting Globalization 413
Features of Organizational Change Process 84
　Collaborative Inquiry and Teamwork 85

Index

Disagreement and Contradictions 84
    Not Always Smooth Sailing 85
    Ongoing and Continuous Process 85
Framing of Hypotheses 533
    Hypothesis Tests 534
    Power and Statistical Errors 535
    Test Null Hypothesis 536
Future Corporate Challenges for Diversity 484

Gap Analysis 446
General Diversity Management 477
Generic Change or Transition Models 59
    John Fisher's Personal Transition Curve 60
    Lewis–Parker Model 60
Globalization 410
    Aligning HR Strategy with Business Goals 415
    OD Process through Human Resources 415
    Organizational Change and Development 411
    Organizational Transformation 426
Globalization Challenges for Managing Organizational Change and Development 421
    Interdependence 422
    Managing Ambiguity 422
    Managing Diversity 421
    Managing HR 421

History or Evolution of OD 338
    Laboratory Stem 339
    Socio-technical Stem 339
    Survey Research Feedback Stem 339
Human Resource Scorecard 301
    Key Benefits 302
    Process of Developing 301
Human Resource Development (HRD) Initiatives and Attitudinal Change 243
    Employee Empowerment 244
    Promoting Quality Circles and Developing the Culture of Total Participation 244
    Team Spirit 245
Human Resource Information Systems 32
    Creating an Environment 34
    Gaining the Support and Commitment 34
    Integration between HRD Processes and other HR Initiatives 34
    Linking HRD with Business Objectives 32
Human Resource Management and Technology Management 213
    Design and Engineering 213
    High Speed Machining 214
    Inspection 214
    Integration and Control 214
    Network Communications 215
    Processing Fabrication and Assembly 214

Implementation Help through Research 511
Implementing Change Improvement Systems 167
Important Triggers for Organizational Development 346
    Changing Composition of the Labour Force 346
    Growing Concern over Personal and Social Issues 346
    Knowledge Explosion 346
    Rapid Product Obsolescence 346
Indian Companies and Knowledge Management Practices 447
Inferential Statistics 532
    Concept of Standard Error 532
ISO Standards and Total Quality Management Systems 313
    Objectives of ISO 9001:2000 Quality Management Systems 314
    Selection and use of the ISO 9000:2000 Family of Standards 313

Key Elements for Success in Organizational Change 57
    Training and Development 58
Knowledge Management 434
    Assumptions 436
    Benefits of 438
    Explicit Knowledge 435
    Integral Components 437
    Organizational Change 449
    Resource-based Competitive Advantage 448
    Tacit Knowledge 435
Knowledge Management Strategy 441
    at Chevron 443
    CRM 442
    Knowledge–Strategy Link 443
    TQM 442

Leadership 425
Lean Practices to Achieve Organizational Excellence 149
    Importance Factors of Consideration for Lean Management 151
    Lean Management at Nestle 151
Leadership Performance-driven Change Process
    Acculturation 95
    Goal-setting 94
    Resource Allocation 94
    Risk Evaluation 94
    Setting Standards of Performance and Behaviour 95
    Supporting Processes and Structure 95
    Trade-off between the Short and Long-term 94
Legitimate Power 192

Literature Review for Organizational Change
  Research 512

Major Institutions Regulating Globalization 418
  International Monetary Fund (IMF) 419
  Organization for Economic Cooperation and
    Development (OECD) 420
  United Nations Conference on Trade and
    Development (UNCTAD) 420
  United Nations Organization (UN) 420
  World Bank 420
  World Trade Organization (WTO) 418
Malcolm Baldrige Model for Organizational
  Excellence 144
  Business Results 145
  Customer and Market Focus 145
  Human Resource Focus 145
  Information and Analysis 145
  Leadership 144
  Process Management 145
  Strategic Planning 144
Management by Objectives (MBO) for Organizational
  Effectiveness and Excellence 133
Management Directed Cultural Change 273
Managerial Roles Theory 135
  Mintzberg's Managerial Roles 136
Managerial Skills and Competencies 135
  Attract and Retain Talent 139
  Balance the Stakeholders Need 140
  Developing Competencies for Effective
    Organizational Change 140
  for the New Millennium 138
  Integrate Technology with the Business 140
  Multi-skilling 138
  Partnerships and Collaboration 139
  Predict the Future 140
  Quick Decision-making 139
  Skill Inventories 137
Managing Change through Balanced Scorecard 297
  Personal Balanced Scorecard for Export Manager
    298
  Perspectives of Balanced Scorecard 297
    Business Process 298
    Customer 298
    Financial 298
    Learning and Growth 297
Measure of Team Effectiveness 497
  Belbin's Team Role Self-perception Inventory 498
  Team Building Quiz 498
Measuring Organizational Effectiveness 121
  Dashboard 122
  Digital Dashboards 123
  OE Cycle 122
  Organizational Effectiveness Inventory (OEI) 122

SAS/GRAPH Dashboard in Version 9.1.3. Service
    Pack 4 125
Mergers and Acquisitions 103
  Change Processes 104
  in India 109
  Integration Phase 105
  Post-merger Phase 105
  Pre-merger Phase 105
  Recent Research 106
  Strategic Focusing in the Organizational Change
    Process 110
Model Building in Organizational Change Research
  513
Models and Tools of OD 382
  Competing Values 384
  Fault-driven 385
  Human Relations 384
  Legitimacy 384
  Open Systems 384
  Rational Goal 384
  Strategic Constituencies 384
Multiple Comparison of Variances 538

Nature and Purpose of Teams 494
  Types of Teams 494
    Cross-functional 495
    Hybrid 494
    Parallel 494
    Process 494
Nature of Change 161
  Responsibility for Managing Change 162

Objectives of T-group 491
  Effectiveness Enhancement through Team
    Interventions 492
Observational Methods of Organizational Diagnosis
  371
  Secondary Data and Unobtrusive Measures 372
OD and Business Process Re-engineering (BPR) 352
  Applications of BPR 353
    Ford Motor Company 353
    Procter & Gamble Corporation (P&G) 353
OD as Action Research Process 335
  OD Interventions at HPC 337
OD in Different Types of Organizations 342
  Transformation at Cisco 343, 350
Open System Concepts and Orchestra Organization
  19
Open Systems Approach in Organization 17
Open Systems Model 126
Optimizing the Cost of Quality 314
  Cost of Appraisal 314
  Cost of Failure 314
  Cost of Prevention 315

Index

Organization 1, 6
    Features of 5
    Principles of 5
Organization Development and Management Development 343
Organization Development Models 387
    ACHIEVE Model 397
    Action Research Model 401
    ADKAR Model of Individual Change 400
    Bridges Transition Model 401
    Burke-Litwin Causal Model 397
    Congruence Model for Organization Analysis 393
    Dannemiller-Tyson Interactive Strategic Planning 402
    Force Field Analysis 388
    Harrison's Model of Diagnosing Individual and Group Behaviour 396
    High Performance Programming 395
        High Performing Organization 396
        Proactive Organization 396
        Reactive Organization 396
        Responsive Organization 396
    IDEAL Model 399
    Leavitt's Model 388
    Likert's System Analysis 389
    McKinsey 7-S Framework 394
    Mobius Model 402
    Open Systems Theory 390
    Organizational Development through Competency Development 404
    PRIMO-F Business Growth Model 398
    Tichy's Technical Political Cultural (TPC) Framework 394
    Weisbord's Six-box Model 390
        Diagnostic Questions for Weisbord's Model 391
    World Healing Model 403
Organizational Analysis for Diagnosis 363
Organizational Change 44
    Content and Process Theories 45
    Guidelines 79
    Management of Manpower Redundancy 102
    Need for 46
    OD and Organizational Change 44
    Personal Examination 83
    Process 83
    through Innovation and Creativity 320
Organizational Change and Total Quality Management 318
Organizational Change Process in Indian Ordnance Factories 116
Organizational Change through Six Sigma 145
    Basic Characteristics 146
    in Organizations 147
    Steps for 148
Organizational Change, Transformation, and Renewal 49
    Different Change Theories and Their Key Features 48
    Kotter's Eight-step Model 47
    Process of Change at LG 50
Organizational Climate 271
Organizational Commitment 270
Organizational Culture 255
    Aspects of 256
    Bureaucratic 257
    Change Process 268
    Characteristics of 261
    Design 35
    Differences in 257
    Jungle-like 257
    Machine-like 257
Organizational Cybernetics 18
Organizational Design 28
    Behavioural Model 29
    Bureaucratic Model 29
Organizational Development 330
    Characteristics of 340
    Definition and Concepts of 331
    Features of 340
    Goals of 344
    Leadership Development 347
    Need for 333
    Organizational Involvement 347
    Person-centred Approach 330
    Relationship Approach 331
    Strategic Aspect of 336
    Structural Approach 331
    Task Forces for 370
Organizational Diagnosis 359
    Objectives of 360
    Questionnaire Development 367
Organizational Diagnostics 269
    Attitudes towards Work 269
Organizational Healthy Survey 366
    Communication 366
    Compensation/Benefits 366
    Customer Service 367
    Empowerment 367
    Equal Employment Opportunity 367
    Fairness 367
Organizational Life Cycle Analysis 350
    Aging Stage 351
    Aspect 37
    Growth Stage 351
    Infant Stage 351
    Model 387
    Prime Stage 351

Organizational Model of Excellence 126
   McKinsey's 7-S Framework 128
   Peters and Waterman 132
   Shared Vision 128
   Staff 129
   Strategy 128
   Stream 130
   Structure 129
   Style 129
   System 129
   Theory Z Concepts 127
   Wal-Mart and the 7-S Framework 131
Organizational Politics 195
Organizational Power and Control 189
   Calculative or Instrumental Systems 191
   Normative or Moral Involvement Systems 191
   Power and Systems of Organizational Membership 190
Organizational Structure 4, 269
   Adhocracy 12
   Adhocracy and Bureaucracy 13
   Components of 11
   Divisional Form 13
   Entrepreneurial Form 13
   Machine Bureaucracy 12
   Organizational Effectiveness 14
   Professional Bureaucracy 12
Organizational Structure and Systems 10
Organizational Transition 58
   Change through Training Initiatives 58
   through Teamwork 501

P-CMM Model for Organizational Excellence 140
   Behavioural Characteristics of Different Maturity Levels 141
   Key Process Areas 142
   Maturity Level 142
   P-CMM and UST 142
   P-CMM and WIPRO 143
Performance Improvement through Knowledge Management Practices 304
   Resource-based Competitive Advantage 305
Performance Management 280
Performance Models 282
Performance-driven Organizational Change 284
   Process 286
Personal Construct Psychology and Organizational Change 70
Personality 544
   Determinants of 544
   Individual Behaviour and Performance 545
   Measurement of Personality Traits 546
   Thinking and Decision-making Process 545
Philosophies of Strategic Change Management 461

Philosophy of Organizational Change 47
Power and Empowerment 193
   Empowerment Definitions and Concepts 193
   Implications in Practice 193
   Process of Empowerment 194
Power and Leadership 186
Principles of Change Management Strategy 459
Principles of OD 341
   Regarding Groups 342
   Regarding Individuals 341
   Regarding Organizations as Human Entities 342
Process Support through Research 511
Processing and Coding of Data 528
   Four Measures of Relative Position 531
   Making Use of Collected Data 528
   Measurers of Central Tendency 528
   Normal Distribution 530
   Range 530
   Standard Deviation 530
   The Pearson r 531
   The Spearman rho 531
   Three Measures of Variability 529
   Two Measures of Relationship 531
Productive Team for Organizational Change and Development 496

Qualitative Research Considerations 539
   Depth Interviews 541
   Document Review 540
   Focus Group 539
   Focus Group Interviews 541
   Interview Technique 540
   Observational Research 540
   One-on-one Interviews 540
   Sample Questionnaire of a Focus Group 542
   Telephone Interviews 541
Qualities of Change Agent 180
Quality Management Principles for Organizational Excellence 135
Quantitative Research
   Budget 521
   Cause-comparative 520
   Correlation 520
   Data Analysis 521
   Descriptive 519
   Drawing a Research Plan 521
   Ethical Considerations in 520
   Experimental 520
   Introduction 521
   Method 521
   Time Schedule 521

Re-engineering 36
   Environmental Aspects 36

Organizational Size and Form Aspects 37
Situational Aspects of Organizational Design 36
Technology Aspects 36
Research Discussion 538
Review of Organizational Purpose and Values 423
Reward Power 192
Role Analysis 493
Role and Significance of HRD in the Organizational
 Change Process 98
 Competencies as Enablers of Organizational
  Change Process 101
 Focus of the HRD System 98
 HRD Culture and Climate 100
 Role of HRD Manager 99
Role of an External Consultant in OD Processes 348
Role of Critical Success Factors in Organizational
 Design 30
Role of Organizational Change and Development
 Research 517
Role of Organizational Change Consultants 73

Scaling Techniques 522
 Guttman's Cumulative Scale 527
 Interval Scales 524
 Likert Scales 525
 Likert's Item Analysis 526
 Likert's Summated Rating Scale 526
 Nominal Scales 523
 Ordinal Scales 523
 Ratio Scales 525
 Semantic Scales 525
 Thurstone Scale 526
 Thurstone's Equal Appearing Intervals Scale 527
Scaling Techniques to Map Attitude 245
 Likert Scales 246
Scenario Planning for Effective Organizational
 Change Process 110
 Application of Delphi Technique in Scenario
  Planning 113
 Forces of Scenario Planning 112
 Nominal Group Method 114
 Steps for Scenario Planning 112
Selection of Organizational Change Strategy 464
Setting Standards of Performance 288
 Checklist for Performance Standards 290
 Guidelines for Performance Standards 288
 Performance Standards for Different Hierarchical
  Levels 289
Shingo Prize Model of Organizational Excellence
 143
Simple Analysis of Variance 537
SMART Objectives 284
Socio-technical Systems Thinking 22
Sources of Power 191

Organizational 191
Personal Sources 192
 Expert Power 192
 Referent (Charismatic) Power 193
Standard Research Tools for Organizational Change
 and Development 515
 FIRO-B (Fundamental Interpersonal Relations
  Orientation-Behaviour) Assessment 516
 Klein Group Instrument (KGI) 515
 Leadership Spectrum Profile (LSP) 516
 Myers-Briggs Type Indicator (MBTI) Assessment
  515
 Pearson-Marr Archetype Indicator (PMAI) 516
 Strength Deployment Inventory (SDI) 515
 Thomas-Kilmann Conflict Mode Instrument (TKI)
  516
 Work Environment Scales (WES) 516
Steps for Strategic Change Management 461
Steps in Organizational Development 345
 Developing of Strategy 345
 Identification and Diagnosis of the Problem 345
 Implementing the Programme 345
 Reviewing the Progress of the Programme 345
Steps in Technology Transitioning Process 232
 Active Management Support and Commitment
  232
 Breaking Down Requirements into Specific Tasks
  232
 Coaching, Managing, and Executing the Transition
  Plans 233
 Training 232
Strategic Approach to Cultural Diversity Management
 474
 General Diversity Management 474
 Globalization 475
 Human Resource Management (HRM) 475
 International Businesses 475
 Multicultural Marketplaces 475
Strategic Framework for Mapping Knowledge 444
 Advanced Knowledge 444
 Core Knowledge 444
 Innovative Knowledge 445
Strategic Knowledge Management in Indian
 Organizations 447
Strategic Organizational Change in the Institutional
 Framework 463
 Four Basic Strategies of Change Management 464
Strategic Technology Management 211
Strategies for Attitudinal Change 239
 Acceptance 241
 Cognitive Dissonance 240
 Compassion 241
 Co-opt 241
 Dialogue 241

Employee Acceptance and Attitude Changes 242
Influence through 360-degree Feedback 240
New Information 240
Positive Use of Fear 240
Release Their Prior Commitment 240
Understand First 241
Strategy 454
Competency Development Programmes 458
Performance Management 456
Strategic Organizational Change and Development 455
Strategic Plans 455
Successful Change Management Strategies 462
SWOT Analysis and the Change Process 95
Environmental Scanning and Feedback-enabled Change Process 97
Opportunities 96
Performing SWOT Analysis 96
Systems Dynamics 23
Systems Theory, Systems Analysis, and Systems Thinking 15
Principles of Systems Theory 16
Systems Thinking and Change 66
Developing a High Performance Work Culture—A Study on Siemens AG 64
Systems View of Organization 6
Feedback Loop 7

Tata Motors Commercial Vehicles Business Unit (CVBU) 153
Team Building 490
Exercises 491
Team Management Wheel—A Model for Teamwork 495
RIDO Scale 495
Teams and Team Work 315
Quality Circles 316
Small Group Forums 316
Structure of a Quality Circle 317
Technology and Organizational Design 218
Thompson's Model 219
Woodward's Study 220
Technology Innovation 218
Technology Management 209
Communication 210
Economic Issues in Technological Change 211
Innovation 209
Organization Structure and Design 210
Social System 210
Sociological Issues in Technology Management 209
Time 210
Technology Planning 216
Principles of 216

Technology Transfer 217
Coordinate 217
Globalization 414
Link 218
Nurture 217
Test of Significance 536
Concept of Significance Level 537
One-tailed and Two-tailed Tests 537
Theories of Organizational Change Process 86
Theories of Power 187
Three Pillars of Organization 6
Tools for Cultural Diversity Management 476
Diversity Management at Tata Steel, India 477
Productivity, Innovation, and Talent Management 476
Total Quality Management 311
Transactional and Transformational Leadership for Organizational Change 196
Contingency Framework of Change 197
Culture and Climate of Leadership 200
Environment and Leadership 199
Leadership and Power 201
Types of Change 62, 171
Developmental 63
Episodic vs Continuous 63
Planned vs Emergent 62
Transformational 64
Transitional 63
Types of Culture 263
Daimler–Chrysler Merger 268
HP–Compaq 267
Merger Mantra 266
Merger and Its Impact on Organizational Culture 266
Organizational Culture from a Global Perspective 265
P&G–Gillette 267
Tata–Corus 267

Understanding Organizational Change Research Tools and Techniques 518
Conducting Quantitative Research 521
Qualitative Paradigm 519
Quantitative Paradigm 518
Types of Quantitative Researches 519
Use of Interview as a Diagnostic Tool 368

Validity and Reliability 521
Various Dimensions of Performance 295
Focus 297
Input 296
Results and Output 296
Time 297
Viable System Model (VSM) 18